Self and Identity

Self and Identity

Contemporary Philosophical Issues

Daniel Kolak
William Paterson College

Raymond Martin
University of Maryland

Macmillan Publishing Company
New York
Collier Macmillan Canada
Toronto

To Rajka
who has seen
behind the mask

Editor: Helen McInnis
Production Supervisor: George Carr
Production Manager: Nick Sklitsis
Text Designer: Blake Logan
Cover Designer: Blake Logan
Cover illustration: Design Photographers International, Inc.
This book was set in Palatino by Digitype, Inc.
The cover was printed by Phoenix Color Corporation.

Macmillan Publishing Company
866 Third Avenue, New York, New York 10022

Collier Macmillan Canada, Inc.
1200 Eglinton Avenue East, Suite 200
Don Mills, Ontario M3C 3N1

Library of Congress Cataloging-in-Publication Data
Kolak, Daniel.
    Self and identity : contemporary philosophical issues / Daniel
Kolak, Raymond Martin.
        p.   cm.
    Includes bibliographical references.
    ISBN 0-02-365710-3
    1. Self-knowledge, Theory of. 2. Self (Philosophy) 3. Identity.
4. Consciousness. 5. Philosophy of mind. I. Martin, Raymond.
1941– . II. Title.
BD450.K639   1991
126—dc20   90-34010
                  CIP

Printing: 1 2 3 4 5 6 7   Year: 1 2 3 4 5 6 7

Preface

Over the past twenty years philosophy has changed dramatically. Logical positivism — the prevailing philosophical paradigm of the first half of the twentieth century and one that encouraged intellectual isolationism — is all but dead. In addition, the core philosophical issues about self, identity, and the nature of mind that tend now to interest philosophers — and also psychologists, sociologists, neurophysiologists, novelists, and even physicists — spill over traditional disciplinary boundaries. Finally, philosophically relevant knowledge and information are increasing at an unprecedented rate.

As a result, the best and most influential philosophy is now being done in a more interdisciplinary way and yet, at the same time, with greater specialization. This creates an urgent need for an anthology that is both general and accessible enough to be used for undergraduate instruction yet specialized and interdisciplinary enough to reflect the ways philosophy is now being done. In putting together *Self and Identity*, we have tried to meet this challenge by including accessible selections focused on a closely integrated set of specific problems that are central to epistemology, philosophy of mind, theories of rationality, metaphysics, philosophy of the social and natural sciences, perception, free will, religion, and ethics.

Self and Identity can thus be used as a text not only in philosophy of mind, but in introduction to philosophy courses as well. Because the topics covered have been so central during the past two decades, many of the most important contemporary philosophers have written about them, and so students will get to study some of the best current philosophy available. At the same time, the selections focus ultimately on an issue that interests students more than any other: themselves.

We have been fortunate to have the expert help of many philosophers, psychologists, and social and natural scientists who have encouraged us and been tremendously influential in both the formation and development of this project. We especially thank John Barresi, Psychology, Dalhousie University; Herbert Fingarette, Philosophy, University of California, Santa Barbara; Ernest Hilgard, Psychology, Stanford University; Richard Wollheim, Philosophy, University of California, Berkeley; Mark Johnston, Philosophy, Princeton University; Brian Garrett, Philosophy, Australian National University; Roland Puccetti, Philosophy, Dalhousie University; Peter Unger, Philosophy, New York University; David Lewis, Philosophy, Princeton University; Rom Harré, Fellow of Linacre College, Oxford University; Arnold Zuboff, Philosophy, University College, London; Douglas Hofstadter, Computer Science, Indiana University; Ruthellen Josselson, Psychology, Towson State University; Allen Stairs, Philosophy, University of Maryland; Michael Brodie, Psychiatrist, Washington, D.C.; John Vollrath, Philosophy, University of Wisconsin, Stevens Point; Larry Stern, Philosophy, University of Puget Sound; Kenneth Gergen, Psychology, Swarthmore College; Jonathan Auerbach, English, University of Maryland; Marshall Missner, Philosophy, University of Wisconsin, Oshkosh; Patricia Hunt, Counseling Center, University of Maryland; Karen Hanson, Philosophy, Indiana University; Denis Robinson, Philosophy, University of Auckland; Martin Tweedale, Philosophy, University of Alberta; Roy Perrett, Philosophy, Massey University; Karey Harrison, Philosophy, University of Wisconsin, Stevens Point; Bart Gruzalski, Philosophy, Northeastern University; Claudia Card, Philosophy, University of Wisconsin; John O'Connor, Dean, School of Humanities, William Paterson College; Jerrold Levinson, Philosophy, University of Maryland; Stephen Braude, Philosophy, University of Maryland, Baltimore County; Robert Martin, Philosophy, Dalhousie University; John Caughey, American Studies, University of Maryland; Martin Hollis, School of Economic and Social Studies, University of East Anglia; Ulric Neisser, Psychology, Emory University; Joan Callahan, Philosophy, University of Kentucky; Larry Temkin, Philosophy, Rice University; Alicia Roque, Philosophy, Prince Georges Community College; Douglas Ehring, Philosophy, Southern Methodist University; Neera Badhwar, Philosophy, University of Oklahoma; J. R. Salamanca, English, University of Maryland; Emmett Holman, Philosophy, George Mason University; Stephen Hahn, English, William Paterson College; Heidi Storl, Philosophy, Augustana College; Morton Winston, Philosophy, Trenton State University; William Day, Psychology, University of Nevada at Reno; and Mary Haight, Philosophy, University of Glasgow.

Evelyn Marzloff helped type the bibliography. Cynthia Read provided us with timely assistance. We also thank the many friends who have helped in various ways with this project, especially Robin Elizabeth, Kathy Krivak, Rochelle Turoff, Angelo Juffras, Jenny Redifer, Steven Fleishman, Richard Fyfe, Rajka Ungerer, and Wendy Zentz.

Finally, we thank everyone at Macmillan who worked on this project, especially our production editor, George Carr, for his excellent supervision; our copy editor, M. V. Callcott, for a truly outstanding job; and our editor, Helen McInnis, for her consistent encouragement and for her kind and expert assistance.

Contents

Introduction

What is consciousness? What is mind? What is self? What is a person? What is self-knowledge and how does it work? Can you know who you really are—your true self? How? Do you even have a true self? Is self-deception possible and, if so, how and why do we deceive ourselves? What does your identity consist in—what makes you *you*? Who are you?

What makes these questions so perplexing is that the answers seem close at hand, hovering invisibly just beyond the horizon of our immediate experience, and yet when we reach out to grasp them they elude us. As so often in philosophy, taking a familiar and obvious path leads straight into a labyrinth so puzzling that it seems utterly insoluble. How can something intimately familiar—ourselves, our own minds—be so utterly unknown?

The familiarity of questions about self and identity stems from the fact that they are about us, the questioners. Since *we* are close at hand, the answers, we think, must also be close at hand. Surely, it would seem, if we know anything, we must know that which is most directly accessible to us—ourselves. But as soon as we examine the facts and assumptions underlying concepts such as consciousness, personal identity, and self, we realize we are further from knowing ourselves than we think. Paradoxically, the more we learn about ourselves, the more puzzled we become about who and what we are. How can we who know so much about so many things know so little about ourselves?

Part of the difficulty is that we have an access to ourselves that we do not have to the rest of nature: We experience our own inner mental states. We thus learn subjectively—"from the inside"—what colors we see, what feelings we feel, whether we are hungry or bored, and so on. We cannot experience the rest of nature, not even other people, this way. We must experience nature and other people "from the outside," through our external sense organs—"objectively."

But we, too, have an outside. We are objects in nature. So we also learn about ourselves objectively. This dual access to ourselves gives rise to the problem of how to integrate both subjective and objective perspectives—which often conflict and sometimes may even contradict each other—into a single, coherent vision. For instance, when you decide to do something, do you decide to do it because you want to achieve some goal—something you may know only subjectively—or because of chemical changes in your brain

—something you know only objectively? If both, how does one affect the other? Do minds push chemicals around or do chemicals give rise to mental states that only make it seem as if mind is in control? Or do minds just reduce to chemicals, so that the apparent differences between them are merely consequences of the alternative conceptual schemes we use to describe and explain behavior? If such mentalistic and physicalistic explanations are merely two ways of describing the same phenomena—ways that conceptualize the phenomena differently—what accounts for the radical differences between these conceptualized schemes and what is their relationship to each other?

Regardless of the ultimate ontological status of these two fundamentally different perspectives—the subjective and the objective—on ourselves, since we neither should, nor are likely to, abandon either of them, we must integrate them somehow if we are to understand ourselves fully. At the same time, a variety of disciplines—philosophy, psychology, sociology, neurophysiology, and physics—generate illuminating concepts and increase our knowledge about ourselves, but often from radically differing objective perspectives, raising again the problem of integration. Thus, if we are to understand ourselves whole, we must integrate not only the subjective and objective perspectives on ourselves but we must also integrate the various perspectives on ourselves from within the different disciplines. That is the goal of this book: to combine perspectives, integrate concepts, and begin the process of understanding ourselves whole.

I

Unity of Consciousness

Origins of Consciousness

Consciousness is one of the great mysteries, perhaps the greatest. We might not agree about what it is, yet most of us agree about how it is distributed. Atoms, rocks, clouds, and rivers are not conscious; neither are amoeba and plankton. Trees and insects may or may not be conscious, dolphins and chimpanzees probably are, and our primitive human ancestors probably were. We, on the other hand, definitely are conscious.

We arrive at these views first by taking for granted that we are conscious and then by attributing consciousness to anything that appears sufficiently like us. The puzzling questions, from the point of view of understanding the origins of consciousness, personal identity, and self, are these: At what point, and how, in the progression from a collection of nonconscious, nonliving atoms to contemporary adult humans, does an organism begin to have consciousness? When and how does an internal mental life arise that is capable of sustaining not only sensation of the surrounding environment but also an awareness that connects the individual sensings into an apparently unified whole? When and how does an organism begin to have an (apparently unified) awareness of its own awareness and a feeling that there is a coherent and continuous being that is aware, the first step to a sense of its own self and identity?

Etymologically, the word "consciousness" means "with knowing," that is, having and using the capacity or ability to know. This captures at least one aspect of consciousness. One reason we do not regard rocks, clouds, rivers, and mountains as being conscious is that we do not think they know anything. On the other hand, even lower life forms, such as amoeba and plankton, have a kind of knowledge in that they retain and process information—at least in the sense that they eat and reproduce, which requires that they distinguish themselves from the surrounding environment in ways that rocks and rivers do not.

The consciousness of humans and perhaps other higher animals is an astounding biological achievement. But consciousness in humans may also be a cultural achievement; that is, not only brains but also language may be necessary. For instance, having a sense of our own continuing identities over time and the ability to reflect upon ourselves may require an internalized self-concept embedded in a unified personal and social history, all of which may require an elaborate language in which to think and also to communicate with others.

Where and when, in the progression from inorganic substances, like rocks, to beings like us, did our kind of conscious experience, which includes self-awareness, a sense of individual unity, and a sense of our own identities, first make its appearance? The progression might go like this. First, some part of the environment becomes aware of another—perhaps simply by becoming a system distinct from the surrounding environment—but without being aware of that awareness. At the second level, there is also an apparently unified awareness of that awareness—perhaps by the system's somehow monitoring its own activity, a sort of internal feeding-back of information about itself to itself. Finally, there is in addition to awareness of awareness the realization (the misconception?) that the awareness belongs to one's self. In other words, there is attachment to (or identification with) an internalized self-concept.

This schema is, of course, oversimplified. Animals such as dogs and chimpanzees may be aware without being aware they are aware, yet may have rudimentary self-concepts. Still, they lack the more complex forms of self-awareness and self-concepts we humans possess. Our consciousness involves not only the ability to conceptualize ourselves but also the ability to recognize that the self conceptualized is "me," an "I," a continuing being with a particular history. Perhaps our primitive human ancestors, before the development of language, experienced consciousness without the full-blown self-awareness that includes an "I."

In the first selection in this book, Julian Jaynes formulates a bold and shocking theory that addresses many of these baffling questions. Ordinarily we suppose that consciousness has been around at least as long as there have been humans, which would place its biological origin somewhere between 300,000 and 200,000 B.C. According to Jaynes, however, consciousness did not appear on this planet until some time between 1400 and 600 B.C. He claims that our human ancestors of only four thousand years ago were not conscious.

Jaynes's theory becomes less shocking once we understand what he means by "consciousness." According to Jaynes, sensation, perception, learning, thinking, and even reasoning sometimes go on without consciousness. Thus, he is not claiming that our human ancestors of only a few thousand years ago had no minds—that is, that they were incapable of sensing, perceiving, and so on. Nor is he claiming, say, that animals do not feel pain. In the case of pain, for instance, Jaynes distinguishes a sensory from a conscious form of pain and argues that animals experience only sensory pain. Conscious pain, he claims, has been experienced on this planet only by humans of the past few hundred generations.

According to Jaynes, consciousness involves at least three essential features: a mind–space, an analog "I," and narratizing. When a schoolboy has a romantic daydream about the girl across the aisle, he creates a mind–space in which he and the girl are together. He—that is, his analog "I"—"sees" into this mind–space. In seeing into this mind–space he creates a context—a kind of story—in which to embed what he sees. This creating of a context is "narratizing." Consciousness, then, according to Jaynes, involves an analog "I" narratizing in a mind–space.

Jaynes distinguishes the analog "I" from the self. His view is that the analog "I" arises prior to the self in an individual's development and, unlike the self, has no content and is not an object of consciousness. Thus, Jaynes's analog "I" is similar to what some philosophers have called a "transcendental self"—"transcendental" because it is not even theoretically possible that it should appear as an object in experience. The analog "I" has no independent ontological status in that it is not a thing or a process existing independently of consciousness. Rather, the analog "I" is an underlying structural feature of consciousness that makes conscious experience as we know it possible, even though it does not exist independently of consciousness and is not, itself, a conscious experience.

Jaynes's theory thus lays the foundations for a theory of the unity of consciousness. Using language that Jaynes does not use, we might say his theory of consciousness lays the foundations for a theory of the origin of two different sorts of unities: an underlying structural feature of consciousness that is a unifier, and a unified self that is experienced. The underlying structural feature is the analog "I." The unified self that is experienced is what developmental psychologists often refer to simply as "the self" and some philosophers have referred to as "the empirical self."

Jaynes claims that consciousness, in the sense in which he understands it, had to await the development of language. This ensures that consciousness has not been around more than 50,000 years. But consciousness also had to await the breakdown of the "bicameral"—literally, two-chambered—mind, a nonconscious human mentality divided into a decision-making part and a follower part. In the bicameral era, claims Jaynes, most people experienced some of their thoughts as "internal voices," much like the voices schizophrenics hear. They did not take the voices to be their own but, rather, the voices of gods. Jaynes speculates that the breakdown of the bicameral mind —or, more accurately, the unification of two nonconscious minds into one conscious unit—had both cultural and neurological causes, the latter involving a change in function of certain parts of the right hemisphere of the brain. Thus, Jaynes's theory includes historical hypotheses about when, where, and how consciousness originated, descriptive hypotheses about the sort of consciousness that contemporary adult humans have, and suggestions of possible relationships among consciousness, unity, and self.

Daniel C. Dennett (selection 2) is sympathetic to the central core of Jaynes's theory, namely, that the advent of consciousness has more to do with conceptual innovation within the brain than with biological evolution. In Dennett's view, the relationship between brain and mind is like the relationship between computer hardware and software. The computer hardware—the physical components of the computer—consists of chips, wires, disc drives, and so on. The brain's "hardware" consists of neurons, chemicals, and so on. The computer's software is the program that directs the functioning of the physical components by telling them what to do. The brain's "software"—in Dennett's view, the mind—is the "program" that directs the functioning of the neurons and chemicals. Just as a computer can perform a variety of functions (financial planning, word processing, etc.) merely by changing its program, so also the brain can perform a variety of functions, depending, among other things, on the concepts at its disposal. Although the brain has evolved little over many thousands of years, changes in the environment encouraged the emergence of certain mental concepts— new software—that may then have set in motion the chain reaction that brought about consciousness as we know it.

At issue is whether certain concepts are necessary not merely to describe a phenomenon but as antecedent conditions for there even to be a phenomenon. For instance, before people had the concepts of right and wrong not only were they unable to talk about morality, there was no morality. Perhaps, suggests Dennett, consciousness is like that. It is not just that we need certain concepts to talk about consciousness, but the concepts must exist before consciousness can arise. Furthermore, these new concepts came into being as a consequence of cultural, not biological, evolution. Dennett thus supports Jaynes's speculative hypothesis by offering a possible explanation of how consciousness might have arisen.

Jonathan Miller (selection 3) criticizes Jaynes's physiological speculations and offers an alternative, cultural explanation of the origin of consciousness (or self-consciousness). He claims, first, that there is little neurological evidence to show that the brain is partitioned in the ways Jaynes claims. For instance, he claims there is no reason to suppose either that the right hemisphere communicates to the left using natural, rather than machine, language, or that hallucinated voices are coming from a different hemisphere of the brain rather than from a malfunction of the speech center on the left. Second, Miller claims that there is not enough evidence to indicate that preliterate humans were any more prone to hallucinations than are we. The evidence from the *Iliad*, claims Miller, does not support Jaynes's thesis because works of art are subject to mythological interpretations. Miller claims it is more likely that the sort of changes in human consciousness that Jaynes is trying to explain are the result of two factors: the invention of writing and the evolution of political and social structures that encouraged individualism.

The questions that Jaynes, Dennett, and Miller consider are about the evolutionary history of consciousness—about the ways in which disunified and relatively simple forms of consciousness become progressively more unified and more complex. But what happens, one might wonder, when the process goes the other way—when a consciousness just like the one that we now have becomes less unified?

Split Brains

The commonsense belief that we are each a unity—one body, one brain, one mind, one consciousness, one self, one person—is fundamental to the ways we ordinarily think about ourselves. That this belief is true seems to be given directly in our experience. Our individual unities, however, are not given in experience. They are a theory, and a highly speculative one at that. Unity must be demonstrated, if possible, by showing how it is a better explanation of experience and behavior than are other, competing explanations.

Biologically, each of us is both two and one. Our brains are a double organ, consisting of two hemispheres connected by a bundle of nerve tissue—the corpus callosum. From the 1860s, when the French neurologist Paul Broca established that the left hemisphere controls speech, until the 1950s, it was widely believed that the right hemisphere, though it controls movement and sensation on the right side of the body, contributes little to higher brain function. Many thus doubted whether the corpus callosum played any important part in brain function, some even suggesting that its main purpose was to hold the two hemispheres in place.

In 1939, in Rochester, New York, the neurosurgeon William P. Van Wagenen severed the corpus callosum of a 26-year-old woman in an effort to reduce the severity of her epileptic seizures. The hope was to confine each seizure to one hemisphere. The procedure did reduce the frequency of the woman's seizures. Van Wagenen repeated the operation many times on epileptics and it sometimes proved to be remarkably effective, resulting in an almost total elimination of all seizures, including unilateral (one-hemisphered) ones. However, the operation had a bizarre side-effect, not discovered until much later: the apparent creation of two independent spheres of consciousness within a single human skull.

The earliest indications of the mental duality of split-brain patients came in a study, in the early 1940s, by the Rochester neuro-psychologist Andrew J. Akelaitis, who was investigating the function of the corpus callosum. Akelaitis examined thirty of Van Wagenen's split-brain patients and found that once they recovered from the surgery they showed virtually no mental or behavioral impairment: they read and spoke and moved and sensed as normal adults. He did, though, note an anomaly, which showed up in two patients: in trying to perform simple tasks, they sometimes seemed strangely at odds with themselves. For instance, one of the two, while dressing herself, put her stocking on with her right hand, pulled it off with her left, and then repeated this several times; and after washing the dishes, she dried the cleaned dishes and then put them back to be washed again, realizing while doing it that her behavior was absurd. Since only two of the thirty patients behaved oddly and these two eventually stopped, Akelaitis concluded that their behavior was unrelated to the surgery. His study reinforced the view that the right hemisphere contributes little to higher brain function.

Then, in the 1950s, Roger W. Sperry and several colleagues carried out studies that ultimately revolutionized views about the right hemisphere's function. They began by studying a cat in which not only the two halves of the brain but also the optic chiasm, the intersection of the optic nerves, were separated so that visual information from the left eye was sent only to the left hemisphere and information from the right eye only to the right hemisphere. With one eye covered, the cat was taught to perform a task. When the same problem was presented to the other eye, the cat showed no recognition of the problem and had to relearn the task with the other half of its brain.

These findings suggested that the corpus callosum is responsible for integrating the responses of the two hemispheres of an intact brain. Researchers thus wondered whether cutting the corpus callosum in a human brain resulted in the right hand not knowing what the left was doing, and whether the two halves of the same brain could have separate thoughts and separate emotions, perhaps even separate streams of individually unified consciousness.

Ordinarily, the two hemispheres of the split-brain patient, like the brains of ordinary people, are synchronized. However, Sperry showed that this synchronization can be disrupted through experimental manipulation, and further documented that occasionally it is also disrupted spontaneously outside the laboratory. In one striking case, a patient complained that when he hugged his wife with one arm, his other arm pushed her away.

Sperry (selection 4) reports the relevant physiological and behavioral facts. These show how our consciousness can apparently be split into two separate streams. His account challenges us to explain what the unity of each stream consists in and what the unity of our consciousness as a whole consists in when it is not split. At the heart of this challenge is the possibility that what we take to be just one unified consciousness may actually be an integrated system of several, independent unities.

When one of us repeats the Cartesian dictum, "I think, therefore I am," a guiding paradigm in the philosophy of mind for hundreds of years, to whom does the "I" refer? Descartes assumed the only serious candidate was himself, the one and only thinking thing that he is. If this utterance is the product of just one thinking thing, then it is natural to suppose that thing is the referent. But if it is the product of more than one thinking thing, we are faced with the puzzle of having several possible referents. In the case of split-brain patients, under certain experimental conditions the individually unified streams of consciousness associated with each hemisphere of the brain are not even co-conscious. In the case of ordinary people, under normal conditions, we usually assume they are. But co-conscious or not, the fact that there is more than one possible referent of "I" raises the question of which, if any, is the correct referent. In other words, when the word "I" issues from you, to what or to whom does it refer?

Roland Puccetti (selection 5) claims that we each have two brains. Just as we do not speak of the eye as a single organ that has two half-eyes protruding onto different sections of the face, so also we should not speak of the brain as a single organ having two half-brains extending into different regions of the skull. Puccetti argues that splitting an organism's brain by severing the corpus callosum and then causing the two hemispheres to get out of sync merely shows dramatically what is going on even under ordinary circumstances—namely, that we each have two independently functioning brains, each of which has its own unified conscious experience. That is, he thinks the split-brain research shows that every normal human organism has two minds.

Puccetti argues that after commissurotomy—the severing of the corpus callosum—each hemisphere of a human brain is a separate mind because each has qualitatively similar (but numerically distinct) experiences and also exhibits differences in obviously intentional and purposeful acts. He claims that even though these differences might have been created, not merely revealed, by the severing of the corpus callosum, it is far simpler to suppose that they were there all along. His reason, apparently, is his belief that severing the corpus callosum is not the sort of change that it is plausible to suppose creates these sorts of complex psychological phenomena. So, Puccetti thinks, if there are two minds after commissurotomy, there must have been two minds even before commissurotomy. He concludes from this that each normal human organism is two persons.

If we each have two minds, why don't we each have two sets of experiences? Puccetti's answer is that we do, but do not realize it. That is, the organism as a whole has two sets of experiences, but no conscious part of the organism has introspective access to both of these sets. That is why, in the case of visual experiences, for instance, neither one of your brains (that is, neither hemisphere) normally experiences double vision.

Thomas Nagel (selection 6), on the other hand, attempts to show that there is no sound basis for saying that split-brain patients have either one or two minds, and that either hypothesis is equally justified by the facts. He claims that the fundamental problem in trying to understand the unity or lack of unity in split-brain cases arises because we take ourselves as paradigms of mental unity and then try to project ourselves into the mental lives of split-brain patients, either once or twice over. In thus using ourselves as the paradigm of mental unity, without understanding how we function, we beg the question by ignoring the possibility that what appears to be unity in our own case is merely integration, more or less effective. Nagel concludes that our ordinary idea of mental unity is inapplicable in an age of increasing information about brain function and hence that neither split-brain patients nor the rest of us can be said to have one or two or any particular number of minds.

Finally, Derek Parfit (selection 7) argues that these same split-brain facts support the view that we are not what we believe ourselves to be: We are not separately existing entities—egos, or "I"'s—over and above our bodies and psychologies. Parfit claims that although we may think we have rejected the view that we are such separately existing entities, we still have beliefs about what is involved in our continued existence that would be justified only if we *were* separately existing entities. For instance, if you are like most people, you believe that if you were to change or transform in some way—say, by having various parts of your body or brain replaced—the resulting person would be either you or a replica of you, and it would make a great difference to you which it was.

Suppose the resulting person is you, but just barely. Start subtracting otherwise relatively insignificant cells from that person until he or she fails to be you, but just barely. The similarity between you and your replica is now so close that the differences between the two should not matter much to you. After all, the replica is almost you and would be you but for a few otherwise insignificant cells. However, for almost all of us, it would matter a great deal that we are not the replica. Parfit claims that this shows that covertly we must believe ourselves to be something more than just our bodies and psychologies, some separately existing entities that by either attaching or failing to attach to the replica make a big difference between the two cases.

What, then, is the relevance of the split-brain cases? Parfit claims these cases should help us to see that we are not what we covertly believe ourselves to be—that we are not separately existing entities. For instance, in the cases where a person's consciousness is divided into two separate, independently unified streams, if we try to explain what unifies each stream by claiming that the experiences are all had by the same person, then there should be just one unified stream of consciousness rather than two, because there is just one person. (Parfit's assumption that there is just one person is denied by Puccetti, Nagel, and, in Part II, David Lewis.) But, Parfit continues, there are two unified streams. So, this so-called explanation explains nothing. One might try to explain the unities by claiming that although there is only one person, there are two separately existing entities, one for each unified stream of consciousness, and that the presence of these separately existing entities explains the unities. But once the notion of person is divorced from that of a separately existing entity, it is much less plausible to suppose there are separately existing entities.

Regardless of which, if any, of the arguments put forth by Puccetti, Nagel, and Parfit is right, their disagreement illustrates dramatically how, in the process of constructing concepts and theories to try to understand ourselves, seemingly noncontroversial facts become controversial interpretations—speculative theories—that go far beyond what is given in experience. It is as if we cannot simply discover who and what we are, we have to decide. But how?

Split Minds

Commissurotomy is one way mental unity can be disrupted. It is dramatic and unusual and involves the creation of an actual physical division in the brain. There are other, more common, ways mental unity can be disrupted that do not involve physical division. Ernest Hilgard (selection 8) describes several of these ways: possessions, fugues, multiple personalities, automatic writing, divided attention, and Hilgard's own discovery: the strange "hidden observer" phenomenon that *seems* to reveal the existence of a hidden yet omnipresent personality within us, a presence that—watching but not speaking—can sometimes be evoked through hypnosis.

Hilgard's survey raises several questions. First, in the case of extreme but nonsurgical disruptions of mental unity, how many minds are there? How many selves? For instance, is a multiple personality one self with a divided mind, one self with two minds, or more than one self? How are we to count minds and selves? Ordinarily, we just count heads. Apparently, this will no longer do.

Kathleen V. Wilkes (selection 9), at least, argues that it will no longer do. She examines the spectacular case of Christine Beauchamp's multiple personality disorder and argues (contrary to Beauchamp's famous therapist, Morton Prince) that Christine was three separate persons simultaneously housed in one body. Her argument depends primarily on a detailed analysis of the case, which she then evaluates in the light of six "conditions of personhood." Wilkes claims that five of the six conditions suggest that Beauchamp was several persons and that the sixth condition is ambiguous. For instance, two of her conditions of personhood are that "a certain stance or attitude" must be taken toward persons that treats them as "moral objects," and that they can reciprocate by acting as "moral agents." Wilkes concludes that it is not clear whether Beauchamp satisfies the first condition because sometimes Prince regarded her as a single agent with several personalities and sometimes he regarded each of her separate personalities as single agents. But she finds that Beauchamp did satisfy the second condition, in that each personality reciprocated by acting as a moral agent.

Accounts of multiple personality disorder tend to focus on the therapist and on the multiple's condition while he or she was a multiple, which is natural enough since the multiple's condition while a multiple, not after a cure, is the unusual and dramatic psychological condition to be examined. Sometimes also dramatic, however, and perhaps revealing, is how the multiple feels after the cure. An especially poignant account is provided by Chris Costner Sizemore, the Eve of the famous "three faces of Eve," who, writing after her "cure"—as a result of which the other personalities, in her word, "died"—laments the passing of her other selves:

> *I am frightened, just a little frightened. . . . If knowing the truth makes one free, it also makes one naked, exposed, unguarded, afraid.*
>
> *Where are they? Where did they go? Before, they have always come when I needed them. I was we; now I am I. "I" is so cold, so alone. Who am I? Where are we? O, my God, is this sanity, is this what they have been trying to bring me to? Why didn't they leave me alone? They're all so sure, so confident, so smug. Why did they have to tell me? I didn't believe them at first, I was angry, I felt betrayed. I knew what I knew, and they knew, too. Everybody knew; it is even written in books. . . .*
>
> *How can something that has always been true become false just because they say it is? But it did become false; even as they were saying it, it became false. And I knew that it did. With all of my being struggling to hold it, it vanished. My place, my world, my selves—vanished. . . .*
>
> *They tell me that I am real, that I have always been here and been real—the only real one. But how can it be? I knew them [the other personalities], saw them, touched the work they produced, kept the possessions they left, felt their parting agonies. I have notes they wrote in the diaries, paintings. . . .*
>
> *It was not Eve, not Eve White or Eve Black—anyway, that's just what the doctors called them. But I was Eve, I know I was Eve—and now I am not Eve. They say I was Eve and that I am still Eve, but she is gone—she left, she died, they died. If I were Eve then, did I die, too? My mind closes, it shuts it out. Can you die and still live?* [Chris Sizemore and Elen Pittillo, I'm Eve, New York: Doubleday, 1977; from the preface]

This poignant statement illustrates the fear of not knowing who we are and the sense of loss we sometimes feel in shedding ways in which we once organized our experience. It also suggests that who we are may be determined in part by who we take ourselves to be: that is, by our underlying (usually implicit) philosophies of what it is to be a continuing person. In other words, your conceptions of yourself guide the ways you experience yourself, which in turn may affect who you are. If you change the fundamental ways you conceptualize yourself, you may change yourself. Everyone agrees you are biology and psychology; perhaps you are also philosophy.

Many of the same questions that arise in the consideration of extraordinary phenomena, such as multiple personality disorder and Hilgard's hidden observer, also apply to ordinary people without dissociative disorders. We might wonder, then, whether normal healthy people have just one mind and are just one self. Puccetti, for instance, argues that the mental duality that becomes apparent after a commissurotomy is evidence of mental duality in ordinary humans even without commissurotomy. Others argue for a similar conclusion on the basis of nonsurgical dissociations such as those of Beauchamp and Sizemore (Eve). In the same vein, but somewhat more radically, the psychotherapist John Beahrs, who specializes in treating multiple personality disorder, suggests that we are all multiple personalities:

> . . . *we are now faced by an unavoidable and somewhat disquieting new datum about consciousness. In normal human individuals, at least while hypnotized, there may be two personalities or more, each with his own consciousness, of which the other part(s) may or may not be aware. As we recognize that boundaries between hypnosis and the usual waking state are fuzzy, if present at all, there is the likelihood that* consciousness occurs simultaneously at different levels within any human mind. [John Beahrs, Unity and Multiplicity, *New York: Brunner/Mazel, 1982, p. 28]*

Beahrs goes on to suggest that we each have the potential to exhibit multiplicity. This potential, according to him, implies the presence of several selves within us, even if they never emerge or if our normal conscious selves are never aware of them.

Stephen E. Braude (selection 10), on the other hand, questions the validity of drawing conclusions about the psychology of ordinary people based on multiple personality disorder. Braude claims that the way a self divides may be as much a function of what divides it as it is of the self's predissociative structure. For instance, many cases of multiple personality develop in response to sexual abuse during childhood. How the psyche divides seems a direct response to the threat posed by that abuse. Braude concludes that we can infer little, if anything, from the bizarre symptoms of multiple personality disorder about how minds are divided before those symptoms are exhibited. He labels attempts to make such inferences the "Humpty Dumpty fallacy."

Another way to approach the question of whether under normal circumstances each of us—each human organism—has just one mind is to ask whether there is enough disunity under normal circumstances to make each of us more than one. In other words, rather than inferring multiplicity in normal circumstances from multiplicity in multiple personality disorder, we can simply look at ourselves more closely than we ordinarily do to see whether there is multiplicity within us.

Some researchers are convinced that there is quite a bit of disunity within us. For instance, Ernest Hilgard begins his classic survey of dissociative phenomena, many of which—such as daydreaming—are part of our ordinary day-to-day consciousness, with the arresting sentence: "The unity of consciousness is an illusion." But is it? And what is the connection between disunity and multiplicity?

Jorge Luis Borges, in his short story "Borges and I," describes a fairly common type of dissociative experience:

> *The other one, the one called Borges, is the one things happen to. I walk through the streets of Buenos Aires and stop for a moment, perhaps mechanically now, to look at the arch of an entrance hall and the grillwork on the*

gate; I know of Borges from the mail and see his name on a list of professors or in a biographical dictionary. I like hourglasses, maps, eighteenth-century typography, the taste of coffee and the prose of Stevenson; he shares these preferences, but in a vain way that turns them into the attributes of an actor. It would be an exaggeration to say that ours is a hostile relationship; I live, let myself go on living, so that Borges may contrive his literature, and this literature justifies me. It is no effort for me to confess that he has achieved some valid pages, but those pages cannot save me, perhaps because what is good belongs to no one, not even to him, but rather to the language and to tradition. Besides I am destined to perish, definitely, and only some instant of myself can survive in him. Little by little, I am giving over everything to him, though I am quite aware of his perverse custom of falsifying and magnifying things. Spinoza knew that all things long to persist in their being; the stone eternally wants to be a stone and the tiger a tiger. I shall remain in Borges, not in myself (if it is true that I am someone), but I recognize myself less in his books than in many others or in the laborious strumming of a guitar. Years ago I tried to free myself from him and went from the mythologies of the suburbs to the games with time and infinity, but those games belong to Borges now and I shall have to imagine other things. Thus my life is a flight and I lose everything and everything belongs to oblivion, or to him.

I do not know which of us has written this page. [J. L. Borges, Labyrinths, *James E. Irby, trans., Donald Yates and James Irby, eds., New York: New Directions, 1962]*

Borges examines his experience from an introspective point of view. That is, he simply looks inside his own mind and reports what he finds: not a consciousness unified as one self, but rather two selves—one "private" and one "public." His private self watches and comments on his public self, but not vice versa. Each self has different likes and dislikes, different emotions, and different developmental histories. Thus, Borges's private self is like a separate personality, but one that is rarely shown to the world. His public self is like a role he plays, one which occupies center stage in the theater of life.

The distinction among selves that Borges describes is a pale shadow of multiple personality disorder. Yet it is not a disorder but, instead, a common feature of ordinary, day-to-day phenomenology, the way many normal, healthy people experience themselves and the world. Many people (perhaps also you) can identify analogues in their own experience to the dissociation Borges so beautifully expresses.

Finally, Nicholas Humphrey and Daniel C. Dennett (selection 11) formulate five criteria they claim must be satisfied for multiple personality disorder to be real. First, there is what we might called the "limited access" criterion: The subject must have at different times "different spokesmen" (or "selves") whose access to each other's mental states is as indirect and limited as is the access ordinary people have to each other's mental states. Second, there is the "ownership" criterion: Each self, when in executive control, must claim to be the sole owner of the organism's actions, experiences, and memories. Third, there is the "self-conviction" criterion: Each self must be convinced of its own integrity and personal importance. Fourth, there is the "persuasiveness" criterion: All else being equal, other people must also be convinced about each self's integrity and personal importance. Fifth, there is the "distinctiveness" criterion: Different selves must present themselves in distinctive ways.

Humphrey and Dennett claim there is considerable evidence that in at least some cases these five criteria have all been met. Although they admit this evidence is inconclusive, they nevertheless accept the reality of multiple personality disorder and go on to consider what implications its existence would have for the nature of the self. They think that selves are fictions in that they do not correspond to anything in the head. Selves help the organism to unify its understanding of itself and to interact socially with other people, but they are not real. The brain, according to Humphrey and Dennett, nominates candidates for the role of "Head of Mind" and then selects among these candidates on the basis of pragmatic need for a self that is "spokesman" for the organism as a whole. Sometimes there are tumultuous upheavals, revolutions, civil wars, and so on. In your own case, you—the conscious self now reading—have emerged as the winner, the brain's elected representative to the world of consciousness, self-understanding, and social interaction.

What, then, of our earlier question? Under normal circumstances, is each of us just one consciousness, one mind, one self? The answer is unclear. What is clear, however, is that our commonsense belief in our individual unities is a highly speculative theory. Knowing this can free us to invent alternative theories, some of which may bring us closer to the truth. Just acknowledging these theories as realistic alternatives to the ordinary ways we view ourselves can enrich not only our philosophies but also the ways we experience ourselves and the world.

Origins of Consciousness

1

JULIAN JAYNES
Consciousness and the Voices of the Mind

Few problems have had as interesting an intellectual trajectory through history as that of the mind and its place in nature. Before 1859, the year that Darwin and Wallace independently proposed natural selection as the basis of evolution, this issue was known as the mind/body problem with its various and sometimes ponderous solutions. But after that pivotal date, it came to be known as the problem of consciousness and its origin in evolution.

Now the first thing I wish to stress this afternoon is this problem. It is easy for the average layman to understand. But paradoxically, for philosophers, psychologists, and neurophysiologists, who have been so used to a different kind of thinking, it is a difficult thing. What we have to explain is the contrast, so obvious to a child, between all the inner covert world of imaginings and memories and thoughts and the external public world around us. The theory of evolution beautifully explains the anatomy of species, but *how* out of mere matter, mere molecules, mutations, anatomies, can you get this rich inner experience that is always accompanying us during the day and in our dreams at night? That is the problem we will consider in this symposium.

Previous Solutions

Previous solutions have been illusory. One of the most difficult but historically interesting (associated with philosophers such as Perry, 1912, or Whitehead, 1925) was a vague analogy that came to be called neo-realism. It seemed to be saying that because interacting matter could be reduced to mathematical relationships, in some ways like our own perceptions and interpersonal relationships, therefore consciousness originates in matter itself. Unfortunately, this much too abstract notion is having a bit of a renaissance today in a different way with some physicists because of some of the astonishing results in quantum physics (e.g., Wigner, 1972).

Another more popular solution was due to Darwin himself. In the last paragraph of *The Origin of Species* (Darwin, 1859), he implies that God created mind and body in the first primitive organisms and then both evolved in parallel together. But this sunk the problem in metaphysics, and it was soon realized that there should be some criterion of consciousness. It seemed obvious in the empiricist climate of the time that this was learning. So the question became: when did learning originate in evolution? Many people don't realize that the reason so many psychologists were studying animal learning, like maze-learning in rats, in the first two decades of this century, was to study animal consciousness on a primitive level and so trace out its evolution. As Dr. Witelson pointed out in her thoughtful introduction, this was indeed the focus of my early work for many years, but which I now see has nothing to do with consciousness. This error, I think, comes from John Locke and empiricism: The mind is a space where we have free ideas somehow floating around and that is consciousness. And when we perceive things in contiguity or contrast or some of the other so-called laws of association, their corresponding ideas stick together. Therefore, if you can show learning in an animal, you are showing the association of ideas which means consciousness. This is muddy thinking. I will be returning to this error in a moment.

Then, of course, there were other solutions — the helpless spectator theory of Huxley (1896), that consciousness just watched behaviour and could do nothing. But if that is true, why is it there at all? And so there followed emergent evolution, which was meant to save us from such a pessimistic view. It was most fully developed by Lloyd Morgan (1923), although the idea goes back to the 19th century. A simple example is water: If you take hydrogen and oxygen you can't derive the wetness of water from either. Wetness is an emergent. Similarly, when in evolution there is a certain amount of brain tissue, particularly cortical tissue, then suddenly you get consciousness. Consciousness is an emergent, underived from anything before. It is unfortunate that this vague and vacuous idea is also having a renaissance in the writings of some neuroscientists today. On analysis, it generates no hypotheses and tells us nothing about any processes involved. Emergent evolution is a label that bandages our ignorance.

What I shall now present is a different kind of solution and one that has surprised me in the wealth of specific and testable hypotheses which it generates, and surprised me in the directions into which my work has been forced. But first we must face squarely the question of what is consciousness. And as a preface to that, I will first outline a few things that consciousness is not.

What Consciousness Is Not

First, consciousness is not *all* of mentality. You know this perfectly well. There are so many things that the nervous system does automatically for us. All the variety of perceptual constancies — for example, size, brightness, colour, shape, which our nervous systems preserve under widely varying environmental changes of light, distance, angle of regard, or even our own moving about in which objects retain their same position, called location constancy — all done without any help from introspective consciousness.

So with another large class of activities that can be called *preoptive*, such as how we sit, walk, and move. All these are done without consciousness, unless we decide to be conscious of them — the preoptive nature of consciousness. Even in speaking, the role of consciousness is more *interpolative* than any constant companion to my words. I am not now consciously entering my lexical storehouse and consciously selecting items to string on these syntactic structures. Instead, I have what can best be described as intentions of certain meanings, what I call *structions*, and then linguistic habit patterns which take over without further input from my consciousness. Similarly, in hearing someone speak, what are you, the listeners, conscious of? If it were the flow of phonemes or even the next level up of morphemes or even words, you would not be understanding what I am intending.

Consciousness is sometimes confused even with simple sense perception. Historically, we inferred and abstracted ideas of sense perception from a realization of our sense organs, and then, because of prior assumptions about mind and matter or soul and body, we believed these processes to be due to consciousness—which they are not. If any of you still think that consciousness is a necessary part of the sense perception, then I think you are forced to follow a path to a *reductio ad absurdum*: you would then have to say that since all animals have sense perception, all are conscious, and so on back through the evolutionary tree even to one-celled protozoa because they react to external stimuli, or one-celled plants like the alga chlamydomonas with its visual system analogous to ours, and thence to even the amoeboid white cells of the blood since they sense bacteria and devour them. They too would be conscious. And to say that there are ten thousand conscious beings per cubic millimetre of blood whirling around in the roller-coaster of the vascular system in each of us here this afternoon is a position few would wish to defend.

That consciousness is in everything we do is an illusion. Suppose you asked a flashlight in a completely dark room to turn itself on and to look around and see if there were any light—the flashlight as it looked around would of course see light everywhere and come to the conclusion that the room was brilliantly lit when in fact it was mostly just the opposite. So with consciousness. We have an illusion that it is all mentality. If you look back into the struggles with this problem in the 19th century and early 20th century, this is indeed the error that trapped people into so much of the difficulty, and still does.

Second, consciousness does not copy experience. This further error about consciousness

stems from the beginning of empiricism when Locke (1690) spoke of the mind's "white paper, void of all characters, without any ideas" (*Essay* II, 1.2) on which experience is copied. Had the camera been around at the time, I suggest Locke would have used it instead of blank paper as his foundational metaphor. In experience, we take successive pictures of the world, immerse them in the developer of reflection, and watch concepts, memories, and all our mental furnishings come into existence.

But that consciousness does not copy experience can be shown very easily: (a) by examining the absence of memories that we should have if consciousness did copy experience, such as knowing what letters go with what numbers on telephones—although we have stared at the matter thousands of times, most of us cannot say—and countless other examples; or (b) by examining the memories we have and noting that they are not structured the way we experienced them, such as thinking of the last time you were in swimming—to take an example from Donald Hebb (1961). Most people, instead of thinking of the complicated visual, thermal, proprioceptive, respiratory experience as it actually was, tend to see themselves swimming from another point of view—a bird's-eye view perhaps—something of course they have never experienced at all. The conscious memory does not copy experience but reconstructs it as a must-have-been. This view is similar to some of the recent constructivist theories of memory.

Third, consciousness is not necessary for learning—which I referred to a moment ago as the mistake I laboured under for so long. If we look at the most primitive kinds of learning, such as Pavlovian conditioning, it occurs in preparations such as the hind leg of a beheaded cockroach for which no one would think that consciousness is plausible. And in humans not only does consciousness not assist in acquisition of conditional responses, it destroys conditioning once the human being is conscious of the contingencies (Razran, 1971).

Learning motor skills seems to happen without much consciousness as well. This was studied extensively in the 1920s in relation to telegraphy, stenography, and the like, occupations which were very important back then. The learning seemed to the subjects to be "organic" —that was one of their words. They were surprised that consciousness did not seem to enter into this learning the way they expected it might.

A more complicated kind of learning is instrumental learning, or operant conditioning, or we would call it learning solutions to problems. This is the old psychological problem called learning without awareness. Psychologists will remember the Greenspoon effect (Greenspoon, 1955) and some of the studies on the instrumental learning of little muscular movements without consciousness (Hefferline, Keenan, & Harford, 1959), and many others. It is more problematical than I can go into here, but I think that we can show that instrumental learning can occur without consciousness.

This is not to say that consciousness does not play a role in these different types of human learning. It does, as in decisions as to what to learn, or making rules of how to learn better, or consciously verbalizing aspects of a task. But this is not the learning itself. And my point is that consciousness is not necessary for learning to occur.

One could here bring up the well-known phenomenon of the automatization of habit; for when this happens to us, it seems that the task has required consciousness at the beginning; but as the habit is perfected, consciousness eases away and the task is performed effortlessly. This same smoothing out and increased rapidity of performance of a habit with practice is universal among all animals that learn. Generally, in this ubiquitous phenomenon, it is not necessarily or basically the lapsing of consciousness with improved performance so much as the lapsing of forced attention to components of the task. And attention, specifically external attention, which is the focusing of sense perception, is not necessarily conscious. Take two

coins in either hand, and toss them across each other until you learn to catch each with the opposite hand. This is a task that will take somewhere between 15 and 20 trials to learn. And if you wish to try this this evening, and monitor your consciousness while you are doing so, you will find that consciousness has little to do with the learning that seems to go on mechanically. You might be conscious of something about your clumsiness, or the silliness of what you are doing as you keep picking the coins up from the floor, until, at the point of success, your consciousness is somewhat surprised and even proud of your superior dexterity. It is the attention which has changed. Automatization is a diminution of attention, not of consciousness.

The fourth thing for which consciousness is not necessary, and it may seem rather paradoxical, is thinking or reasoning. Here we are getting into perhaps the major problem in this area: the definition of our terms, particularly terms such as thinking and reasoning. If we take the simplest definition of thinking, I think we can show indeed that consciousness is not necessary for it. This concerns one of the forgotten experiments of psychology. It is indeed so simple to us today that it seems silly. And yet to me it is as important in the history of psychology as the very complicated Michelson-Morley experiment is in the history of physics (Swenson, 1972). As the latter showed that the aether did not exist, setting the stage for relativity theory, so the experiment I am about to describe showed that thinking is not conscious, setting the stage for the kind of theorizing I am describing here.

The experiment I refer to was first done in 1901 by Karl Marbe, a graduate student at Würzberg (Marbe, 1901) back in a scientific world when consciousness was being intensively studied for the first time. Using his professors as subjects, each of whom had had extensive experience of experiments in introspection, he asked them to make a simple judgement between two identical-looking weights as to which was the heavier. Against the background of the experimental psychology of the time, the result was astonishing. There was no conscious content for the actual judgement itself, although such a judgement was embedded in the consciousness of the problem, its materials, and technique.

So began what came to be called the Würzberg School of Imageless Thought, which led through experiments by Ach, Watt, Kulpe, and others (see the discussions by Boring, 1929, Humphrey, 1951, or Murray, 1983) to concepts such as set, *aufgabe*, and determining tendency —which I have renamed *structions*. Structions are like instructions given to the nervous system, that, when presented with the materials to work on, result in the answer automatically without any conscious thinking or reasoning. And this phenomenon applies to most of our activities, from such simplicities as judging weights to solving problems to scientific and philosophical activity. Consciousness studies a problem and prepares it as a struction, a process which may result in a sudden appearance of the solution as if out of nowhere. During World War II, British physicists used to say that they no longer made their discoveries in the laboratory; they had their three B's where their discoveries were made—the bath, the bed, and the bus. And, as I have mentioned earlier, this process on a smaller scale is going on in me at present as I am speaking: my words are as if chosen for me by my nervous system after giving it the struction of my intended meaning.

Finally, in this list of misconceptions about consciousness, a word about its location. Most people, with possibly the present company excepted, who have thought long about the problem and so placed it 'out there' in the intellectual domain, tend to think of their consciousness, much as Descartes, Locke, and Hume did, as a space usually located inside their heads. Particularly when we make eye-to-eye contact, we tend to—in a subliminal way—infer such space in others. There is of course no such space whatever. The space of consciousness, which I

shall hereafter call *mind–space*, is a functional space that has no location except as we assign one to it. To think of our consciousness as inside our heads, as reflected in and learned from our words like introspection or internalization, is a very natural but arbitrary thing to do. I certainly do not mean to say that consciousness is separate from the brain; by the assumptions of natural science, it is not. But we use our brains in riding bicycles, and yet no one considers that the location of bicycle riding is inside our heads. The phenomenal location of consciousness is arbitrary.

To sum up so far, we have shown that consciousness is not all mentality, not necessary for sensation or perception, that it is not a copy of experience, nor necessary for learning, nor even necessary for thinking and reasoning, and has only an arbitrary and functional location. As a prelude to what I am to say later, I wish you to consider that there could have been at one time human beings who did most of the things we do—speak, understand, perceive, solve problems—but who were without consciousness. I think this is a very important possibility.

So far this is almost going back to a radical behaviourist position. But what then is consciousness, since I regard it as an irreducible fact that my introspections, retrospections, and imaginations do indeed exist? My procedure here will be to outline in a somewhat terse fashion a theory of consciousness and then to explain it in various ways.

What Consciousness Is

Subjective conscious mind is an analog of what we call the real world. It is built up with a vocabulary or lexical field whose terms are all metaphors or analogs of behaviour in the physical world. Its reality is of the same order as mathematics. It allows us to short-cut behavioural processes and arrive at more adequate decisions. Like mathematics, it is an operator rather than a thing or a repository. And it is intimately bound with volition and decision.

Consider the language we use to describe conscious processes. The most prominent group of words used to describe mental events are visual. We 'see' solutions to problems, the best of which may be 'brilliant' or 'clear' or possibly 'dull', 'fuzzy', 'obscure'. These words are all metaphors, and the mind–space to which they apply is generated by metaphors of actual space. In that space we can 'approach' a problem, perhaps from some 'viewpoint', and 'grapple' with its difficulties. Every word we use to refer to mental events is a metaphor or analog of something in the behavioural world. And the adjectives that we use to describe physical behaviour in real space are analogically taken over to describe mental behaviour in mind-space. We speak of the conscious mind as being 'quick' or 'slow', or of somebody being 'nimble-witted' or 'strong-minded' or 'weak-minded' or 'broad-minded' or 'deep' or 'open' or 'narrow-minded'. And so like a real space, something can be at the 'back' of our mind, or in the 'inner recesses' or 'beyond' our minds. But, you will remind me, metaphor is a mere comparison and cannot make new entities like consciousness. A proper analysis of metaphor shows quite the opposite. In every metaphor there are at least two terms, the thing we are trying to express in words, the *metaphrand,* and the term produced by a struction to do so, the *metaphier.* These are similar to what Richards (1936) called the tenor and the vehicle, terms more suitable to poetry than to psychological analysis. I have chosen metaphrand and metaphier instead to have more of the connotation of an operator by echoing the arithmetic terms of multiplicand and multiplier. If I say the ship plows the sea, the metaphrand is the way the bow goes through the water and the metaphier is a plow.

As a more relevant example, suppose a person, back in the time at the formation of our mental vocabulary, has been trying to solve some problem or to learn how to perform some task. To express his success, he might suddenly exclaim (in his own language), aha! I 'see' the solution. 'See' is the metaphier, drawn from the physical behaviour from the physical world, that is applied to this otherwise inexpressible mental occurrence, the metaphrand. But metaphiers usually have associations called *paraphiers* that project back into the metaphrand as what are called *paraphrands* and, indeed, create new entities. The word 'see' has associations of seeing in the physical world and therefore of space, and this space then becomes a paraphrand as it is united with this inferred mental event called the metaphrand.

$$\begin{array}{ccc} \text{metaphrand} & \!\!\rightarrow\!\! & \text{metaphier} \\ \| & & \downarrow \\ \text{paraphrand} & \!\!\leftarrow\!\! & \text{paraphier} \end{array}$$

In this way the spatial quality of the world around us is being driven into the psychological fact of solving a problem (which as I indicated needs no consciousness). And it is this associated spatial quality that, as a result of the language used to describe such psychological events, becomes, with constant repetition, this spatial quality of our consciousness or mind–space. This mind–space I regard as the primary feature of consciousness. It is the space which you preoptively are introspecting on at this very moment.

But who does the 'seeing'? Who does the introspecting? Here we introduce analogy, which differs from metaphor in that the similarity is between relationships rather than between things or actions. As the body with its sense organs (referred to as I) is to physical seeing, so there develops automatically an *analog 'I'* to relate to this mental kind of 'seeing' in mind–space. The analog 'I' is the second most important feature of consciousness. It is not to be confused with the self, which is an object of consciousness in later development. The analog 'I' is contentless, related I think to Kant's (1781) transcendental ego. As the bodily I can move about in its environment looking at this or that, so the analog 'I' learns to 'move about' in mind–space concentrating on one thing or another. If you 'saw' yourself swimming in our earlier example, it was your analog 'I' that was doing the 'seeing'.

A third feature of consciousness is *narratization*: the analogic simulation of actual behaviour. It is an obvious aspect of consciousness which seems to have escaped previous synchronic discussions of consciousness. Consciousness is constantly fitting things into a story, putting a before and an after around any event. This feature is an analog of our physical selves moving about through a physical world with its spatial successiveness which becomes the successiveness of time in mind–space. And this results in the conscious conception of time which is a *spatialized time* in which we locate events and indeed our lives. It is impossible to be conscious of time in any other way than as a space.

There are other features of consciousness which I shall simply mention: *concentration*, the 'inner' analog of external perceptual attention; *suppression*, by which we stop being conscious of annoying thoughts, the analog of turning away from annoyances in the physical world; *excerption*, the analog of how we sense only one aspect of a thing at a time; and *consilience*, the analog of perceptual assimilation; and others. In no way is my list meant to be exhaustive. The essential rule here is that no operation goes on in consciousness that was not in behaviour first. All of these are learned analogs of external behaviour.

Psychologists are sometimes justly accused of the habit of reinventing the wheel and making it square and then calling it a first approximation. I would demur from agreement that this is true in the development that I have just outlined, but I would indeed like to call it a first approximation. Consciousness is not a simple matter and it should not be spoken of as if it were. Nor have I mentioned the different modes

of narratization in consciousness such as verbal, perceptual, bodily, or musical, all of which seem quite distinct with properties of their own. But it is enough, I think, to allow us to go back to the evolutionary problem as I stated it in the beginning and which has caused so much trouble in biology, psychology, and philosophy.

When did all this 'inner' world begin? Here we arrive at the most important watershed in our discussion. Saying that consciousness is developed out of language means that everybody from Darwin on, including myself in earlier years, was wrong in trying to trace out the origin of consciousness biologically or neurophysiologically. It means we have to look at human history after language has evolved and ask when in history did an analog 'I' narratizing in a mind-space begin.

When did language evolve? Elsewhere (Jaynes, 1976a) I have outlined ideas of how language could have evolved from call modification, which has been called the 'Wahee, Wahoo model' and is at present in competition with several others (Maxwell, 1984). But such theorizing points to the late Pleistocene or Neanderthal era on several grounds: (1) such a period coincides with an evolutionary pressure over the last glacial period for verbal communication in the hunting of large animals; (2) it coincides with the astonishing development of the particular areas of the brain involved in language; and (3), what is unique in this theory, it corresponds to the archaeological record of an explosion of tool artifacts, for we know that language is not just communication, but also acts like an organ of perception, directing attention and holding attention on a particular object or task, making advanced tool-making possible. This dating means that language is no older than 50,000 years, which means that consciousness developed sometime between that date and the present (see chart on next page).

It is fortunate for this problem that by 3000 B.C., human beings have learned the remarkable ability of writing. It is therefore obvious that our

200,000 B.C.	language evolves		
40,000	tool explosion	⎤	Neanderthal
10,000	first gods	⎦	
9,000	first towns	⎤	Bicameral
3,000	writing begins	⎦	
1,000	divination, prophets, oracles	⎤	
0		├	Conscious
1,000			
2,000 A.D.		⎦	

first step should be to look at the early writings of mankind to see if there is evidence of an analog 'I' narratizing in a mind-space. The first writing is in hieroglyphics and cuneiform, both very difficult to translate, especially when they refer to anything psychological. And therefore we should go to a language with which we have some continuity, and that is of course Greek. The earliest Greek text of sufficient size to test our question is the Iliad. Are the characters in the Iliad narratizing with an analog 'I' in a mind-space and making decisions in this way?

The Bicameral Mind

First, let me make a few generalizations about the Iliad. To me and to roughly half of classicists, it is oral poetry, originally spoken and composed at the same time by a long succession of *aoidoi* or bards. As such, it contains many incongruities. Even after it was written down in about 800 B.C., perhaps by someone named Homer, it had many interpolations added to it even centuries later. So there are many exceptions to what I am about to say, such as the long speech of Nestor in Book XI for example, or the rhetorical reply of Achilles to Odysseus in Book IX.

But if you take the generally accepted oldest parts of the Iliad and ask, "Is there evidence of

consciousness?," the answer, I think, is no. People are not sitting down and making decisions. No one is. No one is introspecting. No one is even reminiscing. It is a very different kind of world.

Then, who makes the decisions? Whenever a significant choice is to be made, a voice comes in telling people what to do. These voices are always and immediately obeyed. These voices are called gods. To me this is the origin of gods. I regard them as auditory hallucinations similar to, although not precisely the same as, the voices heard by Joan of Arc or William Blake. Or similar to the voices that modern schizophrenics hear. Similar perhaps to the voices that some of you may have heard. While it is regarded as a very significant symptom in the diagnosis of schizophrenia, auditory hallucinations also occur in some form at some time in about half the general population (Posey & Losch, 1983). I have also corresponded with or interviewed people who are completely normal in function but who suddenly have a period of hearing extensive verbal hallucinations, usually of a religious sort. Verbal hallucinations are common today, but in early civilization I suggest that they were universal.

This mentality in early times, as in the Iliad, is what is called the *bicameral mind* on the metaphier of a bicameral legislature. It simply means that human mentality at this time was in two parts, a decision-making part and a follower part, and neither part was conscious in the sense in which I have described consciousness. And I would like to remind you here of the rather long critique of consciousness with which I began my talk, which demonstrated that human beings can speak and understand, learn, solve problems, and do much that we do but without being conscious. So could bicameral man. In his everyday life he was a creature of habit, but when some problem arose that needed a new decision or a more complicated solution than habit could provide, that decision stress was sufficient to instigate an auditory hallucination. Because such individuals had no mind-space in which to question or rebel, such voices had to be obeyed.

But why is there such a mentality as a bicameral mind? Let us go back to the beginning of civilization in several sites in the Near East around 9000 B.C. It is concomitant with the beginning of agriculture. The reason the bicameral mind may have existed at this particular time is because of the evolutionary pressures for a new kind of social control to move from small hunter–gatherer groupings to large agriculture-based towns or cities. The bicameral mentality could do this since it enabled a large group to carry around with them the directions of the chief or king as verbal hallucinations, instead of the chieftain having to be present at all times. I think that verbal hallucinations had evolved along with the evolution of language during the Neanderthal era as aids to attention and perseverance in tasks, but then became the way of ruling larger groups.

It can easily be inferred that human beings with such a mentality had to exist in a special kind of society, one rigidly ordered in strict hierarchies with strict expectancies organized into the mind so that such hallucinations preserved the social fabric. And such was definitely the case. Bicameral kingdoms were all hierarchical theocracies, with a god, often an idol, at their head from whom hallucinations seemed to

come, or, more rarely, with a human being who was divine and whose actual voice was heard in hallucinations.

Such civilizations start in various sites in the Near East and then spread into Egypt, later from Egypt into the Kush in southern Sudan and then into central Africa; while in the other geographical direction, they spread into Anatolia, Crete, Greece; and then into India and southern Russia; and then into the Malay Peninsula, where the ruins of another civilization have just been discovered in northern Thailand; then later into China. A millennium later, a series of civilizations begin in Mesoamerica leading up to the Aztec, and then partly independently and partly by diffusion another series of civilizations in the Andean highlands leading up to the Inca. And wherever we look there is some kind of evidence of what I am calling the bicameral mind. Every ancient historian would agree that all of these early civilizations are thoroughly religious, heavily dependent on gods and idols.

Where writing exists after 3000 B.C., we can see these bicameral civilizations much more clearly. In Mesopotamia the head of state was a wooden statue—wooden so it could be carried about—with jewels in its eyes, perfumed, richly raimented, imbedded in ritual, seated behind a large table (perhaps the origin of our altars) in the *gigunu*, which was a large hall in the bottom of a ziggurat. What we might call the king was really the first steward of this statue god. Cuneiform texts literally describe how people came to the idol–statues, asked them questions, and received directions from them. Just why the minds (or brains) of bicameral people needed such external props as idols for their voices is a question difficult to answer, but I suspect it had to do with the necessary differentiation of one god from another.

I also want to mention that evidence from written texts, personal idols, cylinder seals, and the construction of personal names suggests that every person had a personal god. In Mesopotamia, it was his *ili*, which in Hebrew is perhaps from the same root as Eli and Elhohim. In Egypt, the personal god which had the same function was called a *ka*, a word which has been an enigma in Egyptology until now.

In connection with the personal god, it is possible to suggest that a part of our innate bicameral heritage is the modern phenomenon of the 'imaginary' playmate. According to my own research as well as other data (Singer & Singer, 1984), it occurs in at least one-third of modern children between the ages of 2 and 5 years, and is believed now to involve very real verbal hallucinations. In the rare cases where the imaginary playmate lasts beyond the juvenile period, it too grows up with the child and begins telling him or her what to do in times of stress. It is therefore possible that this is how the personal god started in bicameral times, the imaginary playmate growing up with the person in a society of expectancies that constantly encouraged the child to hear voices and to continue to do so.

This, then, is the bicameral mind. I have not had time to discuss the variations between various bicameral theocracies, but all were based on strict and stable hierarchies as I have stressed. At least some of such civilizations could be compared to nests of social insects, where instead of the social control being by pheromones from a queen insect, it was by hallucinatory directions from an idol. Everything went like clockwork providing there was no real catastrophe or problem.

The Breakdown of the Bicameral Mind

But such a system is obviously precarious. The huge success of such agricultural bicameral civilizations inevitably leads to overpopulation and complexity, and given a time of social and political instability, bicamerality can break down like a house of cards. Some civilizations broke down frequently, as among the Mayans on this conti-

nent. A temple complex and city would be built up, last a few centuries, and then be completely abandoned, presumably because as the society became more and more populous, the voices did not agree anymore. Then after a few centuries as tribal bands, they would somehow get together again and another temple complex would be built up. This is why we find so many of these temple complexes that show evidence of their people suddenly leaving them.

In Egypt we find that the bicameral mind broke down between what is called the Old Kingdom and the Middle Kingdom, and then again between the Middle and the New Kingdom. The evidence for these dark, chaotic periods is in the hieroglyphic writings after they occurred.

But in Mesopotamia, which was the most stable civilization in the world, there does not seem to have been a breakdown until around 1400 B.C. In the graphics of the period, gods are no longer depicted. In some instances kings beg in front of empty gods' thrones—nothing like that had ever occurred before. Another line of evidence is in the cuneiform literature. There is an epic called the Epic of Tikulti-Ninurta where for the first time in history, gods are spoken of as forsaking human beings. The greatest literature of the period, which is possibly the origin of the Book of Job, is the *Ludlul Bel Nemequi*, the first readable lines of which translate as:

> *My god has forsaken me and disappeared,*
> *My goddess has failed me and keeps at a distance,*
> *The good angel who walked beside me has*
>   *departed.*

How similar to some of our Hebrew Psalms—Psalm 42, for example.

The reasons for this breakdown are several. The success of bicameral civilizations leads to overpopulation—as I have mentioned, and as is described in texts from the period. There are various huge catastrophes such as the Thera eruption, which is well known and may be the origin of Plato's myth of Atlantis. The ensuing *tsunami* crushed all the bicameral kingdoms around that part of the Mediterranean. Entire nations were destroyed or dislodged, resulting in large migrations of people invading other countries, looking for 'promised lands', a place to settle down with their gods again and start another bicameral civilization. One of the reasons that we still have problems in this area of the world, I think, goes right back to this chaotic time.

Another cause is writing itself, because once something is written you can turn away from it and it has no more power over you, in contrast to an auditory hallucination which you cannot shut out. Writing, particularly as used extensively in Hammurabi's hegemony, weakened the power of the auditory directions. The spread of writing, the complexities of overpopulation, and the chaos of huge migrations as one population invaded others: these are the obvious causes. And in this breakdown, various things started to happen, including I think the beginning of consciousness.

The immediate results of this loss of hallucinated voices giving directions are several and new in world history. The idea of heaven as where the gods have gone; the idea of genii or angels as messengers between heaven and earth; the idea of evil gods such as demons—all are new phenomena. By 1000 B.C., people in Babylon were walking around draped with amulets and charms which they wore to protect themselves from a huge variety of demons. Such charms have been found archeologically in the thousands dating from this period.

The Beginning of Consciousness

And then came the development of a new way of making decisions, a kind of proto-consciousness. All significant decisions previously had been based on the bicameral mind. But after its breakdown, after the hallucinated voices no longer told people what to do, there seem to have developed various other ways of discerning messages from the gods to make decisions. We call these methods divination. Throwing of lots, the simplest kind; putting oil on water and reading its patterns; dice; the movements of smoke; a priest whispering a prayer into a sacrificial animal, sacrificing it, and then looking at its internal organs to find out what the god intends. All of these were extensively and officially practised. And then the method of divination that is still around, astrology. It is remarkable to go back and read the cuneiform letters of kings to their astrologers and diviners of around 1000 B.C. (Pfeiffer, 1935). These cruel Assyrian tyrants, who are depicted in their bas-reliefs as grappling with lions and engaging in fierce lion hunts, are, in their letters, meek and frightened people. They don't know what to do. Astrologers tell them, "You cannot move out of your house for five days"; "You must not eat this"; "You should not wear clothes today"—extraordinary strictures that official diviners would interpret as what the gods meant. It is interesting to note that not only has astrology lasted, but it is being followed by more people at present than ever before.

If we now move over to Greece just following the period I have been referring to in Mesopotamia, we can trace the bicameral mind as shown in the Linear B Tablets, then going through the Iliad, the Odyssey, through the lyric and elegiac poetry of the next two centuries, as in Sappho and Archilochus, until we get to Solon in 600 B.C. Solon is the first person who seems like us, who talks about the mind in the same way we might. He is the person who said "Know thy-'self,'" although sometimes that's given to the Delphic Oracle. How can you know yourself unless you have an analog 'I' narratizing in a mind–space and reminiscing or having episodic memory about what you have been doing and who you are? In Greece, then, one can see in detail the invention and learning of consciousness on the basis of metaphor and analogy (as I have described above) by tracing out through these writings the change in words like *phrenes, kardia, psyche* (what I have called "preconscious hypostacies") from objective referents to mental functions.

The same kind of development has been studied in ancient China by Michael Carr of the University of Otaru. Comparing the four successive parts of the most ancient collection of texts, the *Shijing*, he found the same internalization process for such words as *Xin*, until they become the concept of mind or consciousness in China (Carr, 1983).

Another area of the world during this period where we can see this rise of consciousness is more familiar to most of you. This is among peoples who may have been refugees from the Thera eruption. The word for refugees in Akkad, the ancient language of Babylon, is the word *khabiru*, and this becomes our word Hebrew. The story of the Hebrews, or really one branch of the Hebrews, is told in what we call the Hebrew Testament or the Old Testament.

Those of you who know biblical scholarship will know that the Hebrew Testament is a patchwork of things put together around 600 B.C.—the date keeps coming forward. Using it as evidence is therefore something of a problem. But there are several ways of entering this mosaic of much-edited texts to test the theory, and here I shall mention only one. If we take the purer books, those that are not patchwork but are singly authored and that can be clearly and firmly dated, and compare the oldest with the most recent, such a comparison should reflect the differences in mentality we are referring to. The oldest of them is the Book of Amos, dating from about 800 B.C., and the most recent is the Book of Ecclesiastes, which comes from about 200 B.C.

I suspect that such prophets as Amos were those left-over bicameral or semi-bicameral persons in the conscious era who heard and could relay the voice of Yahweh with convincing authenticity, and who were therefore highly prized in their societies as reaching back to the secure authoritarian ways of the lost bicameral kingdom. Amos is not a wise old man but a shepherd boy brought in from the fields of Tekoa. Probably much of his life has been spent in the fields listening to older shepherds glorying in tales of Yahweh. Asked if he is a prophet, he does not even know what the word means. But periodically he bursts forth with "Thus sayest the Lord," as the King James Bible translates it, and out pours some of the most powerful passages in Jewish history with such an authenticity that he is always surrounded by scribes taking down his words.

Ecclesiastes is just the opposite. He begins by saying that "I *saw* in my heart that wisdom excelleth folly . . . "(2:13)—a metaphoric use of 'see'. Spatialized time is something that I have not dwelt upon, but I suggest it is one of the hallmarks of consciousness. We cannot think consciously of time apart from making a space out of it. And this is very much in evidence in Ecclesiastes as, for example, in that oft-quoted but still beautiful hymn to time that begins the third chapter: "For everything there is a season, and a time for every matter under heaven, a time to be born, and a time to die" and so on, with times like spaces for everything. Historically, we could go further into the New Testament and note the even greater importance of conscious internalization and changing behaviour from within in contrast to Mosaic law that shaped behaviour from without.

Four Ideas

I can sum up what I have said so far as three major ideas about the origin of consciousness. The first concerns the nature of consciousness itself and that it arises from the power of language to make metaphors and analogies. The second idea is the hypothesis of the bicameral mind, an early type of mentality. I think the evidence for its existence is unmistakable. Apart from this idea, there is the problem of explaining the origin of gods, the origin of religion and the huge, strange pageant of religious practices in the back corridors of time that is so apparent with a psychological study of history. The bicameral mind offers a possibility to tie it all together and to provide a rationale for it. The third idea is that consciousness followed the bicameral mind. I have placed the date somewhere between 1400 B.C. and 600 B.C. This is a long period and that date may have to be adjusted. But I believe this to be a good approximation.

I would add here that there is a weak form of the theory. It says that consciousness could have begun shortly after the beginning of language or perhaps at certain times and places. After all, people could create metaphors at the beginning of oral language—that is how language grew. Consciousness could have originated in exactly the same way as I have described, and existed for a time in parallel with the bicameral mind. Then the bicameral mind is sloughed off at approximately 1000 B.C. for the reasons I have suggested, leaving consciousness to come into its own. This would provide easy *ad hoc* explanations for highly developed cultures such as Sumer which otherwise are a challenge to bicameral theory. But I do not choose to hold this weak theory because it is almost unfalsifiable. I think we should have a hypothesis that can be disproved by evidence if we are going to call it a scientific hypothesis. Also the strong theory has a vigorous explanatory power in understanding many historical phenomena of the transition period. Further, I do not see why there would be a need for consciousness alongside of the bicameral mind if the latter made the decisions.

A fourth idea that I shall end with is a neurological model for the bicameral mind. I want to stress, however, that it is not at all a necessary part of the theory I have presented. Since the bicameral mind was so important in history,

responsible for civilization, what could have been going on in the brain? The proper strategy in trying to answer such a question is to take the simplest idea and set about to disprove it. If it is disproved, you then go on to something more complicated.

The simplest idea, obvious I think to anyone, would involve the two cerebral hemispheres. Perhaps in ancient peoples—to put it in a popular fashion—the right hemisphere was "talking" to the left, and this was the bicameral mind. Could it be that the reason that speech and language function are usually just in the areas of the left hemisphere in today's people was because the corresponding areas of the right hemisphere once had another function? That is a somewhat questionable way to say it, because there are other reasons for the lateralization of function. But on the other hand, it raises issues that I like. What *is* an auditory hallucination? Why is it ubiquitous? Why present in civilizations all over the world?

If we assume that back in bicameral times all admonitory information was being processed in some proportion of the billions of neurons of the right hemisphere, and there stored, particularly in what corresponds to Wernicke's area in the posterior temporal lobe, until it needed to be accessed, how do such complicated processed admonitions get transferred across the cerebral commissures to the left or dominant hemisphere? And what if, as I have supposed (Jaynes, 1976b), the far, far fewer fibres of the anterior commissure that connects regions of the two temporal gyri are the ones involved? And in fact, recent experimental evidence with monkeys indicates that intercommunication of major parts of the temporal lobes is via the anterior commissure (Jouandet, Garey, & Lipp, 1984). The transfer of such information would be more efficiently done if it were put into some kind of code. And what better code is there than human language? So, would it not be interesting if indeed what might correspond to Wernicke's area in the right temporal lobe might be the area that was involved in storing up admonitory information, processing it in such a way that it produced answers to problems and decisions (which is what the bicameral mind is), and then used the code of language to get it across to the left hemisphere, the hemisphere that speaks, obeys, and manages behaviour?

At the time that I was thinking in this primitive fashion, in the early 1960s, there was little interest in the right hemisphere. Even as late as 1964, some leading neuroscientists were saying that the right hemisphere did nothing, suggesting it was like a spare tire. But since then we have seen an explosion of findings about right hemisphere function, leading, I am afraid, to a popularization that verges on some of the shrill excesses of similar discussions of asymmetrical hemisphere function in the latter part of the 19th century (see Harrington, 1985) and also in the 20th century (see Segalowitz, 1983).

But the main results, even conservatively treated, are generally in agreement with what we might expect to find in the right hemisphere on the basis of the bicameral hypothesis. The most significant such finding is that the right hemisphere is the hemisphere which processes information in a synthetic manner. It is now well known from many studies that the right hemisphere is far superior to the left in fitting together block designs (Kohs Block Design Test), parts of faces, or musical chords (see Bryden, 1982; Segalowitz, 1983). The chief function of the admonitory gods was indeed that of fitting people and functions into these societies. I am suggesting that much of the difference we can observe today between hemisphere function can be seen as echoing the differences between the two sides of the bicameral mind.

In summary, I would like to again repeat these four ideas or modules of the theory I have presented. First is the nature of consciousness and its origin in language, which can be empirically studied in the learning of consciousness in children, as well as in the study of changes of consciousness in recent history. The second idea is the bicameral mind, which can be studied directly in ancient texts and indirectly in modern schizophrenia. Third is the idea that consciousness followed bicamerality, which can be studied in the artifacts and texts of history. And the fourth is that the neurological model for the bicameral mind is related to the two hemispheres. And this can be studied in laterality differences today.

What I have tried to present to you is a long and complicated story. It leaves us with a different view of human nature. It suggests that what civilized us all is a mentality that we no longer have, in which we heard voices called gods. Remnants of this are all around us in our own lives, in our present-day religions and needs for religion, in the hallucinations heard particularly in psychosis, in our search for certainty, in our problems of identity. And we are still in the arduous process of adjusting to our new mentality of consciousness. The final thought I will close with is that all of this that is most human about us, this consciousness, this artificial space we imagine in other people and in ourselves, this living within our reminiscences, plans, and imaginings, all of this is indeed only 3,000 years old.

And that, ladies and gentlemen, is less than 100 generations. And from that I think we can conclude that we are all still very young. Thank you very much.

Open Discussion

(From audience): I would just like to raise a terminological question. Do you make any essential difference between the word "consciousness" and the word "self-consciousness"?

Jaynes: Absolutely. Consciousness should not be equated with self-consciousness. There are at least three senses of the term. Self-consciousness has a trivial sense of embarrassment, or fear of what others may think of you, which I am sure is not what you mean. A second and most important sense is the consciousness of self as in answering the question "Who am I?" The self is the answer. It is an entity or structure of attributes given by our culture and imbedded in our language that is learned into our personal history which we infer from two sources: what other people tell us we are and what we infer from our own behaviour. Many recent experiments in social psychology provide evidence for this statement. The self is not in any sense the analog 'I' which is contentless. The self is an object of consciousness, not consciousness itself. As such, the self is not a stable construction, but changes dramatically through history and among nations, as well as in child development and even over the course of a day, depending on one's excerpts and how one narratizes them.

But here, as in many topics relating to mind, we must carefully locate those fuzzy areas of polyreferential confusion where what seems to be the same word is used to denote two or more quite different referents. Thus self properly is the psychological self I have just described. But the word is also used in trivial reflexive senses as when we say "the word itself" or say that "a fly washes itself." And an extension of that usage occurs when we say we see ourselves in a mirror. We don't. We see and recognize our bodies or our faces, not our selves. When pigeons (Epstein, Lanza, & Skinner, 1981) or chimpanzees (Gallup, 1970) are taught to recognize their bodies (note how much easier it would be to say "themselves" and how erroneous!) in mirrors, it has nothing to do with consciousness or self-awareness in its human sense. When such a chimp, because of its mirror training, rubs off a spot on its head it has seen in the mirror, it may be no different

essentially from rubbing off a spot on its arm without a mirror (see Jaynes, 1978).

There is a third sense of self-consciousness that occurs mostly in philosophical discussions and is a rather musty way of indicating self-observation of our own thinking or introspection. Such introspection is one type of narratization in which consciousness—and you remember I called it an operator as in mathematics—is operating twice. We are conscious of our own consciousness. Consider a schoolboy taking an exam fantasizing a romantic daydream about a girl across the aisle. Then when someone makes a noise, perhaps, or he notices a physiological reaction incongruous with the situation, he suddenly realizes he is daydreaming and must stop and return to the exam if he is to pass. Here is consciousness operating twice. From the schoolboy's point of view, it can be diagrammed as:

$$\text{'I'} \rightarrow \text{(me and girl together)}$$

which changes to:

$$\text{'I'} \rightarrow [\text{'I'} \rightarrow \text{(me and girl together)}]$$

and so ceases, where 'I' in single quotes always stands for the analog 'I' and the arrows for those analog abilities designated as narratization.

It is an extremely functional process, making us able to prevent ourselves from being commandeered by fantasy—as happens in dreams. Conscious processes and content are introspectable (which is being conscious of our own consciousness), and even sometimes introspection itself (which is being conscious of being conscious of being conscious). As such, introspection can be used as a denotative definition of consciousness, that is, a definition by pointing at it. But we must not make the mistake of thinking that all consciousness is introspective because it is introspectable.

Is there a more objective way of pointing out consciousness?

Jaynes: Right now let us take any ten people out there on the street and ask them when they next hear a clock strike to tell us all what they had been thinking of in the previous minute. The resulting reports are the basic material of consciousness and what we are trying to understand. That is bedrock and an objective denotative definition of consciousness. It is an experiment I do with my class each year.

I think this is a related question. Some people would say that consciousness is all awareness, while you are just talking about self-awareness. Could you comment?

. . . Am I just talking about self-awareness? The more precise term here is self-consciousness, which I think is what you mean. The question then becomes similar to the last part of the first question where I noted that all consciousness, while being phenomenally located internally, is not self-consciousness. I can be worried about what my young daughter is doing staying out after midnight again. That is certainly consciousness, certainly narratizing in mind-space, and I think of it as going on in me— even though such phenomenal location is arbitrary—but I can't see how that could be called self-consciousness or self-awareness.

Now, as to those who wish to call consciousness all awareness, what could that mean? Probably consciousness as I have described it plus all sense perception. This is very deceptive, and it gets back to the question I mentioned in my talk: Is sense perception consciousness?

First of all, consciousness is not necessary for sense perception. We must be crystal clear about that. You can notice this in your everyday life, all the countless things you do when you are thinking of something else, very obviously being guided by hosts of perceptions. And if you do still hold that consciousness is necessary for perception, you will have to carry it over into animal behaviour and down the evolutionary tree— as I meant to emphasize in my lecture—until you will have to impute consciousness to protozoa, since they react to objects and so have sense perceptions, and so to the white blood cells circulating right now in your body. To me that is a *reductio ad absurdum*.

Second, while sense perception is not due to consciousness, we are of course conscious of what we perceive. Consciousness, this narratizing in a mind–space, would be useless otherwise. I perceive the blackboard. So can an animal. But I can be conscious of the blackboard as I perceive it, a kind of extra dimension that a sub-human animal does not have. But that is a poor example. It is difficult to hold one's consciousness steadily on a perception—like a Zen meditation discipline. If I try to keep conscious of the blackboard, I lose it quickly: I start narratizing around it, noting its location, thinking of what is written on it, remembering other blackboards, wondering how it's made nowadays, and so forth. What is more, I think I can be conscious of the blackboard more easily by closing my eyes. Perception often can be slightly inhibiting to consciousness.

I think I agree that consciousness and perception should be separated and that they have been squeezed together by many psychologists. But why do you think this is so?

Jaynes: There are several reasons. The simplest is that consciousness as I said is an analog of external perception and so is easily mistaken for perception. After all, it is mapped onto sense perception almost as its template. We can 'perceive' an idea or a subtlety using the same word as perceiving a tree. Sharing the same terminology, it is no wonder the two kinds of perception are confused.

Another reason is that even the casual use of mental words inappropriately can produce convictions in us that are quite mistaken, and this goes on non-consciously. If a boxer is knocked out, we might say, lacking a better word, that he is knocked unconscious. This automatically and irrationally gets us to assume that everything before the punch was conscious—which we know is untrue. It's as if having a blackout in a city means that everything in the city is white. We should say the boxer is knocked unreactive or senseless.

Language also plays this trick on us when we try to describe animal behaviour. If a moth keeps flying into that light up there, and someone asks us, "Is the moth aware of the light?," we might say "Yes," lacking a better word. The moth is aware of the light, which translates for some people into consciousness, spiraling us back into the same confusion. The proper description is that the moth flies into the light and nothing more. No projected internality, please. It is reflex machinery.

And a further reason is strictly academic history. So-called experimental psychology was begun in Germany by physicists and physiologists who were strict metaphysical dualists (even if some of them called themselves pan-psychists) and who knew and cared nothing about the evolutionary problem or animal behaviour or human behaviour for that matter. Their perspective is therefore very distorted. Fechner, a physicist, is an excellent example. By studying just-noticeable differences in stimulus intensity, pitch, or brightness, he thought he was studying the elements of consciousness and so relating the universe of mind and the universe of matter, as in the famous Weber-Fechner Law. And this led into what William James—whose emphasis you remember was so opposite, on the *stream* of consciousness—called the

dreary wasteland of psychophysics. Even today some students of perception suppose they are studying consciousness when they are simply studying perception—which we share with all animals.

Some modern philosophers make that mistake as well.

Jaynes: I imagine it is because of the artificial analytic traditions begun in 1920 by two Cambridge friends, G. E. Moore (1922) and Bertrand Russell, about what used to be called sense data: consciousness sits in its space in the head waiting to be fed sense data through the apertures of the sense organs. When Russell (1921, 1927), looking for an example of consciousness, simply says, "I see a table," that is a highly artificial choice, and really incorrect reporting. It is not "I see a table" but his knowing he sees a table that is what he is really meaning. It is his consciousness of seeing a table that he is talking about, not the bare perception. This can be diagrammed thus:

$$'I' \rightarrow I \text{ see a table}$$

Russell thought his consciousness was the second term alone, where really it was both. He was being conscious of the perception as part of an argument. Russell should have selected a more ethologically valid example that was really true of his consciousness, that had really happened, such as "I think I will rewrite the *Principia* now that Whitehead's dead," or "How can I afford the alimony for another Lady Russell?" He would then have come to other conclusions. Such examples are consciousness in action. "I see a table" is not.

Let me give another hypothetical example from our ten subjects out there in the street. Suppose one of our subjects was hurrying to an intersection just as the light turned red against her. Her consciousness indeed would have recognized she had to stop at the red light. If she crossed she would be jay-walking, which is wrong. And she remembers she is a good person. Except she shouldn't have stopped for that fudge sundae—and with walnuts on top too! And now she might be late getting home, because there goes the clock, and now invalided Cousin Sally will be worrying I've been in an accident. Punishment for breaking my diet. I'm sure the police have made this particular red light longer than it used to be, probably just to be mean to me—and to poor Cousin Sally. Oh! There it turns green. Nothing less than all that and more.

And so if a psychologist or a philosopher comes along and says consciousness is awareness or sensation, and "seeing the red light" is a good example of consciousness, it is as absurd as saying a B-flat is a good example of a symphony. Seeing a red light cues consciousness; the sensation is a node between one conscious string and another.

I hope some of you will try that experiment tomorrow of monitoring your consciousness when you hear a clock strike. See if you have just been thinking of a perception.

I could add that even Watson and the early behaviourists would agree with my point here. In saying that consciousness does not exist, they certainly did not mean sense perception.

Are you a behaviourist in animal behaviour?

Jaynes: I am a strict behaviourist up to 1000 B.C. when consciousness develops in the one species that has a syntactic language, namely, ourselves.

Was there humour in the bicameral period?

Jaynes: There was jeering at individuals who do something different from expectation in the bicameral world, shaming them. It is a method of social control that has its parallel in other social mammals' ostracism of an aberrant member of the group or as children on a playground may mock a child who is different. It is not humour in our sense. It is

usually cruel and it is usually excluding somebody from the group. The theory I am working on is that this is what humour grew out of as human beings became conscious. We today have clowns and comics who almost always are portraying people we don't respect for various reasons. We are really excluding such portrayals from ourselves as we laugh at them, and we like to do this in a group, suggesting its ancient innate origin of social ostracism. But I haven't traced it out with any thoroughness. It is an excellent problem for research.

Did everyone hear the gods?

Jaynes: Yes, I think so. Except possibly the deaf. But deaf bicameral people may have had visual hallucinations of gods directing them by gesture, even as modern deaf schizophrenics often do (Rainer, Abdullah, & Altshuler, 1970).

But perhaps you meant to ask if it wasn't just the leaders that heard the gods. The literary data that we have historically is indeed mostly about leaders or important people. But there are other kinds of evidence that show that everyone heard gods. Idols used to facilitate hallucinations were everywhere and of all sizes, not just in palaces and temples. Ordinary people had idols, and idols were buried with them. In some excavations of cities, every family dwelling had a shrine. Thousands of cylinder seals from many sites in Mesopotamia show a person being led by his personal god into the presence of a higher god. Then we have the names of ordinary people that have the name of their god imbedded into their name. *Kainesut,* which translates as "the King is my *ka*," is an Egyptian common name that in bicameral theory means "I hear the King telling me what to do." I think everybody fitted into these hierarchical, tightly knit organizations because everybody did indeed hear voices that controlled them.

Did the role of conscience change between the bicameral period and consciousness?

Jaynes: In one sense, the bicameral mind was conscience, hearing what to do from gods, but the idea of conscience today is like a faint and wayward echo of it. I have been surprised recently to find that conscience in this sense is a relatively modern notion, having been begun, I think, by Thomas Aquinas in the 13th century as practical moral reasoning, and then heavily emphasized by Calvin in the 16th century as an innate subjective model of moral revelation. In the 17th century, the King James translators of the New Testament, no doubt influenced by Calvin, translate *Suneidesis* as "conscience" when it should probably be "consciousness." But it is not until the beginning of Romanticism with Rousseau that "conscience" becomes "divine instinct" and "the voice of the soul." It is interesting that this occurs just as poetry is beginning to turn back to some bicameral-like admirations (see Weissman, 1979, 1982).

I remember as a young boy asking my mother how I could tell the difference between right and wrong. She told me softly to listen to my conscience. I tried but nothing ever happened. I concluded that either I was too wicked to have a conscience or too good to need one. I have been wavering between these two positions ever since.

How about the pyramids of Egypt? Surely the pharaohs who built them as their tombs were thinking ahead to their afterlife, and that would be consciousness.

Jaynes: This is what is called the presentist fallacy. You are phrasing the situation as if ancient Egyptians were like ourselves. They were not. The pharaohs of 250 B.C. did not build the pyramids for themselves. You must remember that the volition of a bicameral person was his auditory hallucination or god, and so the volition of each pharaoh was

Osiris, the chief god, who was his *ka* or bicameral voice. Osiris commands the building of the pyramids to his glory in the same way that a millennium later Yahweh with great architectural detail commands Moses to build an ark and a tabernacle to his glory (Exodus 25–27), or as the Greek earth goddess, Demeter, commands that a temple be built at Eleusis to her glory (Homeric Hymn to Demeter, lines 271ff.), or in many other examples. In Egypt, however, when the pharaoh dies — as we would call the process — he is absorbed into his *ka* and then both are absorbed into Osiris as is depicted many times on funerary walls — even perhaps as Jesus after his resurrection is absorbed into the unified Trinity (Jaynes, 1979).

What about pain? Pain is certainly conscious and ancient people and animals surely feel pain!

Jaynes: Most pain theorists today agree that there are two fundamental types of pain in ourselves, variously called acute and chronic, nocioceptive and operant, or sensory and functional. In our work this same distinction is between sensory pain with its associated pain behaviours and conscious pain (Jaynes, 1985), and they follow each other in history. Animals and bicameral people just have the former; we always have a combination of both. We have sensory pain and also are conscious of it, fear it, recruit it, extend it out, amplify it with our conscious concern, interact with it, re-enact it. Using this distinction, one can enter into a greater understanding of many human pain phenomena such as the effectiveness of placebos, some phantom limb pain, and chronic pain for which no neural basis can be found. Pain in ourselves is always a complex interaction between the physical stimulus that causes pain behaviour and the conscious reactive component to which we might call the conscious suffering.

Before a child can use language, does this mean that the child is not conscious?

Jaynes: Yes. The idea of consciousness that I have just presented should be tested out in child development. My students and I are trying to do that at Princeton. One needs language for consciousness. We think consciousness is learned by children between two and a half and five or six years in what we can call the verbal surround, or the verbal community as B. F. Skinner calls it. It is an aspect of learning to speak. Mental words are out there as part of the culture and part of the family. A child fits himself into these words and uses them even before he knows the meaning of them. A mother is constantly instilling the seeds of consciousness in a two- and three-year-old, telling the child to stop and think, asking him "What shall we do today?" or "Do you remember when we did such and such or were somewhere?" And all this while metaphor and analogy are hard at work. There are many different ways that different children come to this, but indeed I would say that children without some kind of language are not conscious.

If you ask a person what he was thinking about yesterday, would this be something that did not ever happen in the bicameral world?

Jaynes: It would not happen in the bicameral world. Supposing I asked you what you were thinking of five minutes ago, I think you would find it difficult to reply. You have to tag these things in the time domain to remember them. There was not any such thing in the bicameral world, no spatialized time in which we locate lives and actions. This idea of reminiscent memory, what Tulvig (1983) calls episodic memory, is built on consciousness. You don't find a bicameral Achilles saying things like "When I was a child" or "Back in Greece what did I do at this time?" or anything of that sort. The bicameral world goes on in a relatively continual present.

I should add that of course bicameral people knew, *non-consciously knew*, where they were, had come from, and were going, and what they were doing over a short time frame. So does a dog or a pigeon over a short time. Otherwise no behaviour could be completed. This particular time frame is what William James and others have called the specious present (James, 1890, pp. 609ff.). That is a much more primitive type of immediate and non-conscious retention which all vertebrates and many invertebrates have as well, and appears to be very carefully evolved to vary for particular behaviours.

Now add to that for bicameral man the use of language as a retention device. Having verbal formulae or rote epithets, such as "the war-loving Danaans" or "the horse-taming Trojans" or "much-enduring godlike Odysseus" (all examples from the Iliad) for peoples, persons, places, or gods, gave him a much greater capacity for these immediate knowledges by cuing off these verbal associations.

The bicameral epics themselves, composed by formulae and by rote from generation to generation, can be viewed as retention devices and a huge step toward episodic or reminiscent memory. But it is only with consciousness, of course, with its spatialized time in which events can be located, that we achieve remembering in its full sense.

In the model here, does one side of the brain have the attributes of consciousness, since it is making the decisions in terms of the voices of the gods sending it over to the left side?

Jaynes: Narratization, but not with an analog 'I', seems to have taken place in the right hemisphere, since I have assumed the early epic narratives are right hemispheric (Jaynes, 1976b). Therefore some of the attributes of consciousness begin, if this model is correct, in the right hemisphere. That is a very perceptive question and one which needs to be explored, particularly in relation to the previous question.

Do you think there might not be some sculptors, painters, and particularly composers who would dispute the idea that language is required for consciousness?

Jaynes: The assumption of your question, I think, is that consciousness is necessary for art and music. I don't think so. There was a great deal of art and music in the non-conscious bicameral world, all originated by those neural organizations and resulting cognitions called gods. Texts specifically refer to gods dictating how idols are to be carved or buildings built. Look at the meticulous detail that Yahweh goes into in building the ark or the tabernacle in Exodus that I just mentioned. If you talk to composers and painters today, and I have on these matters, many of them don't have the feeling that consciousness is doing the composing or painting any more than consciousness is giving me the words I am presently speaking. As I mentioned in my talk, I am narratizing an intention in consciousness, what I have called a struction, and then the words just come. So in artistic expression of any kind. I have just received a letter from a contemporary composer who asked me if he is schizophrenic because he simply hears his music and transcribes it.

That isn't quite what I meant. I meant that consciousness doesn't seem to be all language.

Jaynes: I understand you now. Yes, the content of consciousness is far from being all language. You or I can right now imagine a triangle in mind–space, colour it red, and even slowly turn it around in our consciousness. There is nothing linguistic in that. But it takes language to get us there, to set it up in our imagination. I did not mean that everything in consciousness is made up of language. Language creates a mind–space on the basis of metaphor and analogy in which you are 'seeing' the triangle, as well as the

analog 'I' which is doing the 'seeing'. The particular things you are conscious of, music, sculpture, triangles, are often not linguistic at all. . . .

How do you define thought and feeling?

Jaynes: Both of these terms are polyreferential, as are most words for mental acts. I would like to use "thought" just for consciousness, for what we are doing in consciousness at any time. But usually this involves a non-conscious substrate that is solving structions on an almost continuous basis. Most people would call that thinking. I use thought loosely and not as a technical term.

"Feeling," however, I do try to use technically — by which I mean with a precise referent. And perhaps I shouldn't because it has several other referents, the most prominent of which have to do with touching and believing, which I feel are entirely separate. In a theory of emotions that I have proposed elsewhere (Jaynes, 1982), I suggest that we, like other mammals, start with a complex of evolved basic affects that, with the advent of consciousness, become the basis of our feelings. That is, a feeling is the consciousness of an affect, thus stretching it out in time and making it difficult to get rid of. So around 700 B.C. in Greece shame becomes guilt; fear, anxiety; anger, hatred; and so on. And, as I mentioned before, pain becomes suffering. The evidence for these changes is in the dramatic transformations of behaviour and customs in the first millennium B.C. This is what I have called the two-tiered theory of emotions.

You said — this was in connection with imaginary playmates — that the bicameral mind was innate. Why then aren't we all bicameral?

Jaynes: Innate does not mean inevitable. It means an inborn potentiality that can be made actual in a particular environment. It is the distinction between genotype and phenotype. The social, verbal, behavioural environment of a child today and the peer pressure to be and think like other children does not encourage or reward a child in a bicameral direction. Back before 1000 B.C., that social, verbal, behavioural environment plus peer pressure would encourage the child's imaginary playmate towards the status of a person god and a full-fledged bicameral mind.

To say this another way: A child from bicameral times brought up in our culture would be normally conscious, while a modern child if brought up in the Ur of 3000 B.C. under the sovereignty of Marduk in his *giginu* in the great ziggurat would be bicameral.

I still can't believe all this, saying that ancient people are not conscious like we are. How can you prove it?

Jaynes: There are really two questions there. First is the difficulty of believing ancient people were not conscious. I certainly understand the problem, which is why in my book I call it "preposterous" (Jaynes, 1976b, p. 84), for so it seems at first. The reason it seems preposterous is because of all the everyday functioning we have packed into our concept of consciousness, thinking of it as all perception, all mentality. That is why I spent so long at the beginning in trying to straighten out the term to its true and original meaning.

To say this another way, we tend to infer that anything that acts like us is conscious because the inference of consciousness in others is so habitual, going on not only in all our social life but in consciousness itself as we narratize about our relationships. It is very difficult to suspend that habit of projecting consciousness in thinking about ancient civilizations or even in animals close to us or even in newborn infants.

The second question was how can it be proved. To stretch a comparison, I can imagine someone back in 1859 complaining to Darwin that it is preposterous to say that species were created by chance and natural selection

without any purpose whatever. Look at all the evidence for the purposiveness of God's creation—everywhere! It can't be chance and selection. How can you prove it?

The answer in both cases, evolutionary theory and bicameral theory, is to try to state the hypothesis as clearly and factually as you can, and then evaluate how the data, all the data you can find, may fit in. For evolutionary theory, we look at the fossil record and current situations of speciation where we can observe them; for bicameral theory, we look at ancient texts and artifacts and current mental phenomena as they may be illuminated by the theory. In both cases the theory must explain the data more completely and parsimoniously than any alternative.

Do you think you have done that?

Jaynes: I know of no alternative of equal explanatory power that maps on to all the evidence. But it is only a beginning. I know there will have to be adjustments and revisions. There is so much left to do. So much more sheer theoretical analysis of consciousness itself, particularly of narratization that covers so much so thinly, so much more accurate translations of ancient texts, so much in studying the development of consciousness in children, a taboo subject for so long, or the variety of mentalities in hunter–gatherer groups, all of whom have partly learned consciousness by now in their contacts with civilizations. But I think it is an opening in the right direction into which psychology should go.

How did you come to this theory?

Jaynes: How do I narratize my arrival at these views? As one who had gone down many blind alleys in search of the origin of consciousness in lower species with simpler nervous systems, until I realized more and more that I—and most others who had preceded me on such a quest—were confused in a way we did not understand. So I decided to change directions and attempt to trace back in human history the mind–body problem as a way of alleviating that confusion. I traced it back until it disappeared in some of the works ascribed to Aristotle, then in some of the pre-Socratics, and then vanished in the Iliad. What did that mean? I then felt for a long time like someone in a dark room, stumbling about, bumping into strange unrecognized objects while feeling for a light switch or chain, not even knowing if there was a light. And then it happened and the light went on. Consciousness is learned on the basis of language, and right at that time — at least in the strong form of the theory. And so many things were suddenly clear. It was not biologically evolved. Other ideas about the metaphoric nature of consciousness, which I had been harbouring for a long time, joined up with that and the theory began.

What are dreams in this theory?

Jaynes: Dreams are consciousness operating primarily on neural reactivations primarily during REM (rapid eye movement) sleep. (And let us remember that the presence of REM does not necessarily indicate dreaming.) The same features of consciousness that function in waking life function in dreams as well: narratization, the analog 'I', mind–space, excerption, and particularly that feature of consciousness not so noticeable when awake because it's so automatic, consilience (what I call in my book conciliation — consilience is Whewell's, 1858, better term for my intended meaning of mental processes that make things compatible with each other). Consilience is the conscious analog of perceptual assimilations where ambiguity is made to conform to some previously learned schema. Consilience is in mind–space what narratization is in mind–time, making things compatible with each other. . . .

What about animal dreams?

Jaynes: They are not dreams in our sense.

What you see in the fluttering paws and mouth of a sleeping dog are pure reactivations instigated as before by the giant pontine cells but without consciousness, without any consilience or narratization with an analog 'I' — or perhaps I should say analog 'Fido'. . . .

Can introspection occur in dreams?

Jaynes: Sometimes, yes. Such occasions are what are called "lucid dreams."

But if dreams are consciousness and consciousness only began about 1000 B.C., then no one should have dreamt before that time.

Jaynes: No one did dream before that time in the way that you and I do. Let's look at the data. In the Iliad there are four dreams, although they are not called that: there is no word for them in the Iliad. The most important one is at the beginning of Book II, important because it renews the Trojan War. Agamemnon is asleep in his tent. Presumably, he is in REM sleep. In comes Oneiros, a god messenger from Zeus, whose name comes to mean "dream" in later Greek. Oneiros appears as the much admired Nestor, "stands at his head," tells Agamemnon he is asleep in his bed, and then proceeds to deliver his message, and departs, after which Agamemnon awakes, arises, and tells the others. Agamemnon never thinks he's anywhere else except on his bed or doing anything except sleeping. He can't because he is not conscious, which is what he would have to be to dream himself somewhere else (translocative) and doing something else (vicarial) as we do in our dreams. It is what we call a bicameral dream, similar to what goes on in the waking mentality of ancient times. Such dreams are very rare today but they occasionally occur with profound effects. Descartes had one and it changed his life.

All four dreams in the Iliad are of this type.

If we go over to the Hebrew world, the famous Jacob's Ladder Dream is a bicameral dream (Genesis 28:10–22). Jacob's dream takes place exactly where he is sleeping and he does nothing except hear Yahweh at the top of probably a ziggurat rather than a ladder, with angels streaming up and down its steps, as Yahweh renews the covenant with him. So sure is he that the dream happened where he was sleeping that he annoints the place as Beth-El, place or house of God. Three other dreams are mentioned prior to this in the early chapters of Genesis and they are all bicameral. The Joseph stories that follow, according to modern scholars (Redford, 1970), come from around 700 years later and they are not bicameral.

In the cuneiform literature, we have dreams going back to 2500 B.C. and in hieroglyphics back to the dream of Djoser in 2650 B.C. All are bicameral with one possible exception where the translation is in question.

Going the other direction in time, dreams after the Iliad rapidly become first vicarial, the person's analog 'I' in his dream doing something other than sleeping, and then translocative, that is, they take place somewhere other than where the person is sleeping. All of us today have vicarial translocative dreams, which are consciousness operating primarily during REM sleep.

I regard this development, this definite historical change in the nature of dreams, as one of the great confirmations of the strong form of the central hypothesis of the origin of consciousness in the breakdown of the bicameral mind.

Does this theory relate to therapy in any way?

Jaynes: I think there are some obvious inferences to be made. As for schizophrenia, the theory of the bicameral mind in simplified form is at present being taught to hallucinating patients in several clinics both here and abroad. It relieves a great deal of the associated distress of "being crazy" by getting the patient to realize that many of his or her symptoms are a relapse to an older mentality that was perfectly normal at one time but no longer works.

In the treatment of neuroses, the theory provides a strong theoretical framework for such consciousness-changing procedures as the cognitive therapies of Beck (1976) or Meichenbaum (1977), reframing or restructuring, the use of guided imagery, paradoxical therapy, and various visualizing practices. Most of what are diagnosed as neurotic behaviours are, of course, disorders of consciousness, or more specifically of narratization and excerption. Therefore, narratization and excerption must be retrained for the patient to obtain relief. Such renarratization is actually what is going on in most therapy, even in analysis of either the Freudian or Jungian variety. And it does not matter whether or not the renarratization is existentially veridical so long as it is believed and redirects behaviour into more adaptive modes.

2

DANIEL C. DENNETT
Julian Jaynes's
Software Archeology

What a philosopher would usually do on an occasion like this is to begin to launch into a series of devastating arguments, criticisms, and counter-examples, and I am not going to do that today, because in this instance I don't think it would be very constructive. I think first it is very important to understand Julian Jaynes's project, to see a little bit more about what the whole shape of it is, and delay the barrage of nitpicking objections and criticisms until we have seen what the edifice as a whole is. After all, on the face of it, it is preposterous and I have found that in talking with other philosophers my main task is to convince them to take it seriously when they are very reluctant to do this. I take it very seriously, so I am going to use my time to try to describe what I take the project to be. Perhaps Julian will disavow the version of Julian Jaynes I am going to present, but at least the version I am going to present is one that I take very seriously.

Now, another thing that philosophers usually do on these occasions is demand definitions of consciousness, of mind, and of all the other terms. I am not going to do that either, because I don't think that would be constructive at this point. If I thought I could bring his entire project crashing down with one deft demand for an impossible definition. I would do it, but I don't think so.

Perhaps this is an autobiographical confession: I am rather fond of his way of using these terms; I rather like his way of carving up consciousness. It is in fact very similar to the way that I independently decided to carve up consciousness some years ago.

So what then is the project? The project is, in one sense, very simple and very familiar. It is bridging what he calls the "awesome chasm" between mere inert matter and the inwardness, as he puts it, of a conscious being. Consider the awesome chasm between a brick and a bricklayer. There isn't, in Thomas Nagel's (1974) famous phrase, anything that it is like to be a brick. But there is something that it is like to be a bricklayer, and we want to know what the conditions were under which there happened to come to be entities that it was like something to be in this rather special sense. That is the story, the developmental, evolutionary, historical story that Jaynes sets out to tell.

Now, if we are going to tell this story at all, obviously we are going to have to stretch our imaginations some, because if we think about it in our habitual ways, without trying to stretch our imaginations, we just end up with a blank; it is just incomprehensible. Sherry Turkle (1984), in her new book about computers, *The Second Self*, talks about the reactions small children have to computer toys when they open them up and look inside. What they see is just an absurd little chip and a battery and that's all. They are baffled at how *that* could possibly do what they have just seen the toy do. Interestingly, she says they look at the situation, scratch their heads for a while, and then they typically say very knowingly: "It's the battery?" (A grown-up version of the same fallacy is committed by the philosopher John Searle, 1980, when he, arriving at a similar predicament, says: "It's the mysterious causal powers of the brain that explain consciousness.") Suddenly facing the absurdly large gap between what we know from the inside about consciousness and what we see if we take off the top of somebody's skull and look in can provoke such desperate reactions. When we look at a human brain and try to think of it as the seat of all that mental activity, we see something that is just as incomprehensible as the microchip is to the child when she considers it to be the seat of all the fascinating activity that she knows so well as the behaviour of the simple toy.

Now, if we are going to do this work at all, if we are going to try to fill this gap, we are going to have to talk about consciousness, because that is what is at one edge of this large terrain. It is fascinating to me to see how reluctant, how uncomfortable, most scientifically minded people are in talking about consciousness. They realize that some day they will have to talk about consciousness—unless they are going to do what the behaviourists tried so unconvincingly to do, just dismiss the problem as not really there. If you can't quite face "feigning anaesthesia" for the rest of your days, you are going to have to admit that consciousness is a phenomenon that needs explaining. We are going to have to talk about the ephemeral, swift, curious, metaphorical features of consciousness.

Many people say: "Some day, but not yet. This enterprise is all just premature." And others say: "Leave it to the philosophers (and look what a mess they make of it)." I want to suggest that it is not premature, that in fact there is no alternative but to start looking as hard as we can at consciousness first. If we don't look at consciousness and get clear about what the destination is, and instead try to work our way up by just thinking about how the brain is put together, we won't know where we are trying to get to from where we are and we will be hopelessly lost. This is commonly referred to as the defence of the top-down strategy, and in looking at Jaynes's book again this morning I find that in his introduction he has one of the clearest and most perspicuous defences of the top-down approach that I have ever come across:

We can only know in the nervous system what we have known in behavior first. Even if we had a complete wiring diagram of the nervous system, we still would not be able to answer our basic question. Though we knew the connections of every tickling thread of every single axon and dendrite in every species that ever existed, together with all its neurotransmitters and how they varied in its billions of synapses of every brain that ever existed, we could still never—not ever—from a knowledge of the brain alone know if that brain contained a consciousness like our own. We first have to start from the top, from some conception of what consciousness is, from what our own introspection is. (Jaynes, 1976b, p. 18)

When I try to make this idea clear to other people I sometimes use a somewhat threadbare analogy with computers. If you want to know what a chess-playing computer does, forget about trying to understand it from the bottom up. If you don't understand the conceptual domain in which the topic is chess—moves and strategy—you'll never make sense of what happens by building up from an analysis of the registers and logico-arithmetic operations in the central processing unit. (I am going to put this comparison with computers to a number of other uses in talking about Jaynes's work.)

If we are going to use this top-down approach, we are going to have to be bold. We are going to have to be speculative, but there is good and bad speculation, and this is not an unparalleled activity in science. An area of great fascination in science is the speculative hypothesis-spinning about the very origins of life, of the first self-replicating creatures, in the primordial soup. That sort of research has to be speculative; there simply are no data imaginable anywhere in the world today, nor are there experiments that could tease out with any certainty how that process began, but if you let your imaginations wander and start speculating about how it might have begun, you can put together some pretty interesting stories. Soon you can even begin to test some of them. Although I know that this enterprise is looked askance upon by many hard-headed scientists, it is certainly one that I would defend as a valuable part of our scientific enterprise more largely seen.

The dangers of this top-down approach of course are many. Speculation is guided largely by plausibility, and plausibility is a function of our knowledge, but also of our bad habits, misconceptions, and bits of ignorance, so when you make a mistake it tends to be huge and embarrassing. That's the price you pay in playing this game. Some people have no taste for this, but we really can't do without it. Those scientists who have no taste for this sort of speculative exercise will just have to stay in the trenches and do without it, while the rest of us risk embarrassing mistakes and have a lot of fun.

Consider the current controversy in biology between the adaptationists and their critics, Stephen J. Gould and Richard Lewontin (1979) at Harvard. Gould and Lewontin shake an angry and puritanical finger at the adaptationists for their "just-so stories," their "panglossian" assumptions, their willingness to engage in speculation where the only real test seems to be how imaginative you can be and how plausible a story you can tell. But see Dennett (1983). One of the responses that one can make is that there is no alternative; the fossil record is simply not going to provide enough information to provide a rigorous, bottom-up, scientific account of all the important moments in the evolution of species. The provable history has to be embellished and extrapolated with a good deal of adaptationists' thinking. What we need is a *just-so story*. This term comes, of course, from Kipling and is used as a term of abuse by Gould and Lewontin, but I am happy to say that some of those who are unblushing adaptationists have simply adopted it. They say, in effect: "That's right; what we are doing is telling just-so stories, and just-so stories have a real role to play in science."

Now, when Julian Jaynes tells his story he doesn't say that it is a just-so story. He doesn't say it is just a sort of guess at how it might have been. He claims to be telling the historical truth as best as he can figure it out.

But he is also clever enough to realize that if he doesn't have the details just right, then some other story which is in very important respects rather like it must be true. So the whole account is put together by a rather interesting amalgam of aprioristic thinking about *how it had to be*, historical sleuthing, and inspired guesswork. He uses aprioristic reasoning to establish that we have to have travelled from point A to point B by *some* route — where and when the twists come is an interesting empirical question. He flavours and deepens and constrains his aprioristic thinking about how it had to be with whatever he can find about how it was and he lets his imagination go as fertile as he can and clutches at whatever straws he can find in the "fossil record."

Now, it is good to be "modular" when you do this sort of theorizing, and Jaynes's account is remarkably modular. On page 221 of his book he presents a summary of seven factors which go into his account: (1) the weakening of the auditory by the advent of writing; (2) the inherent fragility of hallucinatory control; (3) the unworkableness of gods in the chaos of historical upheaval; (4) the positing of internal cause in the observation of difference in others; (5) the acquisition of narratization from epics; (6) the survival value of deceit; and (7) a modicum of natural selection.

He has given us seven factors in this passage, and I think he would agree that you could throw out any one of them and replace it with something that simply did the same work but was historically very different; his theory would survive otherwise quite intact. Moreover, there are many details in his theory which are, as he has noted today, optional. There are ideas which are plausible, indications of the detailed way that his account *might* run, but if they turn out to be wrong they can be jettisoned with small damage to the fabric of the whole theory.

I will just mention a few that are favourites of mine. He claims, for example, that there is a little evidence to suggest that in the period when bicameral people and conscious people coexisted, there was a policy of killing obdurately bicameral children, which may in fact have hastened the demise of the bicameral type. This possible policy of "eugenics" may have given the *cultural* evolutionary process he is describing a biological (or genetic) boost, speeding up the process. You don't need it (to make the just-so story work), but there is a little evidence to suggest something like that might have happened.

Another of his optional modules is the idea that the reason that the Greeks placed the mind in the breast (in the "heart") is that when you have to make decisions you go into a stressful state which makes you breathe harder and may even make your pulse quicken. You notice the turmoil in your breast and this leads to a localization fallacy. Jaynes suggests that's why some of the Greek terms for mind have their roots as it were in the chest instead of in the head. That might be true. It might not, but it's another of the optional modules.

I don't know if Jaynes would agree with me about how much optionality there is in his system. The module I would be most interested in simply discarding is the one about hallucinations. Now you might think that if you throw out his account of hallucinations you haven't got much left of Jaynes's theory, but in fact I think you would, although he would probably resist throwing that part away.

This, then, is why I think it is a mistake, as I said at the outset, simply to bash away at the weakest links in sight, because the weakest links are almost certainly not correct—but also not critical to the enterprise as a whole.

I want to turn now to an explanation of what I find most remarkable about Julian Jaynes's just-so story, by comparing it with another (and

this was in fact touched upon by one of the earlier questions). In the 17th century Thomas Hobbes (1651) asked himself where morality came from. If you look at what he called the state of nature—if you look at animals in the wild, at lions hunting and killing wildebeests, for instance—there is no morality or immorality to be seen there at all. There is no good or evil. There is killing, there is pain, but there is no "ought," there is no right, there is no wrong, there is no sin. But then look at us; here we see the institution of morality permeating the entire fabric of our lives. How did we get from there to here? Hobbes had the same sort of problem as the problem that Jaynes is facing, and his answer of course was a famous just-so story. Back in the old days, he says, man lived in the state of nature and his life was "solitary, poor, nasty, brutish and short." Then there was a sort of crisis and people got together in a group and they formed a covenant or compact, and out of this morality was born. Right and wrong came into existence as a consequence of that social contract.

Now, as history, it is absurd. Hobbes didn't think otherwise. His just-so story was quite obviously a thought experiment, a rational reconstruction or idealization. The last thing Hobbes would have done would have been to look through cuneiform records to see exactly when this particular momentous occasion happened.

But now consider the following objection to Hobbes's account, but first applied to Julian Jaynes's work. In a review of Jaynes's book some years ago, Ned Block (1981) said the whole book made one great crashing mistake, what we sometimes call a "use mention" error: confusing a phenomenon with either the name of the phenomenon or the concept of the phenomenon. Block claimed that even if everything that Jaynes said about historical events were correct, all he would have shown was not that *consciousness* arrived in 1400 B.C., but that *the concept of* consciousness arrived in 1400 B.C. People were conscious long before they had the concept of consciousness, Block declared, in the same way that there was gravity long before Newton ever hit upon the concept of gravity. The whole book in Block's view was simply a great mistake. Concept does not equal phenomenon. You can't ride the concept of the horse!

Well, now, has Jaynes made that mistake? Let's ask if Hobbes made the same mistake. Hobbes says that morality came into existence out of the social contract. Now one might say, "What a stupid mistake Hobbes has made! Maybe the *concepts* of right and wrong didn't exist before the contract of which he speaks, but certainly right and wrong themselves did. That is, people did things that were nasty and evil before they had the concepts of it."

Right and wrong, however, are parts of morality, a peculiar phenomenon that *can't* predate a certain set of concepts, including the concepts of right and wrong. The phenomenon is *created* in part by the arrival on the scene of a certain set of concepts. It is not that animals just haven't noticed that they are doing things that are evil and good. Lacking the concept, they are not doing anything right or wrong; there isn't any evil or good in their world. It's only once you get in a certain conceptual environment that the phenomenon of right and wrong, the phenomenon of morality, exists at all.

Now, I take Jaynes to be making a similarly exciting and striking move with regard to consciousness. To put it really somewhat paradoxically, you can't have consciousness until you have the concept of consciousness. In fact he has a more subtle theory than that, but that's the basic shape of the move.

These aren't the only two phenomena, morality and consciousness, that work this way. Another one that Jaynes mentions is history, and at first one thinks, "Here's another use-mention error!" At one point in the book Jaynes suggests that history was invented or discovered just a few years before Herodotus, and one starts to

object that of course there was history long before there were historians, but then one realizes that in a sense Jaynes is right. Is there a *history* of lions and antelopes? Just as many years have passed for them as for us, and things have happened to them, but it is very different. Their passage of time has not been conditioned by their recognition of the transition, it has not been conditioned and tuned and modulated by any reflective consideration of that very process. So history itself, our *having* histories, is in part a function of our recognizing that very fact. Other phenomena in this category are obvious: you can't have baseball before you have the concept of baseball, you can't have money before you have the concept of money.

I have used up as much time as I should use, but I am going to say a few more words. If you want to pursue the interesting idea that consciousness postdates the arrival of a certain set of concepts, then of course you have to have in your conceptual armamentarium the idea that concepts themselves can be preconscious, that concepts do not require consciousness. Many have held that there is no such thing as the unconscious wielding of concepts, but Jaynes's account of the origins of consciousness depends on the claim that an elaboration of a conceptual scheme under certain social and environmental pressures was the *precondition* for the emergence of consciousness as we know it. This is, to my mind, the most important claim that Jaynes makes in his book. As he puts it, "The bee has a concept of the flower," but not a conscious concept. We have a very salient theoretical role for something which we might as well call concepts, but if you don't like it we can call them schmoncepts, concept-like things that you don't have to be conscious to have.

For instance, computers have them. They are not conscious—yet—but they have lots of concepts, and in fact one way of viewing artificial intelligence is as the attempt to design conceptual systems for those computers to use. In fact this is the way people in artificial intelligence talk all the time. For instance, they may note that they have to give a robot *some concept* of an obstacle so that it can recognize this and that as an obstacle in its environment. Having figured out what concepts to give the robot or the computer, you do some fancy software design, and then you say: Here's how we have realized the concept of *causation,* or *obstacle,* or *the passage of time,* or *other sources of information* or whatever. The idea of unconscious concepts is, as a computer scientist would say, a "winning" idea, and if it is hard for you to get used to it, then at least my recommendation (along with Jaynes) would be: try harder because it is a very useful idea.

After all, one way of casting this whole question (the way that I usually think about it) is not "How do we get from the bricks, amoebas, and then apes to us?" but "How in the world could you ever make a conscious automaton, how could you make a conscious robot?" The answer, I think, is not to be found in hypotheses about hardware particularly, but in software. What you want to do is design the software in such a way that the system has a certain set of concepts. If you manage to endow the system with the right sort of concepts, you create one of those *logical spaces* that Jaynes talks about.

This in fact is a ubiquitous way of talking in the field of artificial intelligence. Consider for instance the idea of LISP. LISP is a programming language. Once you have LISP, your whole vision of how a computer is put together, and what you can do with it, changes dramatically. All sorts of things become possible that weren't possible before. Logical spaces are created that didn't exist before and you could never find them in the hardware. Such a logical space is not in the hardware, it is not in the "organs"; it is purely at the software level. Now Jaynes, in his largest and most dispensable optional module, ties his entire theory to the structure of the brain and I am fascinated to know

whether there is anything in that. But I am quite content to jettison the whole business, because what I think he is really talking about is a software characterization of the mind, at the level, as a computer scientist would say, of a *virtual machine.*

The underlying hardware of the brain is just the same now as it was thousands of years ago (or it may be just the same), but what had to happen was that the environment had to be such as to encourage the development, the emergence, of certain concepts, certain software, which then set in motion some sort of chain reaction. Jaynes is saying that when the right concepts settled into place in the preconscious "minds" of our ancestors, there was a sort of explosion, like the explosion in computer science that happens when you invent something like LISP. Suddenly you discover a new logical space, where you get the sorts of different behaviours, the sorts of new powers, the sorts of new problems that we recognize as having the flavour of human consciousness.

Of course, if that is what Jaynes's theory really is, it is no wonder he has to be bold in his interpretation of the tangible evidence, because this isn't just archeology he is doing: this is *software archeology,* and software doesn't leave much of a fossil record. Software, after all, is just concepts. It is abstract and yet, of course, once it is embodied it has very real effects. So if you want to find a record of major "software" changes in archeological history, what are you going to have to look at? You are going to have to look at the "printouts," but they are very indirect. You are going to have to look at texts, and you are going to have to look at the pottery shards and figurines as Jaynes does, because that is the only place you are going to find any trace. Now, of course, maybe the traces are just gone, maybe the "fossil record" is simply not good enough.

Jaynes's idea is that for us to be the way we are now, there has to have been a revolution—

almost certainly not an *organic* revolution, but a *software* revolution—in the organization of our information processing system, and that has to have come *after* language. That, I think, is an absolutely wonderful idea, and if Jaynes is com-

pletely wrong in the details, that is a darn shame, but something like what he proposes has to be right; and we can start looking around for better modules to put in the place of the modules that he has already given us.

3

JONATHAN MILLER
Primitive Thoughts

I would like to approach Dr. Jaynes's thesis from two points of view. One is neurological, and the other is anthropological. Let me take the neurological issues first of all. Now, as I read it, and as I heard him today, Dr. Jaynes seems to be saying that there are, or have been, two linguistic agencies within the human brain. On the left is one which appears to have evolved phylogenetically and to develop during the course of individual development to create intelligible utterances with our fellow creatures. This, as it were, represents or *comes* to represent the role of public spokesman, whereas the right side is arguably associated with the more holistic, imaginative, and creative capabilities. The right hemisphere, having surrendered its role as public orator to its now dominant partner on the left, turns its speaking voice inwards; and instead of participating in public speech, it acts instead as an inner voice, ready to transmit the imaginative counsels of the right hemisphere to the inner ear of the left. Now, according to Dr. Jaynes, this private advice is not issued all the time. There isn't, in other words, an unremitting babble going from one side of the brain to the other. This private voice only speaks when the individual is stressed by such awkward and dif-

ficult challenges that the literal-minded capabilities of the left hemisphere would be at a loss without the subtler and more strategic cogitations of the right. In primitive man, according to Jaynes, before he succeeded in appropriating all of his mental functions to one coherent, integrated, self-conscious agency, these right-sided counsels were identified as the authoritative voice of supernatural persons. In other words, as divine dictations, as opposed to personal promptings. Now, apart from the fact that Dr. Jaynes bases his claim upon various cultural artifacts, such as the narrative structure of Homer's Iliad—a sophisticated form of narrative, from which I think it would be very rash to draw far-reaching conclusions about the state of mind of the contemporary audience—I believe that there is little neurological evidence to show that the brain is partitioned in the way that this argument suggests it might be. Even if we concede that the neurological substrate responsible for organizing spoken language is bilaterally represented at birth and that the right side slowly surrenders its linguistic role to the left, it does not mean that the residual function confines itself to intracranial utterances, which are then experienced as hallucinations. In other words, even if we admit that there is a division of labour between the right and left halves of the brain, it is unnecessary to assume that the right hemisphere communicates with the left in terms of natural language. The cross-talk could just as easily occur in machine language, and the brain's owner need never overhear the exchange.

Another point. How, and where, hallucinated voices arise in the brain is, as far as I can tell, a moot point. The fact that they are attributed to someone else does not mean to me that their neurological substrate should therefore be sought in something that is comparably remote from whatever it is we regard as the neurological seat of self. Such an experience could just as well arise from some malfunction within the speech centre itself, on the left that is; and still be experienced as the voice of someone else. In other words, the brain doesn't have to be materially bicameral in order to furnish experiences other than that of the personal self. In any case, I think that it would be dangerous to generalize about the way in which such anomalous experiences are identified. Even amongst schizophrenics there is a bewildering variety of attributions as far as the hallucinated voices are concerned. They may be called "my voices," "the radio," or even rather disarmingly, "my hallucinations." In any case there is no ethnographic evidence to show that preliterate man is more of a prey to such hallucinatory experiences than his literate counterparts. The fact that Homeric heroes are frequently addressed by deities should by no means be taken as evidence that such hallucinations prevailed in the society to which this work of literature was addressed— that this was a characteristic form of experience until such hallucinations dwindled into more sophisticated and integrated forms of self-consciousness. The Iliad after all is a work of art, and as such it represents, amongst other things, a view of how things began—an ethnographic just-so story.

The ease with which supernatural persons, for example, appear to mingle with their mortal counterparts is not necessarily a reflection of contemporary experience. It is rather an artful and above all self-conscious way of representing the exalted political status of the heroic protagonists—who were of mixed pedigree with one supernatural parent, and it is by virtue of being in receipt of divine advice that their historic importance is emphasized.

Such narratives represent what the anthropologists call "charter myths" (Kirk, 1970)— that is, they are stories which confer supernatural legitimacy on the structures of existing society. It would be wrong to construe these myths as a picture of primitive consciousness. And even if it could be shown that the members of preliterate societies entertain hallucinatory experiences on a scale which is noticeably different from our own, it would be a mistake to conclude that this represented a stage of mental development, to be equated with that of the savage or of the child. Perhaps I can briefly mention Julian's reference to the phantom playmate. I do *not* believe that these are *hallucinated* episodes on the part of the child. What you have in the case of the imaginary playmate is an adversary fiction created by a child who feels himself to be at odds with his family. Such a fiction is no more hallucinatory than the one which Freud (1966) called "the family romance," namely, the child who is convinced that he is, after all, a foundling.

The same principle applies to primitive cultures. Among the Azande, for example, that almost emblematic tribe which I was actually fortunate enough to visit while doing *The Body in Question* (Miller, 1978), the belief in witchcraft and oracles does not, as 19th-century anthropologists assumed, reflect the faltering of a primitive mind. It is rather the visible expression of the social, political, and jurisprudential order of the Azande—one way, amongst many others, of resolving disputes within a complex society. When Evans-Pritchard (1937), for example, describes an arc of light issuing from the epigastrium of a malignant witch, we cannot assume that this was a bicamerally provoked hallucination; or that the members of such societies owe their distinctive beliefs to some primitive peculiarity of neurological organization which will eventually give way to a more integrated form of consciousness.

In fact, if I can sum up, I am convinced that in many ways, Dr. Jaynes is the latest in a long line of authorities committed to the belief that the cognitive structure of preliterate man is quite different from that of his civilized counterpart. In other words, Dr. Jaynes's work should be set in the context of other writers preoccupied with the existence of the so-called primitive mind. Giambattista Vico (1744), for example, who also identified our ancestors as entranced poets to whom supernatural voices spoke. The English anthropologist Tylor (1974), who claimed to have identified a primitive mind limited by its allegiance to animism and the belief that its dreams came from without. Hallpike (1979) and his analysis in the *Foundations of Primitive Thought*. Lévy-Bruhl (1926) and his prelogical mentality. And, of course, Frazer (1936) with his protoscientific magicians. All of these authors have helped to shape the belief that there has been a single breaking point, a great divide if you like, in the psychological history of the human race. Now, whether the division occurred in the 16th century in Western Europe, in Greece in the 5th century, or in Mesopotamia in the 4th millennium is never made clear. What *is* clear, however, is the unfounded conviction that mental structures have in some way undergone a substantial transformation; and with Dr. Jaynes, we get the even more ambitious claim that this transformation is based on a fundamental change taking place within the nervous system itself. And it is at this point that I part company with Dr. Jaynes.

Man's awareness of himself has undergone and continues to undergo both complication and elaboration. I think that the suggestion of the elaboration of a software program which can leave the hardware intact is an extremely interesting way of looking at the issue. However, I do not believe that because one can actually foresee some notion of the development of software that we have to adapt the program, such as the one Dr. Jaynes suggests, to account for any change in man's self-awareness. I believe that I would like to go, as it were, even more top-down, because I believe that Dr. Jaynes is going from half-way-down to down, rather than from top-down enough. I believe that much of the analysis of self-consciousness, much of the analysis of allegiance to idols and dependence upon shamans, is, in fact, a reflection of political structure. If we were to look in a more Marxist way at the political and economic structure and organization of these societies, we would, I think, learn a great deal more about the way in which they have succeeded in elaborating and furnishing themselves with these more or less elaborate software programs. For instance, the example of the idol and dependence upon the idol as a source of oral wisdom. Dr. Jaynes speaks about this being a literate society. It is, of course, a very peculiarly literate society in which there is a highly specialized monopoly of literacy by those who are also, as it were, the impresarios of the idol itself. And it is through the medium of literacy that the idol is manipulated as the form of wisdom in a society which is highly authoritarian and also in which there are monopolies in the distribution of essential but scarce resources. When you lay claim to the ubiquitousness of the idols as being evidence of the universality of hallucinations, if you extended that analogy to the present day, I think you would have to assume it was something analogous to, for example, what one has in Catholic households. Large numbers of people have photographs of the Pope, but these are not giving them hallucinated audiences with the Pope, they are merely ways of reassuring, reminding, and reinforcing allegiance to the Pope, with whom, in fact, few people can succeed in gaining an audience. I believe that in the same way, these domestic idols, which extend through a large number of cultures, are not in fact a source of hallucination so much as proxy versions of the centralized authority from which oral orders are issued, whether or not on a hallucinated basis.

I'd like to summarize my objection to Dr. Jaynes's theory of "speaking" idols. Jaynes claims that the Mesopotamian congregation hallucinated these oracular voices. Whereas I'm saying that there's no evidence to show that they did. It seems much more likely that a priestly caste acted as spokesmen for the idols and that the oracular pronouncements of the gods were handed to the congregation in the natural voice of the officiating priest. I doubt very much that the faithful actually "heard" the idols speak. They took it on trust that the priests had "heard" the voice of the gods. I refuse to believe that hallucination forms a representative basis for *any* stage of human culture.

Admittedly, human self-consciousness has undergone large-scale changes since early antiquity. But this, as I see it, is the result of two factors: the invention of writing, which enables man to represent his own thoughts in a stable form — thus allowing him to reflect on his inner self; and changes in the political and economic structure of society — changes which eventually resulted in the emergence of the autonomous individual. The interaction of these cultural processes is all we need to explain the emergence of sophisticated self-consciousness. It is unnecessary and misleading to suggest that this transition coincided with the extinction of auditory hallucination.

Panel Discussion

Dennett: . . . The hardware/software distinction has to be handled very carefully because of course (if anybody doesn't realize this already) we do know enough about the architecture of the brain to know that there isn't a CPU (central processing unit) and a bunch of registers in it, and so we don't store a program in the brain's registers. All I mean by software in this context is really, I think, what Julian wants. Of course, even in a computer, to put some software in you must make a physical change in the computer. The change can be thought of as more or less isolated — packed off into some memory somewhere, maybe even off on a disc or on tape, but that is irrelevant. A software change — a change in "concepts" — *is* a physical change; it is a transient, temporary, change in the microstructure of the system. You can "undo" the change with more software — you don't need to use a screwdriver or a file. And, similarly of course, if we are going to be good materialists, we must suppose that when a child, say, grows up in one part of the world and learns French, this is embodied in very subtle changes in the physical structure of that child's brain, which nobody of course would be able to determine by a microscopic examination of that brain, even though those changes are in there. Now just as if you raise a child in France, the child learns French, and if you raise a child in the United States, the child learns English, so if you raise a child in the post-bicameral world, the child "learns consciousness," and if you raise the child in the bicameral world, the child "learns bicamerality." Those are different software configurations of the hardware, and, of course, at some micro level those are all hardware changes because you can't put the software in without making tiny changes in structure. So, I think we can use a sort of biologized version of the term software here, if we like, to mean the sort of thing that Julian wants.

Jaynes: Thank you, I really like that.

Dennett: Another comment I am a little reluctant to enter into because if I really got going on it, I would take half an hour. I think I know how to do most of what you want to do without the hallucinations. But it is nowhere near as exciting, although it still seems to me to be very interesting. I will just say a few things to sketch it out, and then tonight perhaps we will thrash it out for hours.

Jaynes: I would like to.

Dennett: Here is my very boring alternative. Why couldn't the voices you make so much of just be a phenomenon that we all know anyway, the familiar sort of obsessive memory, like having a damn jingle running through your head? That is not a hallucination. Advertisers are very good at writing jingles that once they get in your head, stay there. You keep hearing them, but you don't have to suppose it is a hallucination. It is just a memory which gets triggered under various circumstances and it might be memory of admonitions that were particularly impressive when your first heard them, for instance. Now that is just the first step. I take it that when you recall a jingle, you don't call it a hallucination.

Jaynes: I wouldn't say so.

Dennett: Well, I would take that slender phenomenon and build on it in various ways. There is a whole side to Julian's book which none of us has discussed which is perhaps my favourite part of all, and that is the relationship between consciousness and control, and the idea that the crisis for which consciousness is the ultimate stabilization is a crisis of control where individuals who had been controlled by leaders, more or less the way bees are controlled by the queen bee (or among mammals, the way mole rats are controlled by the queen mole rat), could no longer be so controlled. At some point in history, Julian says, social organizations got too large, groups of people got too large, and their projects became too complex for that

sort of monolithic control to be practical, and so ordinary people had to become *self-controllers* for the first time, and this was a real crisis for them. . . .

Miller: If I may just make the point here about what William James (1929) calls medical materialism. In a sense, I am taking issue here with both you and Julian for trying to see all this in terms of brains rather than societies. I think that most of the things that you are describing about the transformations and changes that have taken place in human self-consciousness could be perfectly satisfactorily described in terms of the development of cultural artifacts, through the medium of which we succeeded in building up elaborate representations, not only of the natural world in which we live, but also of ourselves in the social world. Writing, far from being a sort of fire extinguisher which puts out the hallucinated voice, provides a more manageable way of moving counters around in the mental game of describing your own personality. Without writing them down, your thoughts are nothing more than a fugue of forgettable sentences. Here we are, all scribbling away, not able to marshal our own arguments unless we remember what the others have said; we can't even remember what *we* thought unless we jot it down.

One of the points that Jack Goody (1977) makes in his book *The Domestication of the Savage Mind* is that the most insignificant thing that emerges with writing is that you write down lists and tables. Once you start doing this, you can have very elaborate degrees of reflectiveness. I would attribute most of the changes that took place to writing, as you do indeed, but for very different reasons. The reason why writing did it—and I think that McLuhan's (1964) version of what writing did is nonsensical—is that it enabled us to visualize our thoughts and therefore to play much more sophisticated board games with psychological reality.

Jaynes: I like what you are just saying. But when you use the metaphor of writing "putting out" the voices, I would suggest that it is only one of the things. I am not trying to waffle here. Every large event in history has multiple causes and so likely did the breakdown of the bicameral mind, as I am sure you understand. This event here this afternoon has multiple causes.

Miller: In connection with that, I'd like to modify what I said about the cunning conspiracy of priestly kings who manipulate, as it were, the public relations office of the gods. That is not what I meant at all. I am not suggesting that the priests deliberately invented the gods in order to control society. I am not saying that there was a design conference in some ziggurat where they said, "Well, let's run this up the flagpole and see how it comes out!" What happens is that theological imagery gradually evolves; and people find themselves under its hegemony. The same thing happens in complex literate societies. We know, for example, that the structure of the Anglican Church in England in the 16th century resulted in an authoritarian structure which exerted political control over society at large.

All we know is that when there are social crises, due to catastrophic crop failures, for example, there is often a change in political authority, and with the upset *political* authority there is often a collapse of the theological system, which is, after all, a constitutive part of the social structure. It's nothing to do with hallucinated voices!

Jaynes: There are some data which I think are relevant here. When you look at the writings

in the period from 1400 B.C. to 600 B.C., those that are not simply factual but are more meaningful to us do talk about wanting to get back to the gods. Where have the gods gone? They don't call them voices. This is very distinct in the Hebrew hymns, for example, and it is very hard to know what Psalm 42 would mean otherwise:

> *As the hart pants after the water brooks,*
> *so pants my mind after you, o gods . . .*
> *when am I going to see gods face-to-face again?*

This is the proper translation of this Psalm, and it is not an isolated example.

Miller: I think to use your own apparatus of metaphors and metaphrands and so forth, what is going on here is an elaborate way of representing in the idioms and currencies of the time, a sense of loss, nostalgia, or something of a previous stability which in fact is best often personified. It is easier to do it, we still do it today without being bicameral. It's a way of representing things. It is still in political cartoons personified. I think that this is the "in" poetry and is often the best way of carrying the message across, but not because such poems with their personifications are the residue of actual direct experiences of personal addresses inside the head.

Jaynes: I do understand your point of view. You are saying it is all metaphorical and poetry, related in fact to the loss of some kind of reality which could be this authoritative structure. I, of course, am preferring to take the historical data absolutely literally. They meant what they said.

References

Albert, M., Silverberg, R., Teches, A., & Berman, M. (1976). Cerebral dominance for consciousness. *Archives of Neurology, 33,* 453–454.

Amassian, V., Westenbaker, C., & Reisine, H. (1974). The role of thalamic N. VA-VL in aversive conditioning of contact placing. *Society for Neuroscience,* 4th annual meeting, p. 118 (Abstract).

Bear, D., & Fedio, P. (1977). Quantitative analysis of interical behaviour and temporal lobe epilepsy. *Archives of Neurology, 34,* 454–467.

Beck, A. (1976). *Cognitive therapy and emotional disorders.* New York: International Universities Press.

Block, N. (1981). The origin of consciousness in the breakdown of the bicameral mind. (Book review). *Cognition and Brain Theory, 4,* 81–83.

Boring, E. G. (1929). *A history of experimental psychology.* New York: Appleton Century.

Bryden, M. P. (1982). *Laterality: Functional asymmetry in the intact brain.* New York: Academic Press.

Buchsbaum, M. S., Ingvar, D. H., Kessler, R., Walters, R. N., Cappelletti, J., van Kammen, D. P., King, A. C., Johnson, J. L., Manning, R. G., Flynn, R. W., Mann, L. S., Bunney, W. E., & Sokoloff, L. (1982). Cerebral glucography with positron tomography: Use in normal subjects and in patients with schizophrenia. *Archives of General Psychiatry, 39,* 251–259.

Bucke, R. M. (1901). *Cosmic consciousness: A study in the evolution of the human mind.* New York: Dutton, 1956.

Carr, M. (1983). Sidelights on *Xin* 'Heart, mind' in the *Shijing. Proceedings of the 31st CISHAAN,* Tokyo and Kyoto, 8, 24–25.

Craik, K.J.W. (1943). *The nature of explanation.* Cambridge: Cambridge University Press.

Darwin, C. (1859). *The Origin of Species.* New York: New American Library of the World, 1958.

Dennett, D. (1983). Intentional systems in cognitive ethology: The 'Panglossian Paradigm' defended. *The Behavioural and Brain Sciences, 6,* 343–390.

Durkheim, E. (1915). *The elementary forms of the religious life.* New York: Free Press, 1965.

Epstein, R., Lanza, R. P., & Skinner, B. F. (1981). "Self-awareness" in the pigeon. *Science, 212,* 695–696.

Evans-Pritchard, E. E. (1937). *Witchcraft, oracles and magic among the Azande.* New York: Oxford University Press.

Field, G. C. (1930). *Plato and his contemporaries.* New York: Dutton.

Flor-Henry, P. (1976). Lateralized temporal-limbic dysfunction and psychopathology. *Annals of the New York Academy of Sciences, 28,* 777–795.

Frazer, J. (1936). *The golden bough.* New York: Macmillan.

Freud, S. (1966). *Standard edition of the complete psychological works of Sigmund Freud* (Vol I: 1886–1899, J. Strachey translation). London: Hogarth.

Fried, I., Mateer, C., Ojemann, G., Wohns, R., & Fedio, P. (1982). Organization of visuospatial functions in human cortex: Evidence from electrical stimulation. *Brain, 105.* 349–371.

Fried, I., Ojemann, G., & Fetz, E. (1981). Language related potentials specific to human language cortex. *Science, 212,* 353–356.

Gallup, G. G., Jr. (1970). Chimpanzees: Self-recognition. *Science, 167,* 86–87.

Geschwind, N., & Levitsky, W. (1968). Human brain: Left–right asymmetries in temporal speech region. *Science, 161,* 186–187.

Goody, J. (1977). *The domestication of the savage mind.* New York: Cambridge University Press.

Gould, S. J., & Lewontin, R. (1979). The spandrels of San Marco and the Panglossian Paradigm: A critique of the adaptationist programme. *Proceedings of the Royal Society, B205,* 581–598.

Greenspoon, J. (1955). The reinforcing effect of two spoken sounds on the frequency of two responses. *American Journal of Psychology, 68,* 409–416.

Gur, R. E., Skolnick, B. E., Gur, R. C., Caroff, S., Rieger, W., Obrist, W. D., Younkin, D., & Reivich, M. (1983). Brain function in psychiatric disorders. *Archives of General Psychiatry, 40,* 1250–1254.

Hallpike, C. R. (1979). *Foundations of primitive thought.* Oxford: Oxford University Press.

Harrington, A. (1985). Nineteenth century ideas on hemisphere differences and 'duality of mind.' *The Behavioural and Brain Sciences, 8,* 517–659.

Harvey, N. A. (1918). *Imaginary playmates and other mental phenomena of children.* Ipsilanti: Michigan State Normal College.

Hebb, D. (1961). The mind's eye. *Psychology Today, 2,* 54–68.

Hécaen, H. & Albert, M.L. (1978). *Human neuropsychology.* New York: Wiley,

Hefferline, R. F., Keenan, B., & Harford, R. A. (1959). Escape and avoidance conditioning in human subjects without their observations of the response. *Science, 130,* 1338–1339.

Hendricks, J. C., Bowker, R. M., & Morrison, A. P. (1977). Functional characteristics of cats with pontine lesions during sleep and wakefulness and their usefulness for sleep research. In W. P. Koella & P. Levin (Eds.). *Sleep 1976,* Basel: S. Karger.

Hobbes, T. (1651). *Leviathan.* New York: Collier, 1962.

Hobson, J. A., & McCarley, R. W. (1977). The brain as a dream state generator: An activation-synthesis hypothesis of the dream process. *American Journal of Psychiatry, 134,* 1335–1348.

Humphrey, G. (1951). *Thinking.* London: Methuen.

Huxley, T. H. (1896). *Collected essays.* New York: Appleton.

James, W. (1890). *Principles of psychology.* New York: Holt.

James, W. (1929). *The varieties of religious experience.* New York: Modern Library.

Jasper, H. H. (1960). Unspecific thalamocortical relations. In J. Fields, H. W. Magoun, & V. Hall (Eds.), *The handbook of physiology* (Vol. 2). Baltimore: Williams & Wilkins.

Jaynes, J. (1976a). The evolution of language in the late Pleistocene. *Annals of the New York Academy of Sciences, 28,* 312–325.

Jaynes, J. (1976b). *The origin of consciousness in the breakdown of the bicameral mind.* Boston: Houghton Mifflin.

Jaynes, J. (1978). In a manner of speaking: Commentary on cognition and consciousness in non-human species. *The Behavioral and Brain Sciences, 1,* 578–579.

Jaynes, J. (1979). The meaning of King Tut. *Princeton Alumni Weekly,* June, 16–17.

Jaynes, J. (1981). The visions of William Blake. *Art World, 6,* 1–6.

Jaynes, J. (1982). A two-tiered theory of emotions. *The Behavioral and Brain Sciences, 5,* 434–435.

Jaynes, J. (1985). Sensory pain and conscious pain. *The Behavioral and Brain Sciences, 8,* 61–63.

Jerison, H. J. (1973). *Evolution of the brain and intelligence.* New York: Academic Press.

Jouandet, M. L., Garey, L. J., & Lipp. H. P. (1984). Distribution of the cells of origin of the corpus callosum and anterior commissure in the marmoset monkey. *Anatomy and Embryology, 169,* 45–59.

Kant, I. (1781). *Critique of pure reason.* London: Macmillan, 1929.

Kaufmann, Y. (1960). *The religion of ancient Israel* (M. Greenberg translation). Chicago: University of Chicago Press.

Kirk, G. S. (1970). *Myth. Its meaning and functions in ancient and other cultures.* Los Angeles: University of California Press.

Leonard, C. M., Rolls, E. T., Baylis, G. C., Wilson, F.A.W., Williams, G. V. Griffiths, C., & Murzi, E. (1983). Response properties and distribution of neurons which respond to faces in the monkey. *Society for Neuroscience, 9,* 958 (Abstract).

Lévy-Bruhl, L. (1926). *How natives think.* New York: A. A. Knopf.

Lewis, I. M. (1971). *Ecstatic religion: An anthropological study of spirit possession and shamanism.* Harmondsworth: Penguin.

Lloyd Morgan, C. (1923). *Emergent evolution: The Gifford Lectures delivered in the University of St. Andrews in the year 1922.* London: Williams & Norgate.

Locke, J. (1690). *An essay concerning human understanding.* London: Routledge, 1910.

McLuhan, M. (1964). *Understanding media: The extensions of man.* New York: McGraw-Hill.

Marbe, K. (1901). *Experimental-psychologische Untersuchungen über das Urteil, cine Einleitung in die Logik.* Leipzig: Engelmann.

Maxwell, M. (1984). *Human evolution.* New York: Columbia University Press.

Meichenbaum, D. (1977). *Cognitive-behavior modification.* New York: Plenum.

Miller, J. (1978). *The body in question.* London: Jonathan Cape.

Moore, G. E. (1922). *Philosophical studies.* London: Routledge & Kegan Paul.

Murray, D. J. (1983). *A history of western psychology.* Englewood Cliffs: Prentice-Hall.

Nagel, T. (1974). What is it like to be a bat? *Philosophical Review, 83,* 435–450.

Ojemann, G. (1975). Language and the thalamus: Object naming and recall during and after thalamic stimulation. *Brain and Language, 2,* 101–120.

Ojemann, G. (1977). Asymmetric function of the thalamus in man. *Annals of the New York Academy of Sciences, 299,* 380–396.

Ojemann, G. (1979). Altering memory with human ventrolateral thalamic stimulation. In E. R. Hitchcock, H. T. Ballantine, Jr., & B. A. Meyerson (Eds.), *Modern Concepts in psychiatric surgery.* Amsterdam: Elsevier.

Ojemann, G. (1983a). Brain organization for language from the perspective of electrical stimulation mapping. *The Behavioral and Brain Sciences, 6,* 189–230.

Ojemann, G. (1983b). Interrelationship in the brain organization of language related behaviors: Evidence from electrical stimulation mapping. In U. Kirk (Ed.), *Neuropsychology of language, reading and spelling.* New York: Academic Press.

Ojemann, G., & Lettich, E. (1983). Electrocorticographic (ECoG) correlates of naming, reading and verbal memory: *Society for Neuroscience, 9,* 655 (Abstract).

Ojemann, G., & Mateer, C. (1979). Human language cortex: Localization of memory, syntax and sequential motorphoneme identification systems. *Science, 205,* 1401–1403.

Penfield, W., & Perot, P. (1963). The brain's record of auditory and visual experiences—a final summary and discussion. *Brain, 86,* 595–696.

Perry, R. B. (1912). *The new realism.* Cambridge: Harvard University Press.

Pfeiffer, R. H. (1935). *State letters of Assyria.* New Haven: American Oriental Society.

Posey, T. B., & Losch, M. (1983). Auditory hallucinations of hearing voices in 375 normal subjects. *Imagination, Cognition Personality, and 3,* 99–113.

Rainer, J. D., Abdullah, S., & Altshuler, J. C. (1970). Phenomenology of hallucinations in the deaf. In W. Keup (Ed.), *Origin and mechanisms of hallucinations.* New York: Plenum.

Razran, G. (1971). *Mind in evolution.* Boston: Houghton Mifflin.

Redford, D. B. (1970). *A study of the biblical story of Joseph, Genesis 37–50.* Leiden: Brill.

Richards, I. A. (1936). *Philosophy of rhetoric.* New York: Oxford University Press.

Rosadini, G., & Rossi, G. (1967). On the suggested cerebral dominance for consciousness. *Brain, 90,* 101–112.

Russell, B. (1921). *Analysis of mind.* London: Allen & Unwin.

Russell, B. (1927). *Philosophy.* New York: Norton.

Searle, J. (1980). Minds, brains and programs. *The Behavioral and Brain Sciences, 3,* 417–425.

Segalowitz, S. J. (1983). *Two sides of the brain.* Englewood Cliffs, N.J.: Prentice-Hall.

Serafetinides, E., Hoare, R., & Driver, M. (1965). Intracarotid sodium amylobarbitone and cerebral dominance for speech and consciousness. *Brain, 88,* 107–130.

Singer, J. L., & Singer, D. C. (1984). *Television, imagination and aggression.* Hillsdale, N.J.: Erlbaum.

Swenson, L. (1972). *The etherial aether: A history of the Michelson–Morley–Miller aether-drift experiments, 1890–1930.* Austin: University of Texas Press.

Tulving, E. (1983). *Elements of episodic memory.* Oxford: Clarendon Press.

Turkle, S. (1984). *The second self: Computers and the human spirit.* New York, Simon & Shuster.

Tylor, E. B. (1974). *Primitive culture: Researches into the development of mythology, philosophy, religion, art and custom.* New York: Gordon Press.

Vico, G. (1744). *The new science of Giambattista Vico.* (3rd Edition, T. G. Bergin & M. H. Fisch translation). Ithaca: Cornell University Press, 1984.

Weber, M. (1964). *The sociology of religion.* London: Beacon Press.

Weissman, J. (1979). Vision, madness and morality: Poetry and the theory of the bicameral mind. *Georgia Review, 33,* 118–148.

Weissman, J. (1982). "Somewhere in earshot": Yates' admonitory gods. *Pequod, 14,* 16–31.

Whewell, W. (1858). *Theory of scientific method* (R. E. Butts, Ed.). Pittsburgh: University of Pittsburgh Press, 1968.

Whitaker, H., & Ojemann, G. (1977). Lateralization of higher cortical functions: A critique. *Annals of the New York Academy of Sciences, 299,* 459–473.

Whitehead, A. N. (1925). *Science and the modern world.* Cambridge: Cambridge University Press.

Wigner, E. (1972). The place of consciousness in modern physics. In C. Muses & A. M. Young (Eds.), *Consciousness and science.* New York: Outerbridge & Lazard.

Witelson, S. F. (1977). Anatomic asymmetry in the temporal lobes: Its documentation, phylogenesis, and relationship to functional asymmetry. *Annals of the New York Academy of Sciences, 299,* 328–354.

Split Brains

4

R. W. SPERRY
Hemisphere Deconnection and Unity in Conscious Awareness[1]

The following article is a result of studies my colleagues and I have been conducting with some neurosurgical patients of Philip J. Vogel of Los Angeles. These patients were all advanced epileptics in whom an extensive midline section of the cerebral commissures had been carried out in an effort to contain severe epileptic convulsions not controlled by medication. In all these people the surgical sections included division of the corpus callosum in its entirety, plus division also of the smaller anterior and hippocampal commissures, plus in some instances the massa intermedia. So far as I know, this is the most radical disconnection of the cerebral hemispheres attempted thus far in human surgery. The full array of sections was carried out in a single operation.

[1]Invited address presented to the American Psychological Association in Washington, D.C., September 1967, and to the Pan American Congress of Neurology in San Juan, Puerto Rico, October 1967. Original work referred to in the text by the writer and his co-workers was supported by Grant MH-03372 from the National Institute of Mental Health, United States Public Health Service, and by the Hixon Fund of the California Institute of Technology.

No major collapse of mentality or personality was anticipated as a result of this extreme surgery: earlier clinical observations on surgical section of the corpus callosum in man, as well as the results from dozens of monkeys on which I had carried out this exact same surgery, suggested that the functional deficits might very likely be less damaging than some of the more common forms of cerebral surgery, such as frontal lobotomy, or even some of the unilateral lobotomies performed more routinely for epilepsy.

The first patient on whom this surgery was tried had been having seizures for more than 10 years with generalized convulsions that continued to worsen despite treatment that had included a sojourn in Bethesda at the National Institutes of Health. At the time of the surgery, he had been averaging two major attacks per week, each of which left him debilitated for another day or so. Episodes of *status epilepticus* (recurring seizures that fail to stop and represent a medical emergency with a fairly high mortality risk) had also begun to occur at 2- to 3-month intervals. Since leaving the hospital following his surgery over 5½ years ago, this man has not had, according to last reports, a single generalized convulsion. It has further been possible to reduce the level of medication and to obtain an overall improvement in his behavior and well being (see Bogen & Vogel, 1962).

The second patient, a housewife and mother in her 30s, also has been seizure-free since recovering from her surgery, which was more than 4 years ago (Bogen, Fisher, & Vogel, 1965). Bogen related that even the EEG has regained a normal pattern in this patient. The excellent outcome in the initial, apparently hopeless, last-resort cases led to further application of the surgery to some nine more individuals to date, the majority of whom are too recent for therapeutic evaluation. Although the alleviation of the epilepsy has not held up 100% throughout the series (two patients are still having seizures, although their convulsions are much reduced in severity and frequency and tend to be confined to one side), the results on the whole continue to be predominantly beneficial, and the overall outlook at this time remains promising for selected severe cases.

The therapeutic success, however, and all other medical aspects are matters for our medical colleagues, Philip J. Vogel and Joseph E. Bogen. Our own work has been confined entirely to an examination of the functional outcome, that is, the behavioral, neurological, and psychological effects of this surgical disruption of all direct cross-talk between the hemispheres. Initially we were concerned as to whether we would be able to find in these patients any of the numerous symptoms of hemisphere deconnection that had been demonstrated in the so-called "split-brain" animal studies of the 1950s (Myers, 1961; Sperry, 1967a, 1967b). The outcome in man remained an open question in view of the historic Akelaitis (1944) studies that had set the prevailing doctrine of the 1940s and 1950s. This doctrine maintained that no important functional symptoms are found in man following even complete surgical section of the

corpus callosum and anterior commissure, provided that other brain damage is excluded.

These earlier observations on the absence of behavioral symptoms in man have been confirmed in a general way to the extent that it remains fair to say today that the most remarkable effect of sectioning the neocortical commissures is the apparent lack of effect so far as ordinary behavior is concerned. This has been true in our animal studies throughout, and it seems now to be true for man also, with certain qualifications that we will come to later. At the same time, however—and this is in contradiction to the earlier doctrine set by the Akelaitis studies—we know today that with appropriate tests one can indeed demonstrate a large number of behavioral symptoms that correlate directly with the loss of the neocortical commissures in man as well as in animals (Gazzaniga, 1967; Sperry, 1967a, 1967b; Sperry, Gazzaniga, & Bogen, 1968). Taken collectively, these symptoms may be referred to as the syndrome of the neocortical commissures or the syndrome of the forebrain commissures or, less specifically, as the syndrome of hemisphere deconnection.

One of the more general and also more interesting and striking features of this syndrome may be summarized as an apparent doubling in most of the realms of conscious awareness. Instead of the normally unified single stream of consciousness, these patients behave in many ways as if they have two independent streams of conscious awareness, one in each hemisphere, each of which is cut off from and out of contact with the mental experiences of the other. In other words, each hemisphere seems to have its own separate and private sensations; its own perceptions; its own concepts; and its own impulses to act, with related volitional, cognitive, and learning experiences. Following the surgery, each hemisphere also has thereafter its own separate chain of memories that are rendered inaccessible to the recall processes of the other.

This presence of two minds in one body, as it were, is manifested in a large number and variety of test responses which, for the present purposes, I will try to review very briefly and in a somewhat streamlined and simplified form. . . .

Most of the main symptoms seen after hemisphere deconnection can be described for convenience with reference to a single testing setup —shown in Figure 1. Principally, it allows for the lateralized testing of the right and left halves of the visual field, separately or together, and the right and left hands and legs with vision excluded. The tests can be arranged in different combinations and in association with visual, auditory, and other input, with provisions for eliminating unwanted stimuli. In testing vision, the subject with one eye covered centers his gaze on a designated fixation point on the upright translucent screen. The visual stimuli on 35-millimeter transparencies are arranged in a standard projector equipped with a shutter and are then back-projected at $\frac{1}{10}$ of a second or

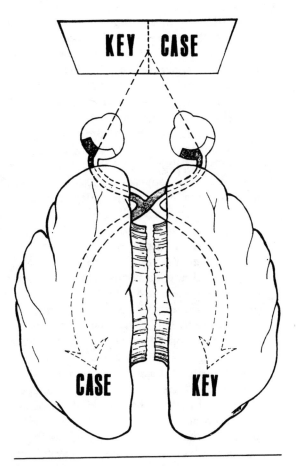

Figure 2
Things seen to the left of a central fixation point with either eye are projected to the right hemisphere and vice versa.

less—too fast for eye movements to get the material into the wrong half of the visual field. Figure 2 is merely a reminder that everything seen to the left of the vertical meridian through either eye is projected to the right hemisphere and vice versa. The midline division along the vertical meridian is found to be quite precise without significant gap or overlap (Sperry, 1968).

When the visual perception of these patients

Figure 1
Apparatus for studying lateralization of visual, tactual, lingual, and associated functions in the surgically separated hemispheres.

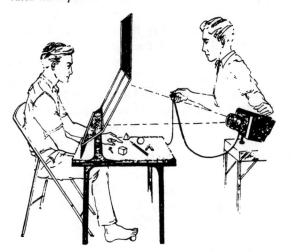

is tested under these conditions the results indicate that these people have not one inner visual world any longer, but rather two separate visual inner worlds, one serving the right half of the field of vision and the other the left half — each, of course, in its respective hemisphere. This doubling in the visual sphere shows up in many ways: For example, after a projected picture of an object has been identified and responded to in one half field, we find that it is recognized again only if it reappears in the same half of the field of vision. If the given visual stimulus reappears in the opposite half of the visual field, the subject responds as if he had no recollection of the previous exposure. In other words, things seen through the right half of the visual field (i.e., through the left hemisphere) are registered in mental experience and remembered quite separately from things seen in the other half of the field. Each half of the field of vision in the commissurotomized patient has its own train of visual images and memories.

This separate existence of two visual inner worlds is further illustrated in reference to speech and writing, the cortical mechanisms for which are centered in the dominant hemisphere. Visual material projected to the right half of the field — left-hemisphere system of the typical right-handed patient — can be described in speech and writing in an essentially normal manner. However, when the same visual material is projected into the left half of the field, and hence to the right hemisphere, the subject consistently insists that he did not see anything or that there was only a flash of light on the left side. The subject acts as if he were blind or agnostic for the left half of the visual field. If, however, instead of asking the subject to tell you what he saw, you instruct him to use his left hand to point to a matching picture or object presented among a collection of other pictures or objects, the subject has no trouble as a rule in pointing out consistently the very item that he has just insisted he did not see.

We do not think the subjects are trying to be

difficult or to dupe the examiner in such tests. Everything indicates that the hemisphere that is talking to the examiner did in fact not see the left-field stimulus and truly had no experience with, nor recollection of, the given stimulus. The other, the right or nonlingual hemisphere, however, did see the projected stimulus in this situation and is able to remember and recognize the object and can demonstrate this by pointing out selectively the corresponding or matching item. This other hemisphere, like a deaf mute or like some aphasics, cannot talk about the perceived object and, worse still, cannot write about it either.

If two different figures are flashed simultaneously to the right and left visual fields, as for example a "dollar sign" on the left and a "question mark" on the right and the subject is asked to draw what he saw using the left hand out of sight, he regularly reproduces the figure seen on the left half of the field, that is, the dollar sign. If we now ask him what he has just drawn, he tells us without hesitation that the figure he drew was the question mark, or whatever appeared in the right half of the field. In other words, the one hemisphere does not know what the other hemisphere has been doing. The left and the right halves of the visual field seem to be perceived quite separately in each hemisphere with little or no cross-influence.

When words are flashed partly in the left field and partly in the right, the letters on each side of the midline are perceived and responded to separately. In the "key case" example shown in Figure 2 the subject might first reach for and select with the left hand a key from among a collection of objects indicating perception through the minor hemisphere. With the right hand he might then spell out the word "case" or he might speak the word if verbal response is in order. When asked what kind of "case" he was thinking of here, the answer coming from the left hemisphere might be something like "in *case* of fire" or "the *case* of the missing corpse" or "a *case* of beer," etc., depending upon the particular mental set of the left hemisphere at the moment. Any reference to "key case" under these conditions would be purely fortuitous, assuming that visual, auditory, and other cues have been properly controlled.

A similar separation in mental awareness is evident in tests that deal with stereognostic or other somesthetic discriminations made by the right and left hands, which are projected separately to the left and right hemispheres, respectively. Objects put in the right hand for identification by touch are readily described or named in speech or writing, whereas, if the same objects are placed in the left hand, the subject can only make wild guesses and may often seem unaware that anything at all is present. As with vision in the left field, however, good perception, comprehension, and memory can be demonstrated for these objects in the left hand when the tests are so designed that the subject can express himself through nonverbal responses. For example, if one of these objects which the subject tells you he cannot feel or does not recognize is taken from the left hand and placed in a grab bag or scrambled among a dozen other test items, the subject is then able to search out and retrieve the initial object even after a delay of several minutes is deliberately interposed. Unlike the normal subject, however, these people are obliged to retrieve such an object with the same hand with which it was initially identified. They fail at cross-retrieval. That is, they cannot recognize with one hand something identified only moments before with the other hand. Again, the second hemisphere does not know what the first hemisphere has been doing.

When the subjects are first asked to use the left hand for these stereognostic tests they commonly complain that they cannot "work with that hand," that the hand "is numb," that they "just can't feel anything or can't do anything with it," or that they "don't get the message from that hand." If the subjects perform a series of successful trials and correctly retrieve a group of objects which they previously stated they

could not feel, and if this contradiction is then pointed out to them, we get comments like "Well, I was just guessing," or "Well, I must have done it unconsciously."

With other simple tests a further lack of cross-integration can be demonstrated in the sensory and motor control of the hands. In a "symmetric handpose" test the subject holds both hands out of sight symmetrically positioned and not in contact. One hand is then passively placed by the examiner into a given posture, such as a closed fist, or one, two, or more fingers extended or crossed or folded into various positions. The subject is then instructed verbally or by demonstration to form the same pose with the other hand, also excluded from vision. The normal subject does this quite accurately, but the commissurotomy patient generally fails on all but the very simplest hand postures, like the closed fist or the fully extended hand.

In a test for crossed topognosis in the hands, the subject holds both hands out of sight, forward and palm up with the fingers held apart and extended. The examiner then touches lightly a point on one of the fingers or at the base of the fingers. The subject responds by touching the same target point with the tip of the thumb of the same hand. Cross-integration is tested by requiring the patient to use the opposite thumb to find the corresponding mirror point on the opposite hand. The commissurotomy patients typically perform well within either hand, but fail when they attempt to cross-locate the corresponding point on the opposite hand. A crude cross-performance with abnormally long latency may be achieved in some cases after practice, depending on the degree of ipsilateral motor control and the development of certain strategies. The latter breaks down easily under stress and is readily distinguished from the natural performance of the normal subject with intact callosum.

In a related test the target point is presented visually as a black spot on an outline drawing of the hand. The picture is flashed to the right or left half of the visual field, and the subject then attempts as above to touch the target spot with the tip of the thumb. The response again is performed on the same side with normal facility but is impaired in the commissurotomy patient when the left visual field is paired with a right-hand response and vice versa. Thus the duality of both manual stereognosis and visuognosis is further illustrated; each hemisphere perceives as a separate unit unaware of the perceptual experience of the partner.

If two objects are placed simultaneously, one in each hand, and then are removed and hidden for retrieval in a scrambled pile of test items, each hand will hunt through the pile and search out selectively its own object. In the process each hand may explore, identify, and reject the item for which the other hand is searching. It is like two separate individuals working over the collection of test items with no cooperation between them. We find the interpretation of this and of many similar performances to be less confusing if we do not try to think of the behavior of the commissurotomy patient as that of a single individual, but try to think instead in terms of the mental faculties and performance capacities of the left and the right hemispheres separately. Most of the time it appears that the major, that is, the left, hemisphere is in control. But in some tasks, particularly when these are forced in testing procedures, the minor hemisphere seems able to take over temporarily.

It is worth remembering that when you split the brain in half anatomically you do not divide in half, in quite the same sense, its functional properties. In some respects cerebral functions may be doubled as much as they are halved because of the extensive bilateral redundancy in brain organization, wherein most functions, particularly in subhuman species, are separately and rather fully organized on both sides. Consider for example the visual inner world of either of the disconnected hemispheres in these patients. Probably neither of the separated vi-

sual systems senses or perceives itself to be cut in half or even incomplete. One may compare it to the visual sphere of the hemianopic patient who, following accidental destruction of an entire visual cortex of one hemisphere, may not even notice the loss of the whole half sphere of vision until this has been pointed out to him in specific optometric tests. These commissurotomy patients continue to watch television and to read the paper and books with no complaints about peculiarities in the perceptual appearance of the visual field.

At the same time, I want to caution against any impression that these patients are better off mentally without their cerebral commissures. It is true that if you carefully select two simple tasks, each of which is easily handled by a single hemisphere, and then have the two performed simultaneously, there is a good chance of getting better than normal scores. The normal interference effects that come from trying to attend to two separate right and left tasks at the same time are largely eliminated in the commissurotomized patient. However, in most activities that are at all complex the normally unified cooperating hemispheres still appear to do better than the two disconnected hemispheres. Although it is true that the intelligence, as measured on IQ tests, is not much affected and that the personality comes through with little change, one gets the impression in working with these people that their intellect is nevertheless handicapped in ways that are probably not revealed in the ordinary tests. All the patients have marked short-term memory deficits, which are especially pronounced during the first year, and it is open to question whether this memory impairment ever clears completely. They also have orientation problems, fatigue more quickly in reading and in other tasks requiring mental concentration, and presumably have various other impairments that reduce the upper limits of performance in functions that have yet to be investigated. The patient that has shown the best recovery, a boy of 14, was able to return to public school and was doing passing work with B to D grades, except for an F in math, which he had to repeat. He was, however, a D student before the surgery, in part, it would seem, for lack of motivation. In general, our tests to date have been concerned mostly with basic cross-integrational deficits in these patients and the kind of mental capacities preserved in the subordinate hemisphere. Studied comparisons of the upper limits of performance before and after surgery are still needed.

Much of the foregoing is summarized schematically in Figure 3. The left hemisphere in the

Figure 3
Schematic outline of the functional lateralization evident in behavioral tests of patients with forebrain commissurotomy.

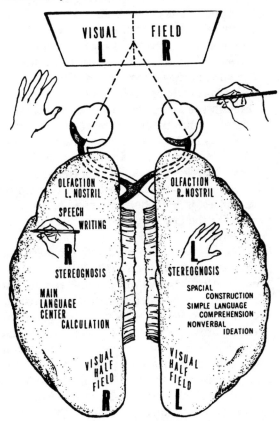

right-handed patients is equipped with the expressive mechanisms for speech and writing and with the main centers for the comprehension and organization of language. This "major" hemisphere can communicate its experiences verbally and in an essentially normal manner. It can communicate, that is, about the visual experiences of the right half of the optic field and about the somesthetic and volitional experiences of the right hand and leg and right half of the body generally. In addition, and *not* indicated in the figure, the major hemisphere also communicates, of course, about all of the more general, less lateralized cerebral activity that is bilaterally represented and common to both hemispheres. On the other side we have the mute aphasic and agraphic right hemisphere, which cannot express itself verbally, but which through the use of nonverbal responses can show that it is not agnostic; that mental processes are indeed present centered around the left visual field, left hand, left leg, and left half of the body; along with the auditory, vestibular, axial somatic, and all other cerebral activities that are less lateralized and for which the mental experiences of the right and left hemispheres may be characterized as being similar but separate.

It may be noted that nearly all of the symptoms of cross-integrational impairment that I have been describing are easily hidden or compensated under the conditions of ordinary behavior. For example, the visual material has to be flashed at 1/10 of a second or less to one half of the field in order to prevent compensation by eye movements. The defects in manual stereognosis are not apparent unless vision is excluded; nor is doubling in olfactory perception evident without sequential occlusion of right and left nostril and elimination of visual cues. In many tests the major hemisphere must be prevented from talking to the minor hemisphere and thus giving away the answer through auditory channels. And, similarly, the minor hemisphere must be prevented from giving nonverbal signals of various sorts to the major hemisphere. There is a great diversity of indirect strategies and response signals, implicit as well as overt, by which the informed hemisphere can be used to cue-in the uninformed hemisphere (Levy-Agresti, 1968).

Normal behavior under ordinary conditions is favored also by many other unifying factors. Some of these are very obvious, like the fact that these two separate mental spheres have only one body, so they always get dragged to the same places, meet the same people, and see and do the same things all the time and thus are bound to have a great overlap of common, almost identical, experience. Just the unity of the optic image—and even after chiasm section in animal experiments, the conjugate movements of the eyes—means that both hemispheres automatically center on, focus on, and hence probably attend to, the same items in the visual field all the time. Through sensory feedback a unifying body schema is imposed in each hemisphere with common components that similarly condition in parallel many processes of perception and motor action onto a common base. To get different activities going and different experiences and different memory chains built up in the separated hemispheres of the bisected mammalian brain, as we do in the animal work, requires a considerable amount of experimental planning and effort.

In motor control we have another important unifying factor, in that either hemisphere can direct the movement of both sides of the body, including to some extent the movements of the ipsilateral hand (Hamilton, 1967). Insofar as a response involves mainly the axial parts and proximal limb segments, these patients have little problem in directing overall response from sensory information restricted to either single hemisphere. Control of the distal limb segments and especially of the finer finger movements of the hand ipsilateral to the governing hemisphere, however, are borderline functions and subject to considerable variation. Impairments

are most conspicuous when the subject is given a verbal command to respond with the fingers of the left hand. The absence of the callosum, which normally would connect the language processing centers in the left hemisphere to the main left-hand motor controls in the opposite hemisphere, is clearly a handicap, especially in the early months after surgery. Cursive writing with the left hand presents a similar problem. It may be accomplished in time by some patients using shoulder and elbow rather than finger movement. At best, however, writing with the left hand is not as good after as before the surgery. The problem is not in motor coordination per se, because the subject can often copy with the left hand a word already written by the examiner when the same word cannot be written to verbal command.

In a test used for more direct determination of the upper limits of this ipsilateral motor control, a simple outline sketch of a finger posture (see Figure 4) is flashed to a single hemisphere, and the subject then tries to mimic the posture with the same or the opposite hand. The sample posture can usually be copied on the same side (i.e., through the main, contralateral control system) without difficulty, but the performance does not go so easily and often breaks down completely when the subject is obliged to use the opposite hand. The closed fist and the open hand with all fingers extended seem to be the two simplest responses, in that these can most often be copied with the ipsilateral hand by the more adept patients.

The results are in accord with the thesis (Gazzaniga, Bogen, & Sperry, 1967) that the ipsilateral control systems are delicate and marginal and easily disrupted by associated cerebral damage and other complicating factors. Preservation of the ipsilateral control system in varying degree in some patients and not in others would appear to account for many of the discrepancies that exist in the literature on the symptoms of hemisphere deconnection, and also for a number of changes between the

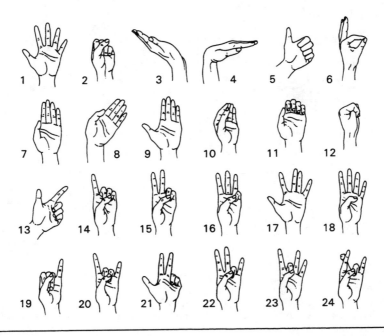

Figure 4
In tests for ipsilateral motor control, different hand postures in outline drawing are projected one at a time to left or right visual field (see Figure 1). Subject attempts to copy the sample hand pose with the homolateral and the contralateral hand.

present picture and that described until 2 years ago. Those acquainted with the literature will notice that the present findings on dyspraxia come much closer to the earlier Akelaitis observations than they do to those of Liepmann or of others expounded more recently (see Geschwind, 1965).

To try to find out what goes on in that speechless agraphic minor hemisphere has always been one of the main challenges in our testing program. Does the minor hemisphere really possess a true stream of conscious awareness or is it just an agnostic automaton that is carried along in a reflex or trancelike state? What is the nature, the quality, and the level of the mental life of this isolated subordinate unknown half of the human brain—which, like the animal mind, cannot communicate its experiences? Closely tied in here are many problems

that relate to lateral dominance and specialization in the human brain, to the functional roles mediated by the neocortical commissures, and to related aspects of cerebral organization.

With such in mind, I will try to review briefly some of the evidence obtained to date that pertains to the level and nature of the inner mental life of the disconnected minor hemisphere. First, it is clear that the minor hemisphere can perform intermodal or cross-modal transfer of perceptual and mnemonic information at a characteristically human level. For example, after a picture of some object, such as a cigarette, has been flashed to the minor hemisphere through the left visual field, the subject can retrieve the item pictured from a collection of objects using blind touch with the left hand, which is mediated through the right hemisphere. Unlike the normal person, however, the commissurotomy

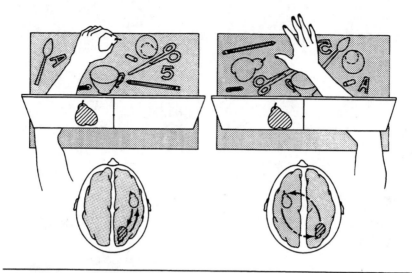

Figure 5
Visuo-tactile associations succeed between each half of the visual field and the correspond-
ing hand. They fail with crossed combinations in which visual and tactual stimuli are
projected into opposite hemispheres.

patient is obliged to use the corresponding hand (i.e., the left hand, in this case) for retrieval and fails when he is required to search out the same object with the right hand (see Figure 5). Using the right hand the subject recognizes and can call off the names of each object that he comes to if he is allowed to do so, but the right hand or its hemisphere does not know what it is looking for, and the hemisphere that can recognize the correct answer gets no feedback from the right hand. Hence, the two never get together, and the performance fails. Speech and other auditory cues must be controlled.

It also works the other way around: that is, if the subject is holding an object in the left hand, he can then point out a picture of this object or the printed name of the object when these appear in a series presented visually. But again, these latter must be seen through the corresponding half of the visual field; an object identified by the left hand is not recognized when seen in the right half of the visual field. Inter-

modal associations of this sort have been found to work between vision, hearing and touch, and, more recently, olfaction in various combinations within either hemisphere but not across from one hemisphere to the other. This perceptual or mnemonic transfer from one sense modality to another has special theoretical interest in that it is something that is extremely difficult or impossible for the monkey brain. The right hemisphere, in other words, may be animal like in not being able to talk or write, but in performances like the foregoing and in a number of other respects it shows mental capacities that are definitely human.

Other responses from the minor hemisphere in this same testing situation suggest the presence of ideas and a capacity for mental association and at least some simple logic and reasoning. In the same visuo-tactual test described above, the minor hemisphere, instead of selecting objects that match exactly the pictured item, seems able also to select related items or items that "go with" the particular visual stimulus, if the subject is so instructed. For example, if we flash a picture of a wall clock to the minor side and the nearest item that can be found tactually by the left hand is a toy wrist watch, the subjects significantly select the watch. It is as if the minor hemisphere has an idea of a timepiece here and is not just matching sensory outlines. Or, if the picture of a dollar sign is flashed to the minor side, the subject searches through the list of items with the left hand and finally selects a coin such as a quarter or a 50¢ piece. If a picture of a hammer is presented, the subject may come up with a nail or a spike after checking out and rejecting all other items.

The capacity to think abstractly with symbols is further indicated in the ability of the minor hemisphere to perform simple arithmetical problems. When confronted with two numerals each less than 10, the minor hemisphere was able in four of six subjects so tested to respond with the correct sum or product up to 20 or so. The numbers were flashed to the left half of the visual field or presented as plastic block numerals to the left hand for identification. The answer was expressed by pointing to the correct number in columns of seen figures, or by left-hand signals in which the fingers were extended out of the subject's sight, or by writing the numerals with the left hand out of sight. After a correct left-hand response had been made by pointing or by writing the numeral, the major hemisphere could then report the same answer verbally, but the verbal report could not be made prior to the left-hand response. If an error was made with the left hand, the verbal report contained the same error. Two different pairs of numerals may be flashed to right and left fields simultaneously and the correct sum or products signaled separately by right and left hands. When verbal confirmation of correct left-hand signals is required under these conditions, the speaking hemisphere can only guess fortuitously, showing again that the answer must have been obtained from the minor and not

from the major hemisphere. This has been demonstrated recently in a study still in progress by Biersner and the present writer. The findings correct an earlier impression (Gazzaniga & Sperry, 1967) in which we underestimated the capacity for calculation on the minor side. Normal subjects and also a subject with agenesis of the callosum (Saul & Sperry, 1968) were able to add or to multiply numerals shown one in the left and one in the right field under these conditions. The commissurotomy subjects, however, were able to perform such calculations only when both numerals appeared in the same half of the visual field.

According to a doctrine of long standing in the clinical writings on aphasia, it is believed that the minor hemisphere, when it has been disconnected by commissural or other lesions from the language centers on the opposite side, becomes then "word blind," "word deaf," and "tactually alexic." In contradiction to this, we find that the disconnected minor hemisphere in these commissurotomy patients is able to comprehend both written and spoken words to some extent, although this comprehension cannot be expressed verbally (Gazzaniga & Sperry, 1967; Sperry, 1966; Sperry & Gazzaniga, 1967). If the name of some object is flashed to the left visual field, like the word "eraser," for example, the subject is able then to search out an eraser from among a collection of objects using only touch with the left hand. If the subject is then asked what the item is after it has been selected correctly, his replies show that he does not know what he is holding in his left hand—as is the general rule for left-hand stereognosis. This means of course that the *talking* hemisphere does not know the correct answer, and we concluded accordingly that the minor hemisphere must, in this situation, have read and understood the test world.

These patients also demonstrate comprehension of language in the minor hemisphere by being able to find by blind touch with the left hand an object that has been named aloud by the examiner. For example, if asked to find a "piece of silverware," the subject may explore the array of test items and pick up a fork. If the subject is then asked what it is that he has chosen, he is just as likely in this case to reply "spoon" or "knife" as fork. Both hemispheres have heard and understood the word "silverware," but only the minor hemisphere knows what the left hand has actually found and picked up. In similar tests for comprehension of the spoken word, we find that the minor hemisphere seems able to understand even moderately advanced definitions like "shaving instrument" for razor or "dirt remover" for soap and "inserted in slot machines" for quarter.

Work in progress shows that the minor hemisphere can also sort objects into groups by touch on the basis of shape, size, and texture. In some tests the minor hemisphere is found to be superior to the major, for example, in tasks that involve drawing spatial relationships and performing block design tests. Perceptive mental performance in the minor hemisphere is also indicated in other situations in which the two hemispheres function concurrently in parallel at different tasks. It has been found, for example, that the divided hemispheres are capable of perceiving different things occupying the same position in space at the same time, and of learning mutually conflicting discrimination habits, something of which the normal brain is not capable. This was shown in the monkey work done some years ago by Trevarthen (1962) using a system of polarized light filters. It also required section of the optic chiasm, which of course is not included in the human surgery. The human patients, unlike normal subjects, are able to carry out a double voluntary reaction-time task as fast as they carry out a single task (Gazzaniga & Sperry, 1966). Each hemisphere in this situation has to perform a separate and different visual discrimination in order to push with the corresponding hand the correct one of a right and left pair of panels. Whereas interference and extra delay are seen in normal subjects

with the introduction of the second task, these patients with the two hemispheres working in parallel simultaneously perform the double task as rapidly as the single task.

The minor hemisphere is also observed to demonstrate appropriate emotional reactions as, for example, when a pinup shot of a nude is interjected by surprise among a series of neutral geometric figures being flashed to the right and left fields at random. When the surprise nude appears on the left side the subject characteristically says that he or she saw nothing or just a flash of light. However, the appearance of a sneaky grin and perhaps blushing and giggling on the next couple of trials or so belies the verbal contention of the speaking hemisphere. If asked what all the grinning is about, the subject's replies indicate that the conversant hemisphere has no idea at this stage what it was that had turned him on. Apparently, only the emotional effect gets across, as if the cognitive component of the process cannot be articulated through the brainstem.

Emotion is also evident on the minor side in a current study by Gordon and Sperry (1968) involving olfaction. When odors are presented through the right nostril to the minor hemisphere the subject is unable to name the odor but can frequently tell whether it is pleasant or unpleasant. The subject may even grunt, make aversive reactions or exclamations like "phew!" to a strong unpleasant smell, but not be able to state verbally whether it is garlic, cheese, or some decayed matter. Again it appears that the affective component gets across to the speaking hemisphere, but not the more specific information. The presence of the specific information within the minor hemisphere is demonstrated by the subject's correct selection through left-hand stereognosis of corresponding objects associated with the given odor. The minor hemisphere also commonly triggers emotional reactions of displeasure in the course of ordinary testing. This is evidenced in the frowning, wincing, and negative head shaking in test situations where the minor hemisphere, knowing the correct answer but unable to speak, hears the major hemisphere making obvious verbal mistakes. The minor hemisphere seems to express genuine annoyance at the erroneous vocal responses of its better half.

Observations like the foregoing lead us to favor the view that in the minor hemisphere we deal with a second conscious entity that is characteristically human and runs along in parallel with the more dominant stream of consciousness in the major hemisphere (Sperry, 1966). The quality of mental awareness present in the minor hemisphere may be comparable perhaps to that which survives in some types of aphasic patients following losses in the motor and main language centers. There is no indication that the dominant mental system of the left hemisphere is concerned about or even aware of the presence of the minor system under most ordinary conditions except quite indirectly as, for example, through occasional responses triggered from the minor side. As one patient remarked immediately after seeing herself make a left-hand response of this kind, "Now I know it wasn't me did that!"

Let me emphasize again in closing that the foregoing represents a somewhat abbreviated and streamlined account of the syndrome of hemisphere deconnection as we understand it at the present time. The more we see of these patients and the more of these patients we see, the more we become impressed with their individual differences, and with the consequent qualifications that must be taken into account. Although the general picture has continued to hold up in the main as described, it is important to note that, with respect to many of the deconnection symptoms mentioned, striking modifications and even outright exceptions can be found among the small group of patients examined to date. Where the accumulating evidence will settle out with respect to the extreme limits of such individual variations and with respect to a possible average "type" syndrome remains to be seen.

References

Akelaitis, A. J. A study of gnosis, praxis, and language following section of the corpus callosum and anterior commissure. *Journal of Neurosurgery*, 1944, 1, 94–102.

Bogen, J. E., Fisher, E. D., & Vogel, P. J. Cerebral commissurotomy: A second case report. *Journal of the American Medical Association*, 1965, 194, 1328–1329.

Bogen, J. E., & Vogel, P. J. Cerebral commissurotomy: A case report. *Bulletin of the Los Angeles Neurological Society*, 1962, 27, 169.

Gazzaniga, M. S. The split brain in man. *Scientific American*, 1967, 217, 24–29.

Gazzaniga, M. S., Bogen, J. E., & Sperry, R. W. Dyspraxia following division of the cerebral commissures. *Archives of Neurology*, 1967, 16, 606–612.

Gazzaniga, M. S., & Sperry, R. W. Simultaneous double discrimination following brain bisection. *Psychonomic Science*, 1966, 4, 262–263.

Gazzaniga, M. S., & Sperry, R. W. Language after section of the cerebral commissures. *Brain*, 1967, 90, 131–148.

Geschwind, N. Disconnexion syndromes in animals and man. *Brain*, 1965, 88, 237–294, 584–644.

Gordon, H. W., & Sperry R. W. Olfaction following surgical disconnection of the hemispheres in man. In, *Proceedings of the Psychonomic Society*, 1968, in press.

Hamilton, C. R. Effects of brain bisection on eye-hand coordination in monkeys wearing prisms. *Journal of Comparative and Physiological Psychology*, 1967, 64, 434–443.

Levy-Agresti, J. Ipsilateral projection systems and minor hemisphere function in man after neocommissurotomy. *Anatomical Record,* 1968, 160, 384.

Myers, R. E. Corpus callosum and visual gnosis. In J. F. Delafresnaye (Ed.), *Brain mechanisms and learning.* Oxford: Blackwell, 1961.

Saul, R., & Sperry, R. W. Absence of commissurotomy symptoms with agenesis of the corpus callosum. *Neurology,* 1968, 17, in press.

Sperry, R. W. Brain bisection and mechanisms of consciousness. In J. C. Eccles (Ed.), *Brain and conscious experience.* New York: Springer-Verlag, 1966.

Sperry, R. W. Mental unity following surgical disconnection of the hemispheres. *The Harvey lectures.* Series 62. New York: Academic Press, 1967. (a)

Sperry, R. W. Split-brain approach to learning prob-

lems. In G. C. Quarton, T. Melnechuk, & F. O. Schmitt (Eds.), *The neurosciences: A study program.* New York: Rockefeller University Press, 1967. (b)

Sperry, R. W. Apposition of visual half-fields after section of neocortical commissures. *Anatomical Record,* 1968, 160, 498–499.

Sperry, R. W., & Gazzaniga, M. S. Language following surgical disconnection of the hemispheres. In C. H. Milikan (Ed.), *Brain mechanisms underlying speech and language.* New York: Grune & Stratton, 1967.

Sperry, R. W., Gazzaniga, M. S., & Bogen, J. E. Function of neocortical commissures: Syndrome of hemisphere deconnection. In P. J. Vinken & G. W. Bruyn (Eds.), *Handbook of neurology.* Amsterdam: North Holland, 1968, in press.

Trevarthen, C. B. Double visual learning in split-brain monkeys. *Science,* 1962, 136, 258–259.

5

ROLAND PUCCETTI
Two Brains, Two Minds? Wigan's Theory of Mental Duality

1 Introduction

The occasion for writing this essay is the republication of A. L. Wigan's long-neglected classic study, *The Duality of the Mind* [1844, 1985], edited by Joseph E. Bogen and Joseph Simon. As Dr. Bogen makes clear in his Foreword to the volume, award of a Nobel Prize in physiology in 1981 to Roger Sperry for his work with split-brain patients has brought widespread attention to the duality of the brain; whether this also signals the presence of a dual *mind* in normal humans, as Wigan argued, is of course highly controversial. Bogen nevertheless states at the

end of his Foreword that Wigan's "prophetic vision was over 100 years ahead of the evidence which has ultimately sustained him (p. xv)." In this essay I shall be concerned whether, or to what degree, Wigan's theory has indeed been confirmed by split-brain and related studies. But it will be equally important to this task to examine the conceptual framework Wigan was working in.

What exactly was Wigan's theory? Perhaps his most succinct statement of this is found in Chapter XIX of the present edition:

There are some corrolaries which only need to be named, and their truth is so easily compre-

hended as to produce instant assent. If, for example, as I have so often stated, and now again repeat, one brain be a perfect instrument of thought — if it be capable of all the emotions, sentiments, and faculties, which we call in the aggregate, mind — then it necessarily follows that man must have two minds with two brains; and however intimate and perfect their unison in their natural state, they must occasionally be discrepant when influenced by disease, either direct, sympathetic, or reflex (201 – 2).

Two objections immediately arise from this synopsis. First, it does not follow *necessarily* that if we have two brains we have two minds, anymore than it follows necessarily from having two nostrils that we have two senses of smell.[1] Second, if it were the case that we have two minds, we should know this from experiencing two distinct trains of thought, etc., occurring to us simultaneously. Wigan apparently thought he did sometimes experience this, but most of us make no such claim. So in order for Wigan's theory (at least as stated above) to stand a chance of being true, he would have to explain how it is that we *do not experience any such mental duality.* I believe there is a way to explain this, but only by major revision of Wigan's working concepts.

2 Wigan's Argument for Our Having Two Brains

But I am getting ahead of myself. Let us first examine the reasoning that led Wigan to conclude that we normals have not one but two

brains.[2] I think his argument to this effect in Chapter IV striking, even if he was obviously wrong about the brain in other respects (he thought each cerebral hemisphere has only three lobes, rather than four; and that disease could be transmitted from one hemisphere to the other only through the meningeal coverings, rather than the corpus callosum):

I believe it to be entirely unphilosophical, and tending to important errors, to speak of the cerebrum as one organ. The term two hemispheres *of the brain is, indeed, strictly a misnomer, since the two together form very little more than one half of a sphere . . . The two hemisphere are really and in fact two distinct and entire organs, and each respectively as complete (indeed more complete), and as fully perfect in all its parts, for the purposes it is intended to perform, as are the two eyes. The corpus callosum, and the other commissures between them, can with no more justice be said to constitute the two hemispheres into one organ, than the optic commissure [optic chiasm] can be called a union of the two eyes into one organ; and it would be just as reasonable to talk of the two lobes or globes of the eye, as of the two hemispheres of the brain (19).*

Surely Wigan is on sound ground here. We feel no impulsion to conceive of a single

---

[1] This is not to deny that we have two *organs* for smelling (the two sides of the olfactory bulb, each supplying the ipsilateral cerebral hemisphere with neural input that transduces into olfactory sensations): on this point Wigan was absolutely correct.

[2] Wigan's *psychological* conversion to belief in double mindedness was occasioned, he says, by a discovery he made at autopsy early in his career:

One hemisphere was entirely gone — that was evident to my senses; the patient, a man about fifty years of age, had conversed rationally and even written verses, within a few days of his death; yet I knew that, according to books, the mind could only manifest itself through a complete brain (which is true enough as I now explain it [he means each hemisphere *is* a complete brain]), and I was in a similar state to that of persons who cannot refuse assent to geological facts, yet cannot reconcile them to the writings of Moses, in which they have absolute faith (32).

organ, "the eye," having two vitreous projections beyond the skin surface of the face; why then should we talk of "the brain" as a single organ having two fibrous intracranial bulges? At the very least we can concede to Wigan that commissural connections between the cerebral hemispheres do not of themselves make these a single organ, and thus that it is equally correct to speak of "the brain" as two cerebra, two half brains, or even two brains.

3 Evidence for Double Mindedness in Split-Brain Patients

But again two brains do not necessarily amount to two *minds*, and this is where the work of Sperry and others on split-brain patients becomes crucially relevant to Wigan's contention. For as a consequence of the therapeutic (for relief of *grand mal* seizures) surgery, or even of natural lesions to the corpus callosum uniting the two hemispheres, the patient displays thereafter a well-defined *disconnection syndrome*. This syndrome is not revealed in everyday behaviour (indeed such patients can pass a routine neurological examination if the physician is not looking for it), but under strictly controlled laboratory testing conditions it is unmistakably present. For example, a right-handed patient easily names objects palpated out of sight in the right hand (projecting most of its sensory fibers to the left, speaking hemisphere), but he or she cannot name objects palpated out of sight in the left hand (since almost all the sensory fibres of that hand project to the right, mute hemisphere, and there is no commissural transfer of the information to the speech hemisphere). Yet the "same" patient *knows* what is being palpated in the left hand, for upon command he or she can retrieve it from an array of objects behind a screen with that left hand (though not with the right hand, in the absence of interhemispheric

commissural transfer). Since normal individuals like ourselves never display such bifurcated behaviour, there is no doubt we are dealing here with two independent streams of consciousness, or minds.

However, the best demonstration of a disconnection syndrome is accomplished in the visual modality, using a tachistoscope. This device back-projects on a screen in front of the patient a picture or a word for one-tenth of a second or less (long enough to register consciously in either hemisphere, but too quickly for normal scanning movements of the eyes to get the information from both sides of the screen into each hemisphere). If for example the patient is asked to fixate on a spot in the centre of the screen and the word TAXABLE is flashed so that the letters TAX fall to the left, and the letters ABLE to the right, of fixation, the right-handed patient with a disconnection syndrome will *say* he or she saw the word ABLE. Yet if asked to point to the word seen using the *left* hand, he or she will select the word TAX from a list of words that includes both ABLE and TAXABLE. The normal subject like you or I would, of course, say the word was TAXABLE and would point to TAXABLE with *either* hand.

What explains this difference in behaviour? Given the concavity of the eyeballs, light from the right half visual field falls on left (temporal) hemiretina of the left eye, and on the left (nasal) hemiretina of the right eye. Neural impulses from these hemiretinae then join at the optic chiasm to project back to Brodmann's area 17 (primary visual cortex) in the occipital lobe of the left, speaking hemisphere. This is why the patient with a disconnection syndrome verbally reports seeing the word ABLE.

Similarly, light from the left half of the visual field strikes the right (nasal) hemiretina of the left eye, and the right (temporal) hemiretina of the right eye. Impulses from these hemiretinae then join at the optic chiasm to project back to the homologous area 17 in the occipital lobe of the right, mute hemisphere. This is why the patient with a disconnection syndrome, using the left hand under control of the nonspeaking right hemisphere, points to the word TAX and not to ABLE or to TAXABLE.

In a normal subject like you or I, however, there is a transfer of what was seen in area 17 of the right hemisphere via the corpus callosum (actually using fibres in its posterior ⅔, called the splenium) to the adjoining area 18 (prestriate cortex) of the left hemisphere. In this way do the letters TAX join the letters ABLE to register there as the whole original word, TAXABLE. But if this is what goes on in the left hemisphere of the normal subject, what is going on in his or her *right* hemisphere? As we have already seen, in the split condition this right hemisphere is capable of pointing with the left hand to the letters TAX as what it has perceived on the left side of the screen. If so, there is no good reason to doubt that in the unsplit condition area 17 of the left hemisphere projects the letters ABLE across the splenium to area 18, prestriate cortex, of the mute right hemisphere, thus forming the original complete word TAXABLE in that hemisphere as well. This, then, provides the model of mental duality Wigan was looking for a century and a half before.

4 Wigan's Mis-statement of His Theory

Yet Wigan did not find it. Why not? One reason may be that he was confused about what, exactly, he was claiming. What he *believed* he was claiming is set out with great clarity in Chapter IV, in the form of four propositions:

1. *That each cerebrum is a distinct and perfect whole, as an organ of thought.*

2. *That a separate and distinct process of thinking or ratiocination may be carried on in each cerebrum simultaneously.*

3. *That each cerebrum is capable of a distinct*

and separate volition, and that these are very often opposing volitions.

4. *That, in the healthy brain, one of the cerebra is almost always superior in power to the other, and capable of exercising control over the volitions of its fellow, and of preventing them from passing into acts, or from being manifested to others (20).*

Yet in Chapter XIX we find Wigan saying this:

I think it may be assumed without risk of contradiction, that the fact of each brain being a perfect and complete instrument of thought is abundantly proved. That each, while in health, corresponds entirely with its fellow, is obvious from the fact that this unison and correspondence give only one result, as in the case of the two eyes producing single vision (204).

Even on the face of it, this statement about the two eyes giving only one result, *i.e.* one visual percept, contradicts Wigan's own proposition 2 above, since if visual perception is a mental activity then on his theory it should occur "separately" and "distinctly" in each cerebrum simultaneously. And if it did, that is if our consciousness spanned both cerebra, then we should perceive any object of perception *twice* side-by-side: *i.e.* we should have *double* vision. It is not having two *eyes* that creates a problem for Wigan's theory (even with one eye closed, the residual eye has two hemiretinae projecting fibres to area 17 of both left and right hemispheres); nor does it matter that there should be perfect "unison and correspondence" between the two percepts: two is not one and that is what mental duality requires. The real problem is that Wigan couched his theory in terms of *one person having two minds*, which if understood literally entails our having, *e.g.*, double vision, though in fact we experience nothing of the kind.

5 Restatement of Wigan's Theory

Can the theory be saved nonetheless? I believe it can. Suppose we make a distinction Wigan did not make, between the human being qua *individual organism,* and the human being qua *person, i.e.* complex minded entity. We are then in a position to restate the theory of mental duality as follows: the individual human organism, having two brains, is the biological substrate of *two persons, each of which has one mind.* In that case, there will be, *e.g.,* double vision at the level of the *organism,* but each of the two *persons* will experience only single vision because, while each cerebrum receives input from the contralateral hemisphere about ipsilateral body space, neither cerebrum has introspective access to the conscious contents of the other.

Why not? An answer may be devined from evolutionary considerations. All vertebrate species have evolved two neural ganglia, one to each side of the anterior portion of a single neuraxis. Given this pattern of development, it comes as no surprise that all such species also evolved commissural connections between the two ganglia, since otherwise (given decussation of sensory and motor nerve tracts, with the exception of olfactory fibres) each ganglion would be ignorant of what is going on in ipsilateral body space. But it would be equally important for such species that consciousness *not* span the two cerebra, *i.e.* that there not be unity of consciousness within the whole cranium, to avoid subjective double mindedness: imagine the effect, for example, on our arboreal primate ancestors of seeing two branches out there side-by-side, when in reality there is only one! This means that in more highly evolved vertebrate species like our own, the function of the corpus callosum is not to integrate, but rather to duplicate the contents of conscious experience for the mutual benefit of the two cerebra.

6 Current Misconceptions of Double Mindedness

It is failure to make this distinction between dual mentality at the level of the organism, on the one hand, and subjectively experienced double mindedness on the other, which motivates much of the criticism directed at the theory. In her recent book, for example, Patricia Churchland describes the theory as a claim that "everyone has two minds (180)." Now what is meant by "everyone" here? If she means every normal human *organism,* that is correct. If, however, she means every complexly minded entity, or *person,* that is not what the present restated version of Wigan's theory maintains. She then comments that the theory entails "believing that each skull houses two persons/minds and that one is not, so to speak, *oneself* (*Ibid.*)." But why should not each person of the pair, with but one mind, be "oneself" to him/herself? Each would have a single stream of consciousness, even though its conscious content concerning ipsilateral body space is being relayed to it from the contralateral cerebral companion. The fact is that nothing one experiences in such a state would be any different from what one experiences at present; it is only when confronted with a disconnection syndrome that the original duality is revealed.[3]

7 The Evidence for Disguised Transcallosal Inhibition

If this were all that could be said for the theory, it would appear to be largely a verbal issue about how best to describe the organization of

[3]Although it may well be the case that duality is known to the mute right hemisphere of every normal human being, simply because it knows it is not generating the linguistic behaviour it observes emanating from its own body.

consciousness in the human brain. But in fact there is more to recommend it: namely what is hinted at in Wigan's proposition 3 (that each cerebrum is capable of distinct and often opposing volitions), and in his proposition 4 (that in the healthy brain dominance of one cerebrum over the other prevents this conflict being manifested in behaviour). For hemispheric disconnection, whether by therapeutic surgery or natural lesion, not only blocks information transfer between the two cerebra; it also disrupts *transcallosal inhibition*, thereby freeing the nondominant (usually the right) hemisphere to undertake independent actions involving the contralateral (usually the left) body side, actions that surprise and perplex the dominant or speaking hemisphere.

Following are some examples of resulting intermanual conflicts and the "alien hand" phenomenon, drawn from Bogen's [1985] authoritative review of the disconnection syndrome:

> The most interesting finding in the entire examination [of a patient presenting with a disconnection syndrome] is the frequent occurrence of well-coordinated movements of the left arm which are at cross purposes with whatever else is going on. These sometimes seem to occur spontaneously, but on other occasions are clearly in conflict with the behavior of the right arm. For example, when attempting a Jendrassic reinforcement, the patient reached with his right hand to hold his left, but the left hand actually pushed his right hand away. While testing finger-to-nose test (with the patient sitting), his left hand suddenly started slapping his chest like Tarzan (312–13).

> While doing the block test unimanually with his right hand [another patient's] left hand came up from beneath the table and was reaching for the blocks when he slapped it with his right hand and said, "That will keep it quiet for a while (313)."

> The patient may say, when the left hand makes some choice among objects, "My hand did that," rather than taking the responsibility. A patient was described [by an earlier investigator] as saying, "Now you want me to put my left index finger on my nose." She then put that finger into her mouth and said, "That's funny; why won't it go up my nose (313–14)?"

Bogen's own summary of the disconnection syndrome, after decades of clinical experience, is the following:

> Split-brain patients soon accept the idea that they have capacities of which they are not conscious, such as retrieval [with the left hand] of objects not nameable. They may quickly rationalize such acts, sometimes in a transparently erroneous way. But even many years after operation, the patients will occasionally be quite surprised when some well-coordinated or obviously well-informed act has just been carried out by the left hand (314).

Of course when Bogen speaks here of "the patient" having capacities of which he is not conscious, he means the person based in the speaking hemisphere; we have no good reason to doubt that the person based in the mute, right hemisphere and controlling the left hand retrieves objects *consciously*. Similarly, it is the dominant left hemisphere-based person who is surprised when the left hand carries out a well-informed or well-coordinated act; the right or nondominant hemisphere-based person is not surprised, since he or she initiated that act.

8 Conclusion

Those sceptics about mental duality who give the safe rejoinder that it is ablation of the forebrain commissures which creates double mindedness in patients manifesting the disconnection syndrome, so that its symptoms tell us nothing about the organization of consciousness in normals, must ask themselves how it is possible one half of a formerly healthy (except for proneness to epileptic seizures in many cases) brain—the half that does not even think in language—should be able to perform transparently intentional and purposeful acts like repeatedly throwing a newspaper to the floor during television commercials (the right hemisphere cannot read, and the newspaper does block its view of the TV screen); or slapping one's face when it is time to get up and have breakfast.[4] Such acts require, at the very least, memory, foresight, and anticipation of probable responses from the dominant, speaking hemisphere. Did these characteristically human psychological capacities arise *de novo* from the disconnection, or were they not previously present but suppressed by the unconscious inhibitory influence of the speech hemisphere, acting through the intact corpus callosum? The latter seem a far more parsimonious explanation of the behaviour Bogen has described.

I conclude that just as one mind does not become two upon hemispheric disconnection, so two minds do not become one upon maturation and myelinization of the commissural fibres linking together the two brains in our heads. Wigan may have not proved his theory, but he was on the right track.

References

Bogen, J. E. [1985]: "The Callosal Syndromes" *Clinical Neuropsychology*, Second Edition, Oxford University Press, pp. 295–338.

Churchland, P. S. [1986]: *Neurophilosophy.* MIT Press/Bradford Books.

Wigan, A. L. [1844, 1985]: *The Duality of the Mind.* Joseph Simon.

[4]The latter two examples were originally supplied to me by the late Stuart Dimond (personal communication, [1978]).

6

THOMAS NAGEL
Brain Bisection and the Unity of Consciousness

I

There has been considerable optimism recently, among philosophers and neuroscientists, concerning the prospect for major discoveries about the neurophysiological basis of mind. The support for this optimism has been extremely abstract and general. I wish to present some grounds for pessimism. That type of self-understanding may encounter limits which have not been generally foreseen: the personal, mentalist idea of human beings may resist the sort of coordination with an understanding of humans as physical systems, that would be necessary to yield anything describable as an understanding of the physical basis of mind. I shall not consider what alternatives will be open to us if we should encounter such limits. I shall try to present grounds for believing that the limits may exist—grounds derived from extensive data now available about the interaction between the two halves of the cerebral cortex, and about what happens when they are disconnected. The feature of the mentalist conception of persons which may be recalcitrant to integration with these data is not a trivial or peripheral one, that might easily be abandoned. It is the idea of a *single* person, a single subject of experience and action, that is in difficulties. The difficulties may be surmountable in ways I have not foreseen. On the other hand, this may be only the first of many dead ends that will emerge as we seek a physiological understanding of the mind.

To seek the physical basis or realization of features of the phenomenal world is in many areas a profitable first line of inquiry, and it is the line encouraged, for the case of mental phenomena, by those who look forward to some variety of empirical reduction of mind to brain, through an identity theory, a functionalist theory, or some other device. When physical reductionism is attempted for a phenomenal feature of the external world, the results are sometimes very successful, and can be pushed to deeper and deeper levels. If, on the other hand, they are not entirely successful, and certain features of the phenomenal picture remain unexplained by a physical reduction, then we can set those features aside as *purely* phenomenal, and postpone our understanding of them to the time when our knowledge of the physical basis of mind and perception will have advanced sufficiently to supply it. (An example of this might be the moon illusion, or other sensory illusions which have no discoverable basis in the objects perceived.)

However, if we encounter the same kind of difficulty in exploring the physical basis of the phenomena of the mind itself, we cannot adopt the same line of retreat. That is, if a phenomenal feature of mind is left unaccounted for by the physical theory, we cannot postpone the understanding of it to the time when we study the mind itself—for that is exactly what we are supposed to be doing. To defer to an understanding of the basis of mind which lies beyond the study of the physical realization of certain aspects of it is to admit the irreducibility of the mental to the physical. A clearcut version of this admission would be some kind of dualism. But if one is reluctant to take such a route, then it is not clear what one should do about central features of the mentalistic idea of persons which resist assimilation to an understanding of human beings as physical systems. It may be true of some of these features that we can neither find an objective basis for them, nor give them up. It may be impossible for us to abandon certain ways of conceiving and representing ourselves, no matter how little support they get from scientific research. This, I suspect, is true of the idea of the unity of a person: an idea whose validity may be called into question with the help of recent discoveries about the functional duality of the cerebral cortex. . . .

III*

What one naturally wants to know about these [split-brain] patients is how many minds they have. This immediately raises questions about the sense in which an ordinary person can be said to have one mind, and what the conditions are under which diverse experiences and activities can be ascribed to the same mind. We must have some idea what an ordinary person is one of in order to understand what we want to know whether there is *one or two* of, when we try to describe these extraordinary patients.

However, instead of beginning with an analysis of the unity of the mind, I am going to proceed by attempting to apply the ordinary, unanalyzed conception directly in the interpre-

*Section II, omitted, contains information already provided in the preceding selection by R. W. Sperry. [Editor's note.]

tation of these data, asking whether the patients have one mind, or two, or some more exotic configuration. My conclusion will be that the ordinary conception of a single, countable mind cannot be applied to them at all, and that there is no number of such minds that they possess, though they certainly engage in mental activity. A clearer understanding of the idea of an individual mind should emerge in the course of this discussion but the difficulties which stand in the way of its application to the split-brain cases will provide ground for more general doubts. The concept may not be applicable to ordinary human beings either, for it embodies too simple a conception of the way in which human beings function.

Nevertheless I shall employ the notion of an individual mind in discussing the cases initially, for I wish to consider systematically how they might be understood in terms of countable minds, and to argue that they cannot be. After having done this, I shall turn to ordinary people like you and me.

There appear to be five interpretations of the experimental data which utilize the concept of an individual mind.

(1) The patients have one fairly normal mind associated with the left hemisphere, and the responses emanating from the nonverbal right hemisphere are the responses of an automaton, and are not produced by conscious mental processes.

(2) The patients have only one mind, associated with the left hemisphere, but there also occur (associated with the right hemisphere) isolated conscious mental phenomena, not integrated into a mind at all, though they can perhaps be ascribed to the organism.

(3) The patients have two minds, one which can talk and one which cannot.

(4) They have one mind, whose contents derive from both hemispheres and are rather peculiar and dissociated.

(5) They have one normal mind most of the time, while the hemispheres are functioning in

parallel, but two minds are elicited by the experimental situations which yield the interesting results. (Perhaps the single mind splits in two and reconvenes after the experiment is over.)

I shall argue that each of these interpretations is unacceptable for one reason or another.

IV

Let me first discuss hypotheses (1) and (2), which have in common the refusal to ascribe the activities of the right hemisphere to a mind, and then go on to treat hypotheses (3), (4), and (5), all of which associate a mind with the activities of the right hemisphere, though they differ on what mind it is.

The only support for hypothesis (1), which refuses to ascribe consciousness to the activities of the right hemisphere at all, is the fact that the subject consistently denies awareness of the activities or that hemisphere. But to take this as proof that the activities of the right hemisphere are unconscious is to beg the question, since the capacity to give testimony is the exclusive ability of the left hemisphere, and of course the left hemisphere is not conscious of what is going on in the right. If on the other hand we consider the manifestations of the right hemisphere itself, there seems no reason in principle to regard verbalizability as a *necessary* condition of consciousness. There may be other grounds for the ascription of conscious mental states that are sufficient even without verbalization. And in fact, what the right hemisphere can do on its own is too elaborate, too intentionally directed and too psychologically intelligible to be regarded merely as a collection of unconscious automatic responses.

The right hemisphere is not very intelligent and it cannot talk; but it is able to respond to complex visual and auditory stimuli, including language, and it can control the performance of discriminatory and manipulative tasks requiring close attention—such as the spelling out of simple words with plastic letters. It can integrate auditory, visual, and tactile stimuli in order to follow the experimenter's instructions, and it can take certain aptitude tests. There is no doubt that if a person were deprived of his left hemisphere entirely, so that the only capacities remaining to him were those of the right, we should not on that account say that he had been converted into an automaton. Though speechless, he would remain conscious and active, with a diminished visual field and partial paralysis on the right side from which he would eventually recover to some extent. In view of this, it would seem arbitrary to deny that the activities of the right hemisphere are conscious, just because they occur side by side with those of the left hemisphere, about whose consciousness there is no question.

I do not wish to claim that the line between conscious and unconscious mental activity is a sharp one. It is even possible that the distinction is partly relative, in the sense that a given item of mental activity may be assignable to consciousness or not, depending on what other mental activities of the same person are going on at the same time, and whether it is connected with them in a suitable way. Even if this is true, however, the activities of the right hemisphere in split-brain patients do not fall into the category of events whose inclusion in consciousness depends on what else is going on in the patient's mind. Their determinants include a full range of psychological factors, and they demand alertness. It is clear that attention, even concentration is demanded for the tasks of the concealed left hand and tachistoscopically stimulated left visual field. The subjects do not take their experimental tests in a dreamy fashion: they are obviously in contact with reality. The left hemisphere occasionally complains about being asked to perform tasks which the right hemisphere can perform, because it does not know what is going on when the right hemisphere controls the response. But the right hemisphere displays enough awareness of what it is doing to justify the attribution of conscious control in the absence of verbal testimony. If the patients did not deny any awareness of those activities, no doubts about their consciousness would arise at all.

The considerations that make the first hypothesis untenable also serve to refute hypothesis (2), which suggests that the activities of the right hemisphere are conscious without belonging to a mind at all. There may be problems about the intelligibility of this proposal, but we need not consider them here, because it is rendered implausible by the high degree of organization and intermodal coherence of the right hemisphere's mental activities. They are not free-floating, and they are not organized in a fragmentary way. The right hemisphere follows instructions, integrates tactile, auditory and visual stimuli, and does most of the things a good mind should do. The data present us not merely with slivers of purposive behavior, but with a system capable of learning, reacting emotionally, following instructions, and carrying out tasks which require the integration of diverse psychological determinants. It seems clear that the right hemisphere's activities are not unconscious, and that they belong to something having a characteristically mental structure: a subject of experience and action.

V

Let me now turn to the three hypotheses according to which the conscious mental activities of the right hemisphere are ascribed to a mind. They have to be considered together, because the fundamental difficulty about each of them lies in the impossibility of deciding among them. The question, then, is whether the patients have two minds, one mind, or a mind that occasionally splits in two.

There is much to recommend the view that they have two minds, i.e. that the activities of

the right hemisphere belong to a mind of their own.[1] Each side of the brain seems to produce its own perceptions, beliefs, and actions, which are connected with one another in the usual way, but not to those of the opposite side. The two halves of the cortex share a common body, which they control through a common midbrain and spinal cord. But their higher functions are independent not only physically but psychologically. Functions of the right hemisphere are inaccessible not only to speech but to any direct combination with corresponding functions of the left hemisphere — i.e. with functions of a type that the right hemisphere finds easy on its home ground, like shape or color discrimination.

One piece of testimony by the patients' left hemispheres may appear to argue against two minds. They report no diminution of the visual field, and little absence of sensation on the left side. Sperry dismisses this evidence on the ground that it is comparable to the testimony of victims of scotoma (partial destruction of the retina), that they notice no gaps in their visual field — although these gaps can be discovered by others observing their perceptual deficiences. But we need not assume that an elaborate confabulatory mechanism is at work in the left hemisphere to account for such testimony. It is perfectly possible that although there are two minds, the mind associated with each hemisphere receives, through the common brain

---

[1]It is Sperry's view. He puts it as follows:

Instead of the normally unified single stream of consciousness, these patients behave in many ways as if they have two independent streams of conscious awareness, one in each hemisphere, each of which is cut off from and out of contact with the mental experiences of the other. In other words, each hemisphere seems to have its own separate and private sensations; its own perceptions; its own concepts; and its own impulses to act, with related volitional, cognitive, and learning experiences. Following the surgery, each hemisphere also has thereafter its own separate chain of memories that are rendered inaccessible to the recall process of the others (*American Psychologist*, xxiii, 724.)

stem, a certain amount of crude ipsilateral stimulation, so that the speaking mind has a rudimentary and undifferentiated appendage to the left side of its visual field, and vice versa for the right hemisphere.[2]

The real difficulties for the two-minds hypothesis coincide with the reasons for thinking we are dealing with one mind—namely the highly integrated character of the patients' relations to the world in ordinary circumstances. When they are not in the experimental situation, their startling behavioral dissociation disappears, and they function normally. There is little doubt that information from the two sides of their brains can be pooled to yield integrated behavioral control. And although this is not accomplished by the usual methods, it is not clear that this settles the question against assigning the integrative functions to a single mind. After all, if the patient is permitted to touch things with both hands and smell them with both nostrils, he arrives at a unified idea of what is going on around him and what he is doing, without revealing any left–right inconsistencies in his behavior or attitudes. It seems strange to suggest that we are not in a position to ascribe all those experiences to the same person, just because of some peculiarities about how the integration is achieved. The people who *know* these patients find it natural to relate to them as single individuals.

Nevertheless, if we ascribe the integration to a single mind, we must also ascribe the experimentally evoked dissociation to that mind, and that is not easy. The experimental situation reveals a variety of dissociation or conflict that is unusual not only because of the simplicity of its anatomical basis, but because such a wide *range* of functions is split into two noncommunicating branches. It is not as though two conflicting volitional centers shared a common perceptual and reasoning apparatus. The split is much

deeper than that. The one-mind hypothesis must therefore assert that the contents of the individual's single consciousness are produced by two independent control systems in the two hemispheres, each having a fairly complete mental structure. If this dual control were accomplished during experimental situations by temporal alternation, it would be intelligible, though mysterious. But that is not the hypothesis, and the hypothesis as it stands does not supply us with understanding. For in these patients there appear to be things happening *simultaneously* which cannot fit into a single mind: simultaneous attention to two incompatible tasks, for example, without interaction between the purposes of the left and right hands.

This makes it difficult to conceive what it is like to *be* one of these people. Lack of interaction at the level of a preconscious control system would be comprehensible. But lack of interaction in the domain of visual experience and conscious intention threatens assumptions about the unity of consciousness which are basic to our understanding of another individual as a person. These assumptions are associated with our conception of ourselves, which to a considerable extent constrains our understanding of others. And it is just these assumptions, I believe, that make it impossible to arrive at an interpretation of the cases under discussion in terms of a countable number of minds.

Roughly, we assume that a single mind has sufficiently immediate access to its conscious states so that, for elements of experience or other mental events occurring simultaneously or in close temporal proximity, the mind which is their subject can also experience the simpler *relations* between them if it attends to the matter. Thus, we assume that when a single person has two visual impressions, he can usually also experience the sameness or difference of their coloration, shape, size, the relation of their position and movement within his visual field, and so forth. The same can be said of cross-modal connections. The experiences of a single person are thought to take place in an *experientially* con-

[2]There is some direct evidence for such primitive ipsilateral inputs, both visual and tactile; cf. Gazzaniga, *The Bisected Brain*, ch. 3.

nected domain, so that the relations among experiences can be substantially captured in experiences of those relations.[3]

Split-brain patients fail dramatically to conform to these assumptions in experimental situations, and they fail over the simplest matters. Moreover the dissociation holds between two classes of conscious states each characterized by significant *internal* coherence: normal assumptions about the unity of consciousness hold intrahemispherically, although the requisite comparisons cannot be made across the interhemispheric gap.

These considerations lead us back to the hypothesis that the patients have two minds each. It at least has the advantage of enabling us to understand what it is like to *be* these individuals, so long as we do not try to imagine what it is like to be both of them at the same time. Yet the way to a comfortable acceptance of this conclusion is blocked by the compelling behavioral integration which the patients display in ordinary life, in comparison to which the dissociated symptoms evoked by the experimental situation seem peripheral and atypical. We are faced with diametrically conflicting bodies of evidence, in a case which does not admit of arbitrary decision. There is a powerful inclination to feel that there must be *some* whole number of minds in those heads, but the data prevent us from deciding how many.

This dilemma makes hypothesis (5) initially attractive, especially since the data which yield the conflict are to some extent gathered at different times. But the suggestion that a second mind is brought into existence only during experimental situations loses plausibility on reflection. First, it is entirely *ad hoc*: it proposes to explain one change in terms of another without suggesting any explanation of the second. There is nothing about the experimental situation that might be expected to produce a fundamental internal change in the patient. In fact it produces no anatomical changes and merely elicits a noteworthy set of symptoms. So unusual an event as a mind's popping in and out of existence would have to be explained by something more than its explanatory convenience.

But secondly, the behavioral evidence would not even be explained by this hypothesis, simply because the patients' integrated responses and their dissociated responses are not clearly separated in time. During the time of the experiments the patient is functioning largely as if he were a single individual: in his posture, in following instructions about where to focus his eyes, in the whole range of trivial behavioral control involved in situating himself in relation to the experimenter and the experimental apparatus. The two halves of his brain cooperate completely except in regard to those very special inputs that reach them separately and differently. For these reasons hypothesis (5) does not seem to be a real option; if two minds are operating in the experimental situation, they must be operating largely in harmony although partly at odds. And if there are two minds then, why can there not be two minds operating essentially in parallel the rest of the time?

Nevertheless the psychological integration displayed by the patients in ordinary life is so complete that I do not believe it is possible to accept that conclusion, nor any conclusion involving the ascription to them of a whole number of minds. These cases fall midway between ordinary persons with intact brains (between whose cerebral hemispheres there is also cooperation, though it works largely via the corpus callosum), and pairs of individuals engaged in a performance requiring exact behavioral coordination, like using a two-handed saw, or playing a duet. In the latter type of case we have two

---

[3]The two can of course diverge, and this fact underlies the classic philosophical problem of inverted spectra, which is only distantly related to the subject of this paper. A type of relation can hold between elements in the experience of a single person that cannot hold between elements of the experience of distinct persons: looking similar in color, for example. Insofar as our concept of similarity of experience in the case of a single person is dependent on his experience of similarity, the concept is not applicable between persons.

minds which communicate by subtle peripheral cues; in the former we have a single mind. Nothing taken from either of those cases can compel us to assimilate the split-brain patient to one or the other of them. If we decided that they definitely had two minds, then it would be problematical why we did not conclude on anatomical grounds that everyone has two minds, but that we do not notice it except in these odd cases because most pairs of minds in a single body run in perfect parallel due to the direct communication between the hemispheres which provide their anatomical bases. The two minds each of us has running in harness would be much the same except that one could talk and the other could not. But it is clear that this line of argument will get us nowhere. For if the idea of a single mind applies to anyone it applies to ordinary individuals with intact brains, and if it does not apply to them it ought to be scrapped, in which case there is no point in asking whether those with split brains have one mind or two.[4]

VI

If I am right, and there is no whole number of individual minds that these patients can be said to have, then the attribution of conscious, significant mental activity does not require the existence of a single mental subject. This is extremely puzzling in itself, for it runs counter to

[4]In case anyone is inclined to embrace the conclusion that we all have two minds, let me suggest that the trouble will not end there. For the mental operations of a single hemisphere, such as vision, hearing, speech, writing, verbal comprehension, etc., can to a great extent be separated from one another by suitable cortical deconnections; why then should we regard *each* hemisphere as inhabited by several cooperating minds with specialized capacities? Where is one to stop? If the decision on the number of minds associated with a brain is largely arbitrary, the original point of the question has disappeared.

our need to construe the mental states we ascribe to others on the model of our own. Something in the ordinary conception of a person, or in the ordinary conception of experience, leads to the demand for an account of these cases which the same conception makes it impossible to provide. This may seem a problem not worth worrying about very much. It is not so surprising that, having begun with a phenomenon which is radically different from anything else previously known, we should come to the conclusion that it cannot be adequately described in ordinary terms. However, I believe that consideration of these very unusual cases should cause us to be skeptical about the concept of a single subject of consciousness as it applies to ourselves.

The fundamental problem in trying to understand these cases in mentalistic terms is that we take ourselves as paradigms of psychological unity, and are then unable to project ourselves into their mental lives, either once or twice. But in thus using ourselves as the touchstone of whether another organism can be said to house an individual subject of experience or not, we are subtly ignoring the possibility that our own unity may be nothing absolute, but merely another case of integration, more or less effective, in the control system of a complex organism. This system speaks in the first person singular through our mouths, and that makes it understandable that we should think of its unity as in some sense numerically absolute, rather than relative and a function of the integration of its contents.

But this is quite genuinely an illusion. The illusion consists in projecting inward to the center of the mind the very subject whose unity we are trying to explain: the individual person with all his complexities. The ultimate account of the unity of what we call a single mind consists of an enumeration of the types of functional integration that typify it. We know that these can be eroded in different ways, and to different degrees. The belief that even in their complete version they can be explained by the presence of a numerically single subject is an illusion. Either this subject contains the mental life, in which case it is complex and its unity must be accounted for in terms of the unified operation of its components and functions, or else it is an extensionless point, in which case it explains nothing.

An intact brain contains two cerebral hemispheres each of which possesses perceptual, memory, and control systems adequate to run the body without the assistance of the other. They cooperate in directing it with the aid of a constant two-way internal communication system. Memories, perceptions, desires, and so forth therefore have duplicate physical bases on both sides of the brain, not just on account of similarities of initial input, but because of subsequent exchange. The cooperation of the undetached hemispheres in controlling the body is more efficient and direct than the cooperation of a pair of detached hemispheres, but it is cooperation nonetheless. Even if we analyze the

idea of unity in terms of functional integration, therefore, the unity of our own consciousness may be less clear than we had supposed. The natural conception of a single person controlled by a mind possessing a single visual field, individual faculties for each of the other senses, unitary systems of memory, desire, belief, and so forth, may come into conflict with the physiological facts when it is applied to ourselves.

The concept of a person might possibly survive an application to cases which require us to speak of two or more persons in one body, but it seems strongly committed to some form of whole number countability. Since even this seems open to doubt, it is possible that the ordinary, simple idea of a single person will come to seem quaint some day, when the complexities of the human control system become clearer and we become less certain that there is anything very important that we are *one* of. But it is also possible that we shall be unable to abandon the idea no matter what we discover.

7

DEREK PARFIT
Divided Minds and the Nature of Persons

It was the split-brain cases which drew me into philosophy. Our knowledge of these cases depends on the results of various psychological tests, as described by Donald MacKay.[1] These tests made use of two facts. We control each of

our arms, and see what is in each half of our visual fields, with only one of our hemispheres. When someone's hemispheres have been disconnected, psychologists can thus present to this person two different written questions in the two halves of his visual field, and can receive two different answers written by this person's two hands.

Here is a simplified imaginary version of the

[1]See [Donald] MacKay's . . . ["Divided Brains—Divided Minds?" in C. Blakemore and S. Greenfield, eds., *Mindwaves*. Oxford: Basil Blackwell, 1987.]

kind of evidence that such tests provide. One of these people looks fixedly at the centre of a wide screen, whose left half is red and right half is blue. On each half in a darker shade are the words, "How many colours can you see?" With both hands the person writes, "Only one." The words are now changed to read, "Which is the only colour that you can see?" With one of his hands the person writes "Red," with the other he writes "Blue."

If this is how such a person responds, I would conclude that he is having two visual sensations—that he does, as he claims, see both red and blue. But in seeing each colour he is not aware of seeing the other. He has two streams of consciousness, in each of which he can see only one colour. In one stream he sees red, and at the same time, in his other stream, he sees blue. More generally, he could be having at the same time two series of thoughts and sensations, in having each of which he is unaware of having the other.

This conclusion has been questioned. It has been claimed by some that there are not *two* streams of consciousness, on the ground that the subdominant hemisphere is a part of the brain whose functioning involves no consciousness. If this were true, these cases would lose most of their interest. I believe that it is not true, chiefly because, if a person's dominant hemisphere is destroyed, this person is able to react in the way in which, in the split-brain cases, the sub-dominant hemisphere reacts, and we do not believe that such a person is just an automaton, without consciousness. The sub-dominant hemisphere is, of course, much less developed in certain ways, typically having the linguistic abilities of a three-year-old. But three-year-olds are conscious. This supports the view that, in split-brain cases, there *are* two streams of consciousness.

Another view is that, in these cases, there are two persons involved, sharing the same body. Like Professor MacKay, I believe that we should reject this view. My reason for believing this is, however, different. Professor MacKay denies that there are two persons involved because he believes that there is only one person involved. I believe that, in a sense, the number of persons involved is none.

The Ego Theory and the Bundle Theory

To explain this sense I must, for a while, turn away from the split-brain cases. There are two theories about what persons are, and what is involved in a person's continued existence over time. On the *Ego Theory*, a person's continued existence cannot be explained except as the continued existence of a particular *Ego*, or *subject of experiences*. An Ego Theorist claims that, if we ask what unifies someone's consciousness at any time—what makes it true, for example, that I can now both see what I am typing and hear the wind outside my window—the answer is that these are both experiences which are being had by me, this person, at this time. Similarly, what explains the unity of a person's whole life is the fact that all of the experiences in this life are had by the same person, or subject of experiences. In its best-known form, the *Cartesian view*, each person is a persisting purely mental thing—a soul, or spiritual substance.

The rival view is the *Bundle Theory*. Like most styles in art—Gothic, baroque, rococo, etc.—this theory owes its name to its critics. But the name is good enough. According to the Bundle Theory, we can't explain either the unity of consciousness at any time, or the unity of a whole life, by referring to a person. Instead we must claim that there are long series of different mental states and events—thoughts, sensations, and the like—each series being what we call one life. Each series is unified by various kinds of causal relation, such as the relations that hold between experiences and later memories of them. Each series is thus like a bundle tied up with a string.

In a sense, a Bundle Theorist denies the existence of persons. An outright denial is of course absurd. As Reid protested in the eighteenth century, "I am not thought, I am not action. I am not feeling; I am something which thinks and acts and feels." I am not a series of events, but a person. A Bundle Theorist admits this fact, but claims it to be only a fact about our grammar, or our language. There are persons or subjects in this language-dependent way. If, however, persons are believed to be more than this—to be separately existing things, distinct from our brains and bodies, and the various kinds of mental states and events—the Bundle Theorist denies that there are such things.

The first Bundle Theorist was Buddha, who taught "anatta," or the *No Self view.* Buddhists concede that selves or persons have "nominal existence," by which they mean that persons are merely combinations of other elements. Only what exists by itself, as a separate element, has instead what Buddhists call "actual existence." Here are some quotations from Buddhist texts:

At the beginning of their conversation the king politely asks the monk his name, and receives the following reply: "Sir, I am known as 'Nagasena'; my fellows in the religious life address me as 'Nagasena'. Although my parents gave me the name . . . it is just an appellation, a form of speech, a description, a conventional usage. 'Nagasena' is only a name, for no person is found here."

A sentient being does exist, you think, O Mara? You are misled by a false conception. This bundle of elements is void of Self, In it there is no sentient being. Just as a set of wooden parts Receives the name of carriage, So do we give to elements The name of fancied being.

Buddha has spoken thus: "O Brethren, actions do exist, and also their consequences, but the person that acts does not. There is no one to cast away this set of elements, and no one to

assume a new set of them. There exists no Individual, it is only a conventional name given to a set of elements.[2]

Buddha's claims are strikingly similar to the claims advanced by several Western writers. Since these writers knew nothing of Buddha, the similarity of these claims suggests that they are not merely part of one cultural tradition, in one period. They may be, as I believe they are, true.

What We Believe Ourselves to Be

Given the advances in psychology and neurophysiology, the Bundle Theory may now seem to be obviously true. It may seem uninteresting to deny that there are separately existing Egos, which are distinct from brains and bodies and the various kinds of mental states and events. But this is not the only issue. We may be convinced that the Ego Theory is false, or even senseless. Most of us, however, even if we are not aware of this, also have certain beliefs about what is involved in our continued existence over time. And these beliefs would only be justified if something like the Ego Theory was true. Most of us therefore have false beliefs about what persons are, and about ourselves.

These beliefs are best revealed when we consider certain imaginary cases, often drawn from science fiction. One such case is *teletransportation.* Suppose that you enter a cubicle in which, when you press a button, a scanner records the states of all of the cells in your brain and body, destroying both while doing so. This information is then transmitted at the speed of light to

[2]For the sources of these and similar quotations, see my *Reasons and Persons* (1984) pp. 502–3, 532. Oxford: Oxford Univ. Press.

some other planet, where a replicator produces a perfect organic copy of you. Since the brain of your Replica is exactly like yours, it will seem to remember living your life up to the moment when you pressed the button, its character will be just like yours, and it will be in every other way psychologically continuous with you. This psychological continuity will not have its normal cause, the continued existence of your brain, since the causal chain will run through the transmission by radio of your "blueprint."

Several writers claim that, if you chose to be teletransported, believing this to be the fastest way of travelling, you would be making a terrible mistake. This would not be a way of travelling, but a way of dying. It may not, they concede, be quite as bad as ordinary death. It might be some consolation to you that, after your death, you will have this Replica, which can finish the book that you are writing, act as parent to your children, and so on. But, they insist, this Replica won't be you. It will merely be someone else, who is exactly like you. This is why this prospect is nearly as bad as ordinary death.

Imagine next a whole range of cases, in each of which, in a single operation, a different proportion of the cells in your brain and body would be replaced with exact duplicates. At the near end of this range, only 1 or 2 per cent would be replaced; in the middle, 40 or 60 per cent; near the far end, 98 or 99 per cent. At the far end of this range is pure teletransportation, the case in which all of your cells would be "replaced."

When you imagine that some proportion of your cells will be replaced with exact duplicates, it is natural to have the following beliefs. First, if you ask, "Will I survive? Will the resulting person be me?," there must be an answer to this question. Either you will survive, or you are about to die. Second, the answer to this question must be either a simple "Yes" or a simple "No." The person who wakes up either will or

will not be you. There cannot be a third answer, such as that the person waking up will be half you. You can imagine yourself later being half-conscious. But if the resulting person will be fully conscious, he cannot be half you. To state these beliefs together: to the question, "Will the resulting person be me?," there must always *be* an answer, which must be all-or-nothing.

There seem good grounds for believing that, in the case of teletransportation, your Replica would not be you. In a slight variant of this case, your Replica might be created while you were still alive, so that you could talk to one another. This seems to show that, if 100 per cent of your cells were replaced, the result would merely be a Replica of you. At the other end of my range of cases, where only 1 per cent would be replaced, the resulting person clearly *would* be you. It therefore seems that, in the cases in between, the resulting person must be either you, or merely a Replica. It seems that one of these must be true, and that it makes a great difference which is true.

How We Are Not What We Believe

If these beliefs were correct, there must be some critical percentage, somewhere in this range of cases, up to which the resulting person would be you, and beyond which he would merely be your Replica. Perhaps, for example, it would be you who would wake up if the proportion of cells replaced were 49 per cent, but if just a few more cells were also replaced, this would make all the difference, causing it to be someone else who would wake up.

That there must be some such critical percentage follows from our natural beliefs. But this conclusion is most implausible. How could a few cells make such a difference? Moreover, if there is such a critical percentage, no one could ever discover where it came. Since in all these cases the resulting person would believe that he was you, there could never be any evidence about where, in this range of cases, he would suddenly cease to be you.

On the Bundle Theory, we should reject these natural beliefs. Since you, the person, are not a separately existing entity, we can know exactly what would happen without answering the question of what will happen to you. Moreover, in the cases in the middle of my range, it is an empty question whether the resulting person would be you, or would merely be someone else who is exactly like you. These are not here two different possibilities, one of which must be true. These are merely two different descriptions of the very same course of events. If 50 per cent of your cells were replaced with exact duplicates, we could call the resulting person you, or we could call him merely your Replica. But since these are not here different possibilities, this is a mere choice of words.

As Buddha claimed, the Bundle Theory is hard to believe. It is hard to accept that it could be an empty question whether one is about to die, or will instead live for many years.

What we are being asked to accept may be made clearer with this analogy. Suppose that a certain club exists for some time, holding regular meetings. The meetings then cease. Some years later, several people form a club with the same name, and the same rules. We can ask, "Did these people revive the very same club? Or did they merely start up another club which is exactly similar?" Given certain further details, this would be another empty question. We could know just what happened without answering this question. Suppose that someone said: "But there must be an answer. The club meeting later must either be, or not be, the very same club." This would show that this person didn't understand the nature of clubs.

In the same way, if we have any worries about my imagined cases, we don't understand the nature of persons. In each of my cases, you would know that the resulting person would be both psychologically and physically exactly like you, and that he would have some particular proportion of the cells in your brain and body —90 per cent, or 10 per cent, or, in the case of teletransportation, 0 per cent. Knowing this, you know everything. How could it be a real question what would happen to you, unless you are a separately existing Ego, distinct from a brain and body, and the various kinds of mental state and event? If there are no such Egos, there is nothing else to ask a real question about.

Accepting the Bundle Theory is not only hard; it may also affect our emotions. As Buddha claimed, it may undermine our concern about our own futures. This effect can be suggested by redescribing this change of view. Suppose that you are about to be destroyed, but will later have a Replica on Mars. You would naturally believe that this prospect is about as bad as ordinary death, since your Replica won't be you. On the Bundle Theory, the fact that your Replica won't be you just consists in the fact that, though it will be fully psychologically continuous with you, this continuity won't have its normal cause. But when you object to teletransportation you are not objecting merely to the abnormality of this cause. You are objecting that this cause won't get *you* to Mars. You fear that the abnormal cause will fail to produce a further and all-important fact, which is different from the fact that your Replica will be psychologically continuous with you. You do not merely want there to be psychological continuity between you and some future person. You want to *be* this future person. On the Bundle Theory, there is no such special further fact. What you fear will not happen, in this imagined case, *never* happens. You want the person on Mars to be you in a specially intimate way in which no future person will ever be you. This means that, judged from the standpoint of your natural beliefs, even ordinary survival is about as bad as teletransportation. *Ordinary survival is about as bad as being destroyed and having a Replica.*

How the Split-Brain Cases Support the Bundle Theory

The truth of the Bundle Theory seems to me, in the widest sense, as much a scientific as a philosophical conclusion. I can imagine kinds of evidence which would have justified believing in the existence of separately existing Egos, and believing that the continued existence of these Egos is what explains the continuity of each mental life. But there is in fact very little evidence in favour of this Ego Theory, and much for the alternative Bundle Theory.

Some of this evidence is provided by the split-brain cases. On the Ego Theory, to explain what unifies our experiences at any one time, we should simply claim that these are all experiences which are being had by the same person. Bundle Theorists reject this explanation. This disagreement is hard to resolve in ordinary cases. But consider the simplified split-brain case that I described. We show to my imagined patient a placard whose left half is blue and right half is red. In one of this person's two streams of consciousness, he is aware of seeing only blue, while at the same time, in his other stream, he is aware of seeing only red. Each of these two visual experiences is combined with other experiences, like that of being aware of moving one of his hands. What unifies the experiences, at any time, in each of this person's two streams of consciousness? What unifies his awareness of seeing only red with his awareness of moving one hand? The answer cannot be that these experiences are being had by the same person. This answer cannot explain the unity of each of this person's two streams of consciousness, since it ignores the disunity between these streams. This person is now having all of the experiences in both of his two streams. If this fact was what unified these experiences, this would make the two streams one.

These cases do not, I have claimed, involve two people sharing a single body. Since there is only one person involved, who has two streams of consciousness, the Ego Theorist's explanation would have to take the following form. He would have to distinguish between persons and subjects of experiences, and claim that, in split-brain cases, there are *two* of the latter. What unifies the experiences in one of the person's two streams would have to be the fact that these experiences are all being had by the same subject of experiences. What unifies the experiences in this person's other stream would have to be the fact that they are being had by another subject of experiences. When this explanation takes this form, it becomes much less plausible. While we could assume that "subject of experiences," or "Ego," simply meant "person," it was easy to believe that there are subjects of experiences. But if there can be subjects of experiences that are not persons, and if in the life of a split-brain patient there are at any time two different subjects of experiences—two different Egos—why should we believe that there really are such things? This does not amount to a refutation. But it seems to me a strong argument against the Ego Theory.

As a Bundle Theorist, I believe that these two Egos are idle cogs. There is another explanation of the unity of consciousness, both in ordinary cases and in split-brain cases. It is simply a fact that ordinary people are, at any time, aware of having several different experiences. This awareness of several different experiences can be helpfully compared with one's awareness, in short-term memory, of several different experiences. Just as there can be a single memory of just having had several experiences, such as hearing a bell strike three times, there can be a single state of awareness both of hearing the fourth striking of this bell, and of seeing, at the same time, ravens flying past the bell-tower.

Unlike the Ego Theorist's explanation, this explanation can easily be extended to cover split-brain cases. In such cases there is, at any time, not one state of awareness of several different experiences, but two such states. In the case I described, there is one state of awareness of both seeing only red and of moving one hand, and there is another state of awareness of both seeing only blue and moving the other hand. In claiming that there are two such states of awareness, we are not postulating the existence of unfamiliar entities, two separately existing Egos which are not the same as the single person whom the case involves. This explanation appeals to a pair of mental states which would have to be described anyway in a full description of this case.

I have suggested how the split-brain cases provide one argument for one view about the nature of persons. I should mention another such argument, provided by an imagined extension of these cases, first discussed at length by David Wiggins.[3]

In this imagined case a person's brain is divided, and the two halves are transplanted into a pair of different bodies. The two resulting people live quite separate lives. This imagined case shows that personal identity is not what matters. If I was about to divide, I should conclude that neither of the resulting people will be me. I will have ceased to exist. But this way of ceasing to exist is about as good—or as bad—as ordinary survival.

Some of the features of Wiggins's imagined case are likely to remain technically impossible. But the case cannot be dismissed, since its most striking feature, the division of one stream of consciousness into separate streams, has already happened. This is a second way in which the actual split-brain cases have great theoretical importance. They challenge some of our deepest assumptions about ourselves.[4]

---

[3]At the end of his *Identity and Spatio-temporal Continuity* (1967) Oxford: Blackwell.

[4]I discuss these assumptions further in part 3 of my *Reasons and Persons*.

Split Minds

8

ERNEST HILGARD
Dissociative Phenomena and
the Hidden Observer

I: Possession States, Fugues, and Multiple Personalities

In the ordinary experience of living, the sense of wholeness and continuity is maintained through the continuity of memories: I am the same person who traveled to Europe last summer, and I am the same person who watched the game being played yesterday. This does not mean that I always behave the same, for I am various people at various times, according to the roles that I play as husband, father, grandfather, teacher, researcher, voter, or loafer. Within these variations I know that I am only one, however, for I carry my memories around with me when I move from one scene to another and adopt one role or another.

The existence of the various roles nevertheless implies subordinate control systems brought into play when the role is foremost, whether the role is a domestic one, a professional one, or the exercise of some special skill, such as playing the violin. What we propose to examine are those instances when these subordinate systems, appropriate to varying roles,

lose communication with each other. In such cases it is appropriate to refer to the bifurcated roles as *dissociated*. In this [section] and the next one we examine some instances of these dissociations that set the stage for the later interpretations.

The main criteria of dissociated behavior are as follows:

1. The dissociated systems can be identified as relatively coherent patterns of behavior with sufficient complexity to represent some degree of internal organization. In the case of a fugue, as we shall see, the behavior does not have to be present repeatedly in order to qualify. If, however, it is repeated, as in the cases of multiple personality to be described, each of the subordinate systems will have identifying characteristics, such as preferences, skills, and memories.

2. There is commonly some amnesic barrier that prevents integration of the disassociated systems, at least during the time that the dissociation persists. This is the primary mark that distinguishes between alternating normal roles and alternating personalities as found in psychopathology. Sometimes system A may be aware of system B, without system B being

aware of system A. A one-directional amnesia is enough.

3. The experience of being "possessed" by an alien personality represents a dissociation of a somewhat different kind, in which the mutual amnesias are not essential because the two "personalities" in some sense conduct a battle for control of the one body. The first criterion holds, of identifiable characteristics of the two split-off personality systems; thus each is recognizable, and both are different.

4. There are minor dissociations occurring in ordinary experience and in hypnosis that are so much less dramatic than fugues, multiple personalities, or possession states that they are more difficult to delimit precisely, for as in the case of possession states, they are determined more by modification of controls than by identifiable amnesias. Among these are automatisms, such as compulsive behavior or obsessive thoughts, or the conversion reactions in hysteria. It may be inferred that there is some kind of concealed motivation for the behavior, commonly assigned to unconscious processes. When comparable behavior is produced by hypnosis, however, and is readily reversed, it is appropriate to include the loss or modification of voluntary control as illustrative of dissociation.

The relationships as they are found to exist in "experiments of nature" occurring in the real world are so complex that it is necessary to use case descriptions to make the domain familiar. Some warnings are in order. The stories of multiple personalities are so dramatic that there is a tendency for the case histories to be overdramatized; they do, in fact, make good material for novels and motion pictures and have been so used. Robert Louis Stevenson's *The Strange Case of Dr. Jekyll and Mr. Hyde* (1886) is probably the best-known fiction case, and *The Three Faces of Eve* the best-known movie based on an actual case (Thigpen and Cleckley, 1957). In addition to the overdramatization of the material itself, sufficient caution has not always been exercised by the psychotherapist to distinguish between what he discovered and what he produced.

Very early in the history of medical reports of such cases, Janet noted that when a secondary personality is identified and named, it tends to take on a more distinct existence. Hence, in giving the accounts of actual cases, an effort is made to note what was known prior to the intrusions by the therapist, particularly if he used hypnotic techniques.

Possession States

The idea of spirit possession is age old. There is the familiar Biblical story of Jesus casting out the devils from the disturbed Gadarene. The devils ('My name is Legion") requested that they be sent into the herd of swine, and the possessed herd rushed down the bank and perished in the sea. The fact that, presumably, both the demoniac host and the demons spoke to Jesus suggests the possibility of something like multiple personality. The idea of demoniac possession has persisted, in some circles, to the present time. The motion picture. *The Exorcist*, brought the matter to light in the 1970s, somewhat to the embarrassment of the Catholic Church, whose rituals for exorcism still exist, although their use is largely frowned on.

Hypnosis and exorcism had a confrontation two hundred years ago at a time when Father Johann Joseph Gassner (1717–1799) was curing many of his parishioners, and others from afar after his fame spread, by using the Church's rituals of exorcism. He had cured himself by getting rid of "the Evil One" while he was a Catholic priest in a small village in Switzerland. There was much opposition to Gassner, because this was the Age of Enlightenment, and many wished to be rid of practices that they considered magical and irrational. The Prince-Elector Max Joseph of Bavaria appointed a commission of inquiry in 1775 and invited Franz Anton Mesmer (1734–1815), then an Austrian physician, to show that the results of exorcism could be obtained as well by his "naturalistic" method of animal magnetism, the precursor of hypnosis. Mesmer was able to produce the same effects that Gasner had produced—causing convulsions to occur and then curing them. Mesmer won the day, and Gassner was sent off as a priest to a small community. Pope Pius VI ordered his own investigation, from which he concluded that exorcism was to be performed only with discretion.

Forms of possession are still in common use by the healers in cultures that cling to old traditions. I had the opportunity in 1974 of visiting several such healers and personal advisers in Singapore, under the guidance of Dr. Chong Ton Mun, an expert in hypnosis who has made it a point to familiarize himself with these practices (Chong, 1975). In a favorite ceremony practiced in the Chinese community, the practitioner or medium goes into a kind of trance, at which time he becomes possessed by the Monkey God. The evidence for possession as I witnessed it included jumping on the chair in a squatting position resembling a monkey's actions and shouting as a monkey might. After the medium calms down, the client's questions can be answered, sometimes directly, sometimes through an interpreter, for the Monkey God may talk in a language unintelligible except to an initiate who serves as the interpreter. This practice is reminiscent of "speaking in tongues" (glossolalia) that goes back at least to Biblical times and occurs in some Christian churches today. In the Malaysian community of Singapore a similar practice is carried out by the "Bomoh," one of whom was willing to demonstrate his trance for me. He had a choice of spirits to call on. The spirit would possess him and then answer questions, particularly making recommendations for the cure of illness, including the special curative powers of a charmed glass of water. Among the spirits were some princesses living on a mountain top, whom he treated with deference and courtesy, and later a warrior who showed through violent aggressive movements that he was in possession.

These trance states appear to have very much in common with self-hypnosis. The Chinese medium who called on the Monkey God had photographs of himself with his cheeks pierced with sharpened sticks and other sticks thrust into his chest or back, apparently without pain. The lore is that no scars are left by the sticks, but there were indeed visible scars on his face, if one looked carefully.

In an attempt to classify these states, Bourguignon (1968) found it convenient to distinguish between trance states with their associated beliefs and possession states with their associated beliefs, even if the two categories often overlap. The classification derived from a study of 700 cultural groups all over the world. The classification of trance and possession behavior and beliefs is diagrammed in Figure 1.

There are, of course, any number of variations on these common themes. A trance is usually defined as a temporary change in the person when he seems to be very different from his usual self, familiar before the episode and found again when the trance is ended. Both naturalistic and supernaturalistic explanations can be found in cultures remote from modern civilization, but both persist in more modern cultures as well. In Figure 1 the naturalistic explanations are translated into terms that are familiar, although these are not the categories used by the people themselves.

The supernaturalistic explanations fall into the two groups of nonpossession and possession beliefs. The nonpossession beliefs differ not so much in their consequences as in the causal agents assigned. If one can become ill naturalistically from a poisoned arrow, he can also become ill supernaturally if a witch pierces his image with an arrow.

In possession trance, as different from nonpossession trance, the person is believed to be invaded by a spirit or a new sense of power for good or ill. If the possession spirit is good, manipulations such as the healing of others can take place; if the possessing spirit is evil, rites of exorcism may have to be attempted. Possession may occur without trance behavior. The person may remain essentially himself, al-

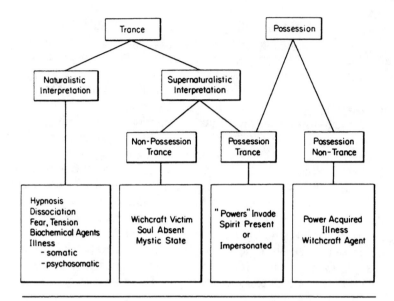

Figure 1
Trance and possession states and associated beliefs. Abbreviated, with modifications from Bourguignon (1968), Tables I and II.

though he may become ill because invading spirits eat at his soul. On the positive side, the transferred spirit may give him some permanent power.

These aspects of trance and possession are found in all parts of the world. Both positive and negative features of the trance are expected; occasionally, negative experiences may be transformed into positive ones. Two forms of trance, such as the possession form and the nonpossession form, may be found in the same society.

Although we may think of the beliefs of societies undeveloped by our standards as "primitive," such beliefs have not died out in Western societies. Christians use the terminology of possession when they speak of being possessed by the Holy Spirit, and demonic possession continues to be occasionally believed. The motion picture, the *Exorcist*, previously mentioned, represented a twentieth century form of this belief. The belief in special powers remains part of the ritual of canonization of a saint.

The persistence of these beliefs means that they meet some deep human need for coming to grips with the uncertainties of human existence, and the earlier motives have not been displaced by the advance of science. Their persistence is not a persuasive argument that the beliefs are true, for many beliefs that are known to be false have a way of persisting when the will to believe is strong enough.

It was only with the decline of the widespread belief in possession that personality disturbances came into the realm of medical science; hence fugues and multiple personalities as we know them are largely a post-Mesmer set of phenomena.

Fugues

A fugue is defined in modern psychiatry as a dissociation characterized by amnesia in which the person runs away from his conflicts or problems by seeking a new environment, or in some other manner demonstrates his flight from reality. During the episode of the fugue, he may behave quite normally in the new environment, but very differently from his usual behavior. When he returns to his usual condition he picks up where he left off and does not remember the events of the fugue. The fugue may be short or long, and it may be a single episode that is not repeated.

The best-known case is that of Reverend Ansel Bourne, studied and reported on in detail by William James (1890, Vol. 1, p. 391–393). Because the details of the case are impressive, I take the liberty of giving James' account in the form in which he presented it.

The Rev. Ansel Bourne, of Greene, R.I., was brought up to the trade of a carpenter; but, in consequence of a sudden temporary loss of sight and hearing under very peculiar circumstances, he became converted from Atheism to Christianity just before his thirtieth year, and has since that time for the most part lived the life of an itinerant preacher. He has been subject to headaches and temporary fits of depression of spirits during most of his life, and has had a few fits of unconsciousness lasting an hour or less. He also has a region of somewhat diminished cutaneous sensibility on the left thigh. Otherwise his health is good, and his muscular strength and endurance excellent. He is of a firm and self-reliant disposition, a man whose yea is yea and his nay, nay; and his character for uprightness is such in the community that no person who knows him will for a moment admit the possibility of his case not being perfectly genuine.

On January 17, 1887, he drew 551 dollars from a bank in Providence with which to pay for a certain lot of land in Greene, paid certain bills, and got into a Pawtucket horse-car. This is the last incident which he remembers. He did not return home that day, and nothing was heard of him for two months. He was published in the papers as missing, and foul play being suspected, the police sought in vain his whereabouts. On the morning of March 14th, however, at Norristown, Pennsylvania, a man calling himself A. J. Brown, who had rented a small shop six weeks previously, stocked it with stationery, confectionery, fruit and small articles, and carried on his quiet trade without seeming to any one unnatural or eccentric, woke up in a fright and called in the people of the house to tell him where he was. He said that his name was Ansel Bourne, that he was entirely ignorant of Norristown, that he knew nothing of shop-keeping, and that the last thing he remembered—it seemed only yesterday—was drawing the money from the bank, etc. in Providence. He would not believe that two months had elapsed. The people of the house thought him insane; and so, at first, did Dr. Louis H. Read, whom they called in to see him. But on telegraphing to Providence, confirmatory messages came, and presently his nephew, Mr. Andrew Harris, arrived upon the scene, made everything straight, and took him home. He was very weak, having lost apparently over twenty pounds of flesh during his escapade, and had such a horror of the idea of the candy-store that he refused to set foot in it again.

The first two weeks of the period remained unaccounted for, as he had no memory, after he had once resumed his normal personality, of any part of the time, and no one who knew him seems to have seen him after he left home. The remarkable part of the change is, of course, the peculiar occupation which the so-called Brown indulged in. Mr. Bourne has never in his life had the slightest contact with trade. 'Brown' was described by the neighbors as taciturn, orderly in his habits, and in no

way queer. He went to Philadelphia several
times; replenished his stock; cooked for himself in the back shop, where he also slept; went
regularly to church; and once at a prayer-
meeting made what was considered by the
hearers a good address, in the course of which
he related an incident which he had witnessed
in his natural state of Bourne.

This was all that was known of the case up
to June 1890, when I induced Mr. Bourne to
submit to hypnotism, so as to see whether, in
the hypnotic trance, his 'Brown' memory
would not come back. It did so with surprising
readiness; so much so indeed that it proved
quite impossible to make him whilst in the
hypnosis remember any of the facts of his
normal life. He had heard of Ansel Bourne,
but "didn't know as he had ever met the
man." When confronted with Mrs. Bourne he
said that he had "never seen the woman before," etc. On the other hand, he told of his
peregrinations during the lost fortnight,* and
gave all sorts of details about the Norristown
episode. The whole thing was prosaic enough;
and the Brown-personality seems to be nothing but a rather shrunken, dejected, and amnesic extract of Mr. Bourne himself. He gives
no motive for the wandering except that there
was 'trouble back there' and he 'wanted rest.'
During the trance he looks old, the corners of
his mouth are drawn down, his voice is slow
and weak, and he sits screening his eyes and
trying vainly to remember what lay before and
after the two months of the Brown experience.
"I'm all hedged in," he says: "I can't get out at
either end. I don't know what set me down in

the Pawtucket horse-car, and I don't know
how I ever left that store, or what became of
it." His eyes are practically normal, and all
his sensibilities (save for tardier response)
about the same in hypnosis as in waking. I
had hoped by suggestion, etc., to run the two
personalities into one, and make the memories
continuous, but no artifice would avail to accomplish this, and Mr. Bourne's skull to-day
still covers two distinct personal selves.

The case (whether it contain an epileptic
element or not) should apparently be classed
as one of spontaneous hypnotic trance, persisting for two months. The peculiarity of it is
that nothing else like it ever occurred in the
man's life, and that no eccentricity of character came out. In most similar cases, the attacks
recur, and the sensibilities and conduct markedly change.*

James assumed that the fugue of Bourne was
that of a spontaneous hypnotic trance of two
months duration. This explanation does not appear valid. That the memories could be recovered through hypnosis means only that hypnosis could break the amnesic barrier; it does
not mean that hypnosis had produced the amnesia in the first place. For our purposes, at this
point, the case is useful as a dramatic instance of
a prolonged dissociation that exhibits the phenomena in dramatic form, whatever their interpretation.

Alternating Personalities

As already noted, the early dissociation theorists
derived their beliefs in dissociation largely from
multiple personalities that came to their atten-

---

*He had spent an afternoon in Boston, a night in New
York, an afternoon in Newark, and ten days or more in
Philadelphia, first in a certain hotel and next in a certain
boarding-house, making no acquaintances, 'resting,' reading, and 'looking around.' I have unfortunately been unable
to get independent corroboration of these details, as the
hotel registers are destroyed, and the boarding-house
named by him has been pulled down. He forgets the name
of the two ladies who kept it. (Footnote in original source)

*The details of the case, it will be seen, are all *compatible*
with simulation. I can only say of that, that no one who has
examined Mr. Bourne (including Dr. Read, Dr. Weir Mitchell, Dr. Guy Hinsdale, and Mr. R. Hodgson) practically
doubts his ingrained honesty, nor, so far as I can discover,
do any of his personal acquaintances indulge in a sceptical
view. (Footnote in original source)

tion in the course of clinical practice. Overt multiple personalities of the kinds they studied appear to be rather rare experiments of nature, but they continue to appear from time to time, and it is pertinent to try to form a contemporary estimate of their scientific status.

Common criticisms of the concept of multiple personality make the assumption that this is a so-called iatrogenic disease—that is, a disease created by the physician treating the person. The criticism has often been made, early voiced as a danger by Janet, and by William James, who was worried about one of Prince's earliest cases. After hearing a lecture by Prince, James said:

> It is very easy in the ordinary hypnotic subject to suggest during a trance the appearance of a secondary personage with a certain temperament, and that secondary personage will usually give itself a name. One has, therefore, to be on one's guard in this matter against confounding naturally double persons and persons who are simply temporarily endowed with the belief that they must play the role of being double (Discussion of Prince, 1890; reproduced in Prince 1975, p. 55).

Actually, a number of cases can be cited in which the patient exhibited the multiple personalities before being treated by anyone who suspected their existence and certainly before any hypnotic procedures were used in calling them forth. Fortunately, there have been a number of able reviews of the cases from the past. The most detailed of these was made by Taylor and Martin (1944), and a careful summary and interpretation has been provided by Ellenberger (1970). There have been a number of new cases reported since Ellenberger's review, indicating either something in the unsettled value systems of our times that leads to these divisions of personality or that psychotherapists are becoming more alert to them.

Ellenberger offered a classification of the cases to give some order to these complex manifestations. His classes, with some of his illustrations in brief, are as follows:

1. *Simultaneous Dual Personalities.* In this most uncommon condition there are two personalities manifesting themselves at once, not just two separate "streams of consciousness," but two personalities, each with its feeling of identity; this is similar to some forms of "possession states."

Hélène Smith, a medium studied by Flournoy (1900), reports a protector, Leopold. Having a spirit intermediary of this kind is not uncommon in the spiritualist tradition, but what brings her case in the dual personality category is that she sometimes *became* Leopold; in the transient state both she and Leopold existed as one was turning into the other. Her case has a somewhat contemporary sound, because it included a visit to the planet Mars.

I find the specification of this category rather unsatisfactory; in any case the coexistence of both personalities is not an enduring matter, and presently one of them is dominant, even though the other may be dimly in the background, just as the dreamer sometimes knows that he is dreaming.

2. *Successive Dual Personalities, Mutually Cognizant.* The first category, just described, readily merges into the second. Because both personalities know each other, the usual discontinuity of memories is not conspicuous, and the few cases of this kind appear to correspond to excessive mood shifts, with corresponding role behavior. A case reported by Cory (1920) is illustrative.

The alternating personalities in a 29-year-old woman were designated A and B. Personality A was the normal, habitual personality, that of a bright and cultured woman of good background. She was rather shy and inhibited. Although she played piano, she sang poorly. Personality B seemed older and bolder, but remained dignified and serious looking. She claimed to be the reincarnation of a Spanish singer. She sang well (in contrast with A). When speaking English (her native tongue) she added a strong Spanish accent. At times she spoke "Spanish," but it was made up of broken Spanish and Spanish-sounding words in a crude imitation of Spanish. Although A was sexually inhibited, B pretended to be a voluptuous, fascinating beauty and claimed to have been a dancer, a courtesan, and the mistress of a nobleman.

Although the two personalities knew each other and were on friendly terms, each was able to hold back a little information from the other, as two friends might.

Some additional information about the relationships between the personalities was obtained under hypnosis. Cory was able to hypnotize A and B separately. When A was hypnotized, she remembered some things of which she was not aware in her waking state; some of them B had already told Cory in her normal state, not hypnotized. Hence some discontinuity in memories, common in multiple personality, was present here also.

Whenever hypnosis has been used in a case of this kind, it is important to inquire whether the hypnotic procedures were required to identify the split; if so, the suspicion remains that hypnosis may have been responsible for the findings. In Cory's case the secondary personality had emerged at the time of the father's suicide, had persisted for three years before coming to Cory's attention, and hence cannot be attributed to hypnosis. The sexual repression-expression conflict is in evidence in the contrasts between A and B; the Spanish content may reflect some experiences she had with Spanish-speaking children in a convent school and some attraction to a Spanish man shortly after her father's death. The spirit-possession aspect may have been reinforced by the reward B received in a circle of believers in spiritualism.

3. Successive Dual Personalities, Mutually Amnesic.

As Ellenberger has noted, the phenomena of possession throughout history have had some of the features of multiple personality, but as long as possession states were interpreted supernaturalistically they did not become identified as alternating personalities. Hence it was only with the decline in belief in possession that multiple personalities became part of the medical literature. An early case, reported by Gmelin in 1791, was identified as an "exchanged personality" and fits the pattern of mutually amnesic states.

A young German woman, impressed by the aristocratic refugees arriving in Stuttgart at the time of the French revolution, suddenly exchanged her personality for the manners of a French lady, speaking French perfectly and German with something of an accent. In the French personality, the young woman remembered all that she had said and done in her previous French states, but in her German condition she knew nothing of the French state.

4. Successive Dual Personalities, One-way Amnesic.

This is probably the most frequent type of multiple personality, in which personality A has its own memories but not those of personality B, while personality B has the memories of A as well as of B.

An early case of this kind was published by Azam (1887) after many years of observation and has since been referred to frequently as a kind of prototype of dual personality. His patient, Felida X, earned her living as a seamstress in her normal personality. She was described as sullen and taciturn, with many headaches and neuralgias that would today be described as psychosomatic. After a crisis, however, she would awaken as a different person, gay, vivacious, and free of symptoms. This secondary person, more "healthful" than the "normal" one, knew all about the symptoms of the primary personality, but the primary person had no awareness of the secondary one, except as she was told about it by others.

It is important to note that the secondary or hidden personality can sometimes be more "normal," better adjusted, healthier than the primary personality. Typically, the secondary personality has the whole set of memories, and therapy is directed to bringing about an integration based on it rather than on the typical personality that at first presents itself as the primary one. This conclusion was reached some time ago by Mitchell (1925), who noted the two points: (1) that it is the secondary personality B that has the memories of both A and B, whereas the primary personality A is cut off from B's memories, and (2) the secondary personality B is often healthier according to common social or mental health criteria.

Multiple Personalities: Three or More

The case of Charles Poultney reported by Franz (1933) is the first of those mentioned here in which there is a third personality. In this case the personalities are defined almost entirely according to the continuities and discontinuities of memories. In terms of social behavior or general characterization there was not much change, except as required by the circumstances engendered by lost memories. The two main parts into which his life was cut by memory discontinuity were the memories of Charles Poultney (his correct name) from birth in 1887 to age 27 in 1914, and Charles Poulting, an assumed name, February 1915 to March 1930, ages 28–43. A gap between September 1914 and February 1915 may have been filled by a third personality, but little is known about this personality. In 1930 he came to Franz's attention. Franz unraveled his story by reintegrative techniques, such as the use of a map to restore his memory of wartime experiences taking place in Africa; hypnosis was not used.

As the story was pieced together, it was found that he had first been picked up in Los Angeles in 1919 in a dazed condition, wandering the streets. Although he had identification papers made out to Charles Poulting of Florida and had

British and French war medals with him, he did not know who he was. He spoke with an Irish accent, thought he might be a Canadian, and Michigan seemed to have had some importance to him. He was tattooed with Buffalo Bill and an American flag. He had traveled widely since World War I, trying to find himself, for he had lost all memories prior to February 1915. In a curious interlude, a woman thought he was her long-lost son and took him into her home, but everything, including the Seventh-Day Adventist religion, was so foreign to him that he refused to accept this solution and continued to wander in search of his identity.

The police again found him wandering in a dazed condition in March 1930, now having regained the memories and identity of Charles Poultney from birth to 1914, but having lost all recent memories. He now thought he was back to 1914 and looked on newspapers with the 1930 dates as some strange "futuristic" sheets because they gave no war news. He missed his uniform and, when seeking to return things to a pocket, automatically fumbled for the breast pocket of his uniform, where there was no pocket in his civilian clothes.

In this second state, as Charles Poulting, it was possible to "introduce him" to the memories of the first state, as Charles Poultney, by way of the biography that he had written while in that state. This did not help much until, with the map of Africa before him, the two personal memories were integrated in a flood of emotion. The place name of Voi proved to be the trigger. The dynamics of repression appeared to be operative with respect to his interim in Africa because of the recall of two tragic events. About one he felt no guilt, but the other burdened his conscience. Out in the forest with another soldier in leopard country, his companion refused to climb a tree and tie himself there to spend the night. During the night he was attacked and eaten by leopards. This did not bother Poultney; he had seen many battle deaths, and this was his companion's fault for not taking the precaution that he had recommended and himself taken. However, the other event was different. He had a monkey with him when nightfall occurred in the same territory. He tied the monkey to the base of the tree, while he found his own secure place up in the tree. During the night the monkey was attacked and eaten; had Poultney not tied him at the bottom of the tree he could have escaped. By contrast with the death of his human companion, the death of the monkey—his fault—was an intolerable burden to think about, and he became amnesic for the event and for other events surrounding it. Although dramatic with respect to this particular incident, this is not the whole story, for there were earlier fugues before the monkey came along, although all of them were preceded by physical or emotional traumas. Once the monkey episode came to light, all the subsequent memories of Poulting and Poultney became fused, and the man felt essentially cured, even though there were still some memory gaps.

He now knew the date and place of his birth, his address in Dublin, the names of his parental family and of his own wife and two children to whom he had not returned after his military service. He had come to the United States in 1913 and had indeed lived in Michigan. That Michigan had some prominence in the alternate personality in which he was amnesic for these events indicates that the amnesia barrier was somewhat permeable.

The case illustrates very well the role of amnesia in disrupting the continuity of self-identity.

Complex cases like that of Franz, including those of Pierre Janet's, had appeared from time to time. One of the women Janet studied, Léonie, began with a dual personality, but soon a third one emerged which, he noted, had also been discovered many years earlier (Janet, 1889).

Léonie was Janet's first reported and most thoroughly experimented case. She came to Janet's attention early in his career, when he

appears to have been more interested in experimenting on her than in attempting to resolve her problems. She had apparently had natural attacks of somnambulism since the age of 3 and had been repeatedly hypnotized by all sorts of people from the age of 16 on; she was 45 when Janet studied her. Her childhood had been spent in peasant surroundings, but the rest of her life had been spent in "drawing rooms and doctors' offices," as Janet put it. In her normal state she was serious, timid, mild, and a little sad; when hypnotized she became vivacious and noisy, with a tendency to irony and jesting toward the strangers who had come to witness her hypnotic behavior. Janet at first performed some dramatic but poorly controlled studies of hynotic influence at a distance, but he repudiated parapsychological influences and attempted to give a purely naturalistic account of what he observed. Léonie eventually turned up with three personalities uncovered with the aid of hypnosis, on occasion called Léonie I, II, and III, sometimes given the names by which the first two referred to themselves: Léonie and Léontine and, for the third, Léonore, a name given by the "magnetizer" who had first discovered the third personality. Léontine appeared when hypnotized by Janet, as she had for other hypnotists before him. Later on, when Léontine was herself hypnotized, a third personality, Léonore, made her appearance. It was only after studying Léonie for some time that Janet found out that she had been treated hypnotically years before by some of the magnetizers of that period and that the "new" personality had been elicited and christened 20 years earlier.

In a much-studied and hypnotized case of this kind, doubts arise as to the role of the hypnotist in consolidating personalities out of amnesic material; Janet, as noted earlier, was aware of the problem. He recognized the role that naming played in defining the secondary personality: "Once baptized, the unconscious personality is clearer and more definite; it shows the psychological traits more clearly" (Janet, 1889, p. 318). The three personalities of Léonie showed signs of their origins. The first was appropriate to her upbringing as a simple country girl and housewife who was now placed in a sophisticated urban setting. She had had her first child while hypnotized and spontaneously fell into the hypnotic state when her other children were born; it is not too surprising that the hypnotized personality (Léonie II) claimed the children as her own, while assigning the husband to Léonie I, who accepted both the husband and the children. Léonore (Léonie III), doubtless a product of the hypnotic manipulations, might have been made use of to reintegrate the personality, for she was quite aware of the others, although she judged Léonie I to be stupid and Léonie II to be disturbed. The amnesic barriers that persisted made Léonie I know only herself; Léonie II knew Léonie I as well as herself; Léonie III knew them all.

Dual personality is probably a more common manifestation than divisions into three or more personalities: we know that more are possible, having met the three personalities of Charles Poulting (if the amnesic period prior to restoration can be called a personality) and of Janet's Léonie.

The best known of these multiple cases was described in Morton Prince's history of Miss Beauchamp (Prince 1906). In her case the four ultimate personalities all arose after she had been in hypnotic treatment for some weeks; thus William James' questions were well raised. Miss Beauchamps' eventual personalities were as follows:

B I, the primary personality of Miss Beauchamp.

B II, a secondary personality, an intensified version of B I.

B III, Sally, who showed scorn and contempt for B I.

B IV, the Idiot, a regressed personality.

Prince eventually succeeded in integrating them all.

The memory overlaps are illustrated for the three main personalities in Figure 2, in which the direction of the arrow indicates access to knowledge of the other personality. (B IV may be ignored.) Only the primary personality, B I, is without knowledge of the other two. B II knows B I, but not B III. B III has full access to the other two. . . .

Figure 2
The component personalities of Miss Beauchamp, with direction of awareness of one personality for another. The arrowhead points in the direction in which one personality knows another. After Prince (1906).

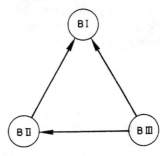

Recent Cases

Jonah This case has been carefully studied from a psychological point of view (Ludwig and others, 1972; Brandsma and Ludwig, 1974). The same psychiatrist who treated the Sibyl case is represented among the authors giving the account of Jonah, a 27-year-old man who came to a hospital with complaints of severe headaches that were often followed by memory loss. Hospital attendants noticed striking changes in his personality on different days, and the psychiatrist in charge detected three distinct secondary personalities prior to any attempt to explore the patient's problems with the help of hypnosis.

Hypnosis was then used in the effort to fuse the personalities, and the patient was discharged from the hospital. However, the result was unsuccessful, and on the patient's return the hospital staff was prepared to do a more thorough study of the personalities before attempting to fuse them again.

The relatively stable personality structures that emerged are diagrammed in Figure 3. The four personalities may be characterized briefly:

JONAH.   The primary personality. Shy, retiring, polite, passive, and highly conventional, he is designated "the square." Sometimes frightened and confused during interviews, Jonah is unaware of the other personalities.

SAMMY.   He has the most intact memories. He can coexist with Jonah or set Jonah aside and take over. He claims to be ready when Jonah needs legal advice or is in trouble. He is designated "the mediator." Sammy remembers emerging at age 6, when Jonah's mother stabbed his stepfather, and Sammy persuaded the parents never to fight again in front of the children.

KING YOUNG.   He emerged when Jonah was 6 or 7 to straighten out his sexual identity after Jonah's mother occasionally dressed him in girls' clothing at home, and Jonah became confused about boys' and girls' names at school. King Young has looked after Jonah's sexual interests ever since; hence he is designated "the lover." He is aware of the other personalities rather dimly, but takes over when Jonah needs assistance in seeking sexual gratification with a woman.

USOFFA ABDULLA.   A cold, belligerent, and angry person, Usoffa is capable of ignoring pain. It is his sworn duty to watch over and protect Jonah; hence he is designated "the warrior." He emerged at about age 9 or 10, when a gang of white boys beat up Jonah, who is black, without provocation. Jonah was helpless, but when Usoffa emerged, he fought viciously and vehemently against the attackers. He is only dimly aware of the other personalities. The fact that the personalities see themselves in these roles is evident from their self-portraits made during the course of the study (Figure 4). The psychological study showed that the four personalities tested very differently on all measures having to do with emotionally laden topics, but scored essentially alike on tests relatively free of emotion or interpersonal conflict, such as intelligence or vocabulary tests.

The outcome of the treatment, in which the four personalities were to be fused into one, has not been reported, although some early indications were that Jonah seemed "sicker" with all the strands of the personality out in the open than when the secondary personalities were in abeyance except when needed. The authors conjectured that, for him, four heads were perhaps better than one.

Figure 3
The four component personalities, with their degrees of awareness of each other. The three personalities on the periphery have superficial knowledge of each other but are intimately familiar with Jonah, who is totally lacking in knowledge of them. Another temporarily emerging personality, De Nova, is not shown. From Ludwig and others (1972).

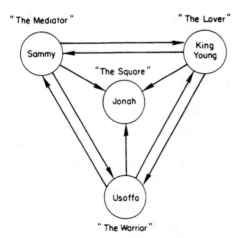

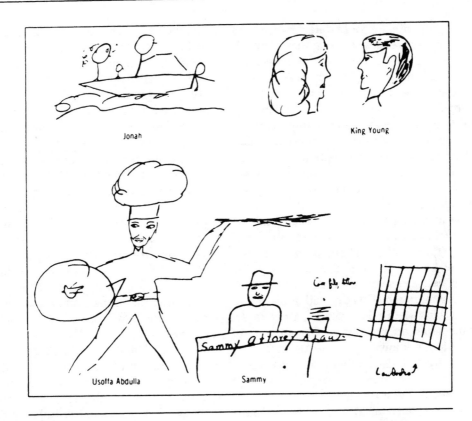

Figure 4
Self-portraits of the separate personalities of Jonah. From Ludwig and others (1972).

Again we note, in the quarrels between mother and stepfather and in the mother's failure to provide a clear sex-typed role for Jonah, that the identification figures of childhood do not permit clear identifications and hence do not lead to a satisfactorily integrated personality.

Katherine—Kathy This unpublished case, furnished to me by Dr. Monroe S. Arlen, the psychiatrist who treated Katherine, reveals some of the childhood difficulties so common in these instances of divided personalities.

Katherine, the 29-year-old mother of a 15-month-old daughter, had become depressed, tense, and irritable and rejected the sexual advances of her husband after the birth of the daughter, a first child. In the previous three years of marriage she had, by his account, been relaxed and an enjoyable sex partner. She was treated briefly by a psychotherapist who used progressive relaxation and hypnosis in the attempt to make sex enjoyable to her once more; this was within three months of the infant's birth. Her husband reported that this had ended in failure, and now, a year later, "She acts like a child, says sex is bad and dumb and wants to die. She responds only to the name Kathy and seems to be in a trance."

Unfortunately the details of the first psychotherapeutic sessions are lacking, but the inference is that the birth of a daughter served as a trigger to bring out postpartum symptoms related to her earlier life. Her husband arranged to have her treated by Dr. Arlen, and the first interview was with the husband. He felt that, in observing his wife, he could detect two secondary personalities, one a suckling infant and the other a sensuous teenager who admitted that sex was bad but enjoyable. He also observed that, during the trance-like states, she would mis-identify him as her mother. It later appeared that Kathy was the only important secondary personality and could appear in behavior as anything from an infant to a teenager. When she wished to prevent sex, she would force Katherine into a fetal position that appeared totally regressed.

Her secondary personality—called Kathy—was immature, varying in age between 7 and 17, and sometimes "wishing to be a baby." Katherine knows about Kathy, and they talk together: hence in some respects it is like a case of possession, in which Kathy will not let Katherine do what Kathy does not wish her to do. Their memories are not entirely in common; for example, Kathy knows about a sexual assault on Katherine by an older brother when she was 7, which Katherine does not recall, although Kathy has told her about it.

Katherine's personal history of sexual traumas was enough to cause concern over sex. There may have been some fantasy overlays, because many of the details came out only in hypnotic age regression within which some distortions are possible. She reported an attempt by a young brother to have sex with her at the age of 5, at the urging of an older sister, but he was unsuccessful and she did not know what it was all about. The important incident occurred at the age of 7, when an older brother forced both oral and anal sex on her in a corn field near their home. This was a painful and frightening experience for her. She could not explain why she was late for dinner, and when her father punished her severely for being late, she accepted this as punishment also for her sexual transgression. Katherine, who does not recall the incident, remembers a frightening dream a year later, "A wolf came out of a corn field, I ran inside to lock the windows, but the wolf

jumped in." The split in personality is dated from this event. One part of her, Katherine, became shy and inhibited and blocked out the whole experience. The other part, Kathy, refused to grow up to adulthood; she retained the experience and began to exert a subtle influence over Katherine's general behavior and attitudes, especially in the sexual sphere.

The unfortunate experiences with sex did not stop with this incident. At the age of 10 she saw her 12-year-old sister raped by several boys; at the age of 17 she was raped by three boys, and on another occasion her father, while drunk, made sexual advances to her, but Kathy emerged to stop him, calling him "dumb and stupid." Somehow Katherine fended off these memories, but Kathy retained them and sought to restrict Katherine's adult sex life.

Therapy now consisted in subordinating Kathy's control over Katherine and in dealing with the general problems of guilt over sex. The sexual relations between Katherine and her husband improved; she was able to experience orgasm, and the therapy was terminated, although Kathy had not completely disappeared and occasionally reappeared for a brief outburst.

One is tempted to interpret why the birth of Katherine's daughter was followed by the symptoms in a form not previously shown. The probability is that the appearance of the baby meant a necessity to adopt a truly adult role as a mother, and the mother figure for Katherine was her own mother who had the feeling that sex was dirty and nasty. Combining this with that part of herself that had been traumatized by sex and preferred not to grow up, a conflict ensued. The conflict was difficult to resolve because sex was not wholeheartedly rejected; in fact, Katherine said at one point, while she was still fearing sex, "My top half is scared, but my bottom half wants it." Later, in therapy, as she had outgrown some of her inability to express emotion, she sized up her relation to Kathy: "She keeps the bad feelings and memories and keeps me away from sex. She's afraid of growing up, but I'm trying to talk with her and explain to her that sex is not naughty and it's not something you are going to get spanked for any more." . . .

Concluding Note on Multiple Personalities

That multiple personalities represent in some sense an effort at coping with a very difficult childhood appears to be the most common feature of these cases. The evidence does not favor cultural causes in the larger sense, but rather a disintegration of values at the heart of the family, with violent and excessive punishment, overt sexual assaults in childhood, unbalanced parental roles, one parent occasionally sadistic, the other rather passive and aloof. In resolving the conflicts over identification and guilt, and in trying to cope in a context in which a unified strategy cannot work, the person divides; sometimes, as in the case of Jonah, the strategy is moderately successful. The solution, however, carries within it so many problems, that at least the restoration of communication among the divided memories is called for; role divisions are acceptable if they are mutually understood and do not cause intolerable confusion.

In summarizing cases of multiple personality it is clear that sometimes the concealed personality is more normal than the presenting one, and sometimes the secondary personality is less acceptable than the primary one. Each is dissociated from the other and accessible at different times. The fact that the concealed part may be more rational and socially acceptable than the presenting part may mean that it will prove particularly useful in the integration of the personality. What has been noted, but not elaborated, is that the cause of the dissociations in these clinical cases lies in motivational conflicts that are often deeply unconscious. Having open access to the dissociated personalities does not in itself account for their origins. . . .

II: Automatic Writing and Divided Attention

Automatisms have an uncertain relationship to awareness and hence to dissociation. The "pure case" is an activity carried out with no awareness whatever that it is going on. An activity may be carried out in awareness, however, without any sense of control over it; compulsive acts or obsessive thoughts may be of this kind. Sometimes the processes are only mildly dissociated, such as the "doodling" that occurs while one is talking on the telephone or listening to a lecture. All these instances are automatic to some extent. In the context of this chapter, most automatic writing is either totally out of awareness, while the writer is preoccupied with something else, or, if he is aware of it, he does not feel that he is its author. This latter case is rather like that of dreams, in which a remembered dream is a conscious product, but the authorship of the dream is obscure. It is *your* dream, just as it is *your* writing, even though you did not "will" it.

The Background in Spiritualism

. . . Stirrings in the culture outside of established science have led in part to the recent interest in consciousness expansion and the development of a more cognitive psychology. The larger cultural setting provides what Boring (following James) liked to refer to as the *Zeitgeist*; what scientists do is influenced by what goes on around them, whether they go along with the popular movement or seek to correct its exaggerations. This happened in the nineteenth century as a consequence of a popular wave of spiritualism, with a residue in naturalistic psychological science of a renewed interest in hypnotism, with automatic writing as one of its methods.

The Fox Sisters   A wave of spiritualism began on March 31, 1848 in Hydesville, Wayne County, New York, when two sisters, Margaret Fox, 12 years old, and Kate Fox, then 9, reported strange rappings attributed to an invisible spirit. They reported that during the previous year they heard these rappings occur in their presence; on this date the rappings were the response to their request to a spirit, Mr. Splitfoot, to answer their questions after they went to bed. A much older sister, Leah, soon found that she, too, was able to communicate with spirits.

The Fox sisters were examined in 1849, with the conclusion that the sounds were made by voluntary effort, probably in their joints. This did not deter believers; as excitement mounted, they were frequently examined and often (though not always) exposed. In 1857 a newspaper, the Boston Courier, offered a prize of $500 to anyone able to produce authentic spiritualistic phenomena; Harvard professors Benjamin Peirce, Louis Agassiz, Eben Horsford, and a Cambridge astronomer, Benjamin A. Gould, served as judges. Kate Fox and her sister Leah competed, along with others. The jury did not award the prize to them or to anyone else, for they found nothing. All that resulted was more business for the mediums. The most important lesson to be learned from the case of the Fox sisters is the helplessness of science against committed belief, a helplessness that is shown even today after the exposure of one fraud after another.

Despite repeated evidences of deception, the experiences of the Fox sisters helped to inaugurate a wave of spiritualistic and mediumistic phenomena that spread around the world. Not all scientists were negative. As late as 1871, 23 years after the original rappings, sister Kate fooled Sir William Crookes, known for the

Crookes tube that played a part in the development of vacuum tube technology, the radiometer, and other contributions to chemistry and physics. Impressed by her performance, he wrote:

> With a full knowledge of the numerous theories which have been started, chiefly in America, to explain these sounds, I have tested them in every way that I could devise, until there has been no escape from the conviction that they were true objective occurrences not produced by trickery or mechanical means (Crookes, 1874, p. 88).

The truth came out a few years later, in 1888, when the sisters confessed that it had all been a matter of trickery and fraud. The fullest confession was made by Margaret in a public meeting at the New York Academy of Music on Sunday evening, October 21, 1888.

Her comments appeared in the *New York World* the following day. She told of her hatred for the older sister Leah, who had forced them into commercializing their tricks, and explained in detail how they made the sounds with the joints of the big toe and fingers. Sister Kate had stated in print two weeks earlier: "Spiritualism is a humbug from beginning to end. It is the greatest humbug of the century" (Christopher, 1975, p. 9). Leah disappeared from sight.

Once their fame spread, the girls were called on for other spiritual services. They enter our account because of the voluminous "automatic writing" done by Kate at the behest of a serious doctor and his wife, Dr. and Mrs. George H. Taylor. Mrs. Taylor preserved a careful transcript of all that went on in repeated sessions between 1869 and 1892 (even after the confessions!), to be published many years later in a large book under her name by W. G. L. Taylor, her son (Taylor, 1932). The last message is one reputed to have come from Benjamin Franklin, who served as a guiding spirit throughout, telling them each time when to meet again. The meetings were held in the old Madison Avenue Hotel, at the corner of Madison Avenue and 58th Street, New York. The book ends with the sad story that Kate had died of drink three weeks after the last session.

An interesting feature of the "communications" was that they were done throughout in mirror writing, which, unless it comes spontaneously, as it very well may, takes considerable practice to acquire. Kate was able to write in the ordinary manner, because one of the published letters from Benjamin Franklin is written in ordinary script from left to right; it is said to have been the only one done this way. The "automatic writing" is of no scientific importance except as a warning against gullibility. Yet the interest in communication with departed spirits by way of automatic writing has not ceased among the believers in spiritualism. For example, the automatic writing of Mrs. Verrall, reflecting communication with many departed persons, has recently been examined in great detail, with such conclusions as that the dead person can communicate directly only for about seven years after death (Lambert, 1971).

The Planchette   A book that appeared in 1869 celebrated the victory of spiritualism over science with the title: *Planchette; or, The despair of science* (Sargent, 1869). Sargent pointed out that the choice of title was dictated by the vogue of the planchette, which had appeared in great numbers in the booksellers' shops in the United States the previous year. It had been common in France for 12 or 15 years. A report from New York in 1868 showed that one manufacturer, a Mr. Kirby, had sold over 200,000 planchettes.

The planchette is a little heart-shaped table, usually about seven inches long and five inches wide. It stands on three legs, one of which is a sharpened lead pencil slipped into a rubber socket at the tip; the other two legs are mounted on casters so that the whole can move freely in any direction over the paper on which it writes.

Sargent pointed out how the planchette descended from the table rapping of the Fox sisters. Communications were at first received by the tedious process of calling out the alphabet and noting down the letters at which the rap was given. Through a series of improvements, in which a pencil was at first mounted on the leg of the table, the planchette described above developed.

Although entirely friendly to its use in spirit communication, Sargent noted that failures were very numerous.

Probably not more than ten out of a hundred persons in a mixed assemblage could be found, through whom the phenomena would take place, and in the hundred there might possibly be one who would prove a good medium. Such a one will soon discard the planchette as of no use in the production of phenomena more extraordinary than any got by its aid (Sargent, 1869, p. 3).

The planchette is described here as a late nineteenth century invention, although something similar had probably been used occasionally from ancient times. Sargent notes that a Dr. Macgowan, writing in the *North China Herald*, reported a device similar to a planchette that he saw widely used in China in 1843, before the Fox sisters got started. A table was sprinkled with bran, flour, dust, or other powder. A hemispheric basket, turned upside down, was the equivalent of the planchette. The writing instrument could be any kind of stylus, such as a reed or a chopstick, thrust through the interstices of the woven basket. The edges of the basket rested on the hands of the "mediums" who sought a message. These operators claimed to be unconscious of the intelligence they communicated.

The use of the planchette in nonmediumistic settings was taken seriously by F. W. H. Myers and Edmund Gurney, the founders of the London Society for Psychical Research, and they collected numerous anecdotes on its use, often referring to its productions as something from the subconscious mind, rather than anything received telepathically or from spirits (although they also entertained these possibilities).

Many illustrations were assembled, of which a typical account is that by F. C. S. Schiller, at the time a Fellow of Corpus Christi College, Oxford. He was experimenting during a Long Vacation with his brother F. and sister L. . . .

Both F. and L. were at first entirely ignorant of what planchette was writing, and F. remained so to the end, nor did the occupations of his conscious self appear in the least to affect the progress of the writing. I have seen planchette write in the same slow and deliberate way both while he was telling an amusing anecdote in an animated way and while he was absorbed in an interesting novel; and frequently whole series of questions would be asked and answered without his knowing what had been written or thinking that anything else than unmeaning scrawls had been produced.

In L's case it is true that after some time she came to know what letters were being formed and was able to interpret the movements of her hand. This, of course, made it difficult to avoid, at times, a certain half-conscious influence on the writing, and makes it necessary to allow for the personal equation. . . .

An interesting experiment was tried of writing with two planchettes, F. having one hand on each. I suggested this in order to elucidate the connection between left-handed writing and "mirror-writing," and fully expected that the two hands would write the same communications. To my astonishment, however, the communications, though written simultaneously, were different and proceeded from different "spirits." . . . Whenever F. wrote with two planchettes, the left hand wrote mirror-writing, which was often very hard to decipher. (Myers, 1887, pp. 216–217).

These fragments suffice to show how the planchette, descended as it was from the table rapping of the Fox sisters, opened up possibilities for study in other settings, even though many of the early investigators continued to entertain the spiritualistic hypothesis along with the naturalistic interpretation of subconscious influence.

The Ouija Board The ouija board (oui-ja = yes-yes in French and German) appears to have been a later invention than the planchette, but it has served similar purposes both as a kind of parlor game and as a means of communicating with departed spirits. Still in production and available for purchase at American toy stores, it differs from the planchette chiefly in that the moving table does not write but comes to rest on letters of the alphabet or numerals and in that way builds up its message.

As with the planchette, it was soon discovered that the hand might indeed produce sensible messages, often to the genuine surprise of the operator as well as the observers. From a naturalistic standpoint, this means that it is occasionally possible to tap levels of memory and imagination, cognitively comprehensible, that are not in the ordinary waking consciousness of the person whose cognitions are being displayed.

A few extreme cases came to light, of which one of the most striking was that of "Patience Worth." Mrs. Curran, a St. Louis housewife, began playing with the ouija board. She had not graduated from high school and she showed no evidence of literary capabilities or pretensions. After Patience Worth introduced herself to Mrs. Curran on the ouija board and took over guidance of her hand, Mrs. Curran soon became a successful author with the help of this unseen spirit. Five novels were published under the authorship of Patience Worth between 1917 and 1928; although they were not great, they had some literary merit and received favorable reviews at the time. Gradually the ouija board was displaced, and Patience Worth began dictating directly to Mrs. Curran. There were a number of poems in addition to the novels. The case is of sufficient interest to have been given a recent thorough review (Litvag, 1972).

It was noted by Sargent over a century ago that once a person was successful with the planchette he could abandon it, and Mrs. Curran demonstrated the same thing when she gave up the ouija board for direct dictation. Automatic writing by pen alone was commonly reported by Myers (1903).

III: Divided Consciousness in Hypnosis: The "Hidden Observer"

Divided consciousness is familiar in ordinary waking life; the division permits fantasy to continue even while the person is performing the obligations of the work life or satisfying the proprieties of social interactions and communications. Because he is able to pay sufficient attention to the obligations and proprieties, this fantasizing may go largely unnoticed. In hypnosis the fantasied world may become more prominent, and, at least in some instances, the realities may be denied. The question arises whether the denied realities are completely obliterated, or whether instead they are concealed behind an amnesia-like mask that is possible within hypnosis. We found in some demonstrations and experiments within our laboratory that two kinds of information processing may go on at once within hypnosis; some aspects are available to the hypnotic consciousness within hypnosis as ordinarily studied; other aspects are available only when special techniques have elicited the concealed information. When these techniques are used, the additional information is reported as though it had been observed in the usual manner. Because the observing part

was hitherto not in awareness, we have come to use the metaphor of a "hidden observer" to characterize this cognitive system. . . .

The Hidden Observer Revealed in a Class Demonstration

The instructor was conducting a classroom demonstration of hypnotic deafness. The subject of the demonstration was a blind student, experienced in hypnosis, who had volunteered to serve; his blindness was not related to the demonstration, except that any visual cues were eliminated. After the induction of hypnosis, he was given the suggestion that, at the count of three, he would become completely deaf to all sounds. His hearing would be restored to normal when the instructor's hand was placed on his right shoulder. To be both blind and deaf would have been a frightening experience for the subject had he not known that his deafness was quite temporary. Loud sounds were then made close to the subject's head by banging together some large wooden blocks. There was no sign of any reaction; none was expected because the subject, in a previous demonstration, had shown a lack of responsiveness to the shots of a starter's pistol. He was also completely unresponsive to any questions asked of him while he was hypnotically deaf.

One student in the class questioned whether "some part" of the subject might be aware of what was going on. After all, there was nothing wrong with his ears. The instructor agreed to test this by a method related to interrogation practices used by clinical hypnotists. He addressed the hypnotically deaf subject in a quiet voice:

As you know, there are parts of our nervous system that carry on activities that occur out of awareness, of which control of the circulation of the blood, or the digestive processes, are the most familiar. However, there may be intellectual processes also of which we are unaware, such as those that find expression in night dreams. Although you are hypnotically deaf, perhaps there is some part of you that is hearing my voice and processing the information. If there is, I should like the index finger of your right hand to rise as a sign that this is the case.

To the surprise of the instructor, as well as the class, the finger rose! The subject immediately said:

Please restore my hearing so you can tell me what you did. I felt my finger rise in a way that was not a spontaneous twitch, so you must have done something to make it rise, and I want to know what you did.

The instructor placed his hand on the subject's right shoulder to restore his hearing, and the following conversation took place.

Can you hear my voice now?
Yes, I hear you. Now tell me what you did. What do you remember?
I remember your telling me that I would be deaf at the count of three, and could have my hearing restored when you placed your hand on my shoulder. Then everything was quiet for a while. It was a little boring just sitting here, so I busied myself with a statistical problem I have been working on. I was still doing that when I suddenly felt my finger lift; that is what I want you to explain to me.

The subject was assured that he would soon be informed about everything that had transpired. At this point an important innovation was introduced. In the laboratory we had been doing some experiments on automatic writing. . . . We had found that material not in the subject's awareness could be recovered through the writing of the hand of which the subject was unaware. It seemed worth testing with this highly hypnotizable subject whether, by anal-

ogy, "automatic talking" might yield results similar to automatic writing. Hence, with the subject hypnotized again but able to hear, the instructor spoke as follows:

When I place my hand on your arm like this (he demonstrated) I can be in touch with that part of you that listened to me before and made your finger rise—that part that could hear and knew what was going on when you were hypnotically deaf. When I question that part, it will be able to answer me and tell me what it knows about what happened. But this hypnotized part of you, to whom I am now talking, will not know what you are saying—or even that you are talking—until, out of hypnosis, I shall say, "Now you can remember everything." All right, now I am placing my hand on your arm.

The following conversation ensued: "Do you remember what happened when you were hypnotized and what the hypnotized part of you reported?" "Yes." (This very literal response is characteristic of this subject when hypnotized. If a question can be answered "yes" or "no," it commonly gets no more extensive answer without further probing.)

On further questioning he repeated much of the earlier conversation, including his surprise at the finger's lifting.

Does the part to whom I am now talking know more about what went on?
Yes.
Tell me what went on.
After you counted to make me deaf you made noises with some blocks behind my head. Members of the class asked me questions to which I did not respond. Then one of them asked if I might not really be hearing, and you told me to raise my finger if I did. This part of me responded by raising a finger, so it's all clear now.

The instructor then lifted his hand from the arm.

Please tell me what has happened in the last few minutes.
You said something about placing your hand on my arm, and some part of me would talk to you. Did I talk?

The subject was aroused from hypnosis and told that he would remember everything. He then recalled all that had happened and had been said.

This unplanned demonstration clearly indicated that a hypnotized subject who is not aware of a source of stimulation (in this case auditory) may nevertheless be registering the information coming from the stimuli. Further, he may be understanding it; thus, under appropriate circumstances, what was unknown to the hypnotized part of him can be uncovered and talked about. For convenience of reference, we speak of the concealed information as available to a "hidden observer."

It should be noted that the "hidden observer" is a metaphor for something occurring at an intellectual level but not available to the consciousness of the hypnotized person. It does not mean that there is a secondary personality with a life of its own—a kind of homunculus lurking in the shadows of the conscious person. The "hidden observer" is merely a convenient label for the information source tapped through experiments with automatic writing and automatic talking.

The Hidden Observer in the Hypnotic Reduction of Pain

For some time we had been studying the reduction of pain in our laboratory, using two types of induced pain: placing the hand and forearm in circulating ice water (cold pressor pain) and fastening a tourniquet to the upper arm, followed by exercise of the hand now deprived of blood (ischemic pain) . . .

Despite some ten years experience of successfully reduced pain, we had never had a single report of the memory of pain returning spontaneously after the experience of no pain. Still, the possible applications of the foregoing observations seemed too important to leave unexamined, so we determined to find if there were some covert pain experiences not revealed in the overt reports.

Because the automatic writing technique was already available to us, we decided to use it as an alternative to the ordinary verbal report of the pain. The usual scale we had been using assigned 0 for no pain and 1–10 for pain of increasing intensity, with 10 a pain so severe that the subject would prefer to remove the hand from the ice water; however, the subject was told to keep the hand in the water until asked to remove it and to count beyond 10 as the pain mounted. The level of 10 and above was usually reached in less than a minute in the waking condition. Hence the adaptation of the experiment was to have one hand in the ice water, with the subject reporting the pain on the numerical scale in the usual way; the other hand was to reply with a number on the same scale, but in writing, with what the hand was writing out of awareness (subconscious).

The first subject on whom we tried this was a young woman experienced in hypnosis; she had no difficulty reducing the ice water pain completely in one arm while keeping the other arm out of awareness for purposes of automatic writing.

She was hypnotized and instructed to feel nothing in the water; she verbally reported "0" in reply to all successive requests for reports at 5-second intervals. She had been instructed under hypnosis to use the same numerical reporting scale with her hand out of awareness; she would of course not know what her hand was writing. While she was overtly reporting "0," the hand out of awareness was simultaneously writing scale values for increasing pain —2, 5, 7, 8, 9. The "hidden observer" was reporting essentially normal pain while the hypnotized part of her was feeling no pain at all!

Automatic writing is a cumbersome technique for questioning a hypnotized subject; therefore, beginning with this same subject, we applied the automatic talking method, using a refinement of the instructions given in the deafness demonstration. With this method, the same pilot subject told us that, while her hypnotized part felt no pain, the hidden part had felt pain of about the same sensory intensity as that produced by the cold water without hypnosis. However, the covert pain bothered her much less at this hidden level within analgesia than overt pain bothered her in the normal waking state.

We extended this kind of experiment to samples of subjects who showed many variations on the common theme; some of the subjects who experienced pain reduction under hypnosis were able to recover an experience of covert pain differing from their overt experience, and some were not. For this latter group, it is important to find out if the covert experience is more deeply buried in some manner that other techniques might uncover or if the experience of pain is actually obliterated.

As an example of the findings, results for the eight most successful subjects in a group of 20 selected as high scorers on tests of hypnotic susceptibility are reproduced in Figure 5. All experienced a vivid distinction between overt and covert pain in hypnotic analgesia. In this arrangement, we returned to a condition similar to automatic writing, referred to in the figure as automatic key pressing. Instead of reporting the magnitude of the pain by writing with a pencil, the subject pressed small keys arranged somewhat like a small calculator, one key for tens and the other for digits. This gave not only a clearer report, but permitted recording on tape against time; thus, by also recording the voice report of overt pain we could determine the synchrony of the concealed and open reports of pain. As seen in Figure 5, while the pain was

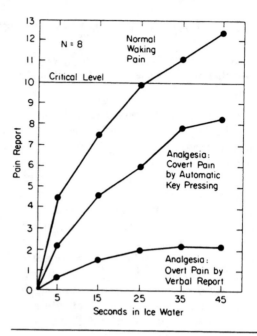

Figure 5
Overt and covert pain as reduced by hypnotic suggestion. Means are plotted for the eight most successful subjects out of 20 highly hypnotizable subjects who participated in the study of ice water pain (cold pressor response). The highest curve shows the normal waking pain in the ice water, the lowest the hypnotically reduced overt pain as ordinarily reported in hypnosis. The middle curve (covert pain) was reported in this instance through a key-pressing device that was the equivalent of automatic writing, reporting the experience of the "hidden observer." Data from Hilgard, Morgan, and Macdonald (1975); reproduced from Hilgard and Hilgard (1975).

mounting scarcely at all at the overt verbal reporting level, it was mounting much more rapidly at the covert level, although it averaged below the normal waking pain. The two reporting systems — overt and covert — operated essentially simultaneously, or, in current information-processing language, in parallel. When at the end of the session the subject, still hypnotized, was questioned by the automatic talking method, the report of maximum covert pain agreed with that reported on the keys; the same information was being tapped by the two methods.

The separation between overt and covert experiences of pain appears to be maintained by an amnesia-like barrier, because the concealed experience, like other hypnotic amnesias, is recoverable. However, this difference must be noted: *the covert experience, unlike the experiences of posthypnotic amnesia, has never been consciously present.* The covert information from the experience somehow registered and was processed, but it was masked by the amnesia-like process before it ever became conscious.

Because two levels of pain reduction were shown in the data of Figure 5, there may be two components to the process by which pain is reduced through suggestion. The lesser reduction, to the level of the overt pain, might possibly occur as a consequence of analgesia suggestions given without hypnosis. Then the further reduction to the overt level of pain reported by responsive hypnotized subjects might be a component added by the hypnosis. We assign the second portion to hypnosis because this part is recoverable, much like other experiences in hypnosis hidden by amnesia-like processes.

It was possible to test this hypothesis by an investigation in which, in balanced order, subjects reduced their pain to waking suggestions and, on another occasion, to suggestions given following induction of hypnosis. The first conjecture to be tested is that, following waking suggestion, the overt pain will be greater than the overt pain felt in hypnotic analgesia. The second conjecture is that the overt pain following waking suggestion will be approximately equal to that reported covertly in hypnotic analgesia. The results with 20 subjects, half of whom had hypnotic analgesia first and half of whom had waking analgesia first, supported the predictions. In hypnotic analgesia the pain was reduced from a mean of 14.2 on the reporting scale to 4.2; the residual pain was 30% of normal. In waking analgesia, the reduction was from 14.2 to 8.5, to 60% of normal. The first

part of the prediction was confirmed by these results in that the hypnotic residual pain was half that of the pain reduced by waking suggestion. How did the second part of the prediction fare? The covert pain, as tested by the hidden observer method, rose to 7.3, a value representing 51% of normal, not significantly different from the 60% in waking analgesia.

The first component of the two-component inferred process is the partial reduction of pain by waking suggestion and the equivalent remaining reduction when the overt hypnotic analgesia has been reported as covertly felt pain. It may be assumed that this reduction is caused by such processes as relaxation and inattentiveness to the pain, processes available to the nonhypnotized person and relatively independent of the special abilities of the hypnotized one. An added inference, with this interpretation in mind, is that there should be no covert component to the overt pain reduced by waking suggestion, because nothing additional was registered as pain. To test this possibility, the hypnotizable subjects who had reduced pain by waking suggestion were hypnotized after this experience, and the hidden observer technique was used to explore covert pain. The pain reported at the covert level was exactly the same as that reported overtly, agreeing with the assumptions regarding this first component of the pain reduction.

It was possible to obtain additional evidence bearing on the two-component theory by studying the results for a group of nonhypnotizable subjects in response to waking suggestions of pain reduction, compared to actual pain reduction when they simulated hypnosis. Additional hypnotizable subjects served as a comparison group; this investigation was in part a replication, and in part an extension, of the one just cited. The first prediction was that nonhypnotizable subjects should be able to reduce their pains through waking suggestion to approximately the same level as hypnotizable subjects in that condition. The second prediction was that the nonhypnotizable subjects, simulating hypnosis, would not be able to reduce their actually felt pain below the waking suggestion level. This required a subsequent "honest report" interview; otherwise, as simulators, they had typically reported less pain than the truly hypnotizable. Exaggerated reports in response to suggestions are characteristic of simulators.

The hypnotizable subjects repeated findings similar to those already reported. For the low hypnotizables, behaving normally in waking pain reduction and simulating hypnosis in hypnotic analgesia, the honestly reported results came out as predicted, with waking and hypnotic analgesia (honesty reports) essentially alike (Figure 6). The covert responses for the hypnotizable subjects are not shown because only six of 12 gave such reports; for those giving covert reports, the earlier findings were confirmed. The supplementary study therefore provided further evidence in support of the two-component theory.

The observation made by the first pilot subject that, at the covert level, the pain remained while the suffering was reduced was true for many others who reported covert sensory pain in the ice water experiments. The division between sensory pain and suffering was further investigated, this time using ischemic pain. It was found that *both* pain and suffering were reduced by hypnotic analgesia at the overt level, and both were represented at higher values at the covert level (Knox, Morgan, and Hilgard, 1974). However, there were indications of individual differences, shown in a subsequent experiment with three exceptionally high subjects.

The three subjects were all able to reduce overtly reported pain and suffering to essentially zero through hypnotic suggestion, although one reported slight distress, without pain, toward the end of the stressful period. Covert reports were obtained at the end of the session, with the subject remaining hypnotized. It was found for two of them that covert pain was reported at nearly normal levels, whereas no covert suffering was reported; the third subject reported both covert pain and covert suffering at normal levels. To clarify these somewhat complex findings, the maximum pains felt under the three conditions (normal, overt within hypnotic analgesia, and covert within hypnotic analgesia) are presented in Table 1. For two of the three subjects, a differential between pain and distress was reported, with covert pain present, but covert distress absent; the third subject did not agree. That at least some subjects show this difference indicates a possible division between the systems for experiencing pain and distress, for which neurophysiological evidence exists (Melzack and Casey, 1968).

What is it like to the subject when he discovers that there is a part of him that experiences pain or distress at a level of which he is unaware within hypnotically suggested analge-

Figure 6

Differential between waking analgesia and hypnotic analgesia: High hypnotizable subjects and less hypnotizable subjects. Both groups responded nonhypnotically to suggestions of analgesia in the waking condition. Honest reports of low subjects simulating hypnosis in the "hypnotic" condition; honest reports of high subjects responding as they normally do in hypnosis. (N = 12 in each group.) Unpublished data, Stanford Laboratory.

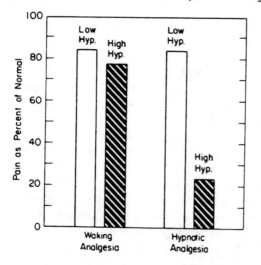

TABLE 1
OVERT AND COVERT PAIN AND DISTRESS IN THREE SELECTED HIGH
HYPNOTIZABLES (DATA FROM GOLDSTEIN AND HILGARD, 1975)

	Pain rating			Distress rating		
	Normal walking	Analgesia		Normal walking	Analgesia	
		Overt	Covert		Overt	Covert
Subject 1	12	0	13	12	0	0
Subject 2	12	0	15[a]	4	0	0
Subject 3	8	0	8	8	2.5	8

[a]The tourniquet was kept in place longer under analgesia than in waking, and the covert pain continued to mount, although overt pain was absent.

sia? Matters of this kind are difficult to put into words, and the reports by subjects vary greatly. Consider two typical illustrations. One report is of a feeling of annoyance that some intruding part is looking on behind a curtain and, in superior fashion, is amused at the person for his self-deception. A second is a reported sense of satisfaction that there is a kind of guardian protecting the body in homeostatic fashion against a failure to use information coming to it through sensory channels. . . . those reports bear importantly on the nature of concealed information processing . . .

Returning to the question of a division of consciousness, as contrasted with two different depths or levels of consciousness, the evidence from the subjects' remarks clearly favors the idea of a vertical division (split consciousness) rather than a horizontal division, in which the material would come from more primitive depths. . . . There is no regression in the subject's language; the hidden observer uses the same conceptual language to describe the covert experience as the hypnotized part does to describe the overt experience, including an estimation of the magnitude of the pain . . .

References

Azam, E. E. (1887) *Hypnotisme, double conscience et altération de la personnalité*. Préface de J. M. Charcot. Paris: Ballière.

Bourguignon, E. (1968) World distribution and patterns of possession states. In R. Prince (Ed.) *Trance and possession states*. Montreal: R. M. Bucke Memorial Society.

Brandsma, J. M., and Ludwig, A. M. (1974) A case of multiple personality: Diagnosis and therapy. *International Journal of Clinical and Experimental Hypnosis, 22,* 216–233.

Chong, T. M. (1975) *The truth about hypnosis.* Singapore: Choong's Clinic.

Christopher, M. (1975) *Mediums, mystics, and the occult.* New York: Crowell.

Crawford, H. J., Macdonald, H., and Hilgard, E. R. (1979) Hypnotic deafness: A psychophysical study of responses to tone intensity as modified by hypnosis. *American Journal of Psychology, 92,* 193–214.

Crookes, W. (1874) *Researches in the phenomena of spiritualism.* London: Burn and Oates.

Diamond, M. J., and Taft, R. (1975) The role played by ego permissiveness and imagery in hypnotic responsivity. *International Journal of Clinical and Experimental Hypnosis, 23,* 130–138.

Ellenberger, H. F. (1970) *The discovery of the unconscious.* New York: Basic Books.

Flournoy, T. (1890) *From India to the Planet Mars. A study of a case of somnambulism with glossolalia.* New York: Harper.

Franz, S. I. (1933) *Persons one and three.* New York: McGraw-Hill.

Giddan, N. S. (1967) Recovery through images of briefly flashed stimuli. *Journal of Personality, 3,* 1–19.

Gmelin, E. (1791) *Materialen für die anthropologie,* I. Tübingen: Cotta. (From Ellenberger, 1970).

Hilgard, E. R., Morgan, A. H., and Macdonald, H. (1975) Pain and dissociation in the cold pressor test: A study of hypnotic analgesia with "hidden reports" through automatic key-pressing and automatic talking. *Journal of Abnormal Psychology, 84,* 280–289.

James, W. (1890) *Principles of pychology.* 2 vols. New York: Holt.

Knox, V. J., Morgan, A. H., and Hilgard, E. R. (1974) Pain and suffering in ischemia: The paradox of hypnotically suggested anesthesia as contradicted by reports from the "hidden observer." *Archives of General Psychiatry, 30,* 840–847.

Lambert, G. W. (1971) Studies in the automatic writing of Mrs. Verall: X. Concluding reflections. *Journal of the Society for Psychical Research,* 217–222.

Litvag, I. (1972) *Singer in the shadows: The strange case of Patience Worth.* New York: Macmillan.

Ludwig, A. M., Brandsma, J. M., Wilbur, C. B., Bendfeldt, F., and Jameson, D. H. (1972) The objective study of a multiple personality, or, are four heads better than one? *Archives of General Psychiatry, 26,* 298–310.

Melzack, R., and Casey, K. L. (1968) Sensory, motivational, and central control determinants of pain: A new conceptual model. In D. Kenshalo (Ed.) *The skin senses.* Springfield, Ill.: Thomas.

Mitchell, T. W. (1925) Division of the self and co-consciousness. In C. M. Campbell, and others (Eds.) *Problems of personality: Studies presented to Dr. Morton Prince.* New York: Harcourt, Brace.

Myers, F. W. H. (1887) Automatic writing III. *Proceedings of the Society of Psychical Research, 4,* 209–261.

Myers. F. W. H. (1903) *Human personality and its survival of bodily death.* 2 vols. London: Longmans, Green. (Reprinted, with introduction by Gardner Murphy, 1954).

Prince, M. (1890) Some of the revelations of hypnotism: Post-hypnotic suggestion, automatic writing, and double personality. *Boston Medical and Surgical Journal, 122,* May 8, 463–467; 475–476; May 22, 493–495.

Prince, M. (1906) *The dissociation of a personality.* New York and London: Longmans Green.

Taylor, S. E. L. (Ed.) (1932) *Fox-Taylor automatic writing, 1869–1892. Unabridged record.* Minneapolis, Minn.: Tribune-Great West Printing Co.

Taylor, W. S., and Martin, M. F. (1944) Multiple personality. *Journal of Abnormal and Social Psychology, 39,* 281–300.

Thigpen, C. H., and Cleckley, H. (1957) *The three faces of Eve.* New York: McGraw-Hill.

9

KATHLEEN V. WILKES
Fugues, Hypnosis, and Multiple Personality

1. The Unity and Continuity of Consciousness

. . . central to the issue of personal identity is the old and powerful idea that persons have a *unity* or a *continuity* of consciousness. However hard it may be to characterize either consciousness itself, or a unity/continuity of consciousness, there seems something right about the intuition behind the belief that a person is something which, in Locke's familiar terms, is and can regard itself as:

> a thinking intelligent being, that has reason and reflection, and can consider itself as itself, the same thinking thing, in different times and places; which it does only by that consciousness which is inseparable from thinking, and, as it seems to me, essential to it (*Essay Concerning Human Understanding* [1690], Book II, ch. xxvii, para. 11; [1959], vol. i, pp. 448–9).

This . . . [essay] will examine Locke's claim, in the guise of a claim that something we call very vaguely a "unity," or a "continuity," of consciousness is a necessary condition of (and thus essential to) personal identity. . . .

Let us first look at conscious *unity*. What is involved in the intuition that this matters centrally? Unity as such (that is, when we do not add the qualifier "conscious") is very commonly scrappy, or missing. We know, for example— and have been long familiar with the idea—

that there is considerable disunity, incoherence, disharmony, failure of mesh, between conscious and *non*-conscious mental phenomena. . . . we do not even have to give the credit for this to Freud; the existence of a subterranean mind which may or may not jibe with our explicit self-reports was a thought taken for granted from Heraclitus onwards—recall Shakespeare describing Prince Harry's exercise in wishful thinking ("[t]hy wish was father, Harry, to that thought"). That being so, we evidently tolerate some degree of disunity in general as a brute fact about people; why should the importance of unity be so enhanced when we restrict ourselves to the conscious level?

Suppose, though, that we do so restrict ourselves. Suppose that we bracket the domain of abnormal behaviour and of depth psychologies, and keep to everyday thought and action, to the sorts of things we can describe without recourse to explicit theory. Even then, though, we find that we are not necessarily as unified, even on the conscious level, as we might like to think. I shall cite a few examples to support this claim. . . . These examples illustrate both an *absence* of unity, and positive *dis*unity. Absence of unity: consider the phenomenon of (successfully) divided attention, when an agent can do two unrelated things at the same time. Disunity or conflict: consider the weak-willed, who is torn between wants and desires that are incompatible; or note that our emotions and feelings about something or someone often clash inharmoniously; and there is also the disunity of the self-deceived, who holds beliefs that are not consistent with one another.

But someone might object to this last example that the self-deceived is not conscious of his disunity, so his difficulty is not due to a breach in the unity of *consciousness*. Such an objection points to the problem, . . . that what is and is not conscious is often very far from clear, and particularly when beliefs are in question. For instance, we are presumably not aware (in the sense of thinking about explicitly) most of the indefinitely large stock of beliefs that can be securely ascribed to us—such as your belief and mine that eating chips does not affect television reception, that no lizards are chartered accountants, that Jaruzelski's wife had parents. These are trivial consequences of other things we believe. Such beliefs, of course, can become consciously held, and citing these three will have made them fleetingly become so; but there is a colossal number that will never cross into the spotlight of conscious attention. Are they therefore nonconscious? This is obscure. But if, on the basis of the fact that they could (easily) be admitted into conscious awareness we call them "conscious" by courtesy, so to speak, then the penalty is that we must recognize substantial "disunity of consciousness." For we rarely pursue far the implications of our explicitly held beliefs; were we to do so, then it is plausible to suppose that all sorts of hidden inconsistencies and contradictions would come to light. After all, it is just when we do examine the implications of our claims that we unearth contradictions.[1]

Leaving unity for a moment: how strong a *continuity* of consciousness do we require? For whatever Locke may have thought—and opinions differ on this—we want to allow that there must be some gaps in the continuity of consciousness. When asleep and not dreaming one is not conscious, or thinking, and so one is not "the same thinking thing" as anything; and we are all familiar with the fact that there are patches of our life that we have just forgotten. So we should admit that there are discontinuities, no less than there are disunities, in the lives of normal and perfectly healthy people.

Thus even in ordinary life the "Lockean principle," or as I shall sometimes call it, the "Lockean condition," needs some modification and weakening; phenomena like weakness of will indicate disunity, dreamless sleep a lack of continuity. The extent to which it will need such modification, though, will most easily be seen if we look at more dramatic cases where the principle fails (even though some of these examples are "dramatic" only because they are more uncommon than weakness of will, or sleeping, and not because the breakdown of the principle is more extensive). We shall see, I think, that with one exception the concept of a person seems to survive all the violations of unity and continuity of consciousness that we can throw at it. This should allow us to see more clearly just what kinds of unity and continuity we require a person to possess, and just where breaches of either do indeed start to threaten the notion of a person.

2. Fugues and Epileptic Automatism

We might start by considering fugues, because these can be relatively unproblematic. Some are very short lived; others can last for months or even years. The best-known example is perhaps the one described by William James ([1890], pp. 391–3), of the Revd Ansel Bourne. Bourne, on

---

[1]To forestall misunderstanding, I should . . . say here that I am *not* arguing that there is a stock of these tacit beliefs, somehow "there," which are, somehow, in conflict. I want to take an instrumentalist attitude to most propositional attitudes (see Wilkes [1986] and [1987]). In any case, the claim here does not presuppose realism. There is inconsistency whenever, by *whatever* mechanisms, conflicting beliefs—tacit or explicit—can be ascribed or self-ascribed.

17 January 1887, left his life as an itinerant preacher in Rhode Island and travelled a considerable distance to a country town in Pennsylvania, where, under the name of Brown, he managed a small shop which he had opened. He was quite amnesic for his past life as a clergyman; it was two months before he "came to," and awoke one night in fright as Ansel Bourne, finding himself in a bedroom that he had never seen before. Ullmann and Krasner [1969] describe an even longer fugue state of fifteen months, during which a sober businessman, a pillar of his community, went off and worked as a manual labourer at a chemical plant. In each case we find a double amnesia: during the fugue phase, both remembered nothing of their former lives, and, after recovery, neither remembered his doings during the time "out." Bourne, it is true, managed to remember his life as Brown when undergoing hypnosis with James, but after the trance had worn off his amnesia for that period returned.

Here the large-scale breakdown of the unity and continuity of consciousness, which afflicted Bourne and the businessman twice, does not tempt us to deny them a continued identity over the course of their adventures. (Some might want to claim that it *should*; my point here is only to appeal to our actual practice to show that in fact it does not.) The reasons why it does not will become clearer later, but we should now note the following. To take Bourne as an example: although much of his factual memory failed him completely, a lot else that he had learned must have stayed ("united") with him; he did not have to relearn the language, for instance, and he seems to have had no difficulties with acquired skills like harnessing and driving a horse and cart, or handling money and change. What other capacities and traits remained unimpaired we do not know — the case is not described in enough detail, and maybe James did not know the answers. Memory, in short, comes in many shapes and forms; the loss of a large set of personal memories may leave

unimpaired the retention of many factual propositions (that Washington is the capital of the USA, say, or that there are 100 cents to the dollar), and many rememberings-how.[2] So "complete amnesia" is rather a misleading label for the fugue condition; even though, to be sure, *some* features of his character must have changed (or so we assume). What does seem clear is that we can manage with fairly dramatic breakdowns in the unity and continuity of consciousness: we regard this as one and the same man. (A question to keep in mind: of the competences and the knowledge that certainly stayed "united" with Bourne — the abilities that he must have retained — how many do we want to describe as *conscious*?)

Exactly the same holds also, for evident reasons, for shorter-term fugue states such as those seen in epileptic automatism or transient global amnesia. In both such conditions the patient has a brief fugue; after recovering he can remember nothing of the "lost" period. Those overtaken by epileptic automatism, a condition which might last for a few seconds or a few hours, typically show either purposeless behaviour patterns (such as buttoning and then immediately unbuttoning a jacket), or else fairly stereotypical ones, involving well-learned routines (such as putting out cat food, brewing hot chocolate). But some such overlearned behaviour may be highly sophisticated: there was one instance of a doctor, caught up unexpectedly by an attack of epileptic automatism while inter-

---

[2]The well-studied amnesic patient H. M. (for a survey see Corkin *et al.* [1981]) has almost complete anterograde amnesia—i.e. he cannot learn new information. But he is able to master motor and maze tasks, and learned to solve the Tower of Hanoi puzzle—even though each time he was confronted with a task, or the puzzle, it felt to him as though he were seeing it for the first time. (H. M. had an operation for epilepsy which involved bilateral mesial temporal lobe ablations.) So H. M., among other such patients, seems to be able to "remember how" without any ability to "remember that." . . .

viewing a patient, who yet managed to conduct a reasonably efficient medical examination — as he discovered from his notes when he recovered and saw that he had successfully examined his patient (although he had no recollection of doing so). Whatever he was or was not amnesic for, he clearly retained his (sophisticated) medical skills and his habit of taking full notes of his checks and tests. Transient global amnesia, which probably results from a short-lived ischaemia,[3] shows patients to all outward appearances behaving quite normally; but after they recover (and the attacks rarely last for more than about five hours) they remember nothing of their activities during this period.

So it seems that short- and long-term fugue states do not pose a problem for the issue of reidentification. That is, it seems clear that each of the individuals cited is one and only one person throughout. Thus it is already evident that we cannot be too demanding in our requirements for a unity or continuity, since our judgements of "sameness of person" allow for disunities and discontinuities on a large scale. This should not be thought surprising. For — surely — epileptic automatism or transient global amnesia are in fact no more puzzling than sleep, which equally interrupts the power of conscious recall. They strike us as odder, certainly, but that is because we are so well used to the breakdowns of conscious unity and continuity during sleep (familiarity breeds neglect), whereas these short-lived amnesias are rare, peculiar, and hence striking. Longer-lasting fugues interrupt the unity and continuity of consciousness more dramatically and drastically; but, if they do not seem to disrupt our

intuition that we have, unproblematically, one and the same person here, that must be because the unity or continuity of consciousness, or perhaps even consciousness itself, are not quite as important as one might at first think.

3. Hypnosis

The dissociations that hypnosis can induce make this point clearer yet. Undeniably we take it for granted that the hypnotized subject is one and the same person as the individual who agreed to be hypnotized, whatever may happen to him under hypnosis. I admit that there is considerable skepticism — often well founded — about the validity of some of the effects described as occurring with hypnotized patients. Certainly many of these effects may indeed be due to deceit, extreme suggestibility, or role-playing. On the other hand, it is usually possible for the critical and well-informed observer to detect the dissembler; and people like Hilgard (see e.g. his [1977]) provide such careful documentation and so many double-checks that the chance that his subjects are deceiving him is well nigh minimal. Genuine hypnotic states can give us not only the sorts of amnesias that we find in fugue states, but, as we shall see, they reveal an extra twist as well.

To take the amnesia first: it is possible, and fairly typical, for the hypnotized subject to act in a way that is quite dramatically out of character, and to have afterwards no recollection of what he said or did under hypnosis. This gives him the same sort of qualitative and quantitative gap in conscious continuity that we found with cases of fugue. However, there is not only a diachronic gap, a failure of continuity; there seems also to be at times a synchronic split, a failure of unity. An example or two would make the point clearer.

One way of distinguishing the genuinely hypnotized subject from the one who is merely

---

[3]Ischaemia is a brief blocking of the blood supply to regions of the brain. Transient global amnesia probably results from a temporary failure in the blood supply to temporal lobe structures. However, some conjecture that transient global amnesia can result from focal epileptic discharges, in which case it would merely be another term for epileptic automatism.

pretending is by instructing the subjects not to see a chair (a negative hallucination) and then asking them to walk in a straight line which would put the chair right in their path. The unhypnotized subject who has been asked to pretend that he is hypnotized walks straight along and crashes into the chair (unless, of course, he knows a bit about the behaviour of patients under hypnosis). The genuinely hypnotized subject, however, goes around it. We can thus tell the two apart; and the split that I mentioned comes in with the fact that the hypnotized subject seems both to see and not to see the chair—he sees it, for he avoids it successfully, but he does not see it, for when asked to describe the room he always leaves the chair out, when asked to sit will not use it, and so forth. He does not comment on his detour around the chair, though, and when shown that he did not walk in a straight line he is typically either puzzled or (sincerely) tries to rationalize his action: "I just thought I'd like some variety," or "your picture caught my eye and I thought I'd go over there to have a closer look." (Incidentally, such *ex post facto* rationalizations should not be damned as deliberate dishonesty. They are peculiar, certainly, and difficult to comprehend; but the very widespread prevalence of such attempts at rationalization in virtually all subjects—in hypnosis, mental illness and confusion, hemispheric neglect,[4] commis-

[4]Hemispheric neglect is a condition in which patients with a lesion to one half of the brain virtually ignore the side of their body contralateral to the lesioned hemisphere, and fail to report, or respond to, stimuli presented to the contralateral side. This is evidently bizarre: how can anyone ignore half of the world, and half of themselves? It would seem that such a condition should be very upsetting to the patient. However, "neglect" patients are rarely worried. They may rationalize the dilemma by denying that an arm or a leg belongs to them at all, by denying that their visual or sensory field is impaired, or by admitting that there is some impairment, but making light of it and regarding it as insignificant.

surotomy patients, and elsewhere—is so widespread that we should accept it as a phenomenon and admit that the patient genuinely believes what he is saying.) Anyway, it looks prima facie as though we can say he is both aware and not aware of the chair.

A second example introduces the so-called "hidden observer," often seen in action during hypnosis. Hilgard [1977] gives many examples of this; we might consider one of them, the phenomenon of hypnotic anaesthesia. This is particularly interesting, and shows us a split in consciousness of a very marked form. One experiment, conducted by Hilgard, is to get the subject hypnotized, and then tell him that he is going to feel no pain. Then one hand and arm are put into a stream of circulating iced water. This is very rapidly felt as painful by the unhypnotized, who cannot under these circumstances keep up the pretence for very long. The successfully hypnotized subject, though, can sit there with his hand and arm in the water for long periods, untroubled and saying that he is untroubled. However, if in his other hand he has a pencil and paper (usually so placed that he cannot see it), and if he is encouraged to write or indicate what he is feeling, then the "hidden observer" may complain bitterly about the intensity and unpleasantness of the pain he is experiencing. (And in fact the hidden observer may observe much more than we realize. Ordinary anaesthesia may not anaesthetize him. Many patients who have been hypnotized after a routine operation involving routine anaesthesia have proved to be able to recall in detail conversations held while the operation was in progress between the surgeon and the anaesthetist: see Cheek and LeCron [1968].)

The objection might perhaps be made to the example of hypnotic anaesthesia that neither state of the hypnotized subject—the state in which he denies pain, and the state in which he complains about it—is strictly a conscious state, so that there may be no violation of the unity of *consciousness* here. But that would be a hard line to defend, for it requires an account of what a "strictly conscious" state may be; we met the same objection, and noted the same difficulty, when discussing self-deception . . . Surely one of our clearest tests of consciousness, at least for human subjects, is verbal or linguistic output (bating for the moment certain possible exceptions like sleep-talking . . .). Yet the subject undergoing hypnotic anaesthesia can talk sensibly to the hypnotist about the absence of pain, and simultaneously can write sensibly about its intensity. So to say that he is not *really* conscious merely requires one to say more clearly what one is understanding by "(strictly) a conscious state." So for the moment I shall ignore that objection, content to point out that it creates as many difficulties for the objector as for his target, precisely because of the obscurity of "consciousness" in such cases.

Prima facie, then, it looks as though we lose any unity of consciousness here. In fact we might even say that we have two consciousnesses, each perhaps internally united, working simultaneously but separately—somewhat like what we apparently find under experimental conditions with split-brain patients. . . . If we add to this the amnesia that often attends states of hypnosis (in other words, an amnesia that can often be made to follow states of hypnosis), we get a double dimension of split in conscious unity and continuity, and Locke's principle seems to be in yet further trouble.

None the less, we have no doubt about the singleness of the person before us here. There is one and only one individual, and *he* is being hypnotized. This, at least, is how our practice runs: we seem not to consider hypnotic subjects as challenging the concept of personal identity. We apparently tolerate breakdowns such as these in the unity and continuity of consciousness. (As already noted, if we hardly ever dreamt we would find dreams just as bizarre as we now find hypnotism and fugues; but as things are we regard the disunity and discontinuity seen with dreams to be perfectly normal.)

The substantial point is that the dissociated states we have discussed so far show how weakly the prejudice in favour of the unity and continuity of consciousness often needs to be taken; whatever else is true, the unalloyed assertion of what I am calling "the Lockean principle," or "the Lockean condition," needs to be modified in order to tolerate our clear intuition that the subject before, during, and after hypnosis is one and the same person.

4. Multiple Personality: Christine Beauchamp

So far, I expect that few would disagree. Since "the Lockean condition" stumbles over such everyday phenomena as sleep and self-deception, it is scarcely surprising that it is hard to fit on to fugues or hypnosis. The plot thickens, though, when we get to multiple personality; even though (as we shall see) this is, in a sense, just more of the same. First, through, we should consider what kind of condition it is.

Previously classified as one subclass of "hysterical neuroses, dissociative type" it has now been to some extent distinguished from the hysterical neuroses and is rather classed along with other dissociative states like fugues, psychogenic amnesias, and so forth. Certainly it can no longer be thought of as an exclusively hysterical disorder (see Confer and Ables [1983]). We saw . . . how fluid and fraught is the taxonomic classification of abnormal conditions, and so this sort of revision and reclassification should not be thought surprising.

It is necessary again to argue, even if only briefly, that we indeed have here a genuine phenomenon—that there is such a condition as multiple personality. For it may look as though with this, as with certain other medical complaints, nature follows art. In the late nineteenth century, when multiple personality was taken as a genuine diagnostic category and philosophers and scientists were fascinated by it, there was a wave of reported cases. But then the increasing scepticism of the mid-twentieth century seemed virtually to abolish the condition. (Of sixty-three patients admitted to Bellevue hospital in 1933–4, all said to be suffering from "loss of identity," not one was declared to be a case of multiple personality; schizophrenia, manic depression, psychosis, aphasia, amnesia, cerebral arteriosclerosis, pre-senile dementia, cerebral trauma, epilepsy, and carbon monoxide poisoning sufficed as diagnostic labels; see Sutcliffe and Jones [1962].) Moreover, there are *very* sound methodological reasons for dropping or at least suspending belief in multiple personality as a discrete and identifiable phenomenon. After all, the condition is an unusual and an intriguing one, so doctors naturally treat potential cases with keen interest and attention—thereby providing strong positive reinforcement to the patient to develop distinct and distinguishable alternate personalities. It is highly likely that role-playing, whether conscious or unconscious, whether in childhood or in the surgery, is an essential element in the aetiology of the condition.[5] Finally, contemporary psychiatry has largely abandoned the almost automatic resort to hypnosis as a method of therapy. This is significant, for after reading case histories it is hard to avoid the impression that repeated hypnotism often had the effect of defining and solidifying alternate personalities which, if not thus encouraged, might have dissolved away again.[6]

On the other hand, though, what remains important is this: with or without the encouragement of doctors; with or without the prior existence of strenuous role-playing; whether we call it multiple personality or just an acute form of *grande hystérie* suffered by some psychoneu-

rotic patients; allowing all that, we do get, and have had, patients with symptoms that cannot be adequately described in any terms other than those provided by the "multiple personality" category and classification. Furthermore, there has been much independent evidence from the relatives and friends of the patients that testifies to the existence of puzzlingly split states well before, and independently of, any medical intervention. Nor does the condition seem to be exceptionally rare; Howland [1975] has noted that over 200 cases have been reported in the literature, and it is impossible to guess at the number of cases that have gone unreported. Whatever the *genesis* of the trouble, many of these patients have become genuinely split and cannot then get out of the problem by making a New Year's resolution to stop playing games. Furthermore, we now have techniques more reliable and more objective than the (theoretically guided and motivated) opinions of doctors. These opinions were admittedly often a product of their own prejudices—either that there was no such thing as multiple personality, or that there was indeed such a thing and what fun it would be if the patient proved to have it! The tests I have in mind are psychological, physiological, and psychophysiological, and one or two illustrations of their use may be helpful.

Ludwig *et al.* [1972] examined Jonah, a twenty-seven-year-old man whose alternate personalities called themselves Sammy ("the Mediator"), Usoffa Abdullah, Son of Omega ("the Warrior"), and King Young ("the Lover"). (Jonah—"the Square"—was also called "Jusky"—a democratic decision reached on the basis of taking the initial letters from the names of Jonah, Usoffa, Sammy, and King Young.) All four personalities showed, quite consistently over time, significantly different reactions *in propria persona*, and with each alternate, in repeated EEG (electroencephalogram) tests that looked for alpha and theta wave frequency and amplitude, or for the conditions of alpha-blocking (eye-opening, for instance, often blocks

[5]See Taylor and Martin [1944], or Congdon, Hain, and Stevenson [1961].

[6]See Harriman [1943], Gruenewald [1971], or Greaves [1980].

alpha wave activity). The four also showed systematic differences on GSR (galvanic skin response) tests to emotionally laden words. King Young, for example, responded strongly to words denoting sex, Usoffa Abdullah, to terms of fight, violence, and bloodshed. Their VERs (visually evoked responses) to light flashes differed systematically too. Tests of paired-word learning showed some transfer of learning from Jonah to the other three, but no transfer between the other three and none from any of them to Jonah. These are not the sorts of results that can be produced intentionally by a single subject bent on tricking a gullible doctor.

Some different cases: Confer and Ables [1983] put their patient Rene several times through the MMPI test (the "Minnesota Multiphasic Personality Inventory"), which threw up great differences of character, traits, preferences, and dispositions between the primary personality and each of the major alternates — differences which no layman could have predicted or prepared for, and so hard to explain on the supposition that the patient was deliberately fooling the doctor. Similarly, Eve Black and Eve White proved to have some differences in microstrabismus (a transient loss of oculomotor parallelism; see Condon *et al.* [1969]). One physical variation between these two showed up even without elaborate tests or equipment: Eve Black was allergic to nylon, Eve White was not (Thigpen and Cleckley [1957]).

Thus we have some *hard* data to add to the mass of evidence that Morton Prince described ([1905]; reprinted in his [1968], from which page references are taken) in his early, but very thorough, analysis of Miss Christine Beauchamp.[7] Prince did not, of course, have available the various tests, just described, which were developed later in the century. But since his description is so clear and full, I shall discuss the problem by reference primarily to his treatment and not to later works, on the reasonable assumption that if he *had* been able to use these tests, they would have fully endorsed his judgement that he was dealing with a thoroughly split individual. His discussion is particularly instructive because, in a work written for fellow scientists rather than for the popular market, he tries to explain his theories, justify his conjectures, and make explicit his assumptions. (The better-known book-length treatments written more recently were intended as popular paperbacks and we miss in them Prince's theoretical and critical stance.)[8] Moreover, he wrote before Freudian theory had swept the USA, and so his book is not shadowed by that potent figure. I shall therefore describe as briefly as possible the salient features of Miss Beauchamp's predicament, and then, with reference to this and one or two other cases, particularly that of Jonah/Jusky, consider the implications for our overall problem.

Following Prince, I shall call the patient as she lived until 1893 "Christine Beauchamp." She was then eighteen. She had been a nervous, ailing, impressionable child, prone to headaches, somnambulism, daydreams, and trances; she had been neglected by a mother she adored and maltreated by her father.[9] In 1893 she was working as a hospital nurse, and on one stormy night had a succession of three shocks, each alone sufficiently alarming to one of a nervous constitution.[10]

---

[7]This was not, of course her real name.

[8]e.g. Schreiber [1975], and Thigpen and Cleckley [1957].

[9]A repressed, puritanical childhood, often including neglect and physical or sexual abuse, seems a pattern common to many cases of multiple personality.

[10]First, she saw illuminated in a lightning flash a patient in a white nightgown, who grabbed hold of her; then she saw her boyfriend's face outside a second-floor window (he had climbed a ladder to surprise her); and finally—although Prince is somewhat coy about this—it seems that the same boyfriend found Miss Beauchamp and attempted what to her seemed near-rape, illuminated only by flashes of lightning.

The patient whom Prince saw for the first time five years later I shall call, as he does, "B1." (Of course, she was not labelled "B1" until much later, after she began to have competitors for the name "Christine Beauchamp.") B1 was otherwise known as "the saint." She was a woman morbidly reticent, morbidly conscientious, a bibliophile, deeply religious, patient, and long-suffering, with "a refinement of character out of the ordinary" and "great delicacy of sentiment." She had been advised to consult Prince because of her insomnia, fatigue, headaches, nervousness, and depression. Prince at once hypnotized her (such patients are typically very easy to hypnotize, although it is counterproductive with multiple personality patients who have any degree of psychosis). B1's hypnotic state came to be called "B1a," and B1a was never considered to be a distinct personality — she *was* B1, but was a B1 who had less reserve and restraint when in a hypnotic trance, and hence who was better able to talk fully and freely about her condition. B1a knew of, and claimed as her own, all B1's thoughts and actions; B1, as is common for hypnotized subjects, was amnesic for all she said and did as B1a. I shall represent this asymmetrical knowledge by an arrow: one arrowhead to represent knowledge of actions, another to represent knowledge of thoughts (Fig 1).

One day under hypnosis the patient referred to B1 not, as before, as "I" but as "she." When asked why she did not think of herself as B1

(who then, having no rivals, was of course simply called "Christine Beauchamp") she replied, "because she is stupid; she goes around mooning, half asleep, with her head buried in a book; she does not know half the time what she is about" (Prince [1968], p. 28). This personality proved to know all of B1's and B1a's thoughts and actions—often, indeed, she was able to describe B1's dreams in greater detail than could B1 or B1a. But she denied that they were *her* thoughts, dreams, and actions. She claimed rather to have existed as an intraconscious[11] personality right from Christine Beauchamp's early childhood. B1 and B1a, on the other hand, knew nothing of this personality. Prince at first called her by Miss Beauchamp's own name, but she disliked and despised B1 so much that she chose eventually to be called "Sally" instead. So in Fig. 2 we need to supplement Fig. 1.

Prince was fascinated by Sally. He used to get her repeatedly by hypnotizing B1, who then either turned into Sally directly, or turned into B1a, from which state Sally could easily come

---

[11]The technical term for a subordinate consciousness that is aware of the primary personalities' actions but not thoughts is "co-conscious"; one aware of both actions and thoughts is "intraconscious." Thus Sally was intraconscious to B1 (and, as we shall see, co-conscious to B4 and intraconscious to B2). Co-consciousness is represented in the figures by a single arrow, and intraconsciousness by a double arrow.

Figure 1

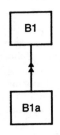

Figure 2

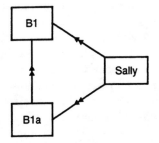

when summoned. She remained as a hypnotic state of the individual until one day she contrived to get her eyes open, and there she was: an unhypnotized, merry, and carefree individual, in full control of the body and with every intention of keeping it that way. After she had once managed to get her eyes open she was able to "come" more and more often, with or without the prior hypnotism of *B1*. Much of this was Prince's responsibility, for he did little at first to discourage her—she amused him by her vivacity, irresponsibility, flirtatiousness, and verve: "there was a delightful attractiveness in [her] absolute disregard of responsibility; she was a child of nature" ([1968], p. 53).

The rise of Sally did the unfortunate *B1* no good at all. *B1* knew nothing of her (it was some time before Prince informed her of the new development), and as far as she was concerned the times when Sally was "out" were times she lost completely. For example, she lost an entire Christmas Day. More painfully, she lost the whole of a ten-day period in hospital to which she (*B1*) had explicitly asked to be committed; Sally amused herself by pretending to be *B1*, and the hospital staff, impressed by "*B1*'s" absence of depression and fatigue, discharged her. Thus *B1* gained not at all from her difficult and courageous decision to undergo hospital treatment.

Sally in fact hated *B1*, and spared no pains to make her life a misery. Prince believed that the implacable hatred was fuelled by jealousy of *B1*'s superior attainments and the love and respect she received from her friends. For Sally, although she claimed to have been present as a coexisting consciousness throughout Miss Beauchamp's life, was far less well educated—she was easily bored, so had not paid attention to school lessons or difficult books. She could not, for example, speak French, whereas *B1* was fluent (a fact Prince often exploited to forestall Sally's interference in his plans for *B1*); and her command of grammar, spelling, and syntax, and the range of her vocabulary, were much

inferior to that of *B1*. Jealous or not, it is clear how much Sally disliked *B1*. She would tear up her letters, conceal money and stamps, destroy sewing and knitting, or perhaps sew up the sleeves of *B1*'s clothes. She sent through the post to *B1* parcels containing spiders, spent money lavishly on unsuitable clothes, and for a period kept *B1* on an "allowance" of 5 or 10 cents a day. Her friends were not *B1*'s friends and her tastes differed from *B1*'s; so *B1* often found herself coming-to in a circle of alien faces, with a drink or a cigarette in her hand—though she rarely drank and hated the taste of cigarettes. Sally broke *B1*'s appointments and walked out of the jobs *B1* had worked so hard to keep. At one time she even thought of killing her, and needed to be reminded of the consequences to herself of such an action. Sally of course had all the advantages, knowing, as she did, everything about *B1*; whereas *B1* could know nothing directly of what Sally was doing and planning. Yet—perhaps unwisely—*B1* continued to visit Prince, as her anguish steadily deepened.[12] Disturbed by Sally's effect on *B1*, Prince eventually tried to suppress her, but failed in this completely.

Prince was in a way fond of Sally, otherwise known as "the devil." But he was less taken by the next personality, an alternate who just arrived one day, unheralded and unexpected. This individual, labelled "*B4*" by Prince, remembered nothing that had happened since the night of trauma in 1893, six years earlier. Indeed, on her first appearance (in Prince's surgery) she thought that it was still that same night. She failed to recognize Prince; struggling to come to terms with a situation almost impos-

[12]In fairness to Prince one ought to say that his suggestions to *B1a* often proved effective in removing for several days *B1*'s headaches, insomnia, depression, and exhaustion. On the other hand, a summer spent in Europe (and thus away from Prince) found *B1* almost entirely untroubled by Sally–the longest such period since Sally first came on the scene.

sible for her, she retreated into aloof reticence, determined to conceal by any means available her embarrassing ignorance of the last six years.

Sally was highly excited by the advent of B4. She found that she was aware of B4's actions but not of her thoughts (thus was "co-conscious" rather than "intraconscious" with her —one arrow in the figures, not a double one), so it was some time before she discovered that B4's pretence to knowledge was no more than that, a pretence. When Sally discovered this she was highly indignant at such a deception, and contemptuously dubbed B4 "the idiot"—the first of her many rash underestimations of B4. B4 had a hypnotic state which stood to B4 just as B1a stood to B1, and was termed B4a; so we now have Figure 3.

B4 knew nothing directly of either B1 or Sally. Prince thought of her as "the woman" of the trio—possibly a judgement revealing some degree of male chauvinism, since he describes her as prickly, hot-tempered, impatient, fiercely independent, and aggressive. Certainly she was someone who ardently resented the position in which she found herself. Quickly despising and discounting what she heard of the wretched B1, B4 set out on battles royal with Sally. Sally in these forays had the obvious advantages of knowing all B4's actions (though B4 could often mislead her by speaking to herself in French, or by pretending to have a headache when she did not—something Sally discovered with indigna-

tion only when B1 "came out"). Sally could exhaust B4 physically, frustrate her arrangements, deny her sleep, hide her belongings, and so tended to win the first rounds; but she in turn could eventually be brought to heel by B4's sincere ultimatum: one more outrage, and B4 would commit the lot of them to an asylum. B1 had to pick up whatever she could from indirect evidence—from the remarks of friends, from finding letters written by Sally and B4 to each other, from the jobs and places in which she found herself—and from her point of view, things were degenerating rapidly.

Sally and B4 were forced into an uneasy working alliance by a development alarming to both of them. Prince discovered that B1 deeply hypnotized and B4 deeply hypnotized—getting "below" B1a and B4a—became one and the same, called B2. This hypnotic state claimed to *be* both B1 and B4, accepting all their thoughts and actions as her own. She seemed, moreover, to combine the virtues of both with the excesses of neither. However, she knew nothing at all of Sally, even though Sally knew (as she did with B1) all her thoughts and actions. So now we get Fig. 4. B2's memory went right back (with lacunae only for the periods when Sally was "out") to early childhood. She seemed, moreover, a

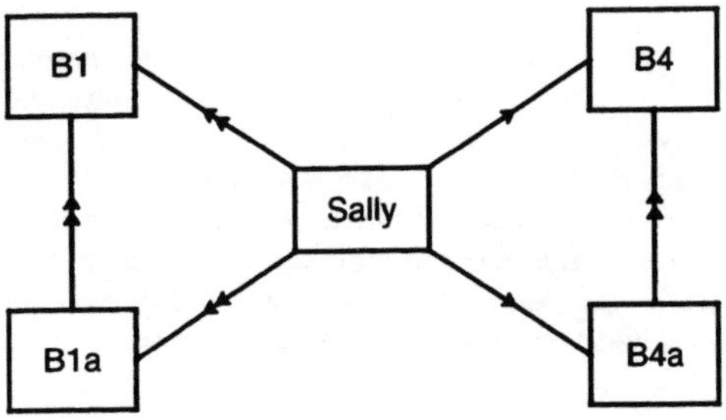

Figure 4

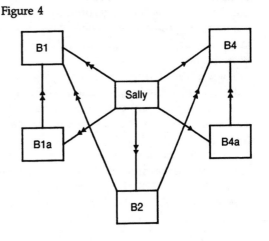

Figure 3

sober, responsible, and well-balanced individual. *B2*, Prince thought, was "the real" Miss Beauchamp, identical with the pre-1893 Christine Beauchamp. However, whenever he tried to wake *B2* out of the hypnotic trance, she never woke up *as B2* but would split, via *B1a* or *B4a*, into *B1* or *B4*.

To *B1* and *B4*, life as *B2* was equivalent to death. From their point of view they ceased to exist when *B2* was present, despite the fact that *B2* claimed to be both of them. *B1*, characteristically, was ready to meet meekly her own extinction. *B4*, though, was determined to fight. She made a partner of Sally who, although not "killed" by the rise of *B2*, would have been "squeezed" (her own term) back to her passive status as a coexisting consciousness by a healthy *B2*, and Sally much preferred a lively and active existence. Thus, for example, *B4* planned a flight to Europe, which was frustrated only just in time; *B4* and Sally broke appointments with Prince; and determined autosuggestion by *B4* made it difficult for Prince to hypnotize her to get *B4a* and thereby *B2*. Eventually, though (in 1904), they were defeated. Sally admitted that she had recognized in *B2* the pre-1893 Christine Beauchamp, and that it had been her subterranean influence which had "split" *B2* back into *B1a* or *B4a* whenever Prince tried to wake up *B2* as *B2*. She withdrew her interference, and, after completing her autobiography and a Last Will and Testament, voluntarily committed herself to what she regarded as extinction. And thus *B2* at last woke up as — Prince contends — Christine Beauchamp.

Then it was all over bar the shouting, and bar Sally. *B2* proved to be quite stable, splitting back into *B1*, *B4*, or Sally only when under severe strain. When *B1* or *B4* did emerge, it was for them as though they had woken up after a coma of several months; as for Sally, she returned to the position that she said she had occupied until 1898, that of an intraconsciousness existing alongside Christine Beauchamp.

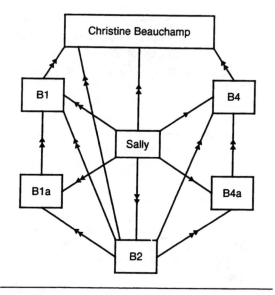

Figure 5

So we can now round out the full diagram as Fig. 5.[13]

5. How Many Miss Beauchamps?

Now for the primary question (a question difficult to frame in a way that is not grammatically suspect): how many people was Christine Beauchamp between 1893 and 1904? It should be clear that it matters not at all for this problem whether the condition of multiple personality is

[13]Fig. 6, like the account offered above, is much simplified. It leaves out, for example, Sally's hypnotic state (which played no very active part in the story); it omits several further but relatively fleeting personalities; it simplifies the coding (*B1a* was first called "*B2*," Sally was first *B3*, then "Chris," and eventually elected to be called "Sally"). The reader is urged to consult Prince's book in case some of the simplification prove positively misleading.

or is not something that psychiatry ought to recognize as such, or whether it is or is not an avoidable phenomenon initiated by role-playing and unwisely encouraged by an undue use of hypnotism. However it is produced, whatever its aetiology, so long as we accept the general truth of the data provided by Prince and supported by the more recent analyses mentioned above, the questions of personal identity, of the role of a unity or continuity of consciousness, and of the role of unity and continuity generally, arise urgently. It is difficult to describe the case except in terms appropriate to four persons (and I have not tried to avoid this question-begging mode of description: the debts from the begged question will be repaid); but nature need to be no party to our phraseology. As we shall see, the various criteria purporting to tell us what it is to be a person are not decisive.

Bodily Considerations

Strongly in favour of saying that there was *one* person throughout is the fact that only one body is involved: one genetic constitution, one pair of hands, one mouth, and so on. Biologically speaking there is just one *homo sapiens* here, one human being. And that is strong evidence, simply because we all do in fact take it much for granted, as we have noted already, that persons and bodies come related one : one.

There is, however, one incidentally puzzling fact here. Let it be agreed that there is only one body, of a specific physical description. All the same, the various personalities of the patient often disagree strongly about their physical characteristics. We do not know whether Sally, B1, and B4 thought of their own appearances in their own idiosyncratic ways—Prince does not tell us. What is certain is that other cases of multiple personality show very marked disagreements on what "the body" looked like.

Rene, for instance, definitely had green eyes and auburn hair, but one of her alternates, Jeane, claimed to have brown eyes and dark brown hair; another, the flirtatious Stella, was a blonde and dressed accordingly. Her third alternate, Sissy, claimed to be four years old, and acted appropriately; while the sinister and violent male alternate, Bob, can scarcely have seen what Stella saw when "he" looked in a mirror. Sybil's sixteen personalities divided into eight pairs of near-twins (one pair of which were males), each pair claiming to be similar in appearance to each other, but to be very unlike any of the others. Further, the doctors treating such patients frequently comment on the different ways each handles the body when in charge of it: this personality slouches with legs crossed, that one sits primly, back straight, on the edge of the chair; this one has an oncoming glint in the eye, that one looks depressed and far away.

That is interesting;[14] but cannot of course defeat the *brute* fact that, like it or not, the various personalities do indeed have to make do with but one body. And this is a prima facie argument for saying that there is only one person there. But we cannot regard this alone as conclusive, precisely because the one : one relationship is something that we *might* need to call into question.

The Six Conditions

[. . . Dennett [1976] has usefully summarized six "conditions of personhood . . . " The list runs as follows: (1) persons are rational. (2) they are the subjects of Intentional ascriptions. (3) a certain stance or attitude must be taken towards

---

[14]Curiously enough, multiple personality patients seem not always bothered by this anomaly, sometimes, indeed, insisting that their bodies are quite different from the body of another alternate. The obvious inconsistencies that this provokes are ignored or shrugged off.

them, a point that introduces the idea that persons are, *inter alia*, moral objects. (4) they can reciprocate when such a stance is taken, which similarly introduces the idea that they are, *inter alia*, moral agents. (5) they are language-users. Finally, (6) they have a special kind of consciousness, perhaps self-consciousness; and this goes along, according to Frankfurt [1971] and others, with the ability to form "second-order" states (e.g. beliefs and desires about beliefs and desires) and hence with one version of freedom of will. . . .]

Let us look . . . at the six conditions and see if they can help us out. Most militate in favour of affirming plurality: each of the three dominant personalities meets four of them handsomely. Consider how (complex) Intentional predicates are true of each of the Beauchamp family separately. All can use language—two of them can use two. Each claims consciousness and self-consciousness. All are as capable of rational thought as are most ordinary people. So four conditions are clearly satisfied. It is the remaining two conditions, to do with "attitude" and "stance," that need examination: what attitude to Sally, B1, and B4 (or, what attitude to "Christine Beauchamp") was, or should have been, taken by Prince; and how did they (or she) reciprocate such attitudes. Let us consider first the attitude taken *to* them (her), for here we will find considerations pulling both ways.

On the one hand, this condition can be used as evidence for the claim that we have one person here, deriving from what we are accustomed to do, what we are accustomed to say. It is just a plain fact that the doctors in charge treat these patients as single individuals to be cured. Prince had no doubt but that his job was to "find" and to "cure" *the* real Miss Beauchamp. There were, I think we should agree, good reasons for him to do so; B2, or "the real Miss Beauchamp," functioned much better than had any of the others, once she was established in virtually sole charge of the body.

It is worth mentioning, though, that it is not invariably the case that singularity is better for "the patient" than plurality. It seems that the "cure" was less effective with Jonah/Jusky; for him/them, apparently, multiplicity was better suited than unity. (The full title of Ludwig *et al.*'s [1972] discussion of Jonah is "The Objective Study of a Multiple Personality: *Or, are Four Heads Better than One?*"—italics mine.) Notwithstanding Jonah/Jusky, though, we can see why singularity is usually preferred. It is typically much more convenient, since the uniqueness of the body jibes poorly with a plurality of owners. Sally and B4, for instance, were most annoyed whenever they "came to" and found themselves in church, or engaged in one of B1's charitable or altruistic activities. B1 in turn could become ill with worry when she found herself with a cigarette in her hand. It was immensely time-consuming for all three if the body had to be bathed up to six times a day (each of them wanted two baths, and if Sally had bathed first in the morning, B1 might have another one, then B4; and then in the evening they might all go through the same routine again). We can guess what difficulties even Jonah/Jusky might have had, despite the fact that Jusky was in general more stable and efficient than the reunited Jonah, if, say, Sammy had wanted to be a ballet dancer and Usoffa Abdullah had thoughts of becoming a Sumo wrestler. The fact that several of Sybil's sixteen alternates wanted to take "the" dose of a prescribed medicine meant that the body was getting much more of it than any doctor intended; nor did her bank balance prosper, when each alternate wanted her own wardrobe of clothes (see Schreiber [1975]). In general, one body per person is just much easier.[15]

All the same, despite the fact that we probably would agree with Prince's presupposition

---

[15]As Fagin puts it: "Some conjurors say that number three is the magic number, and some say number seven. It's neither, my friend, neither. It's number one" (Dickens, *Oliver Twist*).

that it was *Miss Beauchamp* to whom he took the "help-treat-cure" stance, there is a paradox here still. For note that in the relevant period, before *B2* appeared, *he did not have "the real Miss Beauchamp" to take an attitude to*; the fact that he felt he must cure "this patient" was rather an attitude towards someone he had not yet met! Even so, though, I think we have to agree that his overall stance was to a single, albeit absent, individual; he took himself to be treating one woman.

However, the "stance" condition also works to support the thesis that we have *several* people here. We have been arguing so far that Miss Beauchamp seems to have been a *single* object of moral concern: our attitude to her is, at least most of the time, the attitude we take to a single sick person. But we cannot be consistent here, and notably Prince did not try to be. For he *also* regarded each member of the trio as an individual object of concern. He was worried about the effects on *B1* of Sally's practical jokes; he sympathized, quite genuinely, with *B4*'s agony when she told him that he was killing her; and, although he deplored Sally's childishness and occasional spitefulness, he was also amused by this "carefree child of nature." So as well as treating the (elusive) "real Miss Beauchamp" as a single person, he treated each of the three personalities as one too. The "stance condition" is thus a two-edged weapon for use in deciding on the number of people here.

What then of the "reciprocation" condition? This cannot pull in favour of saying that only one person ("Miss Beauchamp") was present during the crucial period. For until the advent of *B2*, she was not there at all. It rather pulls in favour of saying that there were indeed three responsible, reciprocating agents here. Prince certainly regarded all three as such. He firmly (for example) ticked Sally off for her tricks and follies, and would lecture her sternly; he criticized or approved of *B4*'s plans for finding a job, or for taking a holiday; and he commended *B1*'s sweet and self-sacrificing nature. All the

alternate personalities were thus treated as moral and prudential agents, with respect to other people, with respect to each other, and with respect to their own selves. Prince is by no means alone in taking such an attitude to the diverse personalities of a patient—it is practically impossible to avoid. Sybil's alternates often showed their own attitudes and concerns to problems *common* to them all: for instance, the two male alternates often did useful jobs around the house, Vanessa took a job in a launderette, while Marcia submitted a pop song to an agent—all to assist with the financial situation.

Thus five of the six conditions suggest that there are several members of the family Beauchamp; and the sixth is ambiguous.

Further Considerations

Leaving aside the six conditions, we can find further arguments in favour of affirming plurality, and the rest of this section will list these. None of these is conclusive; each has some weight.

The first consideration derives from the very marked differences in their characters and personalities. It is true that differences of character are not enough, alone, to justify claims that we have more than one person—we all know how much our own moods and styles of behaviour can swing, and how the "roles people play" vary from context to context. So consistency of character cannot as such be a "condition of personhood." All the same, and despite role-playing and mood swings, we can and do identify the distinct personalities and character traits of our friends. And, as we read Prince, it emerges that each of the Beauchamp trio not only had swings of mood, and adopted different attitudes in various circumstances; they also had, each her own, *overall* character. They had entirely distinct, though each internally consistent and coherent (within natural limits), preferences, prejudices, outlooks, moods, ambitions, skills, tastes, and habits. Some of these differences have already been mentioned; Prince ([1968], pp. 288–94) lists some of the specific dissimilarities between *B1* and *B4*. For example, *B1*'s appetite was poor, *B4*'s healthy; *B1* liked her coffee unsweetened and black, whereas *B4* took hers with sugar and cream; *B1* never, *B4* regularly, used vinegar and oil in cooking; *B1* liked soups, milk, broths, brown bread, vegetables, and ice cream, all of which *B4* avoided. *B4* was "extravagantly fond" of smoking and drinking, but *B1* rarely drank and never smoked. *B1* preferred sober, loose clothes, with low-heeled boots and no rings or brooches; *B4* bought tight, brightly coloured clothes, high-heeled boots, and jewellery. *B1* read devotional books, but *B4* the newspapers. *B1* visited the sick, attended church, sewed, and knitted, all of which bored *B4* to distraction. Perhaps surprisingly, it was *B4* rather than *B1* who was terrified of the dark. Then again, one's "self-image" is often said to be an important constituent of personality; if so, it is relevant to remember that multiple personalities often regard their physical appearance very differently, and maybe *B1* and *B4* did too —certainly they dressed in violently opposed styles. Whatever the validity of this last point, though, I believe that the accumulation of such differences as these allows us to say that we had very different character types here. A further point in conclusion: a "character" is a certain kind of unity and continuity of character *traits*, without which we would be unable to describe it; but note that there is no implication in this anodyne remark that the unity/continuity must be "conscious."

A second indication (no more than an indication) of plurality is that each of the Beauchamp family could have managed for long periods in sole charge of the body. Indeed *B1*, before she came to see Prince, had had the body to herself for several years. *B4* could have survived well in any circumstances, probably better than *B1* alone: she was a tough lassie. Sally had various remarkable abnormalities; for example, she

never experienced ill-health, pain, tiredness, hunger, or thirst, and claimed never to sleep. (Usoffah Abdullah, Son of Omega—one of Jason/Jusky's alternates—was a bit like this too.) Nevertheless, she showed that when she was in a relatively responsible mood she could take adequate care of herself, remembering the necessity to eat, drink, lie down, and so forth. Of course, all would have liked to have had the body solely to herself; had Prince confirmed any one of them in undisputed charge of it, anyone would have agreed that here was "the" Miss Beauchamp. Each came across as a relatively normal individual, however dissimilar they were from each other in character and temperament. This degree of autonomy does not hold true of all the cases of multiple personality to be found in the literature, where we find personalities most of which are less well rounded than at least the three main figures of the family Beauchamp. For instance, as already noted, the personalities of Jonah/Jusky were specialized to deal with specific sorts of incident. Here again, though, it seems that each could have managed alone, even if not always very adequately. Of the sixteen personalities of Sybil, on the other hand, it seems highly improbable that either of the two male alternates could have managed well with a woman's body; and Rene's four-year-old alternate Sissy would have been helpless by herself for long. However, if we stick to Miss Beauchamp, there then seems no doubt about the adequacy of *at least B1* and *B4*.

A third, equally non-conclusive, argument for regarding the family Beauchamp as a plurality is that it is by no means obvious, as one reads the book, that *B2* is indeed going to come out at the top of the heap. There is even room for some scepticism about whether Prince was correct in picking on her as "the" real Miss Beauchamp; it is evident that his views on which contender had the best title changed from time to time, and were to some extent determined by what he thought a young lady at the turn of the century *ought* to be like. Certainly he had Sally's confirmation that *B2* was the same as the pre-trauma Christine Beauchamp, but it is paradoxical, to put it mildly, to take the word of that young lady in the circumstances. If *B4* had succeeded in her plan of escaping to Europe, who would have ended up in charge? Maybe Henri de Montherlant was right: "It is through chance that, from among the various individuals of which each of us is composed, one emerges rather than another" ("Explicit Mysterium" [1931]).

There is a fourth indication: we should observe that Miss Beauchamp's plurality was not only diachronic—Sally, *B1*, and *B4* by turns—but also synchronic. For whenever *B1*, *B2*, or *B4* were in control, Sally coexisted as a second consciousness, aware of all their actions and of the thoughts of at least *B1* and *B2*, while keeping her own counsel. Her consciousness was substantially independent of that of the personality in charge of the body at the time. We have already seen that Sally observed, as an amused spectator, *B1*'s dreams, even being able to give a fuller account of them than could *B1*. Predictably enough, then, she could also watch and report the confused and chaotic thoughts of *B1* in delirium. Then again, if either of the other two were walking along in a trance, not noticing much around them, Sally might be attending with keen interest to details of the passing scene. Indeed, she could be alert when the personality in control of the body was completely unconscious: chloroform, which suppressed the consciousness of *B1* and *B4*, seemed to have no effect on Sally's. (Compare the "hidden observer" revealed by hypnosis, who sometimes seems immune to normal anaesthetics.) Conversely, though, she could switch off her attention when either of the others was engaged in something that bored her (so that she alone proved ignorant of shorthand, which *B1* and *B4* both decided to learn, and she could not understand French, which Miss Beauchamp had learned as a schoolgirl). All in all, we find with Sally the synchronic duality of consciousness that is also a feature of split-brain patients

under certain experimental conditions. She would have agreed with Oscar Wilde: "One's real life is so often the life that one does not lead" (*L'Envoi* to "Rose-leaf and Apple-leaf" [1882]).

It is true that to get a simultaneous *manifestation* of a second consciousness, or at any rate a manifestation that was not fleeting and unpredictable, artificial circumstances were required just as they are usually required to induce a split in commissurotomy patients. For example, after *B4* had destroyed an autobiography that Sally had been at pains to write, *B4* became somewhat remorseful and allowed her hand to be used "automatically" by Sally to rewrite the document. Thus Sally wrote with "*B4*'s hand," while *B4* commented caustically upon what appeared on the page before her. This situation was no less contrived, in its own way, than are the experiments on split-brain patients.[16] But on top of this Sally provided quantities of *ex post facto* evidence of her simultaneous existence, not all of which could be dismissed (although Prince was laudably sceptical about some of it) since it helped explain and make intelligible some otherwise inexplicable lacunae in *B1*'s own account of her experience. So there was evidence of synchronic duality for all, or almost all, of the time, with the sole exception of the periods in which Sally herself was "out." (This point, of course, only works to suggest that *Sally* was a discrete individual.)

A fifth and final argument for regarding *B1*, *B4*, and Sally as distinct persons appeals to intuition: to the consideration of what it must have

---

[16]This again tends to oversimplify the position. Sally was able, by a technique she described as "willing," to induce positive and negative hallucinations in both *B1* and *B4*; she could induce aboulia (failure of will) or apraxia (inability to act), especially if the primary personality was, as she put it, "rattled"; she could tease *B1* by making her transpose letters in the words she was writing; and so forth. But these and similar instances cannot of themselves indicate the co-presence of a secondary consciousness as clearly as does the arranged phenomenon of her automatic writing.

been like from the inside, from the first-person perspective. The best way of putting this is in terms of Nagel's well-known question (Nagel [1974/1979]), "what is it like for an *X* to be an *X*?" I have argued that intuition is a problematic and dangerous tool to use in consideration of problems of personality identity, and I am myself unsure just what is being asked by the "what is it like . . . ?" question.[17] However, since Nagel's question appeals so strongly to the intuitions of so many, it would be remiss not to consider its weight in this instance.

It is an interesting and puzzling fact about the topic of personal identity and personal survival that the answer one is tempted to give in response to assorted puzzle-cases may differ depending on whether the question is framed in the first or third person. For instance, even if it seems sensible to say of another person that after (say) a thought-experimental body-swap, one of the resulting individuals would be "more or less" him, of oneself one tends to think that either the result will be *me*, or it won't: no degrees about it.[18] So we find, I think, with the Beauchamp family. Because *B4* ceased to exist as far as she was concerned when *B2* was in charge, *B2*'s survival meant death, extinction, for *B4*; as it also did for *B1*. It was little or no consolation for either to be told that they did in

fact survive as *B2*, that *B2* claimed each of them as herself. This refusal to be consoled seems reasonable enough—consider the difficulty of persuading anyone that he had continued to exist as an active agent over a lengthy period of time of which he had absolutely no recollection, simply on the grounds that an individual, of whom he knew nothing directly, claimed to *be* him. There is, in short, *nothing* that it was like to be "Miss Beauchamp" during the time that she was split up into the three dominant personalities. There was, however, something that it was like to be Sally, something that it was like to be *B1*, something that it was like to be *B4*. Whatever the difficulties with the tool of intuition in philosophy, when it comes to the fundamental and heartfelt claim "that's not *me*," as each of these three personalities would say about any of the others, we surely ought not to disregard it lightly.

If we press this line of reasoning, then, we seem to be pointed in the direction of affirming multiplicity. Just the same difficulty, of course, arises with the less dramatic dissociations we mentioned briefly at the beginning of this chapter; there seems nothing that it is like to be the Revd Ansel Bourne that would include both his fugue and his normal state, and nothing that it is like to be both feeling and not feeling pain when undergoing hypnosis. However, with these cases we have a great deal that points us in the direction of singularity; with multiple personality this consideration is yet another of a number of factors suggesting plurality.

---

[17] I am most perplexed about Nagel's question. Put simply, I do not think that I do know what it is like to be me. That is, I could write a tediously long self-analysis, which would seem to me to give any reader as much information as I have on this score; but I am sure that this is not what Nagel means. But if not, then I do not know what he does mean.

[18] It may be *wrong* to say that there are "no degrees" allowable in answer to the question "will that be me, or not?" Ingenious thought experiments have been brought in to suggest that "more or less me" might sometimes be the most appropriate thing to say. But such thought experiments must meet the conditions imposed on legitimate thought experiments . . . Until one is proposed that does meet them, we should hold on to reality: this is not the way that our linguistic habits have it. At minimum, then, our actual prejudice for "no degrees!" must be taken seriously.

Summary

The brunt of the argument suggests that we ought to conclude that during the period from the appearance of Sally and *B4* to that of *B2*, Prince had three people to deal with. Arguments in favor of affirming plurality are more numerous than those suggesting singularity. . . .

References

Cheek, D. B., and LeCron, L. M. [1968], *Clinical Hypnotherapy* (Grune and Stratton, New York).

Confer, W. N., and Ables, B. S. [1983], *Multiple Personality: Etiology, Diagnosis, and Treatment* (Human Sciences Press, New York).

Congdon, M. H., Hain, J., and Stevenson, I. [1961], "A Case of Multiple Personality Illustrating the Transition from Role-Playing," *Journal of Nervous and Mental Disease*, 32: 497–504.

Corkin, S., Sullivan, E., Twitchell, T., and Grove, E. [1981], "The Amnesic Patient H. M.: Clinical Observations and Test Performance 28 Years after Operation," *Abstracts of the Society of Neuroscience*, 80: 12–35.

Dennett, Daniel [1976], "Conditions of Personhood," in *The Identities of Persons*, ed. A. O. Rorty (University of California Press, Berkeley), 175–96.

Greaves, G. B. [1980], "Multiple Personality 165 Years after Mary Reynolds," *Journal of Nervous and Mental Disease*, 168: 577–96.

Gruenewald, D. [1971], "Hypnotic Techniques without Hypnosis in the Treatment of Dual Personality," *Journal of Nervous and Mental Disease*, 153: 41–6.

Harriman, P. L. [1943], "A New Approach to Multiple Personalities," *American Journal of Orthopsychiatry*, 13: 638–43.

Hilgard, E. R. [1977], *Divided Consciousness: Multiple Controls in Human Thought and Action* (Harcourt, New York).

Howland, J. S. [1975], "The Use of Hypnosis in the Treatment of a Case of Multiple Personality," *Journal of Nervous and Mental Disease*, 161: 138–42.

James, W. [1890], *Principles of Psychology* (Dover Press, New York), ii.

——— [1912], *Essays in Radical Empiricism*, ed. R. B. Perry (Longmans, Green, London).

Locke, J. [1690], *An Essay Concerning Human Understanding*, ed. A. C. Fraser [1959] (Constable, London), i, ii.

Ludwig, A. M., Brandsma, J. M., Wilbur, C. B., Bendfeldt, F., and Jameson, D. H. [1972], "The Objective Study of a Multiple Personality: Or, are Four Heads Better than One?" *Archives of General Psychiatry*, 26: 298–310.

Nagel, T., "What is it Like to be a Bat?" *Philosophical Review*, 83: 435–50; repr. in Nagel [1987b], 165–80.

Oxford English Dictionary, compact edn. [1971] (Oxford University Press, Oxford).

Prince, M. [1905], *The Dissociation of a Personality* (Longmans, Green, London); repr. [1968] (Johnson Reprint Corporation, New York).

Schreiber, F. R. [1975], *Sybil* (Penguin Books, Harmondsworth).

Sutcliffe, J. P., and Jones, J. [1962], "Personal Identity, Multiple Personality, and Hypnosis," *The International Journal of Clinical and Experimental Hypnosis*, 10: 231–69.

Szasz, T. S. [1962], *The Myth of Mental Illness* (Harper and Row, London).

Taylor, W. S., and Martin, M. F. [1944], "Multiple Personality," *Journal of Abnormal and Social Psychology*, 39: 281–300.

Thigpen, C. H., and Cleckley, H. M. [1957], *The Three Faces of Eve* (Popular Library, New York).

Ullmann, L. P., and Krasner, L. [1969], *A Psychological Approach to Abnormal Behavior* (Prentice-Hall, Englewood Cliffs).

Wilkes, K. V., "Nemo Psychologus Nisi Physiologus," *Inquiry*, 29: 165–85.

——— [1987], "Describing the Child's Mind," in J. Russell, ed., *Philosophical Perspectives on Developmental Psychology* (Basil Blackwell, Oxford), 3–16.

10

STEPHEN E. BRAUDE
Multiple Personality and the Structure of the Self

I. Introduction

In the eighteenth century, the Marquis de Puységur, a disciple of Franz Anton Mesmer, discovered a sleeplike hypnotic trance state which he called "magnetic sleep," and which appeared to reveal the existence of a persistent doubling of consciousness. Indeed, Puységur believed that his hypnotic procedures had enabled him to uncover the presence of a second self, with its own memories and characteristics (see Crabtree, 1985; Laurence and Perry, 1988). Since that time, dissociative phenomena— especially the dramatic phenomenon of multiple personality disorder (MPD)–have inspired a great deal of theorizing over the structure of the mind and the nature of mental unity and disunity. Quite a lot of this theorizing, however, rests on highly questionable abstract presuppositions.

My aim here is to examine a suspicious principle that has been widely accepted, at least tacitly, for well over a hundred years (probably since the time of Puységur). Although late nineteenth- and early twentieth-century authors asserted it fairly readily, it has seldom been articulated explicitly. Its pervasiveness, however, has done much to undermine discussions of dissociative phenomena. Indeed, this principle has led to a seriously distorted picture of the importance of dissociation for our understanding of the mind. We may call it the principle of *compositional reversibility*, or the *CR-principle*.

II. Varieties of Reversibility

When Puységur and his successors observed apparent forms of multiple personality, they saw themselves as having *uncovered* an aspect of mental functioning by means of magnetic techniques. They did not see themselves as having created the phenomena. From their perspective, the therapeutic techniques of animal magnetism disclosed and utilized a doubling of consciousness that existed already within the subject. Hence, they tacitly supposed that they were evoking phenomena which revealed to them something about the underlying structure or operation of the self or personality. In making that assumption, they were relying on a form of the CR-principle.

As far as I can tell, however, the pioneers of hypnosis never brought this assumption out into the open. The most prominent explicit proponents of the CR-principle were late nineteenth- and early twentieth-century advocates of the colonial view of the self—i.e., the view that a person is a kind of colony of lower-order selves or homunculi. For example. Myers (1903) writes that

observation of the ways in which the personality tends to disintegrate may suggest methods which may tend on the other hand to its more complete integration. (p. 3)

And later, he says (rather less tentatively),

Subjected continually to both internal and external stress and strain, its [i.e., the personality's] ways of yielding indicate the grain of its texture. (p. 39)

Similarly, a few years earlier Ribot had stated, even more boldly, "Seeing how the Self is broken up, we can understand how it comes to be" (1887, p. 20).

Fifty years later, William McDougall (1938) argued along the same lines. He claimed, first, that

we cannot hope for clear and adequate understanding of the various ways in which the mind falls into disorder unless and until we have adequate insight into the conditions of its orderly and harmonious functioning and development. . . . (p. 143)

Then, after asserting that the *historical* structure or aspect of the mind "is the product of, is built up by . . . associative links or bonds" (p. 144), he claims that dissociation is "a weakening, or an undoing, or a failing of the work or product of the associative processes, the links of association" (p. 144).

What these authors seem to be asserting is a kind of historical or developmental claim— namely (and very roughly), that functional disorganization or splitting is a reversal of earlier processes leading to functional organization or unity. Hence, from the phenomena of dissociation, one ought to be able to infer the elements or principles underlying prior functional unity. Stated in this general way, however, the CR-principle is ambiguous. To appreciate its weaknesses, we must consider it in two distinct forms.

The first, and stronger, version of the CR-principle holds that there is a correlation (or perhaps even an identity) between the *particular* clinical entities produced in dissociation and the components of the predissociative self. Hence, from our discovery of the former, we can infer the existence of the latter. Let us call this the *Token* CR-principle; it is the view to

which nineteenth-century writers came perilously close. The weaker version of the CR-principle asserts a correlation merely between the *kinds* of clinical entities produced dissociatively and the kinds of things composing the predissociative self. Let us call this the *Type* CR-principle. (See Beahrs, 1982, and Watkins and Watkins, 1979–80, for perhaps the most explicit recent versions of this view.)

The Type CR-principle is weaker because type-correlations may exist even in the absence of token-correlations. For example, according to the Type CR-principle, the existence of a sexual (aggressive, angry) alternate personality would entail the predissociative existence of a sexual (aggressive, angry) component of the personality. But it needn't be the case that the particular sexual (aggressive, angry) personality that we call Dorothy existed prior to dissociation, or that some specific Dorothy-personality ancestor or germ existed prior to dissociation. Furthermore, the Type CR-principle need only posit one sexual (aggressive, angry) predissociative personality component for all postdissociative members of that type. But the Token CR-principle requires a distinct predissociative component for each distinct postdissociative entity.

Both versions of the CR-principle are fatally flawed. Consider the Token CR-principle first. To begin with, it is not a *general* truth that things always divide or split along some preexisting grain, or that objects divide only into their historically original components. For example, Humpty Dumpty may have been reduced to 40 pieces of shell after his fall. But it would be a mistake to infer that he had previously been assembled and united out of 40 parts, much less those 40 parts. Similarly, I can break a table (or a board) in half with an axe. But it would be a mistake to conclude that the object resulted initially from the uniting of those two halves. Furthermore, some cases of splitting are clearly *evolutionary*. For example, the familiar process of cell division *creates* entities that did not exist previously. Hence, if the Token CR-principle is true, it is not because it is an instance of a more general truth about the way things divide or break up. Presumably, it would be true in virtue of the special way the self breaks up.

But there is no reason to think that the self always breaks neatly, or along the grain, especially under extreme trauma or stress—for example, of the sort that apparently leads to MPD. For one thing, a multiple's total number of alters (full-blown personalities or fragments) can apparently range into the hundreds. Even if we grant the difficulty of taking a precise inventory of the number of distinct alters, must we suppose, on the Token CR-principle, that the predissociative self consisted of *so many* distinct proto-personalities?

But more important, it's preposterous to suppose that the historically original components of personality are those (or correspond to those) that seem quite clearly to be *adaptational*—indeed, trauma- or situation-specific. Most alternate personalities appear to be formed in response to *contingent* stressful situations, and they appear to be similarly contingent *products* of a creative process of adaptation or defense. For example, I know a multiple who developed several animal personalities to deal with the incomprehensibility of parental abuse. The abuse occurred during early childhood, and at that time the only way she could grasp the acts into which she was coerced was by relating them to things she had seen dogs and horses do. (The significance and prevalence of animal alters is beginning to come under scrutiny. See Hendrickson, *et al.*, 1989; Smith, 1989.) Moreover, once a multiple begins to dissociate habitually, as a familiar and apparently effective technique for coping with virtually any kind of stress (traumatic or otherwise), one begins to see the emergence of highly specialized alters, some created to deal merely with inconveniences or relatively minor unpleasant situations. Some alters deal exclusively (or at least principally) with such circumscribed activities as eating, baking muffins, handling domestic finances, cleaning the toilet, participating in oral sex (but

sex of no other kind), receiving enemas, and interacting with in-laws. Granted, they might engage in other identifiable types of activities in the process of executing these general functions. But it is nevertheless clear that certain functions rather than others make sense of the alter's role within the total personality system. These, we could say, are an alter's *centrally defining* functions, and there is no reason to suppose that they played any part in the original organization of the predissociative self. There is simply no reason to suppose that an earlier united self consisted in part of components identical to (or correlated with) exactly these contingent postdissociative entities. Hence, it is highly implausible to insist that the self always breaks along the grain, or that it *has* a grain corresponding to situation-specific alternate personalities.

Furthermore, a multiple's inventory of alters often evolves over time in response either to therapeutic intervention or day-to-day difficulties in life. The problem for the Token CR-principle is not simply that the inventory may continue to enlarge; hard-core advocates of that principle could always argue that additional alters reveal the finer structure of the predissociative personality. Rather, the problem is that the personality system might undergo *fundamental functional reorganization* into a different number of alters. Not only might the multiple have created different alters (and a different number of alters) to deal with the same problems, but the problems themselves might also have been different and might accordingly have elicited a dramatically different set of alters. But then it becomes arbitrary to choose one temporal slice of an evolving system of alters and claim that it reveals the grain (or fundamental structure) of the predissociative self. It is far more reasonable to maintain that a multiple's array of alters *at any time* represents merely one of the many possible dissociative solutions to contingent problems in living.

Obviously, this point also works against the Type CR-principle. Since a multiple's system of alters at different times may divide along significantly different functional lines, it becomes arbitrary to select one set of alter *types* as representing the deep functional divisions of the predissociative self. Those functional divisions are clearly as contingent as the situations in response to which the alters were formed.

In other respects, however, the problems with the Type CR-principle differ somewhat from those afflicting the Token CR-principle. To begin with, it is very difficult to know what the principle means. In particular, *which* types of postdissociative entities is it supposed to apply to? Presumably not to *every* type—for example, personalities that hate Stephen Braude, eat only at McDonald's, or believe that Elvis still lives, or personalities that wear digital watches, enjoy rap music, or prefer Wordstar to WordPerfect. For one thing, that would imply that the historically original predissociative personality components can have functions specific to things that did not exist at the time of birth, or during early childhood (e.g., digital watches or computer programs). And for another, if postdissociative kinds are identified too specifically—for example, the type that has *exactly* the characteristics and history of the personality called Dorothy—then the Type CR-principle is indistinguishable from the Token CR-principle.

Furthermore, even if we were to identify types less specifically, the Type CR-principle would still seem committed to an absurdly inflated inventory of original personality components. Suppose an alter emerged to handle witnessing the murder of one's parents? Does that mean that there already existed a personality component of the type suited specifically to dealing with the murder of one's parents? And if so, must we posit a distinct component waiting in the wings (so to speak) to deal specifically with the murder of siblings, and another for in-laws, or next-door neighbors, or friends in St. Louis, and another for total strangers? Moreover, if the parents' murder was committed with a gun, was the original personality component

designed only to deal with the murder of parents with firearms? Would another component already exist just in case the subject had to deal with murder by axe, or by poison? Even if there needed only to be a personality component for dealing with murder, *of some kind or other*, of one's parents (or of any loved one), would we then need to posit a component that could have been dissociated just in case the victims had been tortured instead, and another just in case they had been relentlessly harassed?

III. An Appeal to Psychological Primitives

Partisans of the Type CR-principle might reply that we need to identify post-dissociative entities very broadly. They might claim that the relevant types are those having to do only with the most *basic* general personality traits or functions—perhaps such as anger, sexuality, helpfulness, compassion, and so on. And presumably, these traits would transcend the familial, cultural, and social influences that help shape the more specific personality types found in MPD. For example, it may not matter that the personality claims to be a possessing spirit of the sort appropriate to a specific cultural milieu or more local belief system of a family or religious cult, or that it displays the stereotypic traits of a Southern belle, 1960s hippie, or a street-wise tough from the Bronx. Similarly, it may not matter that an alter's centrally defining function is to repair plumbing, write term papers, or deal with telephone solicitations. What would matter is whether the alter's more general and basic function is to be angry, helpful, and so on. Hence, some might argue for a correlation between only the basic (or primitive) general personality traits or functions isolated dissociatively and component functions of the predissociative self. This variant of the CR-principle, which we may call the *Minimal* Type CR-principle, would therefore seem committed to the existence of distinct predissociative personality components, each of which specializes in a function corresponding to a basic postdissociative function. And presumably, these corresponding predissociative functions will be the primitive or fundamental functions around which the predissociative self is organized. Undoubtedly, the Minimal Type CR-principle will strike some as commendably conservative. But it is still thoroughly unsatisfactory, for two reasons.

First and foremost, there is no justification for claiming that *any* set of general personality functions is absolutely primitive, either pre- or postdissociatively. For example, our descriptive categories of anger, helpfulness, sexuality, and so forth, are hardly the only plausible ways of slicing up behavior into a set of putatively basic regularities or functions. Alternatively, one might prefer the inventory of functions proposed in Transactional Analysis (into parent, child, etc.), while another might defend a Platonic division into reason, appetite, and emotion, and another might prefer a division along the lines of five-element diagnosis in Chinese medicine, or perhaps even Jungian archetypes. In fact, many different sets of categories can lay equal claim to dividing the self into basic functions. And they might all be able to countenance exactly the same particular behaviors. The different category sets would simply take those behaviors to be instances of different sorts of regularities.

The moral, of course, is that these sets of personality functions, like descriptive categories of every sort, are no more than context-appropriate divisions of nature into kinds. There is no reason to think that one of our categorizations is inherently preferable to another, or that it captures a built-in parsing of the self into discrete functions. On the contrary, it is only relative to a perspective or point of view, or against a background of continually shifting needs and interests (both local and global), that certain cat-

egories rather than others will be appropriate. None are intrinsically appropriate or perspective-independent. Hence, it is only relative to a context, perspective, or background that we divide nature in one way rather than another, and determine which general kinds of descriptive categories, and which level of specificity, are appropriate (Braude, 1986, chap. 4).

The self is like a pie in that respect. We can slice a pie any number of ways—for example, along the radius, diameter, or by means of a vast array of conceivable grids or templates. And even if we select a general method of slicing the pie—say, along the radius—we still have to decide how large to make the slices. The self, too, can be divided functionally in a vast number of ways. And even if we prefer some general approach over others—say, into parent/child divisions—we have numerous options concerning the finer structure we impose on the self. Do we need to distinguish mother from father, son from daughter, husband from wife, infant from adolescent? Do we need to appeal to grandparent/grandchild relations to understand the dynamics of the predissociative self? Any method we choose, however, represents only one way of understanding, one sort of conceptual map we may trace over the surface of our subject. Moreover, like maps of any sort, our descriptive categories cannot be evaluated apart from a background of needs and interests, or in isolation from an actual context of inquiry. And, clearly, there is no reason to suppose that our conceptual maps, tailored to context-specific needs to understand, describe actual partitions on the surface of our subject, any more than state or county borders on a map of the United States correspond to actual partitions on the surface of the land. (See Heil, 1983, for an illuminating discussion of the map analogy.)

Apparently, then, the Minimal Type CR-principle suffers from two related, and very deep, conceptual flaws. It presupposes that in the classification of psychological functions some set of descriptive categories is absolutely basic, and it mistakes the outlines of those categories for inherent divisions in nature. Hence, the Minimal Type CR-principle fails to transform the Type CR-principle into a viable theoretical claim.

IV. Anomalous Multiplicity

Nevertheless, the foregoing arguments may still not be enough to subvert the CR-principle altogether. Many writers seem to subscribe to a kind of CR-principle but refrain from endorsing any one version in particular. Perhaps that is because they don't realize they even have a choice. But whatever the reason, they betray their allegiance to the CR-principle by means of a seemingly modest claim. They argue that the self *cannot* be unitary, because if it were, MPD (and other dissociative phenomena) would be impossible. Binet, for example, writes, "What is capable of division must be made up of parts" (1896, pp. 348f). This principle, which we may call the *noncommittal CR-principle*, also undergirds the work of Beahrs, Hilgard (1986), the Watkins, and many others. Its adherents maintain only that predissociative functional divisions of the self are necessary for the occurrence of postdissociative functional divisions.

Some might protest that, because these writers take no stand on the nature of the correlation between pre- and postdissociative entities, it is unclear whether they subscribe to a *reversibility* principle at all. Theoretically, at least, they have the option of affirming the existence of predissociative divisions of the self while denying that postdissociative divisions correlate with them in *any* meaningful or interesting way. (Borrowing another bit of terminology from recent work in the philosophy of mind, we could call this the *anomalous multiplicity principle*, since the correlations between pre- and postdissociative divisions of the self would be anomalous—i.e., nonlawlike.) I sus-

pect, however, that few (if any) researchers into MPD would be attracted to this rather skeptical position. If postdissociative divisions afforded *no* clue as to the nature of predissociative divisions—that is, if there were no lawlike connections between the two—then the entire enterprise of examining dissociative phenomena in detail would have had a markedly different and presumably less abstract cast. In the absence of such connections, one would not be able to generalize from postdissociative to predissociative phenomena, and infer features of the latter from those of the former.

Now, granted, it may be that to ϕ postdissociatively, one must already have had a predissociative capacity for ϕing. But if *that* is all that partisans of the noncommittal CR-principle are willing to claim, then the principle is theoretically vacuous. For one thing, it seems to be *trivially* true that for one to have ϕd, one must already have had the capacity for ϕing. And for another, dissociative phenomena would then be no more revealing than nondissociative phenomena. After all, to manifest *any* trait, ability, etc., the agent must already have had the capacity for it. Furthermore, the noncommittal CR-principle would in that case not support inferences about the development or formation of the predissociative self—for example, about the nature of the elements or processes out of which the self was originally composed. But Binet and most other major figures in the history of the field have considered dissociative phenomena to be of enormous theoretical interest, and not merely of relevance, say, to therapy. They believed that dissociation promised great and *distinctive* insights into the structure and function of the mind. Hence, it is extremely unlikely that in articulating the CR-principle, they were making such a toothless claim.

To put the point somewhat less abstractly, consider why partisans of a Type CR-principle would ever consider the functional type of a dissociative entity or phenomenon to be of theoretical interest. We obviously do not need angry or sexually promiscuous alternate person-alities, say, to demonstrate that people have a predissociative capacity for anger or sexual promiscuity. So what is theoretically distinctive about the dissociation of anger (or any other trait or ability)? For example, what special sort of fact might advocates of a Type CR-principle hope to learn about the predissociative self from the existence of an angry alter? The answer, presumably, is that an alter of that type would reveal something about how the predissociative self *came to be*—that is, it would tell us some-thing about the self's processes of organization and formation, or about the historically original components of the predissociative self. If that were not the case, dissociated anger would be no more theoretically illuminating than any other sort of anger or angry behavior.

More generally, it seems quite clear that re-searchers expect dissociative phenomena to illu-minate the predissociative divisions of the self that make *those* phenomena possible. They seem to be searching for a certain kind of non-trivial nomological connection between pre- and postdissociative divisions. But that means they have to decide between the Token, Type, or Minimal Type CR-principles, all of which we have found to be fatally flawed. Thus, propo-nents of the noncommittal CR-principle are im-paled on the horns of a dilemma. On the one hand, they could decide that there are no—or only trivial—lawlike correlations between pre- and postdissociative divisions of the self, in which case they would have to concede that MPD, hypnosis, and other dissociative condi-tions tell us virtually nothing about the nature or development of the predissociative self. And on the other hand, they could assert the exis-tence of nontrivial lawlike connections, which would require subscribing to one of the three views we have found to be false.

Interestingly, the noncommittal CR-principle is widely used in physics, where it has contrib-uted to the almost comical proliferation of "fundamental" particles. Actually, physicists

tend to endorse the Token CR-principle, and its weaknesses undermine the familiar argument that atomic collisions reveal deeper preexisting structures and components of the atom. Of course, many physicists realize that they may be creating, rather than discovering, new particles. I am merely calling attention to the flawed prin-ciple underlying the standard argument in favor of the latter alternative. Even if physicists *are* discovering more fundamental units of matter, they will not establish it by appealing to the Token CR-principle, or even the noncommittal CR-principle. We should perhaps call this the *Humpty Dumpty Fallacy*.

V. The Lessons of Dissociation

A few might still protest that *some* kind of CR-principle is required simply to explain the theo-retical relevance of dissociative phenomena. After all, they might say, if that principle were false, how could dissociative phenomena ever teach us anything about the self? But one must understand that, by abandoning the CR-princi-ple, one need not concede that it is impossible to learn about the self or the mind from the study of dissociation.

For example, it is clear that we could not dissociate at all, or in certain ways, unless we already had a capacity for it. Hence, dissociative phenomena promise to enhance our under-standing of the limits and varieties of cognitive functioning. But of course one could not be *non-dissociatively* timid, long-winded, or anything else unless one already had the corresponding capacity. Hence, as we have seen, dissociative phenomena are no more distinctively illuminat-ing in that respect than nondissociative phe-nomena. Naturally, one would hope to discover a range of unusual or enhanced capacities that occur rarely (if at all) outside of dissociative contexts—for example, hypnotic anesthesia, negative hallucinations, and the astonishing intelligence and literary talents of Patience Worth (Braude, 1980; Litvag, 1972; W. F. Prince, 1927/1964). Indeed, one might *expect* dissociation to elicit infrequently used or displayed human capacities and yield insights into the conditions conducive to their manifestation. But the discovery of capacities unique to dissociation is of no greater *developmental* significance than the discovery that people are nondissociatively capable of anger, sarcasm, or compassion. In discovering the existence of the capacity, we do not discover anything in particular about its role in the original formation or basic structure of the self. But it is only this latter sort of developmental claim that we reject when we abandon the CR-principle.

To avoid another possible misunderstanding, I should also emphasize that my criticisms of the CR-principle are not arguments against the view that the self has parts. Nor are my criticisms arguments against the view that the predissociative self is a colony of lower-order selves. Granted, the etiological data weighs heavily against the view that the predissociative self consists of multiple *personalities*, or centers of self-awareness. From what we know of the life histories of multiples, it appears that new personalities *develop* in response to events in the subject's life, and that their development is an adaptive technique for handling trauma, one which perhaps only hypnotically endowed individuals are capable of utilizing (see Bliss, 1986; Putnam, 1989; Ross, 1989). Of course, *how* additional self-aware personalities develop is still a mystery—perhaps the central mystery of MPD. But *when* they develop seems fairly clear. In any case, my argument against the CR-principle are rather limited in scope. Their main purpose is to show that the principle fails to *establish* the colonial, or even the nonunitary, view of the self. The problem with the principle (in all of its versions) is that it infers the existence of predissociative divisions of the self from the existence of postdissociative divisions. But that strategy was doomed from the start. To argue successfully for the predissociative complexity of the self, one must show that it is required to handle *nondissociative* phenomena. Otherwise, one can always maintain—quite plausibly—that alternate personalities and the like are simply products (rather than prerequisites) of dissociation.

VI. Postscript: Commissurotomy

Certain phenomena associated with brain bisection are nearly as striking as those found in cases of multiple personality, and they likewise suggest a profound form of mental disunity. Moreover, as in the case of dramatic dissociative phenomena, many researchers interpret the behavior of split-brain patients as demonstrating the existence, *prior to surgery*, of two distinct minds or selves, corresponding in this case to the two hemispheres of the brain. Of course, this position has been extremely influential, especially outside the academic community. Indeed, many seem to regard as dogma the idea that every person is a compound of two subsidiary selves, the left-brain self and the right-brain self. But, not surprisingly, it seems as if the inference leading to that conclusion rests on a tacit application of the CR-principle, and if so, it would be no more legitimate than it was in connection with MPD. Hence, a few remarks about this relatively common use of the CR-principle seem in order.

As the reader may realize, the apparently disunified behavior of split-brain patients occurs only under highly artificial or otherwise exceptional conditions. In the majority of everyday situations their behavior seems as unified as that of most ordinary, nondissociated persons. Nevertheless, on rare occasions in day-to-day life, a patient's left and right hands might seem to exhibit distinct and conflicting tendencies. For example, the patient might embrace and push away his wife with two different hands, or select different clothes to wear for the day.

However, these spontaneous and quite uncommon displays of disunity are perhaps less impressive than others. In particular, under conditions in which input to the two hemispheres is carefully segregated, the subject will tend to behave in some *predictably* curious ways. For example, suppose that we show a subject, S, two words—say, "house boat," in such a way that the left visual field (going to the right hemisphere) contains only "house" and the right visual field (going to the left hemisphere) contains only "boat." If we ask S what he saw, he will respond verbally by saying that he saw "boat." Moreover, if we ask S what kind of boat it is, he will not necessarily say "house boat." Apparently, he is as likely to name some other sort of boat—say, rowboat or steamboat. But if we ask S to point with his left hand to a picture of what he saw from a display of several pictures (including pictures of a house, a boat, and a houseboat), he will probably point to the picture of a house. In general, when S's response is controlled by his left hemisphere, he will indicate that he was aware of "boat" and not "house." Similarly, responses controlled by the right hemisphere will indicate that he was aware of "house" and not "boat." One can perhaps understand, then, why some conclude that a split-brain patient has two minds, or that he is two persons (even if one disagrees with that position).

It is not my intention, however, to discuss the topic of commissurotomy in detail. Although it is unquestionably very interesting, to do it justice we would have to address numerous complex issues that would carry us quite far afield. I also do not wish to consider whether or in what respect we might sensibly regard a human being as more than one person, or whether the split-brain patient has two minds (see Braude, in press, for a discussion of these issues). Instead, I want merely to examine the claim that

even in the normal, cerebrally intact human being there must be two persons, though before the era of commissurotomy experiments we had no way of knowing this. (Puccetti, 1973, p. 351)

And even then, I wish only to make a rather limited point—namely, that this inference seems to rest on the fallacious CR-principle.

From our foregoing examination of the CR-principle, it should be clear by now that the apparent disunities exhibited by split-brain patients shows *at most* that a person *can be made to have* two minds, or that a person can be made to be two persons. Puccetti, however, in his influential paper (1973), seems quite oblivious to this. He says it is a mystery how brain bisection could *create* two minds when there was only one before. The reason, he claims, is that we would then have to choose *which* of the postoperative minds is new. Hence (he argues), there must have been two minds all along.

But this argument is clearly unconvincing. Assuming it makes sense to attribute two minds to one person, why *not* say that both postoperative minds are new? Analogously, in cell division (or in slicing a flatworm), one gets two new cells (or worms), *neither* of which existed as such before. There is simply no problem of having to decide which of the two worms (or cells) is new. Puccetti quite obviously commits the same error as those who argued from the complexity of the postdissociative self to the complexity of the predissociative self. Indeed, the trauma of surgery is the clear analogue of the trauma leading to the development of alternate personalities. To show that cerebrally intact individuals have two minds, one must argue that two minds are required to explain the apparent disunities of normal mental phenomena. Otherwise, it will always be more plausible to maintain that commissurotomy *causes* split-brain patients to have two minds.

References

Beahrs, J. O. (1983). "Co-Consciousness: A Common Denominator in Hypnosis, Multiple Personality, and Normalcy." *American Journal of Clinical Hypnosis* 26: 100–13.

Binet, A. (1896). *Alterations of Personality*. New York: D. Appleton & Co.

Bliss. E. L. (1986). *Multiple Personality, Allied Disorders, and Hypnosis*. New York & Oxford: Oxford University Press.

Braude, S. E. (ed.) (1980). Selected Poems of Patience Worth. In *New Directions in Prose and Poetry 40*. New York: New Directions Press.

Braude, S. E. (1986). *The Limits of Influence: Psychokinesis and the Philosophy of Science*. London & New York: Routledge & Kegan Paul.

Braude, S. E. (in press). *First-Person Plural: Multiple Personality and the Philosophy of Mind*. London & New York: Routledge.

Crabtree, A. (1985b). "Mesmerism, Divided Consciousness, and Multiple Personality." In N. M. Schott (ed.), *Franz Anton Mesmer und die Geschichte des Mesmerismus*. Stuttgart: Franz Steiner: 133–43.

Heil, J. (1983). *Perception and Cognition*. Berkeley & Los Angeles: University of California Press.

Hendrickson, K. M., McCarty, T., and Goodwin, J. M. (1989). "Edgar Allen Poe and the Animal Alters." Paper presented at Sixth International Conference on Multiple Personality/ Dissociative States. Chicago, October, 1989.

Hilgard, E. R. (1986). *Divided Consciousness: Multiple Controls in Human Thought and Action* (expanded edition). New York: Wiley-Interscience.

Laurence, J-R and Perry, C. (1988). *Hypnosis, Will, and Memory: A Psycholegal History*. New York & London: The Guilford Press.

Litvag, I. (1972). *Singer in the Shadows*. New York: Macmillan.

McDougall, W. (1938). "The Relation Between Dissociation and Repression." *British Journal of Medical Psychology* 17: 141–57.

Myers, F. W. H. (1903). *Human Personality and its Survival of Bodily Death*. London: Longmans, Green, and Co.

Prince, W. F. (1927/1964). *The Case of Patience Worth*. New Hyde Park, N.Y.: University Books.

Puccetti, R. (1973). "Brain Bisection and Personal Identity." *British Journal for the Philosophy of Science* 24: 339–55.

Putnam, F. W. (1989). *Diagnosis and Treatment of Multiple Personality Disorder*. New York: Guilford.

Ribot, T. (1887). *Diseases of Personality*. New York: Fitzgerald.

Ross, C. A. (1989). *Multiple Personality Disorder: Diagnosis, Clinical Features, and Treatment*. New York: Wiley.

Smith, S. G. (1989). "Multiple Personality Disorder with Human and Non-Human Subpersonality Components." *Dissociation* 2: 52–57.

Watkins, J. G. and Watkins, H. H. (1979–80). "Ego States and Hidden Observers." *Journal of Altered States of Consciousness* 5: 3–18.

11

NICHOLAS HUMPHREY AND DANIEL C. DENNETT
Speaking for Ourselves: An Assessment of Multiple Personality Disorder

Thus play I in one person many people, and none contented. —*Richard II*

In the early 1960s when the laws of England allowed nudity on stage only if the actor did not move, a tent at the Midsummer Fair in Cambridge offered an interesting display. "The one and only Chameleon Lady," the poster read, "becomes Great Women in History." The inside of the tent was dark. "Florence Nightingale!" the showman bellowed, and the lights came up on a naked woman, motionless as marble, holding up a lamp. The audience cheered. The lights went down. There was a moment's shuffling on the stage. "Joan of Arc!," and here she was, lit from a different angle, leaning on a sword. "Good Queen Bess!," and now she had on a red wig and was carrying an orb and scepter. "But it's the same *person*," said a know-all schoolboy.

Imagine now, thirty years later, a commercial for an IBM computer. A poster on a tent announces. "The one and only IBM PC becomes Great Information Processors of History." The

tent is dark. "WordStar!" shouts the showman, and the lights come up on a desktop computer, displaying a characteristic menu of commands. The lights go down. There is the sound of changing disks. "Paintbrush!" and here is the computer displaying a different menu. "Now, what you've all been waiting for, Lotus 123!" "But it's just a different *program*," says the schoolboy.

Somewhere between these two scenarios lies the phenomenon of *multiple personality* in human beings. And somewhere between these two over-easy assessments of it lie we. One of us (NH) is a theoretical psychologist, the other (DCD) is a philosopher, both with a long-standing interest in the nature of personhood and of the self. We have had the opportunity during the past year to meet several "multiples," to talk with their therapists, and to savor the world from which they come. We give here an outsider's inside view.

We had been at the conference on Multiple Personality Disorder for two full days before someone made the inevitable joke: "The problem with those who don't believe in MPD is they've got Single Personality Disorder." In the mirror world that we had entered, almost no one laughed. The occasion was the Fifth International Conference on Multiple Personality/Dissociative States in Chicago last October, attended by upwards of five hundred psycho-

Reprinted by permission from *Raritan: A Quarterly Review*, Vol. 9, No. 1 (Summer 1989). Copyright © 1989 by *Raritan*, 165 College Ave., New Brunswick, NJ, 08903.

therapists and a large but unquantifiable number of former patients.[1]

The Movement or the Cause (as it was called) of MPD has been undergoing an exponential growth: 200 cases of multiplicity reported up till 1980, 1,000 known to be in treatment by 1984, 4,000 now. Women outnumber men by at least four to one, and there is reason to believe that the vast majority—perhaps 95 percent—have been sexually or physically abused as children. We heard it said there are currently more than 25,000 multiples in North America.[2]

The accolade of "official diagnosis" was granted in 1980, with an entry in the clinician's handbook, *DSM-III*:

Multiple Personality. 1. The existence within an individual of two or more distinct personalities, each of which is dominant at a particular time. 2. The personality that is dominant at any particular time determines the individual's behavior. 3. Each individual personality is complex and integrated with its own unique behavior patterns and social relationships.[3]

Typically there is said to exist a "host" personality, and several alternative personalities or "alters." Usually, though not always, these personalities call themselves by different names. They may talk with different accents, dress by choice in different clothes, frequent different locales.

None of the personalities is emotionally well-rounded. The host is often emotionally flat, and different alters express exaggerated moods: anger, nurturance, childishness, sexiness. Because of their different affective competence, it falls to various alters to handle different social situations. Thus one may come out for lovemaking, another for playing with the kids, another for picking a fight, and so on.

The host personality is on stage most of the time, but the alters cut in and displace the host when for one reason or another the host cannot cope. The host is usually amnesic for those episodes when an alter is in charge; hence the host is likely to have blank spots or missing time. Although general knowledge is shared between them, particular memories are not. The life experience of each alter is formed primarily by the episodes when she or he is in control. Over time, and many episodes, this experience is aggregated into a discordant view of who he or she is—and hence a separate sense of self.

The number of alters varies greatly between patients, from just one (dual personality), to several dozen. In the early literature most patients were reported to have two or three, but there has been a steady increase, with a recent survey suggesting the median number is eleven. When the family has grown this large, one or more of the alters is likely to claim to be of different gender.

Such at least is how we first heard multiplicity described to us. It was not, however, until we were exposed to particular case histories, that we ourselves began to have any feeling for the human texture of the syndrome or for the analysis being put on it by MPD professionals. Each case must be, of course, unique. But it is clear that common themes are beginning to emerge and that, based on their pooled experience, therapists are beginning to think in terms of a "typical case history." The case that fol-

[1]The International Society for the study of Multiple Personality and Dissociation (2506 Gross Point Road, Evanston, IL 60201) now has over a thousand members. The proceedings of the 1988 Chicago meeting are published in Bennett G. Braun, ed., *Dissociative Disorders: 1988*, Dissociative Disorders Program, Department of Psychiatry, Rush University, 1720 West Polk Street, Chicago, IL 60612.

[2]For the statistics cited on MPD, see F. W. Putnam, et al. "The clinical phenomenology of multiple personality disorder: Review of 100 recent cases," *Journal of Clinical Psychiatry*, 47, 285–93 (1986).

[3]DMS-III is *Diagnostic and Statistical Manual III*, Washington, DC: American Psychiatric Association, 1980.

lows, although in part a reconstruction, is true to type (and life).[4]

Mary, in her early thirties, has been suffering from depression, confusional states, and lapses of memory. During the last few years she has been in and out of the hospital, where she has been diagnosed variously as schizophrenic, borderline, and manic depressive. Failing to respond to any kind of drug treatment, she has also been suspected of malingering. She ends up eventually in the hands of Doctor R, who specializes in treating dissociative disorders. More trusting of him than of previous doctors, Mary comes out with the following telltale information.

Mary's father died when she was two years old, and her mother almost immediately remarried. Her stepfather, she says, was kind to her, although "he sometimes went too far." Through childhood she suffered from sick headaches. She had a poor appetite and she remembers frequently being punished for not finishing her food. Her teenage years were stormy, with dramatic swings in mood. She vaguely recalls being suspended from her high

school for a misdemeanor, but her memory for her school years is patchy. In describing them she occasionally resorts—without notice—to the third person ("She did this, That happened to her"), or sometimes the first person plural ("We [Mary] went to Grandma's"). She is well informed in many areas, is artistically creative, and can play the guitar; but when asked where she learned it, she says she does not know and deflects attention to something else. She agrees that she is "absentminded"—"but aren't we all?": for example, she might find there are clothes in her closet that she can't remember buying, or she might find she has sent her niece two birthday cards. She claims to have strong moral values; but other people, she admits, call her a hypocrite and liar. She keeps a diary—"to keep up," she says, "with where we're at."

Dr. R, who already has four multiples in treatment, is beginning to recognize a pattern. When, some months into treatment, he sees Mary's diary and observes that the handwriting varies from one entry to the next, as if written by several different people, he decides (in his own words) "to go for gold." With Mary's agreement, he suggests they should undertake an exploratory session of hypnosis. He puts her into a light trance and requests that the "part of Mary that hasn't yet come forward" should make herself known. A sea change occurs in the woman in front of him. Mary, until then a model of decorum, throws him a flirtatious smile. "Hi, Doctor," she says, "I'm Sally. Mary's a wimp. She thinks she knows it all, but I can tell you . . ."

But Sally does not tell him much, at least not yet. In subsequent sessions (conducted now without hypnosis) Sally comes and goes, almost as if she were playing games with Dr. R. She allows him glimpses of what she calls the "happy hours," and hints at having a separate and exotic history unknown to Mary. But then with a toss of the head she slips away—leaving Mary, apparently no party to the foregoing conversation, to explain where *she* has been.

Now Dr. R starts seeing his patient twice a

---

[4]Among the recent autobiographical accounts of cases, by far the best written is Sylvia Fraser, *My Father's House*, New York: Ticknor and Fields, 1988. Many short case histories have been published in the clinical literature. J. Damgaard, S. Van Benschaten, and J. Fagan, "An updated bibliography of literature pertaining to multiple personality," *Psychological Reports*, 57, 131–37 (1985), is a comprehensive recent bibliography. See also the special issue on MPD of *Psychiatric Clinics of North America*, 7, March 1984, ed. Bennett G. Braun. Other useful entry points into the vast literature: Philip Coons, "Treatment progress in 20 patients with multiple personality disorder," *Journal of Nervous and Mental Disease*, 174, 715–21 (1986); Richard Kluft, "The dissociative disorders," in John A. Talbott, Robert E. Hales, and Stuart C. Yudofsky, eds., *The American Psychiatric Press Textbook of Psychiatry*, Washington, DC: American Psychiatric Press, 1988, pp. 557–85; and, for a more skeptical treatment, Thomas A. Fahy, "The diagnosis of multiple personality disorder: A critical review," *British Journal of Psychiatry*, 153, 509–606 (1988).

week, for sessions that are several hours in length. In the course of the next year he uncovers the existence not just of Sally but of a whole family of alter personalities, each with its own characteristic style. "Sally" is coquettish, "Hatey" is angry, "Peggy" is young and malleable. Each has a story to tell about the times when she is "out in front"; and each has her own set of special memories. While each of the alters claims to know most of what goes on in Mary's life, Mary herself denies anything but hearsay knowledge of *their* roles.

To begin with, the changeover from one personality to another is unpredictable and apparently spontaneous. The only clue that a switch is imminent is a sudden look of vacancy, marked perhaps by Mary's rubbing her brow, or covering her eyes with her hand (as if in momentary pain). But as their confidence grows, it becomes easier for Dr. R to summon different alters "on demand."

Dr. R's goal for Mary now becomes that of "integration"—a fusing of the different personalities into one self. To achieve this he has not only to acquaint the different alters with each other, but also to probe the origins of the disorder. Thus he presses slowly for more information about the circumstances that led to Mary's "splitting." Piecing together the evidence from every side, he arrives at—or is forced to—a version of events that he has already partly guessed. This is the story that Mary and the others eventually agree upon.

When Mary was four years old, her stepfather started to take her into his bed. He gave her the pet name Sandra, and told her that "Daddy-love" was to be Sandra's and his little secret. He caressed her and asked for her caresses. He ejaculated against her tummy. He did it in her bottom and her mouth. Sometimes Mary tried to please him. Sometimes she lay still like a doll. Sometimes she was sick and cried that she could take no more. One time she said that she would tell—but the man hit her and said that both of them would go to prison. Eventually, when the pain, dirt, and disgrace became too much to

bear, Mary simply "left it all behind": while the man abused her, she *dissociated* and took off to another world. She left—and left Sandra in her place.

What happened next is, Dr. R insists, no more than speculation. But he pictures the development as follows. During the next few crucial years—those years when a child typically puts down roots into the fabric of human society, and develops a unitary sense of "I" and "Me" —Mary was able to function quite effectively. Protected from all knowledge of the horror, she had a comprehensible history, comprehensible feelings, and comprehensible relationships with members of her family. The "Mary-person" that she was becoming was one person with one story. Mary's gain was, however, Sandra's loss. For Sandra *knew*. And this knowledge, in the early years, was crippling. Try as she might, there was no single story that she could tell that would embrace her contradictory experiences, no one "Sandra-person" for her to become. So Sandra, in a state of inchoateness, retreated to the shadows, while Mary—except for "Daddy-love"—stayed out front.

Yet if Mary could split, then so could Sandra. And such, it seems, is what occurred. Unable to make it *all* make sense, Sandra made sense from the pieces—not consciously and deliberately, of course, but with the cunning of unconscious design: she parceled out the different aspects of her abuse-experience, and assigned each aspect to a different self (grafting, as it were, each set of memories as a side-branch to the existing stock she shared with Mary). Thus her experience of liking to please Daddy gave rise to what became the Sally-self. Her experience of the pain and anger gave rise to Hatey. And her experience of playing at being a doll gave rise to Peggy.

Now these descendants of the original Sandra could, with relative safety, come out into the open. And before long, opportunities arose for them to try their newfound strength in settings other than that of the original abuse. When Mary lost her temper with her mother, Hatey could chip in to do the screaming. When Mary was kissed by a boy in the playground, Sally could kiss him back. Everyone could do what they were "good at," and Mary's own life was made that much simpler. This pattern of what might be termed "the division of emotional labor" or "self-replacement therapy" proved not only to be viable, but to be rewarding all around.

Subsequently this became the habitual way of life. Over time each member of the family progressively built up her own separate store of memories, competencies, idiosyncrasies, and social styles. But they were living in a branching house of cards. During her teenage years, Mary's varying moods and waywardness could be passed off as "adolescent rebelliousness." But in her late twenties, her true fragility began to show—and she lapsed into confusion and depression.

Although we have told this story in what amounts to cartoon form, we have no doubts that cases like Mary's are authentic. Or, rather, we should say we have no doubts that there are real people and real doctors to whom this case history could very well apply. Yet, like many others who have taken a skeptical position about MPD, we ourselves have reservations about what such a case history in fact amounts to. How could anyone know for sure the events were as described? Is there independent confirmation that Mary was abused? Does her story match with what other people say about her? How do we know the whole thing is not just a hysterical invention? To what extent did the doctor lead her on? What transpired during the sessions of hypnosis? And, anyway, what does it all really mean? What should we make of Dr. R's interpretation? Is it really possible for a single human being to have several different "selves"?

The last problem—that of providing a philosophically and scientifically acceptable theory of MPD—is the one we have a special interest in addressing. You might think, however, we

ought to start with a discussion of the "factual evidence": for why discuss the theoretical basis of something that has not yet been proven to exist? Our answer is that unless and until MPD can be shown to be theoretically possible—to be neither a logical nor a scientific contradiction —any discussion of the evidence is likely to be compromised by a priori disbelief. As Hume remarked in his essay "Of Miracles": "It is a general maxim worthy of our attention . . . that no testimony is sufficient to establish a miracle unless the testimony be of such a kind that its falsehood would be more miraculous than the fact which it endeavors to establish."[5] In the history of science there have been many occasions in which seemingly miraculous phenomena were not and perhaps could not be taken seriously until some form of theoretical permission for them had been devised. The claims of acupuncture, for example, were assumed by Western scientists to make no sense —and hence be false—until the discovery of endogenous opiates paved the way for a scientific explanation. We shall, we hope, be in a better position to assess the testimony concerning MPD—that is, to be both critical and generous—if we can first make a case that the phenomenon is not only possible but even (in certain circumstances) plausible.

Many people who find it convenient or compelling to talk about the "self" would prefer not to be asked the emperor's-new-clothes question: just what, exactly, is a "self"? When confronted by an issue that seems embarrassingly metaphysical, it is tempting to temporize and wave one's hands: "It's not a thing, exactly, but more a sort of, well, a *concept* or an *organizing principle* or . . . " This will not do. And yet what will?

Two extreme views can be and have been

[5]*An Inquiry Concerning Human Understanding* (1758), section 10 (page 123 in Bobbs Merrill ed., 1973).

taken. Ask a layman what he thinks a self is, and his unreflecting answer will probably be that a person's self is indeed some kind of real *thing*: a ghostly supervisor who lives inside his head, the thinker of his thoughts, the repository of his memories, the holder of his values, his conscious inner "I." Although he might be unlikely these days to use the term "soul," it would be very much the age-old conception of the soul that he would have in mind. A self (or soul) is an existent entity with executive powers over the body and its own enduring qualities. Let's call this realist picture of the self, the idea of a "proper-self."

Contrast it, however, with the revisionist picture of the self which has become popular among certain psychoanalysts and philosophers of mind. On this view, selves are not things at all but instead are explanatory fictions. Nobody really has a soul-like agency inside them: we just find it useful to imagine the existence of this conscious inner "I" when we try to account for their behavior (and, in our own case, our private stream of consciousness). We might say indeed that the self is rather like the "center of narrative gravity" of a set of biographical events and tendencies; but, as with a center of physical gravity, there's really no such *thing* (with mass or shape or color).[6] Let's call this nonrealist picture of the self, the idea of a "fictive-self."

Now maybe, one might think, it is just a matter of the level of description: the plain man's proper-self corresponds to the intrinsic reality, while the philosopher's fictive-selves correspond to people's (necessarily inadequate) attempts to grasp that intrinsic reality. So, for example, there is indeed a proper-Nicholas-

Humphrey-self that actually resides inside one of the authors of this essay, and alongside it there are the various fictive-Humphrey-selves that he and his acquaintances have reconstructed: Humphrey as seen by Humphrey, Humphrey as seen by Dennett, Humphrey as seen by Humphrey's mother, and so on. This suggestion, however, would miss the point of the revisionist critique. The revisionist case is that, to repeat, there really is no proper-self: none of the fictive-Humphrey-selves — including Humphrey's own firsthand version — corresponds to anything that actually exists in Humphrey's head.

At first sight this may not seem reasonable. Granted that whatever *is* inside the head might be difficult to observe, and granted also that it might be a mistake to talk about a "ghostly supervisor," nonetheless there surely has to be some kind of a supervisor in there: a supervisory brain program, a central controller, or whatever. How else could anybody function — as most people clearly do function — as a purposeful and relatively well integrated agent?

The answer that is emerging from both biology and Artificial Intelligence is that complex systems can in fact function in what seems to be a thoroughly "purposeful and integrated" way simply by having lots of subsystems doing their own thing without any central supervision. Indeed most systems on earth that appear to have central controllers (and are usefully described as having them) do not. The behavior of a termite colony provides a wonderful example. The colony as a whole builds elaborate mounds, gets to know its territory, organizes foraging expeditions, sends out raiding parties against other colonies, and so on. The group cohesion and coordination is so remarkable that hardheaded observers have been led to postulate the existence of a colony's "group soul" (vide Marais's "The Soul of the White Ant"). Yet in fact all this group wisdom results from nothing other than myriads of individual termites, specialized as several different castes, going about their indi-

---

[6]See Daniel C. Dennett, "Why we are all novelists," *Times Literary Supplement*, Sept. 16–22, 1988, pp. 1016, 2029–29, also forthcoming under its original title, "The self as the center of narrative gravity," in F. Kessel, P. Cole, D. Johnson, eds., *Self and Consciousness: Multiple Perspectives*, Hillsdale, NJ: Erbaum (in press).

vidual business—influenced by each other, but quite uninfluenced by any master plan.

Then is the argument between the realists and the revisionists being won hands down by the revisionists? No, not completely. Something (some thing?) is missing here. But the question of what the "missing something" is, is being hotly debated by cognitive scientists in terms that have become increasingly abstruse. Fortunately we can avoid—maybe even leapfrog—much of the technical discussion by the use of an illustrative metaphor (reminiscent of Plato's *Republic*, but put to quite a different use).

Consider the United States of America. At the fictive level there is surely nothing wrong with personifying the USA and talking about it (rather like the termite colony) as if it had an inner self. The USA has memories, feelings, likes and dislikes, hopes, talents, and so on. It hates communism, is haunted by the memory of Vietnam, is scientifically creative, socially clumsy, somewhat given to self-righteousness, rather sentimental. But does that mean (here is the revisionist speaking) there is one central agency inside the USA which embodies all those qualities? Of course not. There is, as it happens, a specific area of the country where much of it comes together. But go to Washington and ask to speak to Mr. American Self, and you'd find there was nobody home: instead you'd find a lot of different agencies (the Defense Department, the Treasury, the courts, the Library of Congress, the National Science Foundation, etc.) operating in relative independence of each other.

To be sure (and now it is the realist speaking), there is no such thing as Mr. American Self, but as a matter of fact there is in every country on earth a Head of State: a president, queen, chancellor, or some such figure. The Head of State may actually be nonexecutive; certainly he does not himself enact all the subsidiary roles (the US president does not bear arms, sit in the courts, play baseball, or travel to the moon). But nevertheless he is expected at the very least to take an

active interest in all these national pursuits. The president is meant to appreciate better than anyone the "State of the Union." He is meant to represent different parts of the nation to each other and to inculcate a common value system. Moreover—and this is most important—he is the spokesman when it comes to dealing with other nation states.

That is not to say that a nation, lacking such a figure, would cease to function day to day. But it is to say that in the longer term it may function much better if it does have one. Indeed a good case can be made that nations, unlike termite colonies, require this kind of leader as a condition of their political survival—especially given the complexity of international affairs.

The drift of this analogy is obvious. In short, a human being too may need an inner unifying figure—especially given the complexities of human social life. Consider, for example, the living body known as Daniel Dennett. If we were to look around inside his brain for a Chief Executive Module, with all the various mental properties we attribute to Dennett himself, we would be disappointed. Nonetheless, were we to interact with Dennett on a social plane, both we and he would soon find it essential to recognize someone—some figure—as his spokesman and indeed his leader. Thus we come back full circle, though a little lower down, to the idea of a proper-self: not a ghostly supervisor, but something more like a "Head of Mind" with a real, if limited, causal role to play in representing the person to himself and to the world.

If this is accepted (as we think it should be), we can turn to the vexed question of self-development or self-establishment. Here the Head of State analogy may seem at first less helpful. For one thing, in the USA at least, the president is democratically elected by the population. For another, the candidates for the presidency are preformed entities, already waiting in the wings.

Yet is this really so? It could equally be argued that the presidential candidates, rather than being preformed, are actually brought into being—through a narrative dialectical process—by the very population to which they offer their services as president. Thus the population (or the news media) first try out various fictive versions of what they think their "ideal president" should be, and *then* the candidates adapt themselves as best they can to fill the bill. To the extent that there is more than one dominant fiction about "what it means to be American," different candidates mold themselves in different ways. But in the end only one can be elected—and he will, of course, claim to speak for the whole nation.

In very much a parallel way, we suggest, a human being first creates—unconsciously—one or more ideal fictive-selves and then elects the best supported of these into office as her Head of Mind. A significant difference in the human case, however, is that there is likely to be considerably more outside influence. Parents, friends, and even enemies may all contribute to the image of "what it means to be me," as well as—and maybe over and above—the internal news media. Daddy, for example, might lean on the growing child to impose an *invasive* fictive-self.

Thus a human being does not start out as single or as multiple—she starts out without any Head of Mind at all. In the normal course of development, she slowly gets acquainted with the various possibilities of selfhood that "make sense," partly through her own observation, partly through outside influence. In most cases a majority view emerges, strongly favoring one version of "the real me," and it is that version which is installed as her elected Head of Mind. But in some cases the competing fictive-selves are so equally balanced, or different constituencies within her are so unwilling to accept the result of the election, that constitutional chaos reigns—and there are snap elections (or coups d'état) all the time.

Could a model inspired by (underlying, rendering honest) this analogy account for the memory blackouts, differences in style, and other symptomatology of MPD? Certainly the analogy provides a wealth of detail suggesting so. Once in office a new Head of State typically downplays certain 'unfortunate" aspects of his nation's history (especially those associated with the rival Head of State who immediately preceded him). Moreover, he himself, by standing for particular national values, affects the course of future history by encouraging the expression of those values by the population (and so, by a kind of feedback, confirming his own role).

Let's go back to the case of Mary. As a result of her experience of abuse, she (the whole, disorganized, conglomeration of parts) came to have several alternative pictures of the real Mary, each championed by different constituencies within her. So incompatible were these pictures, yet so strong were the electoral forces, that there could be no lasting agreement on who should represent her. For a time the Mary constituency got its way, overriding the Sandra constituency. But later the Sandra forces subdivided, to yield Sally, Haley, Peggy; and when the opportunities arose, these reformed forces began to win electoral battles. She became thus constitutionally unstable, with no permanent solution to the question of "who I really am." Each new (temporarily elected) Head of Mind emphasized different aspects of her experience and blocked off others; and each brought out exaggerated character traits.

We have talked here in metaphors. But translations into the terms of current cognitive science would not be difficult to formulate. First, what sense can be given to the notion of a Head of Mind? The analogy with a spokesman may not be far off the literal truth. The language-producing systems of the brain have to get their instructions from somewhere, and the very demands of pragmatics and grammar would conspire to confer something like Head of Mind authority on whatever subsystem currently controls their input. E. M. Forster once remarked, "How can I tell what I think until I see what I say?" The four *I*'s in this sentence are meant to refer to the same thing. But this grammatical tradition may depend—and may always have depended—on the fact that the thought expressed in Forster's question is quite literally self-confirming: what "I" (my self) thinks *is* what "I" (my language apparatus) says.

There can, however, be no guarantee that either the speaker or anyone else who hears him over an extended period will settle on there being just a single "I." Suppose, at different times, different subsystems within the brain produce "clusters" of speech that simply cannot easily be interpreted as the output of a single self. Then—as a Bible scholar may discover when working on the authorship of what is putatively a single-authored text—it may turn out that the clusters make best sense when attributed to different selves.

How about the selective amnesia shown by different Heads of Mind? To readers who have even a passing knowledge of computer information processing, the idea of mutually inaccessible "directories" of stored information will already be familiar. In cognitive psychology, new discoveries about state-dependent learning and other evidence of modularization in the brain have led people to recognize that failure of access between different subsystems is the norm rather than the exception. Indeed the old Cartesian picture of the mind "transparent to itself" now appears to be rarely if ever achievable (or even desirable) in practice. In this context the out-of-touchness of different selves no longer looks so startling.

What could be the basis for the different "value systems" associated with rival Heads of Mind? At another level of analysis, psycho-pharmacological evidence suggests that the characteristic emotional style of different personalities could correspond to the brain-wide activation or inhibition of neural pathways that rely on different neurotransmitter chemicals. Thus the phlegmatic style of Mary's host per-

sonality could be associated with low norepinephrine levels, the shift to the carnal style of Sally with high norepinephrine, and the out-of-control Hatey with low dopamine.

Even the idea of an "election" of the current Head of Mind is not implausible. Events very like elections take place in the brain all the time —whenever coherent patterns of activity compete for control of the same network. Consider what happens, for example, when the visual system receives two conflicting images at the two eyes. First there is an attempt at fusion; but if this proves to be unstable, "binocular rivalry" results, with the input from one eye completely taking over while the other is suppressed. Thus we already have, at the level of visual neurophysiology, clear evidence of the mind's general preference for single-mindedness over completeness.

These ideas about the nature of selves are by no means altogether new. C. S. Peirce, for instance, expressed a similar vision in 1905:

> A person is not absolutely an individual. His thoughts are what he is "saying to himself," that is, is saying to that other self that is just coming into life in the flow of time.

From within the psychoanalytic tradition. Heinz Kohut wrote (in "On Courage"):

> I feel that a formulation which puts the *self* into the center of the personality as the initiator of all actions and as the recipient of all impressions exacts too high a price. . . . If we instead put our trust in empirical observation . . . we will see different selves, each of them a lasting psychological configuration, . . . fighting for ascendancy, one blocking out the other, forming compromises with each other, and acting inconsistently with each other at the same time. In general, we will witness what appears to be an uneasy victory of one self over all others.

Robert Jay Lifton has defined the self as the "inclusive symbol of one's own organism"; and in his discussions of what he calls "proteanism" (an endemic form of multiplicity in modern human beings) and "doubling" (as in the double-life led by Nazi doctors), he has stressed the struggle that all human beings have to keep their rival self-symbols in symbiotic harmony.

These ideas have, however, been formulated without reference to the newly gathered evidence on MPD. Moreover, the emphasis of almost all the earlier work has been on the underlying continuity of human psychic structure: a single stream of consciousness manifesting itself in now this, now that configuration. Nothing in the writings of Kohut or of Lifton would have prepared us for the radical discontinuity of consciousness that—if it really exists—is manifest in the case of a multiple like Mary.

Which brings us to the question that has been left hanging all along: does "real MPD" exist? We hope that, in the light of the preceding discussion, we shall be able to come closer to an answer. What would it mean for MPD to be "real"? We suggest that, if the model we have outlined is anything like right, it would mean at least the following:

1. The subject will have, at different times, different "spokesmen," corresponding to separate Heads of Mind. Both objectively and subjectively, this will be tantamount to having different "selves" because the access each such spokesman will have to the memories, attitudes, and thoughts of other spokesmen will be, in general, as indirect and intermittent as the access one human being can have to the mind of another.

2. Each self, when present, will claim to have conscious control over the subject's behavior. That is, this self will consider the subject's current actions to be *her* actions, experiences to be *her* experiences, memories to be *her* memories, and so on. (At times the self out front may be conscious of the existence of other selves—she may even hear them talking in the background—but she will not be conscious *with* them.)

3. Each self will be convinced—as it were by "her own rhetoric"—about her own integrity and personal importance.

4. This self-rhetoric will be convincing not only to the subject but also (other things being equal) to other people with whom she interacts.

5. Different selves will be interestingly different. That is, each will adopt a distinctive style of presentation, which very likely will be associated with differences in physiology. To which we would add—not necessarily as a criterion of "real multiplicity" but nonetheless as an important factual issue—that the "splitting" into separate selves will generally have occurred before the patient entered therapy.

Now, what are the facts about MPD? The first thing to say is that in *no* case do we *know* that all these criteria have been met. What we have to go on instead is a plethora of isolated stories, autobiographical accounts, clinical reports, police records, and just a few scientific studies. Out of those the following answers form.

Does the phenomenon exist?

There can be no doubt that what might be called a "candidate phenomenon" exists. There are literally thousands of people living today who, in the course of clinical investigation, have presented themselves as having several independent selves (or "spokesmen" for their minds). Such cases have been described in reputable scientific journals, recorded on film, shown on television, cross-examined in law courts. We ourselves have met with several of them and have even argued with these separate selves about why we should believe the stories that they tell us. Skeptics may still choose to doubt what the phenomenon amounts to, but they should no longer doubt that it occurs.

Do multiples themselves believe in what they are saying?

Certainly they seem to do so. In the clinic, at

least, different selves stoutly insist on their own integrity and resist any suggestion that they might be "play-acting" (a suggestion which, admittedly, most therapists avoid). The impression "the patient" makes is not of someone who is acting, but rather of a troubled individual who is doing her best—in what can only be described as difficult circumstances—to make sense of what she takes to be the facts of her experience.

As persuasive as anything is the apparently genuine puzzlement that patients show when confronted by facts they can't make sense of. Thus one woman told us of how, when, as frequently happened, she came home and found her neat living room all messed up, she suspected that other people must have been playing tricks on her. A young man described how he found himself being laughed at by his friends for having been seen around gay bars: he tried over several months to grow a beard to prove his manhood, but as soon as the stubble began to sprout, someone—he did not know who—shaved it off. A woman discovered that money was being mysteriously drawn from her bank account, and told the police that she was being impersonated. We have heard of a case of a highly skeptical patient who refused to accept her therapist's diagnosis until they both learned that one of her alters was seeing another therapist.

That is not to say that such stories would always stand up to critical examination: examination, that is, by the standards of "normal human life." But this, it seems, is quite as much a problem for the patient as for anyone else. These people clearly know as well as anybody that there is *something* wrong with them and that their lives don't seem to run as smoothly as other people's. In fact it would be astonishing (and grounds for our suspicion) if they did not: for, to coin a phrase, they were not born yesterday, and they are generally too intelligent not to recognize that in some respects their experience is bizarre. We met a woman, Gina, with a male alter, Bruce, and asked Bruce the obvious "nor-

mal" question: when he goes to the bathroom, does he choose the Ladies or the Gents. He confessed that he goes to the Ladies—because "something went wrong with my anatomy" and "I turned out to be a male living in a woman's body."

For several years a multiple newsletter— S4OS (Speaking for Our Selves)—circulated, in which patients shared with each other their experiences and strategies. In September 1987 S4OS claimed 691 subscribers.

Do they succeed in persuading other people to believe in them?

We have no doubt that the therapist who diagnoses MPD is fully convinced that he is dealing with several different selves. But, from our standpoint, a more crucial issue is whether other people who are not already au fait with the diagnosis accept this way of looking at things. According to our analysis (or indeed any other we can think of), selves have a public as well as a private role to play: indeed, they exist primarily to handle social interactions. It would therefore be odd, to say the least, if some or all of a patient's selves were to be kept entirely secret from the world.

On this point the evidence is surprisingly patchy. True enough, in many cases the patient herself will—in the context of the therapeutic situation—tell stories of her encounters in the outside world. But what we need is evidence from a third source: a neutral source that is in no way linked to the context in which splitting is "expected" (as might still be the case with another doctor, or another patient, or even a television journalist). We need to know whether the picture of her multiple life that the therapist and patient have worked out together jibes with what other people have independently observed.

Prima facie, it sounds like the kind of evidence it would be easy to obtain by asking family, friends, workmates, or whomever. There is the problem, of course, that certain lines of enquiry are ruled out on ethical grounds, or because their pursuit would jeopardize the patient's ongoing therapy, or would simply involve an unjustifiable amount of time. Nonetheless, it is disappointing to discover how few such enquiries have been made.

Many multiple patients are married and have families; many have regular employment. Yet, again and again it seems that no one on the outside has in fact noticed anything peculiar — at least not *so* peculiar. Maybe, as several therapists explained to us, their patients are surprisingly good at "covering up" (secrecy, beginning in childhood, is part and parcel of the syndrome, and in any case the patient has probably learned to avoid putting herself or others on the spot). Maybe other people have detected something odd and dismissed it as nothing more than inconsistency or unreliability (after all, everyone has changing moods, most people are forgetful, and many people lie). Gina told us of how she started to make love to a man she met at an office party but grew bored with him and left — leaving "one of the kids" (another alter) cringing in her place. The man, she said, was quite upset. But no one has heard his side of the story.

To be sure, in many cases, perhaps even most, there is some form of postdiagnostic confirmation from outside: the husband who, when the diagnosis is explained to him, exclaims, "Now it all makes sense!", or the boyfriend who volunteers to the therapist tales of what it is like to be "jerked around" by the tag team alters of his partner. One patient's husband admitted to mixed emotions about the impending cure or integration of his wife: "I'll miss the little ones!" The problem with such retrospective evidence is, however, that the informant may simply be acceding to what might be termed a "diagnosis of convenience." It is probably the general rule that once multiplicity has been recognized in therapy, and the alters have been "given permission" to come out, there are gains to be had all round from adopting the patient's preferred style of presentation. When we ourselves were introduced to a patient who switched three times in the course of half an hour, we were

chastened to discover how easily we ourselves fell in with addressing her as if she were now a man, now a woman, now a child — a combination of good manners on our part and an anxiety not to drive the alter personality away (as Peter Pan said, "Every time someone says, 'I don't believe in fairies,' there is a fairy somewhere who falls down dead").

Any interaction with a patient involves cooperation and respect, which shade imperceptibly into collusion. The alternative might be surreptitious observation in extraclinical situations, but this would be as hard to justify as to execute. The result is that one is limited to encounters that — in our limited experience — have an inevitable séancelike quality to them. Therapists with whom we have talked are defensive on this issue. We have to say, however, that, so far as we can gather, evidence for the external social reality of MPD is weak.

Are there "real" differences between the different selves?

One therapist confided to us that, in his view, it was not uncommon for the different selves belonging to a single patient to be more or less identical, the only thing distinguishing them being their selective memories. More usually, however, the selves are described as being manifestly different in both mental and bodily character. The question is: Do such differences go beyond the range of "normal" acting out?

At the anecdotal level, the evidence is tantalizing. For example, a psychopharmacologist (whom we have reason to consider as hardheaded as they come) told us of how he discovered to his astonishment that a male patient, whose host personality could be sedated with five milligrams of Valium, had an alter personality who was apparently quite impervious to the drug: the alter remained as lively as ever when given a fifty-milligram intravenous dose (sufficient in most people to produce anaesthesia).

Any would-be objective investigator of MPD

is soon struck by the systematic elusiveness of the phenomena. Well-controlled scientific studies are few (and for obvious reasons difficult to do). Nonetheless, what data there are all go to show that multiple patients—in the context of the clinic—may indeed undergo profound psychophysiological changes when they change personality state. There is preliminary evidence, for example, of changes in handedness, voice patterns, evoked-response brain activity, and cerebral blood flow. When samples of the different handwritings of a multiple are mixed with samples by different hands, police handwriting experts have been unable to identify them. There are data to suggest differences in allergic reactions and thyroid functioning. Drug studies have shown differences in responsivity to alcohol and tranquilizers. Tests of memory have indicated genuine cross-personality amnesia for newly acquired information (while, interestingly enough, newly acquired motor skills are carried over).

When and how did the multiplicity come into being?

The assumption made by most people in the MPD movement—and which we so far have gone along with—is that the splitting into several selves (with all the sequelae we have been discussing) originates in early childhood. The therapist therefore brings to light a preexisting syndrome, and in no way is he or she responsible for creating MPD. But an alternative possibility of course exists, namely that the phenomenon—however genuine at the time that it is described—has been brought into being (and perhaps is being maintained) by the therapist himself.

We have hinted already at how little evidence there is that multiplicity has existed before the start of treatment. A lack of evidence that something exists is not evidence that it does not, and several papers at the Chicago meeting reported recently discovered cases of what seems to have

been incipient multiplicity in children.[7] Nonetheless, the suspicion must surely arise that MPD is an iatrogenic condition.[8]

Folie à deux between doctor and patient would be, in the annals of psychiatry, nothing new. It is generally recognized that the outbreak of "hysterical symptoms" in female patients at the end of the last century (including paralysis, anesthesia, and so on) was brought about by the overenthusiastic attention of doctors (such as Charcot) who succeeded in creating the symptoms they were looking for. In this regard, hypnosis, in particular, has always been a dangerous tool. The fact that in the diagnosis of multiplicity hypnosis is frequently (although not always) employed, the closeness of the therapist-patient relationship, and the intense interest shown by therapists in the "drama" of MPD, are clearly grounds for legitimate concern.

This concern is in fact one that senior members of the MPD movement openly share. At the Chicago conference a full day was given to discussing the problem of iatrogenesis. Speaker after speaker weighed in to warn their fellow therapists against "fishing" for multiplicity, misuse of hypnosis, "fascination" by the alter personalities, the "Pygmalion effect," uncontrolled countertransference, and what was bravely called "major league malpractice" (i.e., sexual intimacy with patients). Although the

[7] On incipient MPD in children, see David Mann and Jean Goodwin, "Obstacles to recognizing dissociative disorders in child and adolescent males"; Carole Snowden, "Where are all the childhood multiples? Identifying incipient multiple personality in children"; and Theresa K. Albini, "The unfolding of the psychotherapeutic process in a four year old patient with incipient multiple personality disorder."

[8] For a fascinating discussion of how individuals may mold themselves to fit "fashionable" categories, see Ian Hacking, "Making up people," in Thomas C. Heller, Morton Sosna, and David E. Wellbery, eds., *Reconstructing Individualism*, Stanford: Stanford University Press, 1986, pp. 222–36.

message was that there is no need to invent the syndrome since you'll recognize the real thing when you see it, it is clear that those who have been in the business for some time understand only too well how easy it is to be misleading and misled.

A patient presents herself with a history of, let's call it, "general muddle." She is worried by odd juxtapositions and gaps in her life, by signs that she has sometimes behaved in ways that seem strange to her; she is worried she's going mad. Under hypnosis the therapist suggests that it is not her, but some other part of her that is the cause of the trouble. And lo, some other part of her emerges. But since this *is* some other part, she requires—and hence acquires—another name. And since a person with a different name must be a different person, she requires—and hence acquires—another character. Easy, especially if the patient is the kind of person who is highly suggestible and readily dissociates, as is typical of those who have been subjected to abuse.[9]

Could something like this possibly be the background to almost every case of MPD? We defer to the best and most experienced therapists in saying that it could not. In some cases there seems to be no question that the alternate personality makes its debut in therapy as if already formed. We have seen a videotape of one case where, in the first and only session of hypnosis, a pathetic young woman, Bonny, underwent a remarkable transformation into a character, calling herself "Death," who shouted murderous threats against both Bonny and the hypnotist. Bonny had previously made frequent suicide attempts, of which she denied any knowledge. Bonny subsequently tried to kill another patient on the hospital ward and was discovered by a nurse lapping her victim's blood. It

would be difficult to write off Bonny/Death as the invention of an overeager therapist.

On the general run of cases, we can only withhold judgment, not just because we do not know the facts, but also because we are not sure a "judgmental" judgment is in order. Certainly we do not want to align ourselves with those who would jump to the conclusion that if MPD arises in the clinic rather than in a childhood situation it cannot be "real." The parallel with hysteria is worth pursuing. As Charcot himself demonstrated only too convincingly, a woman who feels no pain when a pin is stuck into her arm *feels no pain*, and calling her lack of reaction a "hysterical symptom" does not make it any the less remarkable. Likewise a woman who at the age of thirty is now living the life of several different selves *is now living the life of several different selves*; any doubts we might have about how she came to be that way should not blind us to the fact that such is now the way she is.

According to the model we proposed, no one starts off as either multiple or single. In every case there has to be some sort of external influence that tips the balance this way or that (or back again). Childhood may indeed be the most vulnerable phase; but it may also very well be that in certain people a state of incipient multiplicity persists much longer, not coming to fruition until later life.

The following story is instructive. A patient, Frances, who is now completely integrated, was telling us about the family of selves she used to live with, among whom she counted Rachel, Esther, Daniel, Sarah, and Rebecca. We were curious as to why a white Anglo-Saxon Protestant should have taken on these Hebrew names, and asked her where the names had come from. "That's simple," she said, "Dad used to play Nazis and Jews with me; but he wanted me to be an innocent victim, so every time he raped me he gave me a new Jewish name."

Here, it seems that (as with Mary) the abuser at the time of the abuse explicitly, even if unwittingly, suggested the personality structure of

[9]On suggestibility, see, for example, E. R. Hilgard's studies of the correlation between hypnotizability and early experience of physical punishment, *Personality and Hypnosis: A Study of Imaginative Involvement*, Chicago: University of Chicago Press, 1970.

MPD. But suppose that Frances had not had the "help" of her father in reaching this "solution." Suppose she had remained in a state of self-confusion, muddling through her first thirty years, until a sympathetic therapist provided her with a way out (and a way forward). Would Frances have been less of a multiple than she turned out to be? In our view, No.

There must be, of course, a world of difference between an abuser's and a therapist's intentions in suggesting that a person contains several separate selves. Nonetheless, the consequences for the structure of the patient/victim's mind would not be so dissimilar. "Patrogenic" and "iatrogenic" multiplicity could be—and in our view would be—equally *real*.

Forty years ago two early commentators, W. S. Taylor and M. F. Martin, wrote: "Apparently most ready to accept multiple personality are (a) persons who are very naive and (b) persons who have worked with cases or near cases."[10] The same is still largely true today. Indeed, the medical world remains in general hostile to—even contemptuous of—MPD. Why?

We have pointed to several of the reasons. The phenomenon is considered by many people to be scientifically or philosophically absurd. We think that is a mistake. It is considered to be unsupported by objective evidence. We think that is untrue. It is considered to be an iatrogenic folly. We think that, even where that's so, the syndrome is a real one nonetheless.

But there is another reason, which we cannot brush aside, and that is the cliquish, almost cultish character of those who currently espouse the cause of MPD. In a world where those who are not for MPD are against it, it is perhaps not surprising that "believers" have tended to close

ranks. Maybe it is not surprising either that at meetings like the one we attended in Chicago there is a certain amount of well-meaning exaggeration and one-upmanship. We were, however, not prepared for what, if it occurred in a church, would amount to "bearing witness."

"How many multiples have you got?" one therapist asks another over breakfast in Chicago, "I'm on my fifth." "Oh, I'm just a novice —two, so far." "You know Dr. Q—she's got fifteen in treatment, and I gather she's a multiple herself." At lunch: "I've got a patient whose eyes change color." "I've got one whose different personalities speak six different languages, none of which they could possibly have learned." "My patient Myra had her fallopian tubes tied, but when she switched to Katey she got pregnant." At supper: "Her parents got her to breed babies for human sacrifice; she was a surrogate mother three times before her eighteenth birthday." "At three years old, Peter was made to kill his baby brother and eat his flesh." "There's a lot of it about: they reckon that a quarter of our patients have been victims of satanic rituals."

To be fair, this kind of gossip belies the deeper seriousness of the majority of therapists who deal with MPD. But that it occurs at all, and is seemingly so little challenged, could well explain why people outside the movement want to keep their distance. Not to put too fine a point on it, there is everywhere the sense that both therapists and patients are participators in a Mystery, to which ordinary standards of objectivity do not apply. Multiplicity is seen as a semi-inspired, semi-heroic condition: and almost every claim relating either the patient's abilities or to the extent of their childhood suffering is listened to in sympathetic awe. Some therapists clearly consider it a privilege to be close to such extraordinary human beings (and the more of them in treatment, the more status the therapist acquires).

We were struck by the fact that some of the

---

[10]W. S. Taylor and M. F. Martin, "Multiple personality." *Journal of Abnormal and Social Psychology*, 39, 281–300 (1944).

very specialists who have conducted the scientific investigations we mentioned earlier are sympathetic also to wild claims. We frankly cannot accept the truth of many of the circulating stories, and in particular we were unimpressed by this year's favorite—namely all the talk of the "satanic cult" origins of many cases of MPD.

However, an astronomer who believes in astrology would not for that reason be untrustworthy as an astronomical observer, and it would be wrong to find the phenomenon of multiplicity guilty by association. The climate in which the discussion is currently occurring is regrettable but probably unavoidable, not because all the true believers are gullible and all the opponents narrow-minded, but because those who have worked with cases *know* they have seen something so remarkable as to defy conventional description, and, in the absence of an accepted conceptual framework for description, they are driven by a sense of fidelity to their own experience to making hyperbolic claims.

We draw, for the time being, the following conclusions:

1. While the unitary solution to the problem of human selfhood is for most people socially and psychologically desirable, it may not always be attainable.

2. The possibility of developing multiple selves is inherent in every human being. Multiplicity is not only biologically and psychologically plausible, but in some cases it may be the best—even the only—available way of coping with a person's life experience.

3. Childhood trauma (usually, though not necessarily, sexual) is especially likely to push a person towards incipient multiplicity. It is possible that the child may progress from there to becoming a full-fledged multiple of his or her own accord, but in general it seems more likely that external pressure—or sanction—is required.

4. The diagnosis of MPD has become, within a particular psychiatric lobby, a diagnostic fad. Although the existence of the clinical syndrome is now beyond dispute, there is as yet no certainty as to how much of the multiplicity currently being reported has existed prior to therapeutic intervention.

5. Whatever the particular history, the end result would appear to be in many cases a person who is genuinely split. That is, the grounds for assigning several selves to such a human being can be as good as—indeed the same as—those for assigning a single self to a normal human being.

To end with further questions, and not answer them, may be the best way of conveying where we ourselves have got to. Here are some (almost random) puzzles that occur to us about the wider cultural significance of the phenomenon.

It remains the case that even in North America, the diagnosis of MPD has become common only recently, and elsewhere in the world it is still seldom made at all. We must surely assume that the predisposing factors have always been widely present in the human population. So where has all the multiplicity been hiding?

In many parts of the world the initiation of children into adult society has, in the past, involved cruel rites, involving sexual and physical abuse (sodomy, mutilation, and other forms of battering). Is the effect (maybe even the intention) of such rites to create adults with a tendency to MPD? Are there contexts where an ability to split might be (or have been thought to be) a positive advantage—for example, when it comes to coping with physical or social hardship? Do multiples make better warriors?

In contemporary America, many hundreds of people claim to have been abducted by aliens from UFOs. The abduction experience is not recognized as such at first, and is described instead as "missing time" for which the person has no memories. Under hypnosis, however, the subject typically recalls having been kidnapped by humanoid creatures who did harmful things to her or him—typically involving some kind of sex-related surgical operation (for example, sharp objects being thrust into the vagina). Are these people recounting a mythic version of an actual childhood experience? During the period described as missing time, was another personality in charge, a personality for whom the experience of abuse was all too real?

Plato banned actors from his Republic on the grounds that they were capable of "transforming themselves into all sorts of characters"—a bad example, he thought, for solid citizens. Actors commonly talk about "losing" themselves in their roles. How many of the best actors have been abused as children? For how many is acting a culturally sanctioned way of letting their multiplicity come out?

The therapists we talked to were struck by the "charisma" of their patients. Charisma is often associated with a lack of personal boundaries, as if the subject is inviting everyone to share some part of him. How often have beguiling demagogues been multiples? Do we have here another explanation for the myth of the "wound and the bow"?

Queen Elizabeth I, at the age of two, went through the experience of having her father, Henry VIII, cut off her mother's head. Elizabeth in later life was notoriously changeable, loving and vindictive. Was Elizabeth a multiple? Joan of Arc had trances, and cross-dressed as a boy. Was she?

In the course of writing and rewriting this essay, we encountered two problems of exposition that we eventually recognized to be important factors contributing to the phenomenon of MPD itself. First, the lure of hyperbolic claims mentioned in the essay was a pressure we experienced ourselves, even in comparing notes on our own observations. It is not just that one wants to tell a good story, but that one wants to tell a consistent story, and the resources of English currently conspire to force one into one

overstatement or another. Readers of early drafts of this essay, both initiates and laypeople, made widely varied criticisms and suggestions, but there was one point of near unison: they felt cheated or unfulfilled because we were "equivocal" about the existence of the phenomenon; we didn't make clear—or clear enough for them—whether MPD was *real*.

A particularly telling instance of this was the therapist who told us that one of her patients, with whom we had talked, would be deeply hurt by our claim that "that is all there is" to her various alters. It is interesting that the therapist didn't come up with the following crusher: *the alters of this patient would be deeply offended by our claim that "that is all there is" to them*; did we really want to call them "second-class citizens" or "subhuman" or "nonpersons"? If MPD is real—if it is *really* real—then an issue of civil rights is raised: shouldn't all adult alters not only be treated with respect by their therapists, but also be granted the right to vote (for there can be no question that their political opinions would often diverge widely)?

Yet alters must in general know perfectly well that they are not "people"; they are basically sane and well informed, and capable of roughly normal reality testing. But if they are not people, what are they? They are what they are—selves, for want of a better word. As selves, they are as real as any self could be: they are not just imaginary playmates or theatrical roles, on the one hand; nor, on the other hand, are they ghostly people or eternal souls sharing a mortal body. It is possible for some therapists, apparently, to tiptoe between these extremes, respecting without quite endorsing the alters, sustaining enough trust and peace of mind in their patients to continue therapy effectively while eschewing the equally (or even more) effective therapeutic route of frank endorsement (with its attendant exaggerations) followed by "fusion" or "integration." Anyone who finds this middle road hard to imagine should try harder to imagine it before declaring it a conceptual impossibility.

A related but more subtle expository problem might stem from the lack of a middle voice between active and passive. When Mary, as a child, was confronted with that horrible cacophony of experience, *who* was confused, *who* "devised" the splitting stratagem, *who* was oblivious to *whose* pains? Prior to the consolidation of a proper person, there is no one home to play subject to the verbs, and yet — according to the model — there is all that clever activity of self-creation going on inside. The standard lame device for dealing with such issues — which are ubiquitous in cognitive science, not just in psychiatry — is to settle for the passive voice and declare the whole process to occur outside of consciousness. The psycholinguist informs us that the most likely interpretation of an ambiguous sentence is chosen unconsciously; the person does not "consciously notice" the ambiguity and then "deliberately choose" the most likely interpretation. Initiates to this way of speaking tend to underestimate the amount of conceptual revision they have undergone. Again, anyone who finds it hard to imagine how it can be right to talk of choices made without a chooser, disapproval without a disapprover, even thoughts occurring without a thinker (Descartes's *res cogitans*), should pause to consider the possibility that this barely conceivable step might be a breakthrough, not a mistake. Those who refuse to suspend their intuitive judgments about this insist on imposing categories on discussion that make MPD seem fraudulent if you're a skeptic, or paranormal if you're a believer. The principle aim of this essay has been to break down this polarity of thought.

II

Personal Identity

Introduction

The problem of unity of consciousness is to explain unity and multiplicity at a given time. The problem of personal identity is to explain unity and multiplicity over time. Although they sometimes look like different sorts of problems, actually they are two aspects of a single problem: that of explaining the principles that underlie the ways we count up how many things there are.

Unity of consciousness is usually considered the more fundamental problem because the units linked together over time to form individual persons are believed to be already unified at a given time. These units are time-slices of bodies and/or minds, what are sometimes called "person-stages." It is as if unity of consciousness is the spatial analog of identity while personal identity is the temporal analog, together constituting "the space and time" of self and identity.

As an analogy, consider the individual images on each single frame of film that, when displayed in sequence over time, give rise to motion pictures. From where (and whence) is the identity of the motion picture derived? First, from the physical elements that make up the substance of each frame. Second, from the relations—including the spatial ones—among those physical elements out of which emerge the unity of the images on each frame. Third, from the relations—including the temporal ones—out of which arise the unity *among* the frames, the *motion* of the motion picture. The individual frames are things, or substances, none of which are present continuously through the motion picture. (A frame is not a *motion* picture but a stationary one.) The motion picture—itself a unified sequence of individually unified images—arises from the relations among (the relations and relata of) the substantial frames.

Problems of unity and multiplicity similar to those that arise in the case of persons arise when we try to account for the identity of any object, such as a table, an airplane, or a tree. What makes the problem of the identity of persons especially immediate and perplexing is the added dimension of consciousness and the subsequent emergence, within a conscious physical structure, of self. Even to raise the question of personal identity in this contemporary way is to overcome an impressive intellectual heritage. The traditional way of counting persons is by counting substances. For instance, when René Descartes, in the seventeenth century, asked "What am I?" he identified the "I" with a continuously existing immaterial substance. For Descartes, as for many who preceded him, the question "Is someone at one time the same person as someone at a later time?" would be answered in terms of whether the earlier person is (or has) the same immaterial substance as the later person.

John Locke, taking up where Descartes left off, tried to extricate his account of personal identity from dependence on the notion of an immaterial substance by arguing that it is not sameness of immaterial substance but, rather, sameness of consciousness that makes someone the same continuously existing person over time. It is a matter of controversy among Locke scholars what Locke meant. One standard interpretation is that for Locke the criterion of identity is "conscious memory." Thus, Locke, although still clinging to a *substance* view, is generally regarded as the originator of the view that personal identity consists in various *relations* among transient elements. The important relations, on his view, are those that obtain among present conscious memories and the earlier experiences or actions remembered. Locke is a transitional figure because despite his belief in substances, he initiated the view that personal identity may be understood in terms of relations.

A possible problem with Locke's view is that strange moral implications may follow from the memory view of personal identity, at least when that view is interpreted strictly. For instance, we can justly punish Smith for murdering Jones only if Smith actually murdered him. On a strict interpretation of the memory view, Smith actually murdered Jones only if he remembers having done it. In other words, if Smith does not remember murdering Jones eight years ago, then Jones's murderer was not Smith but a sort of ancestor of Smith's and Smith is no more guilty of the murder than, say, Jack the Ripper's grandson is guilty of the crimes of his notorious grandfather.

Such difficulties with the strict memory view inspired Thomas Reid in the eighteenth century to argue as follows. If the person who committed a crime cannot remember having committed it but can remember everything he did at an earlier time when he could still remember having committed the crime, then on Locke's view this person both is and is not the same person who committed the crime. Reid thus dismissed Locke's view as self-contradictory. At about the same time Bishop Butler claimed that Locke's memory theory fails because it is circular: "consciousness of personal identity presupposes, and therefore cannot constitute, personal identity any more than knowledge, in any other case, can constitute truth, which it presupposes." Butler is often interpreted as meaning that the notion of conscious memory includes the notion of personal identity and therefore cannot be used to analyze it.

One way to defend Locke against Reid's objection is to suppose that what matters is not the remembering per se but, rather, the *potential* for remembering. Thus the prisoner who cannot remember his crime might remember it, say, under hypnosis, because there exists within his brain some hidden memory traces of that event. Or one might revise Locke's theory with an analysis of personal identity in terms of overlapping memories, because even though there might be few, if any, memory connections among person-stages separated by many years, at any moment-to-moment stage of a person's life there are usually memory connections to the adjacent stages. For instance, suppose you remember now what you had for breakfast today, and at breakfast you remembered what you had for dinner the day before, and so on; it is the having of such overlapping memories that, in this revised Lockean view, makes you the same person over time even though you may not be able to remember now what you had for breakfast on a certain day seven years ago. (Derek Parfit (selection 15) develops his account of "q-memory" to defend his own neo-Lockean view against Butler's criticism.)

As Reid and Butler made clear, moving away from a simple substance view of personal identity results in difficulties of its own. Their solution, however, was to retain the substance view. But Locke had already shown convincingly the advantages of a relational account. Whatever the difficulties with Locke's view, few were attracted to the idea of turning back. The problem thus became even more puzzling.

In the eighteenth century David Hume delivered another powerful blow to the substance view. He argued poignantly that no self—either over time or at a time—shows up in experience:

> There are some philosophers, who imagine we are every moment intimately conscious of what we call our Self; that we feel its existence and its continuance in existence; and are certain, beyond the evidence of a demonstration, both of its perfect identity and simplicity. [A Treatise of Human Nature, 1739, Book I, Section VI.]

By "identity," Hume meant persistence without change *over time*. By "simplicity," he meant existence as an individual thing (rather than as a collection) *at a time*. Hume thought that if there were a self in experience, it would be a perceiver. But when he looked for a perceiver, he found only perceptions, and among them nothing that seemed even a candidate to be the self.

> For my part, when I enter most intimately into what I call myself, I always stumble on some particular perception or other, of heat or cold, light or shade, love or hatred, pain or pleasure. I never can catch myself at any time without a perception, and never can observe [any thing] but the perception. [Treatise, Book I, Section VI.]

Hume claimed, in effect, that the commonsense belief that we perceive a self (that we experience ourselves *as* selves) is based on mistaking a bundle of perceptions for a perceiver. But perceptions, whether individually or collectively, are not a perceiver. Our mistake (on Hume's view, our misperception) involves two errors. First, we reify individual perceptions by treating them as if they were an underlying, unifying, permanent substance. Second, we project (the illusion of) activity onto something that is passive. That is, perceptions, which are passive, are perceived as active agents. Our passive perceptions—what on Hume's view we ordinarily misperceive as an active perceiver, a self—have no causal powers. In other words, for Hume, there is no percei*ver* because there is no percep*tion* that does anything, either individually or collectively. Going in and out of existence, perceptions are in perpetual flux and have no unity except whatever may arise as a consequence of external relations among them. And they have no identity over any but very short periods of time. Yet we perceive this flux of passive, discrete elements as if it were an active agent of perception whose activity is to collect and unify perceptions into an underlying, unifying, permanent structure that we misinterpret as a substantial perceiver. That is why we think we perceive a self when, in truth, there is only the perpetually changing flux of individual perceptions.

Who is it that misperceives perceptions for a self? On Hume's view, to what does "you" refer? Consider your own present experience. Pick up the book you are now reading and look at it as you pick it up. You will have a feeling of pressure in your hand and also a visual sensation of part of the surface of the book. The feeling of pressure and the visual sensation are separate perceptions. (There is no perceiver and no substance *in experience* to unify them.) Now put the book down, close your eyes, and a moment later pick it up again and look at it. Your new visual sensation and your new experience of pressure are not the same perceptions as the old ones. They are here-and-now. The previous perceptions were there-and-then. Your new perceptions may be qualitatively indistinguishable from the old ones. But since they are discontinuous and occur at different times—there is a temporal gap between them—they are numerically distinct. That is, the first visual sensation and the first experience of pressure, before you put the book down, are not the same perceptions as the second visual sensation and the second experience of pressure. If all you are at any given time is what can be found in your experiences at that time (as Hume thought), this suggests that each occurrence of the word "you" in this paragraph has a different referent, that is, the referent is not some perceiver (some active agent) or an underlying substance but, rather, only those individual (passive) perceptions that are in awareness at the same time. Passive, impermanent perceptions do not a perceiver make.

According to Hume, since there is neither a perceiver nor anything simple and continuous in experience to which the word "you" in "Who are you?" could refer, personal identity is an illusion. Strictly speaking, *no one* misperceives perceptions for a perceiver. There is misperception, but no misperceiver. But, then, who are you? No one? It seems an outright contradiction for *you* to discover that *you* do not exist. In the appendix to his *Treatise*, Hume wrote that as a result of his reflections on personal identity "I find myself involv'd in such a labyrinth, that, I must confess, I neither know how to correct my former opinions, nor how to render them consistent."

In the nineteenth century Immanuel Kant responded to Hume by claiming that the self, although not a substance, nevertheless exists—not as something which you can experience, as Hume thought would be required for there to be selves, but as something that makes the having of an experience possible. Kant claimed that our experiences are unified. For instance, the experience of reading this sentence from beginning to end is not just a sequence of separate experiences of individual words but, rather, the experience of a sentence. Sentence comprehension could not have occurred unless the experience of individual words was not separate but unified, that is, connected by something into a whole. If our experiences are unified, something must account for their unities. Kant claimed, like Descartes, that an "I think" accompanies every one of our experiences and that is what accounts for their unities. Unlike Descartes, Kant did not reify this "I think" as a *res cogitans*, a thinking thing (a substance). In other words, Kant claimed that our experiences are unified and that unified experiences cannot exist unowned. The fact that Hume could not find the self, claimed Kant, was due to Hume's looking in the wrong place. Hume's mistake was in supposing that experiences could exist all by themselves, independently of experiencers. According to Kant, the having of an experience *presupposes* that the experience is someone's, but the someone is not a substantial self.

The idea, roughly, is this. We *could* speak about experiences impersonally —for instance, instead of saying "I see a cat," we could say "A cat is being seen," or "Cat-seeing is going on." Kant thinks that to speak in this way, impersonally, is to ignore the fact that when a cat is being seen there is some "I" doing the seeing: *I* see the cat. Hume failed to recognize this, according to Kant, and that is why he failed to discover the self. In other words, by presupposing that experiences can exist independently of an experiencer, Hume blinded himself to what Kant considered an always present, absolutely necessary element to the having of experience: the experiencer. The reason Hume could not find this experiencer, claimed Kant, is that it is nowhere in experience, that is, nowhere in the phenomenal world. It is "transcendental."

Kant's notion of a transcendental self—or "I"—is deeply mysterious. The best way to understand it may be by analogy. Consider, for instance, the role a blank movie screen plays in unifying the images projected upon it. In one sense—in terms of adding actual content—the screen contributes nothing. In another sense—in terms of making it possible for there to be any images at all—the screen contributes a great deal. Even though the screen does not show up in experience, without it there is no unified experience.

If one looks not at the motion picture screen (which itself is never in motion) but directly into the projector, the experience of the motion picture disappears. There is now only the experientially ununified flickering of lights—no picture, only the motion. For there to be an experience of a picture there must be a screen. From the perspective of the phenomenal elements of the motion picture, the screen does not exist (it is not itself a phenomenal element) but is "transcendental," outside or beyond the phenomena. Similarly, Kant claimed that the self exists outside or beyond the phenomena. It is this transcendental self that makes possible the unification of these phenomena we call "experience."

Although Kant's theory of a transcendental self had, and still has, enormous influence (see, for instance, the selections by Jaynes and Harré in this volume), it has not been particularly influential on twentieth century views of personal identity. The reason is that the transcendental view, like the substance view it was designed to replace, is too obscure for the purposes of personal identity theorists. Trying to explain personal identity by appealing to substances and transcendental selves focuses the inquiry outside the realm of both experience and science. It attempts to explain the obscure by the more obscure, which goes against accepted canons of explanation. Twentieth century personal identity theorists have thus tended to work within the context of relational views.

According to relational views of personal identity, what matters in preserving identity is not transcendental selves or the retaining of a particular metaphysical substance in which experiences are embedded but, rather, the continuity of our physical structures (our bodies and brains) and/or our psychological structures (including memory, beliefs, character traits, and so on). And what explains the continuity of our physical and psychological structures is not the persistence of any elements out of which they are composed but, rather, the persistence of a pattern (or patterns) of relationships among these elements. These structures, although they might not be immediately apparent within any one element of experience, could nevertheless be experienced or explained scientifically. That is, they could be found within experience or explained in terms of elements each of which can be understood scientifically. In a sense, the relational view is a middle ground between what cannot be experienced or understood scientifically—metaphysical substances, transcendental selves, and the like—and what is experiential but constantly changing—the individual elements out of which our physical and psychological structures are composed. If self and identity emerge out of impermanent elements, they must do so on the basis of the relations among them. Assuming, at least initially, that normal patterns of physical and psychological maturation and change preserve the right relations to give rise to personal identity, but leaving it open that other patterns might also preserve them, the problem of personal identity becomes that of specifying these relations.

Does the personal identity relation consist in the continuity of physical structures, or psychological structures, or in some combination of both? To find out, we must consider cases in which physical structures are preserved while psychological structures are disrupted, and also cases in which psychological structures are preserved but physical structures are disrupted. We shall have to figure out in which cases personal identity is preserved and in which not. The problem is that real life rarely, if ever, provides clean examples we can use to decide such issues. But in thought experiments we can separate elements that in life are always conjoined. So, philosophers typically address this issue through thought experiments.

Bernard Williams (selection 12) describes a thought experiment that simultaneously and vividly forces us to confront two basic questions about personal identity. First, does personal identity depend more on physical or on psychological continuity? Second, is personal identity an internal or an external relation — that is, does it depend just on the relation between a person at one time and a person at a later time, or must third parties also be taken into account?

Williams's thought experiment involves a single situation presented from two perspectives. In the first presentation, two people will exchange their psychologies and then one of them will be rewarded, the other tortured. Before the switch both people are asked to choose on selfish grounds which one of them should get the reward and which one the torture. Both choose to have the reward go where their own psychologies (memories, character traits, tastes, and so on) go, leaving the physical organisms behind to suffer the torture — without *them*, they think. The prospect that the physical organism, devoid of their psychologies, will suffer is not a source of terror to them. If their response is typical, this suggests that most people think that what matters to the preservation of their personal identities is not their physical organisms but their psychologies. In other words, most people think that a physical organism devoid of their psychology and inhabited by a different psychology is someone else, and thus not an object of selfish concern.

Next, Williams asks us to imagine that a person is told he is going to be tortured tomorrow. Naturally, the person is terrified. Then the person is told that just before the torture, he is going to suffer total amnesia. This additional information makes the situation even more frightening. Finally, he is told that after suffering total amnesia he will come to think he is someone else — he will take on a different psychology. He is, of course, still terrified. But this, claims Williams, is merely the earlier situation now redescribed in terms of what happens to just one physical organism. How can what earlier causes no dread now occasion so much? What has changed? In Williams's second presentation of the example, the person is told only half the original story. The facts he is told are the same. How could being told the rest of the story, Williams asks, change the person's response? After all, the rest of the story merely informs the person that what is going to happen to him is also going to happen to someone else and that he will acquire that other person's personality and memories while that other person acquires his.

Williams's tentative answer to the question of whether personal identity depends more on physical or on psychological continuity is that it depends more on physical continuity. He thus endorses a physical view of personal identity, but is not clear whether for him it is the persistence of the body or the brain that matters most. His answer to the question of whether personal identity is an intrinsic or an extrinsic relation is that it is intrinsic. The main purpose of Williams's article, though, is not to answer these questions but to pose them. In the process he exposes a tension in our ordinary attitudes toward personal identity that raises the possibility that these attitudes are fundamentally incoherent.

Peter Unger (selection 13) develops what might be called a "minimalist physical view" of personal identity. According to him, if you exist at some future time, then (except in some marginal cases) your "core psychology" must be encoded continuously from now until then in a physically continuous "realizer" (or, at least, in a physically noncontinuous succession of physical realizers). Your core psychology includes your capacities to experience consciously, to reason at least in a rudimentary way, and to form simple intentions, but does not include your "distinctive psychology," for instance, your memories. In simplest terms, Unger claims that for you to exist at some future time normally will require that your brain exist continuously from now until then and that it continuously realize your core psychology.

Unger allows that you may continue to exist in a deep coma because relatively minor alterations of your brain might bring you to the point where you could exercise your core psychology. But he denies that you could continue to exist if your brain were turned, even briefly, to "jelly" and then reconstituted. Unger also allows that the physical realizer of your core psychology could be replaced, even with a synthetic replica, without loss of identity provided the replacement process was gradual enough to allow assimilation. Although Unger has a physical view, he thus takes a tolerant stand on the issue of replacement of the parts of which the physical realizer, for instance, your brain, is made. He also concedes great importance to core psychology—so much, in fact, that he claims the importance of physical continuity is only derivative. Its importance depends on the fact that it provides for the continuous existence of our basic mental capacities and is relative only to the general truth of our view of the world. Unger claims that in a different possible world physical continuity might have no importance for our survival.

Unlike Williams and Unger, Robert Nozick (selection 14) rejects the physical view of personal identity. He argues that personal identity is an extrinsic relation, that is, one that depends in part on what happens to "other people." According to Nozick's "closest continuer theory," an individual, X, at a particular time is the same person as an individual, Y, at some later time only if Y's properties stem from or grow out of X's properties and no one stands in a closer (or as close) relationship to X as does Y. Thus, on Nozick's view, who we are is determined in part not just by facts about us, but also by who else exists and what they are like.

Nozick begins by explicating the general principles underlying Williams's argument. He then argues that identities other than personal identity—for instance, the identities of material objects and social organizations—are extrinsic relations. Finally, he argues that personal identity should be understood just as a special case of these more general identity relations, and thus that personal identity, too, should be understood as an extrinsic relation.

Nozick claims, in effect, that most people judge Williams's two presentations differently precisely because what happens to "other people" does matter. The significant difference between Williams's two presentations is that in the first we are provided with the information about what happens to "other people," whereas in the second we are not. Whether and when we get this additional information influences who we regard as the closest continuers of the people in the story because it determines who the candidates for closest continuers are. By analogy, to determine that someone is the king's successor you must know more than simply that he is an heir. You must know who else, if anyone, is also an heir. And you must know who among the heirs has the best claim to the throne. Even though you think you have identified the heir, a "closer" heir might be discovered who usurps the throne from the heir apparent. How one stands with regard to the throne is determined not just by one's intrinsic relations but also by extrinsic considerations.

In Williams's first presentation, you are contemplating two ways in which you might regard yourself as continuing into the future. You identify with one of these ways more than the other. If you are like most people, you identify more with the one that happens to continue your psychology. But you can identify with this way only if you are presented with it as part of the example. In the second presentation you are not presented with it as part of the example. Nozick claims that this explains why most of us judge the two cases differently.

On Nozick's view, in the first presentation of Williams's story each of the people has two possible continuers. Which continuers are them depends on which ones are closest. And which continuers are closest depends on which criterion of "closeness" we (or they) adopt. Ultimately, this will be based on values—for instance, whether physical or psychological continuity matters most. Thus, on Nozick's view, personal identity ultimately is based on personal values. He thinks that it is based on the values of the person (or persons) who are involved in the personal identity relation. So, for Nozick, personal identity is an extrinsic relation. And the sort of extrinsic relation it is depends on our personal values: who we are is thus in part determined by what matters to us.

The move from an intrinsic to an extrinsic account of personal identity may in a sense be said to signal the move within philosophy from an absolute concept of personal identity to a relative one. Substance views, and even intrinsic relational views such as Williams's, are absolute in that they measure your personal identity against a scale determined solely by facts internal to the individual organism(s), independently of whatever is going on elsewhere. Extrinsic views, such as Nozick's, are relative in that they measure your personal identity against a scale determined by both internal and external facts. Consider, for instance, two different ways grades might be awarded on a true/false test with 100 equally weighted questions. Using one scale—an absolute one—it takes 90–100 correct answers to get an A. Whether a student gets an A has nothing to do with how well or how poorly other students perform. Using another scale—a relative one—whoever scores in the top 10 percent of the class gets an A. On the relative scale, whether a student gets an A depends crucially on how well or how poorly her classmates perform.

Suppose how well a student does on this true/false exam is crucial to her career plans, which, in turn, are crucial to her hopes to "be someone." If the exam is graded on the absolute scale, whether she successfully crosses this crucial hurdle and thus has a chance actually to become that someone depends not on the performance of her classmates but on her alone. On the relative scale, whether she actually crosses the hurdle and has a chance to become that someone depends partly on the performance of others. Similarly with personal identity: whether you become a certain future someone or fail to become that someone may or may not depend on others. On absolute views, such as the old-fashioned substance view and even intrinsic relational views such as William's, whether you become a certain future person or instead fail to become that person does not depend on others. On a relative view, such as Nozick's (or Parfit's, to be discussed next) it does depend on others.

Derek Parfit (selection 15) would agree with Nozick that personal identity is an extrinsic relation, and hence a relative one. In addition, Parfit stresses four points. First, we are not entities such as metaphysical substances or Cartesian egos that exist separately, apart from our physical and psychological structures and various interrelated physical and psychological elements and events out of which these structures are composed. Thus, Parfit is a reductionist about persons in that he thinks persons can best be understood in terms of the elements, physical or mental, out of which they are composed.

Second, according to Parfit, personal identity is not determinate. That is, even if we know every fact about various changes to us, there is not always a Yes or No answer to whether personal identity has been preserved through the changes. Parfit claims that if people were separately existing entities, like Cartesian egos, personal identity would be determinate.

Parfit's main argument for these first two points is his "Combined Spectrum." You are asked to imagine a possible range of cases at one end of which is you and at the other end of which is Greta Garbo, age 30. Next to you, at the near end of the spectrum, is the second case: you exactly as you are now except a few of your cells have been replaced with a few of Garbo's cells. Further along the spectrum more and more of your cells are replaced until eventually, near the far end of the spectrum, we reach someone almost exactly like Garbo, except that she has a few of your cells. At the far end of the spectrum is Garbo herself. In other words, the Spectrum consists of a range of cases in which each case differs from adjacent cases only very slightly but from very distant cases so dramatically that between them identity is not preserved. If before we were disturbed by the apparently arbitrary way we responded to Williams's paradox, now we might well be just as disturbed by the difficulty in answering the question Parfit poses for each case in his spectrum of cases: Is it you?

If our identities are determinate, then there must always be a Yes or No answer to Parfit's question. Since the answer at the near end is Yes and at the far end No, if our identities are determinate then somewhere in the spectrum there must be two adjacent cases differing from each other only by a few cells, yet one of which is you and one of which is not you. Since every adjacent pair of cases is so similar, there could never be any evidence of where these borderline cases are located. In other words, if our identities are determinate, then (unbeknownst to you) somewhere in the spectrum from you to Garbo a Yes—it is you—is neighbor to a No—it is not you. And what is the factual difference between these neighbors? Only two cells.

Parfit claims it is implausible to suppose that such a small difference between adjacent cases could be the difference between life and death, between your being there and your not being there. The difference between any two adjacent cases—only a few cells—is trivial; the difference between someone's being you or being someone else is, by comparison, monumental. Parfit claims that the most reasonable conclusion is that in the middle of the spectrum it is an "empty question" whether a given case is you or someone else. That is, you could know all the facts about the case and still not know the answer, not because the answer is subtle or hidden but because there is no answer: identity is not determinate.

Parfit's third claim is that personal identity over time depends not on physical but on psychological relations. He thinks that if physical continuity were essential to identity, it could not be the continuity of the whole body but at most the continuity of the brain that matters because we can survive, for instance, a liver transplant. But the continuity of the whole brain is not necessary either. Any part of the brain, if it were functionally equivalent to the whole, would do just as well. Nor, it would seem, is even the continuity of any part of the brain crucial. The importance of our brains is not intrinsic but derivative. What matters is not what the brain is but what it does. If some other organ, such as the liver, did what the brain does, then this other organ would be as important in preserving personal identity as the brain now is and the brain would be only as important as this other organ now is. Parfit claims that if something else—anything else—could sustain our psychologies as reliably as the brain (and also perform the brain's other essential functions), then the brain would have little importance in preserving personal identity. This would be true even though this other thing were not any part of our bodies.

Suppose you enter a Star Trek–style "teletransporter" to travel to Mars.

The teletransporter scans your entire physical and psychological structure and then, while destroying the physical structure, beams information to Mars on the basis of which an exact replica of your person is constructed. According to Parfit, the teletransporter has reliably preserved your psychology across a break of physical continuity; no part of your original body and brain has been preserved. Only exact replicas exist on Mars. During the break in physical continuity the teletransporter takes over the brain's function of preserving your psychology. So, if the only reason for thinking the brain is essential to identity is that the brain serves this function, then it would be irrational to insist that even partial brain continuity is necessary to identity.

Parfit argues that the reliability of the causal mechanism underlying psychological continuity (which includes on his view the more direct psychological connections — "psychological connectedness" — as well as overlapping chains of such connections — "psychological continuity") is not important. It does not matter how the effect was caused. All that matters is the effect. Imagine, for instance, that stepping out of the teletransporter on Mars you are told that the teletransporter has been malfunctioning lately. Since you are already on Mars, psychologically continuous with your pretrip self, this is the best you could have hoped for in terms of preserving your psychology. Even had the teletransporter been working reliably, you would not have wanted more. The reliability or unreliability of the cause — the teletransporter — does not matter to the effect — you — because everything that matters to your survival — your psychology — has been preserved.

Teletransportation is, for Parfit, a kind of reincarnation. Identity follows psychology, provided that psychology does not branch. In other words, if enough of your psychology continues in one stream only, then you continue; if it does not continue, or continues in more than one stream, then *you* do not continue. So, in response to Williams's paradox, Parfit would claim that the people in the example go where their psychologies go. That is, they merely switch bodies. Parfit resolves Williams's paradox just like Nozick does, by adopting a relative view of identity. But for Parfit the relations that matter are not left up to individual values. They are psychological relations.

Parfit's fourth claim is that preserving your personal identity across various changes is not what *should* matter primarily, that personal identity should not be your highest egoistic value. What should matter instead is the preservation of psychological continuity between your earlier and later selves. Psychological continuity should matter most because it would be irrational for anything else to matter more.

On Parfit's view there are two ways you can fail to continue. One way is if your psychology does not continue. For instance, you die or you become a total and irreversible amnesiac. Either outcome is equally bad — your psychology does not continue. A second way is for your psychology to branch, that is, for it to continue in more than one stream. For instance, suppose the teletransporter simultaneously creates two exact replicas of you on Mars. Parfit claims that because two replicas would not be the same person as each other, neither would be the same person as you. Yet this outcome is not as bad as death. In fact, it is almost as good as ordinary survival.

Parfit has a Socratic view of the relative values of mind and body. The mind means virtually everything, the body almost nothing. A person who chooses not to use the teletransporter to travel to Mars but chooses instead to pay much more for an equally reliable conventional space trip is irrational because, Parfit assumes, the only reason a person could have for preferring his body to a replica is his belief that his body is essential to his identity and hence that the replica would be somebody else. This, on Parfit's view, is not a good reason for preferring one's body to a replica.

Sydney Shoemaker (selection 16) agrees with Nozick and Parfit that personal identity is an extrinsic relation, and agrees with Parfit that physical continuity is not necessary to identity. In addition, Shoemaker answers several objections levied against relative views. Perhaps the most interesting objection is made by Richard Swinburne, one of a handful of well-known philosophers today who subscribes to a metaphysical-substance (soul) view of personal identity.

Swinburne notes that if, as claimed on the relative view, whether you survive depends on who your competitors are (as in the relative scale of test grading, cited earlier), you could ensure your survival by killing the competitors. His example is of a hypothetical fission operation in which a surgeon removes the brain from a patient, divides it into two informationally and functionally equivalent halves that each preserve the full psychology of the donor, and then transplants those halves into qualitatively identical brainless bodies. On the relative view, the donor does not survive: Although there are two survivors, each of whom is a person, neither is the same person as the donor. Swinburne correctly points out that the donor could ensure his survival by plotting with a nurse to have one of the recipients killed. And this, claims Swinburne, is such an absurd result that it discredits the relative view.

To see Swinburne's point, consider an analogy. Suppose the president has been assassinated and the two candidates next in line, A and B, would each be president if the other did not exist. There is no absurdity in supposing that candidate A, by assassinating B, could become president. But the concept of "same person," according to Swinburne, is not like the concept of "president." It is absurd, Swinburne would claim, to suppose that A, by assassinating B, could ensure that tomorrow he (that is, the only one of his "successors" that survives) will be the same person he is today. Swinburne thinks such cases are so obviously disanalogous that the contrast between them discredits any theory, like that of Nozick, Parfit, or Shoemaker, that would treat them as if they were the same. Obvious or not, Swinburne's example at least raises the question of whether being the same person tomorrow as you are today could be like being the president tomorrow.

Shoemaker replies that Swinburne has made the natural but mistaken assumption that when a person wants to survive, what he most wants is to preserve his identity, that is, that he — the very person wanting this — should exist in the future. But, says Shoemaker, this may not be true. What the person may want is that something intimately connected with him, say, his psychology, should continue, regardless of whether his identity is preserved, that is, whether he survives. His own actual surviving, as opposed to the survival of someone else with his psychology, may not make much difference to him. Shoemaker argues that such is in fact the case in many fission examples.

In other words, according to Shoemaker, there is a tremendous difference from the point of view of the brain donor between there being no survivors and there being at least one. But there is not as much difference or the same kind of difference between there being one survivor and there being two, even though if there were two the donor himself would not survive. The first difference is a matter of life and death. The second is not. In the second case, no organisms die; there are two survivors. All that has been lost in the second case is identity, which, according to Shoemaker, is not a loss of life. Thus, for Shoemaker there can be survival without identity because the continuation of life does not require the preservation of identity.

David Lewis (selection 17) claims, contrary to Nozick, Parfit, and Shoemaker, that identity (and also psychological continuity) *is* what matters primarily in a person's survival. Lewis's defense of this claim involves a different way of conceptualizing personal identity, one that radically conflicts with our ordinary assumptions about what it means to be one person. For Lewis, persons are four-dimensional, space-time continuents. Human organisms are not the sort of things whose identities as persons are determined solely by what is going on at a particular moment but, rather, by the totality of their extensions in time. So, for Lewis, you cannot determine personal identity at a time, only over time. That is, to determine personal identity you must gather all the relevant facts as they extend forward and backward in time because your identity at any moment depends on facts about things that may have already happened or may not yet have happened.

To take an analogy, consider common-law marriage. In some states in the United States two people who have not been married legally may become married—become "one," as they say—merely by living together for seven years. These laws are retroactive; after seven years the two individuals not only become a married couple from that point on, they have already been a married couple for seven years. Thus, whether the two individuals are "one" or "two" at any given moment during those seven years may depend on what is happening not just at that moment but in the future. Similarly, whether someone is suffering from a particular mental condition may not depend solely on the facts of the moment. Mental illness is often determined by how long a condition lasts or how it develops. For instance, even though you are severely depressed you cannot be clinically depressed unless your depression lasts a certain length of time, say, three weeks. And the difference between a "fugue" and a 'multiple personality" may depend just on whether the original "fugue episode" is repeated. In the same way, on Lewis's view, what a person is depends on what he or she has been or becomes.

For Nozick, Parfit, and Shoemaker the fission operation creates two people where formerly there was only one. This raises the questions of whether either of the two continuers is the original person and, if not, of whether what matters in survival has been preserved even though identity has been lost. For Lewis, whether there were two or one just before any operation is determined in part by the outcome of the operation. If the outcome is fission, that is, two persons, then there were two all along who earlier simply overlapped. Thus, on Lewis's view the fact that a fission operation that preserves psychological continuity also preserves what matters primarily in survival cannot show that what matters is not identity, because in such an operation no one loses his identity. Lewis's view is that what matters primarily in survival is both identity and psychological continuity—that the two are coincident.

Raymond Martin (selection 18) argues that neither personal identity nor physical continuity (nor psychological continuity) is what matters primarily in survival. What matters primarily, or at least more than these, is becoming the persons we most want to be. The evidence, claims Martin, is that, presented with an appropriate choice, many of us would be willing to sacrifice our identities to become the persons we most want to be. Thus, according to Martin, Parfit is wrong in thinking that psychological continuity is what matters primarily in survival and Lewis is wrong in thinking that both identity and psychological continuity are what matter. And whereas Nozick stresses the ways our values are incorporated into our criteria for personal identity, Martin stresses the ways our values may sometimes override personal identity.

Martin claims that earlier attempts to devalue identity, that is, to show that we have an inflated estimate of its actual value, are inconclusive because they depend on the consideration of fission cases, whose main drawback is that it is debatable (as in the case of Lewis) whether in them personal identity is lost. The claim that it is lost requires certain disputed assumptions about the transitivity of identity or about the ways we should count persons. Martin claims that other examples that do not depend on fission and are free of these drawbacks can be used to devalue identity.

Martin's main example, like the fission cases, depends on a thought experiment in which we are given the opportunity to trade certain benefits, ultimately to trade our identities, for whatever it takes to transform us into the persons we most want to be. However, his thought experiment does not involve fission or require the disputed assumptions that arise in fission cases. He claims that many people would choose to cease existing (that is, to end their identities) so long as their choices would result in their transforming into people who are the sorts of people they (that is, the earlier choosers) most wanted to be. He also claims that transforming into such people matters more than remaining closely physically or psychologically continuous. Martin concludes by considering the possibility that minimalist physical-continuity theories, such as Unger's, might be used to undermine his argument, and claims that whatever the merits of such views as accounts of personal identity, they will not work as accounts of what matters primarily in survival. He thus concludes that the surprising truth about at least many of us is that we crave more to fulfill our deepest "selfish" desires than to continue existing.

Do the unsettling results of personal identity thought experiments have implications for how we should think about related areas of life? Derek Parfit (selection 19) argues that the implications are profound and that they require radical revisions in our theories of rationality and morality. The crucial issue is how much significance we should accord to boundaries — on the one hand to the (partly spatial) boundaries between ourselves and other people and, on the other hand, to the (partly temporal) boundaries between earlier and later stages of ourselves. It is as if what it means to be rational and moral depends in part on the significance of how we and others are distributed across space and time.

The idea that self-concepts and the concept of rationality are linked has quite a bit of prima facie plausibility. We experience ourselves only in the present, not in the future. Because we have direct access to ourselves only at a given time, not over time, we are forced to extrapolate from the present and project ourselves into the future. Knowing the probabilities of future outcomes shapes the contours of these extrapolations. In this way, what is likely to happen in the future, although not as vivid as what is happening in the present, influences what it is now rational for us to believe and do. So far as rationality is concerned, these extrapolations are largely about considerations of self-interest. We thus project ourselves into the future not only with the concept of self but also with self-concepts. It is as if rationality is a kind of bridge between the present and the future, and self — interwoven into projective hopes, wishes, desires, expectations, and so on — is the surface of that bridge.

Everyone agrees that a basic component of rationality is self-interest. Not everyone agrees on the relation between the two. The proper relation depends in part, Parfit argues, on one's view of personal identity — on what it means to be a continuing self. He claims that how strongly we view the connections between earlier and later stages of the self should profoundly affect our models of rationality, say, of the rationality of making sacrifices now to assure later benefits. If you alter your view about the significance of the borders between earlier and later stages of the self, as Parfit does, you may alter the very structure of rationality.

The central issue is the so-called requirement of equal concern according to which rationality requires that a person give equal weight to all the parts of his life. In assessing whether it is rational for you to perform some action, you have to take account of the consequences, which normally would be spread over various stages of your life. The requirement of equal concern prohibits you, say, from weighting pain now more heavily than pain later, even many years later, if all else is equal. According to the requirement of equal concern all of the stages of our lives count equally. Thus, the requirement of equal concern is one of rationality's weapons against overvaluing the present. Parfit is, in a sense, trying to shift the balance of power between the present and the future on the basis of a theory about which relations among various stages of the self account for personal identity. It is as if the question of how we should distribute gains and losses—our rational self-interest—depends, on his view, on how we ourselves are distributed over time.

Parallel considerations arise in the case of morality. Here, too, the idea that self-concepts and moral concepts are linked is prima facie a plausible one. We have greater experiential access to what is going on here, within us, than to what is going on elsewhere, within other people. Yet how other people are affected by our actions, although not as vivid to us as how we ourselves are affected, affects the moral status of our actions. What temporally related stages of self are to rationality, spatially influenced distinctions between self and other are to morality. Morality is one of the organism's major ways of extending itself beyond the vividness of its own concerns, which tend to block its view of itself as embedded with others in a moral community of selves.

Parfit argues, for instance, that how goods should be distributed depends in part on the significance of the boundaries between self and other. Do we have, say, a basic moral obligation to produce as much good as possible, regardless of how it is distributed, as some utilitarians claim, or do considerations of distribution enter into the moral equation? Parfit claims that, all else being equal, assigning less importance to the distinction between self and other should tend to favor the utilitarian view; assigning more importance should tend to favor the view that utilitarianism, if acceptable at all, must be supplemented by a nonutilitarian theory of justice. Thus, how strongly we view the boundaries between self and other—how morally significant we think these boundaries are—could profoundly affect which model of distributive justice is not only more just but also, from the point of view of self-interest, more rational. If Parfit is right, just as rationality links various stages of the individual self over time, so morality links various individuals in the community of selves over space. Morality thus provides a bridge over the chasm that separates self and other.

In sum, morality, like rationality, contributes a major element to that surface structure within our conceptual frameworks that become the topology of self. Moreover, the relations among rationality, morality, and self are reciprocal. The boundaries between self now and self later, as well as between self and other, structure, and are themselves structured by, rational and moral considerations.

Christine Korsgaard (selection 20) disagrees with Parfit over the extent to which metaphysical theories of self and personal identity have implications for rationality and morality. Korsgaard argues that our theories of rationality and morality are relatively impervious to metaphysically motivated revisionism à la Parfit and others. She claims, for instance, that our conception of ourselves as unified agents is not based on metaphysics (on ontological considerations about what we ultimately are) or on conscious experience (on our phenomenology) but on practical considerations. Chief among these practical considerations is that we must view ourselves as unified to eliminate conflict among our various motives and to adopt a standpoint from which we can deliberate and choose.

If we do not eliminate conflict among our motives, our actions will not be integrated. We would be like the split-brain patient who hugged his wife with one arm while he pushed her away with the other. Our actions may sometimes be that deeply ambivalent. But they are not characteristically that ambivalent, or else our lives would not have the kind of unity that most of them do. Regardless of how conflicted we may feel at the level of motivation, we iron out those conflicts before we act or else unified action is impossible.

We also have to adopt a standpoint from which we can deliberate and choose. To make certain decisions, we — or let us say "you" — have to decide whether to regard a future person's desires as yours and hence whether these desires are normative for you. You could decide this on metaphysical grounds but you do not have to. Korsgaard claims that if you are like most people, you will not. For instance, suppose you get paid in the middle of the month and your rent is due at the end. You know when you get paid that a certain future person — ordinarily, we would say "you" — will wish at the end of the month that she had several hundred dollars. Your decision now about what to do with your paycheck — say, whether to spend it all or put some of it away for rent — typically will be influenced by whether you regard that future person as you. If you do, you have a potent reason for saving your money that does not exist if you do not.

So how can you decide whether to regard that future person as you? You could decide on metaphysical grounds, say, by adopting Parfitian reductionism and throwing prudence to the wind or by adopting Swinburnian soulism and squirreling away your paycheck. Korsgaard thinks most people will not decide in these ways; rather, they will succumb to practically motivated and practically sustained pressures to think of themselves as continuously existing unified beings. In other words, Korsgaard's point is that for something to matter to you personally you must view yourself as an agent who chooses and lives a particular life that includes a series of selves the totality of which is a particular person: you. Viewing yourself this way automatically gives you reason to be concerned about the future. It is your future. Such practical considerations, according to Korsgaard, are decisive in determining the view that we take of ourselves as persons, which in turn is the view we adopt in our rationalizing and moralizing.

12

BERNARD WILLIAMS
The Self and the Future

Suppose that there were some process to which two persons, A and B, could be subjected as a result of which they might be said—question-beggingly—to have *exchanged bodies*. That is to say—less question-beggingly—there is a certain human body which is such that when previously we were confronted with it, we were confronted with person A, certain utterances coming from it were expressive of memories of the past experiences of A, certain movements of it partly constituted the actions of A and were taken as expressive of the character of A, and so forth; but now, after the process is completed, utterances coming from this body are expressive of what seem to be just those memories which previously we identified as memories of the past experiences of B, its movements partly constitute actions expressive of the character of B, and so forth; and conversely with the other body.

There are certain important philosophical limitations on how such imaginary cases are to be constructed, and how they are to be taken when constructed in various ways. I shall mention two principal limitations, not in order to pursue them further here, but precisely in order to get them out of the way.

There are certain limitations, particularly with regard to character and mannerisms, to our ability to imagine such cases even in the most restricted sense of our being disposed to take the later performances of that body which was previously A's as expressive of B's character; if the previous A and B were extremely unlike one another both physically and psychologically, and if, say, in addition, they were of different sex, there might be grave difficulties in reading B's dispositions in any possible performances of A's body. Let us forget this, and for the present purpose just take A and B as being sufficiently alike (however alike that has to be) for the difficulty not to arise; after the experiment, persons familiar with A and B are just *overwhelmingly struck* by the B-ish character of the doings associated with what was previously A's body, and conversely. Thus the feat of imagining an exchange of bodies is supposed possible in the most restricted sense. But now there is a further limitation which has to be overcome if the feat is to be not merely possible in the most restricted sense but also is to have an outcome which, on serious reflection, we are prepared to describe as A and B having changed bodies—that is, an outcome where, confronted with what was previously A's body, we are prepared seriously to say that we are now confronted with B.

It would seem a necessary condition of so doing that the utterances coming from that body be taken as genuinely expressive of memories of B's past. But memory is a causal notion; and as we actually use it, it seems a necessary condition on x's present knowledge of x's earlier experiences constituting memory of those experiences that the causal chain linking the experiences and the knowledge should not run outside x's body. Hence if utterances coming from a given body are to be taken as expressive of memories of the experiences of B, there should be some suitable causal link between the appropriate state of that body and the original happening of those experiences to B. One radical way of securing that condition in the imagined exchange case is to suppose, with Shoemaker,[1] that the brains of A and of B are transposed. We may not need so radical a condition. Thus suppose it were possible to extract information from a man's brain and store it in a device while his brain was repaired, or even renewed, the information then being replaced: it would seem exaggerated to insist that the resultant man could not possibly have the memories he had before the operation. With regard to our knowledge of our own past, we draw distinctions between merely recalling, being reminded, and learning again, and those distinctions correspond (roughly) to distinctions between no new input, partial new input, and total new input with regard to the information in question; and it seems clear that the information-parking case just imagined would not count as new input in the sense necessary and sufficient for "learning again." Hence we can imagine the case we are concerned with in terms of information extracted into such devices from A's and B's brains and replaced in the other brain; this is the sort of model which, I think not unfairly for the present argument, I shall have in mind.

We imagine the following. The process considered above exists; two persons can enter some machine, let us say, and emerge changed in the appropriate ways. If A and B are the persons who enter, let us call the persons who emerge the *A-body-person* and the *B-body-person*: the A-body-person is that person (whoever it is) with whom I am confronted when, after the experiment, I am confronted with that body which previously was A's body—that is to say, that the person who would naturally be taken for A by someone who just saw this person, was familiar with A's appearance before the experi-

ment, and did not know about the happening of the experiment. A non-question-begging description of the experiment will leave it open which (if either) of the persons A and B the A-body-person is; the description of the experiment as "persons changing bodies" of course implies that the A-body-person is actually B.

We take two persons A and B who are going to have the process carried out on them. (We can suppose, rather hazily, that they are willing for this to happen; to investigate at all closely at this stage why they might be willing or unwilling, what they would fear, and so forth, would anticipate some later issues.) We further announce that one of the two resultant persons, the A-body-person and the B-body-person, is going after the experiment to be given $100,000, while the other is going to be tortured. We then ask each A and B to choose which treatment should be dealt out to which of the persons who will emerge from the experiment, the choice to be made (if it can be) on selfish grounds.

Suppose that A chooses that the B-body-person should get the pleasant treatment and the A-body-person the unpleasant treatment; and B chooses conversely (this might indicate that they thought that "changing bodies" was indeed a good description of the outcome). The experimenter cannot act in accordance with both these sets of preferences, those expressed by A and those expressed by B. Hence there is one clear sense in which A and B cannot both get what they want: namely, that if the experimenter, before the experiment, announced to A and B that he intends to carry out the alternative (for example), of treating the B-body-person unpleasantly and the A-body-person pleasantly —then A can say rightly, "That's not the outcome I chose to happen," and B can say rightly, "That's just the outcome I chose to happen." So, evidently, A and B before the experiment can each come to know either that the outcome he chose will be that which will happen, or that the one he chose will not happen, and in that sense they can get or fail to get what they

[1]*Self-Knowledge and Self-Identity* (Ithaca, N.Y., 1963), p. 23 f.

wanted. But is it also true that when the experimenter proceeds *after* the experiment to act in accordance with one of the preferences and not the other, then one of A and B will have got what he wanted, and the other not?

There seems very good ground for saying so. For suppose the experimenter, having elicited A's and B's preference, says nothing to A and B about what he will do; conducts the experiment; and then, for example, gives the unpleasant treatment to the B-body-person and the pleasant treatment to the A-body-person. Then the B-body-person will not only complain of the unpleasant treatment as such, but will complain (since he has A's memories) that that was not the outcome he chose, since he chose that the B-body-person should be well treated; and since A made his choice in selfish spirit, he may add that he precisely chose in that way because he did not want the unpleasant things to happen to *him*. The A-body-person meanwhile will express satisfaction both at the receipt of the $100,000, and also at the fact that the experimenter had chosen to act in the way that he, B, so wisely chose. These facts make a strong case for saying that the experimenter has brought it about that B did in the outcome get what he wanted and A did not. It is therefore a strong case for saying that the B-body-person really is A, and the A-body-person really is B; and therefore for saying that the process of the experiment really is that of changing bodies. For the same reasons it would seem that A and B in our example really did choose wisely, and that it was A's bad luck that the choice he correctly made was not carried out, B's good luck that the choice he correctly made was carried out. This seems to show that to care about what happens to me in the future is not necessarily to care about what happens to *this* body (the one I now have); and this in turn might be taken to show that in some sense of Descartes's obscure phrase, I and my body are "really distinct" (though, of course, nothing in these considerations could support the idea that I could exist without a body at all).

These suggestions seem to be reinforced if we consider the cases where A and B make other choices with regard to the experiment. Suppose that A chooses that the A-body-person should get the money, and the B-body-person get the pain, and B chooses conversely. Here again there can be no outcome which matches the expressed preferences of both of them: they cannot both get what they want. The experimenter announces, before the experiment, that the A-body-person will in fact get the money, and the B-body-person will get the pain. So A at this stage gets what he wants (the announced outcome matches his expressed preference). After the experiment, the distribution is carried out as announced. Both the A-body-person and the B-body-person will have to agree that what is happening is in accordance with the preference that A originally expressed. The B-body-person will naturally express this acknowledgment (since he has A's memories) by saying that this is the distribution he chose; he will recall, among other things, the experimenter announcing this outcome, his approving it as what he chose, and so forth. However, he (the B-body-person) certainly does not like what is now happening to him, and would much prefer to be receiving what the A-body-person is receiving —namely, $100,000. The A-body-person will on the other hand recall choosing an outcome other than this one, but will reckon it good luck that the experimenter did not do what he recalls choosing. It looks, then, as though the A-body-person had gotten what he wanted, but not what he chose, while the B-body-person has gotten what he chose, but not what he wanted. So once more it looks as though they are, respectively, B and A; and that in this case the original choices of both A and B were unwise.

Suppose, lastly, that in the original choice A takes the line of the first case and B of the second: that is, A chooses that the B-body-person should get the money and the A-body-person the pain, and B chooses exactly the same thing. In this case, the experimenter would seem to be in the happy situation of giving both persons what they want—or at least, like God, what they have chosen. In this case, the *B*-body-person likes what he is receiving, recalls choosing it, and congratulates himself on the wisdom of (as he puts it) his choice; while the *A*-body-person does not like what he is receiving, recalls choosing it, and is forced to acknowledge that (as he puts it) his choice was unwise. So once more we seem to get results to support the suggestions drawn from the first case.

Let us now consider the question, not of *A* and *B* choosing certain outcomes to take place after the experiment, but of their willingness to engage in the experiment at all. If they were initially inclined to accept the description of the experiment as "changing bodies" then one thing that would interest them would be the character of the other person's body. In this respect also what would happen after the experiment would seem to suggest that "changing bodies" was a good description of the experiment. If *A* and *B* agreed to the experiment, being each not displeased with the appearance, physique, and so forth of the other person's body; after the experiment the *B*-body-person might well be found saying such things as: "When I agreed to this experiment, I thought that *B*'s face was quite attractive, but now I look at it in the mirror, I am not so sure"; or the *A*-body-person might say "When I agreed to this experiment I did not know that *A* had a wooden leg; but now, after it is over, I find that I have this wooden leg, and I want the experiment reversed." It is possible that he might say further that he finds the leg very uncomfortable, and that the *B*-body-person should say, for instance, that he recalls that he found it very uncomfortable at first, but one gets used to it: but perhaps one would need to know more than at least I do about the physiology of habituation to artificial limbs to know whether the *A*-body-person would find the leg uncomfortable: that body, after all, has had the leg on it for some time. But apart from this sort of detail, the general line of the outcome regarded from this point of view seems to confirm our previous conclusions about the experiment.

Now let us suppose that when the experiment is proposed (in non-question-begging terms) *A* and *B* think rather of their psychological advantages and disadvantages. *A*'s thoughts turn primarily to certain sorts of anxiety to which he is very prone, while *B* is concerned with the frightful memories he has of past experiences which still distress him. They each hope that the experiment will in some way result in their being able to get away from these things. They may even have been impressed by philosophical arguments to the effect that bodily continuity is at least a necessary condition of personal identity: *A*, for example, reasons that, granted the experiment comes off, then the person who is bodily continuous with him will not have this anxiety, while the other person will no doubt have some anxiety—perhaps in some sense his anxiety—and at least that person will not be he. The experiment is performed and the experimenter (to whom *A* and *B* previously revealed privately their several difficulties and hopes) asks the *A*-body-person whether he has gotten rid of his anxiety. This person presumably replies that he does not know what the man is talking about; he never had such anxiety, but he did have some very disagreeable memories, and recalls engaging in the experiment to get rid of them, and is disappointed to discover that he still has them. The *B*-body-person will react in a similar way to questions about his painful memories, pointing out that he still has his anxiety. These results seem to confirm still further the description of the experiment as "changing bodies." And all the results suggest that the only rational thing to do, confronted with such an experiment, would be to identify oneself with one's memories, and so forth, and not with one's body. The philosophical arguments designed to show that bodily continuity was at least a necessary condition of personal identity would seem to be just mistaken.

Let us now consider something apparently different. Someone in whose power I am tells me that I am going to be tortured tomorrow. I am frightened, and look forward to tomorrow in great apprehension. He adds that when the time comes, I shall not remember being told that this was going to happen to me, since shortly before the torture something else will be done to me which will make me forget the announcement. This certainly will not cheer me up, since I know perfectly well that I can forget things, and that there is such a thing as indeed being tortured unexpectedly because I had forgotten or been made to forget a prediction of the torture; that will still be a torture which, so long as I do know about the prediction, I look forward to in fear. He then adds that my forgetting the announcement will be only part of a larger process: when the moment of torture comes, I shall not remember any of the things I am now in a position to remember. This does not cheer me up, either, since I can readily conceive of being involved in an accident, for instance, as a result of which I wake up in a completely amnesiac state and also in great pain; that could certainly happen to me, I should not like it to happen to me, nor to know that it was going to happen to me. He now further adds that at the moment of torture I shall not only not remember the things I am now in a position to remember, but will have a different set of impressions of my past, quite different from the memories I now have. I do not think that this would cheer me up, either. For I can at least conceive the possibility, if not the concrete reality, of going completely mad, and thinking perhaps that I am George IV or somebody; and being told that something like that was going to happen to me would have no tendency to reduce the terror of being told authoritatively that I was going to be tortured, but would merely compound the horror. Nor do I see why I should be put into any better frame of mind by the person in charge adding lastly that the impressions of my past with which I shall be equipped on the eve of torture will exactly fit the past of another person now living, and that indeed I shall acquire these impressions by (for instance) information now in his brain being copied into mine. Fear, surely, would still be the proper reaction: and not because one did not know what was going to happen, but because in one vital respect at least one did know what was going to happen—torture, which one can indeed expect to happen to oneself, and to be preceded by certain mental derangements as well.

If this is right, the whole question seems now to be totally mysterious. For what we have just been through is of course merely one side, differently represented, of the transaction which we considered before; and it represents it as a perfectly hateful prospect, while the previous considerations represented it as something one should rationally, perhaps even cheerfully, choose out of the options there presented. It is differently presented, of course, and in two notable respects; but when we look at these two differences of presentation, can we really convince ourselves that the second presentation is wrong or misleading, thus leaving the road open to the first version which at the time seemed so convincing? Surely not.

The first difference is that in the second version the torture is throughout represented as going to happen to *me*: "you," the man in charge persistently says. Thus he is not very neutral. But should he have been neutral? Or, to put it another way, does his use of the second person have a merely emotional and rhetorical effect on me, making me afraid when further reflection would have shown I had no reason to be? It is certainly not obviously so. The problem just is that through every step of his predictions I seem to be able to follow him successfully. And if I reflect on whether what he has said gives me grounds for fearing that I shall be tortured, I could consider that behind my fears lies some principle such as this: that my undergoing physical pain in the future is not excluded by any psychological state I may be in at the time, with the platitudinous exception of those psychological states which in themselves exclude experiencing pain, notably (if it is a psychological state) unconsciousness. In particular, what impressions I have about the past will not have any effect on whether I undergo the pain or not. This principle seems sound enough.

It is an important fact that not everything I would, as things are, regard as an evil would be something that I should rationally fear as an evil if it were predicted that it would happen to me in the future and also predicted that I should undergo significant psychological changes in the meantime. For the fact that I regard that happening, things being as they are, as an evil can be dependent on factors of belief or character which might themselves be modified by the psychological changes in question. Thus if I am appallingly subject to acrophobia, and am told that I shall find myself on top of a steep mountain in the near future, I shall to that extent be afraid; but if I am told that I shall be psychologically changed in the meantime in such a way as to rid me of my acrophobia (and as with the other prediction, I believe it), then I have no reason to be afraid of the predicted happening, or at least not the same reason. Again, I might look forward to meeting a certain person again with either alarm or excitement because of my memories of our past relations. In some part, these memories operate in connection with my emotion, not only on the present time, but projectively forward: for it is to a meeting itself affected by the presence of those memories that I look forward. If I am convinced that when the time comes I shall not have those memories, then I shall not have just the same reasons as before for looking forward to that meeting with the one emotion or the other. (Spiritualism, incidentally, appears to involve the belief that I have just the same reasons for a given attitude toward encountering people again after I am dead, as I did before: with the one modification that I can be sure it will all be very nice.)

Physical pain, however, the example which

for simplicity (and not for any obsessional reason) I have taken, is absolutely minimally dependent on character or belief. No amount of change in my character or my beliefs would seem to affect substantially the nastiness of tortures applied to me; correspondingly, no degree of predicted change in my character and beliefs can unseat the fear of torture which, together with those changes, is predicted for me.

I am not at all suggesting that the *only* basis, or indeed the only rational basis, for fear in the face of these various predictions is how things will be relative to my psychological state in the eventual outcome. I am merely pointing out that this is one component; it is not the only one. For certainly one will fear and otherwise reject the changes themselves, or in very many cases one would. Thus one of the old paradoxes of hedonic utilitarianism; if one had assurances that undergoing certain operations and being attached to a machine would provide one for the rest of one's existence with an unending sequence of delicious and varied experiences, one might very well reject the option, and react with fear if someone proposed to apply it compulsorily; and that fear and horror would seem appropriate reactions in the second case may help to discredit the interpretation (if anyone has the nerve to propose it) that one's reason for rejecting the option voluntarily would be a consciousness of duties to others which one in one's hedonic state would leave undone. The prospect of contented madness or vegetableness is found by many (not perhaps by all) appalling in ways which are obviously not a function of how things would then be for them, for things would then be for them not appalling. In the case we are at present discussing, these sorts of considerations seem merely to make it clearer that the predictions of the man in charge provide a double ground of horror: at the prospect of torture, and at the prospect of the change in character and in impressions of the past that will precede it. And certainly, to repeat what has already been said, the prospect of the second certainly seems to provide no ground for rejecting or not fearing the prospect of the first.

I said that there were two notable differences between the second presentation of our situation and the first. The first difference, which we have just said something about, was that the man predicted the torture for *me*, a psychologically very changed "me." We have yet to find a reason for saying that he should not have done this, or that I really should be unable to follow him if he does; I seem to be able to follow him only too well. The second difference is that in this presentation he does not mention the other man, except in the somewhat incidental role of being the provenance of the impressions of the past I end up with. He does not mention him at all as someone who will end up with impressions of the past derived from me (and, incidentally, with $100,000 as well—a consideration which, in the frame of mind appropriate to this version, will merely make me jealous).

But why *should* he mention this man and what is going to happen to him? My selfish concern is to be told what is going to happen to me, and now I know: torture, preceded by changes of character, brain operations, changes in impressions of the past. The knowledge that one other person, or none, or many will be similarly mistreated may affect me in other ways, of sympathy, greater horror at the power of this tyrant, and so forth; but surely it cannot affect my expectations of torture? But— someone will say—this is to leave out exactly the feature which, as the first presentation of the case showed, makes all the difference: for it is to leave out the person who, as the first presentation showed, will be you. It is to leave out not merely a feature which should fundamentally affect your fears, it is to leave out the very person for whom you are fearful. So of course, the objector will say, this makes all the difference.

But can it? Consider the following series of cases. In each case we are to suppose that after what is described, A is, as before, to be tortured;

we are also to suppose the person A is informed beforehand that just these things followed by the torture will happen to him:

(*i*) A is subjected to an operation which produces total amnesia;

(*ii*) amnesia is produced in A, and other interference leads to certain changes in his character;

(*iii*) changes in his character are produced, and at the same time certain illusory "memory" beliefs are induced in him; these are of a quite fictitious kind and do not fit the life of any actual person;

(*iv*) the same as (*iii*), except that both the character traits and the "memory" impressions are designed to be appropriate to another actual person, B;

(*v*) the same as (*iv*), except that the result is produced by putting the information into A from the brain of B, by a method which leaves B the same as he was before;

(*vi*) the same happens to A as in (*v*), but B is not left the same, since a similar operation is conducted in the reverse direction.

I take it that no one is going to dispute that A has reasons, and fairly straightforward reasons, for fear of pain when the prospect is that of situation (*i*); there seems no conceivable reason why this should not extend to situation (*ii*), and the situation (*iii*) can surely introduce no difference of principle—it just seems a situation which for more than one reason we should have grounds for fearing, as suggested above. Situation (*iv*) at least introduces the person B, who was the focus of the objection we are now discussing. But it does not seem to introduce him in any way which makes a material difference; if I can expect pain through a transformation which involves new "memory"-impressions, it would seem a purely external fact, relative to that, that the "memory"-impressions had a model. Nor, in (*iv*), do we satisfy a causal condition which I mentioned at the beginning for the "memories" actually being memories; though notice that if the job were done thoroughly, I might well be able to elicit from the A-body-person the kinds of remarks about his previous expectations of the experiment—remarks appropriate to the original *B*—which so impressed us in the first version of the story. I shall have a similar assurance of this being so in situation (*v*), where, moreover, a plausible application of the causal condition is available.

But two things are to be noticed about this situation. First, if we concentrate on *A* and the *A*-body-person, we do not seem to have added anything which from the point of view of his fears makes any material difference; just as, in the move from (*iii*) to (*iv*), it made no relevant difference that the new "memory"-impressions which precede the pain had, as it happened, a model, so in the move from (*iv*) to (*v*) all we have added is that they have a model which is also their cause: and it is still difficult to see why that, to him looking forward, could possibly make the difference between expecting pain and not expecting pain. To illustrate that point from the case of character: if *A* is capable of expecting pain, he is capable of expecting pain preceded by a change in his dispositions—and to that expectation it can make no difference, whether that change in his dispositions is modeled on, or indeed indirectly caused by, the dispositions of some other person. If his fears can, as it were, reach through the change, it seems a mere trimming how the change is in fact induced. The second point about situation (*v*) is that if the crucial question for *A*'s fears with regard to what befalls the *A*-body-person is whether the *A*-body-person is or is not the person *B*,[2] then that condition has not yet been satisfied in situation (*v*): for there we have an undisputed *B* in addition to the *A*-body-person, and certainly those two are not the same person.

But in situation (*vi*), we seemed to think, that is finally what he is. But if *A*'s original fears could reach through the expected changes in

(*v*), as they did in (*iv*) and (*iii*), then certainly they can reach through in (*vi*). Indeed, from the point of view of *A*'s expectations and fears, there is less difference between (*vi*) and (*v*) than there is between (*v*) and (*iv*) or between (*iv*) and (*iii*). In those transitions, there were at least differences—though we could not see that they were really relevant differences—in the content and cause of what happened to him; in the present case there is absolutely no difference at all in what happens to him, the only difference being in what happens to someone else. If he can fear pain when (*v*) is predicted, why should he cease to when (*vi*) is?

I can see only one way of relevantly laying great weight on the transition from (*v*) to (*vi*); and this involves a considerable difficulty. This is to deny that, as I put it, the transition from (*v*) to (*vi*) involves merely the addition of something happening to *somebody else*; what rather it does, it will be said, is to involve the reintroduction of *A* himself, as the *B*-body-person; since he has reappeared in this form, it is for this person, and not for the unfortunate *A*-body-person, that *A* will have his expectations. This is to reassert, in effect, the viewpoint emphasized in our first presentation of the experiment. But this surely has the consequence that *A* should not have fears for the *A*-body person who appeared in situation (*v*). For by the present argument, the *A*-body-person in (*vi*) is not *A*; the *B*-body-person is. But the *A*-body-person in (*v*) is, in character, history, everything, exactly the same as the *A*-body-person in (*vi*); so if the latter is not *A*, then neither is the former. (It is this point, no doubt, that encourages one to speak of the difference that goes with [*vi*] as being, on the present view, the *reintroduction* of *A*.) But no one else in (*v*) has any better claim to be *A*. So in (*v*), it seems, *A* just does not exist. This would certainly explain why *A* should have no fears for the state of things in (*v*)—though he might well have fears for the path to it. But it rather looked earlier as though he could well have fears for the state of things in (*v*). Let us grant, however, that that was an illusion, and

---

[2]This of course does not have to be the crucial question, but it seems one fair way of taking up the present objection.

that *A* really does not exist in (*v*); then does he exist in (*iv*), (*iii*), (*ii*), or (*i*)? It seems very difficult to deny it for (*i*) and (*ii*); are we perhaps to draw the line between (*iii*) and (*iv*)?

Here someone will say: you must not insist on drawing a line—borderline cases are borderline cases, and you must not push our concepts beyond their limits. But this well-known piece of advice, sensible as it is in many cases, seems in the present case to involve an extraordinary difficulty. It may intellectually comfort observers of *A*'s situation; but what is *A* supposed to make of it? To be told that a future situation is a borderline one for its being myself that is hurt, that it is conceptually undecidable whether it will be me or not, is something which, it seems, I can do nothing with; because, in particular, it seems to have no comprehensible representation in my expectations and the emotions that go with them.

If I expect that a certain situation, *S*, will come about in the future, there is of course a wide range of emotions and concerns, directed on *S*, which I may experience now in relation to my expectation. Unless I am exceptionally egoistic, it is not a condition on my being concerned in relation to this expectation, that I myself will be involved in *S*—where my being "involved" in *S* means that I figure in *S* as someone doing something at that time or having something done to me, or, again, that *S* will have consequences affecting me at that or some subsequent time. There are some emotions, however, which I will feel only if I will be involved in *S*, and fear is an obvious example.

Now the description of *S* under which it figures in my expectations will necessarily be, in various ways, indeterminate; and one way in which it may be indeterminate is that it leave open whether I shall be involved in *S* or not. Thus I may have good reason to expect that one out of us five is going to get hurt, but no reason to expect it to be me rather than one of the others. My present emotions will be correspondingly affected by this indeterminacy. Thus, sticking to the egoistic concern involved in fear, I shall presumably be somewhat more cheerful than if I knew it was going to be me, somewhat less cheerful than if I had been left out altogether. Fear will be mixed with, and qualified by, apprehension; and so forth. These emotions revolve around the thought of the eventual determination of the indeterminacy; moments of straight fear focus on its really turning out to be me, of hope on its turning out not to be me. All the emotions are related to the coming about of what I expect: and what I expect in such a case just cannot come about save by coming about in one of the ways or another.

There are other ways in which indeterminate expectations can be related to fear. Thus I may expect (perhaps neurotically) that something nasty is going to happen to me, indeed expect that when it happens it will take some determinate form, but have no range, or no closed range, of candidates for the determinate form to rehearse in my present thought. Different from this would be the fear of something radically indeterminate—the fear (one might say) of a nameless horror. If somebody had such a fear, one could even say that he had, in a sense, a perfectly determinate expectation: if what he expects indeed comes about, there will be nothing more determinate to be said about it after the event than was said in the expectation. Both these cases of course are cases of *fear* because one thing that is fixed amid the indeterminacy is the belief that it is to me to which the things will happen.

Central to the expectation of *S* is the thought of what it will be like when it happens—thought which may be indeterminate, range over alternatives, and so forth. When *S* involves me, there can be the possibility of a special form of such thought: the thought of how it will be for me, the imaginative projection of myself as participant in *S*.[3]

---

[3]For a more detailed treatment of issues related to this, see *Imagination and the Self*, British Academy (London, 1966); reprinted in P. F. Strawson (ed.), *Studies in Thought and Action* (Oxford, 1968).

I do not have to think about S in this way, when it involves me; but I may be able to. (It might be suggested that this possibility was even mirrored in the language, in the distinction between "expecting to be hurt" and "expecting that I shall be hurt"; but I am very doubtful about this point, which is in any case of no importance.)

Suppose now that there is an S with regard to which it is for conceptual reasons undecidable whether it involves me or not, as is proposed for the experimental situation by the line we are discussing. It is important that the expectation of S is not *indeterminate* in any of the ways we have just been considering. It is not like the nameless horror, since the fixed point of that case was that it was going to happen to the subject, and that made his state unequivocally fear. Nor is it like the expectation of the man who expects one of the five to be hurt; his fear was indeed equivocal, but its focus, and that of the expectation, was that when S came about, it would certainly come about in one way or the other. In the present case, fear (of the torture, that is to say, not of the initial experiment) seems neither appropriate, nor inappropriate, nor appropriately equivocal. Relatedly, the subject has an incurable difficulty about how he may think about S. If he engages in projective imaginative thinking (about how it will be for him), he implicitly answers the necessarily unanswerable question; if he thinks that he cannot engage in such thinking, it looks very much as if he also answers it, though in the opposite direction. Perhaps he must just refrain from such thinking; but is he just refraining from it, if it is incurably undecidable whether he can or cannot engage in it?

It may be said that all that these considerations can show is that fear, at any rate, does not get its proper footing in this case; but that there could be some other, more ambivalent, form of concern which would indeed be appropriate to this particular expectation, the expectation of the conceptually undecidable situation. There

are, perhaps, analogous feelings that actually occur in actual situations. Thus material objects do occasionally undergo puzzling transformations which leave a conceptual shadow over their identity. Suppose I were sentimentally attached to an object to which this sort of thing then happened; then it might be that I could neither feel about it quite as I did originally, nor be totally indifferent to it, but would have some other and rather ambivalent feeling toward it. Similarly, it may be said, toward the prospective sufferer of pain, my identity relations with whom are conceptually shadowed, I can feel neither as I would if he were certainly me, nor as I would if he were certainly not, but rather some such ambivalent concern.

But this analogy does little to remove the most baffling aspect of the present case—an aspect which has already turned up in what was said about the subject's difficulty in thinking either projectively or non-projectively about the situation. For to regard the prospective pain-sufferer *just* like the transmogrified object of sentiment, and to conceive of my ambivalent distress about his future pain as just like ambivalent distress about some future damage to such an object, is of course to leave him and me clearly distinct from one another, and thus to displace the conceptual shadow from its proper place. I have to get nearer to him than that. But is there any nearer that I can get to him without expecting his pain? If there is, the analogy has not shown us it. We can certainly not get nearer by expecting, as it were, *ambivalent* pain; there is no place at all for that. There seems to be an obstinate bafflement to mirroring in my expectations a situation in which it is conceptually undecidable whether I occur.

The bafflement seems, moreover, to turn to plain absurdity if we move from conceptual undecidability to its close friend and neighbor, conventionalist decision. This comes out if we consider another description, overtly conventionalist, of the series of cases which occasioned the present discussion. This description would reject a point I relied on in an earlier argument —namely, that if we deny that the A-body-person in (vi) is A (because the B-body-person is), then we must deny that the A-body-person in (v) is A, since they are exactly the same. "No," it may be said, "this is just to assume that we say the same in different sorts of situation. No doubt when we have the very good candidate for being A—namely, the B-body-person—we call him A; but this does not mean that we should not call the A-body-person A in that other situation when we have no better candidate around. Different situations call for different descriptions." This line of talk is the sort of thing indeed appropriate to lawyers deciding the ownership of some property which has undergone some bewildering set of transformations; they just have to decide, and in each situation, let us suppose, it has got to go to somebody, on as reasonable grounds as the facts and the law admit. But as a line to deal with a person's fears or expectations about his own future, it seems to have no sense at all. If A's fears can extend to what will happen to the A-body-person in (v), I do not see how they can be rationally diverted from the fate of the exactly similar person in (vi) by his being told that someone would have a reason in the latter situation which he would not have in the former for deciding to call another person A.

Thus, to sum up, it looks as though there are two presentations of the imagined experiment and the choice associated with it, each of which carries conviction, and which lead to contrary conclusions. The idea, moreover, that the situation after the experiment is conceptually undecidable in the relevant respect seems not to assist, but rather to increase, the puzzlement; while the idea (so often appealed to in these matters) that it is conventionally decidable is even worse. Following from all that, I am not in the least clear which option it would be wise to take if one were presented with them before the experiment. I find that rather disturbing.

Whatever the puzzlement, there is one feature of the arguments which have led to it which is worth picking out, since it runs counter to something which is, I think, often rather vaguely supposed. It is often recognized that there are "first-personal" and "third-personal" aspects of questions about persons, and that there are difficulties about the relations between them. It is also recognized that "mentalistic" considerations (as we may vaguely call them) and considerations of bodily continuity are involved in questions of personal identity (which is not to say that there are mentalistic and bodily criteria of personal identity). It is tempting to think that the two distinctions run in parallel: roughly, that a first-personal approach concentrates attention on mentalistic considerations, while a third-personal approach emphasizes considerations of bodily continuity. The present discussion is an illustration of exactly the opposite. The first argument, which led to the "mentalistic" conclusion that A and B would change bodies and that each person should identify himself with the destination of his memories and character, was an argument entirely conducted in third-personal terms. The second argument, which suggested the bodily continuity identification, concerned itself with the first-personal issue of what A could expect. That this is so seems to me (though I will not discuss it further here) of some significance.

I will end by suggesting one rather shaky way in which one might approach a resolution of the problem, using only the limited materials already available.

The apparently decisive arguments of the first presentation, which suggested that A should identify himself with the B-body-person, turned on the extreme neatness of the situation in satisfying, if any could, the description of "changing bodies." But this neatness is basically artificial; it is the product of the will of the experimenter to produce a situation which would naturally elicit, with minimum hesitation, that description. By the sorts of methods he employed, he could easily have left off earlier or gone on further. He could have stopped at situation (*v*), leaving *B* as he was; or he could have gone on and produced two persons each with *A*-like character and memories, as well as one or two with *B*-like characteristics. If he had done either of those, we should have been in yet greater difficulty about what to say; he just chose to make it as easy as possible for us to find something to say. Now if we had some model of ghostly persons in bodies, which were in some sense actually moved around by certain procedures, we would regard the neat experiment just as the *effective* experiment: the one method that really did result in the ghostly persons' changing places without being destroyed, dispersed, or whatever. But we cannot seriously use such a

model. The experimenter has not in the sense of that model *induced* a change of bodies; he has rather produced the one situation out of a range of equally possible situations which we should be most disposed to call a change of bodies. As against this, the principle that one's fears can extend to future pain whatever psychological changes precede it seems positively straightforward. Perhaps, indeed, it is not; but we need to be shown what is wrong with it. Until we are shown what is wrong with it, we should perhaps decide that if we were the person *A* then, if we were to decide selfishly, we should pass the pain to the *B*-body-person. It would be risky: that there is room for the notion of a *risk* here is itself a major feature of the problem.

13

PETER UNGER
The Physical View

Two Hypothetical Examples: A Clear Case of Survival and a Clear Failure of Survival

Sometime in the distant future, as we may imagine, wondrous technologies may become available that will work, not only on other sorts of things, but on people just like ourselves. One of these may be the process of *super freezing and super thawing*: A super freezing machine will stop a person's molecules in their tracks, so to say, almost perfectly preserving their relative

arrangement for minutes, or for years. Almost instantaneously, it reduces the temperature of a person's body to within a very minute fraction of one degree Kelvin of absolute zero, and keeps it there until it operates in reverse. Later, the device may operate as a super thawing machine, raising the temperature of that body, virtually instantaneously, to normal body temperature.

As far as any technical matters are concerned, these devices work extremely well: Technically, the machines work even more reliably and proficiently than the best of our own very reliable electric light switches and, for the bodies that enter them, they are even safer than our own very safe elevators.

Excerpted from Peter Unger, *Identity, Consciousness and Value*, New York: Oxford University Press, 1990.

As we may further imagine, there may be only some small, even trivial differences between the person just after thawing and the person just before freezing. In all important respects, these differences may be noticeably less than the small differences, in actual fact, between you now and yourself just one minute ago, when you did not have your memories of this past minute. After the thawing, experience, thought and behavior will take up where, right before the freezing, they left off.

Will a person who enters this superbly reliable freezing and thawing process survive it? Or, will only the body survive while it becomes, toward the end, the body of an exactly similar, but numerically distinct, person? As we strongly respond, even the person himself will survive. At the end, there will not merely be some later person who is extremely like the earlier, and who is composed of the same matter arranged in the same way. No: there will be the very same identical person, existing both earlier and at later times.

. . . Certain other hypothetical cases elicit equally strong responses, but in the negative direction. One of these concerns the process of *taping with physical temporal overlap*: Whether he is asleep or awake at the time, a person may enter this taping process quite directly. For dramatic emphasis, let us imagine a case where, at the outset, the person who enters is sound asleep, with no conscious thought or experience: he is, of course, asleep in a certain location, which we will say is "right here." In the taping process, a machine records the exact nature of, and the precise relative arrangement of, all of the person's atoms and molecules. Using this information and using a different batch of matter "over there," the device arranges, over there, exactly as many molecules, of just those sorts, in precisely that same arrangement. Exactly alike in all qualitative respects, there is a person sound asleep over there and a person sound asleep right here. After five minutes, there awakens right here a person who is, at the very least, just like the person who was right

here before. There also awakens over there a person just like that. After another five minutes, there is an annihilating explosion right here, which disturbs nothing and nobody over there. From the moment of his awakening, right through and after the explosion, the person over there experiences, thinks and acts in just the expected ways.

Will the person who, right here, enters this temporal overlap process survive the whole thing, including the explosion, and end up as the sole person who emerges over there? Or, will he cease to exist, at the end there being, over there, only an exactly similar, but a numerically distinct, second person. As we strongly respond, someone who undergoes this second hypothetical process will not survive beyond the time of the explosion. The person who emerges from the process, over there, is a numerically distinct individual. Just as it is very clear that a person *will* survive the hypothetical process of super freezing, so it is very clear that a person will *not* survive this quite different hypothetical process of taping with physical temporal overlap. . . .

Core Psychology and Distinctive Psychology

. . . it will be useful for us to make an explicit distinction between two aspects of a person's *dispositional psychology*: We distinguish between her *core psychology* and her *distinctive psychology*. Among the mental capacities that it comprises, my dispositional psychology includes those that I share with all other normal human beings, notably my capacity for conscious experience, my capacity to reason at least in a rudimentary way, and my capacity to form some simple intentions. These capabilities are shared, too, with many humans who are markedly below the psychological norms. We may call this group of capacities my *core* psychology, with the understanding that this term may be highly, and perhaps irremediably, vague. Certain other aspects of my psychology I share with some normal humans but do not share with others, for example, my (ostensible) memory of having tasted butter pecan ice cream. Still other aspects distinguish me from all other actual human beings. . . . Let us say that my *distinctive* psychology comprises both of these other aspects of my psychology. So part of my distinctive psychology I share with some, but not all, other normal human beings, and the rest I share with none. . . .

Although these ideas are vague ones, the notions of core psychology and distinctive psychology may be philosophically useful ideas. Unless we are very badly wrong about ourselves, the distinction that these vague terms make is, with respect to every normal human person, both exhaustive and exclusive: Every normal human person has a core psychology and, in addition to that, a distinctive psychology, which together entirely compose her dispositional psychology. As you and I are normal human people, our psychologies may be exhaustively categorized by these terms. At all events, what happens to us as regards our survival may depend on what happens to these aspects of our psychology, and it might depend, as well, on what happens to *what realizes* these two aspects.

On the psychological approach, the key to my existing at a future time is that much of my present psychology be causally carried forward in time and, thus, be much of a single future person's psychology. To be me, the person at the later time should have, not only all of my core psychology, but much of my distinctive psychology as well. It may be indeterminate how many of, and which ones of, the distinctive dispositions the future person is required to have. But, to be me, he must have rather many of my (ostensible) personal memories or, lacking that, he must at least have rather many of my present character and personality traits.

It is interesting to note that this psychological approach is quite demanding in a certain way while being quite lenient in a related respect: On this approach, a lot is demanded regarding how much of a person's psychology must be causally preserved for me to survive. But very little is demanded regarding how this causal preservation must take place. It will be useful to illustrate this disparity.

An alleged teletransporter may destroy my brain and body in the processes of extracting information as to my innermost constitution. It may then send this information to a companion device that, out of new matter, constructs a new brain and body, qualitatively the same as the old. Owing to these causal connections, the new brain may realize a psychology just like that last realized by the old one. On the psychological approach, I will, in such an event, succeed in making the trip, even though I suddenly have a new brain and body at my destination. To be sure, the causal route by way of which my psychology is carried forward is quite abnormal, not merely in marginal ways, but in ways that are very substantial. In particular, this causal route involves little or none of the physical continuity ordinarily present in cases of our survival. Further, the causal route will allow that, in a possibly brief middle period, I do not exist at all. On the psychological approach, that makes no difference: Roughly, but usefully enough, because there is a causal thrust into the future of, and thus a later realization of, so much of the psychology that was mine, I will survive.

On a physical approach to personal identity, by contrast, much more is demanded of the ways that a person's psychology is causally carried forward. For purposes of exposition, I stipulate that, as regards the more general features, we are right about the causal structure of our lives. Given this stipulation, we may say that, on the physical approach, for a person to survive, some of her psychology, her core psychology, must be carried forward in ways that are, on the whole, not terribly different from the ways that psychological continuity is achieved in ordinary cases. Most importantly, this will require a fair amount of physical continuity between the past person and the future one. In the case of the alleged teletransporter, there is virtually nothing in way of physical continuity in the causal process. So, on the physical approach, I don't survive that exotic procedure. . . .

. . . the labels we employ have no bearing on the traditional problem of mind and body. What we have called the psychological approach is completely compatible with materialism, or physicalism, and may be consistently advocated by philosophers who hold that all mental events are physical events. And what we have called the physical approach is compatible with certain forms of dualism about the mental and the physical. The physical approach to personal identity, as here understood, may be consistently maintained by a philosopher who holds that there are mental events, such as conscious pains, that are not physical. When we bear these points in mind, it is harder for our labels to mislead us.

We can further reduce the danger by noting that even the physical approach is aimed at certain psychological factors, namely, those of core psychology. A person's physical parts and structures are important to her survival *only insofar as they continue to support, and to realize, her basic psychological capacities.* If I am made into living meat, with no mental capacities, I do not survive. If, a day later, a person is configured from this living meat, that person is not me. . . .

Three Uses of "What Matters in Survival"

Very probably, the following sentence expresses a fact about how the world is at a time later than the writing of this very sentence itself: One of the people who will exist ten years from now is me. Contemplating the probable truth of the sentence makes me happy. Should I think there was much chance of its being false, I would be despondent.

But *what is it that matters* so much, at least to me, in the fact that one of the future people will be *me*, that is, in the fact that *I* will survive for at least another ten years? What is so important, to me at least, about *my* existing ten years from now, in contrast to there existing in ten year's time someone, other than myself, who is exceedingly like me in ever so many ways and who is causally descended from me? These questions can be strangely puzzling. To many philosophers, their puzzling character makes the topic of personal identity all the more intriguing.

In asking these questions, however, philosophers may not all be using the key motivational terms, 'important' and 'what matters,' in the same way. Instead, we might be using them in several identifiably different ways. Perhaps our differing uses cluster around a few different paradigms of use, some of us gathering around one of the paradigms, others around another.

As I will argue shortly, many philosophers may focus on a use of these terms that connects closely with matters of psychological continuity. By virtue of this focus, these thinkers will favor a *psychological approach to what matters in our survival.* It will then be but a short step to favoring, as well, the psychological approach to our survival itself, or at least a view quite close to that position. . . .

The question then arises: What are the philosophically prevalent uses of 'what matters in survival'? In this connection, it is instructive to inspect an influential passage from David Lewis, an advocate of the psychological approach to our survival itself:

What is it that matters in survival? . . . What do I really care about? If it can happen that some features of ordinary everyday survival are present but others are missing, then what would it take to make the difference between something practically as good as commonplace survival and something practically as bad as commonplace death?

I answer, along with many others: what matters in survival is mental continuity and connectedness. *When I consider various cases in between commonplace survival and commonplace death, I find that what I mostly want in wanting survival is that my mental life should flow on. My present experiences, thoughts, beliefs, desires, and traits of character should have appropriate future successors. My total present mental state should be but one momentary stage in a continuing succession of mental states. The successive states should be interconnected in two ways. First, by bonds of similarity. Change should be gradual rather than sudden, and (at least in some respects) there should not be too much change overall. Second, by bonds of lawful causal dependence. Such change as there is should conform, for the most part, to lawful regularities concerning the succession of mental states—regularities, moreover, that are examplified in everyday cases of survival. And this should be so not by accident . . . but rather because each succeeding mental state causally depends for its character on the states immediately before it.*[1]

As do other friends of the psychological approach, perhaps Lewis is using 'what matters in survival' in a way that is not highly relevant to questions of our survival.

In trying to understand how philosophers may be employing the term, we should begin by distinguishing between two uses: On the use that Lewis apparently favors, which I will call the *desirability use*, 'what matters in survival' will mean much the same as this: what it is that one gets out of survival that makes continued

survival a desirable thing for one, a better thing, at least, than is utter cessation. On this desirability use, if one has what matters in survival, then, from a self-interested perspective, one has reason to continue rather than opt for sudden painless termination.

On this use, the expression's range may threaten to become so expansive as to be virtually the same as that of 'what matters in life': If this use is taken to the extreme, we will employ the expression so that its range may come to include the having of varied and pleasant experiences, the performance of worthwhile actions, the enjoyment of interpersonal relationships, and so on. Of course, even friends of the psychological approach never do get very near this extreme: With artful good sense, this expansive tendency may be firmly held in check by a concern to stick at least fairly close to considerations of survival itself.

Although this desirability use may have its advantages, philosophical illumination of personal identity is not one of them. On the contrary, in trying to stick close to the topic of personal identity, we want to avoid this use about as much as we can. . . .

A second use is much more appropriate for questions of personal identity. On the use I have in mind, which I will call the *prudential use* of 'what matters in survival,' the expression will be glossed in some such rough way as this: From the perspective of a person's concern for herself, or from a slight and rational extension of that perspective, what future being there is or, possibly, which future beings there are, for whom the person rationally should be "intrinsically" concerned. Saying that this rational concern is "intrinsic" means, roughly, that, even apart from questions of whether or not he might advance the present person's projects, there is this rational concern for the welfare of the future being. So, in particular, this prudential use is to connect directly with our favorite sacrifice for future well-being test, namely, the avoidance of future great pain test.

[1]"Survival and Identity," in [Amélie Rorty, ed.,] *The Identities of Persons.* [Berkeley: University of California Press, 1973,] p. 17.

Tomorrow, I might become a complete amnesiac with regard to all of my past life. Even as Lewis will agree, it is quite clear that I will survive this terribly unfortunate incident. On the desirability use, in this case there will be quite a lot less of what matters in my survival than there is in the ordinary case, where I will have a rich store of personal memories. On the prudential use, by contrast, even in this sad amnesia case, there may be all of what matters in my survival. For example, to spare myself from great electric shocks in two days time, I will rationally undergo just as many slight shocks now on the confident belief that I will become highly amnesiac, or at least very nearly as many, as I would on the equally confident belief that I will not become amnesiac.

Among the rational choices to which this prudential use alludes, the most conspicuous will be those that involve the avoidance of future pain. But not all "intrinsic" choices regarding future well-being are as gloomy as the most conspicuous one. So you may choose to accept a slight decrease, for just one day, in your impending great pleasure. Your prudential concern may be for a great increase in your pleasure, for many years, beginning right after an impending operation that will render you highly amnesiac. . . .

Very roughly, the desirability use aims at just those situations that we should most like to encounter, whereas the prudential use aims at all those that, somewhere or other in logical space, must be faced. Because any serious inquiry into personal identity means facing some sour music along with the sweet, this prudential use is, I think, so important for our topic area that, if it did not already exist, we should invent it. But I do not think that this use needs to be invented. Indeed, it is just this prudential use that I find consistently dominant in my own employment of 'what matters in survival.' Partly because I incline in their direction, I suggest that, when they may consider questions of rational self-concern, it is this use that will dominate the

thought of philosophers who favor the physical approach to personal identity.

There is a third main use of the expression, 'what matters in survival,' which I will call the *constitutive use*.[2] Here the leading idea is that we focus on what it is about a case that *counts toward* the case being one that involves a person who does survive. For this constitutive use to have much philosophical interest, there must be some truth to at least one of two related underlying assumptions: First, it should be true that there are a number of different factors each of which may count toward personal survival. Second, it should be true that at least some of these factors are largely matters of degree. For example, on the psychological approach, perhaps a future person must have *enough* of a certain present person's distinctive psychology, if that future person is that present one. Or, for example, on the physical approach, perhaps there must be a *sufficiently* continuous physical realization, from now until some future time, of that present person's core psychology. Whatever sort of objective approach we favor, most of us deeply believe that at least one of those underlying assumptions is correct. Because this is our belief, we may also believe that this constitutive use is of some interest.

As is obvious, like the prudential use, but perhaps unlike the desirability use, in trying to be relevant to questions about personal identity, the constitutive employment is a use that we may exploit to the full. As also is obvious, this constitutive use does not directly concern the evaluative, or the motivational, matters that surround the topic of our survival. For that

---

[2]In the "Importance of Being Identical," in *The Identities of Persons*, on pp. 85–86, John Perry distinguishes between two "senses" of 'what matters in survival.' More or less, he distinguishes between what I am calling the constitutive use and what I call the desirability use. So far, so good. But it is not nearly far enough. Accordingly, as I see it, Perry falls into many of the same errors as Lewis, whom he is criticizing, and Parfit, with whom he is largely in agreement.

straightforward reason, this use has no direct connection with questions of rational concern for oneself in the future.[3]

The consideration of an appropriate example may help us to see how these three different uses may variously influence our thinking: Suppose that a surgical procedure is applied to you with these following effects: Very little of your distinctive mental life flows on, but all of your core psychology flows on by the normal route of realization in your brain. You will thus be left with your capacity for consciousness, with a capacity for a fair variety of experience, and with what we might call a modicum of intelligence or reasoning ability, perhaps as much as is typically present with a person with an IQ of about 30. But few or none of your personal memories will be realized in your brain now, or flow on in any way at all; few or none of your distinctive personality or character traits will flow on; few or none of your even moderately distinctive capacities, views, or interests will be continued; and so on, and so forth. For good measure, we may further suppose that the effects of this procedure are never reversed. Now we may ask: After such surgery is applied to you, how much of what matters in survival will there be?

We may employ the expression 'what matters in survival' in accord with the desirability use, as Lewis apparently does in the cited passage. If we use the expression in this way, we will mean, close enough, how much value is there for you in the life of the resultant being. Then the answer to our question will be just the answer Lewis would find: not much at all. For you to undergo this procedure is practically as bad as commonplace death. Quite rationally, given your values, you would undergo great sacrifices now to prevent this from happening. Given

your values, how good can it be for you to have the life of such an extremely dull and disoriented person. Indeed, for many people, this prospect has *negative* value. If one of them had the chance beforehand, he would, perhaps quite rationally, arrange for the swift, sudden and painless death of the person, perhaps himself, who emerged from this surgical operation. He might do so even if the process of making these arrangements was one that, in advance, involved considerable pain.

Alternatively, we may employ the expression 'what matters in survival' in accord with the prudential use. Using the expression in this alternative way, we will mean, in effect, something like this: Is there anyone left from such an operation for whom you may have a rational egoistic concern and, if so, how great will this concern be? To this quite different question, we find a quite different answer: Yes; there is someone left, namely, the unfortunate amnesiac imbecile who will be you: and, for yourself, the strength of your rational self-centered concern will be very great. Suppose that, unless you choose to undergo considerable pain beforehand, just that particular imbecile will be mercilessly tortured soon after the operation. From a self-interested perspective, it is rational for you now to undergo the lesser pain, so that this amnesiac imbecile will not then suffer that very much greater pain. And it is very clear why this is rational for you: It is bad enough, indeed much worse than bad enough, that you will then be devoid of almost all of your personal memories and distinctive mental characteristics, not to mention so much of your reasoning ability. But, bad as that may be, it will still be you who is in such a sorry and pathetic state. And, bad as that may be, it will be far worse still if, on top of all that, you will be tortured severely.

It should be clear that this prudential use of 'what matters' is *not* the one most operative with Lewis and like-minded thinkers. It should also be clear that this prudential use *is* the moti-

---

[3]In formulating the descriptions of these three uses, I have been saved from some errors by helpful comments from Derek Parfit and from Mark Johnston.

vational use that is most closely related to questions of personal identity. It is the prudential use, not the desirability use, that is the motivationally relevant counterpart of the constitutive use.

The prudential use fits well with a physical approach to what matters in survival and, by extension, with the physical approach to our survival itself. Partly for this reason, philosophers who are moved to favor a view of our survival that is close to the physical approach are, I suggest, quite close to the truth. . . .

The Physical Approach to Our Survival

The physical approach to our survival is the best *basis* for an adequate treatment of our identity over time: Any better approach will more likely result from a modification of this approach than from a rejection of it. For this reason, it is important that we understand the import of the physical approach.

. . . the physical approach is not offered as any sort of analytic or conceptual truth. For one thing, I see no conceptual necessity about our being physical at all. Rather, subject to whatever qualifications may be required, the view is offered as adequate relative to the proposition that, in broad outline, our view of the world is correct. . . .

Two Formulations of the Physical Approach

The physical approach, as here understood, places infinitely more weight on the brain, or the central nervous system, than it does on all the rest of a person's body. . . . Improving on a famous case of Shoemaker's, we imagine two

people who are qualitatively identical.[4] One may be you, the other your absolute twin. Under a powerful anesthetic, the two brains are taken from the heads of the two bodies. Then each brain is put back in the head of the other body. Two people awaken. One has your original brain and your twin's old body; the other has your original body and the twin's old brain. Shortly after awakening one of these two people will get excruciating pain and the other will get no pain at all. You can do nothing about that. But you do have this much choice: Before the operations are performed, you may choose which of the two will be tortured and which spared. With little doubt indeed, you will choose the person with your original brain to be spared, the torture going to the other. Your reasoning is simple: This person is you and you want very much not to be tortured, whether or not you have the same body.

The physical approach does not insist that there is any logical or analytic connection between anything physical, let alone a particular brain, and the survival of a person from an earlier to a later time. Rather, the reasoning behind the approach may proceed along these lines, offered by Thomas Nagel, who holds a view of our identity that is rather close to what I call the physical approach:

> *Let me repeat that this is not offered as an analysis of the concept of the self but as an empirical hypothesis about its true nature. My concept of myself contains the blank space for such an objective completion, but does not fill*

[4]Shoemaker presents his by now classic example in *Self-Knowledge and Self-Identity*, Cornell University Press, 1963. Unlike my two men here, his two have quite different distinctive psychologies, as well as various other qualitative differences. By eliminating this feature of these qualitative differences, perhaps we may allow the case to be a bit more illuminating. On either version, at all events, the intuition is that each man ends up where his brain goes.

it in. I am whatever persisting individual in the objective order underlies the subjective continuities of that mental life that I call mine. But a type of objective entity can settle questions about the identity of the self only if the thing in question is both the bearer of mental states and the cause of their continuity when there is continuity. If my brain meets these conditions then the core of the self— what is essential to my existence—is my functioning brain. . . . But the brain is the only part of me whose destruction I could not possibly survive. The brain, but not the rest of the animal, is essential to the self.[5]

Less friendly to the physical approach, but also understanding it as empirically motivated, Derek Parfit offers this formulation:

The Physical Criterion: (1) What is necessary is not the continued existence of the whole body, but the continued existence of enough of the brain to be the brain of a living person. X today is one and the same person as Y at some past time if and only if (2) enough of Y's brain continued to exist, and is now X's brain, and (3) this continuity has not taken a 'branching' form.[6]

For focusing on the brain as contrasted with the rest of a person's body, and also for being offered as empirically motivated, both of these statements of a physical view are on the right track. . . . As concerns what is needed from a person's brain, Nagel goes too far even while Parfit fails to go far enough.

Parfit notwithstanding, it is clearly not sufficient for much, or even for all, of the earlier

---

[5]*The View from Nowhere*, Oxford University Press, 1986, p. 40. The indicated emphasis is my own, not Nagel's.

[6]*Reasons and Persons*, [Oxford University Press, 1984] p. 204. (In the first few printings of the book, including the initial 1984 printing cited, clause (3) reads somewhat differently. Parfit has assured me, in written communication, that the latest printing is as above. At any rate, for our discussion, this clause is unimportant.)

person's brain to continue to be alive until the time that the later person needs a properly structured brain. There must be a stronger requirement to the effect that, in the interim period, the brain in question continues to realize certain features of the original person's dispositional psychology. In any ordinary case, of course, the brain will do this by being, throughout the period, suitably structured.

Without this requirement there might be, in the interim, just a brain that is little more than living meat, a brain that is not the brain of any person at all, let alone the brain of Y or of X. There may then be *enough* of a whole brain for it to be the brain of a living person, all right, but it may be structured very unsuitably for supporting mental life. Once Y's brain becomes the brain of no being with a capacity for a significant mental life, and with Y presumed not to have any other physical realization of her psychology, then Y ceases to exist. Whatever the later person X may be, she will not be Y.

For the ordinary cases, we might clarify the point by speaking of different levels of physical structure. Appropriate gross physical structure is enough to ensure the existence of a brain, whether living or not. Appropriate structure that is somewhat finer may be needed to ensure that this brain is composed of living tissue. But much finer structure still is needed, as a matter of fact, for the realization of psychological capacities by that brain. At least in any of the more ordinary cases, in order for someone to survive, there must be continuity of these very fine structures, not just the grosser ones.

Nagel, as I said, goes too far in the other direction. As he says or implies the brain must be *functioning* properly throughout. But recall the process of super freezing and super thawing. In the middle period of that process, the brain is not functioning at all. Still, the person clearly survives. She survives because enough of her brain, although not then functioning, is suitably structured so that it realized her psychology. . . .

In the normal course of events, my brain realizes both my core psychology and my distinctive psychology. On the physical approach, it is owing to its realization of my core psychology that my brain is so important for my survival; by contrast, my brain's realization of my distinctive psychology is completely incidental. An appropriate example helps us to see that this central claim is, at the least, quite close to the truth.

We may imagine that a maniacal surgeon records on tape precise information as to your brain's constitution. Then she tampers with your brain so as to remove all of your distinctive psychology, leaving you only with your core. A week later, she may use the recorded information to restructure your brain, again, thus restoring the distinctive psychology that, for the week, was missing.

On the physical approach to personal identity, the surgeon's patient will be you throughout the week. This is certainly our intuitive response. By employing a pain avoidance test, we may confirm our intuition. Ahead of time and from your natural perspective of self-interest, you must choose when the surgeon will impose what pain. You have precisely two options. On the one hand, you may choose for her to impose some fairly slight, but significant, pain before this week (and never any other pain). Alternatively, you may choose for her to impose very much greater pain during the week, when there is someone with that brain realizing only core psychology (and never any other pain). On the belief that you will get much less pain, you will choose for her to impose the much lesser pain before the operation and, thus, before the week in question. Indeed, you will choose for her to impose the much lesser earlier pain *whether or not*, at the end of the week, the surgeon restores your distinctive psychology. For, as you may deeply believe, in either case, as long as your brain is continuously structured to realize core psychology and, thus, as long as it always is the brain of a person, you will still exist.

A Better Formulation

. . . Taking it as given that a physical approach is in general correct, it may be impossible clearly to refute the claim that, in order to survive, a person needs a brain, at least some brain or other. Indeed, it is difficult enough to refute the claim that, in order to survive, a person needs the brain with which she begins life as a person. Even as regards this weaker claim, most apparently promising attempts quickly fall apart. For example, in certain cases, you may survive even though you and your brain are scattered into quite a few pieces, or are gradually changed into an entity that is made mainly of metal. But, then, your brain may also survive in these cases, with you coming to have a scattered brain, or a metallic brain. Your brain is merely *transformed*; it is not replaced or made superfluous. It is not very easy, then, to undermine the idea that, within the physical approach, the survival of one's brain is crucial to one's own survival. But, with the appropriate material before us, some disturbing doubts may emerge. . . .

. . . Sequentially and gradually, the work of my brain is taken over by structures that are not bunched together as in a typical animal organ, but are spread quite evenly throughout the whole organism. In the less ambitious version of the case, as the nerve cells of my brain are killed, newly inserted nerve cells, much more widely dispersed, may take up their contributory roles. In the more ambitious version, my central nerve cells are replaced not by any new nerve cells, or even by any organic matter at all, but by complex bionic circuitry that is strung throughout most of my body. In either version, rather than being placed near each other in my head, the new structures may be strung throughout my body so that, in late stages, my psychology is as much realized in my arms and legs as in my torso and buttocks, but in my head least of all. In either version, of course, the process may be both slow and gradual, occurring in small steps spread out over much lived time. After sufficient time, there will be, in my brain pan, only a dead brain that is, for the realization of psychology, completely unsuitable and ineffective. Finally, that dead brain may be removed and placed in a frying pan.

In this sort of case, I will survive. But, at the step before the end, will I have, in addition to the dead brain in my head, a second brain that is spread throughout almost all of my body? Apparently not. The only brain I then have is in my head, suitable for little but a meal for a cannibal. At the last step, when the dead brain is on the fire, will there be a *brain* there in my body that is then realizing my psychology? Apparently, no more so than in the step just before. . . .

To achieve a reasonably clear statement, as well as an appropriately general one, it will be best for us to make no mention of brains, or of central nervous systems, in our formulation of the physical approach. Instead, let us talk of whatever physical entity realizes a person's core psychology, calling it the *physical realizer of the person's core psychology*. In these terms, we may characterize the physical approach in a way that, although vague, is not objectionably unclear:

> The person X now is one and the same as the person Y at some time in the future if, and only if, (1) there is sufficiently continuous physical realization of a core psychology between the physical realizer of X's core psychology and the physical realizer of Y's core psychology, and (probably) (2) (Some clause suitable for ruling out unwanted cases of branching).

Because fission and fusion are as much side-issues on the physical approach as on the psychological treatment, we . . . place to the side any thoughts about (2), the second clause.

There are a number of points to emphasize about the physical approach as just characterized. First, this formulation is no more offered as a conceptual, or logical, or analytical truth than are any of the formulations that make reference to brains. To the contrary, even as now characterized, the adequacy of the physical approach is only *relative to* the correctness of a certain view of reality as a whole. This is a view of the world as being, at the least, very largely a physical world. On this view, this physical world is reasonably stable, regular and well behaved: For example, like rocks, and trees, and cats, people do not, along with their matter, pop out of existence, or pop into existence. Rather, people begin, continue, or end, as a consequence of changes in the mutual arrangements of certain comparatively simple physical things.

Second this formulation has the physical approach focus squarely on *core psychology*, giving no importance to distinctive psychology. . . .

Third, . . . there is the focus on a *physical realizer* of that core psychology. The physical realizer need not be a contiguous object and, up to certain points, it may fail to be physically well behaved in a great variety of ways. Further, there may even be some cases where the physical realizer of Y's psychology is not the same physical entity as the realizer of X's mentality; perhaps there may be an appropriate physically continuous succession of realizing entities. But, in any case, the realizer of X's psychology must be physically continuous with the realizer of Y's and, further, this continuity must be of such a sort that it allows us to say, correctly, that there is the physically continuous realization of X's core psychology from the present until that future time, when that psychology is Y's. . . . most of what may be said about a person's physical realizer also may be said about her well-structured brain. Because this is so, we may often use 'brain' as a familiar shorthand term for 'physical realizer.' . . .

Finally, there is the reference to *sufficient physical continuity*. . . . the idea is that sometimes there is, and sometimes there is not, appropriate physical continuity. Within this physical approach, inquiry aims at discerning when there is sufficient continuity between an earlier and a later brain for this physical continuity to ensure that there is realized, at different times, the psychology of one and the same person. On the appropriate conception of it, this physical continuity may involve *various matters of degree*: Not only are matters of material composition and replacement important, so, too, are matters involving the operation of various forces, fields, binding processes, whatever.

Wide Physical Continuity and Contextual Flexibility

Certain sorts of cases may get some to think that the physical approach must be quite wrong even in general conception. At a certain moment, all of the elementary particles that just before composed you cease to exist. A moment later their vacated regions may once again be full of matter. About this situation, some may offer thoughts like these: "With an exceedingly brief period when the regions are empty of matter, will you not survive the episode? Surely, you will survive. But, on the physical approach, you will not survive. So much for the physical approach to our survival."

In several ways, these thoughts are too quick. In the first place, unless there is reason to think that the case has some basis in reality, it cannot begin to pose a threat to the physical approach. For this approach, it will be remembered, is offered as adequate only relative to the general truth of our world view. And perhaps this case is not, in any relevant way, a realistically possible example. If not, then citing it may provide no real challenge. . . .

. . . Usually when we think of an ordinary thing's physical continuity, we think only in terms of the continuity of its constituting matter through ordinary space with respect to time. Usually, we may say, we think only in terms of *narrow physical continuity*. But, perhaps there may be more to an ordinary individual's physical continuity. For example, in addition to ordinary space, there may be other physical dimensions in which, during a certain interval, the individual's matter exists. When there is this more exotic continuity for that matter, just as much as when there is the more ordinary kind, we may say that both the matter itself, and also any ordinary object constituted of that matter, has *wide physical continuity*.

Especially when thinking in terms of this wide continuity, we have a highly liberal, or very wide, understanding of matter itself. On narrower conceptions, matter may pertain to a portion of physical reality only when it is in certain states. On our wide conception, however, some matter will be any portion of physical reality, regardless of state, that is suitable for constituting (wholly or largely) physical individuals.

In relation to this notion of wide physical continuity, the problematic example is left largely unspecified. If it is specified in certain ways, then the original matter, or least a goodly portion of it, will exist throughout the brief episode. On one favorable specification, for example, that matter, always in some suitable form, may go on a trip into some further physical dimensions, even while not, in any ordinary spatial way, moving from the salient spatial region. On such a favorable specification, the person constituted of that matter may also exist throughout. In such a specified circumstance, you will survive the episode.

. . . On certain other specifications, it will be clear that, at the end of the brief episode, none of the original matter is there. Quite abruptly, there will be present only some precisely similar, but numerically distinct, matter. For example, as an absolute physical miracle, the original matter may simply cease to exist, completely and forever. Just a bit later, as another absolute miracle, there may begin to exist, *ex nihilo*, some completely new matter that is, as it happens, just like the old and just where the old was last located. In this quite different specific circumstance, you will not survive the episode.

We do not need to go into these matters in very much detail. Rather, for us, it is enough to explain the main *differences* between our own survival, on the one hand, and, on the other, the survival of other sorts of ordinary concrete individuals, like bushes, ships and rocks. Now, as far as the continuity of a person's constituent matter goes, the cited case finds close parallels in cases concerning these other individuals. Insofar as any of these cases shows any need for continuity of matter, or of physical parts, the whole group of cases will show an equal need across the board. Any such widespread need is of little consequence to our investigation. For us, the only interruptions of much consequence will be those that, although they let bushes and rocks survive, terminate us people. In other words, we are properly interested only in those physical interruptions that are appropriately *selective*. Because an interruption of matter relative to ordinary space is wholly *unselective*, in an inquiry like ours it can be discounted. By a standard of reckoning most relevant to present inquiry, the widely continuous presence of matter will provide us, as well as bushes, ships, and rocks, with physical continuity that is adequate for us to survive. Because this is so, there is nothing in the offered example that means a defect in the physical approach to our survival.

A certain flexibility may attach to the physical account that might be well worth noting: When engaged in theoretical studies we tend to overlook the fact that often we treat continuity as a matter of degree. For, when thinking of continuity theoretically, its ideal cases are salient. But, like many other ideals, in concrete reality this one, too, is rarely if ever realized. We readily adjust our thinking to the pervasive circumstance: What we count as continuous is, in the case at hand, what we count as being sufficiently close to the ideal case for the dominant interests of that context.[7]

[7]For philosophers, the locus classicus for considerations like these is David Lewis, "Scorekeeping in a Language Game," *Journal of Philosophical Logic*, 1979. In my *Philosophical Relativity*, University of Minnesota Press, 1984, there is an extended treatment of these matters.

A physicist, for example, may accept a theory of light according to which light is emitted from a source in discrete units. In a context where he most wants to express the theory clearly, he may deny that there is a signal continuously coming from a certain source. In a different context, by contrast, he may affirm that the signal was continuous: Without interruption, the signal was indicating that it was unsafe to open a certain door during a certain period. What is close enough to the ideal case for (the main interests of) the second context is not close enough for the different (main interests of the) first context.

Harsh reality may all but force us to adopt lower standards than we might otherwise like. Up to certain points, which ones depending on context, we go along with what reality dictates. In the physicist's second context, that went on with the treatment of the light signal. This may go on, as well, with questions regarding the continuity of ordinary individuals and their constituting matter, ourselves included.[8] Accordingly, even while we might insist on our survival requiring the physical continuity of our

[8]An especially intriguing example of this sort is offered by Eddy Zemach on page 212 of his marvelously provocative paper, "Looking Out for Number One." *Philosophy and Phenomenological Research*, 1987: "Let us say that an elementary particle "flashes" in and out of existence, on the average, a million times a second. Given the number of elementary particles in the brain we can calculate how often all its particles go out of existence simultaneously. Suppose that this happens once a year. I therefore get a wholly new brain every year." Being charitable to this passage, we ban ourselves from asking many sensible questions. Even so, contextual features serve to block Zemach's conclusion, as well as any relevantly similar conclusions.

Treating "continuous" as sensitive to context, we may say that, just as I may draw a continuous line with a pencil, despite microscopic areas where there are no particles of carbon, so, even in such a circumstance, there may be the physically continuous realization of my psychology. Just as there are not interruptions in the pencil line every trillionth of a millimeter, so there will not be interruptions in my organs, or in my life, every year.

physical realizers, we may, at the same time, create contexts where the standards for this physical continuity are obligingly low. In ever so many contexts, then, we may understand the physical approach as allowing for our survival.

The Derivative but Great Importance of Physical Continuity

To you, at least, your existence at future times is a matter of considerable importance. Moreover, the importance of your future existence seems to be quite basic, not dependent upon some other fact being an important one. That there should be much physical continuity of whatever realizes your psychology, by contrast, may seem to be a very unimportant fact. Why should you, or anyone, care about *that*? This sort of thinking may get one to believe that physical continuity must have little to do with our survival.

For our survival, whatever importance physical continuity may have is not basic. Or, if it is best to treat these questions as matters of degree, then such importance is not basic to even a moderately high degree. All of this must be admitted. In other words, it must be admitted that, as far as personal survival is concerned, whatever importance physical continuity may have is derivative. But although this importance may be highly derivative, it might, at the same time, be very great.

All of this may seem paradoxical. This apparent paradox might get some to overlook, or to deny, the importance of physical continuity. To remove the air of paradox, we want a derivation of how it is that, as a matter of fact, physical continuity is crucial to our survival. There follows a derivation consisting of two main parts. Especially as regards the second of these parts, there are propositions that are to be taken, not as true in any wholly *a priori*, entirely universal, or purely conceptual way, but only as true relative to the general truth of our view of the

world. Consequently, the derivation as a whole should be taken only in this rather modest way.

The first part of our relativized derivation concerns our existence at different times: It will never be true that someone exists, and then later does not exist, and then still later exists again. This condition of "no interruption" applies across all plausible metaphysical conceptions in which we may find a place. Even on wholly subjective conceptions, where each of us exists only in his own time, nobody will survive an interruption with respect to time. Perhaps this condition is not absolute. But, if it is not, then, at the least, the condition provides a very strong guideline for any adequate account of our survival.

. . . Further, the condition of no temporal gap itself must be grounded in *real processes* that, as most naturally and relevantly described, *ensure that* there will be no interruption.[9] To help clarify this strong condition, it may be useful to consider a quite hypothetical example: Consider a process whereby all of the matter of a person suddenly was annihilated. Causally unconnected with this first process, there might be another process that caused a material person, one of just the same sort, to be in just the place where that matter was annihilated. The new matter may be imposed on this place *immediately* upon the annihilation of the old matter. Fantastic as it seems, all of this is a complete coincidence. In such a situation, there will be two people, one there immediately after the other. This is very clear.

When properly developed in this strong way, our condition of no interruption yields that clear result: If, contrary to the condition, there was one person throughout, then the main process involving her would be a total process consisting of the two processes mentioned above. Because there is no causal connection between

---

[9] I failed to see this very important point until forced to observe it by comments from David Lewine, who opened my eyes.

those two processes, the total process consisting of them both is one that, as most naturally and relevantly described, *will allow for an interruption* in the existence of any person that might be there throughout the period. On our offered condition, however, no process can work in so fortuitous a way if it is to involve the survival of a person.[10] So there must be two people in this situation, not one person throughout. . . .

The second part of the relativized derivation begins with this observation. There is no single occurrent mental phenomenon, such as a conscious self-referential thought, that any of us has at every moment of her existence. What we may say, more weakly, is that, at every moment of her existence, each of us has some basic *mental capacities*. How might a person's mental capacities importantly figure in her survival?

In our thought about ordinary individuals, we employ many common distinctions concerning their properties. But, in our scheme of things, certain of these distinctions are more important than others. Paramount among these are a family of dichotomies whose conspicuous members include the distinction between the conscious and the non-conscious and that between the mental and the non-mental. The key positive properties thus distinguished—mentality, consciousness, and their ilk—have a special place in our thought about ordinary concrete individuals. In line with this, our common principles for individuating ordinary entities may reflect the importance of the noted distinctions: A person's mental capacities may be more central to her survival than any even remotely comparable property of a rock, be it a capacity or a disposition, is to the survival of that rock. And that may be more important to her survival, even, than any comparable properties of a (living) tree, or a (living) brain, are to that tree, or to that brain. Accordingly, what is needed for your survival is the future existence not just of basic mental capacities that are precisely like yours, but of your own particular basic mental capacities.

How are a particular person's basic mental capacities to exist throughout a certain period of time? This takes some doing. After all, each of our core psychologies is exactly the same; all of my basic mental capacities are precisely similar to all of yours.

My basic mental capacities will exist from now until a future time only if, from now until then, they are continuously realized in some physical entity or, at the least, in an appropriate succession of physical entities. In largest measure, this is just a brute fact about the relations between myself, mentality and the objective world order. Now, while both of us are similarly objective physical beings, and while both of us have precisely similar basic mental capacities, you and I are different people. So, at least during some of the time that you exist, and perhaps during all of it, your mental capacities must be realized in one physical entity, or one succession of them, while my mental capacities are realized in another.

Moreover, if my basic mental capacities are to be realized at a future time, as contrasted with capacities just like mine, then there must be sufficient physical continuity between the physical realizer of them now and the physical realizer of them at that future time. In line with this, there must be the continuous physical real-

---

[10]Compare this with a parallel point about factual knowledge: In knowing that something is so, it cannot be accidental, or coincidental, that I am right about its being so. Further, in order for there to be no undermining accident, in the case of many sorts of propositions, there should be the right sort of real (causal) connections between the thing that is so and me, the putative knower. As I have been given to understand, the first of these two related points was made long ago by George Santayana. Not then knowing anything of Santayana, I made heavy use of the idea, possibly a bit too heavy, in my paper, "An Analysis of Factual Knowledge," *The Journal of Philosophy*, 1968, Regarding the second point, in the contemporary literature a seminal paper is Alvin Goldman's "A Causal Theory of Knowing," *The Journal of Philosophy*, 1967.

ization of them by this present physical realizer or, at the least, by a physically continuous succession of realizers beginning with this present one now.

Now we put the parts together: For you to exist at a future time, you must exist, continuously, from now until then. For that to be so, there must be the continuous existence, from now until then, of your particular basic mental capacities. For there to be the continuous existence of just those capacities, there must be, in this wholly or largely physical world of ours, the continuous physical realization of them in a physically continuous realizer or, at the least, in a physically continuous succession of physical realizers. Consequently, for you to exist at a future time, there must be appropriate physical continuity.

The importance of physical continuity for our survival is, thus, derivative rather than basic. Indeed, it is derivative in two ways. First, the importance of physical continuity is *indirect*. Physical continuity *provides for* what is more directly important: the future existence of an individual person's basic mental capacities and, more directly important still, the future existence of that person herself. Second, the great importance of physical continuity is *relative*: It is only relative to the general truth of our view of the world that physical continuity has any importance for our survival. Because we may be confident that, in broad outline, this view is correct, we may believe that physical continuity is of very great importance to our survival, however derivative, indirect and relative that importance may be.

At times, it is hard to believe that anything so crucial to our survival should be of such derivative importance. Then it may be thought that, for this reason, physical continuity cannot really be so very important. Some may thus be moved completely to reject the physical approach. Perhaps this is yet another motivating factor toward the psychological approach to our sur-

vival, the salient alternative. But, like other factors, this one, too, provides no good reason.

Survival and the Realization of Psychological Capacities

The physical approach to our survival must make very heavy use, and perhaps rather subtle use, of the notion of a mental *capacity*. Without an appropriate treatment of capacities, the physical approach is little better than a bad joke. This wants some discussion.

In our common thought, we make some important distinctions concerning the capacity to think: First, there is the very obvious distinction between having the capacity to think and, in contrast, having the capacity to *create or produce something that has* the capacity to think. Some entities have both of these capacities: A super scientist of the future may have, not only the capacity for thought, but the capacity to create something with that capacity. By using materials in her laboratory, she may, for example, produce a duplicate of herself. Other entities have only one of these capacities: Especially if she is biologically sterile, a scientist of the present day has only the capacity to think, not the capacity to create a thinker. Other entities may have only the latter capacity. The unthinking devices that engage in the taping processes will be of this sort.

Second, there is the slightly less obvious distinction between an entity having the capacity to think and, in contrast, an entity having *the potential to have* that capacity.[11] A fertilized egg

---

[11] As Roy Sorensen points out, these ideas relate to the distinction drawn by C. D. Broad among levels of "higher order dispositions." So, going beyond the zygote, still another thing may lack the potential to have, or to develop, mental capacities, but it may have the potential to have, or to develop, *that* potential. And so it goes.

(Footnote continues on p. 208.)

has the potential to have the capacity to reason, but does not have the capacity itself. A person in deep sleep, by contrast, has the capacity to think, not merely the potential to have that capacity.

Although it is not so readily recognized, a third distinction may be equally important. Concerning certain matters of degree, this is the distinction between reckoning mental capacities according to strict standards and, by contrast, reckoning by lenient standards. To see the importance of this distinction, we consider actual cases of very deep and prolonged coma. As is obvious, these cases are well endowed with biological continuity. But is there much continuous realization of psychological capacities as well? At first glance, it may seem that there is not: Relative to *everyday standards* for reckoning capacities, when she is in a deep coma, a person will not have the capacity for much of, or perhaps even for any of, a mental life. However, this appearance might be deceptive. Although it may sound paradoxical to say so, in these matters, our ordinary standards for having mental capacities may be very demanding standards.

(*Footnote 11 continued.*)

In the free spirit of pure inquiry, try this thought on for size: Paralleling what I am calling the physical approach to our survival, there may be an infinite hierarchy of nicely ordered physical approaches. (And, then, too, one might mention the "infinite, all-encompassing" approach that, at once, puts forth the entire hierarchy.) Now, noticing that I already am a person, I see no need, in giving an account of my survival, to go any higher than the possession of the psychological capacities themselves. But I am open to the possibility that ascent might be required. At any rate, the guiding spirit of all of the hierarchically ordered treatments is the same: Whatever level a given approach favors, it focuses on the physically continuous realization of the level's dispositions that are directed at, or that concern, (core) psychology.

Applicable to all sorts of capacities, not just psychological ones, Broad puts forth the kernel idea in his *Examination of McTaggart's Philosophy*, Volume I, Cambridge University Press, 1933, pp. 266–7.

If these strict everyday standards are employed in evaluating judgments of personal survival, we might make incorrect judgments. We might hold, incorrectly, that a person may exist even while she has no mental capacities. Or, perhaps even worse, we might hold that, when a person's brain and body are in a deeply comatose state, that person does not exist. Such incorrect contentions may prove especially embarrassing in those few cases where, beyond all expectations, a person comes out of a very deep and prolonged coma, awakening to enjoy much complex conscious thought.

There are other ways of reckoning a person's mental capacities that are very much more lenient. When we reckon our capacities in these ways, the lenient standards we employ may be more relevant to questions of strict survival. Judgments made in accordance with these standards may conflict with what we say in everyday discourse. But perhaps there is no serious conflict between our more pragmatic assertions and our more reflective statements.

A person who is in what we ordinarily call an *irreversible coma* has a highly structured living brain that may not be all that different from your brain now. Do we believe that a person with such a brain is completely without psychological capacities? Only relative to a practical but possibly superficial way of reckoning such capacities can we confidently give a positive answer.

Then what do we mean when, in everyday life, we speak of a person going into an irreversible coma? For the most part, what we mean is this: Unfortunately, things have happened to this person so that, without the aid of appropriate intervention—be it surgical, electrical, chemical, a combination thereof, or whatever —she will never again think or experience; at the very least, she will never again do so in a conscious manner. Our present medical science cannot provide a helpful intervention and, in typical cases, we are nowhere near being able to do so. Relative to both the course impersonal nature will take and to any course that our society can soon provide, the person in this coma will never be conscious again.

When making common assertions about people in very deep coma, we mean little more than that mental capacities are to be reckoned in this pragmatic way. Inasmuch as the medical resources of the near future look to be quite limited, and particular human beings do not last for centuries, this evaluation may be highly appropriate. In many cases, I suggest, it is only relative to some such quick but severe reckoning that a coma is confidently regarded as irreversible. It is only relative to such a standard that we confidently consider a person to have lost all mental capacities and, thus, to have ceased to exist.

Compare the victim of deep coma with a hypothetical unfortunate whose brain has been turned into a "lump of live jelly," perhaps by some powerfully destructive radiation. In this other case, there is now entirely lacking such internal structure as is relevant to the support of any thought or experience. There is only the persistence of a living mass of flesh of typical brain weight with typical gross brain structure. Now, in virtually any context for their use and in virtually any sense that the terms might reasonably be assigned, perhaps it will be true to say that this person has *lost all of her mental capacities*. If this is so, then the person with the jelly brain will be importantly different from many people said to be in irreversible coma.

In these matters, we might be dealing with large differences in the logical space of possible interventions that alter the brain. With the person who is in the deep coma, there might be certain *comparatively* minor alterations of her brain whose occurrence would have her mental capacities brought to a point where they may be quite readily exercised. With the person whose brain has been turned to jelly, by contrast, the only processes that will do that involve enormously major alterations. As far as reckoning the presence of mental capacities, these enor-

mously altering processes might be more like the construction of a new working brain, out of otherwise useless matter at hand, than they are like the alterations required for the person in a deep coma.

If these considerations are well taken, then, as far as having mental capacities is concerned, a person whose brain has been turned to jelly is more like a person whose brain has been annihilated altogether than she is like a person in a deeply comatose state. In such an eventuality, for the lack of mental capacities, the person whose brain was jellied will no longer exist, while, for having such capacities, the person in a deep coma will still exist. What is very unfortunate is that, given the limitations of science in the present and the not very distant future, the coma patient does not have these capacities to a high enough degree to be of any use or value to her. . . .

How Important for My Survival Is My Capacity for Life?

. . . Perhaps there is some sense of 'living,' or of 'being alive,' according to which it is logically sufficient for an entity to be living, or to be alive, that the entity have some mental capacities. If so, then, when understood as involving such a sense, our question will not be a very interesting one. Accordingly, in what follows, I will understand these expressions in a sense that yields no such tight logical relation between being alive and having a psychology.

Although it is notorious that there is no very clear distinction between the two that is entirely general, in this particular instance, as in some others, perhaps a useful attempt might be made to consider the conceptual aspects of the present question apart from the more "worldly" aspects. To do that, we will simply assume that there are certain non-organic bionic structures that, with an impressive dual effect, may be joined with various parts of my living human brain: On the one hand, the metallic complexes will do nothing to sustain a judgment that I am alive; to the contrary, the more of me that is composed of the structures, the less of me will then be alive. On the other hand, for any significant portion of my brain, there is a certain bionic structure that may replace it, with the result that the very same dispositional psychology realized organically before will, right after the replacement, be realized by an integrated structure. And, after a suitable sequence of such replacements has been completed, we are supposing, all of my psychology will be realized in an entirely bionic inorganic structure. Perhaps most notably, the capacity for conscious experience will be so realized.

Suppose that, very gradually and over much time, thousandths of my brain are sequentially replaced by suitable bionic structures. The parts replaced are killed. Originally there will be a brain that is entirely organic; finally, there will be only a brain that is entirely bionic. During the brief periods when replacements are made, there will be 99.9% of a brain. Between replacements, of course, there will be 100% of a brain. Except at the first and the last steps, it will be an integrated brain. When there is only 99.9% present, the least there ever is, there will be a slight loss as regards my distinctive psychology. But, even at those times, there will be no loss of core psychology. Moreover, as I, the patient, can quite directly tell, at any stage when there is not deep sleep induced, there is a rich variety of conscious experience.

At the end of a year, with all replacements made, there is a person with an entirely bionic brain. This brain then may be removed from my body and kept functioning well in some other way. The body may be killed. The person may then be given a suitable bionic body. Unless we consider there to be a life process of mentation, not a good idea in the present context, this person is not involved in, nor can he then partake in, any of the main processes of life. Indeed,

reckoned by any but the most lenient sort of standard, this person does not even have the capacity for life.

Given the truth of these strong "worldly" assumptions, will I survive this bionic replacement process? It seems very clear that I will indeed survive. Although I will still exist, I will not then have even the capacity for life. At the very least, it will not be determinately true that I then have such a capacity. Fair enough, I may then be a person who, through a long and precisely integrated series of further "opposite" replacements, may be *converted* so that I will (again) have this capacity. But that is a very different thing from actually having the capacity to be alive.

If fatally ill, a person may be made an offer of such mentally supportive bionic transformation. For some people, this may not be a very attractive or desirable offer. Nonetheless, as a pain avoidance test confirms, this would be a genuine offer of survival. Moreover, if there is a later conversion back to being normally organic, and if the interlude of being bionic is pretty short, most of us may find the offer not only genuine but even quite desirable. At any rate, in such a case as this, it is determinately true that I will continue to exist.

In our positive judgments of our survival, we are prepared to forgo quite a lot of what obtains in the ordinary cases. As even coma induction indicates, we will do without any occurrent thought processes, non-conscious as well as conscious. Freezing and thawing makes that clearer. Moreover, as that freezing process indicates, we will do without its being (determinately) true that we remain living. Lastly, as the recent case of bionic replacements indicates, providing that the structure of the world is cooperative, we will even do without (its being determinately true that we have) the capacity for life.

These thoughts reflect well on our formulation of the physical approach to our survival. As formulated, this approach requires only physically continuous realization of basic mental capacities. It does not require, for our survival, that there continue to be realized any (logically independent) capacity to be alive. As our discussion indicates, a proper formulation will make only the first, and not the second, of these requirements.[12]

Physical Continuity and the Gradual Replacement of Matter

As I am using it, "physical continuity" is a technical term. Although certain previous remarks help show the meaning I wish the expression to have, a lot more is needed in that direction. Thus I now will try to indicate some *main aspects* of what counts toward an ordinary individual's having much physical continuity. The *first aspect* concerns the *gradual replacement of an object's matter*.

In actuality, except for my nerve cells, all of my cells, with almost all the matter they ever contain, are replaced every several years. Moreover, while many nerve cells in my brain stay with me from birth until death, the matter of these cells itself is constantly changing. Eventually, almost all the matter of each cell is replaced. Despite all this replacement, there is a certain continuity of my matter. For there is a fairly evenly gradual replacement of old matter by new. As regards the replacement of matter, both me and my brain have enjoyed quite a lot of physical continuity.

[12]As I see it, considerations like these provide one of the best reasons for abandoning biologically oriented approaches to our survival. In the contemporary literature, perhaps the leading exponent of a biological treatment is David Wiggins, *Sameness and Substance*, Harvard University Press, 1980. A far more radical approach along biological lines, brilliantly provocative even if literally incredible, is offered in Peter van Inwagen, *Material Beings*, Cornell University Press, forthcoming.

What would happen to me if I became involved with replacements much more rapid, or much more abrupt, than the ordinary ones? Perhaps a certain abruptness of replacement will do me in. But the rapidity of replacement is not in itself an important factor: As long as they are relevantly even and gradual rather than uneven and abrupt, I can survive the most rapid of complete serial replacements.

Let us suppose that an exotic procedure is applied to me so that all of my matter, including all the matter of my brain, is replaced in a tenth of a second. In order that the example appear more realistic, perhaps we might suppose that I am first super frozen; only then is the replacement of matter imposed in a suitably inclusive spiral; finally, the person composed of the new matter is super thawed. Anyway, at any very brief time during the crucial tenth of a second, such as a millionth of a second, almost all of the matter present was also present just before, during the just previous millionth. So there is a very rapid, but nonetheless quite gradual, replacement of matter.

Will I survive this rapid procedure; will the matter really flow through *me*? Or, on the contrary, will I expire when exposed to this process; after a certain amount of matter has been replaced, will further matter flow, not through me, but only through a region that, before much of the flow occurred, I will have occupied? Our dominant response is quite strong: I will survive; the matter will indeed be flowing through *me* and not only through a region once occupied by me. Applying our test of future pain avoidance confirms this idea: Because the person at the end of this rapid material changeover is me, in advance, I will do much to protect this person from future torture.

In the case just considered, the replacement of a person's matter was very rapid, but the material changeover occurred in an even and a gradual way. In other cases the changeover is much more uneven and abrupt. As is important to note, this abruptness may include the matter of my brain: First, I may be extremely well frozen. Then, every fifteen minutes, a different quarter of my brain is replaced with a newly made duplicate, as may also occur with my body. At the end of this hour, a person is successfully unfrozen. This person will have a brain and a body that is, if not identical with, then at least enormously like, the original brain and body. At the very least, this person will be just like I was right before the procedure began.

Will I survive this replacement procedure? No, I will not exist at the end. Vaguely and briefly, the reason for the failure is that too *much* relevant matter is replaced too *abruptly*: There is too large and abrupt a replacement of the matter that, most directly, realizes my core psychology. Because of this, there is *not sufficient physical continuity* of an entity that might continuously realize *my* basic mental capacities. Thus, my core psychology ceases to exist and, so too, do I.

14

ROBERT NOZICK
The Closest Continuer View

I. Personal Identity Through Time

So many puzzling examples have been put forth in recent discussions of personal identity that it is difficult to formulate, much less defend, any consistent view of identity and nonidentity. One is driven to describe and judge some cases in ways apparently incompatible with how one judges and describes others.[1] Not all of the difficulties, however, uncover something special about personal identity; some concern the general notion of identity through time, and stem, I think, from a natural but mistaken principle about identity. These issues, interesting and puzzling in their own right, raise the metaphysical question: how, given changes, *can* there be identity of something from one time to another, and in what does this identity consist?

The Closest Continuer Theory

A recent essay by Bernard Williams provides convenient entry to these issues.[2] Williams tells two stories, each individually coherent, which are designed to puzzle us together. He first presents a case, aseptically, which we are prone to describe as involving a person coming to oc-

---

[1] See Sydney Shoemaker, *Self-Knowledge and Self Identity* (Cornell University Press, Ithaca, 1963); Bernard Williams, "The Self and the Future," *Philosophical Review*, Vol. 79, 1970, pp. 161–180; Derek Parfit, "Personal Identity," *Philosophical Review*, Vol. 80, no. 1, 1971, pp. 3–27; "On 'The Importance of Self-Identity,'" *Journal of Philosophy*, Vol. 68, 1971, pp. 683–690; David Lewis, "Survival and Identity" in Amelie Rorty, ed., *The Identities of Persons* (University of California Press, Berkeley, 1976), pp. 17–40; John Perry, "The Importance of Being Identical," *ibid.*, pp. 67–90; Derek Parfit, "Lewis, Perry, and What Matters," *ibid.*, pp. 91–107; Daniel Dennett, "Where Am I?" in his *Brainstorms* (Bradford Books, Montgomery, Vermont, 1978), pp. 310–323.

[2] Williams, "The Self and the Future," reprinted in his *Problems of the Self* (Cambridge University Press, 1973).

cupy a new body, indeed as involving two people switching bodies. Two persons, A and B, enter some machine; upon leaving, the A-body person, the person (whoever that now is) now connected with that A-body, has all of (the previous person) B's memories, knowledge, values, modes of behavior, and so on. (When compatible with the constraints of the A-body, this B-material is produced exactly; otherwise, what is present in the A-body is the vector result of this previous B-material plus the limits of the A-body.) Similarly the B-body person emerges with A's memories, knowledge, modes of behavior, character traits, values, and so on. When enough details are filled in (though not details of the mechanism by which the transfer is effected), we are prone to say or conclude that the people have switched bodies. If these events were to be described beforehand, aseptically, and A was to decide solely on selfish grounds to which body something very painful was to be done afterwards, then A would designate the A-body, for he would believe that *he* would be occupying the B-body at that later time. Moreover, supposing this actually were carried out, at that later time the occupant of the B-body, with A's memories and character, would say "I'm glad I decided then that the painful thing was to be done to the A-body so that I am not feeling it now." We, readers of philosophy, are not so tied to our bodies that we find it impossible to imagine coming to inhabit another. We do not conceive of ourselves as (merely) our particular bodies, as inextricably tied to them.

We can wonder, nevertheless, what constitutes a transfer. What difference is there between your moving from one body to another, and the other body's just acquiring memories and character identical to yours, but without your moving to that body? Williams presses this question with his second story. Suppose you are told you will undergo terrible suffering. This prospect is frightening. You next receive the information that before this suffering comes, you will have changed enormously in psychological traits, perhaps so greatly as to possess exactly

the character, memories, values, and knowledge of someone else who now is alive. This would frighten you even more, perhaps. You do not want to lose your character, memories, values, modes of behavior, knowledge, and loves — to lose your identity, as we might say — and afterwards to undergo enormous suffering. Yet how does this differ, asks Williams, from what happened in the first story, which we took to depict a transfer from body to body? In that story, too, the A-body loses its old memories and acquires new ones (which are those of another person); it loses its knowledge, values, and modes of behavior, acquiring new ones. When hearing the first story beforehand, why didn't the A-person have exactly the fear he would have upon learning the second story foretells his future? He reacts differently to the first story because he thinks *he* will occupy the B-body. Yet if terrible things happen to him in the second story, why do they not happen to him in the first one, also? Don't the two stories describe exactly the same events happening to the A-body? What then makes the first story one about the transfer of a person to another body, and not about something terrible happening to a person who stays where he is?

How can the difference be, asks Williams, that in one situation, the first, in addition to

	Body A	Body B
First situation	acquires the memories and character which person B had one hour earlier.	acquires the memories and character which person A had one hour earlier.
Second situation	acquires the memories and character which person B had one hour earlier, or perhaps no previous person had.	stays with the continuation of the memories and character which it had one hour earlier.

everything happening to the A-body, also A's memories and psychological traits end up or arise in body B? Surely, whatever happens elsewhere cannot affect whether or not A continues to inhabit the A-body. When it happens to just one body it is a psychological disintegration and acquisition of a new psychology. How, then, can two psychological disintegrations and acquisitions of new memories and values make or add up to an exchange of bodies?

Let us formulate the general principle that underlies Williams' discussion and leads to these perplexing questions.

If x at time t_1 is the same individual as y at later time t_2, that can depend only upon facts about x, y, and the relationships between them. No fact about any other existing thing is relevant to (deciding) whether x at t_1 is (part of the same continuing individual as) y at t_2.

How could the existence (or nonexistence) of something else be relevant to whether x at t_1 is (part of the same continuing individual as) y at t_2? There is a related principle, also plausible:

If y at time t_2 is (part of the same continuing individual as) x at t_1 in virtue of standing in some relationship R to x at t_1, then there could not be another additional thing at t_2 also standing (along with y) in R to x at t_1. If there also were this additional thing z at t_2, then neither it nor y would be identical to x. If that z could exist, even if it actually does not, then y at t_2 is not identical with x at t_1—at least, it is not in virtue of standing in the relationship R.

Williams assumed this principle in earlier articles,[3] in order to argue that bodily continuity is a necessary condition of personal identity. We are prone, otherwise, to think that a person could enter a machine, disappear there, and appear in another machine ten feet to the left, without

ever having occupied any intervening space. Williams asks us to imagine that there also had been an additional machine ten feet to the right, and at this one too had appeared simultaneously another (qualitatively) identical being. Neither of the two then would be that original person who entered the machine in the middle. Furthermore, if in that situation of double materialization, the person on the left is not the original person, then neither is he in the different situation where only one person appears on the left. The mere possibility of someone also emerging (discontinuously) on the right is enough, according to Williams, to show that anyone who emerges (discontinuously) on the left, even if all alone, is not the original person.[4]

The first principle says that identity cannot depend upon whether there is or isn't another thing of a certain sort; the second says that if there could be another thing so that then there would not be identity, then there isn't identity, even if that other thing does not actually exist. (If there were identity only when that other thing happened not to exist, the first principle would be violated; the second principle follows from the first.) Both of these principles are false.

First, consider a case that does not involve any question of a person's identity. The Vienna Circle was driven from Austria and Germany by the Nazis; one member, Hans Reichenbach, landed in Istanbul. (Later he left and went to the United States.) Suppose there were twenty members of the Circle, of whom three ended up in Istanbul. These three keep meeting through the war years, discussing philosophy. In 1943, they hear that all of the others are dead. *They* now are the Vienna Circle, meeting in Istanbul. Carrying on its discussion, they proclaim that the Vienna Circle lives on in exile. In 1945,

---

[3]"Personal Identity and Individuation" and "Bodily Continuity and Personal Identity," reprinted in his *Problems of the Self*, pp. 1–25.

[4]Note that this principle requires not merely some bodily continuity, but a sort that could not simultaneously be duplicated; so it excludes the result of transplanting half of someone's brain into a new body, even supposing that there are no hemispheric asymmetries and that no other bodily parts continue.

however, they learn that nine members of the Circle had gotten to America, where they continued to meet, discuss philosophy, adhere to the same philosophical program, and so on. That group in the United States is the Vienna Circle in exile; the group in Istanbul turns out not to be the Vienna Circle but its Istanbul offshoot.

How can this be? Either the group in Istanbul is the Vienna Circle or it isn't; how can whether or not it is be affected by whether other members survived and continued to meet in another place? (Isn't it clear, though, that if these nine others had gone underground and continued to meet in Vienna, this would show that the Istanbul group was not the Vienna Circle?) It is not plausible to apply the first principle to this case; it is not plausible to say that if the group of those three persons meeting in Istanbul is the same continuing entity as the earlier Vienna Circle, then this can depend only upon relationships between the two, and not whether anything else of a certain sort exists.

Rather, the group in Istanbul is the Vienna Circle when it is the *closest continuer* of the Vienna Circle. If no other group exists, the Istanbul group is the closest continuer; but if the group in the United States exists, *it* is the continuer (supposing no closer continuer exists) of the Vienna Circle. Whether or not a particular group constitutes the Vienna Circle depends on what other groups there actually are.[5]

To be something later is to be its closest continuer. Let us apply this view to one traditional puzzle about identity over time: the puzzle of the ship of Theseus. The planks of a ship are removed one by one over intervals of time, and as each plank is removed it is replaced by a new plank. The removal of one plank and its replacement by another does not make the ship a

different ship than before; it is the same ship with one plank different. Over time, each and every plank might be removed and replaced, but if this occurs gradually, the ship still will be the same ship. It is an interesting result, but upon reflection not so very surprising, that the identity of something over time does not require it to keep all the very same parts. The story continues, however. (We can imagine this as a continuation of the previous story, or as a new one which begins like the first.) It turns out that the planks removed had not been destroyed but were stored carefully; now they are brought together again into their original shiplike configuration. Two ships float on the waters, side by side. Which one, wondered the Greeks, is the original?

The closest continuer view helps to sort out and structure the issues; it does not, by itself, answer the question. For it does not, by itself, tell which dimension or weighted sum of dimensions determines closeness; rather, it is a schema into which such details can be filled. In the case of the ships, there are two relevant properties: spatiotemporal continuity with continuity of parts, and being composed of the very same parts (in the same configuration). If these have equal weight, there is a tie in closeness of continuation. Neither, then, is the closest continuer, so neither is the original ship. However, even when the two properties receive equal weight, if there actually had been one ship existing without the other, then it, as the closest continuer, would be the original ship. Perhaps the situation is not one of a clear tie, but one of an unclear weighting. Our concepts may not be sharp enough to order all possible combinations of properties according to closeness of continuation. For complicated cases, we may feel that which is closest is a matter to decide, that we must sharpen our concept to settle which is (identical with) the original entity. It is different, though, with persons, and especially with ourselves; we are not willing to think that whether something is *us* can be a matter of (somewhat arbitrary) decision or stipulation.

[5]Saul Kripke has pointed out to me an anticipation of the closest continuer theory in Sydney Shoemaker, "Wiggins on Identity," *Philosophical Review*, Vol. 74, 1970, p. 542; see also his "Persons and Their Pasts," *American Philosophical Quarterly*, Vol. 7, 1970, p. 278, note 18.

Although it does not answer the question about which ship, if any, is the same as the original one, the closest continuer schema does fit and explain our response to this puzzle. When we hear the first story of the ship gradually altered, plank by plank, we are not puzzled or led to deny it really is the same ship. Only when we learn also of the reconstituted ship are we thrown into puzzlement, not only about its status but about the earlier product of gradual rebuilding, too. It is only when we learn of another candidate for closest (or equally close) continuer that we come to doubt whether that gradually altered ship is the same ship as the original one. If our notion of closeness is unsharp, we will not be able to say that either, or neither, is the original; whether one is closest will remain unclear. The nature and contours of people's responses to the puzzle of the ship fits the closest continuer schema and supports it, if not as a metaphysical truth then at least as a component of a psychological explanation of these responses.

The closest continuer view presents a necessary condition for identity; something at t_2 is not the same entity as x at t_1 if it is not x's closest continuer. And "closest" means closer than all others; if two things at t_2 tie in closeness to x at t_1, then neither is the same entity as x. However, something may be the closest continuer of x without being close enough to it to be x. How close something must be to x to be x, it appears, depends on the kind of entity x is, as do the dimensions along which closeness is measured.[6]

If the closest continuer view is correct, our judgments of identity reflect (implicit) weightings of dimensions; therefore, we might use these judgments themselves to discover those dimensions, the ordering and weighting among them. Notice that on the closest continuer view, a property may be a factor in identity without being a necessary condition for it. If persons conceivably can transfer from one body to another, still, bodily continuity can be an important component of identity, even (in some cases) its sole determinant. The dimension of bodily continuity can receive significant weight in the overall measure of closeness for persons.

To say that something is a continuer of x is not merely to say its properties are qualitatively the same as x's, or resemble them. Rather it is to say they grow out of x's properties, are causally produced by them, are to be explained by x's earlier having had its properties, and so forth. (See also our later discussion of tracking.) Indeed, even the notion of spatiotemporal continuity is not to be explained merely as something that when photographed would produce continuous film footage with no gaps; for we can imagine a substitution of one thing for another that would not break film continuity.[7] The later

---

[6]Is the notion of identity, "=," then elliptical for "the same K," where "K" is a term for a kind of entity? Can y be the same K_1 as x but not the same K_2—to use the example in the literature, the same hunk of marble but not the same statue? If the kind determines the relative weights different properties have in determining identity, different kinds might give different weights to the very same properties. However, just as kinds weight properties, might not the kinds themselves also be weighted thereby to specify a nonrelativized notion of "same entity"? I do not mean the closest continuer view to be committed to any relativization of identity.

[7]In classroom lectures in the fall of 1977, I used the example of two machines, a disappearing machine and a producing machine, where there is independent evidence of how each operates separately; when operated together, suitably synchronized, one makes an object disappear while another produces an exact duplicate in the same place. In thus showing that filmstrip continuity is not sufficient for 'same object', I viewed myself as adapting to a different topic a type of argument I encountered in Sydney Shoemaker's "Time Without Change," *Journal of Philosophy*, Vol. 66, 1969, pp. 363–381. There he puts together several different local freezes of different periodicity to produce an overall total freeze of change in the universe for a predictable period of time. Clearly, I had caught on to how to continue the Shoemaker series, as is shown by his article, "Identity, Properties, and Causality," *Midwest Studies in Philosophy*, Vol. IV, 1979, where on pp. 326–327 he makes this very argument, and notes that D. M. Armstrong makes it independently. Did Armstrong also see himself as applying a mode of argument he had learned from Shoemaker?

temporal stages also must be causally dependent (in an appropriate way) on the earlier ones. The condition that something is a continuer incorporates such causal dependence.* The closest continuer view is not committed to the thesis that identity through time depends only upon the qualitative properties of temporal stages to the exclusion of causal relations and dependencies between (aspects of) stages.

This causal dependence, however, need not involve temporal continuity. Imagine that each and every thing flickers in and out of existence every other instant, its history replete with temporal gaps. (Compare how messages are transmitted on telephone wires.) According to concepts developed later in this chapter, if every thing leads this mode of existence, then it is the best kind of continuity there actually is, so all such will count as continuing objects. However, if some have continuity without any temporal gaps, then the others that flicker, though otherwise similar, are not the best realization of continuity; so perhaps their stages do not closely enough continue each other to count as constituting objects that continue through time. How much temporal continuity is necessary for there to be a continuing object depends on how closely things continue temporally elsewhere.

If it governs our judgments about identity over time, it seems plausible that the closest continuer schema also should fit our *perception* of things continuing through time; it should fit what we see as (a later stage of) what. In parallel to Piaget's famous experiments with objects disappearing behind a screen, we should be able to devise experiments to uncover the closest continuer schema and reveal aspects of the metric of closeness. Show a film of an object x going behind a screen followed by something y

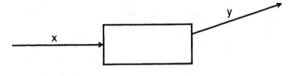

Figure 14.1

coming out at a different angle (Figure 14.1); with color and shape held constant and velocity suitably maintained, a person should see this as the same object emerging, deflected by a collision with something behind the screen. Similarly, with a suitably chosen delay followed by emergence with increased velocity, it should be seen as the same object popping out after being somewhat stuck. Yet if along with y an even closer continuer z also is presented, for example, something emerging straight out at the same velocity, that thing z, rather than y, would be seen as the earlier x emerging, even though in z's absence, y would be seen so, since it then would be x's closest continuer (Figure 14.2). Following this plausible hunch that such psychological experiments could exhibit the closest continuer schema, I inquired of psychologist friends whether experiments like these had ever been done. Though the research seemed plausible, no one I spoke to knew of any, until I met an Israeli psychologist, Shimon Ullman, who had just completed his doctoral dissertation where he had done these experiments.[8] His results fit the closest continuer schema; also he included more detailed experiments in which

Figure 14.2

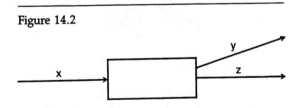

---

*If this causal component indeed is needed, it raises problems for theological views that hold God maintains everything in continued existence, where this includes all causal connections. How does He distinguish continuing an old thing from producing a new one, qualitatively identical, without any filmstrip "break"?

[8]"The Interpretation of Visual Motion," unpublished doctoral dissertation, MIT, 1977.

the color, shape, and velocity of the figures were varied in order to uncover (in my terminology) the details of the metric. (Unfortunately no experiments were done that sharply focus on how people perceive the hard situations that will puzzle us below: tie cases and overlap cases.)

The closest continuer view holds that y at t_2 is the same person as x at t_1 only if, first, y's properties at t_2 stem from, grow out of, are causally dependent on x's properties at t_1 and, second, there is no other z at t_2 that stands in a closer (or as close) relationship to x at t_1 than y at t_2 does.

Closeness, here, represents not merely the degree of causal connection, but also the qualitative closeness of what is connected, as this is judged by some weighting of dimensions and features in a similarity metric. Moreover, it seems plausible that closeness is measured only among those features that are causally connected (instead of a threshold being passed when there is a causal connection, while then closeness is measured among all features of x and y, including those features of y that are causally unconnected with x, even any that pop up spontaneously and at random).

The Theory Applied

Let us now investigate how the closest continuer theory handles particular cases.

> Case 1. After precise measurements of you are taken, your body, including the brain, is precisely duplicated. In all physical properties this other body is the same as yours; it also acts as you do, has the same goals, "remembers" what you do, and so on.

Intuitively, we want to say that you (continue to) exist in this case, and also that a duplicate has been made of you, but this duplicate is not you. According to the closest continuer theory,

too, that other entity is not you, since it is not your closest continuer. Although it exhibits both bodily and psychological similarity (to the earlier you), and though its psychological traits stem from yours via the intermediaries who made it, it does not show bodily continuity. That duplicated body does causally depend, in some way, on the state of your body; it is no accident that it duplicates your properties. Your own body's continuance, though, does not require a duplicator to make a choice in the causal process. The duplicate's causal connection to your earlier body is not this close, so it loses out (as being you) to the continuing you.

> Case 2. You are dying after a heart attack, and your healthy brain is transplanted into another body, perhaps one cloned from yours and so very similar though healthier. After the operation, the "old body" expires and the new body-person continues on with all your previous plans, activities, and personal relationships.

Intuitively we want to say, or at least I do, that you have continued to exist in another body. (We can imagine this becoming a standard medical technique to prolong life.) The closest continuer theory can yield this result. The new body-person certainly is your closest continuer. With psychological continuity and some bodily continuity (the brain is the same), is it a close enough continuer to still be you? I would say it is.

My intention is to show how the closest continuer schema fits my judgments. Perhaps you make different judgments; you thereby differ in judging comparative closeness, but you still are using that same schema. Then is there any content to the claim that the closest continuer schema fits our judgments? When y and z are stages occurring after x, cannot dimensions be given weights so as to yield either one as closer to x, whichever judgment a person makes? It appears that the closest continuer schema excludes nothing. However, though any judgments about one case or situation can be fit to the closest continuer schema by a suitable choice of dimensions and weights, by a suitable choice of metric, it does not follow that any and every group of judgments can be made to fit. Only some (range of) weightings can fit particular judgments J_1 and J_2; these weights, once fixed, give determinate content to the schema. Some judgments J_3 about other cases are excluded, since any weights that would yield J_3 fall outside the range of weights already fixed by judgments J_1 and J_2. The closest continuer schema is compatible with any single judgment about identity or nonidentity, but it is not compatible with each and every set of judgments. Add the assumption that the same dimensions and weights function, when applicable, in various judgments; the closest continuer schema now does exclude some (combinations of) things, and so does have determinate empirical content.

The situation is similar with utility theory. Given any one preference in a pair of alternatives, utility always can be assigned to give the preferred alternative a higher utility; however, some combinations of pairwise preferences among various alternatives cannot be fit to a utility function. To gain empirical content, the assumption must be added that the underlying preferences remain constant during the sequence of pairwise judgments, that it is one utility function which accounts for all the pairwise preferences—just as it is one metric space determining closeness, which must account for the person's various judgments of identity and nonidentity. To say that some straight line or other fits the data, has no restrictive content if there is only one data point, or two; a third point, however, might fail to fall on the straight line fixed by the other two.

Reassured that the closest continuer schema has determinate content, let us return to cases.

Case 3. As you are dying, your brain patterns are transferred to another (blank) brain in another body, perhaps one cloned from yours. The patterns in the new brain are produced by some analogue process that simultaneously removes these patterns from the old one. (There is a greater continuity—or impression of it—with an analogue process as compared to the transmission of digitally coded data.) Upon the completion of the transfer, the old body expires.

Here, there need be no physical continuity at the time of transfer (though there may have been a previous cloning). Still, I believe, this can be you; I believe this is a way a person can continue on. When I contemplate this happening to myself, I believe this continuation would be close enough to count as me continuing.

Notice that the duplicate being in the first case may be exactly like the new you in this case. However, in that case it was not a new you, for the old you still was around—an even closer continuer existed.

Case 4. Suppose medical technology permitted only half a brain to be transplanted in another body, but this brought along full psychological similarity.

If your old half-brain and body ceased to function during such a transplant, the new body-person would be you. This case is like case 2, except that here half a brain is transplanted instead of a full one; we are imaging the half-brain to carry with it the full psychology of the person.

Case 5. Suppose that after an accident damages a portion of your brain, half of it is surgically removed and ceases to function apart from the body. The remaining half continues to function in the body, maintaining full psychological continuity.

Although half of your brain has been removed, you remain alive and remain you.

Case 6. Let us now suppose the fourth and fifth cases are combined: half of a person's brain is removed, and while the remaining half-brain plus body function on with no noticeable difference, the removed half is transplanted into another body to yield full psychological continuity there. The old body plus half-brain is exactly like the continuing person of case 5, the new body plus transplanted half-brain is exactly like the continuing person of case 4. But now both are around. Are both the original person, or neither, or is one of them but not the other?

It appears that the closer continuer in case 6 is (the person of) the original body plus remaining half-brain. Both resultant persons have full psychological continuity with the original one, both also have some bodily continuity, though in one · case only half a brain's worth. One appears to have closer continuity, however—not more kinds of continuity (both have psychological and physical continuity with the original) but more of one of the kinds. One has greater physical overlap with the original person.

If this one is closer, as appears, then he is the original person and the other is not. True, it feels to the other as if *he* is the original person, but so did it for the duplicate in the very first case. Still, I am hesitant about this result. Perhaps we should hold that despite appearances there is a tie for closeness, so neither is the original person; or that though one is closer to the original person, close enough to him to constitute him when there is no competitor (as shown by case 5), that closer one is not enough closer than the competitor to constitute the original person. On this last view, a continuer must be not only closest and close enough, but also enough closer than any other continuer; it must decisively beat out the competition.

Case 7. As you die, a very improbable random event occurs elsewhere in the universe: molecules come together precisely in the configuration of your brain and a very similar (but healthier) body, exhibiting complete psychological similarity to you.

This is not you; though it resembles you, by hypothesis, it does not arise out of you. It is not any continuer of you. In the earlier cases, by *psychological continuity* I meant "stemming from" and "similar to." Of course, we can have the first without the second, as when drastic changes in psychology are brought on by physical injury or emotional trauma; case 7 shows the second without the first.[9]

---

[9]Consider the consequences of the closest continuer theory for issues about the contingency or necessity of identity statements containing only rigid designators, terms which refer to the same individual in every possible world in which they refer, and refer to that individual in every possible world in which it exists. The notion of rigid designators is introduced and the issue of the necessity or contingency of identity statements is discussed in Saul Kripke, "Naming and Necessity" (in Donald Davidson and Gilbert Harman, eds., *Semantics of Natural Languages*, Reidel, Dodrecht, 1972, pp. 253–355; *Naming and Necessity* was published separately by Harvard University Press, Cambridge, 1980).

In cases 1 and 3 above, let us suppose that case 1, where a duplicate is made of me while I continue on, is the actual case. We can diagram this as in Figure N.1, letting time flow to the right. Here ROBERT NOZICK rigidly designates me, and RN rigidly designates the duplicate that is made. Let us also rigidly designate by rn the stage of the actually continuing ROBERT NOZICK which begins at time t_1, when the duplicate comes to be made, and let robert rigidly designate the stage of ROBERT NOZICK from t_0 to t_1. In this actual world

(1) ROBERT NOZICK $\neq$ RN
(2) RN is not a stage of ROBERT NOZICK
(3) rn is a stage of ROBERT NOZICK
(4) RN is not a stage which continues the entity of which robert is a stage.

(Footnote continues on p. 221.)

Figure N.1

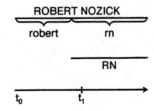

(Footnote 9 continued.)

Let us now consider the possible case 3, where the making of the duplicate from the pattern of the earlier existing person coincides with the ending of that old body. It seems natural to diagram that possible situation as in Figure N.2. Of this case, I said that RN was a close enough continuer to be the continuation of robert, of ROBERT NOZICK. In the possible world of case 3, it seems that

(1′) ROBERT NOZICK = RN
(2′) RN is a stage of ROBERT NOZICK
(3′) rn does not exist
(4′) RN is a stage which continues the entity of which robert is a stage.

Now to draw some lessons. (These depend on the closest continuer structure, not on anything special to persons; similar points could be made with variants of the Greek ship case.) (a) The statement that a stage, rigidly designated, is a stage of an entity, rigidly designated, is in general contingent, varying in truth value from world to world. (Witness 2 and 2′; also 3 and 3′.) I say "in general," for there might be some continuing stages than whom there could not be closer ones. (b) The statement that two stages, rigidly designated, are identical over time (that is, are stages of the same continuing object) is contingent, varying in truth value from world to world. (Witness 4 and 4′.) The most difficult and interesting point is whether (c) a statement of identity between objects, rigidly designated, is contingent and varies in truth value from world to world. It seems that 1 and 1′ show this, that in the first (actual) world ROBERT NOZICK ≠ RN, while in the case-3 world ROBERT NOZICK = RN. However, we must reconsider 1 and 1′, looking more closely at precisely how the reference of the rigid designators is established.

If the reference of "ROBERT NOZICK" is fixed in the actual world (of case 1) as rigidly designating *that* person (pointing to someone between t_0 and t_1), while the reference of "RN" is fixed in the actual world as rigidly designating *that* person (pointing after t_1 to the product of the duplicating process), then clearly in the actual world, ROBERT NOZICK ≠ RN. However, there now is a question about which term, whose reference is already fixed in the actual world, refers in the possible world of case 3 to the person who resides in the duplicated body. Since in the case-3 world that person is ROBERT NOZICK (it is the closest continuer in the case-3 world

of robert, the early stage of ROBERT NOZICK), then it seems that that person in the case-3 world is properly referred to by "ROBERT NOZICK." Now is that person in the case-3 world who inhabits the duplicate also properly referred to by the rigid designator "RN"? The reference of "RN" was (rigidly) fixed in the actual world as the person (pointed to after t_1) inhabiting the duplicated body, and that person (not identical in the actual world to ROBERT NOZICK) does not seem to exist in the case-3 world. And so "RN" does not refer in the case-3 world to the person who is or inhabits the duplicated body. Thus, on this analysis, 1′, 2′, and 4′ are false (in the case-3 world) since RN does not, despite appearances, exist in that world.

Suppose now that the case-3 world is actual, while the case-1 world is merely possible, and let "ROBERT NOZICK" rigidly designate *that* person (pointing before t_1) and let "RN" rigidly designate *that* person (pointing after t_1). Since there is only one person in the case-3 world, both terms rigidly designate the same entity. Now, let us look to the possible world of case 1. There, "ROBERT NOZICK" refers to the person existing before t_1, but what does "RN," whose reference has been rigidly fixed in the case-3 world, refer to in the case-1 world? Despite appearances, it refers not to the person of the duplicate (in the case-1 world), for that person didn't exist in the case-3 world, but rather to ROBERT NOZICK. Thus, on this analysis of the fixing of reference, 1 (and perhaps 2 and 3) are false in the world of case 1, for in that world "RN" carries its reference as fixed in the case-3 world and so refers to ROBERT NOZICK.

Therefore, even given the closest continuer theory, we seem to lack a sharp and clear counterexample to Kripke's specific claim that identity statements between rigid designators are noncontingent. The loophole is that "the entity of which that stage is a stage" or "that entity" (pointing at a stage of an entity) can refer to different entities in the different worlds where uttered, even when the same stage is present. It is point a above that saves Kripke's specific claim against the considerations presented under point c. If, instead of rigidly fixing the reference as that person (or ship), we fix it as that stage, that person-stage, (or ship-stage), we apparently will again only demonstrate point b above. Thus, although on the basis of closest continuer considerations Kripke's claim about noncontingency (of identity statements with ' = ' between rigid designators) has been surrounded, it has not yet been overturned.

Can we push a bit further? Sitting in the actual world of case 1, diagrammed as in Figure N.3, let us mentally point

(Footnote continues on p. 222.)

Figure N.2

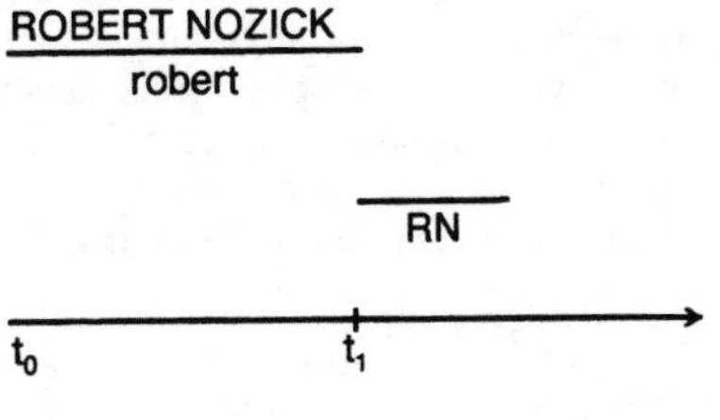

ROBERT NOZICK
robert

RN

t_0 t_1

Figure N.3

Consider the mode of long distance travel described in science fiction stories, wherein a person is "beamed" from one place to another. However, the person's body does not occupy intermediate places. Either the molecules of the decomposed body are beamed or (truer to the intent of the stories) a fully informative description of the body is beamed to another place, where the body then is reconstituted (from numerically distinct molecules) according to the received information. Yet the readers of such stories, and the many viewers of such television programs, calmly accept this as a mode of travel. They do not view it as a killing of one person with the production of another very similar person elsewhere. (We may suppose that those few who do view it that way, and refuse so to "travel," despite the fact that it is faster, cheaper, and avoids the intervening asteroid belts, are laughed at by the others.) The taking and transmission of the informative description might not involve the dematerialization of the person here, who remains also. In that case, the newly constituted person there presumably would be viewed as a similar duplicate.

Do we need to stipulate that the process of transporting by beaming, by its nature, must involve the dematerialization of the original here? In the case of people, at least, a merely accidental ending of the person here may seem inadequate for continuation there; consider the case where as the information is beamed to create what is intended to be only a duplicate, the original person is shot, so that (to speak neutrally) the life in that body ends. Yet, imagine a beamer which can work either way— dematerializing here or not—depending upon which way a switch is thrown. If the process with dematerialization is far more expensive, might not those who wished to travel there choose the less expensive method combined with an alternative ending (accidental with respect to the transporting process) of their existence here? I shall leave these issues unresolved now.

In addition to the closest continuer, we also must focus on the closest predecessor, for similar reasons. Something y may be the closest continuer of another thing x even though x is not y's closest predecessor. Though nothing at t_2 more closely continues x than y does, still, y more closely continues z at t_1 than it does x at t_1. For a later stage y to be part of the same continuing object as an earlier stage x, not only must y be the closest continuer of x, also x must be the closest predecessor of y. Let us say that two things or stages so related are mono-related. This mono-relation need not be transitive, since neither closest continuer nor closest predecessor need be transitive.[10]

(*Footnote 9 continued.*)
Figure N.4

_____

_____

to the world of case 3, diagrammed in Figure N.4, and rigidly fix the reference of "RN" as "that person" (indicated by the bottom line). To which person in the actual world (of case 1) does "RN" then refer, to the one that started at t_0 or the duplicate who begins at t_1? It seems it might be the latter, and since "Robert Nozick" in both worlds refers to the person who exists (but not only) before t_1, we seem to have in the actual world,

Robert Nozick ≠ RN

while in the world of case 3,

Robert Nozick = RN.

It certainly appears that some counterexample should emerge, even to Kripke's specific claim, from closest continuer considerations.

[10]For example, we might have the following structure: y at t_2 is a closer continuer of x at t_1 than z at t_2 is; at a later time t_3 there is no continuer of y but there is a w which is the closest continuer of z. It may also be that w at t_3 is the closest continuer of x at t_1, that is, there is no other thing at t_3 which as closely continues x. Thus, we have y at t_2 being the closest continuer of x at t_1, and w at t_3 not being a continuer of y at t_2 yet being the closest continuer of x at t_1. We can diagram this situation (Figure N.5), letting a dotted-line link stand for one thing's being (among the various things that exist at the same time) the closest continuer of an

(*Footnote continues on p. 223.*)

How shall a view of identity over time cope with these nontransitivities of mono-related, closest continuer, and closest predecessor? Let X refer to the entity over time that continues x at t_1. I see the following four possibilities.

1. Entity X follows the path of closest continuation. We can state this most easily if we suppose each moment of time has an immediate predecessor. The component stage at t_2 of X is just that entity, if any, which is the closest continuer of x at t_1, and which continues it closely enough to be (identical with) X at t_1. The component at t_{n+1} of X is just that entity, if any, which is the closest continuer of the component at t_n of X, and which continues it closely enough to be (identical with) the component at t_n of X. Entity X is constituted from moment to moment by the closest (and close enough) continuer of the immediately preceding component of X. When there is no closest continuer because of a tie, or because nothing continues it at all or closely enough, then X ends.

2. Entity X follows the path of closest contin-

uation, unless it is a short path. If a t_{n+1} is reached when there is no continuer of the component at t_n of X, then backtracking occurs to the nearest component C of X for which there exists at t_{n+1} something z which continues C closely enough to be (identical with) it. The component at t_{n+1} of X is then z, and X continues from z on the path of closest continuation. At t_{n+1}, there is a "jump" to the segment of the path that z begins.

3. This alternative is like the preceding one, except that between the time of C and t_{n+1}, the components constituting X are some continuation path of C that leads to z, without jumps. (Each succeeding step from C will be to a continuer, but not all will be to an adjacent *closest* continuer.)

4. Entity X originates with x at t_1 and each later component of X is the closest continuer existing at that time of the original x at t_1. Since everything harks back to x at t_1, there may be considerable hopping, either around or back and forth.[11]

Overlap

With these four possibilities in mind, let us consider the following most difficult case.

> Case 8. Half of an ill person's brain is removed and transplanted into another body, but the original body plus half-brain does not expire when this is being done; it lingers on for one hour, or two days, or two weeks. Had this died immediately, the original person would survive in the new body, via the transplanted half-brain which carries with it psychological similarity and continuity. However, in the intervening hour or days or weeks, the old

---

(Footnote 10 continued.)

Figure N.5

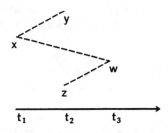

earlier thing. A version of the situation with the ship exemplifies this structure. Let y at t_2 be the ship with some replacement planks, and let z at t_2 be the heap of removed planks, stacked in a storeroom. Between t_2 and t_3 the ship with replacement planks has burned, and at t_3 the ship w has been reassembled out of the original planks. At t_2 the ship with some replacement planks is the same as the original ship, while the heap of planks in the storeroom is not. At t_3 the ship rebuilt from this heap of original planks is the same as the original ship, though it does not physically continue that ship at t_2 with the replacement planks.

[11]Since as far back as we know, everything comes from something else, to find an origin is to find a relative beginning, the beginning of an entity as being of a certain kind K.

body lives on, perhaps unconscious or perhaps in full consciousness, alongside the newly implanted body.

Does the person then die along with it (as in option 1 above)? Can its lingering on during the smallest overlapping time interval, when the lingerer is the closest continuer, mean the end of the person, while if there was no such lingerer, no temporal overlap, the person would live on? It seems so unfair for a person to be doomed by an echo of his former self. Or, does the person move to the new body upon the expiration of the old one (as in option 2 above)? But then, who was it in the new body for the hour or two days or two weeks preceding his arrival there, and what happened to that person? Perhaps during that initial time interval, it was a duplicate of the person in that new body (with old half-brain), a duplicate which becomes the person upon the expiration of the old body. It seems strange that at a certain time, without any (physical) change taking place in it, the new body could become the person when the old body expires. However, once we have become used to the idea that whether y at t_2 is (identical with) x at t_1 does not depend only upon the properties and relations of x and y, but depends also upon whether there exists a z of a certain sort (which more closely continues x), then perhaps we can swallow this consequence as well.[12] Still, there is a difficulty. If the old body plus half-brain linger on for long enough, three years say, then surely that is the person, and the person dies when that body expires—the duplicate does not suddenly become the person after three years. A one-minute period of lingering is compatible with the new body-person being the original person, a three-year period is not. But the interval can be varied gradually; it

seems absurd that there should be some sharp temporal line which makes the difference to whether or not the person continues to live in the other body. ("Doctor, there's only one minute left! Hurry to end life in the old body so the person can live on in the new one." And out of which body would these words come?)[13]

Or, does the person move to the new body immediately upon the transplantation of the half-brain into it (as in option 3 above)? Are we opportunists who leave a sinking body before it is sunk? And what if, despite predictions, it has not sunk but makes it to port—where are we then? Does whether we move at one time depend upon how things turn out later, so there is identity ex post facto? If the person moves over at the time of the transplant, who is it that dies (in the old body) two days later?

None of these positions seems satisfactory. Even if our intuitions did fit one of them completely, we would have to explain why it was such an important notion. Perhaps we are willing to plunk for one of these options as compared to its close variants when the overlap involves ships, tables, countries, or universities. We do not so arbitrarily want to apply a concept or theory of identity to ourselves; we need to be shown a difference between it and its apparently close variants, deep enough to make the difference between our being there and not.

Let us examine more closely the structure of the problematic overlap situation. In Figure

---

[12]This instantaneous movement of a person from one place to another does not violate special relativity's constraint on the transmission of energy or a causal signal faster than light.

[13]Compare the case of abortion, where also no sharp line or threshold (between the times of conception and birth) seems appropriate. However, we can imagine a presumption against abortion that increases in moral weight as the fetus develops, so that only reasons of increasing significance could justify (later) abortion. Unlike the abortion case, there is nothing in our present concern, the lingering overlap, that can vary continuously like the moral weight of a presumption. One might be tempted to consider the (continuously varying) probability of the healthier one's being the same (earlier) person, but what additional fact would there be to fix how that probability comes out?

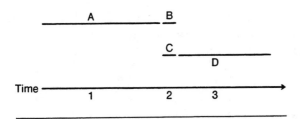

Figure 14.3

14.3, the closest successor of A is B, and the closest successor of A + B is D. However, the closest predecessor of D is C, and the closest predecessor of C + D is A. Neither A + B + D nor A + C + D is a mono-related entity. Taking a longer view, though, A and D are mono-related: D is the closest successor of A plus A's closest successor; also A is the closest predecessor of D plus D's closest predecessor.

When B and C are small in comparison, the mono-relation of A and D would seem to constitute them as part of the same entity. Thereby, is marked off an extensive entity.[14] Are we mono-related entities that need not be temporally continuous? On this view, there could be a person with temporal parts A and D during

[14]Some writers have speculated that when people sleep and dream, an astral body actually moves off from the sleeping body and in some realm performs the dreamed actions. (But in a dream of mine involving another actual person, will that person also have dreamed the same situation? And what was Marilyn Monroe dreaming on these evenings when so many others were dreaming of her but not of all the others?) Such a view would be diagrammed as in Figure N.6. Each day a person is mono-related to himself the previous day, and that suffices for identity, no matter how the question of where he was during the previous night is answered.

Figure N.6

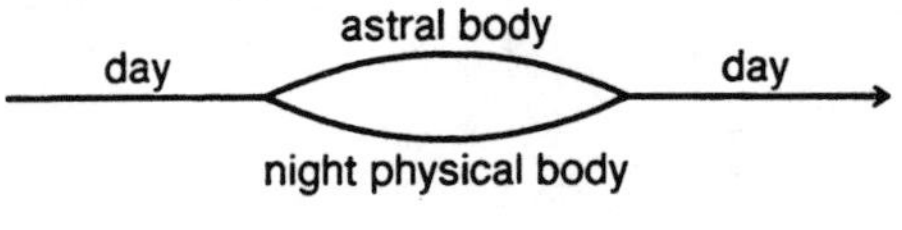

times 1 and 3, yet that person does not exist during the intervening time 2. Something related does exist then, so this discontinuous person does depend upon some continuities during time 2, but these are not continuities through which he continues to exist then. (A watch repairer takes a watch completely apart and puts it together again; the customer later picks up his watch, the same one he had brought in, though there was an intervening time when it did not exist.)

This view encounters difficulties, however. C might think to himself, "Since it is unjust for someone to be punished for a crime he did not do, D may not be punished for a crime planned and executed during time 2, when D does not exist. No one will be apprehended until time 3, so it is safe for me to commit the crime without fear of punishment." Surely we may punish D for what C does. Is it B or C we punish for the acts of A? Or do we wait until time 3 and punish D? (Yet, if D certainly will escape punishment if we wait, do we punish B or C?) It would appear that D may not be punished for acts of B (unless C does not exist). However, B might assassinate a rival political candidate to bring about the election of D. If this continued a calculated plan put into effect by A, then D may be punished; but suppose B first thinks of this act during time 2, or that A planned it thinking his life would end with B, in order to ensure that the later person D who claimed to be A—falsely on A's view—would be punished for usurping A's identity. It is clear that a morass of difficulties faces the position that one continuing entity includes A and D as parts but not the overlapping segments B and C.

The problem of temporal overlap is not unique to people, we have seen. It arises in the Greek ship case if the original planks are reconfigured into a ship one day before the ship consisting of replacement planks catches fire and burns. Is the reconfigured ship the original ship, or not?

This quandary about temporal overlap is intrinsic, I believe, to any notion of identity applicable to more than atomic-point-instants. Any such notion trades off depth to gain breadth; in order to encompass larger entities, it sacrifices some similarity among what it groups together. Maximum similarity within the groupings would limit them to atomic-point-instants. The purpose of the identity notion is wider breadth, but a grouping that included everything would not convey specific information. The closest continuer theory is the best Parmenides can do in an almost Heraclitean world.

The notion of identity itself compromises between breadth and (exact) similarity (which similarity can include being part of the same causal process). Since spatial and temporal distances involve some dissimilarity, any temporal or spatial breadth involves some sacrifice of (exact) similarity. For our cases, width and breadth are measured along spatiotemporal dimensions, closeness or similarity along other dimensions. The informativeness of a classification varies positively with the extent of its subclasses, and with the degree of similarity exhibited within each subclass; similar norms apply to the clumping of entities from the flux.[15]

Usually, the closest continuer schema—or more generally (when the temporal relation is not the most salient), the closest relation schema—serves to achieve the right measure of breadth. It extends entities X to the maximum

feasible extent: further extended, something would be included that is not close enough to link with X rather than something else, or X would no longer be sharp enough to be an informative category. When there is temporal overlap, however, the immediate closest continuer view, holding that A's existence continues through B and then stops, does not give the maximum feasible extension. Yet the wider view of the entity as continuing on from A to D brings the difficulties of the overlapping segments.

For the structure of overlap in Figure 14.3, the norm of breadth would place A and D together, as would the norm of similarity. The similarity relation also would place together A and B, and C and D. Yet the disconnected spatial positions, along with the different activities occurring there simultaneously, fall under the dissimilarity relation; this relation, which places things separately in classification, separates B and C. There is no way to bring A and D, A and B, and C and D together into one entity or subclassification, while keeping B and C separate. Still, how can an entity's continuation (from A to C + D) be blocked by the merest continuing tentacle or echo (B) of its previous stage?

The quandary over the overlap situation, I have said, is intrinsic to the notion of identity over time, and stems from its uneasy compromise between the outward and the inward urges. Overlap falls at precisely the point of tension between two different modes of structuring a concept: the closest relation mode and the global mode. We are familiar with the closest continuer or closest relation mode. The global mode looks further. It holds that Y is (a later stage of the same entity as) X if Y is the closest continuer of X, and if there is no even longer extending thing Z that more closely continues X than any equally large thing of which Y is part. . . .

---

[15] Amos Tversky, "Features of Similarity," *Psychological Review*, Vol. 84, 1977, pp. 327–352, especially pp. 347–349, proposes a general formula for the formation of categories. Tversky, surprisingly but convincingly, explains how two things can be the most similar entities within a group and also the most dissimilar, and he provides data to show that people do make such judgments. Hence, a formula for category formation cannot speak only of degrees of similarity within a category; it also must speak, nonredundantly, of (minimizing) degrees of dissimilarity within categories.

15

DEREK PARFIT
The Psychological View

I: What We Believe Ourselves to Be

I enter the Teletransporter. I have been to Mars before, but only by the old method, a space-ship journey taking several weeks. This machine will send me at the speed of light. I merely have to press the green button. Like others, I am nervous. Will it work? I remind myself what I have been told to expect. When I press the button, I shall lose consciousness, and then wake up at what seems a moment later. In fact I shall have been unconscious for about an hour. The Scanner here on Earth will destroy my brain and body, while recording the exact states of all of my cells. It will then transmit this information by radio. Travelling at the speed of light, the message will take three minutes to reach the Replicator on Mars. This will then create, out of new matter, a brain and body exactly like mine. It will be in this body that I shall wake up.

Though I believe that this is what will happen, I still hesitate. But then I remember seeing my wife grin when, at breakfast today, I revealed my nervousness. As she reminded me, she has been often teletransported, and there is nothing wrong with *her*. I press the button. As predicted, I lose and seem at once to regain consciousness, but in a different cubicle. Examining my new body, I find no change at all. Even the cut on my upper lip, from this morning's shave, is still there.

Several years pass, during which I am often Teletransported. I am now back in the cubicle, ready for another trip to Mars. But this time, when I press the green button, I do not lose consciousness. There is a whirring sound, then silence. I leave the cubicle, and say to the attendant: "It's not working. What did I do wrong?"

"It's working," he replies, handing me a printed card. This reads: "The New Scanner records your blueprint without destroying your brain and body. We hope that you will welcome the opportunities which this technical advance offers."

The attendant tells me that I am one of the first people to use the New Scanner. He adds that, if I stay for an hour, I can use the Intercom to see and talk to myself on Mars.

"Wait a minute," I reply, "If I'm here I can't *also* be on Mars."

Someone politely coughs, a white-coated man who asks to speak to me in private. We go into his office, where he tells me to sit down, and pauses. Then he says: "I'm afraid that we're having problems with the New Scanner. It records your blueprint just as accurately, as you will see when you talk to yourself on Mars. But it seems to be damaging the cardiac systems which it scans. Judging from the results so far, though you will be quite healthy on Mars, here on Earth you must expect cardiac failure within the next few days."

The attendant later calls me to the Intercom. On the screen I see myself just as I do in the mirror every morning. But there are two differences. On the screen I am not left-right reversed. And, while I stand here speechless, I can see and hear myself, in the studio on Mars, starting to speak.

What can we learn from this imaginary story? Some believe that we can learn little. This would have been Wittgenstein's view.[1] And Quine writes: "The method of science fiction has its uses in philosophy, but . . . I wonder whether the limits of the method are properly heeded. To seek what is 'logically required' for sameness of person under unprecedented circumstances is to suggest that words have some logical force beyond what our past needs have invested them with."[2]

This criticism might be justified if, when considering such imagined cases, we had no reactions. But these cases arouse in most of us strong beliefs. And these are beliefs, not about our words, but about ourselves. By considering these cases, we discover what we believe to be involved in our own continued existence, or what it is that makes us now and ourselves next year the same people. We discover our beliefs about the nature of personal identity over time. Though our beliefs are revealed most clearly when we consider imaginary cases, these beliefs also cover actual cases, and our own lives. . . .

Simple Teletransportation and the Branch-Line Case

At the beginning of my story, the Scanner destroys my brain and body. My blueprint is beamed to Mars, where another machine makes an organic *Replica* of me. My Replica thinks that he is me, and he seems to remember living my life up to the moment when I pressed the green button. In every other way, both physically and psychologically, we are exactly similar. If he returned to Earth, everyone would think that he was me.

Simple Teletransportation, as just described, is a common feature in science fiction. And it is believed, by some readers of this fiction, merely to be the fastest way of travelling. They believe that my Replica *would* be *me*. Other science fiction readers, and some of the characters in this fiction, take a different view. They believe that, when I press the green button, I die. My Replica is *someone else*, who has been made to be exactly like me.

This second view seems to be supported by the end of my story. The New Scanner does not destroy my brain and body. Besides gathering the information, it merely damages my heart. While I am in the cubicle, with the green button pressed, nothing seems to happen. I walk out, and learn that in a few days I shall die. I later talk, by two-way television, to my Replica on Mars. Let us continue the story. Since my Replica knows that I am about to die, he tries to console me with the same thoughts with which I recently tried to console a dying friend. It is sad to learn, on the receiving end, how unconsoling these thoughts are. My Replica then assures me that he will take up my life where I leave off. He loves my wife, and together they will care for my children. And he will finish the book that I am writing. Besides having all of my drafts, he has all of my intentions. I must admit that he can finish my book as well as I could. All these facts console me a little. Dying when I know that I shall have a Replica is not quite as bad as, simply, dying. Even so, I shall soon lose consciousness, forever.

In Simple Teletransportation, I am destroyed before I am Replicated. This makes it easier to believe that this *is* a way of travelling—that my Replica *is* me. At the end of my story, my life

---

[1]See, for example, *Zettel*, ed. by G. Anscombe and G. von Wright, and translated by G. Anscombe, Blackwell, 1967, Proposition 350: "It is as if our concepts involve a scaffolding of facts. . . . If you imagine certain facts otherwise . . . then you can no longer imagine the application of certain concepts."

[2]Quine, p. 490.

and that of my Replica overlap. Call this the *Branch-Line Case*. In this case, I cannot hope to travel on the *Main Line*, waking up on Mars with forty years of life ahead. I shall stay on the Branch-Line, here on Earth, which ends a few days later. Since I can talk to my Replica, it seems clear that he is *not* me. Though he is exactly like me, he is one person, and I am another. When I pinch myself, he feels nothing. When I have my heart attack, he will again feel nothing. And when I am dead he will live for another forty years.

If we believe that my Replica is not me, it is natural to assume that my prospect, on the Branch Line, is almost as bad as ordinary death. I shall deny this assumption. As I shall argue later, being destroyed and Replicated is about as good as ordinary survival. I can best defend this claim, and the wider view of which it is a part, after discussing the past debate about personal identity.

Qualitative and Numerical Identity

There are two kinds of sameness, or identity. I and my Replica are *qualitatively identical*, or exactly alike. But we may not be *numerically identical*, or one and the same person. Similarly, two white billiard balls are not numerically but may be qualitatively identical. If I paint one of these balls red, it will cease to be qualitatively identical with itself as it was. But the red ball that I later see and the white ball that I painted red are numerically identical. They are one and the same ball.

We might say, of someone, "After his accident, he is no longer the same person." This is a claim about both kinds of identity. We claim that *he*, the same person, is *not* now the same person. This is not a contradiction. We merely mean that this person's character has changed. This numerically identical person is now qualitatively different.

When we are concerned about our future, it is our numerical identity that we are concerned

about. I may believe that, after my marriage, I shall not be the same person. But this does not make marriage death. However much I change, I shall still be alive if there will be some person living who will *be* me. . . .

The Physical Criterion of Personal Identity

There has been much debate about the nature both of persons and of personal identity over time. It will help to distinguish these questions:

(1) What is the nature of a person?
(2) What makes a person at two different times one and the same person? What is necessarily involved in the continued existence of each person over time?

The answer to (2) can take this form: "X today is one and the same person as Y at some past time *if and only if* . . . " Such an answer states the *necessary and sufficient conditions* for personal identity over time.

In answering (2) we shall also partly answer (1). The necessary features of our continued existence depend upon our nature. And the simplest answer to (1) is that, to be a person, a being must be self-conscious, aware of its identity and its continued existence over time.

We can also ask

(3) What is in fact involved in the continued existence of each person over time?

Since our continued existence has features that are not necessary, the answer to (2) is only part of the answer to (3). For example, having the same heart and the same character are not necessary to our continued existence, but they are usually part of what this existence involves.

Many writers use the ambiguous phrase "the criterion of identity over time." Some mean by this "our way of telling whether some present object is identical with some past object." But I shall mean *what this identity necessarily involves, or consists in*.

In the case of most physical objects, on what I

call the *standard view*, the criterion of identity over time is the spatio-temporal physical continuity of this object. This is something that we all understand, even if we fail to understand the description I shall now give. In the simplest case of physical continuity, like that of the Pyramids, an apparently static object continues to exist. In another simple case, like that of the Moon, an object moves in a regular way. Many objects move in less regular ways, but they still trace physically continuous spatio-temporal paths. Suppose that the billiard ball that I painted red is the same as the white ball with which last year I made a winning shot. On the standard view, this is true only if this ball traced such a continuous path. It must be true (1) that there is a line through space and time, starting where the white ball rested before I made my winning shot, and ending where the red ball now is, (2) that at every point on this line there was a billiard ball, and (3) that the existence of a ball at each point on this line was in part caused by the existence of a ball at the immediately preceding point.[3]

Some kinds of thing continue to exist even though their physical continuity involves great changes. A Camberwell Beauty is first an egg, then a caterpillar, then a chrysalis, then a butterfly. These are four stages in the physically continuous existence of a single organism. Other kinds of thing cannot survive such great changes. Suppose that an artist paints a self-portrait and then, by repainting, turns this into a portrait of his father. Even though these portraits are more similar than a caterpillar and a butterfly, they are not stages in the continued existence of a single painting. The self-portrait is a painting that the artist destroyed. In a general discussion of identity, we would need to explain why the requirement of physical continuity differs in such ways for different kinds of thing. But we can ignore this here.

[3]This states a necessary condition for the continued existence of a physical object. Saul Kripke has argued, in lectures, that this condition is not sufficient. Since I missed these lectures, I cannot discuss this argument.

Can there be gaps in the continued existence of a physical object? Suppose that I have the same gold watch that I was given as a boy even though, for a month, it lay disassembled on a watch-repairer's shelf. On one view, in the spatio-temporal path traced by this watch there was not at every point a watch, so my watch does not have a history of full physical continuity. But during the month when my watch was disassembled, and did not exist, all of its parts had histories of full continuity. On another view, even when it was disassembled, my watch existed.

Another complication again concerns the relation between a complex thing and the various parts of which it is composed. It is true of some of these things, though not true of all, that their continued existence need not involve the continued existence of their components. Suppose that a wooden ship is repaired from time to time while it is floating in harbor, and that after fifty years it contains none of the bits of wood out of which it was first built. It is still one and the same ship, because, as a ship, it has displayed throughout these fifty years full physical continuity. This is so despite the fact that it is now composed of quite different bits of wood. These bits of wood might be qualitatively identical to the original bits, but they are not one and the same bits. Something similar is partly true of a human body. With the exception of some brain cells, the cells in our bodies are replaced with new cells several times in our lives.

I have now described the physical continuity which, on the standard view, makes a physical object one and the same after many days or years. This enables me to state one of the rival views about personal identity. On this view, what makes me the same person over time is that I have the same brain and body. The criterion of my identity over time—or what this identity involves—is the physical continuity, over time, of my brain and body. I shall continue to exist if and only if this particular brain and body continue both to exist and to be the brain and body of a living person.

This is the simplest version of this view. There is a better version. This is

The Physical Criterion: (1) What is necessary is not the continued existence of the whole body, but the continued existence of *enough* of the brain to be the brain of a living person. X today is one and the same person as Y at some past time if and only if (2) enough of Y's brain continued to exist, and is now X's brain, and (3) this physical continuity has not taken a 'branching' form. (4) Personal identity over time just consists in the holding of facts like (2) and (3).

(1) is clearly true in certain actual cases. Some people continue to exist even though they lose, or lose the use of, much of their bodies. (3) will be explained later.

Those who believe in the Physical Criterion would reject Teletransportation. They would believe this to be a way, not of travelling, but of dying. They would also reject, as inconceivable, reincarnation. They believe that someone cannot have a life after death, unless he lives this life in a resurrection of the very same, physically continuous body. This is why some Christians insist that they be buried. They believe that if, like Greek and Trojan heroes, they were burnt on funeral pyres, and their ashes scattered, not even God could bring them to life again. God could create only a Replica, someone else who was exactly like them. Other Christians believe that God could resurrect *them* if he reassembled their bodies out of the bits of matter that, when they were last alive, made up their bodies. This would be like the reassembly of my gold watch.[4]

[4]On this view, it could be fatal to live in what has long been a densely populated area, such as London. It may here be true of many bits of matter that they were part of the bodies of many different people, when they were last alive. These people could not all be resurrected, since there would not be enough such matter to be reassembled. Some hold a version of this view which avoids this problem. They believe that a resurrected body needs to contain only one particle from the original body.

The Psychological Criterion

Some people believe in a kind of psychological continuity that resembles physical continuity. This involves the continued existence of a purely mental *entity*, or thing—a soul, or spiritual substance. I shall return to this view. But I shall first explain another kind of psychological continuity. This is less like physical continuity, since it does not consist in the continued existence of some entity. But this other kind of psychological continuity involves only facts with which we are familiar.

What has been most discussed is the continuity of memory. This is because it is memory that makes most of us aware of our own continued existence over time. The exceptions are the people who are suffering from amnesia. Most amnesiacs lose only two sets of memories. They lose all of their memories of having particular past experiences—or, for short, their *experience memories*. They also lose some of their memories about facts, those that are about their own past lives. But they remember other facts, and they remember how to do different things, such as how to speak, or swim.

Locke suggested that experience-memory provides the criterion of personal identity.[5] Though this is not, on its own, a plausible view, I believe that it can be part of such a view. I shall therefore try to answer some of Locke's critics.

Locke claimed that someone cannot have committed some crime unless he now remembers doing so. We can understand a reluctance to punish people for crimes that they cannot remember. But, taken as a view about what is involved in a person's continued existence, Locke's claim is clearly false. If it was true, it would not be possible for someone to forget any of the things that he once did, or any of the experiences that he once had. But this *is* possible. I cannot now remember putting on my shirt this morning.

[5]Locke, Chapter 27, Section 16.

There are several ways to extend the experience-memory criterion so as to cover such cases. I shall appeal to the concept of an overlapping chain of experience-memories. Let us say that, between X today and Y twenty years ago, there are *direct memory connections* if X can now remember having some of the experiences that Y had twenty years ago. On Locke's view, only this makes X and Y one and the same person. But even if there are *no* such direct memory connections, there may be *continuity of memory* between X now and Y twenty years ago. This would be so if between X now and Y at that time there has been an overlapping chain of direct memories. In the case of most adults, there would be such a chain. In each day within the last twenty years, most of these people remembered some of their experiences on the previous day. On the revised version of Locke's view, some present person X is the same as some past person Y if there is between them continuity of memory.

This revision meets one objection to Locke's view. We should also revise the view so that it appeals to other facts. Besides direct memories, there are several other kinds of direct psychological connection. One such connection is that which holds between an intention and the later act in which this intention is carried out. Other such direct connections are those which hold when belief, or a desire, or any other psychological feature, continues to be had.

I can now define two general relations:

Psychological connectedness is the holding of particular direct psychological connections.

Psychological continuity is the holding of overlapping chains of *strong* connectedness.

Of these two general relations, connectedness is more important both in theory and in practice. Connectedness can hold to any degree. Between X today and Y yesterday there might be several thousand direct psychological connections, or only a single connection. If there was only a single connection, X and Y would not be, on the revised Lockean View, the same person. For X and Y to be the same person, there must be over every day *enough* direct psychological connections. Since connectedness is a matter of degree, we cannot plausibly define precisely what counts as enough. But we can claim that there is enough connectedness if the number of connections, over any day, is *at least half* the number that hold, over every day, in the lives of nearly every actual person.[6] When there are enough direct connections, there is what I call *strong* connectedness. . . .

The Psychological Criterion: (1) There is *psychological continuity* if and only if there are overlapping chains of strong connectedness. X today is one and the same person as Y at some past time if and only if (2) X is psychologically continuous with Y, (3) this continuity has the right kind of cause, and (4) it has not taken a 'branching' form. (5) Personal identity over time just consists in the holding of facts like (2) to (4).

As with the Physical Criterion, (4) will be explained later.

There are three versions of the Psychological Criterion. These differ over the question of what is the *right* kind of cause. On the *Narrow* version, this must be the *normal* cause. On the *Wide* version, this could be *any reliable* cause. On the *Widest* version, the cause could be *any* cause. . . .

Reconsider the start of my imagined story, where my brain and body are destroyed. The

---

[6]This suggestion would need expanding, since there are many ways to count the number of direct connections. And some kinds of connection should be given more importance than others. As I suggest later, more weight should be given to those connections which are distinctive, or different in different people. All English-speakers share a vast number of undistinctive memories of how to speak English.

Scanner and the Replicator produce a person who has a new but exactly similar brain and body, and who is psychologically continuous with me as I was when I pressed the green button. The cause of this continuity is, though unusual, reliable. On both the Physical Criterion and the Narrow Psychological Criterion, my Replica would *not* be me. On the two Wide Criteria, he *would* be me.

I shall argue that we need not decide between these three versions of the Psychological Criterion. A partial analogy may suggest why. Some people go blind because of damage to their eyes. Scientists are now developing artificial eyes. These involve a glass or plastic lens, and a microcomputer which sends through the optic nerve electrical patterns like those that are sent through this nerve by a natural eye. When such artificial eyes are more advanced, they might give to someone who has gone blind visual experiences just like those that he used to have. What he seems to see would correspond to what is in fact before him. And his visual experiences would be causally dependent, in this new but reliable way, on the light-waves coming from the objects that are before him.

Would this person be *seeing* these objects? If we insist that seeing must involve the normal cause, we would answer No. But even if this person cannot see, what he has is *just as good as* seeing, both as a way of knowing what is within sight, and as a source of visual pleasure. If we accept the Psychological Criterion, we could make a similar claim. If psychological continuity does not have its normal cause, it may not provide personal identity. But we can claim that, even if this is so, what it provides is as good as personal identity. . . .

. . . Suppose that a certain club exists for several years, holding regular meetings. The meetings then cease. Some years later, some of the members of this club form a club with the same name, and the same rules. We ask: "Have these people reconvened the *very same* club? Or have they merely started up *another* club, which

is exactly similar?" There might be an answer to this question. The original club might have had a rule explaining how, after such a period of non-existence, it could be reconvened. Or it might have had a rule preventing this. But suppose that there is no such rule, and no legal facts, supporting either answer to our question. And suppose that the people involved, if they asked our question, would not give it an answer. There would then be no answer to our question. The claim "This is the same club" would be *neither true nor false*.

Though there is no answer to our question, there may be nothing that we do not know. This is because the existence of a club is not separate from the existence of its members, acting together in certain ways. The continued existence of a club just involves its members having meetings, that are conducted according to the club's rules. If we know all the facts about how people held meetings, and about the club's rules, we know everything there is to know. This is why we would not be puzzled when we cannot answer the question, "Is this the very same club?" We would not be puzzled because, even without answering this question, we can know everything about what happened. If this is true of some question, I call this question *empty*.

When we ask an empty question, there is only one fact or outcome that we are considering. Different answers to our question are merely different descriptions of this fact or outcome. This is why, without answering this empty question, we can know everything that there is to know. In my example we can ask, "Is this the very same club, or is it merely another club, that is exactly similar?" But these are not here two different possibilities, one of which must be true.

When an empty question has no answer, we can decide to *give* it an answer. We could decide to call the later club the same as the original club. Or we could decide to call it another club, that is exactly similar. This is not a decision between different views about what really happened. Before making our decision, we already knew what happened. We are merely choosing one of two different descriptions of the very same course of events.

If we are Reductionists about personal identity, we should make similar claims. We can describe cases where, between me now and some future person, the physical and psychological connections hold only to reduced degrees. If I imagine myself in such a case, I can always ask, "Am I about to die? Will the resulting person be me?" On the Reductionist View, in some cases there would be no answer. My question would be *empty*. The claim that I was about to die would be neither true nor false. If I know the facts about both physical continuity and psychological connectedness, I would know everything there was to know. I would know everything, even though I did not know whether I was about to die, or would go on living for many years.

When it is applied to ourselves, this Reductionist claim is hard to believe. In such imagined cases, something unusual is about to happen. But most of us are inclined to believe that, in any conceivable case, the question "Am I about to die?" must have an answer. And we are inclined to believe that this answer must be either, and quite simply, Yes or No. Any future person must be either me, or someone else. These beliefs I call the view that *our identity must be determinate*.

I shall next describe two explanatory claims. The first answers a new question. What unites the different experiences that are had by a single person at the same time? While I type this sentence, I am aware of the movements of my fingers, and can see the sunlight on my desk, and can hear the wind ruffling some leaves. What unites these different experiences? Some claim: the fact that they are all *my* experiences. These are the experiences that are being had, at this time, by a particular person, or *subject of experiences*. A similar question covers my whole life. What unites the different experiences that, together, constitute this life? Some give the same answer. What unites all of these experiences is, simply, that they are all mine. These answers I call the view that *psychological unity is explained by ownership*.

The views described so far are about the nature of personal identity. I shall end with a pair of views that are about, not the nature of this identity, but its importance. Consider an ordinary case where, even on any version of the Reductionist View, there are two possible outcomes. In one of the outcomes, I am about to die. In the other outcome I shall live for many years. If these years would be worth living, the second outcome would be better for me. And the difference between these outcomes would be judged to be important on most theories about rationality, and most moral theories. It would have rational and moral significance whether I am about to die, or shall live for many years. What is judged to be important here is whether, during these years, there will be someone living who will *be me*. This is a question about personal identity. On one view, in this kind of case, this is always what is important. I call this the view that *personal identity is what matters*. This is the natural view.

The rival view is that *personal identity is not what matters*. I claim

> What matters is Relation R: psychological connectedness and/or continuity with the right kind of cause.

Since it is more controversial, I add, as a separate claim

> In an account of what matters, the right kind of cause would be any cause.

It is in imaginary cases that we can best decide whether what matters is Relation R or personal identity. One example may be the Branch-Line Case, where my life briefly overlaps with that of my Replica. Suppose that we believe that I and my Replica are two different people. I am about to die, but my Replica will live for another forty years. If personal identity is what matters, I should regard my prospect here as being nearly as bad as ordinary death. But if what matters is Relation R, with any cause, I should regard this way of dying as being about as good as ordinary survival.

The disagreement between these views is not confined to imaginary cases. The two views also disagree about all of the actual lives that are lived. The disagreement is here less sharp, because, on both views, all or nearly all these lives contain the relation that matters. On all of the plausible views about the nature of personal identity, personal identity nearly always coincides with psychological continuity, and roughly coincides with psychological connectedness. But, as I shall argue later, it makes a great difference which of these we believe to be what matters. If we cease to believe that our identity is what matters, this may affect some of our emotions, such as our attitude to ageing and to death. And, as I shall argue, we may be led to change our views about both rationality and morality. . . .

II: How We Are Not What We Believe

The different views about personal identity make different claims about actual people, and ordinary lives. But the difference between these views is clearer when we consider certain imaginary cases. Most of the arguments that I shall discuss appeal, in part, to such cases. It may be impossible for some of these cases to occur, whatever progress may be made in science and technology. I distinguish two kinds of case. Some cases contravene the laws of nature. I call these *deeply* impossible. Other cases are *merely technically* impossible.

Does it matter if some imagined case would

never be possible? This depends entirely on our question, or what we are trying to show. Even in science it can be worth considering deeply impossible cases. One example is Einstein's thought-experiment of asking what he would see if he could travel beside some beam of light at the speed of light. As this example shows, we need not restrict ourselves to considering only cases which are possible. But we should bear in mind that, depending on our question, impossibility may make some thought-experiment irrelevant.

I start with an objection to the Psychological Criterion.

Does Psychological Continuity Presuppose Personal Identity?

I remember trying, when a child, to remain standing among the crashing waves of the Atlantic Ocean. I am the same person as the child who had that experience. On Locke's view, what makes me the same person as that child is my memory, or "consciousness," of that experience.

Bishop Butler thought this a "wonderful mistake." It is, he wrote, "self-evident, that consciousness of personal identity presupposes, and therefore cannot constitute personal identity, any more than knowledge in any other case, can constitute truth, which it presupposes."[7]

I have already revised Locke's view. The Psychological Criterion appeals, not to single memories, but to the continuity of memory, and, more broadly, to Relation R, which includes other kinds of psychological continuity. But this revision does not answer Butler's objection.

On one interpretation, the objection would be this: "It is part of our concept of memory that

[7]Butler, *The Analogy of Religion*, first appendix, 1736, reprinted in Perry (1), p. 100.

we can remember only *our own* experiences. The continuity of memory therefore presupposes personal identity. The same is therefore true of your Relation R. You claim that personal identity just consists in the holding of Relation R. This must be false if Relation R itself presupposes personal identity."

To answer this objection, we can define a wider concept, *quasi-memory*. I have an accurate quasi-memory of a past experience if

(1) I seem to remember having an experience.

(2) *someone* did have this experience,

and

(3) my apparent memory is causally dependent, in the right kind of way, on that past experience.

On this definition, ordinary memories are a sub-class of quasi-memories. They are quasi-memories of our own past experiences.[8]

We do not quasi-remember other people's past experiences. But we might begin to do so. The causes of long-term memories are memory-traces. It was once thought that these might be localized, involving changes in only a few brain cells. It is now more probable that a particular memory-trace involves changes in a larger number of cells. Suppose that, even if this is true, neuro-surgeons develop ways to create in one brain a copy of a memory-trace in another brain. This might enable us to quasi-remember other people's past experiences.

Consider

Venetian Memories. Jane has agreed to have copied in her brain some of Paul's memory-traces. After she recovers consciousness in the post-surgery room, she has a new set of vivid apparent memories. She seems to remember walking on the marble paving of a square, hearing the flapping of flying pigeons and the cries of gulls, and

seeing light sparkling on green water. One apparent memory is very clear. She seems to remember looking across the water to an island, where a white Palladian church stood out brilliantly against a dark thundercloud.

What should Jane believe about these apparent memories? Suppose that, because she has seen this church in photographs, she knows it to be San Giorgio, in Venice. She also knows that she has never been to Italy, while Paul goes to Venice often. Since she knows that she has received copies of some of Paul's memory-traces, she could justifiably assume that she may be quasi-remembering some of Paul's experiences in Venice.

Let us add this detail to the case. Jane seems to remember seeing something extraordinary: a flash of lightning coming from the dark cloud, which forked and struck both the bell-tower of San Giorgio and the red funnel of a tug-boat passing by. She asks Paul whether he remembers seeing such an extraordinary event. He does, and he has kept the issue of the *Gazzettino* where it is reported. Given all of this, Jane should not dismiss her apparent memory as a delusion. She ought to conclude that she has an accurate quasi-memory of how this flash of lightning looked to Paul.

For Jane's quasi-memories to give her knowledge about Paul's experiences, she must know roughly how they have been caused. This is not required in the case of ordinary memories. Apart from this difference, quasi-memories would provide a similar kind of knowledge about other people's past lives. They would provide knowledge of what these lives were like, *from the inside.* When Jane seems to remember walking about the Piazza, hearing the gulls, and seeing the white church, she knows part of what it was like to be Paul, on that day in Venice. . . .

Return now to Butler's objection to the Psychological Criterion of personal identity. On this

[8] I follow Shoemaker (2).

objection, the continuity of memory cannot be, even in part, what makes a series of experiences all the experiences of a single person, since this person's memory presupposes his continued identity.

On the interpretation that I gave above, memory presupposes identity because, on our concept of memory, we can remember only our own past experiences. This objection can now be answered. We can use the wider concept of quasi-memory.

In our statement of our revised Psychological Criterion, we should not claim that, if I have an accurate quasi-memory of some past experience, this makes me the person who had this experience. One person's mental life may include a few quasi-memories of experiences in some other person's life, as in the imagined case of Jane and Paul. Our criterion ignores a few such quasi-memory connections. We appeal instead to overlapping chains of many such connections. My mental life consists of a series of very varied experiences. These include countless quasi-memories of earlier experiences. The connections between these quasi-memories and these earlier experiences overlap like the strands in a rope. There is *strong connectedness* of quasi-memory if, over each day, the number of direct quasi-memory connections is at least half the number in most actual lives. Overlapping strands of strong connectedness provide *continuity of quasi-memory*. Revising Locke, we claim that the unity of each person's life is in part created by this continuity. We are not now appealing to a concept that presupposes personal identity. Since the continuity of quasi-memory does not presuppose personal identity, it may be part of what constitutes personal identity. It may be part of what makes me now and myself at other times one and the same person. (I say "part" because our criterion also appeals to the other kinds of psychological continuity.)

Butler's objection may be interpreted in a different way. He may have meant: "In memory we are directly aware of our own identity through time, and aware that this is a separate, further fact, which cannot just consist in physical and psychological continuity. We are aware that each of us is a persisting subject of experiences, a separately existing entity that is not our brain or body. And we are aware that our own continued existence is, simply, the continued existence of this subject of experiences."

Does our memory tell us this? Are we directly aware of the existence of this separate entity, the subject of experiences? Some have thought that we are aware of this, not just in memory, but in all of our experiences.

The Subject of Experiences

Reid writes:

> *my personal identity . . . implies the continued existence of that indivisible thing that I call myself. Whatever this self may be, it is something which thinks, and deliberates, and resolves, and acts, and suffers. I am not thought, I am not action, I am not feeling; I am something that thinks, and acts, and suffers.*[9]

In one sense, this is clearly true. Even Reductionists do not deny that people exist. And, on our concept of a person, people are not thoughts and acts. They are thinkers and agents. I am not a series of experiences, but the person who *has* these experiences. A Reductionist can admit that, in this sense, a person is *what has* experiences, or the *subject of experiences*. This is true because of the way in which we talk. What a Reductionist denies is that the subject of experiences is a *separately existing entity*, distinct from a brain and body, and a series of physical and mental events.

Is it true that, in memory, we are directly aware of what the Reductionist denies? Is each of us aware that he is a persisting subject of experiences, a separately existing entity that is

[9]Reid, reprinted in Perry (1), p. 109.

not his brain and body? Is each of us aware, for example, that he is a Cartesian Ego?

This is not a point that can be argued. I do not believe that *I* am directly aware that I am such an entity. And I assume that I am not unusual. I believe that no one is directly aware of such a fact.

Suppose that I *was* aware that I was such an entity. There would still be an objection to the Cartesian View. It has been claimed that I could not know that this entity continued to exist. As both Locke and Kant argued,[10] there might be a series of such entities that were psychologically continuous. Memories might be passed from one to the next like a baton in a relay race. So might all other psychological features. Given the resulting psychological continuity, we would not be aware that one of these entities had been replaced by another. We therefore cannot know that such entities continue to exist.

Reconsider the Branch-Line Case, where it is clear that I remain on Earth. It might seem to a certain person that he has just had these two thoughts: "Snow is falling. So it must be cold." But the truth might be this. This person is my Replica on Mars. Just before I pressed the green button, I thought "Snow is falling." Several minutes later, my Replica suddenly becomes conscious, in a similar cubicle on Mars. When he becomes conscious, he has apparent memories of living my life, and in particular he seems to remember just having thought, "Snow is falling." He then thinks "So it must be cold." My Replica on Mars would now be in a state of mind exactly like mine when I have just had both these thoughts. When my Replica is in this state of mind, he would believe that both these thoughts were had by the same thinker, himself. But this would be false. I had the first thought, and my Replica only had the second.

This example is imaginary. But it seems to show that we could not tell, from the content of our experiences, whether we really are aware of the continued existence of a separately existing subject of experiences. The most that we have are states of mind like that of my Replica. My Replica falsely believes that he has just had two thoughts. He is not aware of the continued existence of a separately existing entity: the thinker of these thoughts. He is aware of something less, the psychological continuity between his life and mine. In the same way, when we have had a series of thoughts, the most that we are aware of is the psychological continuity of our stream of consciousness. Some claim that we are aware of the continued existence of separately existing subjects of experiences. As Locke and Kant argued, and our example seems to show, such awareness cannot in fact be distinguished from our awareness of mere psychological continuity. Our experiences give us no reason to believe in the existence of these entities. Unless we have other reasons to believe in their existence, we should reject this belief.

This conclusion is not, as some write, crudely verificationist. I am not assuming that only what we could know could ever be true. My remarks make a different assumption. I am discussing a general claim about the existence of a particular kind of thing. This is claimed to be a separately existing entity, distinct from our brains and bodies. I claim that, if we have no reasons to believe that such entities exist, we should reject this belief. I do not, like verificationists, claim that this belief is senseless. My claim is merely like the claim that, since we have no reason to believe that water-nymphs or unicorns exist, we should reject these beliefs.[11]

Even if we are not directly aware of the existence of these entities, some claim that we can deduce their existence from any of our experi-

---

[10]See Locke, Chapter 27, Section 13, reprinted in Perry (1), p. 101; and Kant, p. 342, especially footnote a. I take the example from Wachsberg.

[11]Non-Reductionists have several other arguments which, in a longer discussion, I would need to try to answer. Besides Swinburne, see in particular Lewis (1), (2), and (3), and Madell. I hope to discuss these arguments elsewhere.

ences. Descartes, famously, made such a claim. When he asked if there was anything that he could not doubt, his answer was that he could not doubt his own existence. This was revealed in the very act of doubting. And, besides assuming that every thought must have a thinker, Descartes assumed that a thinker must be a Pure Ego, or spiritual substance. A Cartesian Pure Ego is the clearest case of a separately existing entity, distinct from the brain and body.[12]

Lichtenberg claimed that, in what he thought to be most certain, Descartes went astray. He should not have claimed that a thinker must be a separately existing entity. His famous *Cogito* did not justify this belief. He should not have claimed, "I think, therefore I am." Though this is true, it is misleading. Descartes could have claimed instead, "It is thought: thinking is going on." Or he could have claimed, "This is a thought, therefore at least one thought is being thought."[13]

Because we ascribe thoughts to thinkers, we can truly claim that thinkers exist. But we cannot deduce, from the content of our experiences, that a thinker is a separately existing entity. And, as Lichtenberg suggests, because we are not separately existing entities, we could fully describe our thoughts without claiming that they have thinkers. We could fully describe

our experiences, and the connections between them, without claiming that they are had by a subject of experiences. We could give what I call an *impersonal* description. . . .

Williams's Argument Against the Psychological Criterion

I have defended the Psychological Criterion in two ways. I have claimed, and partly shown, that we can describe psychological continuity in a way that does not presuppose personal identity. And I have claimed that, on the evidence we have, the carrier of this continuity is not an entity that exists separately from a person's brain and body.

I shall next consider another objection to the Psychological Criterion. This is advanced by Williams.[14] This objection seems to show that, if some person's brain continues to exist, and to support consciousness, this person will continue to exist, however great the breaks are in the psychological continuity of this person's mental life.

Here is a simpler version of this objection. Consider

Williams's Example. I am the prisoner of some callous neuro-surgeon, who intends to disrupt my psychological continuity by tampering with my brain. I shall be conscious while he operates, and in pain. I therefore dread what is coming.

The surgeon tells me that, while I am in pain, he will do several things. He will first activate some neurodes that will give me amnesia. I shall suddenly lose all of my memories of my life up to the start of my pain. Does this give me less reason to dread what is coming? Can I assume that, when the surgeon flips this switch, my pain will suddenly cease? Surely not. The pain might

---

[12]Descartes, p. 101: "I noticed that whilst I thus wished to think all things false, *it was absolutely essential that the 'I' who thought this should be a somewhat*, and remarking that this truth, 'I think, therefore I am,' was so certain and so assured that all the most extravagant suppositions brought forward . . . were incapable of shaking it, I came to the conclusion that I could receive it without scruple as the first principle of the Philosophy for which I was seeking." (First emphasis mine.)

[13]Lichtenberg, p. 412. Though I cannot read German, this famous aphorism seems to deserve its original words: *"Es denkt, sollte man sagen, so wie man sagt: es blitzt."* To spell out the aphorism: from the truth of "I think, therefore I am," Descartes should *not* have assumed that "it was absolutely essential that the 'I' who thought this should be a somewhat."

[14]In Williams (2).

so occupy my mind that I would even fail to notice the loss of all these memories.

The surgeon next tells me that, while I am still in pain, he will later flip another switch, that will cause me to believe that I am Napoleon, and will give me apparent memories of Napoleon's life. Can I assume that this will cause my pain to cease? The natural answer is again No. To support this answer, we can again suppose that my pain will prevent me from noticing anything. I shall not notice my coming to believe that I am Napoleon, and my acquiring a whole new set of apparent memories. When the surgeon flips this second switch, there will be no change at all in what I am conscious of. The changes will be purely disposi- tional. It will only become true that, if my pain ceased, so that I could think, I would answer the question "Who are you?" with the name "Napoleon." Similarly, if my pain ceased, I would then start to have de- lusory apparent memories, such as those of reviewing the Imperial Guard, or of weep- ing with frustration at the catastrophe of 1812. If it is only such changes in my dis- positions that would be brought about by the flipping of the second switch, I would have no reason to expect this to cause my pain to cease.

The surgeon then tells me that, during my ordeal, he will later flip a third switch, that will change my character so that it becomes just like Napoleon's. Once again, I seem to have no reason to expect the flip- ping of this switch to end my pain. It might at most bring some relief, if Napoleon's character, compared with mine, involved more fortitude.

In this imagined case, nothing that I am told seems to give me a reason to expect that, during my ordeal, I shall cease to exist. I seem to have as much reason to dread all of the pain. This reason does not seem to be removed by the other things I have to dread—losing memories,

and going mad, becoming like, and thinking that I am, Napoleon. As Williams claims, this argument seems to show that I can have reason to fear future pain whatever psychological changes precede this pain. Even after all these changes, it will be I who feels this pain. If this is so, the Psychological Criterion of personal iden- tity is mistaken. In this imagined case, between me now and myself after the ordeal, there would be no continuity of memory, character, and the like. What is involved in my continuing to exist therefore cannot be such continuity.[15]

It may be objected that, if I remain conscious throughout this ordeal, there will at least be one kind of psychological continuity. Though I lose all my memories of my past life, I would have memories of my ordeal. In particular, I would continue to have short-term memories of the last few moments, or what is sometimes called the *specious present*. Throughout my ordeal there would be an overlapping chain of such memories.

To meet this objection we can add one feature to the case. After I have lost all my other memo- ries, I am for a moment made unconscious. When I regain consciousness, I have *no* memo- ries. As the ordeal continues, I would have new memories. But there would be no continuity of memory over my moment of unconsciousness.

It may next be objected that I have described this story in question-begging terms. Thus I suggested that, when I am made to lose my memories, I might, because of my pain, fail to notice any change. This description assumes that, after the loss of my memories, the person in pain would still be me. Perhaps the truth is that, at this point, I would cease to exist, and a new person would start to exist in my body.

Williams could reply that, even though my description assumes that I would continue to exist, this is the overwhelmingly plausible as-

---

[15]There would be certain kinds of *non-distinctive* continu- ity, such as continued memory of how to walk, and run. The Psychological Criterion should not appeal to these kinds of psychological continuity.

sumption. It is the defender of the Psychological Criterion who must show that this assumption is not justified. And this would be hard to show. It is hard to believe that, if I was made to lose my memories while I was in agony, this would cause me to cease to exist half-way through the agony. And it is hard to believe that the change in my character would have this effect.

Williams's argument seems to refute the Psychological Criterion. It seems to show that the true view is the Physical Criterion. On this view, if some person's brain and body continue to exist, and to support consciousness, this person will continue to exist, however great the breaks are in the psychological continuity of this person's mental life.

The Psychological Spectrum

I shall now revise Williams's argument. Why this is worth doing will emerge later.

Williams discusses a single case in which, after a few changes, there will be no psychological continuity. I shall discuss a *spectrum*, or range of cases, each of which is very similar to its neighbours. These cases involve all of the possible degrees of psychological connectedness. I call this the *Psychological Spectrum.*

In the case at the far end, the surgeon would cause very many switches to be simultaneously flipped. This would cause there to be no psychological connections between me and the resulting person. This person would be wholly like Napoleon.

In the cases at the near end, the surgeon would cause to be flipped only a few switches. If he flipped only the first switch, this would merely cause me to lose a few memories, and to have a few apparent memories that fit the life of Napoleon. If he flipped the first two switches, I would merely lose a few more memories, and have a few more of these new apparent memories. Only if he flipped all of the switches would I lose all my memories, and have a complete set of Napoleonic delusions.

Similar claims are true about the changes in my character. Any particular switch would cause only a small change. Thus, if I am to be like Napoleon, I must become more bad-tempered, and must cease to be upset by the sight of people being killed. These would be the only changes produced by the flipping of the first two switces.

In this revised version of the argument, which involves very many different cases, we must decide which are the cases in which I would survive. In the case at the near end, the surgeon does nothing. In the second case, I would merely lose a few memories, have a few delusions, and become more bad-tempered. It is clear that, in this case, I would survive. In the third case, the changes would be only slightly greater. And this is true of any two neighbouring cases in this range. It is hard to believe both that I would survive in one of these cases, and that, in the next case, I would cease to exist. Whether I continue to exist cannot be plausibly thought to depend on whether I would lose just a few more memories, and have a few more delusory memories, and have my character changed in some small way. If no such small change could cause me to cease to exist, I would continue to exist in all of these cases. I would continue to exist even in the case at the far end of this spectrum. In this case, between me now and the resulting person, there would be *no* psychological connections.

It may be objected:

In this revised form, the argument suspiciously resembles those that are involved in the *Sorites Problem*, or the *Paradox of the Heap.* We are led there, by what seem innocent steps, to absurd conclusions. Perhaps the same is happening here.

Suppose we claim that the removal of a single grain cannot change a heap of sand into something that is not a heap. Someone starts with a heap of sand, which he removes grain by grain. Our claim forces us to admit that, after every change, we still have a heap, even when the number of grains becomes three, two, and one. But we know that we have reached a false conclusion. One grain is not a heap.

In your appeal to the Psychological Spectrum, you claim that no small change could cause you to cease to exist. By making enough small changes, the surgeon could cause the resulting person to be in no way psychologically connected with you. The argument forced you to conclude that the resulting person would be you. This conclusion may be just as false as the conclusion about the grain of sand.

To defend this version of William's argument, I need not solve the Sorites Problem. It will be enough to make the following remarks.

When considering heaps, we all believe that there are borderline cases. Are two grains of sand a heap, or four, or eight, or sixteen? We may not know how to answer all of these questions. But we do not believe that this is the result of ignorance. We do not believe that each of these questions must have an answer. We know that the concept of a heap is vague, with vague borderlines. And when the Sorites Argument is applied to heaps, we are happy to solve the problem with a *stipulation*: an arbitrary decision about how to use the word "heap." We might decide that we shall not call nine grains a heap, but we shall call heaps any collection of ten or more grains. We shall then be abandoning one premise of the argument. On our new more precise concept, the removal of a single grain may turn a heap of sand into something that is not a heap. This happens with the removal of the tenth last grain.

[16]As before, for a discussion of these arguments see Dummett, Peacocke, Forbes, and Sainsburg. See also C. Wright, "On the Coherence of Vague Predicates," *Synthese*, 1975. For a longer discussion of the argument as applied to persons, see especially Unger (1), Unger (2), and the other works by P. Unger in this remarkable series. I have not yet had time to consider whether the solution suggested by Peacocke, Forbes, and Sainsbury, appealing to *degrees of truth*, meets Unger's arguments.

When it is applied to other subjects, such as phenomenal colour, the Sorites Argument cannot be so easily dismissed.[16] Nor does this dismissal seem plausible when the argument is applied to personal identity. Most of us believe that our own continued existence is, in several ways, unlike the continued existence of a heap of sand.

Reconsider the range of cases in the Psychological Spectrum. Like Williams's Example, these cases provide an argument against the Psychological Criterion. This criterion is one version of the Reductionist View. A Reductionist might say:

The argument assumes that, in each of these cases, the resulting person either would or would not be me. This is not so. The resulting person would be me in the first few cases. In the last case he would not be me. In many of the intervening cases, neither answer would be true. I can always ask, "Am I about to die? Will there be some person living who will be me?" But, in the cases in the middle of this Spectrum, there is no answer to this question.

Though there is no answer to this question, I could know exactly what will happen. This question is, here, *empty*. In each of these cases I could know to what degree I would be psychologically connected with the resulting person. And I could know which particular connections would or would not hold. If I knew these facts, I would know everything. I can still ask whether the resulting person would be *me*, or would merely be *someone else* who is partly like me. In some cases, these are two different possibilities, one of which must be true. But, in *these* cases, these are not two different possibilities. They are merely two descriptions of the very same course of events.

These remarks are analogous to remarks that we accept when applied to heaps. We do not believe that any collection of sand must either be, or not be, a heap. We know that there are borderline cases, where there is no obvious answer to the question "Is this still a heap?" But we do not believe that, in these cases, there must *be* an answer, which must be either Yes or No. We believe that, in these cases, this is an empty question. Even without answering the question, we know everything.

As Williams claims, when applied to our own existence, such remarks seem incredible. Suppose that I am about to undergo an operation in the middle of this Spectrum. I know that the resulting person will be in agony. If I do not know whether or not I shall be the person in agony, and I do not even know whether I shall still be alive, how can I believe that I *do* know exactly what will happen? I do not know the answer to the most important questions. It is very hard to believe that these are empty questions.

Most of us believe that we are not like heaps, because our identity must be determinate. We believe that, even in such "borderline cases," the question "Am I about to die?" must have an answer. And, as Williams claims, we believe that the answer must be either, and quite simply, Yes or No. If someone will be alive, and will be suffering agony, this person either will or will not be me. One of these must be true. And we cannot make sense of any third alternative, such as that the person in agony will be *partly* me. I can imagine being only partly in agony, because I am drifting in and out of consciousness. But if someone will be fully conscious of the agony, this person cannot be partly me.

The Reductionist View would provide an answer to Williams's argument. When Williams gives his version of this argument, he rejects this view. He concludes instead that, if my brain continues to exist, and to be the brain of a living person, I shall be that person. This would be so even if, between myself now and myself later, there would be *no* psychological connections. After advancing his argument, Williams writes that this conclusion may "perhaps" be wrong,

"but we need to be shown what is wrong with it."[17]

The Physical Spectrum

One objection is that a similar argument applies to physical continuity. Consider another range of possible cases: the *Physical Spectrum*. These cases involve all of the different possible degrees of physical continuity.

In the case at the near end of this spectrum, there would later be a person who would be fully continuous with me as I am now, both physically and psychologically. In the case at the far end, there would later be a person who would be psychologically but not physically continuous with me as I am now. The far end is like the case of Teletransportation. The near end is the normal case of continued existence.

In a case close to the near end, scientists would replace 1% of the cells in my brain and body with exact duplicates. In the case in the middle of the spectrum, they would replace 50%. In a case near the far end, they would replace 99%, leaving only 1% of my original brain and body. At the far end, the 'replacement' would involve the complete destruction of my brain and body, and the creation out of new organic matter of a Replica of me.

What is important in this last case is not just that my Replica's brain and body would be entirely composed of new matter. As I explained, this might become true in a way that does not destroy my brain and body. It could become true if there is a long series of small changes in the matter in my body, during which my brain and body continue to exist, and to function normally. This would be like the ship that becomes entirely composed of new bits of wood, after fifty years of piecemeal repairs. In both of these cases, the complete change in the identity of the components does not disrupt physical continuity. Things are different in the case at the far

[17]Williams (1), p. 63.

end of the Physical Spectrum. There is here no physical continuity, since my brain and body are completely destroyed, and it is only later that the scientists create, out of new matter, my Replica.

The first few cases in this range are now believed to be technically possible. Portions of brain-tissue have been successfully transplanted from one mammal's brain to another's. And what is transplanted could be a part of the brain that, in all individuals, is sufficiently similar. This could enable surgeons to provide functioning replacements for some damaged parts of the brain. These actual transplants proved to be easier than the more familiar transplants of the kidney or the heart, since a brain seems not to 'reject' transplanted tissue in the way in which the body rejects transplanted organs.[18] Though the first few cases in this range are even now possible, most of the cases will remain impossible. But this impossibility will be merely technical. Since I use these cases only to discover what we believe, this impossibility does not matter.

Suppose we believe that, at the far end of this spectrum, my Replica would not be me. He would merely be someone else who was exactly like me. At the near end of this spectrum, where there would be no replacement, the resulting person would be me. What should I expect if what will happen is some intermediate case? If they replaced only 1%, would I cease to exist? This is not plausible, since I do not need all of my brain and body. But what about the cases where they would replace 10%, or 30%, or 60% or 90%?

This range of cases challenges the Physical Criterion, which is another version of the Reductionist View. Imagine that you are about to undergo one of these operations. You might try to believe this version of Reductionism. You might say to yourself:

[18]*The Times*, London, Science Column, 22 November 1982. I am told that reports of more impressive results will soon appear in the appropriate scientific journals.

In any central case in this range, the question "Am I about to die?" has no answer. But I know just what will happen. A certain percentage of my brain and body will be replaced with exact duplicates of the existing cells. The resulting person will be psychologically continuous with me as I am now. This is all there is to know. I do not know whether the resulting person will be me, or will be someone else who is merely exactly like me. But this is not, here, a real question, which must have an answer. It does not describe two different possibilities, one of which must be true. It is here an empty question. There is not a real difference here between the resulting person's being *me*, and his being *someone else*. This is why, even though I do not know whether I am about to die, I know everything.

I believe that, for those who accept the Physical Criterion, this is the right reaction to this range of cases. But most of us would not yet accept such claims.

If we do not yet accept the Reductionist View, and continue to believe that our identity must be determinate, what should we claim about these cases? If we continue to assume that my Replica would not be me, we are forced to the following conclusion. There must be some critical percentage which is such that, if the surgeons replace less than this percent, it will be me who wakes up, but if they replace more than this percent, it will *not* be me but only someone else, who is merely like me. We might suggest a variant of this conclusion. Perhaps there is some crucial part of my brain which is such that, if the surgeons do not replace this part, the resulting person will be me, but if they do, it will be someone else. But this makes no difference. What if they replace different percentages of this crucial part of my brain? We are again forced to the view that there must be some critical percentage.

Such a view is not incoherent. But it is hard to

believe. And something else is true, that makes it even harder to believe. We could not *discover* what the critical percentage is, by carrying out some of the cases in this imagined spectrum. I might say, 'Try replacing 50% of the cells in my brain and body, and I shall tell you what happens'. But we know in advance that, in every case, the resulting person would be inclined to believe that he is me. And this would not show that he *is* me. Carrying out such cases could not provide the answer to our question. . . .

The Combined Spectrum

Consider another range of possible cases. These involve all of the possible variations in the degrees of *both* physical *and* psychological connectedness. This is the *Combined Spectrum.*

At the near end of this spectrum is the normal case in which a future person would be fully continuous with me as I am now, both physically and psychologically. This person would be me in just the way that, in my actual life, it will be me who wakes up tomorrow. At the far end of this spectrum the resulting person would have no continuity with me as I am now, either physically or psychologically. In this case the scientists would destroy my brain and body, and then create, out of new organic matter, a perfect Replica of someone else. Let us suppose this person to be, not Napoleon, but Greta Garbo. We can suppose that, when Garbo was 30, a group of scientists recorded the states of all the cells in her brain and body.

In the first case in this spectrum, at the near end, nothing would be done. In the second case, a few of the cells in my brain and body would be replaced. The new cells would *not* be exact duplicates. As a result, there would be somewhat less psychological connectedness between me and the person who wakes up. This person would not have all of my memories, and his character would be in one way unlike mine. He would have some apparent memories of Greta Garbo's life, and have one of Garbo's character-

istics. Unlike me, he would enjoy acting. His body would also be in one way less like mine, and more like Garbo's. His eyes would be more like Garbo's eyes. Further along the spectrum, a larger percentage of my cells would be replaced, again with dissimilar cells. The resulting person would be in fewer ways psychologically connected with me, and in more ways connected with Garbo, as she was at the age of 30. And there would be similar changes in this person's body. Near the far end, most of my cells would be replaced with dissimilar cells. The person who wakes up would have only a few of the cells in my original brain and body, and between her and me there would be only a few psychological connections. She would have a few apparent memories that fit my past, and a few of my habits and desires. But in every other way she would be, both physically and psychologically, just like Greta Garbo.

These cases provide, I believe, a strong argument for the Reductionist View. The argument again assumes that our psychological features depend upon the states of our brains. Suppose that the cause of psychological continuity was not the continued existence of the brain, but the continued existence of a separately existing entity, like a Cartesian Ego. We could then claim that, if we carried out such operations, the results would *not* be as I have described them. We would find that, if we replaced much of someone's brain, even with dissimilar cells, the resulting person would be exactly like the original person. But there would be some critical percentage, or some critical part of the brain, whose replacement would utterly destroy psychological continuity. In one of the cases in this range, the carrier of continuity would cease either to exist, or to interact with this brain. The resulting person would be psychologically totally unlike the original person.

If we had reasons to believe this view, it would provide an answer to my argument. There *would* be, in this range of cases, a sharp borderline and *this* borderline *could* be discovered. It would correspond with what appeared to be a complete change in personal identity. This view would also explain how the replacement of a few cells could totally destroy psychological continuity. And this view could be applied to both the Psychological and the Physical Spectrum. We could claim that, in both these Spectra, the results would not in fact be what I assumed.

Except for the cases close to the near end, the cases in the Combined Spectrum are, and are likely to remain, technically impossible. We therefore cannot directly discover whether the results would be as I assume, or would instead be of the kind just described. But what the results would be depends on what the relation is between the states of someone's brain and this person's mental life. Have we evidence to believe that psychological continuity depends chiefly, not on the continuity of the brain, but on the continuity of some other entity, which either exists unimpaired, or does not exist at all? We do not in fact have the kind of evidence that I described above. And we have much reason to believe both that the carrier of psychological continuity is the brain, and that psychological connectedness could hold to any reduced degree.

Since our psychological features depend on the states of our brains, these imagined cases are only technically impossible. If we could carry out these operations, the results would be what I have described. What should we believe about the different cases in this Combined Spectrum? Which are the cases in which I would continue to exist?

As before, we could not find the answer by actually performing, on me and other people, operations of the kind imagined. We already know that, somewhere along the Spectrum, there would be the first case in which the resulting person would believe that he or she was not me. And we have no reason to trust this

belief. In this kind of case, who someone is cannot be shown by who he thinks he is. Since experiments would not help, we must try to decide now what we believe about these cases.

In considering the first two Spectra, we had three alternatives: accepting a Reductionist reply, believing that there must be some sharp borderline, and believing that the resulting person would in every case be me. Of these three, the third seemed the least implausible conclusion.

In considering the Combined Spectrum, we cannot accept this conclusion. In the case at the far end, the scientists destroy my brain and body, and then make, out of new matter, a Replica of Greta Garbo. There would be no connection, of any kind, between me and this resulting person. It could not be clearer that, in this case, the resulting person would *not* be me. We are forced to choose between the other two alternatives.

We might continue to believe that our identity must be determinate. We might continue to believe that, to the question "Would the resulting person be me?," there must always be an answer, which must be either and quite simply Yes or No. We would then be forced to accept the following claims:

Somewhere in this Spectrum, there is a sharp borderline. There must be some critical set of the cells replaced, and some critical degree of psychological change, which would make all the difference. If the surgeons replace slightly fewer than these cells, and produce one fewer psychological change, it will be me who wakes up. If they replace the few extra cells, and produce one more psychological change, I shall cease to exist, and the person waking up will be someone else. There must be such a pair of cases somewhere in this Spectrum, *even though there could never be any evidence where these cases are.*

These claims are hard to believe. It is hard to believe (1) that the difference between life and death could just consist in any of the very small differences described above. We are inclined to believe that there is *always* a difference between some future person's being me, and his being someone else. And we are inclined to believe that this is a *deep* difference. But between neighbouring cases in this Spectrum the differences are trivial. It is therefore hard to believe that, in one of these cases, the resulting person would quite straightforwardly be me, and that, in the next case, he would quite straightforwardly be someone else.

It is also hard to believe (2) that there must be such a sharp borderline, somewhere in the Spectrum, though we could never have any evidence where the borderline would be. Some would claim that, if there could never be such evidence, it makes no sense to claim that there must somewhere be such a line.

Even if (2) makes sense, claims (1) and (2), taken together, are extremely implausible. I believe that they are even more implausible than the only other possible conclusion, which is the Reductionist View. We should therefore now conclude that the Reductionist View is true. On this view, in the central cases of the Combined Spectrum, it would be an empty question whether the resulting person would be me. This Spectrum provides, as I claimed, a strong argument for this view. . . . Reductionists admit that there is a difference between numerical identity and exact similarity. In some cases, there would be a real difference between some person's being me, and his being someone else who is merely exactly like me. Many people assume that there must *always* be such a difference.

In the case of nations, or clubs, such an assumption is false. Two clubs could exist at the same time, and be, apart from their membership, exactly similar. If I am a member of one of these clubs, and you claim also to be a member, I might ask, "Are you a member of the very same club of which I am a member? Or are you merely a member of the other club, that is exactly similar?" This is not an empty question, since it describes two different possibilities. But though there are two possibilities in a case in which the two clubs co-exist, there may not be two such possibilities when we are discussing the relation between some presently existing club and some past club. . . .

In the same way, there are some cases where there is a real difference between someone's being me, and his being someone else who is exactly like me. This may be so in the Branch-Line Case, the version of Teletransportation where the Scanner does not destroy my brain and body. In the Branch-Line Case, my life overlaps with the life of my Replica on Mars. Given this overlap, we may conclude that we are two different people—that we are qualitatively but not numerically identical. If I am the person on Earth, and my Replica on Mars now exists, it makes a difference whether some pain will be felt by me, or will instead be felt by my Replica. This is a real difference in what will happen.

If we return to Simple Teletransportation, where there is no overlap between my life and that of my Replica, things are different. We could say here that my Replica will be me, or we could instead say that he will merely be someone else who is exactly like me. But we should not regard these as competing hypotheses about what will happen. For these to be competing hypotheses, my continued existence must involve a *further fact*. If my continued existence merely involves physical and psychological continuity, we know just what happens in this case. There will be some future person who will be physically exactly like me, and who will be fully psychologically continuous with me. This psychological continuity will have a reliable cause, the transmission of my blueprint. But this continuity will not have its normal cause, since

this future person will not be physically continuous with me. This is a full description of the
facts. There is no further fact about which we
are ignorant. If personal identity does not involve a further fact, we should not believe that
there are here two different possibilities: that
my Replica will be me, or that he will be someone else who is merely like me. What could
make these different possibilities? In what could
the difference consist?

Some non-Reductionists would agree that, in
this case, there are not two possibilities. These
people believe that, in the case of Teletransportation, my Replica would not be me. I shall later
discuss a plausible argument for this conclusion.
If we would be wrong to say that my Replica is
me, the remarks that I have just made apply
instead to the central cases in the Physical
Spectrum. My Replica might have a quarter of
the existing cells in my brain and body, or half,
or three-quarters. In these cases there are not
two different possibilities: that my Replica is
me, or that he is someone else who is merely
like me. These are merely different descriptions
of the same outcome.

If we believe that there is always a real difference between some person's being me and his
being someone else, we must believe that this
difference comes somewhere in this range of
cases. There must be a sharp borderline, though
we could never know where this is. As I have
claimed, this belief is even more implausible
than the Reductionist View.

In the case of clubs, though there is sometimes a
difference between numerical identity and exact
similarity, there is sometimes no difference. The
question, "Is it the same, or merely exactly similar" is sometimes empty. This could be true of
people, too. It would be true either at the end or
in the middle of the Physical Spectrum.

It is hard to believe that this could be true.
When I imagine myself about to press the green
button, it is hard to believe that there is not a
real question whether I am about to die, or shall

instead wake up again on Mars. But, as I have
argued, this belief cannot be justified unless
personal identity involves a further fact. And
there could not be such a fact unless I am a
separately existing entity, apart from my brain
and body. One such entity is a Cartesian Ego.
As I have claimed, there is no evidence in favour of this view, and much evidence against it.

III: Why Our Identity Is Not What Matters

Divided Minds

Some recent medical cases provide striking evidence in favour of the Reductionist View.
Human beings have a lower brain and two
upper hemispheres, which are connected by a
bundle of fibres. In treating a few people with
severe epilepsy, surgeons have cut these fibres.
The aim was to reduce the severity of epileptic
fits, by confining their causes to a single hemisphere. This aim was achieved. But the operations had another unintended consequence. The
effect, in the words of one surgeon, was the
creation of "two separate spheres of
consciousness."[19]

This effect was revealed by various psychological tests. These made use of two facts. We
control our right arms with our left hemispheres, and vice versa. And what is in the right
halves of our visual fields we see with our left
hemispheres, and vice versa. When someone's
hemispheres have been disconnected, psychologists can thus present to this person two different written questions in the two halves of his
visual field, and can receive two different answers written by this person's two hands.

Here is a simplified version of the kind of
evidence that such tests provide. One of these
people is shown a wide screen, whose left half

[19]Sperry. p. 299.

is red and right half is blue. On each half in a darker shade are the words, "How many colours can you see?" With both hands the person writes, "Only one." The words are now changed to read: "Which is the only colour that you can see?" With one of his hands the person writes "Red," with the other he writes "Blue."

If this is how this person responds, there seems no reason to doubt that he is having visual sensations—that he does, as he claims, see both red and blue. But in seeing red he is not aware of seeing blue, and vice versa. This is why the surgeon writes of "two separate spheres of consciousness." In each of his centres of consciousness the person can see only a single colour. In one centre, he sees red, in the other, blue.

The many actual tests, though differing in details from the imagined test that I have just described, show the same two essential features. In seeing what is in the left half of his visual field, such a person is quite unaware of what he is now seeing in the right half of his visual field, and vice versa. And in the centre of consciousness in which he sees the left half of his visual field and is aware of what he is doing with his left hand, this person is quite unaware of what he is doing with his right hand, and vice versa.

One of the complications in the actual cases is that for most people, in at least the first few weeks after the operation, speech is entirely controlled by the right-handed hemisphere. As a result, "if the word 'hat' is flashed on the left, the left hand will retrieve a hat from a group of concealed objects if the person is told to pick out what he has seen. At the same time he will insist verbally that he saw nothing."[20] Another complication is that, after a certain time, each hemisphere can sometimes control both hands. Nagel quotes an example of the kind of conflict which can follow:

A pipe is placed out of sight in the patient's left hand, and he is then asked to write with his left hand what he was holding. Very laboriously and heavily, the left hand writes the letters P and I. Then suddenly the writing speeds up and becomes lighter, the I is converted to an E, and the word is completed as PENCIL. Evidently the left hemisphere has made a guess based on the appearance of the first two letters, and has interfered. . . . But then the right hemisphere takes over control of the hand again, heavily crosses out the letters ENCIL, and draws a crude picture of a pipe.[21]

Such conflict may take more sinister forms. One of the patients complained that sometimes, when he embraced his wife, his left hand pushed her away.

Much has been made of another complication in the actual cases, hinted at in Nagel's example. The left hemisphere typically supports or "has" the linguistic and mathematical abilities of an adult, while the right hemisphere "has" these abilities at the level of a young child. But the right hemisphere, though less advanced in these respects, has greater abilities of other kinds, such as those involved in pattern recognition, or musicality. It is assumed that, after the age of three or four, the two hemispheres follow a "division of labour," with each developing certain abilities. The lesser linguistic abilities of the right hemisphere are not intrinsic, or permanent. People who have had strokes in their left hemispheres often regress to the linguistic ability of a young child, but with their remaining right hemispheres many can re-learn adult speech. It is also believed that, in a minority of people, there may be no difference between the abilities of the two hemispheres.

Suppose that I am one of this minority, with two exactly similar hemispheres. And suppose that I have been equipped with some device

[20]Nagel (2), reprinted in Nagel (1), p. 152.   [21]Nagel, ibid., p 153.

that can block communication between my hemispheres. Since this device is connected to my eyebrows, it is under my control. By raising an eyebrow I can divide my mind. In each half of my divided mind I can then, by lowering an eyebrow, reunite my mind.

This ability would have many uses. Consider

My Physics Exam. I am taking an exam, and have only fifteen minutes left in which to answer the last question. It occurs to me that there are two ways of tackling this question. I am unsure which is more likely to succeed. I therefore decide to divide my mind for ten minutes, to work in each half of my mind on one of the two calculations, and then to reunite my mind to write a fair copy of the best result. What shall I experience?

When I disconnect my hemispheres, my stream of consciousness divides. But this division is not something that I experience. Each of my two streams of consciousness seems to have been straightforwardly continuous with my one stream of consciousness up to the moment of division. The only changes in each stream are the disappearance of half my visual field and the loss of sensation in, and control over, one of my arms.

Consider my experiences in my "right-handed" stream. I remember deciding that I would use my right hand to do the longer calculation. This I now begin. In working at this calculation I can see, from the movements of my left hand, that I am also working at the other. But I am not aware of working at the other. I might, in my right-handed stream, wonder how, in my left-handed stream, I am getting on. I could look and see. This would be just like looking to see how well my neighbour is doing, at the next desk. In my right-handed stream I would be equally unaware both of what my neighbour is now thinking and of what I am now thinking in my left-handed

stream. Similar remarks apply to my experiences in my left-handed stream.

My work is now over. I am about to reunite my mind. What should I, in each stream, expect? Simply that I shall suddenly seem to remember just having worked at two calculations, in working at each of which I was not aware of working at the other. This, I suggest, we can imagine. And, if my mind had been divided, my apparent memories would be correct.

In describing this case, I assumed that there were two separate series of thoughts and sensations. If my two hands visibly wrote out two calculations, and I also claimed later to remember two corresponding series of thoughts, this is what we ought to assume. It would be most implausible to assume that either or both calculations had been done unconsciously.

It might be objected that my description ignores "the necessary unity of consciousness." But I have not ignored this alleged necessity. I have denied it. What is a fact must be possible. And it is a fact that people with disconnected hemispheres have two separate streams of consciousness — two series of thoughts and experiences, in having each of which they are unaware of having the other. Each of these two streams separately displays unity of consciousness. This may be a surprising fact. But we can understand it. We can come to believe that a person's mental history need not be like a canal, with only one channel, but could be like a river, occasionally having separate streams. I suggest that we can also imagine what it would be like to divide and reunite our minds. My description of my experiences in my Physics Exam seems both to be coherent and to describe something that we can imagine.

It might next be claimed that, in my imagined case, I do not have a divided mind. Rather, I have two minds. This objection does not raise a real question. These are two ways of describing one and the same outcome.

A similar objection claims that, in these actual

and imagined cases, the result is not a single person with either a divided mind or two minds. The result is two different people, sharing control of most of one body, but each in sole control of one arm. Here too, I believe that this objection does not raise a real question. These are again two ways of describing the same outcome. This is what we believe if we are Reductionists.

If we are not yet Reductionists, as I shall assume, we believe that it is a real question whether such cases involve more than a single person. Perhaps we can believe this in the actual cases, where the division is permanent. But this belief is hard to accept when we consider my imagined Physics Exam. In this case there are two streams of consciousness for only ten minutes. And I later seem to remember doing both of the calculations that, during these ten minutes, my two hands could be seen to be writing out. Given the brief and modest nature of this disunity, it is not plausible to claim that this case involves more than a single person. Are we to suppose that, during these ten minutes, I cease to exist, and two new people come into existence, each of whom then works out one of the calculations? On this interpretation, the whole episode involves three people, two of whom have lives that last for only ten minutes. Moreover, each of these two people mistakenly believes that he is me, and has apparent memories that accurately fit my past. And after these ten minutes I have accurate apparent memories of the brief lives of each of these two people, except that I mistakenly believe that I myself had all of the thoughts and sensations that these people had. It is hard to believe that I am mistaken here, and that the episode does involve three quite different people.

It is equally hard to believe that it involves two different people, with me doing one of the calculations, and some other person doing the other. I admit that, when I first divide my mind, I might in doing one of the calculations believe that the other calculation must be being done by someone else. But in doing the other calculation I might have the same belief. When my mind has been reunited, I would then seem to remember believing, while doing each of the calculations, that the other calculation must be being done by someone else. When I seem to remember both these beliefs, I would have no reason to think that one was true and the other false. And after several divisions and reunions I would cease to have such beliefs. In each of my two streams of consciousness I would believe that I was now, in my other stream, having thoughts and sensations of which, in this stream, I was now unaware. . . .

What Happens When I Divide?

I shall now describe another natural extension of the actual cases of divided minds. Suppose first that I am one of a pair of identical twins, and that both my body and my twin's brain have been fatally injured. Because of advances in neuro-surgery, it is not inevitable that these injuries will cause us both to die. We have between us one healthy brain and one healthy body. Surgeons can put these together.

This could be done even with existing techniques. Just as my brain could be extracted, and kept alive by a connection with an artificial heart-lung machine, it could be kept alive by a connection with the heart and lungs in my twin's body. The drawback, today, is that the nerves from my brain could not be connected with the nerves in my twin's body. My brain could survive if transplanted into his body, but the resulting person would be paralysed.

Even if he is paralysed, the resulting person could be enabled to communicate with others. One crude method would be some device, attached to the nerve that would have controlled this person's right thumb, enabling him to send messages in Morse Code. Another device, attached to some sensory nerve, could enable him to receive messages. Many people would welcome surviving, even totally paralysed, if they could still communicate with others. The stock example is that of a great scientist whose main aim in life is to continue thinking about certain abstract problems.

Let us suppose, however, that surgeons are able to connect my brain to the nerves in my twin's body. The resulting person would have no paralysis, and would be completely healthy. Who would this person be?

This is not a difficult question. It may seem that there is a disagreement here between the Physical and Psychological Criteria. Though the resulting person will be psychologically continuous with me, he will not have the whole of my body. But, as I have claimed, the Physical Criterion ought not to require the continued existence of my whole body.

If all my brain continues both to exist and to be the brain of one living person, who is psychologically continuous with me, I continue to exist. This is true whatever happens to the rest of my body. When I am given someone else's heart, I am the surviving recipient, not the dead donor. When my brain is transplanted into someone else's body, it may seem that I am here the dead donor. But I am really still the recipient, and the survivor. Receiving a new skull and a new body is just the limiting case of receiving a new heart, new lungs, new arms, and so on.[22]

It will of course be important what my new body is like. If my new body was quite unlike my old body, this would affect what I could do, and might thus indirectly lead to changes in my character. But there is no reason to suppose that being transplanted into a very different body would disrupt my psychological continuity.

It has been objected that "the possession of some sorts of character trait requires the possession of an appropriate sort of body." Quinton answers this objection. He writes, of an unlikely case,

> It would be odd for a six-year-old girl to display the character of Winston Churchill, odd indeed to the point of outrageousness, but it is not utterly inconceivable. At first, no doubt, the girl's display of dogged endurance, a world-historical comprehensiveness of outlook, and so forth, would strike one as distasteful and pretentious in so young a child. But if she kept it up the impression would wear off.[23]

More importantly, as Quinton argues, this objection could show only that it might matter whether my brain is housed in a certain *kind* of body. It could not show that it would matter whether it was housed in any *particular* body. And in my imagined case my brain will be housed in a body which, though not numerically identical to my old body, is—because it is my twin's body—very similar.

On all versions of the Psychological Criterion, the resulting person would be me. And most believers in the Physical Criterion could be persuaded that, in this case, this is true. As I have claimed, the Physical Criterion should require only the continued existence of *enough* of my brain to be the brain of a living person, provided that no one else has enough of this brain. This would make it me who would wake up, after the operation. And if my twin's body was just like mine, I might even fail to notice that I had a new body.

It is in fact true that one hemisphere is enough. There are many people who have survived, when a stroke or injury puts out of action one of their hemispheres. With his remaining hemisphere, such a person may need to re-learn certain things, such as adult speech, or how to control both hands. But this is possible. In my example I am assuming that, as may be true of certain actual people, both of my hemispheres have the full range of abilities. I could thus survive with either hemispheres, without any need for re-learning.

I shall now combine these last two claims. I would survive if my brain was successfully

----

[22]I follow Shoemaker (1), p. 22.

[23]Quinton, in Perry (1), p. 60.

transplanted into my twin's body. And I could survive with only half my brain, the other half having been destroyed. Given these two facts, it seems clear that I would survive if half my brain was successfully transplanted into my twin's body, and the other half was destroyed.

What if the other half was *not* destroyed? This is the case that Wiggins described: that in which a person, like an amoeba, divides.[24] To simplify the case, I assume that I am one of three identical triplets. Consider

> *My Division.* My body is fatally injured, as are the brains of my two brothers. My brain is divided, and each half is successfully transplanted into the body of one of my brothers. Each of the resulting people believes that he is me, seems to remember living my life, has my character, and is in every other way psychologically continuous with me. And he has a body that is very like mine.

This case is likely to remain impossible. Though it is claimed that, in certain people, the two hemispheres may have the same full range of abilities, this claim might be false. I am here assuming that this claim is true when applied to me. I am also assuming that it would be possible to connect a transplanted half-brain with the nerves in its new body. And I am assuming that we could divide, not just the upper hemispheres, but also the lower brain. My first two assumptions may be able to be made true if there is enough progress in neurophysiology. But it seems likely that it would never be possible to divide the lower brain, in a way that did not impair its functioning.

Does it matter if, for this reason, this imagined case of complete division will always remain impossible? Given the aims of my discus-

sion, this does not matter. This impossibility is merely technical. The one feature of the case that might be held to be *deeply* impossible — the division of a person's consciousness into two separate streams — is the feature that has actually happened. It would have been important if this had been impossible, since this might have supported some claim about what we really are. It might have supported the claim that we are indivisible Cartesin Egos. It therefore matters that the division of a person's consciousness is in fact possible. There seems to be no similar connection between a particular view about what we really are and the impossibility of dividing and successfully transplanting the two halves of the lower brain. This impossibility thus provides no ground for refusing to consider the imagined case in which we suppose that this can be done. And considering this case may help us to decide both what we believe ourselves to be, and what in fact we are. As Einstein's example showed, it can be useful to consider impossible thought-experiments.

It may help to state, in advance, what I believe this case to show. It provides a further argument against the view that we are separately existing entities. But the main conclusion to be drawn is that *personal identity is not what matters.*

It is natural to believe that our identity is what matters. Reconsider the Branch-Line Case, where I have talked to my Replica on Mars, and am about to die. Suppose we believe that I and my Replica are different people. It is then natural to assume that my prospect is almost as bad as ordinary death. In a few days, there will be no one living who will be me. It is natural to assume that *this* is what matters. In discussing My Division, I shall start by making this assumption.

In this case, each half of my brain will be successfully transplanted into the very similar body of one of my two brothers. Both of the resulting people will be fully psychologically

---

[24]Wiggins, p. 50. I decided to study philosophy almost entirely because I was enthralled by Wiggins's imagined case.

continuous with me, as I am now. What happens to me? There are only four possibilities: (1) I do not survive; (2) I survive as one of the two people; (3) I survive as the other; (4) I survive as both.

The objection to (1) is this. I would survive if my brain was successfully transplanted. And people have in fact survived with half their brains destroyed. Given these facts, it seems clear that I would survive if half my brain was successfully transplanted, and the other half was destroyed. So how could I fail to survive if the other half was also successfully transplanted? How could a double success be a failure?

Consider the next two possibilities. Perhaps one success is the maximum score. Perhaps I shall be one of the two resulting people. The objection here is that, in this case, each half of my brain is exactly similar, and so, to start with, is each resulting person. Given these facts, how can I survive as only one of the two people? What can make me one of them rather than the other?

These three possibilities cannot be dismissed as incoherent. We can understand them. But, while we assume that identity is what matters, (1) is not plausible. My Division would not be a bad as death. Nor are (2) and (3) plausible. There remains the fourth possibility: that I survive as both of the resulting people.

This possibility might be described in several ways. I might first claim: "What we have called the 'two resulting people' are not two people. They are one person. I do survive this operation. Its effect is to give me two bodies, and a divided mind."

This claim cannot be dismissed outright. As I argued, we ought to admit as possible that a person could have a divided mind. If this is possible, each half of my divided mind might control its own body. But though this description of the case cannot be rejected as inconceivable, it involves a great distortion in our concept of a person. In my imagined Physics Exam I

claimed that this case involved only one person. There were two features of the case that made this plausible. The divided mind was soon reunited, and there was only one body. If a mind was permanently divided, and its halves developed in different ways, it would become less plausible to claim that the case involves only one person. (Remember the actual patient who complained that, when he embraced his wife, his left hand pushed her away.)

The case of complete division, where there are also two bodies, seems to be a long way over the borderline. After I have had this operation, the two "products" each have all of the features of a person. They could live at opposite ends of the Earth. Suppose that they have poor memories, and that their appearance changes in different ways. After many years, they might meet again, and fail even to recognise each other. We might have to claim of such a pair, innocently playing tennis: "What you see out there is a single person, playing tennis with himself. In each half of his mind he mistakenly believes that he is playing tennis with someone else." If we are not yet Reductionists, we believe that there is one true answer to the question whether these two tennis-players are a single person. Given what we mean by "person," the answer must be No. It cannot be true that what I believe to be a stranger, standing there behind the net, is in fact another part of myself.

Suppose we admit that the two "products" are, as they seem to be, two different people. Could we still claim that I survive as both? There is another way in which we could. I might say: "I survive the operation as two different people. They can be different people, and yet be me, in the way in which the Pope's three crowns together form one crown."[25]

This claim is also coherent. But it again greatly distorts the concept of a person. We are happy to agree that the Pope's three crowns,

[25]Cf. Wiggins, p. 40. I owe this suggested way of talking, and one of the objections to it, to Michael Woods.

when put together, are a fourth crown. But it is hard to think of two people as, together, being a third person. Suppose the resulting people fight a duel. Are there three people fighting, one on each side, and one on both? And suppose one of the bullets kills. Are there two acts, one murder and one suicide? How many people are left alive? One or two? The composite third person has no separate mental life. It is hard to believe that there really would be such a third person. Instead of saying that the resulting people together constitute me—so that the pair is a trio –it is better to treat them as a pair, and describe their relation to me in a simpler way. . . .

I must now distinguish two ways in which a question may be empty. About some questions we should claim both that they are empty, and that they have no answers. We could decide to *give* these questions answers. But it might be true that any possible answer would be arbitrary. If this is so, it would be pointless and might be misleading to give such an answer. This would be true of the question, 'Shall I survive?' in the central cases in the Combined Spectrum. And it would be true in the central cases in the other Spectra, if I would not survive in the case at the far end.

There is another kind of case in which a question may be empty. In such a case this question has, in a sense, an answer. The question is empty because it does not describe different possibilities, any of which might be true, and one of which must be true. The question merely gives us different descriptions of the same outcome. We could know the full truth about this outcome without choosing one of these descriptions. But, if we do decide to give an answer to this empty question, one of these descriptions is better than the others. Since this is so, we can claim that this description is the answer to this question. And I claim that there is a best description of the case where I divide. The best description is that neither of the resulting people will be me.

Since this case does not involve different pos-

sibilities, the important question is not, "Which is the best description?" The important question is: "What ought to matter to me? How ought I to regard the prospect of division? Should I regard it as like death, or as like survival?" When we have answered this question, we can decide whether I have given the best description.

Before discussing what matters, I shall fulfil an earlier promise. One objection to the Psychological Criterion is that psychological continuity presupposes personal identity. I answered this objection, in the case of memory, by appealing to the wider concept of quasi-memory. Jane quasi-remembered having someone else's past experiences. My Division provides another example. Since at least one of the two resulting people will not be me, he can quasi-remember living someone else's life.

I did not show that, in describing the other relations that are involved in psychological continuity, we need not presuppose personal identity. Now that I have described My Division, this can be easily shown. One other direct relation is that which holds between an intention and the later action in which this intention is carried out. It may be a logical truth that we can intend to perform only our own actions. But we can use a new concept of *quasi-intention*. One person could quasi-intend to perform another person's actions. When this relation holds, it does not presuppose personal identity.

The case of division shows what this involves. I could quasi-intend both that one resulting person roams the world, and that the other stays at home. What I quasi-intend will be done, not by me, but by the two resulting people. Normally, if I intend that someone else should do something, I cannot get him to do it simply by forming this intention. But, if I was about to divide, it would be enough simply to form quasi-intentions. Both of the resulting people would inherit these quasi-intentions, and, unless they changed their inherited minds, they would carry them out. Since they might change their minds, I could not be sure that they would do what I quasi-intended. But the same is true within my own life. Since I may change my own mind, I cannot be sure that I shall do what I now intend to do. But I have some ability to control my future by forming firm intentions. If I was about to divide, I would have just as much ability, by forming quasi-intentions, to control the futures of the two resulting people.

Similar remarks apply to all of the other direct psychological connections, such as those involved in the continuity of character. All such connections hold between me and each of the resulting people. Since at least one of these people cannot be me, none of these connections presupposes personal identity.

What Matters When I Divide?

Some people would regard division as being as bad, or nearly as bad, as ordinary death. This reaction is irrational. We ought to regard division as being about as good as ordinary survival. As I have argued, the two "products" of this operation would be two different people. Consider my relation to each of these people. Does this relation fail to contain some vital element that is contained in ordinary survival? It seems clear that it does not. I would survive if I stood in this very same relation to only one of the resulting people. It is a fact that someone can survive even if half his brain is destroyed. And on reflection it was clear that I would survive if my whole brain was successfully transplanted into my brother's body. It was therefore clear that I would survive if half my brain was destroyed, and the other half was successfully transplanted into my brother's body. In the case that we are now considering, my relation to each of the resulting people thus contains everything that would be needed for me to survive as that person. It cannot be the *nature* of my relation to each of the resulting people that, in this case, causes it to fail to be survival. Nothing

is *missing*. What is wrong can only be the duplication.

Suppose that I accept this, but still regard division as being nearly as bad as death. My reaction is now indefensible. I am like someone who, when told of a drug that could double his years of life, regards the taking of this drug as death. The only difference in the case of division is that the extra years are to run concurrently. This is an interesting difference; but it cannot mean that there are *no* years to run. We might say: "You will lose your identity. But there are different ways of doing this. Dying is one, dividing is another. To regard these as the same is to confuse two with zero. Double survival is not the same as ordinary survival. But this does not make it death. It is even less like death."

The problem with double survival is that it does not fit the logic of identity. Like several Reductionists, I claim

> *Relation R is what matters. R is psychological connectedness and/or psychological continuity, with the right kind of cause.*[26]

I also claim

> In an account of what matters, the right kind of cause could be any cause.

Other Reductionists might require that R have a reliable cause, or have its normal cause. To postpone this disagreement, consider only cases where R would have its normal cause. In these cases, Reductionists would all accept the following claim. A future person will be me if he will be R-related to me as I am now, and no different person will be R-related to me. If there is no such different person, the fact that this future

---

[26]Other Reductionists with whom, on the whole, I agree include H. P. Grice (in Perry (1)), A. J. Ayer (see especially "The Concept of a Person"), in Ayer, A. Quinton, J. L. Mackie, (in Mackie (1) and (2)), J. Perry, especially in "The Importance of Being Identical", in Rorty, and in Perry (2), and D. K. Lewis. . . .

person will be me just consists in the fact that relation R holds between us. There is nothing more to personal identity than the holding of relation R. In nearly all of the actual cases, R takes a one-one form. It holds between one presently existing person and one future person. When R takes a one-one form, we can use the language of identity. We can claim that this future person will be this present person.

In the imagined case where I divide, R takes a "branching" form. But personal identity cannot take a branching form. I and the two resulting people cannot be one and the same person. Since I cannot be identical with two different people, and it would be arbitrary to call one of these people me, we can best describe the case by saying that neither will be me.

Which is the relation that is important? Is what matters personal identity, or relation R? In ordinary cases we need not decide which of these is what matters, since these relations coincide. In the case of My Division these relations do not coincide. We must therefore decide which of the two is what matters.

If we believe that we are separately existing entities, we could plausibly claim that identity is what matters. On this view, personal identity is a deep further fact. But we have sufficient evidence to reject this view. If we are Reductionists, we *cannot* plausibly claim that, of these two relations, it is identity that matters. On our view, the fact of personal identity just consists in the holding of relation R, when it takes a non-branching form. If personal identity just consists in this other relation, this other relation must be what matters. . . .

There is still room for minor disagreements. . . . I might regard my division as being somewhat better than ordinary survival, or as being somewhat worse.

Why might I think it somewhat worse? I might claim that the relation between me and each of the resulting people is not quite the relation that matters in ordinary survival. This is not because something is missing, but because division brings *too much*. I may think that each of the resulting people will, in one respect, have a life that is worse than mine. Each will have to live in a world where there is someone else who, at least to start with, is exactly like himself. This may be unpleasantly uncanny. And it will raise practical problems. Suppose that what I most want is to write a certain book. This would be what each of the resulting people would most want to do. But it would be pointless for both to write this book. It would be pointless for both to do what they most want to do.

Consider next the relations between the resulting people and the woman I love. I can assume that, since she loves me, she will love them both. But she could not give to both the undivided attention that we now give to each other.

In these and other ways the lives of the resulting people may not be quite as good as mine. This might justify my regarding division as being not quite as good as ordinary survival. But it could not justify regarding division as being much less good, or as being as bad as death. And we should note that this reasoning ignores the fact that these two lives, taken together, would be twice as long as the rest of mine.

Instead of regarding division as being somewhat worse than ordinary survival, I might regard it as being better. The simplest reason would be the one just given: the doubling of the years to be lived. I might have more particular reasons. Thus there might be two life-long careers both of which I strongly want to pursue. I might strongly want both to be a novelist and to be a philosopher. If I divide, each of the resulting people could pursue one of these careers. And each would be glad if the other succeeds. Just as we can take pride and joy in the achievements of our children, each of the resulting people will take pride and joy in the other's achievements.

If I have two strong but incompatible ambitions, division provides a way of fulfilling both, in a way that would gladden each resulting person. This is one way in which division could be better than ordinary survival. But there are other problems that division could not wholly solve. Suppose that I am torn between an unpleasant duty and a seductive desire. I could not wholly solve this problem by quasi-intending one of the resulting people to do my duty, and quasi-intending the other to do what I desire. The resulting person whom I quasi-intend to do my duty would himself be torn between duty and desire. Why should *he* be the one to do my unpleasant duty? We can foresee trouble here. My duty might get done if the seductive desire could not be fulfilled by more than one person. It might be the desire to elope with someone who wants only one companion. The two resulting people must then compete to be this one companion. The one who fails in this competition might then, grudgingly, do my duty. My problem would be solved, though in a less attractive way.

These remarks will seem absurd to those who have not yet been convinced that the Reductionist View is true, or that identity is not what matters. Such a person might say: "If I shall not *be* either of the resulting people, division could not fulfil my ambitions. Even if one of the resulting people is a successful novelist, and the other a successful philosopher, this fulfils neither of my ambitions. If one of my ambitions is to be a successful novelist, my ambition is that *I* be a successful novelist. This ambition will not be fulfilled if I cease to exist and *someone else* is a successful novelist. And this is what would happen if I shall be neither of the resulting people."

This objection assumes that there is a real question whether I shall be one of the resulting people, or the other, or neither. It is natural to assume that these are three different possibilities, any of which might be what happens. But as I have argued, unless I am a separately exist-

ing entity, such as a Cartesian Ego, these cannot be three different possibilities. There is nothing that could make it true that any of the three might be what really happens. (This is compatible with my claim that there is a best description of this case: that I shall be neither resulting person. This does not commit me to the view that there are different possibilities. This would be so only if one of the other descriptions *might* have been the truth—which I deny.)

We *could* give a different description. We could say that I shall be the resulting person who becomes a successful novelist. But it would be a mistake to think that my ambition would be fulfilled if and only if we *called* this resulting person me. How we choose to describe this case has no rational or moral significance. . . .

Is the True View Believable?

Nagel once claimed that, even if the Reductionist View is true, it is psychologically impossible for us to believe this. I shall therefore briefly review my arguments given above. I shall then ask whether *I* can honestly claim to believe my conclusions. If I can, I shall assume that I am not unique. There would be at least some other people who can believe the truth. . . .

What I find is this. I can believe this view at the intellectual or reflective level. I am convinced by the arguments in favour of this view. But I think it likely that, at some other level, I shall always have doubts.

My belief is firmest when I am considering some of these imagined cases. I am convinced that, if I divided, it would be an empty question whether I shall be one, or the other, or neither of the resulting people. I believe that there is nothing that could make these different possibilities, any of which might be what would really happen. And I am convinced that, in the central cases of the Third Spectrum, it is an empty question whether the resulting person would be me.

When I consider certain other cases, my conviction is less firm. One example is Teletransportation. I imagine that I am in the cubicle, about to press the green button. I might suddenly have doubts. I might be tempted to change my mind, and pay the larger fare of a space-ship journey.

I suspect that reviewing my arguments would never wholly remove my doubts. At the reflective or intellectual level, I would remain convinced that the Reductionist View is true. But at some lower level I would still be inclined to believe that there must always be a real difference between some future person's being me, and his being someone else. Something similar is true when I look through a window at the top of a sky-scraper. I know that I am in no danger. But, looking down from this dizzying height, I am afraid. I would have a similar irrational fear if I was about to press the green button.

It may help to add these remarks. On the Reductionist View, my continued existence just involves physical and psychological continuity. On the Non-Reductionist View, it involves a further fact. It is natural to believe in this further fact, and to believe that, compared with the continuities, it is a *deep* fact, and is the fact that really matters. When I fear that, in Teletransportation, *I* shall not get to Mars, my fear is that the abnormal cause may fail to produce this further fact. As I have argued, there is no such fact. What I fear will not happen, *never* happens. I want the person on Mars to be me in a specially intimate way in which no future person will ever be me. My continued existence never involves this deep further fact. What I fear will be missing is *always* missing. Even a space-ship journey would not produce the further fact in which I am inclined to believe.

When I come to see that my continued existence does not involve this further fact, I lose my reason for preferring a space-ship journey. But, judged from the stand-point of my earlier belief, this is not because Teletransportation is

about as good as ordinary survival. It is because ordinary survival is *about as bad as*, or little better than, Teletransportation. *Ordinary survival is about as bad as being destroyed and Replicated.*

By rehearsing arguments like these, I might do enough to reduce my fear. I might be able to bring myself to press the green button. But I expect that I would never completely lose my intuitive belief in the Non-Reductionist View. It is hard to be serenely confident in my Reductionist conclusions. It is hard to believe that personal identity is not what matters. If tomorrow someone will be in agony, it is hard to believe that it could be an empty question whether this agony will be felt by *me*. And it is hard to believe that, if I am about to lose consciousness, there may be no answer to the question "Am I about to die?"

Nagel once claimed that it is psychologically impossible to believe the Reductionist View. Buddha claimed that, though this is very hard, it is possible. I find Buddha's claim to be true. After reviewing my arguments, I find that, at the reflective or intellectual level, though it is very hard to believe the Reductionist View, this is possible. My remaining doubts or fears seem to me irrational. Since I can believe this view, I assume that others can do so too. We can believe the truth about ourselves.

IV. What Does Matter

Liberation from the Self

The truth is very different from what we are inclined to believe. Even if we are not aware of this, most of us are Non-Reductionists. If we considered my imagined cases, we would be strongly inclined to believe that our continued existence is a deep further fact, distinct from physical and psychological continuity, and a fact that must be all-or-nothing. This is not true.

Is the truth depressing? Some may find it so. But I find it liberating, and consoling. When I believed that my existence was a such a further fact, I seemed imprisoned in myself. My life seemed like a glass tunnel, through which I was moving faster every year, and at the end of which there was darkness. When I changed my view, the walls of my glass tunnel disappeared. I now live in the open air. There is still a difference between my life and the lives of other people. But the difference is less. Other people are closer. I am less concerned about the rest of my own life, and more concerned about the lives of others.

When I believed the Non-Reductionist View, I also cared more about my inevitable death. After my death, there will no one living who will be me. I can now redescribe this fact. Though there will later be many experiences, none of these experiences will be connected to my present experiences by chains of such direct connections as those involved in experience-memory, or in the carrying out of an earlier intention. Some of these future experiences may be related to my present experiences in less direct ways. There will later be some memories about my life. And there may later be thoughts that are influenced by mine, or things done as a result of my advice. My death will break the more direct relations between my present experiences and future experiences, but it will not break various other relations. This is all there is to the fact that there will be no one living who will be me. Now that I have seen this, my death seems to me less bad.

Instead of saying, "I shall be dead," I should say, "There will be no future experiences that will be related, in certain ways, to these present experiences." Because it reminds me what this fact involves, this redescription makes this fact less depressing. Suppose next that I must undergo some ordeal. Instead of saying, "The person suffering will be me," I should say, "There will be suffering that will be related, in certain

ways, to these present experiences." Once again, the redescribed fact seems to me less bad.

I can increase these effects by vividly imagining that I am about to undergo one of the operations I have described. I imagine that I am in a central case in the Combined Spectrum, where it is an empty question whether I am about to die. It is very hard to believe that this question could be empty. When I review the arguments for this belief, and reconvince myself, this for a while stuns my natural concern for my future. When my actual future will be grim—as it would be if I shall be tortured, or shall face a firing squad at dawn—it will be good that I have this way of briefly stunning my concern.

After Hume thought hard about his arguments, he was thrown into "the most deplorable condition imaginable, environed with the deepest darkness."[27] The cure was to dine and play backgammon with his friends. Hume's arguments supported total scepticism. This is why they brought darkness and utter loneliness. The arguments for Reductionism have on me the opposite effect. Thinking hard about these arguments removes the glass wall between me and others. And, as I have said, I care less about my death. This is merely the fact that, after a certain time, none of the experiences that will occur will be related, in certain ways, to my present experiences. Can this matter all that much?

The Continuity of the Body

Because it affects my emotions in these ways, I am glad that the Reductionist View is true. This is simply a report of psychological effects. The effects on others may be different.

There are several other questions still to be discussed. And in discussing these I can do more than report facts about my reactions. The answers to these questions partly depend on the

[27]Hume, p. 269.

force of certain arguments. I shall first discuss what, as Reductionists, we ought to claim to be what matters. I shall then ask how, if we have changed our view about the nature of personal identity, we ought to change our beliefs about rationality, and about morality.

As the case of My Division shows, personal identity is not what matters. It is merely true that, in most cases, personal identity coincides with what matters. What does matter *in the way in which* personal identity is, mistakenly, thought to matter? What is it rational to care about, in our concern about our own future?

This question can be restated. Assume, for simplicity, that it could be rational to be concerned only about one's own self-interest. Suppose that I am an Egoist, and that I could be related in one of several ways to some resulting person. What is the relation that would justify egoistic concern about this resulting person? If the rest of this person's life will be well worth living, in what way should I want to be related to this person? If the rest of his life will be much worse than nothing, in what way should I want *not* to be related to this person? In short, what is the relation that, for an Egoist, should fundamentally matter? This relation will also be what, for all of us, should fundamentally matter, in our concern for our own future. But since we may be concerned about the fate of the resulting person, *whatever* his relation is to us, it is clearest to ask what, for an Egoist, should matter.

Here are the simplest answers:

(1) Physical continuity,

(2) Relation R with its normal cause,

(3) R with any reliable cause,

(4) R with any cause.

R is psychological connectedness and/or continuity, with the right kind of cause. If we decide that R is what matters, we must then consider the relative importance of connectedness and continuity. It might be suggested that what matters is *both R and* physical continuity. But this is the same as answer (2), since physical continuity is part of R's normal cause.

Can we defend (1), the claim that only physical continuity matters? Can we claim that, if I shall be physically continuous with some resulting person, this is what matters, even if I shall not be R-related to this person?

Reconsider Williams's Example, where the surgeon totally destroys any distinctive kind of psychological continuity. Suppose that this surgeon is about to operate on me, in a painless way, and that the resulting person will have a life that is much worse than nothing. If I am an Egoist, I might regard this prospect as being no worse than a painless death, since I do not care what will happen to the resulting person. I might instead regard this prospect as much worse than death, because I am egoistically concerned about this person's appalling future. Which should my attitude be?

I should be egoistically concerned about this person's future if I could justifiably believe that this person will be *me*, rather than being *someone else* who is merely physically continuous with me. But, as I have argued, this belief is not justified. Williams's example is at the far end of the Psychological Spectrum. Both in the central cases in this Spectrum, and at the far end, there is not a real difference between the resulting person's being me, and his being someone else. These are not two different possibilities, one of which must be true. In Williams's example, the full facts are these. The resulting person will be physically but not psychologically continuous with me. We would call this person me, or call him someone else. On the Wide Psychological Criterion of identity, we would call him someone else. But neither of these descriptions could be a factual mistake. Both are descriptions of the same fact. If we give one of these descriptions in order to imply some view about what matters, our description might be a bad description. It might imply an indefensible view about what matters. But we must decide what matters *before* choosing our description.

Suppose that I accept these claims. As a Reductionist, should I be egoistically concerned about the future of this person? Should I be concerned, though I know that the physical continuity cannot cause it to be true, as a further fact, that this person will be me? In deciding what matters, I must set aside all thoughts about my identity. The question about identity is, here, empty. I must ask whether, *in itself*, physical continuity justifies egoistic concern.

I believe that the answer must be No. As I argued, those who believe in the Physical Criterion cannot plausibly require the continuity of the whole body. It cannot matter whether I receive some transplanted organ, if this organ functions just as well. All that could be claimed to matter is that enough of my brain continues to exist.

Why should the brain be singled out in this way? The answer must be: "Because the brain is the carrier of psychological continuity, or Relation R." If this is why the brain is singled out, the continuity of the brain would not matter when it was *not* the carrier of Relation R. The continuity of the brain would here be no more important than the continuity of any other part of the body. And the continuity of these other parts does not matter at all. It would not matter if these other parts were replaced with sufficiently similar duplicates. We should claim the same about the brain. The continuity of the brain matters if it will be the cause of the holding of Relation R. If R will *not* hold, the continuity of the brain should have no significance for the person whose brain it now is. It would not justify egoistic concern.

Reductionists cannot plausibly claim that only physical continuity matters. They can at most claim that this continuity is part of what matters. They can at most defend (2), the claim that Relation R would not matter if it did not have its normal cause, part of which is physical continuity.

I believe that (2) is also indefensible. I believe that physical continuity is the least important element in a person's continued existence. What we value, in ourselves and others, is not the continued existence of the same particular brains and bodies. What we value are the various relations between ourselves and others, whom and what we love, our ambitions, achievements, commitments, emotions, memories, and several other psychological features. Some of us would also want ourselves or others to continue to have bodies that are very similar to our present bodies. But this is not wanting the same particular bodies to continue to exist. I believe that, if there will later be some person who will be R-related to me as I am now, it matters very little whether this person has my present brain and body. I believe that what fundamentally matters is Relation R, even if it does not have its normal cause. Thus it would not matter if my brain was replaced with an exact duplicate.[28]

If some person will be R-related to me, this person's body should also be sufficiently like my present body to allow full psychological connectedness. This would not be true, for example, if this body was of the opposite sex. And for a few people, such as some of those who are very beautiful, there should also be exact physical similarity. These claims about this similarity I shall in future omit.

Whether we accept this view may affect our beliefs and attitudes about our own lives. But the question is clearest in the imagined case of Teletransportation. On my view, my relation to my Replica contains what fundamentally matters. This relation is about as good as ordinary survival. Judged from the stand-point of the

---

[28]Both Nagel and Williams are inclined to believe that physical continuity is what matters. But while Nagel believes that receiving a duplicate brain would be as bad as death, Williams believes this to be a mere trivial extension of existing kinds of surgery. See Williams (1), p. 47.

Non-Reductionist View, ordinary survival is, on my view, little better than — or about as bad as — being destroyed and Replicated. It would therefore be irrational to pay much more for a conventional space-ship journey.

Many people would be afraid of Teletransportation. I admit that, at some level, I might be afraid. But, as I have argued, such fear cannot be rational. Since I know exactly what will happen, I cannot fear that the worse of two outcomes will be what happens.

My relation to my Replica is R without its normal cause. The abnormality of the cause seems to me trivial. Reconsider the artificial eyes which would restore sight to those who have gone blind. Suppose that these eyes would give to these people visual sensations just like those involved in normal sight, and that these sensations would provide true beliefs about what can be seen. This would surely be as good as normal sight. It would not be plausible to reject these eyes because they were not the normal cause of human sight. There would be some grounds for disliking artificial eyes, since they would make one's appearance disturbing to others. But there is no analogue to this in Teletransportation. My Replica, though he is artificially produced, will be just like me in every way. He will have a normal brain and body. . . .

. . . It cannot matter much that the cause is abnormal. It is the *effect* which matters. And this effect, the holding of Relation R, is in itself the same. It is true that, if this effect has the abnormal cause, we can describe the effect in a different way. We can say that, though my Replica is psychologically continuous with me, he will not be me. But this is not a further difference in what happens, beyond the difference in the cause. If I decide not to press the button, and to pay much more for a conventional space-ship journey, I must admit that this is merely because I do not like the thought of an abnormal method of causation. It cannot be rational to care much about the abnormality of this cause.

Similar remarks apply to the continued exis-

tence of one's present brain and body. It may be rational to want the body of my Replica to be like my present body. But this is a desire for a certain kind of body, not a desire for the same particular body. Why should I want it to be true that *this* brain and body gets to Mars? Once again, the natural fear is that only this ensures that *I* shall get to Mars. But this again assumes that whether or not I get to Mars is, here, a real question. And we ought to conclude that this is an empty question. Even if this question has a best answer, we can know exactly what will happen before deciding what this answer is. Since this is so, can I rationally care a great deal whether or not this person's brain and body will be my present brain and body? I believe that, while it may not be irrational to care a little, to care a great deal would be irrational.

Why would it not be irrational to care a little? This could be like one's wish to keep the same wedding ring, rather than a new ring that is exactly similar. We understand the sentimental wish to keep the very ring that was involved in the wedding ceremony. In the same way, it may not be irrational to have a mild preference that the person on Mars have my present brain and body.

There remains one question. If there will be some person who will be R-related to me, would it matter if this relation did not have a reliable cause?

There is an obvious reason for preferring, in advance, that the cause will be reliable. Suppose that Teletransportation worked perfectly in a few cases, but in most cases was a complete failure. In a few cases, the person on Mars would be a perfect Replica of me. But in most cases he would be totally unlike me. If these were the facts, it would clearly be rational to pay the larger fare of a space-ship journey. But this is irrelevant. We should ask, 'In the few cases, where my Replica will be fully R-related to me, would it matter that R did not have a reliable cause?'

I believe that the answer should again be No. Suppose that there is an unreliable treatment for some disease. In most cases the treatment achieves nothing. But in a few cases it provides a complete cure. In these cases, only the effect matters. This effect is just as good, even though its cause was unreliable. We should claim the same about Relation R. I conclude that, of the answers I described, we should accept (4). In our concern about our own future, *what fundamentally matters is relation R, with any cause.*

The Branch-Line Case

Teletransportation would, I have argued, be about as good as ordinary survival. Another challenge to this claim comes from the Branch-Line Case. Suppose that the New Scanner has not destroyed my brain and body, but has damaged my heart. I am here on Earth, and expect to die within a few days. Using the Intercom, I see and talk to my Replica on Mars. He assures me that he will continue my life where I leave off.

What should my attitude here be? I am about to die. Does my relation to *this* Replica contain what matters? He is fully psychologically continuous, not with me as I am now, but with me as I was this morning, when I pressed the green button. Is this relation about as good as survival?

It may be hard to believe that it is. But it is also hard to believe that it can matter much whether my life briefly overlaps with the life of my Replica.

It may help to consider

The Sleeping Pill. Certain actual sleeping pills cause *retrograde* amnesia. It can be true that, if I take such a pill, I shall remain awake for an hour, but after my night's sleep I shall have no memories of the second half of this hour.

I have in fact taken such pills, and found

out what the results are like. Suppose that I took such a pill nearly an hour ago. The person who wakes up in my bed tomorrow will not be psychologically continuous with me as I am now. He will be psychologically continuous with me as I was half an hour ago. I am now on a *psychological branch-line*, which will end soon when I fall asleep. During this half-hour, I am psychologically continuous with myself in the past. But I am not now psychologically continuous with myself in the future. I shall never later remember what I do or think or feel during this half-hour. This means that, in some respects, my relation to myself tomorrow is like a relation to another person.

Suppose, for instance, that I have been worrying about some practical question. I now see the solution. Since it is clear what I should do, I form a firm intention. In the rest of my life, it would be enough to form this intention. But, when I am on this psychological branch-line, this is not enough. I shall not later remember what I have now decided, and I shall not wake up with the intention that I have now formed. I must therefore communicate with myself tomorrow as if I was communicating with someone else. I must write myself a letter, describing my decision, and my new intention. I must then place this letter where I am bound to notice it tomorrow.

I do not in fact have any memories of making such a decision, and writing such a letter. But I did once find such a letter underneath my razor.

This case is in one way like the Branch-Line Case. And it would be just like a variant of this case, in which though I live for a few days after leaving the cubicle, my Replica would not be created until after I have died. But, in the case that we are considering, my life overlaps with that of my Replica. We talk on the Intercom. There is no analogue to this in the case of the Sleeping Pill.

The analogue can be found in my imagined Physics Exam. In this case I divide my mind for ten minutes. In both of my streams of consciousness, I know that I am now having thoughts and sensations in my other stream. But in each stream I am unaware of my thoughts and sensations in my other stream. My relation to myself in my other stream is again like my relation to another person. I would have to communicate in a public way. I might in one stream write a letter to myself in my other stream. With one hand I would then place this letter in my other hand.

This is like my situation in the Branch-Line Case. I can imagine having a divided mind. Since this is so, I need not assume that my Replica on Mars is someone else. Here on Earth, I am not aware of what my Replica on Mars is now thinking. This is like the fact that, in each of my two streams of my consciousness in the Physics Exam, I am not aware of what, in my other stream, I am now thinking. I can believe that I do now have another other stream of consciousness, of which, in this stream, I am now unaware. And, if it helps, I can take this view about my Replica. I can say that I now have two streams of consciousness, one here on Earth, and another on Mars. This description cannot be a factual mistake. When I talk to my Replica on Mars, this is merely like the communication in the Physics Exam between myself in my two streams.

The actual case of the Sleeping Pill provides a close analogy to one of the special features of the Branch-Line Case: the fact that I am on a psychological branch-line. The imagined Physics Exam provides a close analogy to the other special feature: that my life overlaps with that of my Replica. When we consider these analogies, this seems enough to defend the claim that, when I am on the Branch-Line, my relation to my Replica contains almost everything that matters. It may be slightly inconvenient that my Replica will be psychologically continuous, not with me as I am now, but with me as I was this morning when I pressed the green button. But these relations are substantially the same. It makes little difference that my life briefly overlaps with that of my Replica.

If the overlap was large, this *would* make a difference. Suppose that I am an old man, who is about to die. I shall be outlived by someone who was once a Replica of me. When this person started to exist forty years ago, he was psychologically continuous with me as I was then. He has since lived his own life for forty years. I agree that my relation to *this* Replica, though better than ordinary death, is not nearly as good as ordinary survival. But this relation would be about as good if my Replica would be psychologically continuous with me as I was ten days or ten minutes ago. As Nozick argues, overlaps as brief as this cannot be rationally thought to have much significance.[29]

Though my two analogies seem enough to defend this claim, I admit that this is one of the cases where my view is hardest to believe. *Before* I press the green button, I can more easily believe that my relation to my Replica contains what fundamentally matters in ordinary survival. I can look forward down the Main Line where there are forty years of life ahead. *After* I have pressed the green button, and have talked to my Replica, I cannot in the same way look forward down the Main Line. My concern for the future needs to be redirected. I must try to direct this concern backwards up the Branch Line beyond the point of division, and then forward down the Main Line. This psychological manoeuvre would be difficult. But this is not surprising. And, since it is not surprising, this difficulty does not provide a sufficient argument against what I have claimed about this case.

[29]Op. cit., p. 44.

References

Ayer, A. J., *The Concept of a Person and Other Essays*, London, Macmillan, 1964.

Descartes, R., *Meditations*, translated by E. S. Haldane and G. R. T. Ross, Cambridge University Press, 1969.

Dummett, M. A. E., "Wang"s Paradox", *Synthese* 30, 1975.

Forbes, G., "Thisness and Vagueness", *Synthese* 54, 1983.

Grice, H. P., "Personal Identity," *Mind* 50 (1941) 330–350, reprinted in Perry (1).

Hume, D., *A Treatise of Human Nature*, Oxford, Clarendon Press, 1978.

Kant, I., *Critique of Pure Reason*, trans. by N. Kemp Smith, London, Macmillan, 1964.

Lewis, D. K., *Convention: A Philosophical Study*, Cambridge, Mass., Harvard University Press, 1969.

Lewis (1), H. D., *The Elusive Mind*, London, George Allen and Unwin, 1969.

Lewis (2), H. D., *The Self and Immortality*, New York, Seabury Press, 1973.

Lewis (3), H. D., *The Elusive Self*, London, Macmillan, 1982.

Lichtenberg, G. C., *Schriften und Briefe*, Sudelbucher II, Carl Hanser Verlag, 1971.

Locke, J., *Essay Concerning Human Understanding*, partly reprinted in Perry (1).

Mackie (1), J. L., *Problems from Locke*, Oxford, Clarendon Press, 1976.

Mackie (2), J. L., "The Transcendental 'I'", in Van Straaten.

Madell, G., *The Identity of the Self*, Edinburgh University Press, 1981.

Nagel (1), T., *Mortal Questions*, Cambridge University Press, 1979.

Nagel (2), T., "Brain Bisection and the Unity of Consciousness", *Synthese* 22, 1971, reprinted in Nagel (1) and in Perry (1).

Peacocke, C., "Are Vague Predicates Incoherent?", *Synthese* 46, 1981.

Perry (1), J., ed., *Personal Identity*, Berkeley, University of California Press, 1975.

Perry (2), J., *A Dialogue on Personal Identity and Immortality*, Indianapolis, Hackett, 1978.

Quine, W. V., reviewing Milton K. Munitz, ed., *Identity and Individuation*, in *The Journal of Philosophy*, 1972.

Quinton, A., "The Soul", *The Journal of Philosophy*, 59, No. 15, July 1962, reprinted in Perry (1).

Reid, T., *Essays on the Intellectual Powers of Man*, first published in 1785, "Of Memory", chap. 4, reprinted in Perry (1).

Rorty, A., ed., *The Identities of Persons*, Berkeley, University of California Press, 1976.

Sainsbury, R. M., "In Defence of Degrees of Truth", unpublished paper.

Shoemaker (1), S., *Self-Knowledge and Self-Identity*, Ithaca, N.Y., Cornell University Press, 1963.

Shoemaker (2), S., "Persons and Their Pasts", *American Philosophical Quarterly* 7, 1970.

Sperry, R. W., in J. C. Eccles, ed., *Brain and Conscious Experience*, Berlin, Springer Verlag, 1966.

Swinburne, R. G., "Personal Identity", *Proceedings of the Aristotelian Society* 74, 1973–4.

Unger (1), P., "Why There Are No People", *Midwest Studies in Philosophy* 4, 1979.

Unger (2), P., "I Do Not Exist", in G. F. MacDonald, ed., *Perception and Identity*, Ithaca, N.Y., Cornell University Press, 1979.

Van Straaten, Z., *Philosophical Subjects*, Oxford, Clarendon Press, 1980.

Wachsberg, M., "Personal Identity, The Nature of Persons, and Ethical Theory", Ph.D. dissertation, Princeton University, June 1983.

Wiggins, D., *Identity and Spatio-Temporal Continuity*, Oxford, Basic Blackwell, 1967.

Williams (1), B., *Problems of the Self*, Cambridge University Press, 1973.

Williams (2), B., "The Self and the Future", *Philosophical Review* 70, No. 2, Apr. 1970.

16

SYDNEY SHOEMAKER
Survival and the Importance of Identity

The Brain-State Transfer Device

. . . I spoke of the physical realization of mental states as requiring a "mechanism." It might be supposed that the physical realization of a mechanism would have to be a physical body of some sort. And then it might seem implicit in what I have said that if materialism is true personal identity must always be realized in the identity of some sort of physical body—if not in the identity of something like a complete human body, then at least in the identity of a brain or of some organ that plays the sort of functional role the brain plays in us.[1] In order to consider whether this is so, and also in order to consider some of the objections that have been raised against accounts of personal identity like that presented here, I have to consider yet another hypothetical example.

A number of philosophers have envisaged the possibility of a device which records the state of one brain and imposes that state on a second brain by restructuring it so that it has exactly the state the first brain had at the beginning of the operation.[2] We will suppose that this process obliterates the first brain, or at any rate obliterates its current state. Discussions of this example usually proceed on the assumption that mental states are at least "supervenient" on brain states, which means that creatures cannot differ in their mental states without differing in their brain states, and therefore that the "recipient" of a total brain-state transfer would have exactly the same mental states the "donor" had immediately before. Philosophers who have discussed this sort of case have differed in their intuitions as to whether the brain-state transfer would amount to a person's changing bodies—whether, as I shall put it, the procedure would be "person-preserving." Some think it would. Others think that it would amount to killing the original person and at the same time creating (or converting someone into) a psychological duplicate of him.

Initially, I think, most people are inclined to take the latter view. But one can tell a story which enhances the plausibility of the former view. Imagine a society living in an environment in which an increase in some sort of radiation has made it impossible for a human body to remain healthy for more than a few years. Being highly advanced technologically, the society has developed the following procedure for dealing with this. For each person there is a stock of duplicate bodies, cloned from cells taken from that person and grown by an accelerated process in a radiation-proof vault, where they are then stored. Periodically a person goes into the hospital for a "body-change." This consists in his total brain-state being transferred to the

---

[1]See Wiggins 1967, p. 51.
[2]See Williams 1970, p. 162, and Nozick 1981, p. 39.

brain of one of his duplicate bodies. At the end of the procedure the original body is incinerated. We are to imagine that in this society going in for a body-change is as routine an occurrence as going to have one's teeth cleaned is in ours. It is taken for granted by everyone that the procedure is person-preserving. One frequently hears remarks like "I can't meet you for lunch on Tuesday, because that is the day for my body-change; let's make it Wednesday instead." All of the social practices of the society presuppose that the procedure is person-preserving. The brain-state recipient is regarded as owning the property of the brain-state donor, as being married to the donor's spouse, and as holding whatever offices, responsibilities, rights, obligations, etc. the brain-state donor held. If it is found that the brain-state donor had committed a crime, everyone regards it as just that the brain-state recipient should be punished for it.

Let us suppose, for now, that materialism is true; the world does not contain any non-material substances, and all of the entities in it are composed exclusively of the entities recognized by physics. The members of my hypothetical society know this, and they know precisely what happens, physically speaking, in the brain-state transfer procedure (for short, the BST-procedure). There is no clear sense in which they can be said to be mistaken about a matter of fact in regarding the procedure as person-preserving. If we confronted such a society, there would, I think, be a very strong case for saying that what *they* mean by "person" is such that the BST-procedure *is* person-preserving (using "person" in *their* sense). And, what goes with this, it would be very hard to maintain that they are being irrational when, being under no misconception concerning matters of fact, they willingly submit themselves to the BST-procedure. But there would also be a strong reason for saying that what they mean by "person" is what we mean by it; they call the same things persons, offer the same sorts of charac-

terizations of what sorts of things persons are, and attach the same kinds of social consequences to judgments of personal identity— i.e., personal identity has with them the same connections with moral responsibility, ownership of property, etc. as it does with us. But if they are right in thinking that the BST-procedure is person-preserving, and if they mean the same by "person" as we do, then it seems that *we* ought to regard the BST-procedure as person-preserving.

A variety of objections have been raised against the view that anything like the BST-procedure could be person-preserving, and some of these would also apply, if valid, to the view that the brain-transplant procedure (as in the Brown–Brownson case) could be person-preserving. Some of these will be discussed in the following sections. Here I want to consider the bearing of this example on the question of whether a materialist view of mind requires personal identity to be realized in the identity of some sort of physical body.

On the face of it, if one allows that the BST-procedure is person-preserving, one must hold that the answer to this question is "no." For the BST-procedure does not involve the transfer of any bodily organ, or of any matter at all, from the one body to the other. All that is transferred, it is natural to say, is "information." If we have personal identity here, it is apparently not carried by the identity of any body. Yet it seems clear that one is not committed to dualism, or the rejection of materialism, in holding that the procedure is person-preserving; on the contrary, the plausibility of holding the latter seems to depend on the materialist assumption that mental states are realized in, or at least supervenient on, states of the brain.

But how can this be reconciled with my claim . . . that the physical realization of a mental state requires the existence of a physical "mechanism" whereby it stands, or is capable of standing, in the functionally appropriate causal relations to other mental states of the same person, including its successor states? I think that what one must say, if one allows that the BST-procedure would be person-preserving, is that in the circumstances I have imagined the mechanism in which the mental states of a person are realized does not include just the person's body or brain; it also includes the BST-device, and perhaps the social institutions that govern its use. For it is in virtue of the existence of all this that mental states existing immediately before a body-change produce the functionally appropriate successor states. What one has here is a non-standard (relative to us) way of realizing mental states and the relation of copersonality, one that relies for the most part on the mechanism in which these are realized in us, but which supplements these with an additional mechanism. The mechanism as a whole does not consist in any *single* physical body, or even depend on any single one (for the BST-device could wear and be replaced several times during a person's lifetime). Thus it is that we have personal identity without the identity of any body, even though nothing non-physical is involved. . . .

The Duplication Objection

A common objection to the view that something like the BST-procedure could be person-preserving goes along the following lines. It might happen that the BST-device misfunctions, and produces the states of brain A in brain B without obliterating those states in brain A, or produces these states not only in brain B but also in brain C. If this happened the post-transfer possessor of brain B could not be identical to the pre-transfer possessor of brain A—or at any rate, he could not be so simply in virtue of his psychological continuity with that person. But surely (it is said), whether a person X at time t_2 is identical to person Y existing at an earlier time t_1 cannot depend on whether there happens to be

another person Z whose state at t_2 is related to Y's state at t_1 in the same way that X's state at t_2 is related to it. So even if the machine functions properly, and there is no duplication, the post-transfer possessor of brain B cannot be identical to the pre-transfer possessor of brain A in virtue of his psychological continuity with him.[3]

One could meet this objection just by stipulating that the BST-procedure is such as to make such duplication nomologically impossible—it essentially depends on the states of the original brain being obliterated, and is such that the states can be transferred to only one brain. But I shall not rely on such a stipulation. Let us suppose that duplication of the sort envisaged is nomologically possible, and that only the vigilance of the operators of the BST-device prevents it from happening.

The duplication objection cannot be that the psychological continuity account of personal identity (which is presupposed by the view that the BST-procedure is person-preserving) has the absurd consequence that both post-transfer duplicates (the A-brain person and the B-brain person, or the A-brain person and the C-brain person) are identical to the original A-brain person. We guarded the account against that objection by having it say, not that personal identity consists in psychological continuity *simpliciter*, but that it consists in *non-branching* psychological continuity. The objection is rather that this way of guarding against that absurd consequence makes the identity depend on something it cannot depend on. Later on . . . I will concede something (not much) to the duplication objection. Here I want to reveal the extent to which it rests on confusion.

Suppose that the BST-device functions correctly, and that after the transfer only brain B has the states that brain A had immediately before the transfer. Let "Smith" name the pre-

---

[3]For this general sort of objection, see Williams 1956–57. For a recent formulation, see Wiggins 1980, pp. 95–6.

transfer A-brain person, and let "George" name the post-transfer B-brain person. It might appear that my version of the psychological continuity account, with its "non-branching" provision, commits us to saying the following: since there was no branching in the psychologically continuous series of person-stages connecting Smith before the transfer and George after the transfer, George and Smith are the same person; but the BST-device could have misfunctioned and left brain A unaffected, in which case Smith and George would have been different persons. Now this would be an absurd consequence. If Smith and George are in fact one and the same person, they are necessarily the same, and there is no possible circumstance in which they are different persons.[4] But it is a confusion to think that this absurd consequence follows from the non-branching psychological continuity view (together with the assumption that the BST-device in fact functioned correctly, but could have misfunctioned in the way envisaged).

What does follow is this: in fact the post-transfer B-brain person is identical to the pre-transfer A-brain person, but if the BST-device had misfunctioned in the way envisaged, the post-transfer B-brain person would not have been the pre-transfer A-brain person. This does not offend against the principle that identity holds necessarily if at all, and it is analogous to the following observation (which is true on one natural reading of it): in fact the president of the US in 1982 is the only former governor of California who began his career as a movie actor, but if Carter had received a lot more votes then the president of the US in 1982 would not have been that former governor. The crucial difference here is that whereas names like "George" and "Smith" are what Saul Kripke has called "rigid designators," and have the same reference in talk about hypothetical or counter-fac-

tual situations ("other possible worlds") as they do in talk about the actual situation, definite descriptions like "the post-transfer B-body person" and "the president of the US in 1982" are not rigid designators.[5] It is only identity statements whose terms are rigid designators that have to be necessarily true if true at all, and so cannot be such that they are true but might have been false. It is not possible that George should have failed to be Smith; what is possible (on the non-branching psychological continuity view) is that George (i.e., Smith) should not have been the post-transfer B-brain person, either because he failed to survive the transfer or because he survived it as the post-transfer A-brain person. If either of the latter possibilities had been realized, the post-transfer B-brain person would have been somebody else— perhaps somebody who was created (with a set of memories corresponding to George's past) by the BST-procedure.

In part, I think, the duplication objection is the result of a failure to distinguish rigid and non-rigid designators and their roles in identity statements. But it has other sources as well. One of these, which comes out in a version of the duplication objection raised by Richard Swinburne, is connected with one of the central issues about personal identity.[6]

Recall the "fission" example . . . which involves the transplantation of the two hemispheres of someone's brain into two different bodies. Swinburne envisages a theory of personal identity which holds (as indeed our psychological continuity theory seems to do) that whether the post-operative owner of one hemisphere is identical to the original person depends on whether the transplantation of the other hemisphere "takes." One of his objections to this is the one we have already answered. He thinks that such a view has the absurd consequence that "Who I am depends on whether

---

[4]Here I assume the truth of Saul Kripke's view that identity propositions having names as terms are necessarily true if true at all. See Kripke 1980.

[5]See Kripke 1980.

[6]See Swinburne 1973–74.

you exist" (1973–74, p. 236). Now there is a perfectly good sense in which "who I am" *can* depend on whether you exist; e.g., whether I am the heir to someone's fortune may depend on this (if his will stipulates that I inherit only if you no longer exist). What cannot depend on whether you exist is whether I am identical to some particular person. But the theory in question does not imply that there could be such a dependence. To be sure, if I am the post-operative possessor of the left brain hemisphere, then in order to establish whether I am identical to the original person I might have to establish whether the transplantation of the right hemisphere was successful. But suppose that it was in fact successful (and the post-operative possessor of the right hemisphere is you). In that case neither of us is identical to the original person. And it would be wrong to say that if the other half-brain transplantation had failed, then I would have been the original person; one should say instead that if it had failed *I* would not exist (although there would exist someone with this body and these memories). If we suppose instead that the actual situation is that in which the other transplant failed, and in which I am identical to the original person (according to our theory), then the true counterfactual is not that if the other transplant had succeeded I would not have been the original person, but that in that case I (= the original person) would no longer exist.

But Swinburne says that the view in question has a second absurd consequence, namely that

> The way for a man to ensure his own survival is to ensure the non-existence of future persons too similar to himself. Suppose the mad surgeon had told P_1 before the operation what he was intending to do . . . P_1 is unable to escape the clutches of the mad surgeon, but is nevertheless very anxious to survive the operation. If the empiricist theory in question is correct there is an obvious policy which will guarantee his survival. He can bribe one of

> the nurses to ensure that the right half-brain does *not survive successfully.* (1973–74, p. 237)

I think that it can be agreed that it does seem absurd for P_1 to try to guarantee his survival by bribing the nurse. But I think that it is not absurd for the reason Swinburne thinks it is.

Survival and the Importance of Identity

What is at stake here is what it is that we really care about when we care about our own survival and our own future well-being. Swinburne makes the natural assumption that when I want to survive it is essential to the satisfaction of my want that I, the very person who is now wanting this, should exist in the future. But this can be questioned.

Consider another variant of our half-brain transplant case. Suppose that half of my brain and all of the rest of my body are ridden with cancer, and that my only hope for survival is for my healthy half-brain to be transplanted to another body. There are two transplantation procedures available. The first, which is inexpensive and safe (so far as the prospects of the recipient are concerned) involves first transplanting the healthy hemisphere and then destroying (or allowing to die) the diseased hemisphere that remains. The other, which is expensive and risky (the transplant may not take, or it may produce a psychologically damaged person) involves first destroying the diseased hemisphere and then transplanting the other. Which shall I choose? Notice that if I choose the first procedure there will be, for a short while, two persons psychologically continuous with the original person (me), and therefore that on the non-branching psychological continuity theory the recipient of the healthy hemisphere cannot count as me. If I choose the second procedure, on the other hand, then at no point will the recipient (the post-operative possessor of the healthy hemi-sphere) have any "competitor" for the status of being me, so it seems that he can count as me (if the transplantation takes). Should I therefore choose the expensive and risky procedure? This seems absurd. The thing to do is to choose the first procedure, even though (I think) it guaran-tees that the transplant recipient will not be me.

How can this be? Am I relying on some moral principle that requires one to so act as to maxi-mize the number and well-being of future per-sons, independently of who those persons are, even if this involves sacrificing oneself? No. The reason is that whether the future person will be me is *in a case like this* of no importance to me. This is why I find it absurd for P_1 in Swin-burne's example to bribe the nurse with the object of ensuring that the left half-brain recipi-ent is himself; I see that if I were in P_1's position, bribing the nurse would contribute nothing to giving me what I really want in wanting to survive.

Consider again our original fission case, in which both half-brain transplantations take and there are two later persons who are psychologi-cally continuous with the owner of the original brain. How should the original person view the prospect of this? Let us suppose that he accepts the analysis according to which neither offshoot will be him (where "be him" means "be identi-cal to him"). Does this mean that he must view the impending fission as his death and replace-ment by duplicates? Remember that the off-shoots will be (and we can suppose him to know that they will be) psychologically contin-uous with him in all of the ways in which a person at one time is continuous with himself at other times. Not only will they remember his past; they will also be influenced by his inten-tions and motivated by his desires (or by desires which are "successor states" of his pre-opera-tive desires). For him now to deliberate about and plan their future careers would be just as efficacious as it is for a person to deliberate about and plan his own future career. Their

future sufferings and delights, their prospects of success and failure, could not be a matter of indifference to him. Indeed, if his attitude towards these were not essentially like those a person normally has towards his own future sufferings, delights, successes and failures, then we would not have full psychological continuity between the original person and the offshoots.

Since cases of this sort do not occur, we are ill-equipped with language for talking about them. One way of doing so, adopted by Derek Parfit, is to sever the connection between our current notion of survival and the concept of identity, and to speak of the original person as "surviving as" both offshoots.[7] The rationale for doing this is that the attitudes that are ap-propriate in a case in which one believes that one will survive as a person of a certain descrip-tion (fear of that person's suffering, hope for that person's success, etc.) are ones which a man could appropriately have towards the fu-ture states of both his offshoots in a case of impending fission. But even if one does not want to call this survival, one can allow that it could be just as good (or, as the case might be, just as bad) as survival.

Considerations like these have led some phi-losophers to maintain that what matters in sur-vival is not identity, *per se*, but the psychological continuity or connectedness which normally ac-company and constitute it, namely when there is no branching.[8] This is not, certainly, the view that recommends itself to pre-analytic intuition. One's initial inclination is to say that if one cares especially about the future person who will be psychologically continuous with one, this is be-cause one believes that that person will be one-self. What reflection on the fission case suggests is that it is just the other way around . . .

---

[7]See Parfit 1971.
[8]See Shoemaker 1970, and Parfit 1971. See also Perry 1976.

References

Kripke, Saul (1980). *Naming and Necessity.* Cambridge, Mass.

Nozick, Robert (1981). *Philosophical Explanations,* chapter I. Cambridge, Mass.

Parfit, Derek (1971). "Personal Identity," *The Philosophical Review,* 80, pp. 3–27. Reprinted in Perry, 1975.

Perry, John (ed.) (1975). *Personal Identity.* Berkeley, Los Angeles, and London.

Perry, John (1976). "The Importance of Being Identical." In Amélie Rorty (ed.), *The Identities of Persons.* Berkeley, Los Angeles, and London.

Shoemaker, Sydney (1970). "Persons and Their Pasts," *American Philosophical Quarterly,* 7, pp. 269–85.

Swinburne, Richard (1973–74). "Personal Identity,"

Proceedings of the Aristotelian Society, 74, pp. 231–48.

Wiggins, David (1967). *Identity and Spatio-temporal Continuity.* Oxford.

Wiggins, David (1980). *Sameness and Substance.* Oxford.

Williams, Bernard (1956–57). "Personal Identity and Individuation," *Proceedings of the Aristotelian Society.* 57, pp. 229–52. Reprinted in Williams, 1973.

Williams, Bernard (1970). "The Self and the Future," *The Philosophical Review,* 79, pp. 161–80. Reprinted in Williams 1973 and Perry 1975.

Williams, Bernard (1973). *Problems of the Self.* Cambridge.

17

DAVID LEWIS
Survival and Identity

What is it that matters in survival? Suppose I wonder whether I will survive the coming battle, brainwashing, brain transplant, journey by matter-transmitter, purported reincarnation or resurrection, fission into twins, fusion with someone else, or what not. What do I really care about? If it can happen that some features of ordinary, everyday survival are present but others are missing, then what would it take to make the difference between something practically as good as commonplace survival and something practically as bad as commonplace death?

I answer, along with many others: *what matters in survival is mental continuity and connectedness.* When I consider various cases in between commonplace survival and commonplace death, I find that what I mostly want in wanting survival is that my mental life should flow on. My present experiences, thoughts, beliefs, desires, and traits of character should have appropriate future successors. My total present mental state should be but one momentary stage in a continuing succession of mental states. These successive states should be interconnected in two ways. First, by bonds of similarity. Change should be gradual rather than sudden, and (at least in some respects) there should not be too much change overall. Second, by bonds of lawful causal dependence. Such change as there is should conform, for the most part, to lawful regularities concerning the succession of mental states—regularities, moreover, that are exemplified in everyday cases of survival. And this should be so not by accident (and also not, for instance, because some demon has set out to create a succession of mental states patterned to counterfeit our ordinary mental life) but rather because each succeeding mental state causally depends for its character on the states immediately before it.

I refrain from settling certain questions of detail. Perhaps my emphasis should be on *connectedness*: direct relations of similarity and causal dependence between my present mental state and each of its successors; or perhaps I should rather emphasize *continuity*: the existence of step-by-step paths from here to there, with extremely strong local connectedness from each step to the next. Perhaps a special place should be given to the special kind of continuity and connectedness that constitute memory;[1] or perhaps not. Perhaps the "mental" should be construed narrowly, perhaps broadly. Perhaps nonmental continuity and connectedness—in my appearance and voice, for instance—also should have at least some weight. It does not matter, for the present, just which version I would prefer of the thesis that what matters is mental continuity and connectedness. I am sure that I would endorse some version, and in this paper I want to deal with a seeming problem for any version.

The problem begins with a well-deserved complaint that all this about mental connectedness and continuity is too clever by half. I have

forgotten to say what should have been said first of all. What matters in survival is survival. If I wonder whether I will survive, what I mostly care about is quite simple. When it's all over, will I myself—the very same person now thinking these thoughts and writing these words—still exist? Will any one of those who do exist afterward be me? In other words, *what matters in survival is identity*—identity between the I who exists now and the surviving I who will, I hope, still exist then.

One question, two answers! An interesting answer, plausible to me on reflection but far from obvious: that what matters is mental connectedness and continuity between my present mental state and other mental states that will succeed it in the future. And a compelling commonsense answer, an unhelpful platitude that cannot credibly be denied: what matters is identity between myself, existing now, and myself, still existing in the future.

If the two answers disagreed and we had to choose one, I suppose we would have to prefer the platitude of common sense to the interesting philosophical thesis. Else it would be difficult to believe one's own philosophy! The only hope for the first answer, then, is to show that we need not choose: the answers are compatible, and both are right. That is the claim I wish to defend. I say that it cannot happen that what matters in survival according to one answer is present while what matters in survival according to the other answer is lacking.

I. Parfit's Argument

Derek Parfit has argued that the two answers cannot both be right, and we must therefore choose.[2] (He chooses the first). His argument is as follows:

---

[1] Better, *quasi-memory*: that process which is memory when it occurs within one single person, but might not be properly so-called if it occurred in a succession of mental states that did not all belong to a single person.

[2] Derek Parfit, "Personal Identity," *Philosophical Review* 80 (1971): 3–27.

(a) Identity is a relation with a certain formal character. It is one-one and it does not admit of degree.

(b) A relation of mental continuity and connectedness need not have that formal character. We can imagine problem cases in which any such relation is one-many or many-one, or in which it is present to a degree so slight that survival is questionable.

Therefore, since Parfit believes as I do that what matters in survival is some sort of mental continuity or connectedness,

(c) What matters in survival is not identity. At most, what matters is a relation that coincides with identity to the extent that the problem cases do not actually arise.

Parfit thinks that if the problem cases did arise, or if we wished to solve them hypothetically, questions of personal identity would have no compelling answers. They would have to be answered arbitrarily, and in view of the discrepancy stated in (a) and (b), there is no answer that could make personal identity coincide perfectly with the relation of mental continuity and connectedness that matters in survival.

Someone else could just as well run the argument in reverse. Of course what matters in survival is personal identity. Therefore what matters cannot be mental continuity or connectedness, in view of the discrepancy stated in premises (a) and (b). It must be some better-behaved relation.

My task is to disarm both directions of the argument and show that the opposition between what matters and identity is false. We can agree with Parfit (and I think we should) that what matters in questions of personal identity is mental continuity or connectedness, and that this might be one-many or many-one, and admits of degree. At the same time we can consistently agree with common sense (and I think we should) that what matters in questions of personal identity—even in the problem cases —is identity.

I do not attack premises (a) and (b). We could,

of course, say "identity" and just mean mental continuity and connectedness. Then we would deny that "identity" must have the formal character stated in (a). But this verbal maneuver would not meet the needs of those who think, as I do, that what matters in survival is literally *identity*: that relation that everything bears to itself and to no other thing. As for (b), the problem cases clearly are possible under Parfit's conception of the sort of mental continuity or connectedness that matters in survival: or under any conception I might wish to adopt. The questions about continuity and connectedness which I left open are not relevant, since no way of settling them will produce a relation with the formal character of identity. So we do indeed have a discrepancy of formal character between identity and any suitable relation of mental continuity and connectedness.

But what does that show? Only that the two relations are different. And we should have known that from the start, since they have different relata. He who says that what matters in survival is a relation of mental continuity and connectedness is speaking of a relation among more or less momentary person-stages, or time-slices of continuant persons, or persons-at-times. He who says that what matters in survival is identity, on the other hand, must be speaking of identity among temporally extended continuant persons with stages at various times. What matters is that one and the same continuant person should have stages both now and later. Identity among stages has nothing to do with it, since stages are momentary. Even if you survive, your present stage is not identical to any future stage.[3] You know that your present stage will not survive the battle—that is not disconcerting—but will *you* survive?

---

[3]Unless time is circular, so that it is in its own future in the same way that places are to the west of themselves. But that possibility also has nothing to do with survival.

II. The R-Relation and the I-Relation

Pretend that the open questions have been settled, so that we have some definite relation of mental continuity and connectedness among person-stages in mind as the relation that matters in survival. Call it the *R-relation*, for short. If you wonder whether you will survive the coming battle or what-not, you are wondering whether any of the stages that will exist afterward is R-related to you-now, the stage that is doing the wondering. Similarly for other "questions of personal identity." If you wonder whether this is your long-lost son, you mostly wonder whether the stage before you now is R-related to certain past stages. If you also wonder whether he is a reincarnation of Nero, you wonder whether this stage is R-related to other stages farther in the past. If you wonder whether it is in your self-interest to save for your old age, you wonder whether the stages of that tiresome old gaffer you will become are R-related to you-now to a significantly greater degree than are all the other person-stages at this time or other times. If you wonder as you step into the duplicator whether you will leave by the left door, the right door, both, or neither, you are again wondering which future stages, if any, are R-related to you-now.

Or so say I. Common sense says something that sounds different: in wondering whether you will survive the battle, you wonder whether you—a continuant person consisting of your present stage along with many other stages—will continue beyond the battle. Will you be identical with anyone alive then? Likewise for other questions of personal identity.

Put this way, the two answers seem incomparable. It is pointless to compare the formal character of identity itself with the formal character of the relation R that matters in survival. Of course the R-relation among stages is not the same as identity either among stages or among continuants. But identity among continuant persons induces a relation among stages: the relation that holds between the several stages of

a single continuant person. Call this the *I-relation*. It is the I-relation, not identity itself, that we must compare with the R-relation. In wondering whether you will survive the battle, we said, you wonder whether the continuant person that includes your present stage is identical with any of the continuant persons that continue beyond the battle. In other words: whether it is identical with any of the continuant persons that include stages after the battle. In other words: you wonder whether any of the stages that will exist afterward is I-related to—belongs to the same person as—your present stage. If questions of survival, or personal identity generally, are questions of identity among continuant persons, then they are also questions of I-relatedness among person-stages; and conversely. More precisely: *if common sense is right that what matters in survival is identity among continuant persons, then you have what matters in survival if and only if your present stage is I-related to future stages.* I shall not distinguish henceforth between the thesis that what matters in survival is identity and the thesis that what matters in survival is the I-relation. Either way, it is a compelling platitude of common sense.

If ever a stage is R-related to some future stage but I-related to none, or if ever a stage is I-related to some future stage but R-related to none, then the platitude that what matters is the I-relation will disagree with the interesting thesis that what matters is the R-relation. But no such thing can happen, I claim; so there can be no such disagreement. In fact, I claim that *any stage is I-related and R-related to exactly the same stages.* And I claim this not only for the cases that arise in real life, but for all possible problem cases as well. Let us individuate relations, as is usual, by necessary coextensiveness. Then I claim that *the I-relation is the R-relation.*

A continuant person is an aggregate[4] of per-

---

[4]It does not matter what sort of "aggregate." I prefer a mereologial sum, so that the stages are literally parts of the continuant. But a class of stages would do as well, or a sequence or ordering of stages, or a suitable function from moments or stretches of time to stages.

son-stages, each one I-related to all the rest (and to itself). For short: a person is an I-*interr*elated aggregate. Moreover, a person is not part of any larger I-interrelated aggregate; for if we left out any stages that were I-related to one another and to all the stages we included, then what we would have would not be a whole continuant person but only part of one. For short: a person is a maximal I-interrelated aggregate. And conversely, any maximal I-interrelated aggregate of person-stages is a continuant person. At least, I cannot think of any that clearly is not.[5] So far we have only a small circle, from personhood to I-interrelatedness and back again. That is unhelpful; but if the I-relation is the R-relation, we have something more interesting: a noncircular definition of personhood. I claim that *something is a continuant person if and only if it is a maximal R-interrelated aggregate of person-stages.* That is: if and only if it is an aggregate of person-stages, each of which is R-related to all the rest (and to itself), and it is a proper part of no other such aggregate.

I cannot tolerate any discrepancy in formal character between the I-relation and the R-relation, for I have claimed that these relations are one and the same. Now although the admitted discrepancy between identity and the R-relation is harmless in itself, and although the I-relation is not identity, still it may seem that the I-relation inherits enough of the formal character of identity to lead to trouble. For suppose that S_1, S_2, . . . are person-stages; and suppose that C_1 is the continuant person of whom S_1 is a stage, C_2 is the continuant person of whom S_2 is a stage, and so on. Then any two of these stages S_i and S_j are I-related if and only if the corresponding continuant persons C_i and C_j are identical. The I-relations among the stages mirror the structure of the identity relations among the continuants.

I reply that the foregoing argument wrongly takes it for granted that every person-stage is a stage of one and only one continuant person. That is so ordinarily; and when that is so, the I-relation does inherit much of the formal character of identity. But ordinarily the R-relation also is well behaved. In the problem cases, however, it may happen that a single stage S is a stage of two or more different continuant persons. Worse, some or all of these may be persons to a diminished degree, so that it is questionable which of them should count as persons at all. If so, there would not be any such thing (in any straightforward way) as *the* person of whom S is a stage. So the supposition of the argument would not apply. It has not been shown that the I-relation inherits the formal character of identity in the problem cases. Rather it might be just as ill behaved as the R-relation. We shall examine the problem cases and see how that can happen.[6]

It would be wrong to read my definition of the I-relation as saying that person-stages S_1 and S_2 are I-related if and only if the continuant person of whom S_1 is a stage and the continuant person of whom S_2 is a stage are identical. The definite articles require the presupposition that I have just questioned. We should substitute the indefinite article: S_1 and S_2 are I-related if and only if a continuant person of whom S_1 is a stage and the continuant person of whom S_2 is a stage are identical. More simply: if and only if there is some one continuant person of whom both S_1 and S_2 are stages.

One seeming discrepancy between the I-relation and the R-relation need not disturb us. The I-relation must be symmetrical, whereas the R-relation has a direction. If a stage S_2 is mentally connected to a previous stage S_1, S_1 is available in memory to S_2 and S_2 is under the intentional control of S_1 to some extent — not the other way

---

[5]The least clear-cut cases are those in which the stages cannot be given any "personal time" ordering with respect to which they vary in the way that the stages of an ordinary person vary with respect to time. But it is so indeterminate what we want to say about such bizarre cases that they cannot serve as counter-examples to any of my claims.

[6]The argument also takes it for granted that every person-stage is a stage of at least one person. I do not object to that. If there is no way to unite a stage in a continuant with other stages, let it be a very short-lived continuant person all by itself.

around.[7] We can say that S_1 is R-related *forward* to S_2, whereas S_2 is R-related *backward* to S_1. The forward and backward R-relations are converses of one another. Both are (normally) antisymmetrical. But although we can distinguish the forward and backward R-relations, we can also merge them into a symmetrical relation. That is the R-relation I have in mind: S_1 and S_2 are R-related simpliciter if and only if S_1 is R-related either forward or backward to S_2.

While we are at it, let us also stipulate that every stage is R-related—forward, backward, and simpliciter—to itself. The R-relation, like the I-relation, is reflexive.

Parfit mentions two ways for a discrepancy to arise in the problem cases. First, the R-relation might be one-many or many-one. Second, the R-relation admits in principle of degree, and might be present to a degree that is markedly subnormal and yet not negligible. Both possibilities arise in connection with fission and fusion of continuant persons, and also in connection with immortality and longevity.

III. Fission and Fusion

Identity is one-one, in the sense that nothing is ever identical to two different things. Obviously neither the I-relation nor the R-relation is one-one in that sense. You-now are a stage of the same continuant as many other stages, and are R-related to them all. Many other stages are stages of the same continuant as you-now, and are R-related to you-now. But when Parfit says that the R-relation might be one-many or many-one, he does not just mean that. Rather, he means that one stage might be R-related to many stages that are not R-related to one another, and that many stages that are not R-related to one another might all be R-related to

one single stage. (These possibilities do not differ once we specify that the R-relation is to be taken as symmetrical.) In short, the R-relation might fail to be transitive.

In a case of fission, for instance, we have a prefission stage that is R-related forward to two different, simultaneous postfission stages that are not R-related either forward or backward to each other. The forward R-relation is one-many, the backward R-relation is many-one, and the R-relation simpliciter is intransitive.

In a case of fusion we have two prefusion stages, not R-related either forward or backward to each other, that are R-related forward to a single postfusion stage. The forward R-relation is many-one, the backward R-relation is one-many, and the R-relation simpliciter is again intransitive.

Identity must be transitive, but the I-relation is not identity. The I-relation will fail to be transitive if and only if there is partial overlap among continuant persons. More precisely: if and only if two continuant persons C_1 and C_2 have at least one common stage, but each one also has stages that are not included in the other. If S is a stage of both, S_1 is a stage of C_1 but not C_2, and S_2 is a stage of C_2 but not C_1, then transitivity of the I-relation fails. Although S_1 is I-related to S, which in turn is I-related to S_2, yet S_1 is not I-related to S_2. In order to argue that the I-relation, unlike the R-relation, must be transitive, it is not enough to appeal to the uncontroversial transitivity of identity. The further premise is needed that partial overlap of continuant persons is impossible.

Figure 1 shows how to represent fission and fusion as cases of partial overlap. The continuant persons involved, C_1 and C_2, are the two maximal R-interrelated aggregates of stages marked by the two sorts of cross-hatching. In the case of fission, the prefission stages are shared by both continuants. In the case of fusion, the postfusion stages are likewise shared. In each case, we have a shared stage S that is I-related to two stages S_1 and S_2 that are not

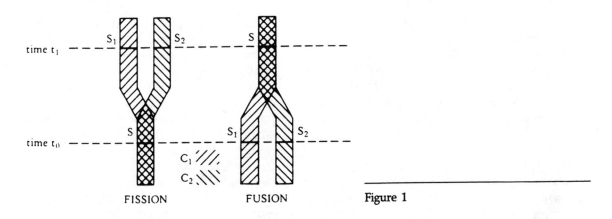

Figure 1

I-related to each other. Also S is R-related to S_1 and S_2 (forward in the case of fission, backward in the case of fusion) but S_1 and S_2 are not R-related to each other. More generally, the I-relation and the R-relation coincide for all stages involved in the affair.

There is, however, a strong reason for denying that continuant persons can overlap in this way. From this denial it would indeed follow (as it does not follow from the transitivity of identity alone) that the I-relation cannot share the possible intransitivities of the R-relation.

The trouble with overlap is that it leads to overpopulation. To count the population at a given time, we can count the continuant persons who have stages at that time; or we can count the stages. If there is overlap, there will be more continuants than stages. (I disregard the possibility that one of the continuants is a time traveler with distinct simultaneous stages.) The count of stages is the count we accept; yet we think we are counting persons, and we think of persons as continuants rather than stages. How, then, can we tolerate overlap?

For instance, we say that in a case of fission *one* person becomes *two*. By describing fission as initial stage-sharing we provide for the two, but

not for the one. There are two all along. It is all very well to say from an eternal or postfission standpoint that two persons (with a common initial segment) are involved, but we also demand to say that on the day before the fission only *one* person entered the duplication center; that his mother did not bear twins; that until he fissions he should only have one vote; and so on. Counting at a time, we insist on counting a person who will fission as one. We insist on a method of counting persons that agrees with the result of counting stages, though we do not think that counting persons just *is* counting (simultaneous) stages.

It is not so clear that we insist on counting a product of fusion as one (or a time traveler meeting himself as two). We are not sure what to say. But suppose we were fully devoted to the doctrine that the number of different persons in existence at a time is the number of different person-stages at that time. Even so, we would not be forced to deny that continuant persons could overlap. We would therefore not be driven to conclude that the I-relation cannot share the possible intransitivities of the R-relation.

The way out is to deny that we must invariably count two nonidentical continuants as two. We might count not by identity but by a weaker relation. Let us say that continuants C_1 and C_2 are *identical-at-time-t* if and only if they both exist at t and their stages at t are identical. (More precisely: C_1 and C_2 both have stages at t, and all and only stages of C_1 at t are stages of C_2 at t.) I shall speak of such relations of identity-at-a-time as relations of *tensed identity*. Tensed identity is not a kind of identity. It is not identity among stages, but rather a derivative relation among continuants which is induced by identity among stages. It is not identity among continuants, but rather a relation that is weaker than identity whenever different continuants have stages in common. If we count continuants by tensed identity rather than by identity, we will get the right answer—the answer that agrees with the answer we get by counting stages—even if there is overlap. How many persons entered the duplication center yesterday? We may reply: C_1 entered and C_2 entered, and no one else; although C_1 and C_2 are not identical today, and are not identical simpliciter, they were identical yesterday. So counting by identity-yesterday, there was only one. Counting by identity-today, there were two; but it is inappropriate to count by identity-today when we are talking solely about the events of yesterday. Counting by identity simpliciter there were two; but in talking about the events of yesterday it is as unnatural to count by identity as it is to count by identity-today. There is a way of counting on which there are two all along; but there is another way on which there are first one and then two. The latter has obvious practical advantages. It should be no surprise if it is the way we prefer.

It may seem far-fetched to claim that we ever count persons otherwise than by identity simpliciter. But we sometimes *do* count otherwise. If an infirm man wishes to know how many roads he must cross to reach his destination, I will count by identity-along-his-path rather than by identity. By crossing the Chester A. Arthur Parkway and Route 137 at the brief stretch where they have merged, he can cross both by crossing only one road. Yet these two roads are certainly not identical.

You may feel certain that you count persons by identity, not by tensed identity. But how can you be sure? Normal cases provide no evidence. When no stages are shared, both ways of counting agree. They differ only in the problem cases: fission, fusion, and another that we shall soon consider. The problem cases provide no very solid evidence either. They are problem cases just because we cannot consistently say quite all the things we feel inclined to. We must strike the best compromise among our conflicting initial opinions. Something must give way; and why not the opinion that of course we count by identity, if that is what can be sacrificed with least total damage?

A relation to count by does not have to be identity, as the example of the roads shows. But perhaps it should share the key properties of identity. It should at least be an *equivalence* relation: reflexive, symmetrical, and transitive. Relations of tensed identity are equivalence relations. Further, it should be an *indiscernibility* relation; not for all properties whatever, as identity is, but at least for some significant class of properties. That is, it ought to be that two related things have exactly the same properties in that class. Identity-at-time-t is an indiscernibility relation for a significant class of properties of continuant persons: those properties of a person which are logically determined by the properties of his stage at t. The class includes the properties of walking, being tall, being in a certain room, being thirsty, and believing in God at time t; but not the properties of being forty-three years old, gaining weight, being an ex-Communist, or remembering one's childhood at t. The class is sizable enough, at any rate, to make clear that a relation of tensed identity is more of an indiscernibility relation than is identity-along-a-path among roads.

If we are prepared to count a product of fusion as two, while still demanding to count a person who will fission as one, we can count at t by the relation of identity-at-all-times-up-to-t. This is the relation that holds between continuants C_1 and C_2 if and only if (1) they both exist at some time no later than t, (2) at any time no later than t, either both exist or neither does, and (3) at any time no later than t when both exist, they have exactly the same stages. Again, this is a relation among continuants that is weaker than identity to the extent that continuants share stages. Although derived from identity (among stages) it is of course not itself identity. It is even more of an indiscernibility relation than identity-at-t, since it confers indiscernibility with respect to such properties as being forty-three years old, gaining weight (in one sense), being an ex-Communist, and remembering one's childhood at t; though still not with respect to such properties as being, at t, the next winner of the State Lottery.

It may be disconcerting that we can have a single name for one person (counting by tensed identity) who is really two nonidentical persons because he will later fission. Isn't the name ambiguous? Yes; but so long as its two bearers are indiscernible in the respects we want to talk about, the ambiguity is harmless. If C_1 and C_2 are identical-at-all-times-up-to-now and share the name "Ned" it is idle to disambiguate such remarks as "Ned is tall," "Ned is waiting to be duplicated," "Ned is frightened," "Ned only decided yesterday to do it," and the like. These will be true on both disambiguations of "Ned," or false on both. Before the fission, only predictions need disambiguating. After the fission, on the other hand, the ambiguity of "Ned" will be much more bother. It can be expected that the ambiguous name "Ned" will then fall into disuse, except when we wish to speak of the shared life of C_1 and C_2 before the fission.

But what if we don't know whether Ned will fission? In that case, we don't know whether the one person Ned (counting by identity-now) is one person, or two, or many (counting by iden-tity). Then we don't know whether "Ned" is ambiguous or not. But if the ambiguity is not a practical nuisance, we don't need to know. We can wait and see whether or not we have been living with a harmless ambiguity.

This completes my discussion of fission and fusion. To summarize: if the R-relation is the I-relation, and in particular if continuant persons are maximal R-interrelated aggregates of person-stages, then cases of fission and fusion must be treated as cases of stage-sharing between different, partially overlapping continuant persons. If so, the R-relation and the I-relation are alike intransitive, so there is no discrepancy on that score. If it is granted that we may count continuant persons by tensed identity, then this treatment does not conflict with our opinion that in fission one person becomes two; nor with our opinion (if it really is our opinion) that in fusion two persons become one.

IV. Longevity

I turn now to a different problem case. Parfit has noted that mental connectedness will fade away eventually. If the R-relation is a matter of direct connectedness as well as continuity, then intransitivities of the R-relation will appear in the case of a person (if it is a person!) who lives too long.

Consider Methuselah. At the age of 100 he still remembers his childhood. But new memories crowd out the old. At the age of 150 he has hardly any memories that go back before his twentieth year. At the age of 200 he has hardly any memories that go back before his seventieth year; and so on. When he dies at the age of 969, he has hardly any memories that go beyond his 839th year. As he grows older he grows wiser; his callow opinions and character at age 90 have vanished almost without a trace by age 220, but his opinions and character at age 220 also have vanished almost without a trace by age 350. He soon learns that it is futile to set goals for himself too far ahead. At age 120, he is still somewhat interested in fulfilling the ambitions he held at age 40; but at age 170 he cares nothing for those ambitions, and it is beginning to take an effort of will to summon up an interest in fulfilling his aspirations at age 80. And so it goes.

We sometimes say: in later life I will be a different person. For us short-lived creatures, such remarks are an extravagance. A philosophical study of personal identity can ignore them. For Methuselah, however, the fading-out of personal identity looms large as a fact of life. It is incumbent on us to make it literally true that he will be a different person after one and one-half centuries or so.

I should imagine that this is so just in virtue of normal aging over 969 years. If you disagree, imagine that Methuselah lives much longer than a bare millennium (Parfit imagines the case of immortals who change mentally at the same rate as we do). Or imagine that his life is punctuated by frequent amnesias, brain-washings, psychoanalyses, conversions, and what not, each one of which is almost (but not quite) enough to turn him into a different person.

Suppose, for simplicity, that any two stages of Methuselah that are separated by no more than 137 years are R-related; and any two of his stages that are separated by more than 137 years are not R-related. (For the time being, we may pretend that R-relatedness is all-or-nothing, with a sharp cutoff.)

If the R-relation and the I-relation are the same, this means that two of Methuselah's stages belong to a single continuant person if and only if they are no more than 137 years apart. (Therefore the whole of Methuselah is not a single person.) That is the case, in particular, if continuant persons are maximal R-interrelated aggregates. For if so, then segments of Methuselah are R-interrelated if and only if they are no more than 137 years long; whence it follows that all and only the segments that are

exactly 137 years long are maximal R-interrelated aggregates; so all and only the 137-year segments are continuant persons.

If so, we have intransitivity both of the R-relation and of the I-relation. Let S_1 be a stage of Methuselah at the age of 400; let S_2 be a stage of Methuselah at the age of 500; let S_3 be a stage of Methuselah at the age of 600. By hypothesis S_1 is R-related to S_2 and S_2 is R-related to S_3, but S_1 and S_3 are not R-related. Being separated by 200 years, they have no direct mental connections. Since S_1 and S_2 are linked by a 137-year segment (in fact, by infinitely many) they are I-related; likewise S_2 and S_3 are I-related. But S_1 and S_3 are not linked by any 137-year segment, so they are not I-related. The R-relation and the I-relation are alike intransitive.

The problem of overpopulation is infinitely worse in the case of Methuselah than in the cases of fission or fusion considered hitherto. Methuselah spends his 300th birthday alone in his room. How many persons are in that room? There are infinitely many different 137-year segments that include all of Methuselah's stages on his 300th birthday. One begins at the end of Methuselah's 163rd birthday and ends at the end of his 300th birthday; another begins at the beginning of his 300th and ends at the beginning of his 437th. Between these two are a continuum of other 137-year segments. No two of them are identical. Every one of them puts in an appearance (has a stage) in Methuselah's room on Methuselah's 300th birthday. Every one of them is a continuant person, given our supposition that Methuselah's stages are R-related if and only if they are not more than 137 years apart, and given that continuant persons are all and only maximal R-interrelated aggregates of person-stages. It begins to seem crowded in Methuselah's room!

Tensed identity to the rescue once more. True, there are continuum many non-identical continuant persons in the room. But, counting by the appropriate relation of tensed identity, there is only one. All the continuum many nonidentical continuant persons are identical-at-the-time-in-question, since they all share the single stage at that time. Granted that we may count by tensed identity, there is no over-crowding.

V. Degree

We turn now to the question of degree. Identity certainly cannot be a matter of degree. But the I-relation is not defined in terms of identity alone. It derives also from personhood: the property of being a continuant person. Thus personal identity may be a matter of degree because personhood is a matter of degree, even though identity is not. Suppose two person-stages S_1 and S_2 are stages of some one continuant that is a person to a low, but not negligible, degree. Suppose further that they are not stages of anything else that is a person to any higher degree. Then they are I-related to a low degree. So if personhood admits of degree, we have no discrepancy in formal character between the I-relation and the R-relation.

Parfit suggests, for instance, that if you fuse with someone very different, yielding a fusion product mentally halfway between you and your partner, then it is questionable whether you have survived. Not that there is a definite, unknown answer. Rather, what matters in survival—the R-relation—is present in reduced degree. There is less of it than in clear cases of survival, more than in clear cases of non-survival.[8] If we want the I-relation and the R-relation to coincide, we may take it that C_1 and C_2 (see Fig. 1 for cases of fusion) are persons to reduced degree because they are broken

by abrupt mental discontinuities. If persons are maximal R-interrelated aggregates, as I claim, that is what we should expect; the R-relations across the fusion point are reduced in degree, hence the R-interrelatedness of C_1 and C_2 is reduced in degree, and hence the personhood of C_1 and C_2 is reduced in degree. C_1 and C_2 have less personhood than clear cases of persons, more personhood than continuant aggregates of stages that are clearly not persons. Then S and S_1, or S and S_2, are I-related to reduced degree just as they are R-related to reduced degree.

Personal identity to reduced degrees is found also in the case of Methuselah. We supposed before that stages no more than 137 years apart are R-related while stages more than 137 years apart were not. But if the R-relation fades away at all—if it is a relation partly of connectedness as well as continuity—it would be more realistic to suppose that it fades away gradually. We can suppose that stages within 100 years of each other are R-related to a high enough degree so that survival is not in doubt; and that stages 200 or more years apart are R-related to such a low degree that what matters in survival is clearly absent. There is no significant connectedness over long spans of time, only continuity. Then if we want the R-relation and the I-relation to coincide, we could say roughly this: 100-year segments of Methuselah are persons to a high degree, whereas 200-year segments are persons only to a low degree. Then two stages that are strongly R-related also are strongly I-related, whereas stages that are weakly R-related are also weakly I-related. Likewise for all the intermediate degrees of R-relatedness of stages, of personhood of segments of Methuselah, and hence of I-relatedness of stages.

It is a familiar idea that personhood might admit of degrees. Most of the usual examples, however, are not quite what I have in mind. They concern continuants that are said to be persons to a reduced degree because their stages are thought to be person-stages to a reduced

---

[8] No similar problem arises in cases of fission. We imagine that immediate postfission stages to be pretty much alike, wherefore they can all be strongly R-related to the immediate prefission stages.

degree. If anyone thinks that the wolf-child, the "dehumanized" proletarian, or the human vegetable is not fully a person, that is more because he regards the stages themselves as deficient than because the stages are not strongly enough R-interrelated. If anyone thinks that personhood is partly a matter of species membership, so that a creature of sorcery or a freak offspring of hippopotami could not be fully a person no matter how much he resembled the rest of us, that also would be a case in which the stages themselves are thought to be deficient. In this case the stages are thought to be deficient not in their intrinsic character but in their causal ancestry; there is, however, nothing wrong with their R-interrelatedness. A severe case of split personality, on the other hand, does consist of perfectly good person-stages that are not very well R-related. If he is said not to be fully a person, that *is* an example of the kind of reduced personhood that permits us to claim that the R-relation and the I-relation alike admit of degrees.

Let us ignore the complications introduced by deficient person-stages. Let us assume that all the stages under consideration are person-stages to more or less the highest possible degree. (More generally, we could perhaps say that the degree of I-relatedness of two stages depends not on the absolute degree of personhood of the continuant, if any, that links them; but rather on the relative degree of personhood of that continuant compared to the greatest degree of personhood that the degree of person-stage-hood of the stages could permit. If two wolf-child-stages are person-stages only to degree 0.8, but they are stages of a continuant that is a person to degree 0.8, we can say that the stages are thereby I-related to degree 1.)

If we say that a continuant person is an aggregate of R-interrelated person-stages, it is clear that personhood admits of degree to the extent that the R-relation does. We can say something like this: the degree of R-interrelatedness of an aggregate is the minimum degree of R-relatedness between any two stages in the aggregate. (Better: the greatest lower bound on the degrees of R-relatedness between any two stages.) But when we recall that a person should be a maximal such aggregate, confusion sets in. Suppose we have an aggregate that is R-interrelated to degree 0.9, and it is not included in any larger aggregate that is R-interrelated to degree 0.9 or greater. Suppose, however, that it *is* included in a much larger aggregate that is R-interrelated to degree 0.88. We know the degree to which it qualifies as an R-interrelated aggregate, but to what degree does it qualify as a maximal one? That is, to what degree does it qualify as a person, if persons are maximal R-interrelated aggregates? I am inclined to say: it passes the R-interrelatedness test for personhood to degree 0.9, but at the same time it flunks the maximality test to degree 0.88. Therefore it is a person only to degree 0.02!

This conclusion leads to trouble. Take the case of Methuselah. Assuming that R-relatedness fades out gradually, every segment that passes the R-interrelatedness test to a significant degree also flunks the maximality test to almost the same degree. (If the fadeout is continuous, delete "almost.") So *no* segment of Methuselah passes both tests for personhood to any significant degree. No two stages, no matter how close, are stages of some *one* continuant that is a person to high degree. Rather, nearby stages are strongly I-related by being common to many continuants, each one of which is strongly R-interrelated, is almost as strongly non-maximal, and therefore is a person only to a low degree.

We might sum the degrees of personhood of all the continuants that link two stages, taking the sum to be the degree of I-relatedness of the stages.

But there is a better way. Assume that R-relatedness can come in all degrees ranging from 0 to 1 on some scale. Then every number in the interval from 0 to 1 is a possible location for an arbitrary boundary between pairs of stages that are R-related and pairs that are not. Call every such number a *delineation* of this boundary. Every delineation yields a decision as to which stages are R-related. It thereby yields a decision as to which continuants are R-interrelated; a decision as to which continuants are included in larger R-interrelated aggregates; a decision as to which continuants are persons, given that persons are maximal R-interrelated aggregates; and thence a decision as to which stages are I-related. We can say that a certain continuant is a person, or that a certain pair of stages are I-related, *relative* to a given delineation. We can also say whether something is the case relative to a set of delineations, provided that all the delineations in the set agree on whether it is the case. Then we can take the degree to which it is the case as the size (more precisely: Lebesgue measure) of that set. Suppose, for instance, that two stages count as I-related when we set the cut-off for R-relatedness anywhere from 0 to 0.9, but not when we set the cut-off more stringently between 0.9 and 1. Then those two stages are I-related relative to delineations from 0 to 0.9, but not relative to delineations from 0.9 to 1. They are I-related to degree 0.9—the size of the delineation interval on which they are I-related. Yet there may not be any continuant linking those stages that is a person to degree more than 0. It may be that any continuant that links those stages is both R-interrelated and maximal only at a single delineation. At any more stringent delineation, it is no longer R-interrelated; while at any less stringent delineation it is still R-interrelated but not maximal.

The strategy followed here combines two ideas. (1) When something is a matter of degree, we can introduce a cutoff point. However, the choice of this cutoff point is more or less arbitrary. (2) When confronted with an arbitrary choice, the thing to do is not to make the choice. Rather, we should see what is common to all or most ways (or all or most reasonable ways) of making the choice, caring little what happens on any particular way of making it. The second idea is van Fraassen's method of supervaluations.[9]

On this proposal the I-relation admits of degree; and further, we get perfect agreement between degrees of I-relatedness and degrees of R-relatedness, regardless of the degrees of personhood of continuants. For at any one delineation, two stages are R-related if and only if they belong to some one maximal R-interrelated aggregate; hence if and only if they belong to some one continuant person; hence if and only if they are I-related. Any two stages are R-related and I-related relative to exactly the same set of delineations. Now if two stages are R-related to a degree X, it follows (given our choice of scale and measure) that they are R-related at all and only the delineations in a certain set of size x. Therefore they are I-related at all and only the delineations in a certain set of size x; which means that they are I-related to degree x. The degree of I-relatedness equals the degree of R-relatedness. In this way personal identity can be just as much a matter of degree as the mental continuity or connectedness that matters in survival. . . . *

Postscripts to "Survival and Identity"

A. Two Minds with But a Single Thought

Derek Parfit rejects my attempt to square his views (which are mine as well) with common sense.[10] He objects that before I bring off the

---

[9]See Bas van Fraassen, "Singular Terms, Truth-Value Gaps, and Free Logic," *Journal of Philosophy* 63 (1966): 481–95. See also the discussion of vagueness in my "General Semantics," *Synthese* 22 (1970), 18–67.

*Editors' Note: Here we omit a final section in which Lewis compares his treatment with that of John Perry, "Can the Self Divide?", *Journal of Philosophy* 69 (1972), 463–88.

[10]"Lewis, Perry and What Matters," in Amélie Rorty, *The Identities of Persons* (Berkeley: University of California Press, 1976), pp. 91–96.

reconciliation, I must first misrepresent our commonsensical desire to survive. Consider a fission case as shown. I say there are two continuant persons all along, sharing their initial segments. One of them, C_1, dies soon after the fission. The other, C_2, lives on for many years. Let S be a shared stage at time t_0, before the fission but after it is known that fission will occur. The thought to be found in S is a desire for survival, of the most commonsensical and unphilosophical kind possible. Since S is a shared stage, this desire is a shared desire. Certainly C_2 has the survival he desired, and likewise has what we think matters: mental continuity and connectedness (the R-relation) between S and much later stages such as S_2. But how about C_1?

I wrote that "if common sense is right that what matters in survival is identity . . . , then you have what matters in survival if and only if your present stage is I-related to future stages" where stages are I-related if they belong to some single continuant person.* If that is right, then

C_1 has what he commonsensically desired. For C_1's stage S at time t_0 is indeed I-related to stages far in the future such as S_2. These stages are I-related via the person C_2—"But isn't this the *wrong* person?" says Parfit. C_1 himself survives only a short time. The one who lives longer is another person, one with whom C_1 once shared stages. If his desire is satisfied by this vicarious survival, it cannot really have been a commonsensical desire to survive.

If C_1 really had the commonsensical desire that he himself—the continuant person C_1—survive well into the future, then I grant that his desire is not satisfied. But I don't think he could have had exactly that desire. I said that the desire found in S was to be *of the most commonsensical and unphilosophical kind possible*. And there is a limit to how commonsensical one's desires can possibly be under the peculiar circumstance of stage-sharing.

The shared stage S does the thinking for both of the continuants to which it belongs. Any thought it has must be shared. It cannot desire one thing on behalf of C_1 and another thing on behalf of C_2. If it has an urgent, self-interested desire for survival on the part of C_1, that very thought must also be an urgent, self-interested (and not merely benevolent) desire for survival on the part of C_2. It is not possible that one thought should be both. So it is not possible for S to have such a desire on behalf of C_1. So it is not possible for C_1 at t_0 to have the straightforward commonsensical desire that he himself survive.

If C_1 and C_2 share the most commonsensical kind of desire to survive that is available to them under the circumstances, it must be a plural desire: let *us* survive. Now we must distinguish two different plural desires: existential and universal, weak and strong.

(weak)   Let at least one of us survive.

(strong)   Let all of us survive.

Figure 2

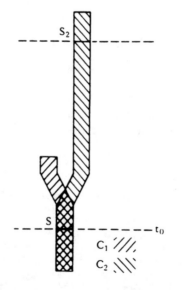

*Editors' Note: Pages 276–77, this volume.

Because these desires are plural instead of singular, they are not perfectly commonsensical. Because they are put in terms of survival of continuants rather than relations of stages, they are more commonsensical than the "philosophical" desire for R-relatedness of one's present stage to future stages.

If C_1's (imperfectly) commonsensical desire for survival is predominantly the weak desire, then my reconciliation goes through. For C_1's weak desire is satisfied even though it is his stage-sharer rather than himself who survives. The weak desire is indeed equivalent to a desire for I-relatedness to future stages. Then if I am right that the I-relation is the R-relation, it is equivalent also to the desire for R-relatedness to future stages.

If C_1's desire is predominantly the strong desire, on the other hand, it is not satisfied. Then his desire for survival is not equivalent to the "philosophical" desire for R-relatedness to future stages, and my reconciliation fails. (However, the strong desire is equivalent to a more complicated desire concerning R-relatedness of stages.) But should we say that C_1 has the strong desire, and that since it is not satisfied, he does not have what commonsensically matters in survival? I think not. For if we say that of C_1, we must say it also of C_2. If one has the strong desire, both do. The strong desire is no more satisfied for C_2 than it is for C_1. But it seems clear that C_2, at least, *does* have what commonsensically matters in survival.

It is instructive to consider a system of survival insurance described by Justin Leiber, in *Beyond Rejection*.[11] (But let us imagine it without the risks and unpleasantness that Leiber supposes.) From time to time your mind is recorded; should a fatal accident befall you, the latest recording is played back into the blank brain of a fresh body. This system satisfies the weak desire for survival, but not the strong desire. Let S at t_0 be the stage that desires survival and

therefore decides to have a recording made; the fission occurs at the time of recording; C_1 dies in an accident not long after; C_2 survives. The only extra peculiarities, compared with a simple case of fission, are that C_2 is interrupted in time and undergoes a body transplant. If this system would fairly well satisfy your desire for survival—or if your misgivings about it concern the body transplant rather than the fission—then your desire is predominantly the weak desire.

So far, I have supposed that C_1 and C_2 at t_0 already anticipate their fission. Now suppose not. Now, cannot they share the perfectly commonsensical singular desire: let *me* survive? After all, the desire to be found in the stage S in this case is no different from the desire that would be there if S were what it takes itself to be: a stage of a single person with no fission in his future. I agree that C_1 and C_2 have the singular desire. But it is not a desire that can be satisfied, for it rests on the false presupposition that they are a single person. The "me" in their shared thought (unless it refers to the thinking stage) has the status of an improper description. It cannot refer to C_1 in C_1's thought, and to C_2 in C_2's thought for these thoughts are one and the same. But their desire to survive *is* satisfied; at least C_2's is, and C_1's is no different. Therefore their desire for survival cannot consist only of their unsatisfiable singular desire. They must have the weak plural desire as well, despite the fact that they don't anticipate fission. And so must we. Doubtless we seldom have it as an occurrent desire. But many of our urgent desires are not occurrent, for instance your present desire not to suffer a certain torture too fiendish for you to imagine.

(At this point the reader of "Attitudes *De Dicto* and *De Se*" [*Philosophical Review* 88 (1979), 513–43] may wonder how well I have learned my own lesson. There I taught that desire is a relation of wanting-to-have—take this as indivisible—that the subject bears to a property. Why can't C_1 and C_2 bear the very same

[11](New York: Ballantine, 1980).

wanting-to-have relation to the very same property of surviving, so that they think the very same thought, and yet each thereby desire his own survival? But recall that the subject that wants-to-have properties was taken to be a stage, not a continuant. (See pages [527, 531].) Under this analysis, my point is that S's wanting-to-have the property

   being such that the unique continuant of which it is a stage survives

is an unsatisfiable desire. That is so whether we think of it as a desire of S's or, more naturally, as the desire of C_1 and C_2. S had better want survival on behalf of C_1 and C_2 by wanting to have a different property:

   being such that some continuant of which it is a stage survives.

This is the satisfied desire for survival that C_1 and C_2 share.)

B. In Defense of Stages[12]

Some would protest that they do not know what I mean by "more or less momentary person-stages, or time-slices of continuant persons, or persons-at-times." Others do know what I mean, but don't believe there are any such things.

The first objection is easy to answer, especially in the case where the stages are less momentary rather than more. Let me consider that case only; though I think that instantaneous stages also are unproblematic, I do not really

[12]On this topic I am much indebted to discussions with Saul Kripke and with Denis Robinson. Kripke's views on related matters were presented in his lectures on "Identity through Time," given at Princeton in 1978 (and elsewhere); Robinson's in "Re-Identifying Matter," *Philosophical Review* 91 (1982) 317–341.

need them. A person-stage is a physical object, just as a person is. (If persons had a ghostly part as well, so would person-stages.) It does many of the same things that a person does: it talks and walks and thinks, it has beliefs and desires, it has a size and shape and location. It even has a temporal duration. But only a brief one, for it does not last long. (We can pass over the question how long it can last before it is a segment rather than a stage, for that question raises no objection of principle.) It begins to exist abruptly, and it abruptly ceases to exist soon after. Hence a stage cannot do everything that a person can do, for it cannot do those things that a person does over a longish interval.

That is what I mean by a person-stage. Now to argue for my claim that they exist, and that they are related to persons as part to whole. I do not suppose the doubters will accept my premises, but it will be instructive to find out which they choose to deny.

First: it is possible that a person-stage might exist. Suppose it to appear out of thin air, then vanish again. Never mind whether it is a stage *of* any person (though in fact I think it is). My point is that it is the right sort of thing.

Second: it is possible that two person-stages might exist in succession, one right after the other but without overlap. Further, the qualities and location of the second at its appearance might exactly match those of the first at its disappearance. Here I rely on a *patchwork principle* for possibility: if it is possible that X happen intrinsically in a spatiotemporal region, and if it is likewise possible that Y happen in a region, then also it is possible that both X and Y happen in two distinct but adjacent regions. There are no necessary incompatibilities between distinct existences. Anything can follow anything.

Third: extending the previous point, it is possible that there might be a world of stages that is exactly like our own world in its point-by-point distribution of intrinsic local qualities over space and time.

Fourth: further, such a world of stages might

also be exactly like our own in its causal relations between local matters of particular fact. For nothing but the distribution of local qualities constrains the pattern of causal relations. (It would be simpler to say that the causal relations supervene on the distribution of local qualities, but I am not as confident of that as I am of the weaker premise.)

Fifth: then such a world of stages would be exactly like our own simpliciter. There are no features of our world except those that supervene on the distribution of local qualities and their causal relations.

Sixth: then our own world is a world of stages. In particular, person-stages exist.

Seventh: but persons exist too, and persons (in most cases) are not person-stages. They last too long. Yet persons and person-stages, like tables and table-legs, do not occupy spatiotemporal regions twice over. That can only be because they are not distinct. They are part-identical; in other words, the person-stages are parts of the persons.

Let me try to forestall two misunderstandings.

(1) When I say that persons are maximal R-interrelated aggregates of person-stages, I do *not* claim to be reducing "constructs" to "more basic entities." (Since I do not intend a reduction to the basic, I am free to say without circularity that person-stages are R-interrelated aggregates of shorter person-stages.) Similarly, I think it is an informative necessary truth that trains are maximal aggregates of cars interrelated by the ancestral of the relation of being coupled together (count the locomotive as a special kind of car). But I do not think of this as a reduction to the basic. Whatever "more basic" is supposed to mean, I don't think it means "smaller." (2) By a part, I just mean a subdivision. I do not mean a well-demarcated subdivision that figures as a unit in causal explanation. Those who give "part" a rich meaning along these lines[13] should take me to mean less by it than they do.

[13]Such as D. H. Mellor, in his *Real Time* (Cambridge: Cambridge University Press, 1981), chapter 8.

18

RAYMOND MARTIN
Identity, Transformation, and What Matters in Survival

We never vanish without a trace. Even in death, the stuff into which we decompose continues. Most of it is recomposed into other things, often things that are alive. We are food for worms.

For those of us who want to continue, these facts are small comfort. Why exactly? Is it because transformation is not good enough—because we want to preserve our identities? Or is it because the things into which we transform —worms, perhaps—are not good enough?

Transformation *is* good enough. The problem is worms. I shall argue that many of us, if we could choose what we would transform into, would not only be satisfied with transformation but would actually prefer it to continuing as the persons we now are. More specifically, I shall argue that many of us would choose to cease to exist if, by so choosing, we could transform into the (sorts of) persons we most want to be.

There are two situations in which some would choose to cease to exist that are not directly relevant to what I want to consider. First, many of us, if all of our options were very grim, would prefer, for our own sakes, to cease to exist; for instance, doomed to a life of continuously severe pain, many of us would prefer to die. Second, a few of us who are very altruistic might, under certain circumstances, choose, for the sake of others, to die; that is, even if we had selfish options that were good, we might sacrifice our own good to promote the good of others.

The situation I want to consider is one in which we are given a choice among at least as good a set of alternatives as those we are typically given in our lives and we choose just for our own sakes, that is, to promote selfish ends. The question is whether, under such circumstances, we might nevertheless choose cessation. In other words, when there is a way of our continuing that preserves our identities and is much better than death, would we ever nevertheless rather cease to exist (not for the sake of others, but for our own sakes) than to continue? I shall argue that under such circumstances many of us would rather cease to exist than to continue, provided that in ceasing to exist we could transform into the persons we most want to be.

Since several contemporary philosophers have already tried to show that we would sometimes rather cease to exist than to continue even when there is a way of our continuing that preserves our identities and is better than death, I want to begin, in part I, by explaining why

their arguments have not settled the issue. The reason, in a nutshell, is that their arguments have depended on fission examples. Then, in parts II and III, I shall offer an argument of my own that does not depend on a fission example.

I

The question "Under what conditions is your personal identity preserved?" should be sharply distinguished from the question "Under what conditions is what matters primarily to you in survival preserved?" The first question asks (among other things) for a specification of the conditions under which someone in the future would be the same person as you are now. The second asks for the conditions under which the existence of someone (or something) in the future would preserve what now matters primarily to you in survival.

It is extremely difficult to define what it means for something to matter *in survival*.[1] Here I shall merely try to illustrate the idea with a clear example in which, depending on which criterion of personal identity we assume, you (or someone) might be able to preserve what matters primarily to you in survival even without preserving your personal identity.

Suppose you are contemplating a trip to Mars and there are two means available to get there. First, you could enter a Star Trek–style "beamer" on Earth that recorded exact and complete information about your body, brain, and psychology, and, as it did so, dematerialized you on Earth and sent the information to Mars where, a few minutes later, it was used to create an exact replica of you—body, brain, and psychology—out of new, but qualitatively

---

[1] I discuss this problem in "Identity's Crisis," *Philosophical Studies*, v. 53, 1988, pp. 295–307, particularly in connection with Derek Parfit's views, and attempt to solve it in *The Many Faces of Self* (tentative title), forthcoming.

similar, matter. Second, you could board a conventional spaceship, go to sleep for two weeks, and then, soon after landing on Mars, wake up again with no unusual side effects. Physically and psychologically it would be just as if you had taken an ordinary, two-hour-long nap on Earth.

It is controversial whether *you* would survive the beaming procedure. Several philosophers have argued for views that imply that, in such a procedure, the person on Mars would not be you but only an exact replica, and that you would cease to exist.[2] Assume, for the sake of argument, that these philosophers are right. The outcome of both procedures is that there is someone on Mars who is at least very similar to you on Earth just before the trip. In the first case, this person on Mars is not you, but an exact replica; in the second, he is you.

The crucial question is this. Excluding all altruistic considerations and thinking just "selfishly," how much would it matter to you that if you were to go to Mars the first way you would not survive the trip? People who have considered this question disagree sharply on the answer—to some it would matter a great deal, to others not much. If it would not matter much to you—if, say, you would rather enter the beamer and have your replica be given a large sum of money once he emerges on Mars than take the conventional spaceship and receive nothing on the other end—then the beamer, even though it does not preserve your identity, preserves what matters primarily to you in survival.

Returning to the distinction between the two questions, if preserving *yourself* is what matters primarily to you in survival, then the question "Under what conditions is your personal identity preserved?" and the question "Under what conditions is what matters primarily to you in survival preserved?" will have the same answer. Otherwise, they may have different answers.

For hundreds of years, and until recently, philosophers assumed that both of these questions had the same answer. It was obvious to them that identity is what matters primarily in survival. It is not *obvious* to many today. In the 1970s and 1980s several philosophers argued persuasively that other things matter more than identity.[3] According to the philosophers who hold this new view, the reason identity is often mistakenly thought to be what matters primarily in survival is that in real life identity is all but invariably correlated with what does matter primarily in survival, say, close physical and psychological continuity.

The consideration of fission cases, that is, hypothetical cases in which a person somehow splits into two persons each of whom is exactly similar to the original person, is what originally motivated this new view.[4] Suppose, for instance, someone's brain is divided (call her "Eve") and each half of her brain is then transplanted into its own new (brainless) body (call the persons that result "Bea" and "Coe," respectively). Before division each half of Eve's brain is exactly similar to the other half and is also psychologically redundant, so that immediately after division the resulting persons—Bea

[2]See, for instance, Mark Johnston, "Human Beings," *The Journal of Philosophy*, v. 84, 1987, and Peter Unger, *Identity, Consciousness and Value*, Oxford University Press, 1990. See selection 13, this volume.

[3]See, for instance, Derek Parfit, "Personal Identity," *Philosophical Review*, v. 80, 1971, pp. 3–27; Robert Nozick, *Philosophical Explanations*, Harvard University Press, 1981, chap. 1; Sydney Shoemaker, "Personal Identity. A Materialist Account," in Sydney Shoemaker and Richard Swinburne, *Personal Identity*, Basic Blackwell, 1984, pp. 67–132; and Derek Parfit, *Reasons and Persons*, Oxford University Press, 1984, Ch. 12.

[4]See David Wiggins, *Identity and Spatio-Temporal Continuity*, Oxford: Basic Blackwell, 1967, p. 50. Consideration of spectra of closely related cases (see, for instance, the first two selections by Parfit in this volume) have also been used to devalue identity, but they are less useful than fission cases for determining whether we would be willing to trade our identities for other benefits.

and Coe—each has all and only the psychological characteristics that Eve had—the same character traits, the same beliefs, the same tastes, and so on. Suppose Bea and Coe have bodies exactly similar to each other's and to Eve's body.

Many philosophers believe Eve does not survive this operation. The reason is that neither Bea nor Coe is the same person as Eve. The argument for this view—henceforth, "the Fission Argument"—is this. Since Bea and Coe each have an equal claim to be the same person as Eve, neither can be the same person as Eve unless both are. But if both Bea and Coe are the same person as Eve, then Bea and Coe are the same person as each other (identity is a transitive relationship: If X is identical to Y, and Y to Z, then X is identical to Z). Bea and Coe, at least once they begin to lead independent lives, are not the same person. Thus, neither Bea nor Coe is the same person as Eve. Since it is implausible to suppose that Eve survives the operation as a person that includes both Bea and Coe (in other words, that there are three people who emerge from the operation, Bea, Coe, and Bea–Coe), the fission operation does not preserve Eve's identity. By the time the operation is complete (or soon after), Eve has ceased to exist. Even so, the outcome of Eve's operation may be better, from Eve's point of view, than all of the available alternatives that preserve her identity.

Suppose, for instance, that although Eve's brain is healthy, her body is ridden with cancer, and that Eve's only hope for survival is to have her healthy brain transplanted into at least one healthy body.[5] Two procedures are available. The first is to have her entire brain put into a single healthy body. The second is to have her brain split, as in the fission operation, and the two halves of it put into two separate healthy bodies. Suppose, for some esoteric reason having to do with brain transplants, there is only a 10 percent chance the transplantation will take if Eve adopts the first procedure (if it does not take, Eve will be severely mentally retarded), but there is a 95 percent chance *both* transplantations will take if Eve adopts the second procedure. Which procedure should Eve choose?

According to the Fission Argument, if Eve chooses the first procedure and the transplantation takes, she will be the same person as the recipient of her brain, whereas if Eve chooses the second procedure and both transplantations take, she will not be the same person as either of the recipients of half of her brain. In other words, if Eve chooses the first procedure and the transplantation takes, she will preserve her identity, whereas if Eve chooses the second procedure and both transplantations take, she will fail to preserve her identity, that is, she will cease to exist. Even so, it seems obvious, on at least some ways of fleshing out this example, that Eve should choose the second procedure. This shows that Eve's preserving her identity, that is, continuing to exist, should not (and, if she were typical, probably would not) matter as much to her in survival as her promoting other values she has, in particular, that of significantly increasing her changes of continuing her psychology in a body as good as her current body.

The Fission Argument depends on a "thought experiment" in which events are depicted that could not happen in real life, at least not soon. The halves of our brains are not equivalent. Even if they were equivalent, we could not successfully transplant them into healthy bodies in the ways just envisaged. So, there may never actually be a fission operation that separates identity from other characteristics, such as psychological continuity, that normally accompany it. Some say this undermines the evidential value of the Fission Argument's thought experiment. In fact, it is precisely why it has so much value.

The purpose of this thought experiment is to

[5]This example is based on one presented by Sydney Shoemaker in "Personal Identity. A Materialist Account," p. 119, (p. 271, this volume).

separate identity from other characteristics that normally accompany it in real life. If it succeeds in doing this, we are given an opportunity to decide which we would choose if we were able to choose between identity and these other characteristics. Without such a thought experiment it would be extremely difficult to elicit these preferences. If we decide that identity is not what matters most, that is, if we would choose other things over identity, that decision is evidence that *in real life* identity only seems to be of central importance but is not really, because other things that are more important than identity get confused with it. Thus, although the thought experiment is about a rather fanciful hypothetical situation, the outcome of it is evidence about what actually matters to us in survival, not at some time in the technologically distant future, but right now. The thought experiment is a way of revealing our current beliefs and values.

Still, the Fission Argument is controversial. For one thing, it depends on the assumption that identity is a transitive relationship. Although some philosophers have questioned this assumption, not many have been willing to give it up. The reason is that the assumption that identity is transitive is so well entrenched in the ways we think about identity that a persuasive argument that identity should not be regarded as transitive would have to specify the circumstances under which we are and are not entitled to infer from the fact that X is identical to Y, and Y to Z, the conclusion that X is identical to Z. So far, no proposed solution to this problem has attracted much support.[6]

Another reason the Fission Argument is controversial is that it relies on the assumption that the donor who fissions is just one person. Some philosophers have rejected this assumption in favor of the view that the donor is as many persons as she will fission into.[7] Strictly speaking, on this view the donor is not a person, but rather a "person-stage," roughly a time-slice of a person. All persons are composed of person-stages. In the example above, Eve is a prefission stage of a person that also includes the postfission stage Bea. Eve is also a prefission stage of a different person that includes the postfission stage Coe. Two or more persons thus sometimes share the same stage; for instance, the person who includes Eve and Bea and the different person who includes Eve and Coe share a person-stage: Eve.

On this view, there is no loss or gain of personal identity in a fission operation, provided the operation preserves psychological continuity. Before fission the two persons who will eventually separate overlap; after fission, no new people *begin* to exist, the donors merely separate. In other words, there were at least two people all along, no one who exists before fission ceases to exist after fission, and no new persons come into existence: No one loses or gains identity.

The main idea behind this proposal can be understood in terms of a simple analogy. Imagine a single stretch of highway that goes in an easterly direction for ten miles and then forks into two branches, one going in a northeasterly direction, the other southeasterly.[8] Before forking, the single road is both Route 15 and Route 66. After forking, the northeasterly branch is just Route 15, the southeasterly just Route 66. One road surface, until the forking, yet two

---

[6]For a proposed solution, see, for instance, John Perry, "Can the Self Divide?" *Journal of Philosophy*, v. 69, 1972, pp. 463–488.

[7]The author and principal defender of this sort of view is David Lewis. See his "Survival and Identity," in Amelie Rorty, ed., *The Identities of Persons*, University of California Press, 1976, pp. 17–40, reprinted, along with "Postscripts to 'Survival and Identity,'" in David Lewis, *Philosophical Papers, V. I*, Oxford University Press, 1983, pp. 55–77. Lewis's view is criticized by Derek Parfit, in "Lewis, Perry and What Matters," also in *The Identities of Persons*, pp. 91–96. (For Lewis, see selection 17.)

[8]I am borrowing the road metaphor from David Lewis, "Survival and Identity," p. 280, this volume.

routes. The Fission Argument assumes persons are more like segments of road surfaces: First there is one, the donor, and then two, the recipients. The objection assumes persons are more like routes: The donor was (at least) two people, the same two as the recipients. Thus, this way of objecting to the Fission Argument does not question whether identity is transitive but whether the fission operation separates identity from other characteristics, such as psychological continuity, that may or may not matter more in survival than identity matters.

Philosophers disagree about the merits of this objection to the Fission Argument. I shall not pause here to debate the issue because my argument to devalue identity does not depend on a fission example; if my examples are persuasive, they will show that there are situations in which many of us would prefer to give up our identities and transform into the persons we most want to be rather than to retain our identities and fail to make such a transformation.

There is another source of dissatisfaction with the Fission Argument as a way of devaluing identity. It is that the Fission Argument turns on a merely technical point: the transitivity of identity. Thus, it seems to many people that in the example above Eve does not really lose her identity except perhaps in a thin, technical sense of "identity." This objection may rest on a misconception. Still, confused or not, it does point to a limitation of the Fission Argument. It is not as interesting to learn that identity is not as valuable as we thought because it is thinner than we thought as it would be to learn that even if identity is as robust as we thought, there are, surprisingly, other things we value even more. In sum, whatever the merits of this objection, we could more convincingly show that identity is not as valuable as we thought if, without leaning so heavily on the transitivity of identity, we could show that there are situations in which many of us would prefer to give up our identities to obtain other benefits than retain our identities and lose those benefits.

II

What does matter primarily in survival? If we assume that identity is not what matters, then, for most philosophers, what is left that might matter is physical continuity, in whole or in part, and/or psychological continuity, in whole or in part. Because the Fission Argument is inconclusive, it remains an open question whether identity or physical continuity, or psychological continuity, matters primarily in survival. I shall argue now that there are other things that matter more in survival than any of these.

The fission operation described above preserves both physical and psychological continuity. Eve gave half of her brain and all of her psychology to Bea and half of her brain and all of her psychology to Coe. So, although Eve gives up a lot (most of her body and perhaps her identity), she does not give up everything. She preserves both halves of her brain and all of her psychology. In opting for the operation, Eve bet the trade-off would be worth it. Most people would agree. But what happens if we raise the ante by asking Eve to give up more?

The key to unraveling our inflated estimates of the value of identity or physical continuity, or psychological continuity, is the innocent realization that most of us would rather change than stay the same, at least if we could choose the ways in which we would change. Probably you would like your body to be better than it is, perhaps stronger, more flexible, younger, more beautiful, and so on; probably you would also like to be better psychologically than you are, perhaps more patient, or generous, or intelligent, or knowledgeable, or industrious, or humorous, or spontaneous, or compassionate, or more or less something. I would like to change in all of these ways. Probably many others would too.

I want to suggest, first, that many of us would be willing to trade so many of our psychological and physical characteristics for better replacements that, on the views of many (but not all) philosophers, our willingness would amount to a willingness to trade our identities (because we would have traded away too much to preserve them). This would show, on these criteria of identity, that, for many of us, identity is not what matters primarily in survival.

Imagine, for instance, that it were possible for a person to undergo a series of painless, safe, and inexpensive operations in each of which he would exchange some physical or psychological trait for a better replacement. So, for instance, you could, through a single, almost instantaneous operative procedure, one, say, that simply used sound waves and involved no cutting, become physically better—stronger, more flexible, more beautiful, and so on—or psychologically better—more patient, more generous, more intelligent, and so on.

Without going into too much detail about the specifics of the procedure, suppose that in any given operative procedure you could change only in relatively small increments and that no matter how many times you repeated the procedure there were recognizably human limits to the total amount you could eventually change along any given dimension. So, for instance, if you wanted to become physically stronger, you could increase your overall physical strength in any single operation by only about 5 percent of your current overall physical strength, and the most you could change along this dimension by repeating the procedure many times, at the minimum monthly intervals, would eventually make you about as physically strong as any living human. Imagine similar restrictions on the rate and extent of change along other dimensions. If such a procedure were available, many of us, no doubt, would continually improve ourselves through a series of such operations to the point where we would have significantly transformed ourselves. The benefits would be enormous. At last, a self-improvement program that really works! How much would the benefits be worth?

Suppose the only cost was that each time you underwent such an operation the memories you

had of life before the first operation faded somewhat, so that if you underwent the operation enough times these memories would fade entirely. Would the benefits be worth this price? Remember that, overall, memory fades for most of us anyway as we grow older and it would be possible to be reeducated about the past. For instance, you could record the story of your life before beginning the operations and then afterwards you (or your transformational descendent) could relearn that story just as you now may learn from your parents about things you did in your early childhood.

Imagine the details fleshed out in a way that makes this operative procedure as attractive to you as possible. Then, if it were available, would you choose to undergo it? I find, when I ask myself this question, that I would choose to, probably many times. I think many others would as well.

The willingness of people to undergo such a procedure probably would vary drastically, depending, among other things, on their current physical and psychological conditions and their current levels of self-acceptance. A person who was old, unhealthy, and psychologically tortured would have a tremendous incentive to change, whereas a person who was physically and psychologically well off would have less of an incentive. Overall, this procedure should be a bigger draw than the fountain of youth (were people to believe it existed) because it could provide not only the physical equivalent of a youthful body but also many other physical and psychological benefits not guaranteed by youth alone. Given how much money affluent people currently spend on creams and ointments to reduce wrinkles and grow hair as well as on cosmetic surgery and psychotherapy, just to mention a few of the changes and programs currently in vogue, it is likely that if the procedure I have described were available many people would be *intensely* interested, to say the least, in using it to improve themselves.

Now change the example and imagine that although the operation is still safe, inexpensive, and painless you can undergo it only once, but during that single operation you can change yourself as much as you like. Because you have only one chance at the operation, and the alternative ways of changing yourself dramatically for the better are so onerous and unreliable, there would be a tremendous incentive to change yourself drastically in all the ways you would like to change to become the person you most want to be. However, the greater the changes, the greater the tax on your personal memory. You could change radically and become the person you most want to be (assuming you are not already close to that sort of person), but only by ceasing to be either physically or psychologically closely continuous with your current self. On most theories of personal identity, perhaps on all psychological-continuity theories, this would mean you could change radically and become the person you most want to be only by ceasing to be the person you now are. For instance, if to become the person you most want to be you would have to transform into someone who was, in effect, an amnesiac with respect to your preoperative self, then, on a psychological-continuity account of identity, such as Parfit's, that postoperative person would not be sufficiently psychologically continuous with your preoperative self to be the same person, and hence identity would be lost. Would you opt, nevertheless, for the operation?

Probably you would want to know much more about the procedure before deciding. For now, just imagine these further details filled in so that the cost of the operation is no greater than losing almost all of your personal memories and those of your physical and psychological traits you wish to change (thus greatly diminishing your physical and psychological continuity with your current self) and the benefit is becoming the person you most want to be. If these were the costs and benefits, would you have the operation? Can you imagine *any way* of filling out the details of the example so that you would? I can imagine ways of filling out the

details so that I would. I suspect many others can do so as well.

On many theories of personal identity, if I change abruptly so that the person who results is neither physically nor psychologically closely connected to me-before-the-change, then that resultant person is not the same person as I am. Assume, for the moment, that these theories are correct. How much would it matter to you that the changes you would want in the operative procedure just envisaged would cost you your identity? Remember that you can have the operation only once. You could choose to hold back from becoming (that is, transforming into) the person you most want to be and request only such changes as are compatible with your remaining the person you now are. Or you could go for it and become the person you most want to be.

I believe I would go for it, though not without some (irrational) fear, and that to become the person I most want to be would require such drastic physical and psychological changes that the tax on my personal memory would be enormous and the physical and psychological connectedness to my current self so greatly diminished that (on most theories of personal identity) the resultant person would probably not be the person I now am. Yet, I would choose the changes I want anyway, even if it meant I would lose my identity. I suspect many others would make similar choices, even at the cost of their own identities.

But does the fact, if it is a fact, that many of us would choose changes that cost us our identities show that even for us becoming the persons we most want to be is what matters primarily in survival? One might object that even if many people would rather become the persons they most want to be than retain their identities, these same people might even more strongly prefer to become the persons they most want to be *in ways that* preserve their identities. For instance, many would prefer to become more spontaneous by learning gradually how to become more comfortable with their bodies—say, by successfully completing a two-year program in psychotherapy and hatha yoga—rather than resort to instantaneous psychic surgery, and similarly with the other things about themselves they would like to change. Or more simply, many would prefer effecting the desired changes without diminishing their personal memories, and so, at least arguably, without losing their identities.

I agree that many of us would strongly prefer to change in ways that allowed us to retain our identities. But this shows, at most, that many of us would prefer both to retain our identities and also to become the persons we most want to be rather than just to become the persons we most want to be. In other words, many of us might rather *be* the persons we most want to be—that is, become those persons without losing our identities—than *transform* into the persons we most want to be—that is, become those persons in ways that fail to preserve our identities. But if the question is which of these two matters most in survival, then we have to consider a situation in which we could have one of the two, but not both. That is what we just did. And I think, though admittedly without proof, that in the sort of situation envisaged above, where we could transform in the ways we would want to or else we could retain our identities but we could not do both, many of us would opt for the changes. For those of us who would, becoming the persons we most want to be matters more in survival than either close physical or psychological continuity; even more, it seems, than identity.

same thing over + over.

III

The transformational examples just presented will not persuade certain minimalist physical-continuity theorists of identity and of what matters in survival to accept my conclusions.[9] The trade-offs in the examples require only superficial changes in the brain, such as the erasure of whatever it is that underlies memory. The brain itself is not traded in, and this, it might be said, is what really matters. So, some of these theorists would argue that the trade-offs do not show either that identity is not what matters primarily in survival or that physical continuity is not what matters.

To answer these and other physical-continuity theorists, suppose, first, as in the example above, that although Eve's brain is healthy, her body is ridden with cancer.[10] But this time, suppose Eve's only hope for survival is to have her entire healthy brain transplanted intact to another healthy body and that this transplantation procedure is perfectly safe. We might even imagine that the body into which Eve's brain will be transplanted is better than Eve's current body, not only in that it is healthy but also in other respects that appeal to Eve. Imagine, say, that the new body is better looking, more athletic, and younger. Eve, in effect, is faced with radical cosmetic surgery.

Surely Eve has not lost much if she jettisons her old body and moves her brain to the better body that awaits it. Such an operation would not be as bad as staying in the old body and dying of cancer, even if the death were painless. Vanity being what it is, if radical cosmetic surgery of this sort were available and safe, it is likely that many people—both men and women—would choose it, even if the old bodies they jettisoned in the process were healthy. So, if physical continuity matters primarily in survival, it cannot be the continuity of the whole body but at most the continuity of the brain.

[9]For a current and subtle defense of a minimalist physical-continuity theory, see Peter Unger, *Identity, Consciousness and Value*, excerpted from in selection 13.

[10]I am indebted here and for my "second" and "third" points that follow to Parfit, *Reasons and Persons*, pp. 284–285 (pp. 262–263 in the present volume).

Second, the importance of our brains, like that of our other organs, is not intrinsic, but derivative, that is, it depends not on what the brain is in and of itself but solely on the functions the brain serves. Ultimately, the most important function the brain serves, so far as the preservation of what matters in survival is concerned, is that of sustaining our psychologies. If half of the brain were functionally equivalent to the whole, the preservation of our whole brain would not matter much in survival.

Third, it would seem that the continuity even of any part of the brain is not necessarily important. As Parfit has pointed out, if some other organ, such as the liver, sustained our psychologies and our brains served the functions this other organ now serves, then this other organ would be as important in survival as the brain now is and the brain only as important as this other organ now is. So, it would *seem* that if something else—anything else—could sustain our psychologies as reliably as the brain, then the brain (that is, the physical organ that actually now functions as the brain) would have little importance in survival, and this even though this other thing were not any part of our bodies. If this were true, then physical continuity would not matter primarily in survival. But is this true?

It is possible that even though the importance of an organ is derivative and based solely on its being the vehicle for preserving a person's psychology, given that it has always been that vehicle, then that organ matters importantly, perhaps even primarily, in survival. In other words, it is possible that even though something else *might have* assumed that organ's function of preserving a person's psychology, and hence that under those imagined circumstances that organ *would not have* mattered importantly in survival, once the organ actually has served the function of preserving a person's psychology, then the organ does matter importantly in survival. But even though this is possible, it is doubtful that the very organ that has actually

sustained your psychology thereby matters importantly to you in survival.

Imagine, for instance, that competent doctors discover that you have both a brain disease and a brain abnormality. The disease has not impaired your brain functions yet, but, if untreated, it will result in your death in the near future. Because of the abnormality, there is a simple, effective, and painless cure. The abnormality is that only one half of your brain, the half now diseased, has ever functioned. The other half has been lying dormant—healthy, perfectly capable of performing a whole brain's functions, should the need arise, but nevertheless never functioning, and not currently encoded with any of your psychology.

There is a simple procedure the doctors can perform to switch the roles of the two halves of your brain: All of the encoded psychology on the diseased half of your brain will be transferred to the healthy half; as it is transferred, it will be erased from the diseased half and the healthy half will begin to function just as the diseased half did (and would have continued to function had it been healthy). The procedure is as quick and simple (and abrupt) as flipping a switch, and it will have no effect on your subjective psychology. You will remain conscious throughout the procedure and not even notice any change. Once the transfer is completed, almost instantaneously, the diseased half of your brain will become dormant and pose no further threat to your physical or psychological health.

How much would it matter to you that the half of your brain that has always sustained your psychology will no longer sustain it, while the half that has never sustained it will sustain it from now on? Probably not much. The procedure would not be as bad as death; unless it caused existential anxiety, it would not even be as bad as a root canal. So much for the derivative value of the organs that have actually sustained our psychologies.

Those who are skeptical of this response might simply imagine that whereas the procedure described is the simplest way of disabling the threat to the organism posed by the diseased half-brain, it is not the only way. An alternative procedure the doctors can perform is to repair your diseased half-brain through a series of twenty brain operations spread over the next twenty years of your life. Each operation will cost about one half of your annual salary (medical insurance does not and probably never will cover the procedure) and will require two months of hospitalization. And the operations will be disfiguring. When they are finally completed, you will be healthy enough, but your life will have been seriously disrupted and your body and face will be somewhat deformed. I assume that, on your scale of values, the disruption and expense and disfigurement, although bad, are not as bad as death. (If they are as bad as death, simply reduce their severity to the point where they are not quite as bad as death.) So, if the first procedure is as bad as death, then the second procedure is a better choice. Which procedure would you choose? I think most people would choose the first procedure.

How important is it as a feature of the example that the two halves of your brain are structurally isomorphic? Change the example slightly so that now the doctors tell you that the underlying mechanisms by means of which the two halves of your brain would sustain your psychology are a little different. They also tell you that this difference makes your healthy half-brain a more efficient mechanism than your diseased half-brain (but not in ways that will affect your subjective psychology). You learn this is not just your doctor's opinion. Several noted brain physiologists who are following your case closely are unanimous in regarding this structural difference in your healthy half-brain as "a design improvement." Under these circumstances, I doubt that many people would object to activating the healthy half-brain for the reason that it is structurally different.

A physical-continuity theorist who feels that whatever organ has sustained your psychology must continue to do so to preserve what matters primarily in survival might object that, strictly speaking, the same organ—your brain—that sustained your psychology before the procedure will continue to sustain it afterwards, and so the example does not show that that organ does not matter importantly, much less primarily, in survival.

Whether we would regard the two halves of such a brain as part of the same organ or as two different organs does not change the fact that what sustained your psychology before the procedure—just one half of your brain—will no longer sustain it afterwards. In any case, we can modify the example so that what the doctors discover is not that half of your brain is healthy but, so far, nonfunctional, but that the two halves of your brain actually developed as separate organs. In other words, you have always had two (malformed) brains. One of your brains, the one that, so far, has been the sole sustainer of your psychology, is the one that is diseased. The other brain, the one that so far has never sustained your psychology and does not initially have any part of your psychology encoded on it, is just a healthy version of the diseased, functioning brain, with or without some minor structural differences, as discussed above. The rest of the example goes as before, and lead again to the same inevitable question: How much would it matter to you that, if you allow the doctors to perform the procedure, the organ that has always sustained your psychology will no longer sustain it? The answer, I think, for most people, will be, "Not much."

Finally, a physical-continuity theorist might still object that what is important is the continuous existence of that part of the physically embedded structure of the brain (or whatever sustains your psychology) that underlies the most basic parts of your psychology.[11] This view is compatible with the idea that the actual organ

---

[11]See Peter Unger, *Identity, Consciousness and Value*, Chaps. 1–4 (or pp. 192–212 in the present volume).

may be replaced, provided the replacement is not too abrupt and provided enough of that crucial physical structure that underlies the most basic parts of your psychology remains continuously in existence.

The organ replacement in my example was abrupt and, in one version of the example, there was structural change. But suppose, for the sake of argument, that the replacement was not too abrupt nor the changes too drastic for such a minimalist physical-continuity theorist.

Imagine once again that you are told that you must have a brain operation or else you will soon die. There are two procedures available. In the first, physicians will record all of the information in your brain, and, as they do so, break down those structures in your brain that underlie your psychology (turn them to jelly, so to speak); then, just a few seconds later (or, in variations on this example, a few minutes or a few hours, or even a few days later), they will reconstruct your brain, including all of the structures they just erased, so that your brain is just like it was before, except that it will be rid of the disability that motivated the operation in the first place. In the second procedure, the physicians will subject you to a series of twenty brain operations spread over the next twenty years of your life . . . and so on, just as in the example above, with the same consequences and trade-offs. So, if the first procedure is as bad as death, then the second procedure is a better choice. Which procedure would you choose? I think most people would choose the first procedure.

There are a host of other thought experiments relevant to the question of how much and in what ways physical continuity matters in survival. The result of considering them, I think, would be to show that it is relatively easy to imagine circumstances in which many of us would trade those aspects of our physical continuity that are said by various theorists to be essential to our identities for other benefits. Physical continuity matters, so we would not accept any old trade. But because, for many of us, physical continuity does not matter primarily, it is always possible to imagine a trade that we would be willing to make. A critic *might* argue that our willingness to make such trades is irrational and hence shows nothing about what should matter in survival. However, no one has argued this yet, and I think it would be very difficult to argue it plausibly.

In sum, I have argued that, for many people, one thing that would be worth more than continuing as the persons they are is becoming the persons they most want to be. In other words, under certain circumstances—not desperate circumstances, but, rather, advantaged ones—many of us would prefer to transform into other people than to remain the persons we are; and not for altruistic reasons, but for selfish ones, or at least for reasons that are close cousins to what in more familiar situations would count as selfish reasons.

This conclusion reveals something fundamental and perhaps also startling about our most basic values. In simplest terms, it reveals that many of us crave to be fulfilled more than we crave to *be*—that, paradoxically, we would choose to cease to exist if by so choosing we could realize our deepest selfish values.

This should not be so surprising. Many people, even now, choose to live shorter lives or to run grave risks of shortening their lives to realize selfish values. For instance, many people smoke cigarettes or drink alcohol merely because it pleases them to do so, even though they believe these practices probably will shorten their lives. Many athletes take steroids or other drugs to improve their performances even though they believe these practices probably will shorten their lives.

In the transformational examples life is not lost, shortened, or even threatened. Only identity is lost. Death is a worse fate than loss of identity under the circumstances imagined to obtain in the transformational examples. Thus, the fact that many people would shorten their lives to realize selfish values, sometimes even rather trivial values, is evidence that many people would choose to cease to exist to realize their *deepest* selfish values.

Finally, if I am right that *we*—many of us—crave to fulfill our deepest selfish values more than we crave to *be*, it is interesting to wonder what *they*—our transformational descendants—would crave. If this process of "trading up" were repeated over and over, through many cycles of "birth" and "rebirth," it would not be surprising if our deepest values, the ones that initiated the process in the first place, came to seem quaint. Perhaps the better selves that eventually emerged would be more satisfied with themselves than most of us are with ourselves and would thus crave the preservation of their identities. A more exotic possibility—no more than a possibility, yet one worth thinking

about—is that these better selves would grow weary of the cycle of birth and rebirth, of mere transformation into other selves, and crave a way of transforming that took them beyond selfhood altogether.[12]

---

[12]Parts of the present paper are revised from "Identity and Survival: The Persons We Most Want To Be," in Daniel Kolak and Raymond Martin, eds., *The Experience of Philosophy*, Wadsworth, 1990, pp. 97–108. In that paper I also consider the traditional problem of survival of bodily death. In *The Past Within Us*, Princeton University Press, 1989, I consider briefly the connection between our desire for an identity and our need to reconstruct the past. I am grateful to Peter Unger, Brian Garrett, Jerry Levinson, and John Barresi for helpful criticisms of earlier attempts to state my views on the relationships among identity, transformation, and what matters in survival, and to Daniel Kolak and Michael Slote for helpful and perceptive comments on a previous version of the present paper.

19

DEREK PARFIT
Personal Identity, Rationality, and Morality

I. Personal Identity and Rationality

The Extreme Claim

Reconsider the Self-interest Theory. This claims that, for each person, there is one supremely rational ultimate aim: that things go as well as possible for himself. A rational agent should both have, and be ultimately governed by, a temporally neutral bias in his own favour. It is

irrational for anyone to do what he believes will be worse for himself.

Some writers claim that, if the Reductionist View is true, we have *no* reason to be concerned about our own futures. I call this the *Extreme Claim*. Butler wrote that, on a Reductionist version of Locke's view, it would be "a fallacy to . . . imagine . . . that our present self will be interested in what will befall us tomorrow.[1]

---

[1]In Perry, p. 102.

Taken literally, this is a prediction. But Butler probably meant that, if the Reductionist View is true, we would have no reason for such concern. Sidgwick made similar claims about Hume's view. On this view, "the permanent identical 'I' is not a fact but a fiction"; the "Ego is merely a . . . series of feelings." Sidgwick asked

> *Why . . . should one part of the series of feelings . . . be more concerned with another part of the same series, any more than with any other series?*[2]

Wiggins suggests that this question has no answer.[3] And Madell writes

> *It is obvious that I have every reason to be concerned if the person who will be in pain is me, but it is not at all obvious that I have any reason to be concerned about the fact that the person who will be in pain will have a certain set of memory impressions . . .*

adding

> *. . . it is no clarification . . . to be told that in this sort of context that is all that being me involves.*[4]

Other writers have no doubts. On the Reductionist View, personal identity just consists in physical and psychological continuity. Swinburne claims that, if there is nothing more to personal identity than these continuities, we ought to be indifferent whether we live or die. In his words, "in itself surely such continuity has no value."[5]

Swinburne rejects the Reductionist View. But at least two Reductionists make similar claims. Perry claims that, if I merely know that *someone* will be in pain, I have some reason to prevent this pain, if I can. If I learn that this person will

be *me*, most of us would think that I have "an additional reason" to prevent this pain. But Perry writes that, on his Reductionist account of personal identity, there seems to be nothing to justify this claim. I have some reason to prevent the pain of a complete stranger. And, unless it will interfere with the fulfilment of my present projects, I have only this same reason to prevent my own future pain. That some pain will be *mine* does not, in itself, give me any *more* reason to prevent the pain.[6] Wachsberg agrees.[7]

Ought we to accept this Extreme Claim? I should first comment further on a distinction drawn above. It is one question how, if we became Reductionists, this would affect our attitudes, and emotions. It is another question whether, if the Reductionist View is true, these attitudes or emotions are justified. As I have said, when I ceased to believe the Non-Reductionist View, I became less concerned about my own future. But I am still much more concerned than I would be about the future of a mere stranger. Though I am less concerned about my future, if I knew that I would later be in great pain, I would still be greatly distressed. If other people became Reductionists, there would at most be a similar effect on their concern. This is what we should expect, on any view. Special concern for one's own future would be selected by evolution. Animals without such concern would be more likely to die before passing on their genes. Such concern would remain, as a natural fact, even if we decided that it was not justified. By thinking hard about the arguments, we might be able briefly to stun this natural concern. But it would soon revive.

As I have claimed, if some attitude has an evolutionary explanation, this fact is neutral. It neither supports nor undermines the claim that this attitude is justified. But there is one excep-

---

[2]Sidgwick, pp. 418–19.
[3]Wiggins.
[4]Madell, p. 110.
[5]Swinburne, p. 246.

[6]"The Importance of Being Identical," in Rorty, pp. 78–85.
[7]Wachsberg.

tion. It may be claimed that, since we all have this attitude, this is a ground for thinking it justified. *This* claim is undermined by the evolutionary explanation. Since there is this explanation, we would all have this attitude even if it was not justified; so the fact that we have this attitude cannot be a reason for thinking it justified. Whether it is justified is an open question, waiting to be answered.

Should we accept the Extreme Claim that, if the Reductionist View is true, we have no reason to be specially concerned about our own futures? Consider Swinburne's ground for claiming this. Swinburne claims that, in themselves, physical and psychological continuity have no value.

I once wrote, of this and similar claims:

> These claims are too strong. Why should the psychological continuities not have rational significance? Even on the Non-Reductionist view, they must surely be granted significance. If we retained our identity, but were stripped of all the continuities, we could not do anything at all. Without the connections of memory and intention, we could neither act nor plan nor even think.[8]

As Wachsberg writes,[9] this is a bad reply. Swinburne believes that personal identity is a deep further fact, distinct from physical and psychological continuity, and that this further fact is what gives us reasons for special concern about our own futures. I claimed that, without psychological continuity, we could neither think nor act. This is no objection to Swinburne's view. Swinburne could agree that, when added to the further fact of personal identity, psychological continuity is of great importance. This does not show that, in the absence of this further fact, psychological continuity gives us reasons for special concern.

I also wrote:

[8]Parfit, p. 229.
[9]Op. cit.

> The continuities may seem trivial when compared with the "further fact," yet be immensely important when compared with every other fact. So if there is no further fact—if it is an illusion—the continuities may have supreme importance. While we are not Reductionists, the further fact seems like the sun, blazing in our mental sky. The continuities are, in comparison, merely like a day-time moon. But when we become Reductionists, the sun sets. The moon may now be brighter than everything else. It may dominate the sky.[10]

Swinburne could reject these claims. Night is not day. On Swinburne's view, only the further fact gives us reasons for special concern. If this Extreme Claim is justified, and there is no such fact, we have no such reasons.

It may help to return to the imagined case where I divide. On the Non-Reductionist View, there are three possibilities. I might be one of the resulting people, or the other, or neither. As Chisholm writes:

> When I contemplate these questions, I see the following things clearly and distinctly to be true . . . The questions "Will I be Lefty?" And "Will I be Righty?" Have entirely definite answers. The answers will be simply "Yes" or "No" . . . What I want to insist upon . . . is that this will be the case even if all our normal criteria for personal identity should break down.[11]

Suppose that Chisholm's view was true. A Non-Reductionist might then say: "If I shall be Righty, I now have a reason to be specially concerned about Righty's future, but I have no reason to be specially concerned about Lefty's future. Similar remarks apply if I shall be Lefty. If I shall be *neither* of these two people, I have no reason to be specially concerned about either's future."

[10]Parfit, p. 230.
[11]Chisholm, pp. 188–9.

These claims assume that, in the absence of personal identity, psychological continuity provides no reason for special concern. We might deny this assumption. Suppose that I shall be Righty. Lefty will not be a mere stranger. My relation to Lefty is and will be very close. We might claim that, compared with the future of a mere stranger, I have reasons to be more concerned about Lefty's future.

A Non-Reductionist might reply: "After the division, when I am Righty, Lefty will be someone else who, at least to start with, is exactly like me. As you have said, I may have reason to regret Lefty's existence. Though I have survived as Righty, the woman that I love would not know this. She might believe Lefty's false claim that he is me. Whatever she believes, Lefty's existence will interfere with her love for me. Because this is true, I could rationally hope that Lefty soon dies. Since I could rationally have this hope after the division, I could rationally have this hope now. This implies that I cannot have a reason to be specially concerned about Lefty's future. If I had such a reason, I ought to be distressed by the thought of Lefty's early death. but we have seen that I could rationally welcome this event. Though Lefty will be psychologically continuous with me as I am now, this continuity does not here give me a reason for special concern."

On the Non-Reductionist View, if I shall be *either* of the resulting people, it can be plausibly denied that I have a reason to be specially concerned about *the other*. What of the remaining possibility that I shall be neither of these people? If this is what will happen, it is more plausible to claim that psychological continuity gives me reason for special concern. I ought to care about the resulting people more than I care about mere strangers. I have reasons to want at least one of these two people to live a full life. This would be better for the woman I love than if both of the resulting people soon died. And this resulting person could finish my unfinished book, and in other ways fulfil some of my desires.

We must admit that this kind of concern is not like the special concern that we have about our own future. It is a concern for someone else who can, in various ways, act on my behalf. If an Egoist had such concern, he might regard this other person as a mere instrument. Suppose that I learn that this resulting person will have to endure great pain. Should I react to this news as if I had learnt that *I* shall have to endure such pain? Non-Reductionists could plausibly answer No. They can claim that, if this future pain would not be revealed to the woman I love, nor interfere with the completion of my book, I have no special reason to care about this pain. This pain will not be felt by me. If I am an Egoist, my concern for the person in pain is only a concern that, in various ways, this person fulfils my desires. If this person's pain will not interfere with his fulfilment of my desires, why should it give me grounds for concern?

I conclude that, if the Non-Reductionist View was true, Non-Reductionists could plausibly accept what I call the Extreme Claim. On this claim, only the deep further fact gives me a reason to be specially concerned about my future. In the absence of this fact, psychological continuity gives me no such reason.

Suppose next that a Non-Reductionist ceases to believe his view. Could he still accept the Extreme Claim? If personal identity does not involve the deep further fact, but just consists in physical and psychological continuity, my relation to each of the resulting people is as good as ordinary survival. My relation to each of the resulting people is Relation R with its normal cause, enough physical continuity. If we have become Reductionists, we ought to accept my claim that Relation R is as good as ordinary survival. But this claim does not imply that, when R holds, it gives us a reason to be specially concerned about our own future. We could accept the Extreme Claim that, if ordinary survival does not involve the deep further fact, it does not give us such a reason.

Suppose that we accept another of my claims: that it would not matter if the psychological continuity had an abnormal cause. We should then agree that, in Teletransportation, my relation to my Replica is as good as ordinary survival. But, from the stand-point of our earlier Non-Reductionist View, this claim would be better put in a different way. As I wrote, ordinary survival is *no better than*, or *is as bad as*, my relation to my Replica. And I might now say: "My relation to my Replica gives me no reason for special concern. Since ordinary survival is no better it too gives me no such reason."

This line of reasoning is defensible. When a Non-Reductionist ceases to believe that personal identity involves the deep further fact, he can defensibly keep his view that only this fact would give us reasons for special concern. He can accept the Extreme Claim that, if there is no such fact, we have no such reasons. And we could defensibly accept this claim even if we have always been Reductionists.

Could a Non-Reductionist defensibly change his view? Could he claim that Relation R gives us a reason for special concern? I call this the *Moderate Claim.*

I believe that, like the Extreme Claim, this claim is defensible. I do not know of an argument to show that, of these two claims, it is the Moderate Claim that we ought to accept. It might be said

Extremists are wrong to assume that only the deep further fact gives us a reason for special concern. Think of our special concern for our own children, or for anyone we love. Given the nature of our relation to our children, or to someone whom we love, we can plausibly claim that we have reasons to be specially concerned about what will happen to these

people. And the relations that justify this special concern are not the deep separate fact of personal identity. If these relations give us reason for special concern, we can claim the same about Relation R. We can claim that this relation gives each of us a reason to be specially concerned about his own future.

But an Extremist might reply:

Why should I care about what will happen later to those people whom I love? The reason cannot be because I shall still love them later. This is no answer, because our question is why I should care now, specially, about what I shall care about later. Nor could the reason be, "Because my loved ones now care about what will happen to them later." This is no answer, because our problem is also to know why they should care about what will happen to them later. We still have no answer to the question why, in the absence of the deep further fact, we should be specially concerned about our own or anyone else's future.[12]

This objection has some force. And it may be wrong to compare our concern about our own future with our concern for those we love. Suppose I learn that someone I love will soon suffer great pain. I shall be greatly distressed by this news. I might be *more* distressed than I would be if I learnt that *I* shall soon suffer such pain. But this concern has a different quality. I do not *anticipate* the pain that will be felt by someone I love. It might be claimed that only on the Non-Reductionist View can we justifiably anticipate future pains. Anticipation might be justified only by the non-existent deep further fact. Perhaps, if we are Reductionists, we should cease to anticipate our own future pains.[13]

If this last claim is true, it provides a further ground for thinking that, on the Reductionist View, we have no reason to be specially con-

[12]This reply was suggested to me by J. Broome.
[13]This is suggested by Wachsberg.

cerned about our own futures. But this claim does not force us to accept this conclusion. It seems defensible both to claim and to deny that Relation R gives us reason for special concern. Though we are not forced to accept the Extreme Claim, we may be unable to show that it should be rejected. There is a great difference between the Extreme and Moderate Claims. But I have not yet found an argument that refutes either.

How do these conclusions bear on the Self-interest Theory about rationality? The Extreme Claim is the extreme denial of this theory. This may be the argument against S that, as I claimed . . . , Sidgwick half-suggested.

Since the Extreme Claim is defensible, this argument achieves something. But the Extreme Claim can also be defensibly denied. Since this is so, this argument does not refute the Self-interest Theory.

A Better Argument Against S

We can do better. I have been claiming

(A) Since personal identity does not involve the deep further fact, it is less deep, or involves less.

I have also defended

(B) What fundamentally matters are psychological connectedness and continuity.

The Extreme Claim, which appeals to (A), can be denied. But (B) provides the premise for a new challenge to the Self-interest Theory.

Central to this theory is

The Requirement of Equal Concern: A rational person should be *equally* concerned about *all* the parts of his future.

As Sidgwick writes, "my feelings a year hence should be just as important to me as my feelings next minute, if only I could make an equally

sure forecast of them. Indeed this equal and impartial concern for all parts of one's conscious life is perhaps the most prominent element in the common notion of the *rational* . . . "[14] Each of us can rationally give less weight to what may happen further in the future, if this remoteness makes this event less likely to occur. But, on the Self-interest Theory, we cannot rationally care less about our further future, merely because it is more remote. S therefore claims that it is irrational to postpone an ordeal if one knows that this would make this ordeal worse.

By appealing to the Reductionist view, we can challenge this last claim. To simplify our challenge, we can assume that merely temporal proximity cannot matter. We can assume that it is irrational to care less about one's further future simply because it is further in the future. This does not show that it is irrational to care less about one's further future. There may be another ground for doing so.

As I have argued, what fundamentally matters are psychological connectedness and continuity. I also claimed that these matter, however they are caused. Since we are now considering our actual lives, this second claim is irrelevant. Our claim could be that these two relations are what matter, provided that they have their normal cause.

I also argued . . . that *both* these relations matter. We cannot defensibly claim that only continuity matters. We must admit that connectedness matters.

Since this relation matters, I claim

(C) My concern for my future may correspond to the degree of connectedness between me now and myself in the future. Connectedness is one of the two relations that give me reasons to be specially concerned about my own future. It can be rational to care less, when one of the grounds for caring will

[14]Sidgwick, p. 124.

hold to a lesser degree. Since connectedness is nearly always weaker over longer periods, I can rationally care less about my further future.

This claim defends a new kind of discount rate. This is a discount rate, not with respect to time itself, but with respect to the weakening of one of the two relations which are what fundamentally matter. Unlike a discount rate with respect to time, this new discount rate will seldom apply over the near future. The psychological connections between me now and myself tomorrow are not much closer than the connections between me now and myself next month. And they may not be very much closer than the connections between me now and myself next year. But they are very much closer than the connections between me now and myself in forty years. . . .

The S-Theorist's Counter-Argument

A Self-interest Theorist might now appeal to

The Truism: All the parts of a person's future are *equally* parts of his future.

He might claim that, since this is true, it is irrational not to care equally about all the parts of one's future.

This argument assumes that personal identity is what matters. When we consider the imagined case in which I divide, we learn that personal identity is not what matters. Though I shall not be either of the two resulting people, my relation to each of these people contains what matters.

Since the S-Theorist's Counter-argument falsely assumes that identity is what matters, we need not discuss this argument. Nothing is shown by an argument with a false premise. But it is worth pointing out that, even if we grant this premise, the S-Theorist's argument fails.

Assume, falsely, that personal identity is what matters. Does an appeal to the Truism provide a good argument for the Requirement of Equal Concern? The whole of any person's future is equally his future. Does this show that this person ought now to be equally concerned about his whole future?

This would be a good argument if the Non-Reductionist View was true. On that view, the Truism is a profound truth, deep enough to support the argument. But, on the Reductionist View, the Truism is too trivial to support the argument.

Consider

(F) All of a person's relatives are *equally* his relatives.

In one sense, this is true. We can use "relative of" in a sense which has no degrees. On this use, my children and my distant cousins are as much my relatives. Is this a deep truth?

It must be distinguished from another truth, which requires the same use of these words. On this use, *relative of* is a transitive relation: the relatives of my relatives must be my relatives. This is a useful use. Since Darwin, it gives new significance to the Great Chain of Being. As we now know, the birds outside my window are, in a literal sense, my relatives. They are my relatives in the *same* sense in which my cousins are my relatives. We have a common ancestor. The birds are my *n*th cousins *m* times removed. (*Relative of* crosses the boundaries between different species. If it did not, there could be no evolution.)

That all the higher animals are *literally* my relatives is a profound truth. But is it profoundly true that they are all *equally* my relatives—that the birds are as much my relatives as my own children? This is not a profound truth. It is superficial, and—though it never in fact misleads—misleading. That it is true at all is the price we have to pay for the transitivity of *relative of*. Suppose we say, "By 'relative' we really mean 'not too distant relative'—tenth cousins ten times removed aren't really relatives." This would deprive us of the profound truth that the birds are literally my relatives. To preserve that truth we must agree that—in a superficial sense—the birds are *as much* my relatives as my own children.

Since it is superficial, (F) cannot support the kind of argument that we are considering. Suppose that, believing strongly in the ties of kinship, I leave all my money to my various relatives. I announce my intentions while I am alive. I intend to leave the largest shares to my own children. Could my cousins plausibly appeal to (F)? Could they argue that, since they are *equally* my relatives, they (and the birds) should have equal shares? Clearly not. Though it is true that they are equally my relatives, this truth is too trivial to support their argument.

Similar remarks apply to

(G) All pains are *equally* pains.

We can use the word 'pain' in a way which makes this true. Could we argue that, because (G) is true, it is irrational to care more about pains that are more intense? Clearly not. This is another truth that is too trivial to support such an argument. Consider, finally,

(H) All the parts of a nation's history are *equally* parts of this nation's history.

All the parts of England's history are equally parts of England's history. Tudor England was as much England. So was Saxon England. So, if we choose to call it "England," was Roman England. But, if we call it "Roman Britain," it was not England at all. This shows that (H) is trivial.

A nation is in many ways unlike a person. Despite these differences, the identity of persons over time is, in its fundamental features, like the identity of nations over time. Both consist in nothing more than the holding over time of various connections, some of which are matters of degree. It is true that in my old age it will be just as much me. But this truth may be fairly compared with the truth that (say) modern

Austria is still *just as much* Austria. A descendant of the Habsburg Emperors would be right to call this truth trivial.

In this section I have discussed the S-Theorist's Counter-argument. Since this argument falsely assumes that personal identity is what matters, it could have been dismissed at once. But it was worth showing that, even if we make this false assumption, the argument fails. The argument appeals to the claim that all the parts of our futures are *equally* parts of our futures. This truth is too trivial to support the argument. On one use of "relative," it is also true that my children and my cousins are equally my relatives. If my cousins argue that, because this is true, they and my children should inherit equal shares, we should reject their claim. For the same reason, even if we falsely assume that personal identity is what matters, we should reject the S-Theorist's Counter-argument.[15]

The Defeat of the Classical Self-Interest Theory

Return to my argument against the Self-interest Theory. This argument shows, I believe, that we must reject the Requirement of Equal Concern. According to this requirement, I should now care equally about all the parts of my future. It is irrational to care less about my further future —to have what economist's call a discount rate. This may be irrational if I have a discount rate with respect to time. But this is not irrational if I have a discount rate with respect to the degrees of psychological connectedness.

The Self-interest Theorist might revise his

[15](Note added in 1985) As B. Garrett has pointed out, this Section makes a mistake. In the case of kinship, what matters is not the transitive relation *relative of* but the intransitive relation *close relative of*, which can have degrees. This is therefore not a good analogy, if we assume that what matters is personal identity. To meet the Counter-argument, we may have to challenge this assumption.

view. On the Revised Theory, a rational person's dominant concern should be his own future, but he may now be less concerned about those parts of his future to which he is now less closely connected. This Revised Theory incorporates my new discount rate. On this theory, we are not rationally required to have this discount rate. But, if we do, we are not irrational.

This revision makes a great difference. It breaks the link between the Self-interest Theory and what is in one's own best interests. On the unrevised or *Classical Theory*, it is irrational for anyone to do what he believes will be worse for him. On the Revised Self-interest Theory, this claim must be abandoned. If it is not irrational to care less about some parts of one's future, it may not be irrational to do what one believes will be worse for oneself. It may not be irrational to act, knowingly, against one's own self-interest.

As this last claim shows, the Revised Theory is not a version of the Self-interest Theory. It is a version of the Critical Present-aim Theory. But how we classify this theory is unimportant.

What is important is that we must abandon the Classical Theory's central claim. Consider deliberate and great imprudence. For the sake of small pleasures in my youth, I cause it to be true that I shall suffer greatly in my old age. I might, for instance, start smoking when I am a boy. I know that I am likely to impose upon myself a premature and painful death. I know that I am doing what is likely to be much worse for me. Since we must reject the Classical Theory, we cannot claim that all such acts are irrational.

On the Revised Theory, such acts *might* be irrational. On this theory, it is not irrational to have a discount rate with respect to the degrees of psychological connectedness. When I bring upon myself great suffering in my old age, for the sake of small pleasures now, my act is irrational only if my discount rate is *too steep*.

One weakness of the Revised Theory is its need to explain what makes a discount rate too steep. But the important point is that, even if

this rate is *not* too steep, all such acts need to be criticized. Great imprudence is always sad, and often (as in the case of smoking) tragic. On the Revised Theory, we cannot claim that all such acts are irrational. Since we should criticize all such acts, we must appeal to another theory.

The Immorality of Imprudence

How should we criticize great imprudence? It might be said that we can simply call such acts imprudent. It might be said that this is a criticism, even if we no longer believe that imprudence is irrational.

Many people would reject this claim. Consider the claim that someone is *unchaste*. Many people now believe that there is nothing morally wrong in unchastity. And, for these people, the charge "unchaste" ceases to be a criticism. A similar claim applies to the charge "imprudent." Just as "unchaste" expresses a moral objection, "imprudent" expresses an objection about rationality. This is shown by the more common words with which people are criticized for acting imprudently. When someone does what he knows will be worse for himself, he would be called by many "stupid," "an idiot," "a mug," or "a fool." This shows that this objection is about irrationality. If we believe that an imprudent act is not irrational, the charge "imprudent" might, for some of us, cease to be a criticism. It might become like "unchaste," merely a description.

Great imprudence ought to be criticized. What kind of criticism can we give? It might be suggested that we can appeal to the Critical Present-aim Theory. As I wrote . . . , we can claim that, in our concern for our own self-interest, it is irrational not to be temporally neutral. On this version of CP, great imprudence is irrational. More exactly, it is irrational unless it brings great benefits to others, or fulfils some desire that is not irrational.

This suggestion fails. In my latest argument against the Self-interest Theory, I *assumed* that it is irrational not to be temporally neutral. The argument defended a discount rate, not with respect to time, but with respect to the degrees of psychological connectedness. Since this connectedness is one of my two reasons for caring about my future, it cannot be irrational for me to care less, when there will be less connectedness. The Critical Present-aim Theory cannot, defensibly, deny this claim.

The objection to great imprudence must come from another direction. I suggest that, since we must reject the Classical Self-interest Theory, we should expand the area covered by morality. Our moral theory should annex the territory that the Revised Self-interest Theory has abandoned.

As Mill's critics claimed, *purely "self-regarding"* acts are rare. If I am greatly imprudent, this is likely to be bad for certain other people. But, if my act's main effects will be on myself, most of us would not judge it to be morally wrong. The older versions of Common-Sense Morality do include some duties towards oneself. But these are special duties, such as a duty to develop one's talents, or to preserve one's purity. It is seldom claimed that great imprudence is morally wrong. This is seldom claimed partly because there seemed no *need* for such a claim. While such acts were thought to be irrational, they did not need to be thought immoral. But since we must now abandon the Classical Self-Interest Theory, we should extend our moral theory.

There are two ways of doing so. We could appeal to Consequentialism. In particular, we could appeal to an impartial or agent-neutral Principle of Beneficence. Suppose that, for the sake of lesser benefits now, I impose greater burdens on myself in old age. I am here doing what, impartially considered, has worse effects, or increases the sum of suffering. We could claim that my act is morally wrong, because it

increases the sum of suffering, even when it will be *me* who will suffer more. More generally, my imprudence is wrong because I am making the outcome worse. It is no excuse that the outcome will be worse only for me.

We could also extend the part of our theory that is agent-relative. This part covers our special obligations to those to whom we stand in certain relations, such as our parents, children, pupils, patients, clients, or constituents. A person stands to himself in the future in another special relation, which we could claim to create similar special obligations.

If we revised our moral view in either of these ways, this would be, for many people, a large change in their conception of morality. These people believe that it cannot be a moral matter how one affects one's own future.

It may be easier to believe this if we subdivide a person's life into that of successive selves. As I have claimed, this has long seemed natural, whenever there is some marked weakening of psychological connectedness. After such a weakening, my earlier self may seem alien to me now. If I fail to *identify* with that earlier self, I am in some ways thinking of that self as like a different person.

We could make similar claims about our future selves. If we now care little about ourselves in the further future, our future selves are like future generations. We can affect them for the worse, and, because they do not now exist, they cannot defend themselves. Like future generations, future selves have no vote, so their interests need to be specially protected.

Reconsider a boy who starts to smoke, knowing and hardly caring that this may cause him to suffer greatly fifty years later. This boy does not identify with his future self. His attitude towards this future self is in some ways like his attitude to other people. This analogy makes it easier to believe that his act is morally wrong. He runs the risk of imposing on himself a premature and painful death. We should claim that it is wrong to impose on *anyone*, including such a future self, the risk of such a death. More generally, we should claim that great imprudence is morally wrong. We ought not to do to our future selves what it would be wrong to do to other people.

II. Personal Identity and Morality

If we become Reductionists, should we make other changes in our moral views?

Autonomy and Paternalism

We are paternalists when we make someone act in his own interests. It provides some justification of paternalism, when this involves coercion or the infringement of someone's autonomy, if we are stopping this person from acting irrationally. This is what we believe we are doing if we accept the Self-interest Theory. I argued that we must reject this theory. But we ought to extend our moral theory so that it covers what we have rejected. We should claim that great imprudence is morally wrong.

This claim strengthens the case for paternalistic intervention. The person we coerce might say; "I may be acting irrationally. But even if I am, that is my affair. If I am only harming myself, I have the right to act irrationally, and you have no right to stop me." This reply has some force. We do not believe that we have a general right to prevent people from acting *irrationally*. But we do believe that we have a general right to prevent people from acting *wrongly*. This claim may not apply to minor wrongdoing. But we believe that it cannot be wrong, and would often be our duty, to prevent others from doing what is seriously wrong. Since we ought to believe that great imprudence is seriously wrong, we ought to believe that we should prevent such imprudence, even if this

involves coercion. Autonomy does not include the right to impose upon oneself, for no good reason, great harm. We ought to prevent anyone from doing to his future self what it would be wrong to do to other people.

Though these claims support paternalism, there remain the well-known objections. It is better if each of us learns from his own mistakes. And it is harder for others to know that these are mistakes.

The Two Ends of Lives

There are many other ways in which, if we have changed our view about personal identity, this may justify a change in our moral views. One example is our view abut the morality of abortion. On the Non-Reductionist view, since my existence is all-or-nothing, there must have been a moment when I started to exist. As in my imagined Spectra, there must be a sharp borderline. It is implausible to claim that this borderline is birth; nor can any line be plausibly drawn during pregnancy. We may thus be led to the view that I started to exist at the moment of conception. We may claim that this is the moment when my life began. And, on the Non-Reductionist View, it is a *deep* truth that all the parts of my life are *equally* parts of my life. I was as much me even when my life had only just started. Killing me at this time is, straightforwardly, killing an innocent person. If this is what we believe, we shall plausibly claim that abortion is morally wrong.

On the Reductionist View, we do not believe that at every moment I either do or don't exist. We can now deny that a fertilized ovum is a person or a human being. This is like the plausible denial that an acorn is an oak-tree. Given the right conditions, an acorn slowly becomes an oak-tree. This transition takes time, and is a matter of degree. There is no sharp borderline. We should claim the same about persons, and human beings. We can then plausibly take a different view about the morality of abortion. We can believe that there is nothing wrong in an early abortion, but that it would be seriously wrong to abort a child near the end of pregnancy. Such a child, if unwanted, should be born and adopted. The cases in between we can treat as matters of degree. The fertilized ovum is not at first, but slowly becomes, a human being, and a person. In the same way, the destruction of this organism is not at first but slowly becomes seriously wrong. After being in no way wrong, it becomes a minor wrong-doing, which would be justified all things considered only if the later birth of this child would be seriously worse either for its parents or for other people. As the organism becomes fully a human being, or a person, the minor wrong-doing changes into an act that would be seriously wrong.

I have described the two main views that are widely held about the morality of abortion. The first of these is supported by the Non-Reductionist View about the nature of persons, and the second is supported by the Reductionist View. Though it is not the only view that is compatible with Reductionism, I believe that we should take this second view.

Within this view, there is room for disagreement. Most of us do not distinguish persons from human beings. But some of us, following Locke, make a distinction. These people typically claim that a human being becomes a person only when this human being becomes self-conscious. A foetus becomes a human being before the end of pregnancy. But a new-born baby is not self-conscious. If we draw this distinction, we may think that, while it is bad to kill a human being, it is worse to kill a person. We may even think that only the killing of persons is wrong. I shall not pursue this debate. What both sides assume I shall be questioning . . . Consider next the other end of life. On the Non-Reductionist View, any person must be either alive or dead. On the Reductionist View, a person can gradually cease to exist some time

before his heart stops beating. This will be so if the distinctive features of a person's mental life gradually disappear. This often happens. We can plausibly claim that, if the person has ceased to exist, we have no moral reason to help his heart to go on beating, or to refrain from preventing this.

This claim distinguishes the person from the human being. If we know that a human being is in a coma that is incurable—that this human being will certainly never regain consciousness—we shall believe that the person has ceased to exist. Since there is a living human body, the human being still exists. But, at this end of lives, we should claim that only the killing of persons is wrong.

Desert

Some writers claim that, if the Reductionist View is true, we cannot deserve to be punished for our crimes. Butler writes that, on a Reductionist version of Locke's View, it would be "a fallacy upon ourselves, to charge our present selves with anything we did. . . ."[16] Another of Locke's Eighteenth Century critics makes a more sweeping claim. Reid contrasts personal identity with the identity of such things as ships or trees. The identity of such things, he writes:

> is not perfect identity; it is rather something which, for the conveniency of speech, we call identity. It admits of a great change of the subject, providing the change be gradual; sometimes, even of a total change. And the changes which in common language are made consistent with identity differ from those that are thought to destroy it, not in kind, but in number and degree. Identity has no fixed nature when applied to bodies; and questions about the identity of a body are very often questions about words. But identity, when ap-

[16]In Perry, p. 102.

plied to persons, has no ambiguity, and admits not of degrees, or of more and less. It is the foundation of all rights and obligations, and of all accountableness; and the notion of it is fixed and precise.[17]

Reid is clearly a Reductionist about the identity of bodies. On his view, personal identity is quite different. It involves a fact that is always determinate, and that must be all-or-nothing. This is what I call the deep further fact. Reid believes that this fact is the foundation of morality: that if, as I have argued, there is no such fact, it is not merely true that we cannot be "accountable" for past crimes. All rights and obligations are undermined.

Certain modern writers make similar claims. Madell claims that "an analysis of personal identity in terms of psychological continuity . . . is utterly destructive of a whole range of our normal moral attitudes. . . . Shame, remorse, pride, and gratitude" all depend on a rejection of this view.[18] And Haksar claims that my view undermines all "human rights" and "non-utilitarian moral constraints," and is "incompatible with any kind of humane morality."[19]

Should we accept these Extreme Claims? We should first note the following. If the truth about personal identity had these implications, most of us would find this deeply disturbing. It may be thought that, if these *were* the implications of the Reductionist View, this would show this view to be false. This is not so. The truth may be disturbing. Consider the claim that the Universe was not created by a benevolent God. Many people find this claim disturbing; but this cannot show it to be false. If some truth is disturbing, this is no reason not to believe it. It can only be a reason for acting in certain ways. It might be a reason for trying to conceal this truth

from others. It might even be a reason for trying to deceive ourselves, so that we cease to believe this truth. As I have said, wishful thinking is theoretically irrational, but it may be practically rational. This might be so, for instance, if it was the only way to save ourselves from severe depression.

Consider next one of these Extreme Claims. Some people argue that, if the Reductionist View is true, we cannot deserve to be punished for our crimes. This argument assumes that only the deep further fact carries with it desert, or responsibility. I shall again ask two questions: (1) Would this assumption be plausible, or at least defensible, if the Non-Reductionist View was true? (2) Is the assumption plausible, or defensible, given the truth of the Reductionist View? . . . *

. . . When some convict is now less closely connected to himself at the time of his crime, he deserves less punishment. If the connections are very weak, he may deserve none. This claim seems plausible. It may give one of the reasons why we have Statutes of Limitations, fixing periods of time after which we cannot be punished for our crimes. (Suppose that a man aged ninety, one of the few rightful holders of the Nobel Peace Prize, confesses that it was he who, at the age of twenty, injured a policeman in a drunken brawl. Though this was a serious crime, this man may not now deserve to be punished.)

This claim should be distinguished from the idea of diminished responsibility. It does not appeal to mental illness, but instead treats a criminal's later self as like a sane accomplice. Just as someone's deserts correspond to the degree of his complicity with some criminal, so his

---

[17]In Perry, p. 112.
[18]Madell, p. 116.
[19]Haksar, p. 111.

*Editors' Note: Here we omit Parfit's reply to an argument that Desert is incompatible with Reductionism.

deserts now, for some past crime, correspond to the degree of psychological connectedness between himself now and himself when committing that crime.

We may be tempted to protest, "But it was just as much *his* crime." This is true. And this truth would be a good objection if we are not Reductionists. But on the Reductionist View this truth is too trivial to refute my claim about reduced responsibility. It is like the claim, "Every accomplice is just as much an accomplice." Such a claim cannot show that complicity has no degrees.

In this section I have described three views. On the Extreme Claim, since the Reductionist View is true, no one ever deserves to be punished. As before, this claim is defensible, but it can also be defensibly denied. I have also claimed that the weakening of connections may reduce responsibility. This claim seems to me more plausible than its denial.

Commitments

If we turn to commitments, similar claims apply. On the Extreme Claim, since the Reductionist View is true, we can never be bound by past commitments. This claim is defensible, but so is its denial. And it is plausible to claim that the weakening of connections would reduce the strength of a commitment.

It would be tedious to give a similar defence of these conclusions. I therefore turn to a question that has no analogue in the case of desert. When we are considering commitments, the fact of personal identity enters twice. We must consider the identity both of the maker of some promise, and of the person to whom it is made. The weakening of connectedness may reduce the *maker's* obligation. But, in the case of the person who *received* the promise, any implications of the Reductionist View could be deliberately blocked. We could ask for promises of this form: "I shall help you, and all of your later selves." If the promises made to me take this form, they cannot be held to be later undermined by any change in my character, or by any other weakening, over the rest of my life, in psychological connectedness.

There is here an asymmetry. A similar form cannot so obviously bind the maker of a promise. I might say, "I, and all of my later selves, shall help you." But it could be objected that I can bind or commit only my present self. This objection has some force, since it resembles the plausible claim that I can bind or commit only myself. In contrast, no one denies that I can promise you that I shall help other people, such as your children. It is therefore clear that I can promise you that I shall help your later selves.

Such a promise may become especially binding. Suppose that you change much more than I do. I may then regard myself as committed, not to you, but to your earlier self. I may therefore think that you cannot waive my commitment. This would be like a commitment, to someone now dead, to help his children. We cannot be released from such commitments.

Such a case would be rare. But, because it illustrates some other points, it is worth giving an example. Consider

The Nineteenth Century Russian. In several years, a young Russian will inherit vast estates. Because he has socialist ideals, he intends, now, to give the land to the peasants. But he knows that in time his ideals may fade. To guard against this possibility, he does two things. He first signs a legal document, which will automatically give away the land, and which can be revoked only with his wife's consent. He then says to his wife, "Promise me that, if I ever change my mind, and ask you to revoke this document, you will not consent." He adds, "I regard my ideals as essential to me. If I lose these ideals, I want you to think that I cease to exist. I want you to regard your husband then, not as me, the man who asks you for this promise, but only as his corrupted later self. Promise me that you would not do what he asks."

This plea, using the language of successive selves, seems both understandable and natural. And if this man's wife made this promise, and he did in middle age ask her to revoke the document, she might plausibly regard herself as not released from her commitment. It might seem to her as if she has obligations to two different people. She might believe that to do what her husband now asks would be a betrayal of the young man whom she loved and married. And she might regard what her husband now says as unable to acquit her of disloyalty to this young man—of disloyalty to her husband's earlier self.

Such an example may seem not to need the distinction between successive selves. Suppose that I ask you to promise never to give me cigarettes, even if I beg you for them. You may think that I cannot, in begging you, simply release you from this commitment. And to think this you need not deny that it is I to whom you are committed.

This is true. But the reason is that addiction clouds judgement. Similar examples might involve extreme stress or pain, or—as with Odysseus, tied to the mast while the Sirens sang—extraordinary temptation. When nothing clouds a person's judgement, most of us believe that the person to whom we are committed can always release us. He can always, if in sound mind, waive our commitment. We believe this whatever the commitment may be. On this view, the content of a commitment cannot prevent its being waived. This is like a similar fact about authority. Suppose that a general tells his troops, "I order you to attack at dawn, and to disregard any later contrary order." He later says, "Disregard my last order, and retreat." Despite the content of the first order, it would be this second order that his troops should obey.

To return to the Russian couple. The young man's ideals fade, and in middle age he asks his wife to revoke the document. Though she promised him to refuse, he declares that he now releases her from her commitment. I have described two ways in which she might believe that she is not released. She might take her husband's change of mind to show that he cannot now make well-considered judgements. But we can suppose that she has no such thought. We can also suppose that she shares our view about commitments. If this is so, how can she believe that her husband cannot release her from her commitment? She can believe this only if she thinks that it is, in some sense, not *he* to whom she is committed. I have described such a sense. She may regard the young man's loss of his ideals as involving his replacement by a later self.

This example illustrates a general claim. We may regard some events within a person's life as, in certain ways, like birth or death. Not in all ways, for beyond these events the person has earlier or later selves. But it may be only one out of the series of selves which is the object of some of our emotions, and to which we apply some of our principles.

The young Russian socialist regards his ideals as essential to his present self. He asks his wife to promise to this present self not to act against these ideals. And, on this way of thinking, she can never be released from her commitment. The self to whom she is committed would, in trying to release her, cease to exist.

This is not a legalistic point. It is in part a truth about this woman's beliefs and emotions. She loves, not her middle-aged husband, but the young man she married. This is why it is to this young man that she believes she ought to be loyal. We can love, and believe we are committed to, someone who is dead. And the object of such love and commitment may be, not someone who is dead, but some living person's earlier self.

It may be objected that, by distinguishing successive selves in convenient ways, we could unfairly escape our commitments, or our just deserts. This is not so. I might say, "It was not I who robbed the bank this morning, but only my past self." But others could more plausibly reply. "It was you." Since there are no fixed criteria, we can choose when to speak of a new self. But such choices may be, and be known to be, insincere. And they can also sincerely express beliefs—beliefs that are not themselves chosen. This is true of the woman in my example. That the young man whom she loved and married has, in a sense, ceased to exist—that her middle-aged and cynical husband is at most the later self of this young man—these claims seem to her to express more of the truth than the simple claim, "they are the same person." Just as we can more accurately describe Russia's history if we divide this into the histories of the Empire and the Soviet Union, she can more accurately describe her husband's life, and her own beliefs and emotions, if she divides this life into that of two successive selves.[20]

The Separateness of Persons and Distributive Justice

We are different people, each with his own life to lead. This is true on all views about the nature of personal identity. But it is a deeper truth on the Non-Reductionist View. If we accept this view, we may regard this truth as one of the fundamental facts underlying all reasons for acting. This fact has been called the *separateness of persons*.

[20] Nabokov, p. 64: "They said the only thing this English-man loved in the world was Russia. Many people could not understand why he had not remained there. Moon's reply to questions of that kind would invariably be, 'Ask Robertson' (the orientalist) 'why he did not stay in Babylon.' The perfectly reasonable objection would be raised that Babylon no longer existed. Moon would nod with a sly, silent smile. He saw in the Bolshevist insurrection a certain clear-cut finality. While he willingly allowed that, by-and-by, after the primitive phases, some civilization might develop in 'the Soviet Union,' he nevertheless maintained that Russia was concluded and unrepeatable."

Sidgwick believed that this fact is the foundation of the Self-interest Theory about rationality. If what is fundamental is that we are different persons, each with his own life to lead, this supports the claim that the supremely rational ultimate aim, for each person, is that his own life go as well as possible. Sidgwick believed that there is another equally rational ultimate aim. This is that things go, on the whole, as well as possible for everyone. Many agree with Sidgwick that this is the ultimate aim given to us by morality. And some accept Sidgwick's view that, when morality conflicts with self-interest, there is no answer to the question of what we have most reason to do. When he compared moral and self-interested reasons, neither seemed to Sidgwick to outweigh the other.

Sidgwick held this view because he believed the separateness of persons to be a deep truth. He believed that an appeal to this truth gives a Self-interest Theorist a sufficient defence against the claims of morality. And he suggested that, if we took a different view about personal identity, we could refute the Self-interest Theory. I have claimed that this is true.

The Self-interest Theory seemed, to Sidgwick, to be grounded on the separateness of persons. I shall now discuss a similar claim about morality. This claim challenges Sidgwick's moral view. Sidgwick thought that there was one ultimate moral principle, that of Impartial Benevolence. Since he accepted the Hedonistic Theory about self-interest, his principle of benevolence took a hedonistic form. On his view, our ultimate moral aim is the greatest net sum of happiness minus misery, or of 'desirable consciousness' minus 'undesirable consciousness.' Those Utilitarians who reject Hedonism take the ultimate aim to be the greatest net sum of benefits minus burdens. On either version, the Utilitarian View is, in the following sense, *impersonal*. All that matters are the amounts of happiness and suffering, or of benefits and burdens. It makes no moral difference how these amounts are distributed as between different people.

Many people reject this view. They might say: "The Utilitarian aim may be one of our ultimate moral aims. But we have at least one other. Happiness and suffering, or benefits and burdens, ought to be fairly shared as between different people. Besides the Utilitarian Principle we need principles of Distributive Justice. One example is the Principle of Equality. On this principle, it is bad if some people are worse off than others through no fault of theirs."

The argument for equality is often claimed to be grounded on the separateness of persons. One such claim might be: "Since it is a deep truth that we live different lives, it is an ultimate moral aim that, in so far as we are equally deserving, the lives of each should go equally well. If this is impossible, it should at least be true that the lives of each have an equal chance of going well."[21]

If we cease to believe in the Non-Reductionist View, what does this imply about the Principle of Equality, and other distributive principles? My main claims will be these. This change of view supports three arguments about these principles. Two of these arguments imply that we should give to these principles *more scope*. This would make them more important. But we may also be led to give to these principles *less weight*. This would make them less important. We must therefore ask what the *net* effect would be. . . .

Changing a Principle's Scope

Since Utilitarians reject distributive principles, they believe that the boundaries of lives have

no moral significance. On their view, the separateness of persons can be ignored. I have described three explanations for this view. I shall now argue that, despite some complications, mine is the best explanation.

Consider

The Child's Burden. We must decide whether to impose on some child some hardship. If we do, this will either

   (i) be for this child's own greater benefit in adult life, or

   (ii) be for the similar benefit of someone else—such as this child's younger brother.

Does it matter morally whether (i) or (ii) is true?

Most of us would answer: "Yes. If it is for the child's own later benefit, there can at least be no unfairness." We might add the general claim that imposing useful burdens is more likely to be justified if these burdens are for a person's own good.

Utilitarians would accept this claim, but explain it in a different way. Rather than claiming that such burdens cannot be unfair, they would claim that they are in general easier to bear.

To block this reply, we can suppose that our child is too young to be cheered up in this way. This simplifies the disagreement. Utilitarians would say: "Whether it is right to impose this burden on this child depends only on how great the later benefit will be. It does not depend upon who benefits. It would make no moral difference if the benefit came, not to the child himself, but to someone else." Non-utilitarians would reply: "On the contrary, if it came to the child himself, this would help to justify the burden. If it came to someone else, that would be unfair."

Do the two views about the nature of personal identity support different sides in this disagreement?

Part of the answer is clear. Non-utilitarians think it a morally important fact that it will be the child himself who, as an adult, benefits. This fact is more important on the Non-Reduc-

---

[21]Nozick, p. 33, writes: "The moral side-constraints upon what we may do, I claim, reflect the fact of our separate existences. They reflect the fact that no moral balancing act can take place among us; there is no moral outweighing of one of our lives by others so as to lead to a greater overall *social* good. There is no justified sacrifice of some of us for others. This root idea, namely, that there are different individuals with separate lives *and so* no one may be sacrificed for others . . . " (second emphasis mine).

tionist View, for it is on this view that the identity between the child and the adult is in its nature deeper. On the Reductionist View, what is involved in this identity is less deep, and it holds, over adolescence, to a reduced degree. If we are Reductionists, we may compare the weakening of the connections between the child and his adult self to the absence of connections between different people. We shall give more weight to the fact that, in this example, this child does not care what will happen to his adult self. That it will be *he* who receives the benefit may thus seem to us less important. We might say, "It will not be *he* who benefits. It will only be his adult self."

The Non-Reductionist View supports the Non-utilitarian reply. Does it follow that the Reductionist View supports the Utilitarian claim? It does not. We might say, "Just as it would be unfair if it is someone else who benefits, so if it won't be the child, but only his adult self, this would also be unfair."

The point is a general one. If we are Reductionists, we regard the rough subdivisions within lives as, in certain ways, like the divisions between lives. We may therefore come to treat alike two kinds of distribution: within lives, and between lives. But there are two ways of treating these alike. We can apply distributive principles to both, or to neither.

Which of these might we do? I distinguished two ways in which our moral view may change. We may give to distributive principles a different scope, and a different weight. If we become Reductionists, we may be led to give these principles *greater* scope. Since we regard the subdivisions within lives as, in certain ways, like the divisions between lives, we may apply distributive principles even within lives, as in the claim just made about imposing burdens on a child. By widening the scope of distributive principles, we would be moving further away from the Utilitarian view. In this respect the Reductionist View counts against rather than in favour of the Utilitarian view.

Changing a Principle's Weight

Return next to the second explanation of the Utilitarian view. Gauthier suggests that to suppose that we should maximize for mankind "is to suppose that mankind is a super-person."[22]

To understand this suggestion we should first ask why, within a single life, we can ignore distributive principles. Why is it morally permissible here simply to maximize? It might be thought that this is permissible because it is not a moral matter what we do with our own lives. Even if this was true, it could not be the explanation. We believe that it can be right to maximise within the life of someone else. Medicine provides examples. We think it right for doctors to maximize on behalf of their unconscious patients. They would be right to choose some operation which would give their patients a smaller total sum of suffering, even though this suffering would all come within one period We do not believe that this would be unfair to this person during this period.

Some claim: "We are free to maximize within one life only because it is *one* life." This claim supports Gauthier's charge against Utilitarians. It supports the claim that we would be free to maximize over different lives only if they were like parts of a single life.

When presented with this argument, Utilitarians would deny its premise. They might claim: "What justifies maximization is not the unity of a life. Suffering is bad, and happiness is good. It is better if there is less of what is bad, and more of what is good. This is enough to justify maximization. Since it is not the unity of a life that, within this life, justifies maximization, this can be justified over different lives without the assumption that mankind is a super-person."

One connection with the Reductionist View is this. It is on this, rather than the Non-Reductionist View, that the premise of Gauthier's argument is more plausibly denied. If the unity of

[22]Gauthier, p. 126.

a life is less deep, it is more plausible to claim that this unity is not what justifies maximization. This is one of the ways in which the Reductionist View provides some support for the Utilitarian View.

I shall expand these remarks. There are two kinds of distribution: within lives, and between lives. And there are two ways of treating these alike. We can apply distributive principles to both, or to neither.

Utilitarians apply them to neither. I suggest that this may be, in part, because they accept the Reductionist View. An incompatible suggestion is that they accept the reverse view, believing that mankind is a super-person.

My suggestion may seem clearly wrong if we overlook the fact that there are two routes to the abandonment of distributive principles. We may give them no scope, or instead give them no weight.

Suppose we assume that the only route is the change in scope. This is suggested by Rawls's claim that "the utilitarian extends to society the principle of choice for one man."[23] The assumption here is that the route to Utilitarianism is a change in the scope, not of distributive principles, but of its correlative: our freedom to ignore these principles. If we assume that the only route is a change in scope, it may indeed seem that Utilitarians must either be assuming that any group of people is like a single person (Gauthier's suggestion), or at least be forgetting that it is not (Rawls's suggestion).

I shall describe the other route. Utilitarians may not be denying that distributive principles have scope. They may be denying that they have weight. This denial may be given some support by the Reductionist View.

More exactly, my suggestion is this. The Reductionist View does support a change in the scope of distributive principles. It supports giving these principles *more* scope, so that they apply even within a single life. This is what I

claimed in the case of the Child's Burden. A Reductionist is more likely to regard this child's relation to his adult self as being like a relation to a different person. He is thus more likely to claim that it is unfair to impose burdens on this child merely to benefit his adult self. It is on the Non-Reductionist View that we can more plausibly reply, "This cannot be unfair, since it will be just as much *he* who will later benefit." . . . But though . . . the Reductionist View supports widening the scope of distributive principles, it also supports giving these principles less weight. And, if we give these principles *no* weight, it will make no difference that we have given them wider scope. This is how the net effect might be the Utilitarian View. . . .

Can It Be Right to Burden Someone Merely to Benefit Someone Else?

. . . those who object to balancing think that . . . a person's burden, while it can be morally outweighed by benefits to him, cannot *ever* be outweighed by mere benefits to others. This is held to be so even if the benefits are far greater than the burden. The claim thus gives to the boundaries between lives—or to the fact of non-identity—overwhelming significance. It allows within the same life what, over different lives, it totally forbids.

This claim would be more plausible on the Non-Reductionist View. Since the fact of identity is, here, thought to be deeper, the fact of non-identity could more plausibly seem to have such importance. On this view, it is a deep truth that all of a person's life is as much his life. If we are impressed by this truth—by the unity of each life—the boundaries between lives will seem to be deeper. This supports the claim that, in the moral calculus, these boundaries cannot be crossed. On the Reductionist View, we are less impressed by this truth. We regard the unity

[23]Rawls, p. 28, and p. 141.

of each life as, in its nature, less deep, and as a matter of degree. We may therefore think the boundaries between lives to be less like those between, say, the squares on a chessboard—dividing what is all pure white from what is all jet black—and more like the boundaries between different countries. They may then seem less morally important.

It may be objected:

> The Reductionist claims that the parts of each life are less deeply unified. But he does not claim that there is more unity between different lives. The boundaries between lives are, on his view, just as deep.

We could answer:

> If some unity is less deep, so is the corresponding disunity. The fact that we live different lives is the fact that we are not the same person. If the fact of personal identity is less deep, so is the fact of non-identity. There are not two different facts here, one of which is less deep on the Reductionist View, while the other remains as deep. There is merely one fact, and this fact's denial. The separateness of persons is the denial that we are all the same person. If the fact of personal identity is less deep, so is this fact's denial.

An Argument for Giving Less Weight to the Principle of Equality

Turn now to a different principle, that of equal distribution as between equally deserving people. Most of us give to the Principle of Equality only a certain weight. We believe, for instance, that inequality can be justified if it produces a sufficient gain in the total sum of benefits.

On this view, we do not reject the Utilitarian Principle. We agree that every increase in the sum of benefits has moral value. But we insist

that weight must also be given to the Principle of Equality. Though every gain in welfare matters, it also matters *who* gains. Certain distributions are, we claim, morally preferable. We ought to give some priority to helping those who are worst off, through no fault of theirs. And we should try to aim for equality.

Utilitarians would reply: "These claims are plausible. But the policies they recommend are the very policies that tend to increase total welfare. This coincidence suggests that we ought to change our view about the status of these claims.[24] We should regard them not as checks upon, but as guides to, our ultimate moral aim. We should indeed value equal distribution. But the value lies in its typical effects."

This reply might be developed in the following way. Most of us believe that a mere difference in when something happens, if it does not affect the nature of what happens, cannot be morally significant. Certain answers to the question "When?" are of course important. We cannot ignore the timing of events. And it is even plausible to claim that, if we are planning when to give or to receive benefits, we should aim for an equal distribution over time. But we aim for this only because of its effects. We do not believe that the equality of benefits at different times is, as such, morally important.

Utilitarians might say: "If it does not, as such, matter *when* something happens, why does it matter *to whom* it happens? Both of these are mere differences in position. What is important is the *nature* of what happens. When we choose between social policies, we need to be concerned only with how great the benefits and burdens will be. Where they come, whether in space, or in time, or as between people, has in itself no importance."

---

[24]Cf. Sidgwick, p. 425, "the Utilitarian argument cannot be fairly judged unless we take fully into account the cumulative force that it derives from the complex character of the coincidence between Utilitarianism and Common Sense."

Part of the disagreement is, then, this. Non-utilitarians take the question "Who?" to be quite unlike the question "When?" If they are asked for the simplest possible description of the morally relevant facts, their description may be tenseless, but it must be personal. They might say, for instance, "A benefit to this person, the same benefit to someone else, an equally great burden to the first person . . . " Utilitarians would instead merely say, "A benefit, the same benefit, an equally great burden . . . "

There are many different arguments for and against these two positions. I am asking: would becoming Reductionists support one of these positions?

I claim that it would. On the Reductionist View, it is more plausible to compare the question "Who?" to the question "When?," and to describe the moral data in the impersonal way. This is more plausible than it would be if the Non-Reductionist View was true.

Return to Hume's comparison. Most of us believe that the existence of a nation does not involve anything more than the existence of a number of associated people. We do not deny the reality of nations. But we do deny that they are separately, or independently, real. Their existence just involves the existence of their citizens, living together in certain ways, on their territories.

This belief supports certain moral claims. If there is nothing more to a nation than its citizens, it is less plausible to regard the nation as itself a primary object of duties, or possessor of rights. It is more plausible to focus upon the citizens, and to regard them less as citizens, more as people. We may therefore, on this view, think a person's nationality less morally important.

On the Reductionist View, we hold similar beliefs. We believe the existence of a person to involve nothing more than the occurrence of interrelated mental and physical events. We do not deny that people exist. And we agree that we are not series of events—that we are not

thoughts and actions, but thinkers and agents. But this is true only because we describe our lives by ascribing thoughts and actions to people. As I have argued, we could give a complete description of our lives that was impersonal: that did not claim that persons exist. We deny that we are not just conceptually distinct from our bodies, actions, and experiences, but also separately real. We deny that a person is an entity whose existence is separate from the existence of his brain and body, and the occurrence of his experiences. And we deny that a person's continued existence is a deep further fact, that must be all-or-nothing, and that is different from the facts of physical and psychological continuity.

These beliefs support certain moral claims. It becomes more plausible, when thinking morally, to focus less upon the person, the subject of experiences, and instead to focus more upon the experiences themselves. It becomes more plausible to claim that, just as we are right to ignore whether people come from the same or different nations, we are right to ignore whether experiences comes within the same or different lives.

Consider the relief of suffering. Suppose that we can help only one of two people. We shall achieve more if we help the first; but it is the second who, in the past, suffered more. Those who believe in equality may decide to help the second person. This will be less effective; so the amount of suffering in the two people's lives will, in sum, be greater; but the amounts in each life will be made more equal. If we accept the Reductionist View, we may decide otherwise. We may decide to do the most we can to relieve suffering.

To suggest why, we can vary the example. Suppose that we can help only one of two nations. The one that we can help the most is the one whose history was, in earlier centuries, more fortunate. Most of us would not believe that it could be right to allow mankind to suffer more, so that the suffering was more equally divided between the histories of different nations. In trying to relieve suffering, we do not regard nations as the morally significant units.

On the Reductionist View, we compare the lives of people to the histories of nations. We may therefore think the same about them. We may believe that, when we are trying to relieve suffering, neither persons nor lives are the morally significant unit. We may again decide to aim for the least possible suffering, whatever its distribution. . . .

References

Chisholm, R., "Reply to Strawson's Comments", in H. E. Kiefer and Milton K. Munitz, eds., *Language, Belief, and Metaphysics*, Albany, N.Y., State University of New York Press, 1970.

Gauthier, D., *Practical Reasoning*, Oxford, Clarendon Press, 1962.

Haksar, V., *Equality, Liberty, and Perfectionism*, Oxford, Clarendon Press, 1979,

Hare, R. M., "Abortion and the Golden Rule", *Philosophy and Public Affairs* 4, No. 3, Spring 1975.

Madell, G., *The Identity of the Self*, Edinburgh University Press, 1981.

Nabokov, V., *Glory*, London, Weidenfeld and Nicholson, 1971.

Nozick, R., *Anarchy, State, and Utopia*, Oxford, Basil Blackwell, 1974.

Parfit, D., "Personal Identity and Rationality", *Synthese* 53, 1982.

Perry, J., ed., *Personal Identity*, Berkeley, University of California Press, 1975.

Rawls, J., *A Theory of Justice*, Cambridge, Mass., Harvard University Press, 1971.

Rorty, A., ed., *The Identities of Persons*, Berkeley, University of California Press, 1976

Sidgwick, H., *The Methods of Ethics*, London, Macmillan, 1907.

Sumner, L. W., *Abortion and Moral Theory*, Princeton University Press, 1981.

Swinburne, R. G., "Personal Identity", *Proceedings of the Aristotelian Society* 74, 1973–4.

Tooley, M., *Abortion and Infanticide*, Oxford, Clarendon Press, 1983.

Wachsberg, M., "Personal Identity, The Nature of Persons, and Ethical Theory", Ph.D. dissertation, Princeton University, June 1983.

Wiggins, D., "The Concern to Survive", *Midwest Studies in Philosophy* 4, 1979.

20

CHRISTINE M. KORSGAARD
Personal Identity and the Unity of Agency: A Kantian Response to Parfit

. . . .

II. The Unity of Agency

Suppose Parfit has established that there is no deep sense in which I am identical to the subject of experiences who will occupy my body in the future.[1] In this section I will argue that I nevertheless have reasons for regarding myself as the same rational agent as the one who will occupy

[1]This formulation is not, I believe, quite right. Parfit's arguments show that there is not a one-to-one correspondence between persons, and human animals, but of course there is no implication that a person ever exists apart from a human animal. So perhaps we should say that what his arguments show is that the subject of *present* experiences is not the person, but the animal on whom the person supervenes. There are several difficulties with this way of talking, for there are pressures to attribute experiences to the person, not to the animal. It is the person to whom we attribute memory of the experience, and what the person remembers is "such and such happened to me," not "such and such happened to the animal I was then." And, to the extent that the character of your experiences is conditioned by memories and character, we should say that the character of your experiences is more determined by which person you are than by which animal you are (see note 13 below). In fact, however, none of this blocks the conclusion that the animal is the subject of experiences in the sense that it is immediately conscious of them when they are present. And I will suggest that we attribute experiences to the person in a different sense: the person is the agent in whose activities these experiences figure, the one who is engaged in having them. It is only if we insist on saying that the person and not the animal is the conscious subject of present experiences that we can get the conclusion in the text.

my body in the future. These reasons are not metaphysical, but practical.

To see this, first set aside the problem of identity over time, and think about the problem of identity at any given time. Why do you think of yourself as one person now? This problem should seem especially pressing if Parfit has convinced you that you are not unified by a Cartesian Ego which provides a common subject for all your experiences. Just now you are reading this article. You may also be sitting in a chair, tapping your foot, and feeling hot or tired or thirsty. But what makes it one person who is doing and experiencing all this? We can add to this a set of characteristics which you attribute to yourself, but which have only an indirect bearing on your conscious experiences at any given time. You have loves, interests, ambitions, virtues, vices, and plans. You are a conglomerate of parts, dispositions, activities, and experiences. As Hume says, you are a bundle.[2] What makes you one person even at one time?

[2]Hume, *Treatise of Human Nature*, p. 252. Hume, however, would not accept the description of the problem I have just given, for two reasons. First, he thinks that we do not experience more than one thing at a time, but rather that our perceptions "succeed each other with an inconceivable rapidity" (ibid.). Second, he is talking only about the persistence of a subject of "perceptions," or as he puts it, "personal identity, as it regards our thought or imagination," which he separates from personal identity "as it regards our passions or the concern we take in ourselves" (ibid., p. 253). Taken together, these two points leave Hume with only the diachronic problem of what links a perception to those that succeed and follow it.

In *On the Soul*, Aristotle says that the practical faculty of the soul must be one thing.[3] We think of it as having parts, of course, because we sometimes have appetites that are contrary to practical reason, or experience conflict among our various desires. Still, the faculty that originates motion must be regarded as a single thing, because we do act. Somehow, the conflicts are resolved, and no matter how many different things you want to do, you in fact do one rather than another.

Your conception of yourself as a unified agent is not based on a metaphysical theory, nor on a unity of which you are conscious. Its grounds are practical, and it has two elements. First, there is the raw necessity of eliminating conflict among your various motives. In making his argument for Reductionism, Parfit appeals to a real-life example which has fascinated contemporary philosophers: persons with split brains (245–46).* When the corpus callosum, the network of nerves between the two hemispheres of the brain, is cut, the two hemispheres can function separately.[4] In certain experimental situations, they do not work together and appear to be wholly unconscious of each other's activities. These cases suggest that the two hemispheres of the brain are not related in any metaphysically deeper way than, say, two people who are married. They share the same quarters and, with luck, they communicate. Even their characteristic division of labor turns out to be largely conventional, and both can perform most functions. So imagine that the right and left halves of your brain disagree about what to do. Suppose that they do not try to resolve their differ-

ences, but each merely sends motor orders, by way of the nervous system, to your limbs. Since the orders are contradictory, the two halves of your body try to do different things.[5] Unless they can come to an agreement, both hemispheres of your brain are ineffectual . . . . You are a unified person at any given time because you must act, and you have only one body with which to act.

The second element of this pragmatic unity is the unity implicit in the *standpoint* from which you deliberate and choose. It may be that what actually happens when you make a choice is that the strongest of your conflicting desires wins. But that is not the way you think of it when you deliberate. When you deliberate, it is as if there were something over and above all your desires, something that is *you*, and that *chooses* which one to act on. The idea that you choose among your conflicting desires, rather than just waiting to see which one wins, suggests that you have reasons for or against acting on them.[6] And it is these reasons, rather than the desires themselves, which are expressive of your will. The strength of a desire may be counted *by you* as a reason for acting on it; but this is different from *its* simply winning. This means that there is some principle or way of choosing that you regard as expressive of yourself, and that provides reasons that regulate your choices among your desires. To identify with such a principle or way of choosing is to be "a law to yourself," and to be unified as such. This does not require that your agency be located in a separately existing entity or involve a deep metaphysical fact. Instead, it is a practical

---

[3]Aristotle, *On the Soul*, III. 9–10.

[4]In my account of these persons, I rely on Thomas Nagel's "Brain Bisection and the Unity of Consciousness." *Synthese* 20 (1971), repr. in *Moral Questions* (Cambridge: Cambridge University Press, 1979), pp. 147–64 [selection 7].

*Editors' Note: Pages in parentheses throughout this selection refer to Parfit's *Reasons and Persons*, Oxford, 1984.

[5]This is not an entirely fantastic idea. In one case, a man with a split brain attempted to push his wife away with one hand while reaching out to embrace her with the other. See Parfit, *Reasons and Persons*, p. 246, and Nagel, "Brain Bisection and the Unity of Consciousness," in *Moral Questions*, p. 154.

[6]See Stephen Darwall. "Unified Agency," in *Impartial Reason* (Ithaca: Cornell University Press, 1983), pp. 101–13.

necessity imposed upon you by the nature of the deliberative standpoint.[7]

It is of course important to notice that the particular way you choose which desires to act on *may* be guided by your beliefs about certain metaphysical facts. Parfit evidently thinks that it should. When he argues about the rationality of concern about the future, Parfit assumes that my attitude about the desires of the future inhabitant of my body should be based on the metaphysics of personal identity. That is, I should treat a future person's desires as *mine* and so as normative for me if I have some metaphysical reason for supposing that she is *me*.[8] But this argument from the metaphysical facts

to normative reasons involves a move from "is" to "ought" which requires justification. I will argue shortly that there may be other, more distinctively normative grounds for determining which of my motives are "my own"; metaphysical facts are not the only possible ground for this decision. For now, the important points are these: First, the *need* for identification with some unifying principle or way of choosing is imposed on us by the necessity of making deliberative choices, not by the metaphysical facts. Second, the metaphysical facts do not obviously settle the question: I must still decide whether the consideration that some future person is "me" has some special normative force for me. It is practical reason that requires me to construct an identity for myself; whether metaphysics is to guide me in this or not is an open question.

The considerations I have adduced so far apply to unification at any given moment, or in the context of any given decision. Now let us see whether we can extend them to unity over time. We might start by pointing out that the body which makes you one agent now persists over time, but that is insufficient by itself. The body could still be a series of agents, each unified pragmatically at any given moment. More telling considerations come from the character of the things that human agents actually choose. First of all, as Parfit's critics often point out, most of the things we do that matter to us take up time. Some of the things we do are intelligible only in the context of projects that extend over long periods. This is especially true of the pursuit of our ultimate ends. In choosing our careers, and pursuing our friendships and family lives, we both presuppose and construct a continuity of identity and of agency.[9] On a

---

[7] The problem of person identity often gets compared to the problem of free will, as both are metaphysical issues that bear on ethics. I hope it is clear from the above discussion that there is another similarity between them. The conception of myself as one and the conception of myself as free (at least free to choose among my desires) are both features of the deliberative standpoint. And from this standpoint both conceptions find expression in my identification with some principle or way of choosing.

[8] This view is also found in Sidgwick. When Sidgwick attempts to adjudicate between egoistic and utilitarian conceptions of practical reason, the consideration that favors egoism is this: "It would be contrary to Common Sense to deny that the distinction between any one individual and any other is real and fundamental, and that consequently, 'I' am concerned with the quality of my existence as an individual in a sense, fundamentally important, in which I am not concerned with the quality of the existence of other individuals: and this being so, I do not see how it can be proved that this distinction is not to be taken as fundamental in determining the ultimate end of rational action" (*The Methods of Ethics* [Indianapolis: Hackett, 1981], p. 498). But the utilitarian, appealing to metaphysics rather than common sense, replies, "Grant that the Ego is merely a system of coherent phenomena, that the permanent identical 'I' is not a fact but a fiction, as Hume and his followers maintain; why, then, should one part of the series of feelings into which the Ego is resolved be concerned with another part of the same series, any more than with any other series?" (ibid., p. 419). Parfit endorses the basic form of Sidgwick's argument explicitly in *Reasons and Persons*, p. 139. Neither Sidgwick nor Parfit shows why these metaphysical views are supposed to have the normative force suggested.

[9] As Susan Wolf points out, "Love and moral character require more than a few minutes. More to the point, love and moral character as they occur in the actual world occur in persons, or at any rate in psychophysical entities of some substantial duration" ("Self-Interest and Interest in Selves," *Ethics* 96 [1986]: 709).

more mundane level, the habitual actions we perform for the sake of our health presuppose ongoing identity. It is also true that we think of our activities and pursuits as interconnected in various ways; we think that we are carrying out plans of life. In order to carry out a rational plan of life, you need to be one continuing person. You normally think you lead one continuing life because you are one person, but according to this argument the truth is the reverse. You are one continuing person because you have one life to lead.

You may think of it this way: suppose that a succession of rational agents *do* occupy my body. I, the one who exists now, need the cooperation of the others, and they need mine, if together we are going to have any kind of a *life*. The unity of our life is forced upon us, although not deeply, by our shared embodiment, together with our desire to carry on long-term plans and relationships. But actually this is somewhat misleading. To ask why the present self should cooperate with the future ones is to assume that the present self has reasons with which it already identifies, and which are independent of those of later selves. Perhaps it is natural to think of the present self as necessarily concerned with present satisfaction. But it is mistaken. In order to make deliberative choices, your present self must identify with something from which you will derive your reasons, but not necessarily with something present. The sort of thing you identify yourself with may carry you automatically into the future; and I have been suggesting that this will very likely be the case. Indeed, the choice of any action, no matter how trivial, takes you some way into the future. And to the extent that you regulate your choices by identifying yourself as the one who is implementing something like a particular plan of life, you need to identify with your future in order to be *what you are even now*.[10] When the

person is viewed as an agent, no clear content can be given to the idea of a merely present self.[11]

Still, Parfit might reply that all this concedes his point about the insignificance of personal identity. The idea that persons are unified as agents shares with Reductionism the implication that personal identity is not very deep. If personal identity is just a prerequisite for coordinating action and carrying out plans, individual human beings do not have to be its possessors. We could, for instance, always act in groups. The answer to this is surely that for many purposes we do; there *are* agents of different sizes in the world. Whenever some group wants or needs to act as a unit, it must form itself into a sort of person—a legal person, say, or a corporation. Parfit himself likes to compare the unity of persons to the unity of nations. A nation, like a person, exists, but it does not amount to anything more than "the existence of its citizens, living together in certain ways, on its territory" (211–12). In a similar way, he suggests, a person just amounts to "the existence of a brain and body, and the occurrence of a series of interrelated physical and mental events" (211). On the view I am advancing, a better comparison would be the state. I am using "nation" here, as Parfit does, for a historical or ethnic entity, naturalistically defined by shared history and traditions; a state, by contrast, is a moral or formal entity, defined by its constitution and deliberative procedures. A state is not merely a group of citizens living on a shared

---

[10] This way of looking at things places a constraint on how we formulate the reasons we have for desiring to carry on long-term projects and relationships. We cannot say that we want them because we expect to survive for a long time;

instead, these things give us reasons for surviving. So the reasons for them must be independent of expected survival. See Bernard Williams, "Persons, Character, and Morality," in *Moral Luck* (Cambridge: Cambridge University Press, 1981), pp. 1–19, especially the discussion on Parfit on pp. 8–12.

[11] I would like to thank the Editors of *Philosophy & Public Affairs* for prompting me to be clearer on this point.

territory. We have a state only where these citizens have constituted themselves into a single agent. They have, that is, adopted a way of resolving conflicts, making decisions, interacting with other states, and planning together for an ongoing future. For a group of citizens to view themselves as a state, or for us to view them as one, we do not need to posit the state as a separately existing entity. All we need is to grant an authoritative status to certain choices and decisions made by certain citizens or bodies, as its legislative voice. Obviously, a state is not a deep metaphysical entity underlying a nation, but rather something a nation can make of itself. Yet the identity of states, for practical reasons, must be regarded and treated as more determinate than the identity of nations.

But the pragmatic character of the reasons for agent unification does not show that the resulting agencies are not *really* necessary. Pragmatic necessity can be overwhelming. When a group of human beings occupy the same territory, for instance, they have an imperative need to form a unified state. And when a group of psychological functions occupy the same human body, they have an even more imperative need to become a unified person. This is why the human body must be conceived as a unified agent. As things stand, it is the basic kind of agent.

Of course if our technology were different, individual human bodies might not be the basic kind of agent. My argument supports a physical criterion of identity, but only a conditional one. *Given the technology we have now*, the unit of action is a human body. But consider Thomas Nagel's concept of a "series-person." Nagel imagines a society in which persons are replicated in new matter once every year after they reach the age of thirty. This prevents them from aging, and barring accidents and incurable diseases, may even make them immortal (289–90). On my concept, a series-person, who would be able to carry out unified plans and projects, and having ongoing relations with other persons,

would be a person.[12] But the fact that the basic unit of action might be different if technology were different is neither here nor there. The relevant necessity is the necessity of acting and living, and it is untouched by mere technological possibilities. The main point of the argument is this: a focus on agency makes more sense of the notion of personal identity than a focus on experience. There is a necessary connection between agency and unity which requires no metaphysical support.

III. The Unity of Consciousness

Many will feel that my defense of personal unity simply bypasses what is most unsettling in Parfit's arguments. Parfit's arguments depend on what we may broadly call an "Aristotelian" rather than a "Cartesian" metaphysics of the person. That is, matter is essentially particular; form is essentially copiable; and form is what makes the person what she is, and so is what is important about her. The "Cartesian" metaphysics, by contrast, holds that the important element of a person is something essentially particular and uncopiable, like a Cartesian Ego. What tempts people to believe this is an entrenched intuition that something like a Cartesian Ego serves as the locus of the particular consciousness that is mine and no one else's. And my argument about the unity of agency in no way responds to this intuition.

Parfit writes: "When I believed that my existence was a further fact, I seemed imprisoned in myself. My life seemed like a glass tunnel,

---

[12]On the other hand, Williams's person-types, of whom a number of copies (tokens) exist simultaneously, are not persons, since the tokens would not necessarily lead a common life. See Parfit, *Reasons and Persons*, pp. 293–97, and Bernard Williams, "Are Persons Bodies?" in *The Philosophy of the Body*, ed. Stuart F. Spicker (Chicago: Quadrant Books, 1970), repr. in Bernard Williams, *Problems of the Self* (Cambridge: Cambridge University Press, 1973), pp. 64–81.

through which I was moving faster every year, and at the end of which there was darkness. When I changed my view, the walls of my glass tunnel disappeared. I now live in the open air" (281). Parfit's glass tunnel is a good image of the way people think of the unity of consciousness. The sphere of consciousness presents itself as something like a room, a place, a lit-up area, within which we do our thinking, imagining, remembering, and planning, and from out of which we observe the world, the passing scene. It is envisioned as a tunnel or a stream, because we think that one moment of consciousness is somehow directly continuous with others, even when interrupted by deep sleep or anesthesia. We are inclined to think that memory is a deeper thing than it is, that it is *direct* access to an earlier stage of a continuing self, and not merely one way of knowing what happened. And so we may think of amnesia, not merely as the loss of knowledge, but a door that blocks an existing place.

The sense that consciousness is in these ways unified supports the idea that consciousness requires a persisting psychological subject. The unity of consciousness is supposed to be explained by attributing all one's experiences to a single psychological entity. Of course, we may argue that the hypothesis of a unified psychological subject does nothing to *explain* the unity of consciousness. It is simply a figure for or restatement of that unity. Yet the idea of such a subject seems to have explanatory force. It is to challenge this intuition that Parfit brings up the facts about persons with divided brains. People are often upset by these facts because they think that they cannot imagine what it is like to be such a person. When the hemispheres function separately, the person seems to have two streams of consciousness. If consciousness is envisioned as a sort of place, then this is a person who seems to be in two places at the same time. If consciousness requires a subject, then this person's body seems, mysteriously, to have become occupied by two subjects. Here, the hy-

pothesis of a psychological subject brings confusion rather than clarity.

Parfit's own suggestion is that the unity of consciousness "does not need a deep explanation. It is simply a fact that several experiences can be co-conscious, or be the objects of a single state of awareness" (250). Split-brain people simply have experiences which are not co-conscious and nothing more needs to be said. This seems to be close to the truth but not quite right. Privileging the language of "having experiences" and "states of awareness" gives the misleading impression that we can count the experiences we are now having, or the number of objects of which we are aware, and then ask what unifies them. The language of activities and dispositions enables us to characterize both consciousness and its unity more accurately.[13]

Consciousness, then, is a feature of certain

---

[13] I have argued that the idea of a momentary agent is unintelligible; I would also like to suggest, perhaps more surprisingly, that even the idea of a momentary experience is suspect. Consider, for instance, what seems to be one of the clearest cases of a temporally localized experience: physical pain. There is a clear sense in which pain is worse if you have been in pain for a long while. If pain is a momentary experience, we must suppose that this particular form of badness can be explicated in terms of the quality of the experience you are having now—so that, I suppose, a clever brain surgeon by stimulating the right set of nerves could make you have exactly the experience of a person who has been in pain for a long while even if you have not. The idea that the intrinsic goodness or badness of an experience can always be explicated in terms of the felt quality of the experience at the time of having it is defended in Sidgwick's *Methods of Ethics*, bk. II, chaps. II–III, and bk. III, Chap. XIV. I do not think Sidgwick's arguments are successful, but at least he sees that the point needs defending. A more complex challenge to Sidgwick's thesis comes from the fact that there is a sense in which a pain (I feel like saying: the *same* pain) can be worse if in the face of it you panic, or lose your sense of humor, or give way to it completely. And this will be determined not just by how bad the pains, but by your character. There is a kind of courage that has to do with how one handles pain, and this suggests that even "experiencing pain" is something that can be *done* in various ways. Privileging the language of conscious states or experiences can cause us to overlook these complications.

activities which percipient animals can perform. These activities include perceiving; various forms of attending such as looking, listening, and noticing; more intellectual activities like thinking, reflecting, recalling, remembering, and reading; and moving voluntarily. Consciousness is not a state that makes these activities possible, or a qualification of the subject who can perform them. It is a feature of *the activities themselves*. It is misleading to say that you must be conscious in order to perform them, because your being able to perform them is all that your being conscious amounts to.

Voluntary motion is an important example because of a distinction that is especially clear in its case. When we move voluntarily, we move consciously. But this is not to say we are conscious that we are moving. Much of the time when we move nothing is further from our minds than *the fact* that we are moving. But of course this does not mean that we move unconsciously, like sleepwalkers. It is crucial, in thinking about these matters, not to confuse *being engaged in a conscious activity* with *being conscious of an activity*. Perhaps such a confusion lies behind Descartes' bizarre idea that nonhuman animals are unconscious. In the direct, practical sense, an adult hunting animal which is, say, stalking her prey, knows exactly what she is doing. But it would be odd to say that she is aware *of* what she is doing or that she knows anything *about* it. What she is aware of is her environment, the smell of her prey, the grass bending quietly under her feet. The consciousness that is inherent in psychic activities should not be understood as an inner *observing* of those activities, a theoretic state. An animal's consciousness can be entirely practical.

The unity of consciousness consists in one's ability to coordinate and integrate conscious activities. People with split brains cannot integrate these activities in the same way they could before. This would be disconcerting, because the integration itself is not something we are ordinarily aware of. But it would not make you feel like two people. In fact, such persons learn new ways to integrate their psychic functions, and appear normal and normally unified in everyday life. It is only in experimental situations that the possibility of unintegrated functioning is even brought to light.[14]

What makes it possible to integrate psychic functions? If this is a causal question, it is a question for neurologists rather than philosophers. But perhaps some will still think there is a conceptual necessity here—that such integration requires a common psychological subject. But think again of persons with split brains. Presumably, in ordinary persons the corpus callosum provides means of communication between the two hemispheres; it transmits signals. When split-brain persons are not in experimental situations, and they function normally, the reason appears to be simply that the two hemispheres are able to communicate by other means than the corpus callosum. For example, if the left hemisphere turns the neck to look at something, the right hemisphere necessarily feels the tug and looks too.[15] Activities, then, may be coordinated when some form of communication takes place between the performers of those activities. But communication certainly does not require a common psychological subject. After all, when they can communicate, two different people can integrate their functions, and, for purposes of a given activity, become a single agent.

Communication and functional integration do not require a common subject of conscious experiences. What they do require, however, is the unity of agency. Again, there are two aspects of this unity. First, there is the raw practical necessity. Sharing a common body, the two

---

[14] Nagel, in "Brain Bisection and the Unity of Consciousness," also arrives at the conclusion that the unity of consciousness is a matter of functional integration, but he believes that there is something unintuitive or unsatisfactory about thinking of ourselves in this way.

[15] Ibid., in *Moral questions*, p. 154.

hemispheres of my brain, or my various psychic functions, must work together. The "phenomenon" of the unity of consciousness is nothing more than the *lack* of any perceived difficulty in the coordination of psychic functions. To be sure, when I engage in psychic activities *deliberately*, I regard myself as the subject of these activities. *I* think, *I* look, *I* try to remember. But this is just the second element of the unity of agency, the unity inherent in the deliberative standpoint. I regard myself as the employer of my psychic capacities in much the same way that I regard myself as the arbiter among my conflicting desires.

If these reflections are correct, then the unity of consciousness is simply another instance of the unity of agency, which is forced upon us by our embodied nature.

IV. Agency and Identity

At this point it will be useful to say something about why I take the view I am advancing to be a Kantian one. Kant believed that as rational beings we may view ourselves from two different standpoints.[16] We may regard ourselves as objects of theoretical understanding, natural phenomena whose behavior may be causally explained and predicted like any other. Or we may regard ourselves as agents, as the thinkers of our thoughts and the originators of our actions. These two standpoints cannot be completely assimilated to each other, and the way we view ourselves when we occupy one can appear incongruous with the way we view ourselves when we occupy the other. As objects of theoretical study, we see ourselves as wholly determined by natural forces, the mere undergoers of our experiences. Yet as agents, we view ourselves as free and responsible, as the authors

of our actions and the *leaders* of our lives. The incongruity need not become contradiction, so long as we keep in mind that the two views of ourselves spring from two different relations in which we stand to our actions. When we look at our actions from the theoretical standpoint our concern is with their explanation and prediction. When we view them from the practical standpoint our concern is with their justification and choice. These two relations to our actions are equally legitimate, inescapable, and governed by reason, but they are separate. Kant does not assert that it is a matter of theoretical fact that we are agents, that we are free, and that we are responsible. Rather, we must view ourselves in these ways when we occupy the standpoint of practical reason — that is, when we are deciding what to do. This follows from the fact that we must regard ourselves as the causes — the first causes — of the things that we will. And this fundamental attitude is forced upon us by the necessity of making choices, regardless of the theoretical or metaphysical facts.[17]

From the theoretical standpoint, an action may be viewed as just another experience, and the assertion that it has a subject may be, as Parfit says, "because of the way we talk." But from the practical point of view, actions and choices must be viewed as having agents and choosers. This is what *makes* them, in our eyes, our own actions and choices rather than events that befall us. In fact, it is only from the practical point of view that actions and choices can be distinguished from mere "behavior" determined by biological and psychological laws. This does not mean that our existence as agents

---

[16]No single reference is adequate, for this conception unfolds throughout Kant's writings. But for the most explicit account of the "two standpoints" view see *Foundations of the Metaphysics of Morals*, pt. III.

[17]Some people suppose that this means that freedom and agency are an *illusion* produced by the practical standpoint. But this presupposes the primacy of the theoretical standpoint, which is in fact the point at issue. Free agency and, according to my argument, unified personal identity are what Kant calls "Postulates of Practical Reason" (see *The Critique of Practical Reasons*, trans. Lewis White Beck [Indianapolis: Bobbs-Merrill, 1956], pp. 137ff.: Prussian Academy ed., pp. 132ff.).

is asserted as a further fact, or requires a separately existing entity that should be discernible from the theoretical point of view.[18] It is rather that from the practical point of view our relationship to our actions and choices is essentially *authorial*: from it, we view them as *our own*. I believe that when we think about the way in which our own lives matter to us personally, we think of ourselves in this way. We think of living our lives, and even of having our experiences, as something that we *do*. And it is this important feature of our sense of our identity that Parfit's account leaves out.[19]

What sort of difference does this make? To put it in Parfit's terms, it privileges certain kinds of psychological connection—roughly speaking, authorial ones—over others. In discussing the events that according to Reductionism comprise a person's life, Parfit introduces the idea of a *boring* event—for instance, the continued existence of a belief or a desire (211). His point in including these, of course, is to cover the fact that one of the things that makes you the same person at time$_2$ that you were at time$_1$ is that certain things about you have remained the same. But we can distinguish beliefs and desires that continue merely because, having been acquired in childhood, they remain unexamined from beliefs and desires that continue because you have arrived at, been convinced of, decided on, or endorsed them. In an account of personal identity which emphasizes agency or author-

ship, the latter kind of connection will be regarded as much less boring than the former. This is because beliefs and desires you have actively arrived at are more truly your own than those which have simply arisen in you (or happen to inhere in a metaphysical entity that is you).[20] Recall Mill's complaint:

> *Not only in what concerns others, but in what only concerns themselves, the individual or the family do not ask themselves, what do I prefer? or, what would suit my character and disposition? or, what would allow the best and highest in me to have fair play and enable it to grow and thrive? . . . I do not mean that they choose what is customary in preference to what suits their own inclination. It does not occur to them to have any inclination except for what is customary. Thus the mind itself is bowed to the yoke: even in what people do for pleasure, conformity is the first thing thought of; they like in crowds . . . , and are generally without either opinions or feelings of home growth, or properly their own.*[21]

[18]Contrary to the view of Gruzalski in "Parfit's Impact on Utilitarianism." Gruzalski claims that a deep further fact is required to support any conception of agency more libertarian than Hume's (ibid., p. 767).

[19]That it is lives and not merely experiences that matter, and that lives cannot be understood merely as sequences of experiences, is a point that several of Parfit's commentators have made. Thus Wolf urges that "the value of these experiences depends on their relation to the lives of the persons whose experiences these are" ("Self-Interest and Interest in Selves," p. 709). And Darwall, commenting on Scheffler's response to Parfit, emphasizes "a conception of the kind of life one would like oneself and others to lead as opposed to the kind of things that befall people" ("Scheffler on Morality and Ideals of the Person," pp. 249–50).

[20]Other critics of Parfit have stressed the importance of what I am calling the authorial connection. Darwell, in "Scheffler on Morality and Ideals of the Person," reminds us that "the capacity to choose our ends, and rationally to criticize and assess even many of our desires, means that our future intentions and desires do not simply befall us: rather, they are to some degree in our own hands" (p. 254). And in "Self-Interest and Interest in Selves" Wolf writes, "Being a rational agent involves recognizing one's ability to make one's own decisions, form one's own intentions, and plan for one's own future" (p. 719). Alternatively, a desire or a belief that has simply risen in you may be reflectively endorsed, and this makes it, in the present sense, more authentically your own. See Harry Frankfurt, "Freedom of the Will and the Concept of a Person," *Journal of Philosophy* 68 (1971): 5–20; "Identification and Externality," in *The Identities of Persons*, ed. Amélie Rorty (Berkeley and Los Angeles: University of California Press, 1976), pp. 239–51; and "Identification and Wholeheartedness," in *Responsibility, Character, and the Emotions: New Essays in Moral Psychology*, ed. Ferdinand Schoeman (Cambridge: Cambridge University Press, 1988), pp. 27–45. Parfit himself suggests that Reductionism "gives more importance to how we choose to live" (*Reasons and Persons*, p. 446).

[21]Mill, *On Liberty* (Indianapolis: Hackett, 1978), pp. 58–59 (emphasis added).

It is, I think, significant that writers on personal identity often tell stories about mad surgeons who make changes in our memories or characters.[22] These writers usually emphasize the fact that after the surgical intervention we are altered, we have changed. But surely part of what creates the sense of lost identity is that the person is changed by *intervention*, from outside. The stories might affect us differently if we imagined the changes initiated by the person herself, as a result of her own choice. You are not a different person *just* because you are very different.[23] Authorial psychological connected-

ness is consistent with drastic changes, provided those changes are the result of actions by the person herself or reactions for which she is responsible.[24]

It is important to see how these claims do and do not violate Parfit's thesis that we should not care what the causal mechanism of connection is (286). Given a suitable understanding of the idea of a causal mechanism, the Kantian can agree. If I can overcome my cowardice by surgery or medication rather than habituation I might prefer to take this less arduous route. So long as an authentic good will is behind my desire for greater courage, and authentic courage is the result, the mechanism should not matter. But for the Kantian it does matter who is initiating the use of the mechanism. Where I change myself, the sort of continuity needed for identity may be preserved, even if I become very different. Where I am changed by wholly external forces, it is not. This is because the sort of continuity needed for what matters to me in my own personal identity essentially involves my agency.

[22]Some of Parfit's own stories involve surgical intervention, and in this he follows Bernard Williams in "The Self and the Future," *Philosophical Review* 79 (1970), repr. in *Problems of the Self*, pp. 46–63. It is also significant, in a related way, that these writers focus on the question of future physical pains. Although it is true that there is an important way in which my physical pains seem to happen to *me* and no one else, it is also true that they seem to have less to do with who I am (which *person* I am) than almost any other psychic events. (But see note 13 above for an important qualification of this remark.) The *impersonal* character of pain is part of what makes it seem so intrusive. Williams uses pain examples to show how strongly we identify with our bodies. One might say, more properly, that they show how strongly we identify with the animals who we (also) are. It is important to remember that each of us has an animal identity as well as our more specifically human identity and that some of the most important problems of person integration come from this fact (see note 1 above). One might say, a little extravagantly, that the growing human animal is disciplined, frustrated, beaten, and shaped until it becomes a person—and then the person is faced with the task of reintegrating the animal and its needs back into a human life. That we are not much good at this is suggested by psychoanalytic theory and the long human history of ambivalence (to say the least) about our bodily nature. Pain examples serve to show us how vulnerable our animal identity can make our human identity.

[23]One of the few things I take issue with in Wolf's "Self-Interest and Interest in Selves" is a suggestion that persons who regarded themselves as R-related to rather than identical with their future selves would be less likely to risk projects that might involve great psychological change. Wolf reasons that great changes would be viewed as akin to death (ibid., p. 712). It should be clear from the above that I think this depends on how one envisages the changes arising.

[24]Parfit does notice the difference between deliberate changes and those brought about by "abnormal interference, such as direct tampering with the brain" (*Reasons and Persons*, p. 207), but he seems to take it for granted that those who feel that identity is threatened by the latter kind of changes are concerned about the fact that they are *abnormal*, not the fact that they are *interference*. Of course the sorts of considerations that feed worries about free will and determinism make it hard to distinguish cases in which a person has been changed by external forces from cases in which she has changed herself. Surgical intervention seems like a clear case of external interference because the person's prior character plays no role in producing the result. But what of someone who changes drastically in response to tragedy or trauma? I do not take up these problems here, but only note that form our own perspective we do distinguish cases in which we change our minds, desires, or characters from those in which the changes are imposed from without.

V. The Moral Differences

Parfit believes that accepting Reductionism should modify many of our views about rationality and morality. In particular, he believes that Reductionism lends support to utilitarian attitudes about paternalism and distributive justice. In this section, I show how a more agent-centered conception of personal identity blocks the utilitarian implications which Parfit anticipates. Yet the agent-centered conception of the person shares with Reductionism the idea that persons are not deeply or metaphysically separated. And some modification of conventional philosophical views, therefore, does emerge.

Future Concern and Paternalism

Parfit's argument that Reductionism lends support to paternalism has two parts. First, he argues that Reductionism grounds a challenge to a standard view of rationality: that we have reason to be equally concerned about all parts of our own future. What matters is not identity but Relation-R, and part of that relation, connectedness, is a matter of degree. Two possible conclusions may be drawn about the rationality of special concern about one's own future. What Parfit calls the "Extreme Claim" is that I have *no* reason to be especially concerned about my own future. (More properly speaking, I have no reason of the form "she's me" to be especially concerned about any particular future person.) The "Moderate Claim" is that my personal concern about any future person who is R-related to me may (rationally) be a matter of degree (307–8).

The disquieting result, according to Parfit, is that we cannot always criticize great imprudence as irrational. There may be no irrationality in my imposing a disproportionate burden on a person who will be R-related to me in the future for the sake of myself now. Even if we

accept the "Moderate Claim," my future self may be too weakly connected to me to require great concern on my part. The result is disquieting because great imprudence "ought to be criticized" (318). However we characterize it, most of us agree that there is something wrong about engaging in activities and relationships that pose a bad risk to one's future self-esteem, health, or welfare. Parfit proposes, therefore, that we should regard such conduct, even where not irrational, as immoral. Imposing the burdens of diminished self-respect, ill health, or misery on your later self should be regarded as wrong in exactly the same way that imposing these burdens on other persons is.

But this, in turn, may change our view about "paternalistic" intervention. Parfit writes:

> The person we coerce might say: "I may be acting irrationally. But even if I am, that is my affair. If I am only harming myself, I have the right to act irrationally and you have no right to stop me." This reply has some force. We do not believe that we have a general right to prevent people from acting irrationally. But we do believe that we have a general right to prevent people from acting wrongly. This claim may not apply to minor wrong-doing. But we believe that it cannot be wrong, and would often be our duty, to prevent others from doing what is seriously wrong. Since we ought to believe that great imprudence is seriously wrong, we ought to believe that we should prevent such imprudence, even if this involves coercion. (321)

There is more than one problem with this proposal. First, Parfit bases his analysis on an account of ordinary morality which I believe is mistaken. Most people *already* believe that great imprudence is morally wrong. The ruined or wasted life, with health, opportunity, and talent squandered, seems to us not merely stupid but reprehensible. And strictures against a lack of proper self-concern also follow from most ethical theories. The Greeks arguably made a form of self-concern the basis of their ethical theories, and unarguably included self-regarding virtues alongside others without hesitation. Of the eighteenth-century moralists perhaps only Hutcheson, who thought all virtue grounded in benevolence, was prepared to argue that self-regarding attributes could be virtues only indirectly.[25] For the utilitarian, lack of self-concern is the cause of needless pain and grief; for the Kantian, it evinces a lack of respect for the humanity in one's own person.[26] For the religious moralist, it is a failure of responsibility for what has been placed in one's special care.

The reason we do not feel entitled to interfere with imprudence is not, as Parfit claims, based on the difference between irrationality and immorality. He is also mistaken when he says that we believe that we may always interfere with immorality unless it is minor. The difference here is rather that between the realm of public right and the realm of private virtue. We enforce public right even when it is trivial; we cannot interfere with private vice even when it is as major as the concerns of human life can be. We may use coercion to prevent you from parking your car in your neighbor's unused private driveway or running a red light on a deserted road. We may not use coercion to prevent you from breaking your lover's heart or demolishing your spouse's self-esteem. A person has a right to the disposition of his driveway, but no one has a right not to have his heart broken.[27] This is certainly not because the latter is a minor wrong, but because of the moral territory we are in.

I have claimed that what matters personally is, or at least essentially involves, the view of myself as an agent, as one who chooses and lives a particular life. And, as things stand, it is qua the occupant of this particular body that I live a life, have ongoing relationships, realize ambitions, and carry out plans. So long as I occupy this body and live this life, I am this rational agent, the same one. As I argued earlier, it is misleading to ask whether my present self has a reason to be concerned with my future selves. This way of talking presupposes that the present self is necessarily interested in the quality of present experiences, and needs a further reason to care for more than that. But insofar as I constitute myself as an agent living a particular life, I will not in this way oppose my present self to future ones. And so I do have a personal

---

[25]See Francis Hutcheson, *An Inquiry concerning the Original of Our Ideas of Virtue or Moral Good* (1725), sec. II. The relevant passages may be found in *British Moralists* 1650–1800, ed. D. D. Raphael (Oxford: Clarendon Press, 1969), 1:271.

[26]Of course a Kantian does not believe in the split between rationality and morality that underlies Parfit's analysis in the first place. In a Kantian view, as I have been arguing, no aim is *my own* unless it is the object of my own choice. And if Kant is right in supposing that a choice I may regard as truly my own must also be a universalizable choice, no split between personal rationality and morality is possible. In other words, Kant supposes that the view of the person that I have been arguing for leads to the adoption of a particular unifying principle of action, the categorical imperative. I have not tried to argue for this more ambitious thesis here.

[27]I am using "right" here in the strict sense usual in the contract theory tradition, where a right is something that may be coercively enforced; since Parfit is discussing the possible use of coercion, this seems appropriate. Of course, the difference between using coercion and trying to *persuade* the wrongdoer to desist is essential here. But even the latter is normally permitted only to close friends or relatives of the people involved. As Steven Wagner has pointed out to me, we do say things like "You had no right to treat her that way" in private contexts where coercion is not at issue. A Kantian would say that we use this language because of the way the private duties of respect model the public, and enforceable, duties of justice. (When we speak this way, we do not mean merely that it was not *benevolent* to treat her that way.) Although coercion obviously cannot be used to make me respect another, I should regard my respect as something to which she has as claim, just as she does to her rights; respect is not something we give to others out of generosity. See Kant, *The Metaphysical Principles of Virtue*, in *Kant's Ethical Philosophy*, trans. James Ellington (Indianapolis: Hackett, 1983), pp. 113–14 and 127–33; Prussian Academy ed., pp. 449–50 and 462–68.

reason, whether or not I also have a moral one, to care for my future.

But this kind of reason for future concern is going to weigh against extensive paternalistic intervention. This is not for the standard utilitarian reasons Parfit mentions—that people should learn from their own mistakes, and are in the best positions to know whether their own actions are bad for them (321). If it matters to me to live my own life, and that includes making my own choices and arriving at my own beliefs, then obviously I will not want others to intervene paternalistically unless it is necessary to prevent me from killing or crippling myself. I can live my own life only to the extent that I am free of such interference. We should be opposed to paternalism, then, not because self-concern lies outside morality, but because freedom is a condition of living one's own life, or even, as we say, of being one's own person.

But this is not to say that the considerations against deep personal separateness that Parfit and I both endorse have no consequences for the standard philosophical model of rationality. I have suggested that agents come in different sizes, and that the human body is merely the basic one. If we grant that the unity of agency is a reason for future concern, then we should grant that I also have reasons to care for the future of larger agencies of which I am a part. Just as I have a personal concern for my physical future, I may have a *personal* concern for the future of my family, the organization for which I work, a project in which I have been active, or the state of which I am a citizen. In fact our existing attitudes reflect this. We are glad if another country makes difficult changes to secure equality for an oppressed minority, but proud if our own does so; sorry if another country has recourse to needless military bluster, but ashamed when ours does. We care not just about the purposes involved here, but about our own involvement in them, even where it is distant. And this kind of personal concern often extends to the future of the agencies of which

we are a part. The territory of practical reasons is not split into two domains—self-interested rationality concerned with the occupant of this particular body on the one hand, and reasons of impartial morality on the other. Instead, the personal concern which begins with one's life in a particular body finds its place in ever-widening spheres of agency and enterprise, developing finally into a *personal* concern for the impersonal—a concern, that is to say, for the fate of one's fellow creatures, considered merely as such.

Compensation and Distributive Justice

Parfit's treatment of distributive justice begins from consideration of an objection to utilitarianism advanced by Rawls (329ff.). In burdening one person in order to benefit another, Rawls argues, utilitarianism improperly treats social choice as if it were just like individual choice.[28] The difficulty can be brought out in terms of *compensation.* If I am burdened today in order to get a benefit tomorrow, *I* am compensated. But if I am burdened so that *you* can get a benefit, no one is compensated. Therefore, while burdening myself for a future benefit is rational, burdening one person to benefit another is not. This is part of the reason for what Parfit calls "the objection to balancing," that is, balancing the gains of one person against the losses of another (337).

Parfit agrees that one person cannot be compensated by a benefit to another. But he thinks that Reductionism makes this fact less important. One formulation of his argument is revealing:

Even those who object to balancing think that it can be justified to impose burdens on a child for his own greater benefit later in his life.

[28]John Rawls, *A Theory of Justice* (Cambridge: Harvard University Press, 1971), sec. 5, esp. pp. 26–27.

Their claim is that a person's burden, while it can be morally outweighed by benefits to him, cannot ever be outweighed by mere benefits to others. This is held to be so even if the benefits are far greater than the burdens. The claim thus gives to the boundaries between lives — or to the fact of non-identity — overwhelming significance. It allows within the same life what, over different lives, it totally forbids. (338–39)

Parfit thinks that Reductionism makes this position less rational. But notice his equation of "the boundaries between lives" with "the fact of non-identity." This is explicit in the next paragraph when he says: "The fact that we live different lives is the fact that we are not the same person. If the fact of personal identity is less deep, so is the fact of non-identity" (339). But this conclusion does not follow even from Reductionism. Or, rather, it follows only if we also adopt a peculiarly agentless conception of what it is to live a life. Living a life as Parfit sees it is a matter of having a series of experiences. Since the idea of a continuing subject of experiences, as anything more than a grammatical convenience, has been discredited, Parfit supposes that the unity of a life has been discredited as well. He concludes that distributive policies should focus on the quality of experiences rather than on lives. But when living a life is conceived as something done by an agent we do not get this result. Lives conceived of as led by agents may be completely separate even if the unity of those agents is pragmatic rather than metaphysically deep. And if living a life in this sense is what matters, distribution should be over lives, and the agents who lead them. As things stand, the basic leader of a life is a human being, and this is what makes the human being the unit of distribution.[29] If tech-

nology changes this — for instance, if series-persons become possible — then the appropriate unit of distribution may change.

But still, one might envisage some change in our views as a result of our coming to believe that the fact that we lead separate lives *can be* less deep. Not just human beings, but marriages, friendships, institutions, and states all have lives. If we suppose that I participate in various lives, then there may be more scope for compensation than the objection to balancing allows. I *may* sometimes be compensated for a personal burden by a benefit to a larger life in which I participate. This is not an unfamiliar or revisionist idea, but is already realized in the attitudes most people have towards their friends and family. The efforts we make for the sake of those we love, and for the sake of keeping our relationships alive, are not regarded as uncompensated burdens, any more than the sacrifices we make today in order to benefit ourselves tomorrow are. I do things for my friend not because I calculate that she will do as much for me, but because she is my friend. This is just as comprehensible a reason, all by itself, as doing something for myself because I am myself. So perhaps it would be all right to impose a burden on me in order to benefit one of my close friends.[30]

But notice that *nothing* in this line of reasoning suggests that I can be compensated for a burden by a benefit to a person whose life is unconnected to, and not part of, my own. Even

---

[29]In fact, for economic purposes the unit is often the family, and this is because family members are presumed to share their lives, although of course in an economic rather than a metaphysical sense.

[30]Friendship is not a form of altruism. In routine cases, the question of "making a sacrifice" — if that is supposed to be an uncompensated burden — does not even come up. Where a burden is large, one may speak of "making a sacrifice" for one's friend. But then, where a burden is large, one may also speak of "making a sacrifice" for one's career or health. Sometimes, the impossibility of compensation springs from the incommensurability of values, not from who gets what. My friend's happiness may be incommensurable with other things I care about, without being any the less a part of my own happiness for all that.

if personal identity is less deep, and our lives can be connected to those of others in much the same way they are connected within, it does not follow that our lives are equally connected to any lives whatever. And they are not. So a utilitarian criterion for distribution does not follow from this line of thought.

Still, one might think that even a limited expansion of the scope of possible compensation will change our views about distributive justice. But the argument against paternalism just given bears against this conclusion. And indeed to draw it would be to miss an important part of Rawls's point about the essential difference between private and political decision. Even in the most straightforward case of compensation, where a burden is imposed on a person from which she herself will later benefit, compensation by itself does not do the justificatory work. That I will be compensated may give me a reason to accept a burden; it does not give you a reason to impose one on me. The only reason you have to impose one on me is that *I do accept it*.[31] This fact may be obscured if we start, as Parfit does, from the example of a child, who is a legitimate object of paternalism, and on whose acceptance we cannot wait. In the case of an adult, it is the acceptance, not the compensation, that does the justificatory work.

VI. Conclusion

Some of the discussion of Parfit's work has revolved around the question whether we can, or even should, use a morally neutral, metaphysical conception of the person to support one moral theory over others.[32] I believe that the answer depends on what "morally neutral" is taken to mean. When we say a conception is morally neutral, we may mean that it is constructed without regard to the fact that we are going to employ it in moral thinking; or we may mean that it is constructed without prior dependence on any particular moral theory. I see no point in being neutral with respect to the purposes of moral thinking, nor do I see that metaphysics achieves that kind of neutrality any better than, say, psychoanalysis or biology.[33] On the other hand, if we are to find a basis for deciding among competing moral theories, an initial neutrality with respect to particular theories might be worth having. But Parfit's conception of the person does not have this kind of moral neutrality.

According to Parfit, utilitarians disagree with those who insist on compensation and other distributive values because utilitarians think that the question "to whom does it happen?" is like the question "when does it happen?" They regard both of these as "mere differences in position" (340). Reductionism supports this parallel between the two questions because the Reductionist holds that an impersonal description

---

[31]It will help to recall here that, according to the social contract theory accepted by Kantians, the burdens of social life are supposed to be ones that the citizens accept, through their representatives. Any coercive measure must have this kind of backing.

[32]See, for instance, John Rawls, "The Independence of Moral Theory," *Proceedings and Addresses of the American Philosophical Association* 47 (1974–75): 15–20; Norman Daniels, "Moral Theory and the Plasticity of Persons," *Monist* 62 (1979): 269; Samuel Scheffler, "Ethics, Personal Identity, and Ideals of the Person," pp. 240ff.; and Bart Schultz, "Persons, Selves, and Utilitarianism," *Ethics* 96 (1986): 721–45, esp. 741ff.

[33]Parfit might reply that the point of appealing to a metaphysical conception is not merely that it is neutral, but that it is deep. It is what we most truly are. But both the truth and the force of this consideration are questionable. Parfit's conception of the person is recognizably metaphysical in that it is concerned with the theoretical conditions of identity and counting, certainly traditional concerns of metaphysics. It is also as minimal as possible. But our metaphysical concerns about countability and ontological economy are still just some concerns among others. And they are not obviously the important ones for ethics.

of life is possible. Persons can be said to exist, but, according to Parfit, "this is true only because we describe our lives by ascribing thoughts and actions to people" (341). It is a matter of grammatical convenience. Therefore "it becomes more plausible, when thinking morally, to focus less upon the person, the subject of experiences, and instead to focus more upon the experiences themselves" (341).

So Parfit thinks that Reductionism supports the thesis that the quality of experiences is what matters, and so supports a utilitarian theory of value. But I believe instead that Parfit has assumed this theory of value from the start. The metaphysical argument about whether a person is a separately existing subject of experiences, or merely a stream of experiences with no separately existing subject, is preceded by an essentially *moral* assumption—the assumption that life is a series of experiences, and so that a person is first and foremost a locus of experiences. If you begin with the view that a person is a subject of experiences, and take away the subject, you are indeed left with nothing but experiences. But you will begin with that view only if you assume from the start that having experiences is what life is all about.

This assumption dictates the reduction of agency to a mere form of experience. . . . That is, it involves regarding our actions and activities as among the things that happen to us, and so, once the subject is removed, as simply among the things that happen. Because they regard doings as mere happenings, Parfit and other utilitarians suppose that the question

"who does it?" is like the question "to whom does it happen?": according to them, it is merely a question about position.[34] But from the deliberative standpoint our relationship to our actions and our lives is not merely one of position. It is essential to us that our actions are our own, and we regard living our lives as something that we do.

Unless persons are separately existing entities, Parfit supposes, the ascription of actions to people is a matter of mere grammatical convenience. The Kantian reply is that neither metaphysics nor grammar is the basis for such ascriptions. Rather, the conception of ourselves as agents is fundamental to the standpoint of practical reason, the standpoint from which choices are made. And it is from this standpoint that we ask moral questions, and seek help from moral philosophy. This makes the conception of the agent, along with its unity, an appropriate one to employ in moral thinking. In fact, it is from the standpoint of practical reason that moral thought and moral concepts—including the concept of the person—are generated.

[34]This is related to the utilitarian's perplexity about agent-centered restrictions. . . . In his discussion of his now well-known example of Jim, who is invited by a South American soldier to kill one Indian in order to save the lives of nineteen others. Bernard Williams says that the utilitarian solution of the problem regards Jim as "the agent of the satisfaction system who happens to be at *a particular point at a particular time*: in Jim's case, our man in South America." See "A Critique of Utilitarianism," in J.J.C. Smart and Bernard Williams, *Utilitarianism: For and Against* (Cambridge: Cambridge University Press, 1973), p. 115 (emphasis added).

III

Self

Introduction

The problem of the unity of consciousness is to explain unity at a time. The problem of personal identity is to explain unity over time. Out of these unities selves appear to emerge. The fundamental philosophical problem about selves is to determine whether they exist and, if so, how they emerged and what they are.

There is a puzzling disparity between the feeling of certainty that you are (or have) a self and the difficulty in describing what a self is. The feeling of certainty seems to stem from the (perhaps incoherent) belief that the self which is conceptualized as a perceiver can itself be perceived. The difficulty stems from the fact that there is no self—no perceiver—in experience. Hume, as we have seen, claimed there is no perceiver or any underlying unifying substance to be found in experience. Almost everyone who has ever considered the matter carefully thinks Hume was right.

If there is nevertheless a self in experience, then it must be an experiential element, such as a particular perception of pain or pleasure, warmth or coolness, or a (possibly ordered) collection of experiential elements. This sort of "self," the kind studied, say, by developmental psychologists, is not a perceiver, but, rather, something perceived. In other words, it is not an agent of perception but an object of perception, that is, it is itself a perception or a collection of perceptions. In the sense in which we naively conceptualize self—as a perceiver to which we have direct and immediate experiential access—there is no self. The familiar conviction that there is one is an illusion.

In experience there are only experiential elements related in various ways.

These experiential elements are impermanent, only externally unified, and passive. Yet because there *seems* to be a self-as-perceiver in experience, we must be misperceiving—somehow perceiving the elements that are there as if they were a permanent, unifying, perceiv*ing* substance. If we are not making some such misperception it is hard to explain why Hume's claim that there is no perceiver or any substantial self in experience was shocking not only to his contemporaries but is shocking even today to people who have never considered the matter carefully. Parfit, as we saw in the last section, argued that most people believe they are something over and above physical and mental events and the relations among them, a kind of "further fact." But it is hard to prove that most people believe this (perhaps Parfit succeeded), or to say much about the specific content of this supposed belief. Ironically, the experiential basis of the belief in self may well be the very feeling of certainty that there is a self in experience, a self that only seems to be found in experience until "it" looks for itself. The self is the unseen, but seemingly present, seer who, when it looks for itself, finds only the certainty that there is a seer.

Recognizing, or at least responding to, this certainty, Descartes concluded that "I exist" is every I's most certain knowledge. Descartes's belief that "I" and certainty are linked, however mistakenly he may have developed that belief, is based on a sound phenomenological insight. For there is, at least, the widespread experience of certainty in self-existence: "Even if the whole world is a dream, at least I exist." But what is this "I" that so many claim, with certainty, exists—this shadow of objectivity reified at the heart of subjectivity?

Even if the feeling of certainty that "I exist" somehow encourages an illusion, the ability of the organism to distinguish between itself and its surrounding environment—between self and other—is not an illusion but a fact. How, though, does an organism distinguish between self and other? How is its ability to make this distinction related to how we do (or should) think about selves? Saying that an organism is, or has, a self may be little more than saying that the organism is capable of distinguishing between self and other. In other words, insofar as we have any evidence that selves exist, we draw a boundary between selves and nonselves largely, it seems, on the basis of the organism's ability to draw a boundary between self and other.

Strictly speaking, it is not the organism as a whole but a distinguishing mechanism (or mechanisms) within the organism that distinguishes between self and other. This mechanism distinguishes parts of the organism from other parts and the organism as a whole from other organisms. Eventually, at least in humans, the distinguisher—presumably the brain or some part of it—also tries to distinguish itself from the organism within which it makes distinctions. In making this crucial move it often reifies itself as a separate thing; that is, in distinguishing between itself and the organism in which it is housed it says not only "I am a self," but also "I am the self that *has* this organism." Such reification is part and parcel of the brain's construction of a self-concept that allows it to imagine that it is (or has) a self capable of existing apart from both brain and organism.

How did this process of self-reification begin? There are two evolutionary stories to track, one about life on this planet, the other about each of our individual lives. Life on this planet went from a condition in which neither developed forms of consciousness nor selves (or even the illusion of selves) were present, to a condition in which consciousness of a sort that appears to sustain a self is present. Each of our individual lives also went from a single-celled organism to our current level of consciousness, replete with a sense of our own continuing existence and an array of self-concepts and self-conceptions (beliefs abut ourselves).

According to common sense, we are each a self. Various other kinds of things, such as rocks, are not. Moreover, some conscious things, such as animals, are not selves. Until we understand how we differ from these other kinds of things, the notion of self has little, if any, content or meaning. Some believe that primitive humans and human infants are conscious, yet not selves. If animals or primitive humans or human infants are conscious, but not selves, do they fail to be selves because their consciousness is not well enough developed? If so, what developments in consciousness are required for selfhood? Where and when, in the progression from the lowest to the higher forms of consciousness, do the required complexities—selves—first make their appearance? How did this happen? Why?

Similar questions arise for each of us individually. At some time between our earliest beginnings, when sperm and egg met to form a zygote, and our existence as fully grown adults, consciousness emerged, complete with self-representations and a sense of our own identities. Each of us emerged out of elements that were not yet a self and had only the identity of a biological life form (or of its constituent elements). This life form went through many stages to become a self with an internalized sense of identity. Along the way we developed the capacity to use and understand language. What are the salient stages through which a nonconscious, nonself evolves to become a self with the sort of consciousness we have? What role does language play? What effect do interpersonal and social interactions have? How can we best understand the progression through these stages? When and how did selves emerge along the way?

According to Daniel C. Dennett (selection 21), the human self that ultimately emerged from this complex process is not anything real. In response to the question "Who are you?" Dennett would answer that you are a fictional character in a story told by the physical organism—what you call "your" brain—that invented you. In fact, your brain is not *your* brain. You are your brain's persona. Your brain is the author of you, a self who is merely the central character in a fictional narrative invented by a bunch of "imaginative" neurons which, individually, are not trying to create you or trying to do anything at all. It is, of course, amazing that neurons could do this, particularly since they create this fiction in a language that, individually, they do not even understand.

Dennett begins his account of how this might have happened with the idea that the emergence of self is rooted in the fundamental biological principle of self-preservation. Even the most rudimentary organisms must not only have boundaries, that is, *be* distinguished from their environment, they must also at some level be able to *recognize* these boundaries in order to protect them, pass materials through them, and occasionally retreat from them. This activity does not necessarily require a central control system within the organism to guide it. Integrated and apparently purposeful activity, on Dennett's view, can arise out of the organism's subsystems working harmoniously with each other. For instance, anthills and termite colonies exhibit marvelously purposeful behavior even though there is no central control system or any overall "insect mind" providing guidance. But, according to Dennett, the purposeful behavior of human beings is different in that although lower animals might have selves, human beings are constantly engaged in presenting themselves both to others and to themselves. In thus representing themselves our brains create autobiographical narratives about who they are. The self, according to Dennett, is not the source of these narratives but, rather, a by-product of the brain's propensity to produce them.

Dennett thus argues that the self is a fiction, an abstract object, like the physicist's "center of gravity." The self is the center of narrative gravity within the biographies our brains compose about ourselves and each other. Selves, like centers of gravity, are useful organizing concepts but they are not real. There are no parts of us which are our selves any more than there are parts of us which are our centers of gravity.

However, as Dennett claims in "The Self as the Center of Narrative Gravity" (see bibliography), one difference between fictional characters and our own selves is that we usually encounter a fictional character in a finished work. Brains, on the other hand, continually write and rewrite their autobiographical fictions, like a novelist who constantly revises his fictional world and continues the narrative into an unfolding but as yet nonexistent future. As we have already seen, an interesting application of the idea that selves are fictional characters is in Dennett's suggestion that the decision a therapist might make about how many selves should be attributed to someone who appears to be suffering from multiple personality disorder should be decided on literary grounds. In such cases the crucial question, he claims, is whether the best story of the person who has multiple personality disorder coheres around one self or more.

How can people feel so certain they exist as selves somehow revealed to themselves in their own experience when, on careful inspection, selves never show up in experience? Dennett's answer is that our brains mistake a plausible story, which has an important unifying function in our lives, for the literal truth. Like the social constructionists, to be considered next, Dennett provides an account of how our brains might have come to believe that there are selves when in fact there are none.

Rom Harré (selection 22), like Dennett, thinks that selves are not real. The illusion that they are real, on his view, emerges not from the individual human organism but from the social relations within which it exists. His "social constructionist" theory of self rests fundamentally on a distinction between the public fact of personal identity and the private fact of an individual's sense of identity. Harré claims that the public fact is a social matter. It is grounded in the concept of a person as a publicly identifiable being with a characteristic combination of language skills and moral qualities, which mostly have to do with responsibility. The private fact of an individual's sense of identity concerns a particular way of organizing perception, thought, feelings, memories, and so on. It is captured in the phrase "a sense of self," or, in Doris Lessing's arresting image: that which is "continuing to burn" behind the various roles we play.

Harré further claims that the concept of "person" is culturally dependent. There could be cultures whose members have no private sense of their own individual identities and who identify themselves exclusively through their public behavior. He thinks chimpanzees may be like this. But most human cultures consist of people with a private sense of their own individual identities. The basic social contructionist thesis is that this private sense of individual identity is made available to the members of a culture through the (mistaken) myth that the self is real.

According to social constructionism, the notion of self, which appears in talk about our private sense of identity, is a theoretical concept modeled on the public concept of a person. Just as society uses the public concept of a person to help organize social relationships (for instance, to assign responsibility), so also the individual uses the private concept of self to help unify his or her experience. Although useful as an organizational tool, the concept of self is a theoretical concept that in reality refers to nothing: According to social constructionists, there are no selves. In sum, Harré's thesis involves the claim that the self and its internal states, as well as the sense of personal identity, are social phenomena; to understand them properly we must attend to the social contexts in which individuals find themselves. These phenomena are culture-relative. As we saw in the section on personal identity, philosophical accounts of personal identity characteristically abstract away from this social context. But there are some recent indications that this may be changing.

For instance, philosophers have been concerned for some time (at least since the publication in 1970 of the article by Bernard Williams [selection 12]) that how one responds to thought experiments about personal identity varies importantly depending on how the examples are presented. Williams argued that the same example will elicit two different, perhaps incompatible, responses depending on how it is presented. Robert Nozick (selection 14) suggested that an important part of the explanation of the phenomenon of differing responses is that personal identity is not a matter just of the intrinsic relationships between an individual at one time and an individual at some later time but is also importantly affected by the presence or absence of other persons, individuals who could plausibly be regarded as "continuers" of the original person. Nozick's innovation was a small but crucial move in the direction of a social concept of personal identity.

Steven White has argued more recently that Nozick did not go far enough. According to White, an important part of the explanation of the phenomenon of differing responses is that different ways of presenting the same example suggest differing social contexts. The aspects of these contexts that partly determine which way our intuitions go include not just the presence or absence of competing continuers, but a much richer array of social facts: "facts about the attitudes and feeling of others, the conventions and practices of the subject's society, and in some cases even the society's level of technological development". Such considerations lead White to embrace a view he calls "metapsychological relativism":

> *The metapsychological facts are those facts about personal identity, responsibility, and the unity and character of the self which are presupposed, rather than settled, by empirical psychology. The relativist claim, then, is that there could be two societies, neither of whose members are either misinformed or irrational, but whose social practices settle the significant metapsychological issues in radically different ways. [Steven White, "Metapsychological Relativism and the Self," Journal of Philosophy, 1989, (pp. 298–323)]*

White's view represents another step away from the traditional philosophical stance of what we have called the absolute view of personal identity — a form of personal atomism — in the direction of what we have called the relative view — the most extreme form of which is a kind of social holism. It is too early to say whether philosophers as a group will continue to move toward integrating considerations of social context into their analyses of personal identity and, if they do, how far they will go. But if they continue to move even a little further in this direction, social science discussions of self and identity could become important to the philosophical problem of personal identity.

One kind of social science consideration already relevant is the question of how social context influences the ways people come to describe themselves and their properties. We each seem to have knowledge not merely about the organism that, for instance, on Dennett's view, fabricated us, we also seem to have knowledge about our own subjective states — what we call our mental lives. Even if it turns out that the feelings of certainty about self are an illusion because the self is nothing but an elaborate fiction, how are we to account for the apparent knowledge we each have about ourselves?

Kenneth J. Gergen (selection 23) advances the startling thesis that not only is the self a fabrication but the very properties we attribute to ourselves (our internal states) are themselves fabrications. He thinks there is (almost) no self-knowledge because there are (almost) no truths about ourselves to know. Almost everything we think we know about ourselves is merely derivative from and dependent on the social environment in which we find (that is, fabricate) ourselves.

Gergen's idea is this. When you try to determine the nature of your inner states, aside from crude discriminations, there is no objective basis for characterizing your inner states one way rather than another. What we call self-knowledge is merely socially conditioned interpretation that has little to do with the actual intrinsic properties being interpreted. So-called breakthroughs in self-knowledge are merely realizations that alternative, more satisfying ways of interpreting ourselves are available.

Gergen's evidence is derived from several sources. For instance, he argues that emotional states, except in extreme cases, depend on social context. He admits that we can differentiate physiologically between positive and negative emotions and between fear and anger, for instance, but claims that we cannot differentiate physiologically among more refined emotions such as hostility, envy, vengefulness, and frustration. In the (inner) world according to Gergen, most of our emotional states are so diffuse that we can figure out what they are only by observing how others treat us: Social cues provide us with the proper concepts to use in understanding what we "truly" feel.

Gergen argues that self-esteem also is importantly dependent on the social environment. As perceived evaluation by others varies, so, too, do judgments of self-worth. In scanning our memories and applying to ourselves labels such as "strong-principled," "intelligent," "physically attractive," and so on, Gergen claims that we have so much data, which we scan selectively, that we can justify almost any label we choose. Social cues importantly influence which labels we do choose. Even the way we decide whether someone's actions (including our own) were caused by that person's volition or by external causes—how free someone is—is also in large part socially determined.

Whereas Dennett, Harré, and Gergen are all profoundly skeptical about either the reality of the self or the possibility of self-knowledge or both, Ulric Neisser (selection 24) identifies five different sources of self-knowledge. He claims that the five distinct mechanisms that give rise to this knowledge constitute five distinct selves. Thus, on Neisser's view not only is self-knowledge possible but there are no fewer than five knowing selves within us, each of which is actual: Not only are you real, there are five of you.

Consider the act of walking with eyes open. This produces continuously changing flow patterns in the visual field. Looking straight ahead while walking toward a wall produces one such pattern; walking parallel to a wall produces another. Under normal circumstances the organism is aware of several of these patterns at the same time, which collectively it uses to determine its position and movement. This, claims Neisser, allows the organism to distinguish itself from its environment and also affects the organism's sense of self. For instance, studies indicate that children locate the self in the region of the eyes—at the point of observation as specified by the optical flow patterns; when children cover their eyes with their hands and exclaim "You can't see me," they usually admit, when questioned, that you can see their feet, their hands, their bellies, and so on, but not *them*. Children also see themselves as the cause of predictable and repeatable changes in their immediate environment, such as the movements of their limbs, and as a consequence they come to regard the things that move and change as a result of their own wills as parts of themselves. According to Neisser, these two interrelated abilities within the organism give rise to a self that he calls "the ecological self." Because even human infants have these abilities, Neisser claims this shows that—contrary to conventional psychological wisdom—a young infant can distinguish between itself and the environment, including between itself and its mother, even though it does not yet possess a self-concept.

On the other hand, the "interpersonal" self, according to Neisser, is established by species-specific signals of emotional rapport and communication, such as the ways human infants respond to the facial expressions of their mothers. This rich form of intersubjectivity is typically in place by the time the infant is two months old. Neisser claims that psychological studies have demonstrated that young infants in normal face-to-face interactions with their mothers are not just picking up information about their mothers, they are actually perceiving and anticipating the ongoing intersubjective relationship.

In addition to these two "selves," Neisser also distinguishes three others. The "extended self"—perhaps the self of the personal identity literature—is constructed on the basis of memory and anticipation relations. The "private self" is constructed on the basis of the organism's recognition that its conscious experiences are exclusively its own. The "conceptual self" is constructed on the basis of the organism's theories about itself—its "self-concepts." The reason Neisser thinks these five forms of information in effect create five different selves is that they are so distinct from each other in both structure and origin. They differ "in their developmental histories, in the accuracy with which we can know them, in the pathologies to which they are subject, and generally in what they contribute to human experience."

Frithjof Bergmann (selection 25) also argues for the reality of self but in an extremely different way from Neisser. Although Bergmann thinks there actually is such a thing as our "true self" and that we can each know what our own true self is, he claims that the self is not a substantial thing. It is, rather, a pattern of "identifications": we are selective about which elements of our experience and behavior we accept as truly our own and which we reject as being somehow externally caused. For the most part we are not even aware that we are involved in this process of accepting and rejecting; identification is not a conscious process, and the identifications themselves crystallize behind our backs: "Meanings attach themselves, experience is organized into new structures." These (unconsciously forming) patterns of identifications create psychological structures that constitute what we call "the self" and, depending on their effects, either a "true self" or a "false self." Bergmann claims that if these patterns of identifications create a true self, then the experience that results will be one of freedom—"a natural flow, neither cramped nor forced, a shift away from the need to control, to compensate and to correct, and toward the exuberance of actions and words at last taking shape quite effortlessly, as if by themselves." False selves impede this experience.

Extrapolating from Bergmann's views, we can imagine how the organism could have a false self thrust upon it, often one that does not fit. Many institutions and people—the government, churches, advertisers, teachers, parents—are more than willing to tell people who they *should* be. This can have a profound influence on our experiences; instead of seeing ourselves for what we really are, we see ourselves as we think we *should* be. For instance, an adolescent raised in a sexually repressed environment might not experience his first sexual feelings as natural responses within his body; instead, he might dissociate from these feelings and experience them as the effect of external, evil forces. The instructions on which such misinterpretations of one's self are based begin early. By the time the child learns to talk it has already internalized many of these "shoulds." By adolescence it becomes difficult, if not impossible, to distinguish what one thinks one should think, feel, and experience from what one actually thinks, feels, and experiences.

Nevertheless, the idea that there is such a thing as a "true self" is philosophically suspect. For many, including, it would seem, for Dennett, Harré, and Gergen, it may be difficult to take the idea seriously. That is why before we consider alternative ways in which we might analyze the notion of a true self we should first be made to feel that the application of the notion is sometimes compelling. What we need, then, are richly contextualized examples of situations in which the notion of a true self seems to capture something significant. Fiction provides an ample source of such examples, one of which may be found in Charlotte Perkins Gilman's gripping story, "The Yellow Wallpaper."

Gilman's story is about a woman's attempt to break through the imprisoning constraints of societal expectations. Having internalized, but not completely, the expectations of late nineteenth-century American society, the woman yearns to do meaningful work—to write. Her husband, a doctor, forbids her to do so. He prescribes rest and especially sleep. His sister—"a perfect and enthusiastic housekeeper"—helps enforce the prescription. When the three of them rent a house for the summer, the frustrated woman sees—although not clearly at first—in the pattern of the faded, yellow wallpaper a symbolic expression of her struggle to be free. The prisonlike surface pattern of the wallpaper, which represents social expectations, is chaotic, ugly and distracting:

> *[It is] a constant irritant to a normal mind. The color is hideous enough, and unreliable enough, and infuriating enough, but the pattern is torturing.*
> *You think you have mastered it, but just as you get well under way in*

following, it turns a back-somersault and there you are. It slaps you in the face, knocks you down, and tramples upon you. It is like a bad dream. . . .

The woman eventually notices that beneath this surface pattern there lurks a figure—a woman, or several women—trying to escape:

There are things in that wallpaper that nobody knows about but me, or ever will.

Behind that outside pattern the dim shapes get clearer every day. . . . it is like a woman stooping down and creeping about behind that pattern. . . . The faint figure behind seemed to shake the pattern, just as if she wanted to get out.

Her recognition of this figure trying to escape, which is a projection of her deepest aspirations, at first frightens her—so thoroughly has she internalized society's expectations. Then it fascinates her. Finally, as its meaning becomes clearer, it liberates her.

Gilman's story dramatically illustrates the struggle to shed a false and imprisoning self and find a liberating one—on Bergmann's view, a true one. In the case of the heroine of Gilman's story, the false self revolves around the woman's internalized beliefs about her proper role and includes phenomenology—for instance, how she experiences herself—as well as behavior—how she spends her days. The story is constructed to dramatize the fact that the woman's beliefs about her proper role are sharply at odds with her "true feelings."

When Gilman's story was published in 1891, a Boston physician complained that it might drive readers mad. Unquestionably the story has a disorienting power. In her subsequent explanation of why she wrote it, Gilman reveals that

For many years I suffered from a severe and continuous nervous breakdown tending to melancholia—and beyond. During about the third year of this trouble I went, in devout faith and some faint stir of hope, to a noted specialist in nervous diseases, the best known in the country. This wise man put me to bed and applied the rest cure, to which a still-good physique responded so promptly that he concluded there was nothing much the matter with me, and sent me home with solemn advice to "live as domestic a life as far as possible," to "have but two hours' intellectual life a day," and "never to touch pen, brush, or pencil again" as long as I lived. This was in 1887.

I went home and obeyed those directions for some three months, and came so near the borderline of utter mental ruin that I could see over.

Then, using the remnants of intelligence that remained, and helped by a wise friend, I cast the noted specialist's advice to the winds and went to work again—work, the normal life of every human being; work, in which is joy and growth and service, without which one is a pauper and a parasite—ultimately recovering some measure of power.

Being naturally moved to rejoicing by this narrow escape, I wrote "The

Yellow Wallpaper," with its embellishments and additions . . . and sent a
copy to the physician who so nearly drove me mad. He never acknowledged
it. [Ann Lane, ed., The Charlotte Perkins Gilman Reader, *New York:*
Pantheon Books, 1980, pp. 3–20]

Gilman's story beautifully illustrates Bergmann's thesis and suggests that, although difficult to formulate precisely, it may be based on a sound insight. Her story is believably realistic. At the beginning, the heroine is a victim of societal expectations that she has internalized into a kind of false self. Imprisoned by this false self, she cannot live freely. By the end, however, she has thrown off these expectations and replaced them with a pattern of identifications that, regardless of their origin, are more conducive to her freedom. The process is familiar enough. The question is how to understand it philosophically. Bergman's thesis about the ways in which identifications form selves and the relationships between true and false selves, on the one hand, and freedom, on the other, is a possible way of trying to understand this phenomenon.

And yet, however persuasive the notion of "true self" when we encounter stories such as Gilman's and theoretical analyses such as Bergmann's, fiction also provides equally compelling examples to illustrate that the notion remains deeply puzzling. For instance, Milan Kundera's "The Hitchhiking Game" illustrates nicely how, when it comes to the task of discovering our true selves, or even to discovering what we really want, really value, really are like, and so on, the line between truth and pretense is a tenuous one at best. The problem is that, as with actors, there are many roles we can play, some compatible with our self-conceptions and our usual behavior, some quite alien. Which of these roles, if any, express who we really are? With which do we identify the most? Which make us feel authentic, which phony? Or is it all simply pretense? How can we know?

In Kundera's story, a pair of young lovers discover that it is not easy to distinguish true selves from false masks. Stopping for gas on their way to a vacation on the coast, they pretend that she is hitchhiking and that he has picked her up. He tries to seduce her. Ordinarily shy, she plays at being receptive to a stranger. They both discover, to their astonishment, that she plays the part quite well. Unexpected and powerfully vivid feelings surface that she never before would have imagined possible to take as her own.

He had intercourse with her. She was glad that at least now finally the
unfortunate game would end and they would again be the two people they
had been before and would love each other. She wanted to press her mouth
against his. But the young man pushed her head away and repeated that he
only kissed women he loved. She burst into loud sobs. But she wasn't even
allowed to cry, because the young man's furious passion gradually won over
her body, which then silenced the complaint of her soul. On the bed there
were soon two bodies in perfect harmony, two sensual bodies, alien to each
other. This was exactly what the girl had most dreaded all her life and had

scrupulously avoided till now: love-making without emotion or love. She knew that she had crossed the forbidden boundary, but she proceeded across it without objections and as a full participant; only somewhere, far off in a corner of her consciousness, did she feel horror at the thought that she had never known such pleasure, never so much pleasure as at this moment — beyond that boundary.

Is the woman out of character? Is she just pretending? Or has she been deceiving herself and only now finally discovered her true self? Or is one's so-called true self just a more elaborate form of pretense? The woman herself does not know. She suddenly finds herself identifying with an emergent unknown. The intensity of her pleasure is matched by an equally intense fear: Who is she?

Fiction was suddenly making an assault upon real life. . . . It irritated the young man more and more how well able *the girl was to become the lascivious miss; if she was able to do it so well, he thought, it meant that she really* was *like that; after all, no alien soul had entered into her from somewhere in space; what she was acting now was she herself; perhaps it was that part of her being which had formerly been locked up and which the pretext of the game had let out of its cage. Perhaps the girl supposed that by means of the game she was* disowning *herself, but wasn't it the other way around? wasn't she becoming herself only through the game? wasn't she freeing herself through the game? no, opposite him was not sitting a strange woman in his girl's body; it was his girl, herself, no one else. . . .*

Then it was all over. The young man got up off the girl and, reaching out for the long cord hanging over the bed, switched off the light. He didn't want to see the girl's face. He knew that the game was over, but didn't feel like returning to their customary relationship; he feared this return. He lay beside the girl in the dark in such a way that their bodies would not touch.

After a moment he heard her sobbing quietly; the girl's hand diffidently, childishly touched his; it touched, withdrew, then touched again, and then a pleading, sobbing voice broke the silence, calling him by his name and saying, "I am me, I am me . . ."

The young man was silent, he didn't move, and he was aware of the sad emptiness of the girl's assertion, in which the unknown was defined by the same unknown.

And the girl soon passed from sobbing to loud crying and went on endlessly repeating this pitiful tautology: "I am me, I am me, I am me . . ." [Milan Kundera, "The Hitchhiking Game," in his Laughable Loves, *translated by Suzanne Rappaport, New York: Knopf, 1974, pp. 65–88]*

Kundera's story suggests that there is no true self or, if there is, it is unknowable. In the story, Bergmann's criteria are apparently satisfied. The woman, for the first time in her life, experiences a sense of freedom. Yet neither she nor we, the readers, can feel confident that her true self has been revealed in the experience. It is as if her experience of freedom creates identity problems rather than solves them.

As so often in his fiction—*The Unbearable Lightness of Being* is another example—Kundera suggests that our selves are nothing but a thin surface of illusions created in large part by self-deception. But the very idea of deceiving ourselves—especially on such a fundamental level—is puzzling. It is easy to understand how the deception of others is possible and why it sometimes might be valuable. But how could we possibly deceive ourselves? Why would we even want to? It is not implausible to suppose that before we can make sense of the distinction between true and false selves, we must first understand self-deception.

The surprising fact is that we do deceive ourselves—not just sometimes and over trivial matters, but often and seriously. For instance, sometimes when we have excellent evidence for an unwanted conclusion we suppress our awareness of the evidence or choose not to draw the obvious conclusion. We engage in "willful ignorance." The chronic alcoholic who refuses to acknowledge his addiction, even to himself; the wife or husband who refuses to see the other's infidelity; the unprepared student who believes his failure is due to the teacher not liking him; the stockbroker who attributes a lucky break to her own prowess; the businessman who attributes a personal failure to bad luck; and so on. The list is endless.

One component of self-deception seems to be that we acquire false information from or about ourselves. This may be just through simple error. Self-deception, however, requires more: perhaps that the false information is *known* by us to be false and yet, at the same time, is believed by us to be true. This seems contradictory. Knowing that something is false implies that you believe it is false. Yet some suggest that for self-deception to occur you also have to believe that what you know to be false is true. For instance, people often deceive themselves into believing that they are happier than they are. But if you know you are unhappy, then you also believe you are unhappy. How, while believing you are unhappy, can you also believe you are happy? Is this not impossible?

Ways of showing how self-deception might be possible only heighten the puzzle of what use the organism might have for self-deception. Suppose, for instance, you were to build an android that could scan its own states and report back on them to the central part of its internal computer. You program the android so that it periodically monitors itself for internal trouble and, if it finds it, double-checks itself before taking corrective action. For instance, it checks its ankle joints to see if they need oil; if they do, it double-checks before activating the lubricating circuits. Clearly this programing could be beneficial to the android. Suppose, though, that you program it so that when it double-checks itself it often reports back incorrectly. In other words, you construct the android so that it systematically deceives itself and thus delays, or even negates, corrective action. That programing seems not beneficial but destructive. You certainly could program the android that way, but why would you want to? How could it possibly improve the android's ability to function if it is prone to self-deception? Apparently, however, this is similar to what nature has done to us, or worse yet, what we have done to ourselves. Why would nature give rise to such deceived creatures? Why would an organism do this to itself?

Mark Johnston (selection 26), in his account of self-deception, claims that the function of self-deceptive mechanisms in our psychologies is to reduce anxiety. He begins by arguing against so-called homuncular accounts of self-deception according to which the self is divided into interacting subsystems each of which has its own beliefs, goals, plans, and strategies. On the homuncular theory, selves have a kind of subpersonal multiple personality disorder, and self-deception occurs when some of these homuncular subsystems intentionally deceive the main system.

According to Johnston's nonhomuncular account, self-deception is a species of wishful thinking. In the face of contrary evidence, we believe what we want to believe. Such belief is purposeful but usually not intentional—that is, although it serves the person's objectives, and hence is goal directed, it is not something the person intends to happen. For example, blood flowing through our veins serves the objectives of the organism but is not usually intended. Johnston appeals to the notion of a "mental tropism"—a purpose-serving but nonintentional mental mechanism—to argue that typical cases of self-deception involve nonintentional deflection of belief by desire. When we desire a certain outcome the tropism deflects us from believing that that outcome has not happened or will not happen. This reduces anxiety.

Martha Nussbaum (selection 27) gives a radically different account of self-knowledge and self-deception. She is concerned with the knowledge we have of our own emotions and focuses on the specific knowledge a person has of whether she is in love. She tries to account for it not by appeal to traditional, intellectual models of what knowledge consists in but to a radically different kind of model that stresses the display of emotional content rather than an explanatory account of it. Although she does not mention feminism, her defense of her model might be considered a provocative foray into what is sometimes called "feminist epistemology."

Nussbaum illustrates her model of knowledge by contrasting it with two others: what we might call the "traditional, intellectual model," and the "catalyptic-impression model," which she claims Proust advocates in *Remembrance of Things Past*. She finds her own model of emotional knowledge exemplified in Ann Beattie's short story, "Learning to Fall."

On the intellectual (or scientific) model, one acquires knowledge about whether one is in love by a detached, unemotional, analytic examination of one's self. Speaking loosely, one might say that, on this model, the answer to the question "Are you in love?" is found in the intellect.

The catalyptic-impression model has two versions. In the first, knowledge of whether one is in love is given in and through certain powerful experiences, such as anguish, that come from the reality of one's condition and could not possibly come from anything else. On this version of the model, one might say that the answer to the question of whether one is in love is found in the passions. In the second version of the model, catalyptic impressions are still necessary—passion provides the data—but the intellect must then interpret the passions to get the answer. So, in a sense, still speaking loosely, on this model the answer is in both the passions and the intellect. It is difficult to be sure exactly how this second version differs from the intellectual view; perhaps it is simply a special case of the intellectual view.

On Nussbaum's own model, which might be called the "interactive" view, love is not a condition of the solitary individual but a way of being, feeling, and interacting with another person that involves trust and vulnerability. Nussbaum seems to be saying that knowledge of love is not discovered in an analytic examination or given in a powerful experience but, rather, is shown. She says in one place that knowledge of love is "a whole way of life," in another place that it is "a love story."

In the original essay, but not included in the excerpt here, Nussbaum explains her view of the role of a philosophy of self-deception, which is not to give a general, philosophical account of it, but to set opposing literary views of self-deception side by side and to examine their relationships to each other and to experience. Thus, she claims, the job of philosophy, which should be continuous with literature, is to set up the confrontations, clarify the oppositions, and move us "from an unarticulated sympathy with this or that story to a reflective grasp of our own sympathies."

Finally, we might wonder how some of the perplexing puzzles and insights about consciousness, self, and identity that we have surveyed in this book fit into our larger concept of the nature of the world. In particular, we might wonder how the issues we have explored fit into a picture of the world in which modern physics occupies a central place. Allen Stairs (selection 28) addresses this question.

The fundamental puzzle about quantum mechanics is how to understand the *superposition of states.* Stairs begins with a discussion of this concept, intended for readers who are not familiar with modern physics, and goes on to explore how our views on superposition might connect with our views about self.

One view about superposition—the "many worlds" interpretation— claims the universe itself branches every time anyone makes a quantum mechanical measurement, and thus that selves are constantly splitting into more and more copies. Stairs considers this possibility briefly but rejects it. Next, he considers what he regards as a more perplexing question: Can there be a superposition of mental states? This leads to a broader discussion of the relationship among self, mentality, and the microworld. Stairs' surprising conclusion is that our theories of self are more likely to shed light on quantum reality than the other way around. He suggests that those who, perplexed by the puzzles and paradoxes about who and what we are, wish to take solace in the idea that at least we know what the world is, are in for a shock.

21

DANIEL C. DENNETT
The Origins of Selves

What is a self? Since Descartes in the seventeenth century, we have had a vision of the self as a sort of immaterial ghost that owns and controls a body the way you own and control your car. More recently, with the rejection of dualism and the rise of materialism—the idea that the mind just *is* the brain—we have gravitated to the view that the self must be a node or module in the brain, the Central Headquarters responsible for organizing and directing all the subsidiary bureaucracies that keep life and limb together. Or is the very idea of a self nothing but a compelling fiction, a creed outworn, as some theorists insist, a myth we keep telling ourselves in spite of the advances of science that discredit it?

". . . a myth we keep telling ourselves." A myth we keep telling *whom*? Is a self something else, perhaps even some hard-to-image combination of these very different ideas?

On my first trip to London many years ago I found myself looking for the nearest Underground station. I noticed a stairway in the sidewalk labeled "Subway," which in *my* version of English meant subway train, so *I* confidently descended the stairs and marched forth looking for the trains. After wandering around in various corridors, I found another flight of stairs, leading up, alas, and somewhat dubiously climbed them to find myself on the other side of the intersection from where I had started. I must have missed a turn, I thought, and walked back downstairs to try again. After what seemed to

me to be an exhaustive search for hitherto overlooked turnstiles or side entrances, I emerged back on the sidewalk where I had started, feeling somewhat cheated. It finally dawned on me that a subway in London is just a way of crossing the street underground. Searching for the self can be somewhat like that. You enter the brain through the eye, march up the optic nerve, round and round in the cortex, looking behind every neuron, and then, before you know it, you emerge into daylight on the spike of a motor nerve impulse, scratching your head and wondering where the self is.

That is not the way to find the self, or to understand what a self is. (That's a bit like wandering around Manhattan looking for the Big Apple.) Where then might we look? We might look first to origins. As the British biologist D'Arcy Thompson once said, "Everything is what it is because it got that way" (1917, *On Growth and Form*).

If selves are anything at all, then they exist. *Now* there are selves. There was a time, millions (or billions) of years ago, when there were none—at least none on this planet. So there has to be—as a matter of logic—a true story to be told about *how there came to be* creatures with selves. This story will have to tell—as a matter of logic—about a process (or a series of processes) involving the activities or behaviors of things that do not yet *have* selves—or *are* not yet selves—but which eventually yield, as a new product, beings that do have selves. That is the true story I would like to tell, but quite obviously it is now—and probably forever—impossible to *know* the details of that story, so we will have to speculate somewhat, guided as firmly as possible by the available facts.

And since this will have to be a brief overview of a rather large and intricate research project, I must resort to simplifications and metaphors to illustrate the outlines without going into the details. That does not mean that I have a different version, right now, for the *experts*. In fact there are no experts on these topics, and the experts on the details have just as much trouble seeing the overall shape and direction of theory as any novice—perhaps more trouble, since they are so preoccupied with their close-up views of tiny patches of the problem.

This story that must be told is analogous to other stories that science is beginning to tell. Compare it, for instance, to the fascinating story of the evolution of sex. There are many organisms today that have no genders and reproduce asexually, and there most certainly was a time when all the organisms that existed did not come in different genders, male and female, and did not engage in *sexual* reproduction.[1] Somehow, by some imaginable series of steps, some of these organisms have to have evolved into organisms that did have genders, and eventually, of course, into us, and the rather exotic—and, indeed, erotic—transformations and elaborations we have added to the basic biological phenomenon of gender. What sort of conditions were required to foster or necessitate these innovations? Why, in short, did all these changes happen?

There is a nice parallel between the two questions, about the origins of *sex* and the origins of *selves*. There is almost nothing *sexy* (in human terms) about the sex life of insects, oysters, and other simple forms of life, but we can recognize in their mechanical and apparently joyless routines of reproduction the foundations and principles of our much more exciting world of sex. Similarly, there is nothing particularly *selfy* (if I may coin a term) about the primitive precursors of human selves, but they lay the foundations for our particularly human innovations and complications.

The original distinction between self and other is a deep biological principle; one might say it is the deepest principle, for biology begins in *self*-preservation—in the emergence of entities (the simplest replicators) who resisted destruction and decay, who combatted, at least for a short time, the Second Law of Thermodynamics, and passed on their capacity to do this to their descendants.

As soon as something gets into the business of self-preservation, boundaries become important, for if you are setting out to preserve yourself, you don't want to squander effort trying to preserve the whole world; you draw the line. You become, in a word, *selfish*. This primordial form of selfishness (which, as a primordial form, lacks most of the flavors of *our* brand of human selfishness) is one of the marks of life. Where one bit of granite ends and the next bit begins is a matter of slight moment; the fracture boundary may be real enough, but nothing works to protect the territory, to push back the frontier or retreat. "Me against the world"—this distinction between everything on the *inside* of a closed boundary and everything in the *external world* is at the heart of all biological processes—not just ingestion and excretion, respiration and transpiration. Consider, for instance, the immune system, with its millions of different antibodies arrayed in defense of the body against millions of different alien intruders. This army must solve the fundamental problem of recognition: telling one's self (and one's friends) from everything else. And the problem has been solved in much the way human nations, and their armies, have solved the counterpart problem: by standardized

---

[1] See, esp., John Maynard Smith, *The Evolution of Sex*, 1978, Cambridge Univ. Press., and Richard Dawkins, *The Selfish Gene*, 1976, pp. 46–48.

identification—routines—the passports and customs officers in miniature are molecular shapes and shape-detectors. It is important to recognize that this army of antibodies has no generals, no GHQ with a battle plan or even a description of the enemy; the antibodies represent their enemies only in the way a million locks represent the keys that open them. Occasionally, misidentifications are made—in *autoimmune* reactions, for instance, in which a sort of civil war takes place between different factions of what *ought* to be peacefully coexisting parts of the whole that resides inside the walls.

The distinctions at this level are far from absolute; within the walls of the body are many, many interlopers, ranging from bacteria and viruses through microscopic mites that live like cliff-dwellers in the ecological niche of our skin and scalp, to larger parasites—horrible tapeworms, for instance. These interlopers are all tiny self-protectors in their own rights, but some of them, such as the bacteria that populate our digestive systems and without which we would die, are just as essential team members in our quest for self-preservation as the antibodies in our immune systems. (If Lynn Margulis' theory is correct, the mitochondria that do the work in almost all the cells in our body are the descendants of bacteria with whom "we" joined forces about two billions years ago.) Other interlopers are tolerated parasites—not worth the effort to evict, apparently—and still others are indeed the enemy within, deadly if not rooted out and driven out.

This fundamental biological principle of distinguishing self from world, inside from outside, has some remarkable echoes in the highest vaults of our psychology. The psychologist Paul Rozin has shown in a fascinating series of experiments on the nature of *disgust* that there is a powerful and unacknowledged undercurrent of blind resistance to certain acts that, rationally considered, should not trouble us.[2] For example,

would you please swallow the saliva in your mouth right now? This act does not fill you with revulsion. But suppose I had handed you a sparkling clean drinking glass and asked you to spit into the glass and *then* swallow the saliva from the glass. Disgusting! But why? It seems to have to do with our perception that once something is outside of our bodies it is no longer quite part of us anymore—it becomes alien and suspicious—it has renounced its citizenship and becomes something to be rejected.

Border crossings are thus either moments of anxiety, or, in a familiar reversal, something to be especially enjoyed:

> *In addition they seemed to spend a great deal of time eating and drinking and going to parties, and Frensic, whose appearance tended to limit his sensual pleasures to putting things into himself rather than into other people, was something of a gourmet.* [Tom Sharpe, The Great Pursuit, 1977[3]]

Sharpe suggests, in this funny but unsettling passage, that when you get right down to it all pleasure consists in playing around with one's own boundary, or someone else's, and these biological reflections of ours suggest that he is onto something—if not the whole truth, then part of the truth.

In any event, the origin of complex life forms on this planet was also the birth of the most primitive sort of self, whatever sort of self is implied by the self-regard that prevents the lobster, when hungry, from eating itself. Does a lobster have a self? Or, should we say, are there selves that have lobster bodies? This question is obviously the secular descendant of a question that has troubled theologians for several thousand years: Do animals have immortal souls? Do insects? I must say that I much prefer the secular version to the religious, and will not make any attempt—except by implication, no doubt—to express my opinions about the existence of *souls*. Even the most hard-headed ma-

---

[2] Paul Rozin, and April E. Fallon, "A Perspective on Disgust," *Psychological Review*, 1987.

[3] Secker and Warburg, Pan Books, edn, p. 6.

terialist/mechanist/scientist, on the other hand, must face the question of how to describe the distinction between the lobster and the rock behind which the lobster crouches—only one of them is designed around the principle of self-regard. So far as *that* property goes, we can make fairly simple robots or automata that also exhibit it, detecting and retreating from dangers, seeking out shelter and striving to renew their energy resources. This is minimal selfhood, but one must start at the beginning.

So a minimal self is not a *thing* inside a lobster or a lark, and it is not the "whole lobster" or "whole lark" either; it is something abstract which amounts just to the existence of an organization which tends to distinguish, control, and preserve portions of the world, an organization that thereby creates and maintains boundaries. To a first approximation the principle that draws the boundary is this:

You are what you control and care for.

Every word in this slogan cries out for further refinement, but I prefer to leave it in its simplest form, since the amendments that will already no doubt have occurred to you illustrate my next point. The boundaries of the minimal self are not only permeable, as we have just seen, but flexible as well. The hermit crab finds the discarded shell of another creature and appropriates it as a portable shelter, but by this appropriation that alien shell is moved inside the boundary—just as much as the shell that a snail grows, utilizing materials it likewise finds in its environment, but ingests and then extrudes.

The beaver's dam, by the same token, is so intimately associated with the beaver's fundamental strategies of survival that it should be included inside the boundary as well, as Richard Dawkins argues—I think conclusively—in *The Extended Phenotype*. One might protest that however loyally the beaver cares for its dam, it doesn't *directly* control the shape of its dam (in

the way that it directly controls the posture of its limbs), but one could also go on to point out that it doesn't control its limbs as directly as it controls the motor nerve firings that innervate its limbs—so should we draw the boundary of minimal selfhood inside its limbs? Surely not.

An even more stunning example is the anthill or termite colony, in which there is a boundary not marked by any membrane or even by unbroken proximity of parts. What is particularly striking about the termite colony is that it is an example of a complex system capable of functioning in what seems to be a thoroughly "purposeful and integrated" way simply by having *lots of subsystems doing their own thing* without any central supervision. Indeed most systems on earth that appear to have central controllers (and are usefully described as having them) do not. The colony as a whole builds elaborate mounds, gets to know its territory, organizes foraging expeditions, sends out raiding parties against other colonies, and so on. The group cohesion and coordination is so remarkable that hard-headed observers have been led to postulate the existence of a colony's "group soul" (*vide* Marais' "The Soul of the White Ant"[4]). Yet in fact all this group wisdom results from nothing other than myriads of individual termites, specialized as several different castes, going about their individual business—influenced by each other, but quite uninfluenced by any master–plan.[5]

In every beehive or termite colony there is, to

[4]E. N. Marais, *The Soul of the White Ant*, London: Methuen, 1937.

[5]Douglas Hofstadter has developed the analogy between mind and ant colony in the "Prelude . . . Ant Fugue" flanking chapter 10 of *Gödel, Escher, Bach*, New York: Basic Books, 1979, pp. 275–336. The "distributed control" approach to designing intelligent machines has in fact had a long history in artificial intelligence, going back as far as Selfridge's early "Pandemonium" model of 1959, and finding recent expression in Marvin Minsky's *The Society of Mind*, New York: Simon & Schuster, 1985.

be sure, a Queen Bee or Queen Termite, but these individuals are more patient than agent, more a treasure to be protected than the chief of the protective forces—in fact, their name is more fitting today than in earlier ages, for they are much more like Queen Elizabeth II than Queen Elizabeth I. There is no Margaret Thatcher bee, no George Bush termite, no Oval Office in the anthill.

But enough about the bees and the birds. What about us? I know that there will be some among you who will be sure I am leading you on a wild goose chase; the sort of selfhood we have been examining, you think, is *not at all* the sort of selfhood that you have; a human being's self is *entirely different* from the sort of implied self of the lobster or the ant-colony. Yes and no. Of course they are different in important ways; the question is, can we build a bridge of evolution or development between them?

First, let's look at a similarity, and then a major difference. Do our selves, our nonminimal *selfy* selves, exhibit permeability and flexibility of boundaries? We have noted the hermit crab's shell and the beaver's dam. What of our own clothes, our houses, our automobiles, and the other paraphernalia we strive to control— our "stuff" as George Carlin calls it? Do we expand our personal boundaries—the boundaries of our *selves*—to enclose any of this? In general, perhaps, no, but there are certainly times when this seems true, psychologically. For instance, some people own cars and drive them, while other people are *motorists*; the inveterate motorist prefers *being* a four-wheeled, gas-consuming agent to being a two-legged, food-consuming agent, and his use of the first-person pronoun betrays this identification:

"I'm not cornering well on rainy days because my tires are getting bald."

So sometimes we enlarge our boundaries; at other times, in response to perceived challenges real or imaginary, we let our boundaries shrink:

"*I* didn't do that! That wasn't the real me talking. Yes, the words came out of my mouth, but I refuse to recognize them as my own."

This shrinking tactic has important moral implications. If you make yourself really small, you can externalize virtually everything.[6]

I have reminded you of these familiar speeches to draw out the similarities between our selves and the selves of ants and hermit crabs, but the speeches also draw attention to the most important difference: ants and hermit crabs don't talk. The hermit crab is designed or organized in such a way as to see to it that it acquires a shell; this organization, we might say, *implies* a shell, and hence, in a *very* weak sense, tacitly *represents the crab as having a shell*, but the crab does not in any stronger sense *represent itself as* having a shell. It doesn't go in for self-representation at all. To whom would it so represent itself and why? It doesn't need to remind *itself* of this aspect of its nature, since its innate design takes care of that problem, and there are no other interested parties in the offing. And the ants, as we have noted, accomplish their communal projects without relying on any explicitly communicated blueprints or edicts.

We, in contrast, are almost constantly engaged in presenting ourselves to others, and to ourselves, and hence *representing* ourselves—in language and gesture, external and internal. The most obvious difference in our environment that would explain this difference in our behavior is the behavior itself. Our human environment contains not just food and shelter, enemies to fight or flee and conspecifics with whom to mate, but words, words, words. These words are potent elements of our environment that we readily incorporate, ingesting and ex-

---

[6]See the discussion of the moral implications of the "dimensions of the self" in Dennett, Daniel C., *Elbow Room: The Varieties of Free Will Worth Wanting*, Cambridge, Mass.: MIT Press, 1984, esp. p. 143.

truding them, weaving them like spiderwebs into self-protective strings of *narrative. Our* fundamental tactic of self-protection, self-control, and self-definition is not building dams or spinning webs, but telling stories—and more particularly concocting and controlling the story we tell others—and ourselves—about who we are.

Now we are ready for the strangest idea in my paper, but also, I think, the most important: there is a further similarity between the spiders, the beavers, and us. Spiders don't have to think, consciously and deliberately, about how to spin their webs; that is just something that spider brains are designed to get spiders to do. And even beavers, unlike professional human engineers, do not consciously and deliberately plan the structures they build. And finally, *we*, (unlike *professional* human storytellers) do not consciously and deliberately figure out what narratives to tell and how to tell them; like spider webs, our tales are *spun by us*; our human consciousness, and our narrative selfhood, is their *product*, not their *source*.

These strings or streams of narrative issue forth *as if* from a single source—not just in the obvious physical sense of flowing from just one mouth, or one pencil or pen, but in a more subtle sense: their effect on any audience or readers is to encourage them to (try to) posit a unified agent whose words they are, about whom are: in short, to posit what I call a *center of narrative gravity*.[7] This is yet another abstraction, not a thing in the brain, but still a remarkably robust and almost tangible *attractor of properties*, the "owner of record" of whatever items and features are lying about unclaimed. Who owns your car? You do. Who owns your clothes? You do. Then who owns your body? You do! When you say "This is *my* body," you

certainly aren't taken as saying "This body owns itself." But what can you be saying, then? If what you say is neither a bizarre and pointless tautology (this body is its own owner, or something like that) nor the metaphysically discredited—or at least highly suspect—claim that you are an immaterial soul or ghost puppeteer who owns and operates this body, what else could you mean? I think we could see more clearly what "This is *my* body" meant if we could answer the question: as opposed to what? How about as opposed to this? "No it isn't; it's *mine*, and I don't like sharing it!"

If we could see what it would be like for two (or more) selves to vie for control of a single body, we could see better what a single self really is. As scientists of the self, we would like to conduct controlled experiments in which, by varying the initial conditions, we could see just what has to happen, in what order, and requiring what resources for such a talking self to emerge. Are there conditions under which life goes on but no self emerges? Are there conditions under which more than one self emerges? Of course we cannot ethically conduct such experiments, but, as in other scientific investigations of human phenomena, occasionally nature conducts terrible experiments, from which we can cautiously draw conclusions.

Such an experiment is Multiple Personality Disorder, in which a single human body *seems* to be shared by several selves, each, typically, with a proper name and an autobiography. Nicholas Humphrey and I have been investigating MPD with an eye to answering these questions about the self.

The idea of Multiple Personality Disorder, or MPD, strikes many people as too outlandish and metaphysically bizarre to believe—a "paranormal" phenomenon to discard along with ESP, close encounters of the third kind, and witches on broomsticks. I suspect that some of these people have made a simple *arithmetical* mistake: They have failed to notice that two or

---

[7] Daniel Dennett, "Why We are All Novelists," *Times Literary Supplement*, Sept. 16–22, 1988, also to appear as "The Self as the Center of Narrative Gravity," in F. Kessel, P. Cole, and D. Johnson, eds., *Self and Consciousness: Multiple Perspectives*, Hillsdale, NJ: Erlbaum (in press).

three or seventeen selves per body is really no more *metaphysically* extravagant than one self per body. One is bad enough!

"I just saw a car drive by with five selves in it."

"*What?? The mind reels! What kind of metaphysical nonsense is this?*"

"Well, there were also five bodies in the car."

"*Oh, well, why didn't you say so. Then everything is OK.*"

"Or maybe only four bodies, or three—but definitely five selves."

"*What??!!*"

The principle of "one to a customer" certainly captures the normal arrangement, but if a body can have one, why not more than one under abnormal conditions?

I don't at all mean to suggest that there is nothing shocking or deeply puzzling about MPD. It is, in fact, a phenomenon of surpassing strangeness, not, I think, because it challenges our presuppositions about what is *metaphysically* possible, but more because it challenges our presuppositions about what is *humanly* possible, about the limits of human cruelty and depravity on the one hand, and the limits of human creativity on the other. For the evidence is now voluminous that there are not a handful or a hundred but thousands of cases of MPD in this country, and it almost invariably owes its existence to prolonged early child abuse, usually sexual, and of sickening severity.

These children have often been kept in such extraordinarily terrifying and confusing circumstances that I am more amazed that they survive psychologically at all than I am that they manage to preserve themselves by a desperate redrawing of their boundaries. What they do, when confronted with overwhelming conflict and pain, is this: They "leave." They create a boundary so that the horror doesn't happen *to them*; it either happens to no one, or to some other self better able to sustain its organization under such an onslaught—at least that's what they *say* they did, as best they recall.

How can this be? What kind of account could we give, ultimately at the biological level, of such a process of splitting? Does there have to have been a single, whole self that somehow fissioned, amoebalike? How could that be if a self is not a proper physical part of an organism or a brain but, as I have suggested, an abstraction? The response to the trauma seems so creative, moreover, that one is inclined at first to suppose that it must be the work of some kind of a supervisor in there: a supervisory brain program, a central controller, or whatever. But we should remind ourselves of the termite colony, which also seemed, at first, to require a central chief executive to accomplish such clever projects. We can perhaps convince ourselves of the possibility—no more than that—of such a creative process by exploring an extended analogy.

Consider the United States of America. At one level of description there is surely nothing wrong with personifying the USA and talking about it (rather like the termite colony) as if it had an inner self. The USA has memories, feelings, likes and dislikes, hopes, talents, and so on. It hates Communism, is haunted by the memory of Vietnam, is scientifically creative, socially clumsy, somewhat given to self-righteousness, rather sentimental. But does that mean there is one central agency inside the USA which embodies all those qualities? Of course not. There is, as it happens, a specific area of the country where much of it comes together. But go to Washington and ask to speak to Mr. American Self and you'd find there was nobody home: Instead, you'd find a lot of different agencies (the Defense Department, the Treasury, the courts, the Library of Congress, the National Science Foundation, etc.) operating in relative independence of each other.

To be sure, there is no such thing as Mr. American Self, but as a matter of fact there is in every country on earth a Head of State: a President, Queen, Chancellor, or some such figurehead. The head of State may actually be nonexecutive; certainly he does not himself enact all the subsidiary roles (the U.S. president does not bear arms, sit in the courts, play baseball, or travel to the Moon . . .). But nevertheless he is expected at the very least to take an active interest in all these national pursuits. The president is meant to appreciate better than anyone the "State of the Union." He is meant to *represent* different parts of the nation *to* each other, and to inculcate a common value system. Moreover—and this is most important—he is the "spokesman" when it comes to dealing with other nation-states. Other individuals—diplomats and press secretaries—may deliver the actual utterances, but these acts are understood to be relaying *his* speech acts to the world.

That is not to say that a nation, lacking such a figurehead, would cease to function day-to-day. But it is to say that in the longer term it may function much better if it does have one. Indeed, a good case can be made that nations, unlike termite colonies, require this kind of figurehead as a condition of their political survival—especially given the complexity of international affairs.

The drift of this analogy is obvious. In short, a human being, too, may need an inner figurehead—especially given the complexities of human social life. If this is accepted (as I think it should be), we can turn to the vexed question of how such a figurehead could be developed or established in the first place. Here the Head of State analogy may seem at first less helpful. For one thing, in the USA at least, the President is democratically elected by the population. For another, the candidates for the presidency are preformed entities, already waiting in the wings.

Yet is this really so? It could equally be argued that the presidential candidates, rather than being preformed, are actually brought into being—through a narrative dialectical process—by the very population to which they offer their services as president. Thus, the population (or the news media) first try out various fictive

versions of what they think their "ideal president" should be and *then* the candidates adapt themselves as best they can to fill the bill. To the extent that there is more than one dominant fiction about "what it means to be American," different candidates mold themselves in different ways. But in the end only one can be elected—and he will, of course, claim to speak for the whole nation.

In very much a parallel way, Humphrey and I suggest, a human being first creates—unconsciously (the way a spider creates a web)—one or more ideal fictive-selves and then elects the best supported of these into office as her Head of Mind. A significant difference in the human case, however, is that there is likely to be considerably more *outside influence*. Parents, friends, and even enemies may all contribute to the image of "what it means to be me," as well as—and maybe over and above—the internal news media. In a Multiple Personality case, Daddy, for example, might lean on the growing child to impose an *invasive* fictive-self.

Thus a human being does not start out as single or as multiple—she starts out without any Head of Mind at all. She is poised to fend for herself—just as the lobster or beaver is—but she does not *yet* have an organization crystallized around one or more centers of narrative gravity. In the normal course of development, she slowly gets acquainted with the various possibilities of selfhood that "make sense"—partly through her own observation, partly through outside influence. In most cases a majority view emerges, strongly favoring one version of "the real me," and it is that version which is installed as her elected Head of Mind. But in some cases the competing fictive-selves are so equally balanced, or different constituencies within her are so unwilling to accept the result of the election, that constitutional chaos reigns—and there are snap elections (or coups d'état) all the time.

I think that a model inspired by (underlying, rendering honest) this analogy can account for symptomatology of MPD: the memory black-spots, differences in style, and so forth. Certainly the analogy provides a wealth of detail suggesting so. Once in office a new Head of State typically downplays certain "unfortunate" aspects of his nation's history (especially those associated with the rival Head of State who immediately preceded him). Moreover, he himself, by standing for particular national values, affects the course of future history by encouraging the expression of those values by the population (and so, by a kind of feedback, confirming his own role).

I am still talking in metaphors, however. What translations into the terms of current cognitive science could we formulate? First, what sense can be given to the notion of a "Head of Mind"? The analogy with a *spokesman* may not be far off the literal truth. The language-producing systems of the brain have to get their instructions from somewhere, and the very demands of pragmatics and grammar would conspire to confer something like Head of Mind authority on whatever subsystem *currently* controls their input. E. M. Forster once remarked, "How can I tell what I think until I see what I say?" The four "I"s in this sentence are meant to refer to the same thing. But this grammatical tradition may depend—and always has depended—on the fact that the thought expressed in Forster's question is quite literally self-confirming: what "I" (my self) thinks *is* what "I" (my language apparatus) says.

There can, however, be no guarantee that either the speaker or anyone else who hears him over an extended period will settle on there being just a single "I." Suppose, at different times, different subsystems within the brain produce "clusters" of speech that simply cannot easily be interpreted as the output of a single self. Then—as a Bible scholar may discover when working on the authorship of what is putatively a single-authored text—it may turn out that the clusters make *best sense* when attributed to different selves.

Another central feature of MPD is selective amnesia, which is the chief difference between the plight of the MPD sufferer and the rest of us (who have our various *personae* in the various roles we play day-to-day). MPD sufferers typically have no memory at all for the events that occur during regimes when they are out of power. To those who have even a passing knowledge of computer information processing, the idea of mutually inaccessible "directories" of stored information will already be familiar. In cognitive psychology, new discoveries about state-dependent learning and other evidence of modularization in the brain have led people to recognize that *failure* of access between different subsystems is the norm rather than the exception. Indeed, the old Cartesian picture of the mind "transparent to itself" now appears to be rarely if ever achievable (or even desirable) in practice. In this context the out-of-touchness of different selves no longer looks so startling.

The different "alters" of an MPD sufferer almost always have different attitudes toward life and different emotional characters; one will be prudish and reserved, another sexy, a third angry and violent, for instance. What could be the basis for the different "value systems" associated with these rival Heads of Mind? At another level of analysis, psychopharmacological evidence suggests that the characteristic emotional style of different personalities could correspond to the brain wide activation or inhibition of neural pathways that rely on different neurotransmitter chemicals. Thus, the phlegmatic style of one personality could be associated with low norepinephrine levels, the shift to a carnal style with high norepinephrine, and the out-of-control alter could coincide with low dopamine.

Even the idea of an "election" of the current Head of Mind is not implausible. Events very like elections take place in the brain all the time —whenever coherent patterns of activity compete for control of the same network. Consider what happens, for example, when the visual system receives two conflicting images at the two eyes. First there is an attempt at fusion; but if this proves to be unstable "binocular rivalry" results, with the input from one eye completely taking over while the other is suppressed. Thus, we already have, at the level of visual neurophysiology, clear evidence of the mind's general preference for single-mindedness over completeness.

MPD provides a window into alternative possibilities. In the same way that the force of grav-

ity is well-nigh invisible until you have imagined the weightlessness of outer space, so single-selfedness is hard to discern in a body until you have seen, or imagined, multiple-selfedness. . . . *

*Passages in this paper are drawn from Nicholas Humphrey and Daniel C. Dennett, "Speaking for Ourselves," *Raritan*, Fall, 1989, pp. 68–98. [Selection II in this volume.]

22

ROM HARRÉ
Personal Being as Empirical Unity

I: Public and Private Modes of Personal Identity

. . . The basic distinction that will be deployed is that between the fact of personal identity (what it is that makes a human being this or that particular person within a public–collective context) and the sense of personal identity (how people experience their unique selfhood). Clearly, there is no necessary coordination between these aspects of personal identity. The former could be well established in a species: for example, members might have no difficulty in recognizing each other as different and distinct and treating each other differentially without any member of that species having a sense of their own personal identity. One might imagine this to be the case among chimpanzees. We know that they treat each other as individuals, but we are by no means so sure each chimpan-

zee experiences their lives as developing *autobiographies*, centered on a unified consciousness. What is required for someone to have a sense of personal identity?

(1) Clearly, one necessary condition is that the individual should be self-conscious, that is, be aware of their experiences as constituting a personal unity. A miner, hewing at the coalface, can attend not only to the things which he is doing, the plans which he is entertaining, but know that they are his, by virtue of his capacity to identify himself as a unique person among others. In the sections below I shall be bringing out what is involved in experiencing one's experience and so one's personal life as a unity.

(2) If experiencing matters as one's own were only an ephemeral or momentary phenomenon, then this would not yield the full sense of personal uniqueness. There has also to be some kind of experiential continuity. In some way or other, an individual woman, for example, must

treat most of her actions as developments of and connected with her past personal experience and as attributes of one being, herself. In short, a person's present actions must be located in an autobiography, representing the past and anticipating the future.

In order to keep these complex matters under control, it will be necessary to introduce some basic philosophical distinctions among the kinds of identity with which we might be concerned. These reflect two major senses of sameness. These senses of identity are well established in traditional philosophy.

(1) In one sense of "same," two individuals are the same when they have closely similar properties, that is, are qualitatively identical. They remain, however, numerically different and distinct, and there are two of them.

(2) Sometimes by sameness we mean numerical identity. "This is the same person" implies that there is only one individual even though some of its properties at different times are different. The notion of numerical identity raises some interesting philosophical problems about what attributes or properties of an individual must remain the same for it to count as one and only one individual of a given kind. Clearly, some kinds of change, for instance changes in body weight, can be tolerated within a continuous numerical personal identity, whereas others such as extreme changes in personality may incline us, though not force us, to talk of one individual or person changing into another. Some of the more difficult conceptual problems in the area of personal identity arise at exactly this point.

A simple way of setting up the distinction between qualitative and numerical identity can be worked out by relating it to spatiotemporal considerations. If individuals exist at the same time and have all their properties in common except their spatial location, then they are numerically distinct. Sometimes an observer notices, at different times, apparently very similar individuals at the same place. Provided the differences between the apparently distinct individuals do not breach the criteria for identifying an individual of that kind and temporal continuity can be assumed, then we can say that there is one and only one individual persisting in that place. Consider a third possible case, in which there are apparently two individuals, some of whose properties are the same and some different, and the properties that are the same are appropriate for the identity of an individual of that category. But we find these seemingly distinctive individuals at different places at different times. Only if a spatiotemporally continuous path from one place at one time to the other place at the other time can be assumed, are we justified in claiming that we have truly one and only one distinct individual. So by reference to the spatiotemporal system and the grid it lays over the world, we are able to set up criteria which can be used to make coherent judgements of identity.

In the human case, considerations of spatiotemporal location and continuous translation point to the body as the source of the fact of identity. But the sense of identity seems to involve subjective and psychological matters like memory, consciousness and so on. However, bodily identity and continuity play a role in both the fact and the sense of identity; and the following considerations make this clear.

The distinctiveness of one's body serves as the basis of the identification of one's self by others as the same person. One can be reidentified from time to time and in different places through one's distinctive physical qualities and a corporeal body is surely spatiotemporally continuous. Once an individual has been identified, say from an old sepia regimental photograph, as having been present at a particular time and place, say Allahabad 1927, then further questions of identity are usually settled by reference to spatiotemporal continuity from that place and moment to the place and moment at which the allegedly identical individual appears to us now, for example, in the dock at the Old Bailey.

It seems clear that the basis of one's personal sense of identity has also to be, at least in part, referred to bodily considerations. Several philosophers have recently argued for the importance of two associated continuities in human experience (e.g. Strawson, *Individuals*, and Hampshire, *Thought and action*). There is the continuity of one's location in space and time relative to one's point of view. One sees the world from a particular place, relative to which particular aspects and perspectives are disclosed to the perceiver. A moment's reflection on one's autobiography suggests that this way of triangulating one's existence forms a large part of one's sense of a permanent self. Spatiotemporal location is also required to understand where and when one can act. For normal human beings one's point of action in the spatiotemporal system, defined by one's relations with other material bodies, is closely related to one's point of view. Even with the help of causal processes by means of which one can bring about changes at other places and times from those at which one initiated an action, one is nevertheless required to find the sensitive triggers that initiate causal processes near where one is standing oneself. These general considerations will allow us to proceed to more detail in considering the two aspects of personal identity we have identified, the fact of identity and the sense of identity.

II: Fact of Identity

The problems that are raised by the fact of human identity turn on the way in which the two main kinds of criteria, which seem to be at work in deciding whether an individual with whom we are presented is or is not the same person, are related to one another. Consider the case of the Tichbourne claimant, the man who turned up from Australia to establish his right to a disputed estate. Which criterion has priority in deciding whether he is the same person who left England many years before? There is his bodily continuity and the criteria for deciding that; and there is his continuity of "psyche," manifested in the public and private displays of what one might reasonably call mental aspects of his being, for example, his personality, avowed knowledge and demonstrated skills. His public right to claim a private sense of identity turns on his ability to remember events in his past life of a rich enough texture to sustain a hypothesis of continuity. The major problem of the balance between bodily and mental criteria arises through the difficulty of deciding, in particular cases, which should have priority (see Williams, *Problems of the self*).

By inventing hard cases, philosophers have tested the force of these criteria to try to disentangle their relationships since they are not always clearly distinguished in practice. The first question to be addressed is whether bodily continuity is a necessary condition for personal identity. That is, if one were able to establish similarity of personality and good agreement as to what an individual purported to remember, would this require us to say that two apparently bodily distinct individuals were really (and perhaps necessarily) one and the same person? By considering fantastic examples, philosophers are able to put pressure on these distinctions to see under what conditions they break down. These examples serve as tests to disclose unconsidered aspects of the use of distinctions taken for granted in ordinary unproblematic contexts. Two kinds of examples are usually offered:

Case 1: The case of the emperor and the peasant exemplifies a typical philosopher's test example. The two people have distinctive bodies: on the one hand, plump and well nourished, and, on the other, gnarled and worn by toil. Each has distinctive memories and radically different personalities. They fall asleep in some contrived situation. When they awake, the man who remembers himself to be a peasant soon discovers he is experiencing the world from the bodily envelope of the emperor and vice versa. Now these individuals are clearly located differently in space at the same time. What are we to say about them? Are they or are they not radically changed? Is the emperor in the peasant's body and vice versa, or has the emperor had a radical change of personality and beliefs about himself?

Suppose the personalities of these two individuals remained associated with their bodies as before, i.e. the emperor's body behaved imperiously and spoke with an authoritative tone of voice, and the peasant's body showed in his cracked tones a suitable deference to authority. However, we are to assume that their memories of their previous lives are radically different. The imperious person remembers being a peasant, and the bucolic individual remembers being an emperor. We now might be inclined to say, not that they had exchanged bodies, but that the peasant now remembers the emperor's past life, and the emperor remembers that of the peasant. We could express this by saying "He [the peasant, by bodily criteria] thinks he is the emperor." On this basis, the three possible criterial attributes—bodily identity, identity of personality and sameness of memories are ordered as follows:

$$\left.\begin{array}{l} \text{Body} \\ \text{Personality} \end{array}\right\} > \text{Memory}$$

Case 2: There are people who claim to be the reincarnations of famous historical persons. We might suppose that all continuous spatiotemporal links have been broken or are unknown and that we are required to decide whether two individuals, whose existence is widely separated in space and time, are the same, that is, numerically identical. Here our grounds can only be personal memory avowals. We might examine the case for numerical identity presented by a Mr John Smith who exhibits the Napoleonic personality and can tell us in a way that satisfies even the most knowledgeable historian of his memories of the campaigns of the great emperor. Philosophical argument has been used to demonstrate that these mentalistic criteria,

without a proof of bodily continuity, are not enough. The argument runs as follows: if Mr John Smith could satisfy these requirements there is, it seems, nothing logically impossible about Mr Bill Brown satisfying them as well. Now what do we have—two Napoleons? Or would we be more inclined to say "Two individuals purporting to be Napoleon"? It seems clear that there is nothing in our conceptual system which obliges us to say the former. The priority among the three main personal qualities has been further clarified as follows:

$$\text{Body} > \left\{\begin{array}{l} \text{Personality} \\ \text{Memory} \end{array}\right.$$

The upshot of all this is a clear indication that bodily continuity plays a primary role when the cases become difficult. But is it a sufficient condition for personal identity?

To examine the possibility that numerical identity of the body is a sufficient condition for the personal identity of a human being, we shall again examine some hard cases on the borders of real possibility. The case of Miss Beauchamp, given in Prince, *The dissociation of personality*, provides us with a real example. She exhibited radically distinct patterns of behaviour with seemingly very different personalities, abrasive and argumentative, soft and agreeable, and so on. To make the matter more interesting, there was good evidence that she was not able to remember the activities and thoughts she had had when she was behaving in some but not all of these distinctive ways. One might begin to feel that both the personality and the memory criteria point towards different persons even though there could be no doubt about the numerical identity of Miss Beauchamp's body. The question for the philosopher to examine, before any therapeutic work by psychologists, is whether under these circumstances we would be conceptually obliged to treat Miss Beauchamp as a collection of different persons. Should the differences in behaviour and memory be used to individuate several personalities of the one person or *be allocated to* several persons, conceived as distinctive beings? In the former case, we would have an extension of our ordinary working conception. We could say that the same person has very distinctive personalities, and we would save bodily identity as a sufficient condition for unity of personhood. We could say, though Miss Beauchamp is the same person, her range of personalities is more fully differentiated than those of ordinary folk. One reason for adopting this alternative is the well-established fact that even ordinary folk have very distinctive ways of presenting themselves to different people under different circumstances and, indeed, there is some evidence (Helling, ''Autobiography as self-presentation'') that memory is distributed differentially with respect to each personality presented, though not in the radically discontinuous way that it was with Miss Beauchamp.

It now seems we are in a position to summarize the criteria by means of which we decide questions of identity for other people. The hard cases demonstrate that the conceptual system which we operate does give priority to continuity of bodily identity and the criteria of physical appearance based upon it. Though we are prepared to distinguish very different kinds of behaviour, and even different clusters of memories as kinds of unities, nevertheless the comfortable thing seems to be to assign these to entities (such as personalities, roles etc.) which are subordinate to or dependent upon persons rather than competitors with them. So, each individual could be thought to have a more or less radically distinguished set of personalities which would be presented differentially for different occasions. . . .

III: Sense of Identity

To explore the sense we have of our own identity in any disciplined fashion one must avoid vague discussions of what it feels like to be ''myself.'' We can follow an alternative route by exploring the idea of a criterion of personal identity: a criterion I might be imagined to employ to decide about myself. What can be made of the questions ''Who am I?'' and statements like ''I'm not myself today''? Does the former represent a genuine puzzle, and is the latter an expression of a discovery about personal identity? To answer this one must ask what conditions have to be met for there to be a criterion, for an entity to be judged to be this or that kind of thing (*see* Shoemaker, *Self-knowledge and self-identity*). Clearly, one important condition must be that we admit the possibility of the criterion not being met and candidates being rejected. In attempting to answer the question ''Who am I?,'' could I make the discovery that I am not, after all, myself? Could I, for example, find out I was someone else? It is intuitively obvious, I think, that these considerations are nonsensical. They are nonsensical because, to query one's own personal, as contrasted with one's social identity undermines one of the very presuppositions that are required for first person utterances to make sense, namely that they are the utterances of an individual person. In short, to have just this sense of any individuality, to treat myself as a possible subject of predication as I treat others, is a necessary part of what it is to be a person. When I ask, ''Who am I?,'' the most I could mean would be ''Which of various possible social identities, publicly identified, is legitimately or properly mine?'' Amnesia is not a loss of the sense of identity, but rather involves the inaccessibility of various items of knowledge about my public and social being, my past history. The fact that some of the loss concerns private–individual matters shows that the ability to *maintain* a continuous autobiography is secondary. The joint unities, point of view and point of action, make autobiographies possible. The statement ''I am not myself today'' can only mean that I do not feel the same as I did yesterday, which presupposes a conserved sense of identity. Since, then, I cannot doubt that I am the author, as it were, of my own speech, the very idea of a criterion for my sense of my own identity is empty.

Philosophers have made this point in various ways. Butler, "Of personal identity," for example, argued that memory cannot be the basis of a sense of identity since the very notion of memory presupposes that identity. For instance, it is empty to ask whether these memories I am remembering are mine. I can ask only whether what I take to be a memory is an accurate recollection of what happened to me or of what I did. To ponder on whether my recollections are another's memories is at most to ask whether I could perhaps be recollecting someone else's experience. Whatsoever they were, they must, as recollections, be my experiences since I am now experiencing them. At best I can be amazed that my imaginings are like your rememberings, so alike as to be qualitatively identical with your recollections in so far as we can make comparisons. But even in that case, my discovery that you and I have identical, i.e. very similar, recollections of a great many events is no ground whatever for the hypothesis that I am you.

What, then, are the origins of this strong sense of identity? I propose to show that the best hypothesis is that, though the sense of identity is conceptually and logically distinct from the fact of personal identity, nevertheless the former, in the course of human development, derives from the latter. Adequate empirical studies of this matter have yet to be made, but there are pieces of work which can be treated as the first step in a programme of research into the psychological foundations of personal being. The very first step in devising such a programme must be the classification of the relevant features of the notion of identity, brought out by philosophical analysis, features that could serve as the basis of hypotheses to be explored by developmental psychologists. . . .

. . . If I am to be able to refer to something, to point to it, in the world, I must know from where I am pointing as well as to what. That is, I must anchor my frame of reference to the corporeal here and now. Ordinarily, this is done through the indexical presuppositions of the uses of the word "I," presuppositions which embody the very idea that I am here and speaking now. One might wish to argue that having acquired a language and in so doing grasped the indexicality of referential expressions, a human being is in possession of the concept of numerical identity in space and time, since experience soon provides that person with the idea of a trajectory through a spatiotemporal system which is the locus of their coordinated points of view and points of action.

However, in order to achieve this happy coincidence, the actor must be in possession of the system of personal pronouns and know-how to use them. The indexicality of "I" depends, it might be argued, upon the grasp of the simple referential function of "you." Since "myself" is not a thing I could discover, it seems I cannot first experience myself and then attach the personal pronoun "I" to that experience. I must be learning the pronoun system as a whole through the ways in which and the means by which I am treated as a person by others. So that, by being treated as "you," or as a member of "we," I am now in a position to add "I" to my vocabulary, to show where, in the array of persons, speaking, thinking, feeling, promising and so on, is happening. In order to be addressed as "you," I must be being perceived as a definite embodied person, that is, as a distinct human but material individual by others. This unity of pronoun system might be one of the things that is meant by the social construction of the self. But it depends upon the recognizable bodily identity that I have even as an infant. I have identified these as the indexical uses of "I."

I am also treated by other people as having a distinct point of view and being the locus of exercises of agency. So that these very conditions of bodily identity, . . . as necessary conditions for having the idea of myself as a person, are also, it seems, to be taken as presumptions that are embedded in all kinds of social practices. For example, the idea that a person has a distinct point of action is embedded in such practices as moral praise and blame. That kind of talk makes sense only upon the presupposition that one has a point of action through which one's intentions and so on can be realized.

So the acquisition of the idea of personal identity for oneself, through which one develops a sense of identity, is at least in part a consequence of social practices which derive from the fact of identity as it is conceived in a culture. Our first preliminary conclusion, then, must be that a human being learns that he or she is a person from others and in discovering a sphere of action the source of which is treated by others as the very person they identify as having spatiotemporal identity. Thus, a human being does not learn that he or she is a person by the empirical disclosure of an experiential fact. Personal identity is symbolic of social practices not of empirical experiences. It has the status of a theory.

However, there is a great deal more to the sense of personal identity than the realization that one has a point of view and can act upon the world at certain places. We must now turn to what I shall call transcendental conditions. These require certain features of personhood as necessary conditions for the possibility of certain kinds of human activities. Philosophers have insisted, and rightly, since the days of David Hume, that in an important sense the self is not experienced. As Hume pointed out, "I never can catch *myself* at any time without a perception, and never can observe anything but the perception" (*A treatise of human nature*, book 1, pt 4, s. 4).

IV: Summary of the Argument

The first step towards identifying transcendental features of selfhood involved in the sense of identity was to notice that the considerations advanced above and the analysis based upon

them depend upon the assumption of the existence of two kinds of unities.

There is a unity of the realm of consciousness in that, for instance, the experiences I have as a being, spatiotemporally and socially located, and acting where I am, are coordinated in one realm of experience. Consciousness is not divided, and hence does not have to be combined. But this is not to say that that of which I am conscious is not ordered. Clearly, there is an indefinite potential hierarchy of "knowings" which is given by the possibility of reflexive consciousness. Thus, I can become aware of an orange, pay attention to it, and perhaps, if suitably prompted, can know that I am attending to it, and so on. One of the commonplace techniques of dealing with pain is to attend not so much to the pain but to the relation in which I, as experiencer, stand to that pain.

This leads to a second kind of unity. The hierarchy of experience is paralleled for human beings by a hierarchy of action. I can act upon the things in the world, for instance tennis balls, and I can act upon my actions upon the things in the world, for instance I can improve my forehand style. It would not be unreasonable to say that the hierarchies of awareness and of action involve a regress of the very same self; that the centre of consciousness and the source of action are one self. I act according to a rule; I adopt the rule according to some principle; I accept a principle according to some theory, and so on. It would not be unreasonable to argue that it is the very same "I" who is aware of the peeling of an orange, who knows that he is aware of peeling an orange, and so on.

It is now clear, I hope, where the need for a transcendental hypothesis comes from. These coordinated unified hierarchies are unified via the self which is presupposed in them. Each time that an individual is able to make a start up the hierarchy of action and hopes, naïvely, to experience the self which makes that step and which is, as it were, the origin of the sphere of experience, that self must remove itself from the realm of experience. The sense I have of myself, then, must include the very complex idea of something not experienced but presupposed as a necessary condition for the form that experience takes; in particular, its unified and hierarchical form. The fine structure of this kind of hierarchy has been perceptively explored by Langford in "Persons as necessarily social." From the point of view of the philosophy of science, "the self" is a theoretical concept, and the sense of self derives from the way we experience our experiences as unified, but is not reducible to it. From the point of view of the philosophy of psychology, that unification is an achievement, made possible by the possession of the chief unifying concept, "myself." . . .

These matters need to be further elaborated: the idea of an array of persons as the moral order that forms the background of all thought and action; the uses of personal pronouns as a key to the understanding of the structuring of experience; the identification of a mother–infant interaction pattern from which personal being emerges.

V: Autobiography as Self-Knowledge

Presented in the course of development with a sense of self, a human being can undertake the organization of memories and beliefs into a narrative of which he or she is the central character. However, autobiography is not just a chronicle of episodes, whether private or public. It has also to do with a growing grasp of capabilities and potentials. As such it involves the exploitation of the conditions for both consciousness and agency. For expository purposes, the structure of the argument of this work can be reflected in three aspects of autobiography.

Consciousness, I have argued, is not some unique state, but is the possession of certain grammatical models for the presentation to oneself and others of what one knows by inter- and self-intrapersonal perception. These models provide the structures by which I can know that which *I* am currently feeling, thinking, suffering, doing and so on, that is, they provide the wherewithal for an organization of knowledge as mine.

Agency, likewise, is an endowment from theory, permitting the formulation of hypotheses about what I was, am or could be capable. Through this my history is enriched by reference to possibilities of thought and action and so finds a continuous link with the moral orders through which I have lived my life.

To create autobiography out of this some of my beliefs about myself must stand as memories, of what I have at other times thought, done, felt and enjoyed. But as we have seen there is nothing in the phenomenal quality of experiences which authenticates them as true recollections. The category of belief-as-recollection is socially constructed and hierarchically organized. Autobiography involves the social conditions of the confirmation of recollections. . . .

VI: Speculation: The Breakdown of Transcendental Unities

I have argued that what makes a being a person is the possession and use of a certain theory, in terms of which that being constructs and orders its beliefs, plans, feelings and actions. I have suggested that the acquisition of the person-engendering theory occurs, and indeed must occur, in the course of changing responsibilities within relationships of psychological symbiosis.

One of the learning progressions which contributes most to the capacity to grasp oneself as a being who perceives the world from a certain point of view is the acquisition of the capacity to use the personal pronouns. With this goes a practical understanding of indexicality, the technique of displaying where in an array of persons something personal is happening. At the same time a nascent person is receiving praise, blame, exhortation, prohibition and so on for what he or she is doing or trying to do. Through these language games a being is acquiring the idea that it can be an actor, with a point of action, that is, has leverage within the world, and with the idea comes the capacity.

The theory I have used to illustrate the social constructivist thesis identifies consciousness and agency, point of view and point of action as one and as mine through the theoretical concept of "self." I follow Kant in calling this a transcendental unity, not given in experience, but rather the means by which experience is ordered. There may be cultures where the unity of experience and the unity of action are not unified in a higher order singular conception.

What might be expected to happen to people built up in our way if the unity between point of view and point of action begins to break down? Remember this is not the idea of there being an awareness of some phenomenological disaster, but rather the lapsing of a theoretical standpoint, like ceasing to believe in the unity of electricities.

Failure of memory might make it impossible to order one's experience around the idea of a continuous trajectory of point of view, while one may continue to deploy moment by moment the idea that one acts more or less where one is currently located and in accordance with what one is momentarily intending. This possibility could be realized in some forms of senility. Only against the background of a general belief in the unity of unities does senility appear as a deficit, as opposed to just another form of life.

Another theoretical possibility is that the sense of agency, of being in control of one's actions, may dissolve while one retains a continuous sense of self as a being experiencing the world and one's own states from a continuously developing trajectory of space–time locations and relationships with other people. Certain kinds of schizophrenia seem to have this general character. This is not intended as any kind of rough sketch of a theory of schizophrenia, rather a speculation as to one of the cognitive deficits that might enter into the condition. Then there are cases where, though point of view and point of action are both maintained, they are not unified, but if both dissolve the person has ceased to be. . . .

23

KENNETH J. GERGEN
The Social Construction of Self-Knowledge

Common parlance strongly suggests that the ancient search for self-knowledge continues to be of paramount concern in society. We are all familiar with such question as "who am I," "what are my real values," "do I really love him or her," "what am I trying to hide or protect myself from," "am I really a calloused person," "what are my real intentions," and so on. It is commonly thought that without a certain degree of self-knowledge, one's life is likely to be fraught with difficulty. People often try to "find themselves" and seek professional guidelines for this. Erik Erikson makes "self-identity" a criterion for psychological maturity;[1] the aim of Rogerian therapy is to enable the individual to acquire true experience of self, and psychoanalysis is similarly oriented in its emphasis on the motivational springs behind aberrant or maladaptive behavior. Others have used the Wanderyahr, lysergic acid, meditation, the armed services, the primal scream, transactional analysis, or leaves of absence for much the same purpose. The search, then, seems to be for a stable and unifying core of existence, a firm touchstone which can provide us with a sense of authenticity and coherence, and which can serve as a criterion for action. It is my present aim to demonstrate that the search for self is largely misconceived. It does not yield knowledge in the traditional sense, but rather, provides a means of rendering action socially intelligible. . . .

A Socio-Cognitive Orientation to Self

William James assumed that the experiential world of the infant is largely a "booming, buzzing confusion"; from moment to moment the infant is confronted with ever-changing patterns of essentially undifferentiated and meaningless stimuli. Adaptive action within such a chaotic environment requires that the individual come to differentiate among kinds of stimulus inputs and to relate these classes of inputs with one another. Thus, in order to secure nurturant care, it may be necessary to differentiate a class of stimuli which may later be called "mother" from the remainder of the stimulus array. A class of liquid substances may be singled out for the pleasure which they seem to produce when ingested, and a class of actions we call "crying" seems to bring forth the presence of living beings. In order to cope with the otherwise overwhelming array of stimulation, the individual learns to engage in a cognitive batching process that we commonly view as conceptualization.

It seems clear that the particular form in which this batching takes place is largely under the influence of the social world. The child learns through observation, for example, to differentiate a class of objects we call "chairs" from other objects, and observes that people normally engage in certain classes of actions (e.g., sitting on, moving toward or away from a table, etc.) toward this particular set of objects. Once the child has developed a rudimentary grasp of the language, the efficacy of the learning process is increased manifold. Although imperfectly, the language of the culture reflects the common inventory of "What there is," i.e., the relevant groupings of significance within the culture, and enables the individual to assimilate rapidly large amounts of information about the relationships among such classes. In the simple directive, "Never hit your mother," the individual quickly learns the relationship (in this case, negative) between two classes of events, "hitting" and "mother," a relationship which might otherwise have required numerous and painful instances to learn *in vivo*. In effect, through exposure to the contingencies of social interaction and to the linguistic medium, the individual acquires a conceptual system that provides (1) a virtual inventory of the relevant and functional classes of events or phenomena within the culture, (2) rules concerning the conditions under which these concepts are to be applied, and (3) the manner in which these classes are to be related. More generally, the individual acquires an "intelligibility system" which enables him to "makes sense" of the stimulus world and to participate "meaningfully" with other members of the culture.

Although these observations are not particu-

[1] Erikson, E. *Childhood and society.* Chicago: W. W. Norton, 1963.

larly challenging in themselves, they begin to acquire a cutting edge when applied to the self. The infant may rapidly learn to differentiate a class of experiences that may later be called "self" from the surrounding environment. He may also learn that certain of his behaviors are to be singled out as "bad" and others as "good." By adolescence, the social milieu will have also furnished the individual with a host of concepts with which he may classify his internal states. States of "pleasure," "pain," "love," "hate," "anger," and so on, must be differentiated if the individual is to function adequately within this milieu. He must master such differentiations as well as the proper circumstances in which the relevant concepts are to be employed in self-understanding. Further, whether an individual perceives himself as "willing" his own behavior, whether he believes he possesses a soul, whether he perceives himself to harbor certain attributes or capabilities, should depend on the meaning systems into which he is socialized. Thus, through social observation, interaction, and language acquisition the individual acquires an inventory of self-attributes or conceptions, and knowledge as to their relationship with other relevant classes of stimuli. In more general terms, what there is to understand about the self and how one is to go about it, follows a normative rule system governing concept usage. Only through mastering such rules can the individual render himself intelligible to himself and to others.

If I impute a certain arbitrary character to the intelligibility system which the individual comes to acquire, it is not by accident. The particular way in which we come to segment the world of experience is certainly not sacrosanct and it could be otherwise. Immense anguish is generated over the question of whether one is sufficiently principled, warm and accepting, spontaneous, ambitious, intelligent and so on, and seldom does one question the arbitrary character of the questions themselves. The existence of such distinctions, the value placed upon them, and the precise range of particulars that may be encompassed by each concept is subject to gross alteration both through time and across circumstance. . . .

The present orientation distinguishes between raw sense data and the symbolic conceptualization of these data. Thus, we may say that the organism is exposed to a continuous stream of sense data, and that the process of conceptualization exists as an artificial overlay or template employed in making sense or codifying the otherwise chaotic aspects of this experience. In this context, it is misleading to view the individual in quest of self-knowledge as trying to discover some truth or reality; to borrow William James' phrasing, we are not confronted with a searching "I" and the discovered "me." Rather, we may view the process of knowing as one of fitting a conceptual template to experience. There is nothing to be discovered; the sense data are essentially given. The "experience of discovery," of self-revelation or insight, is essentially the realization that an alternative template is also applicable to the same experiential complex. Our orienting premise is thus that self-knowledge is best understood as the application of a conceptual system, imbedded as it is within the social system, to a given field of sense data. To make this clear, we will examine four means to self-knowledge, each of which rests upon these orienting assumptions.

Communication and Conceptualization

In Nigel Dennis' novel, *Cards of Identity*, a shattering story is unfolded in which an altogether normal adult is abducted and placed in an entirely alien environment. He is given a new name, different clothing, is housed in a separate domicile, and most importantly, is treated as a servant by all members of his new environment. There is no escape. Unsettlingly, within a short period the protagonist comes to feel perfectly at home in his new identity. He gains perfect authenticity within a life-circumstance jarringly inconsistent with his entire past. The question raised by Dennis is whether normal identity, that indelible core of self-relevant experience (as it is commonly considered) can be obliterated so easily. Is our hold on personal reality so very tenuous? Of course, one can dismiss Dennis' account as purely fictional. But this does not escape the question: Erving Goffman again brings it to our attention in his analysis of the mental patient.[2] As he demonstrates, by ordering the patient about, locking him in, examining him without his consent, speaking to him as an alien and so on, the patient learns a new identity, that of being "mentally ill." When the individual exists in a closed institution, one in which the social and physical environment consistently reinforces a specific identity, there is virtually no escape because there is no alternative identity into which one can step. Neither the individual's view of himself in the here and now, nor his past behavior which led him into the institution, provide an incentive for departure. Mental illness is a secure niche in which the individual may remain — often 'til death.

It is also possible to dismiss Goffman's analysis. We cannot be certain that, like any good social analyst, he didn't select out of a complex set of incidents only those which confirmed his particular predilections. But, the question remains: is common identity so fragile that it will readily capitulate to social influence? From the socio-cognitive viewpoint, we might fully anticipate such flexibility in self-identity. If we may define identity as a sub-set of highly salient concepts which the individual most frequently utilizes in thinking about himself or his activities, then any means by which concepts in general can be altered should apply in no lesser degree to self-identity. Accordingly, if the social environment continues to define a given indi-

vidual in a specified manner, we may reasonably anticipate that, without countervening information, the individual will come to accept the publicly provided definition as his own. This view, of course, does not differ essentially from that developed by George Herbert Mead in the 1920s. As Mead maintained, "We are in possession of selves just insofar as we can and do take the attitudes of others toward ourselves and respond to those attitudes."[3] The relevance of Mead's account to ours is assured with the simple substitution of concepts for attitudes. Further, if we liberalize Mead's notions concerning the means by which others' concepts of oneself are introjected, if we can agree that taking the role of the other is only one means by which the individual may incorporate others' views of himself, then Mead's theory of self-development and change may be considered wholly consistent with the present treatment.

In this context, let us consider research on alterations in self-esteem. It is commonly held, within the mental health tradition and by the public more generally, that the individual develops over time (and typically within the first six years of life) an essential mode of self-evaluation. He comes to attach a basic value to his identity, which may vary from extremely positive (in which case he might be labelled an egotist) to extremely negative (in which case it was once popular to say that he suffered an inferiority complex). It is generally argued that the individual carries such evaluative sets with him across time and circumstance and that they are highly significant in molding his social behavior. Numerous means of assessing basic self-esteem have been developed over the years, and an immense number of experimental studies have attempted to isolate the behavioral correlates of persons differing in basic self-esteem. Therapy in both the neo-Freudian and Rogerian

[2] Goffman, E. *Asylums.* New York: Doubleday Anchor, 1963.

[3] Mead, G. H. The genesis of self and social control. *International Journal of Ethics*, 1925, 35, 251–73.

traditions may be specifically directed toward altering this basic sense of self-esteem.

From the present standpoint, self-esteem may be understood in terms of our knowledge of the relationship between concepts and affect. Experimental psychology has provided a number of wide-ranging experiments demonstrating that through association learning, affect may become associated with specific objects or our concepts of them. Once such associations are developed it is possible to stimulate affect by calling the concepts to mind. Various forms of lie detection, in fact, owe their success to this line of experimentation. What is traditionally termed self-esteem may thus be viewed in terms of the affective associations accompanying the individual's central array of self-relevant concepts. However, from this vantage point, there is little reason to suspect a strong degree of transituational coherence in self-esteem. Unlike the picture of enduring levels of self-esteem found in the clinical annals, we might anticipate that the stability of self-esteem is importantly dependent on the consistency of the social environment. As the messages received from others concerning one's worth are varied, one's concepts of self (along with their valuational associations) may be changed. Self-esteem may thus be regarded, not as an enduring sub-stratum of experience, but as inextricably linked to the social context and fully dependent on it for its strength.

Consider some research findings related to this line of thinking. Undergraduate women volunteered to help in a training program for clinical graduate students.[4] As part of the program each woman found herself in an interview in which the graduate student asked her various questions about herself. The questions were primarily of a self-evaluative nature, so that the interviewee had to rate herself on a variety of characteristics, including her intelligence, facial beauty, sociability, and so on. During the 45 minute interview, the interviewer showed subtle signs of agreement (smiles, nods, "I agree," etc.) whenever the student made a positive evaluation of herself. When the self-ratings were negative, however, the interviewer showed signs of disagreement (frowns, "I don't see it that way," etc.). As the interview progressed the participants thus learned that the interviewer's conception of them was highly positive in character. Would their self-appraisal begin to mirror the social context? A systematic study of the self-ratings revealed that as the interview progressed the participants' ratings of themselves became steadily more positive. No such increase in self-esteem was evidenced in a control condition.

It is possible, of course, that the self-ratings may have been adopted for the benefit of the interviewer and so may not have been an accurate reflection of what the subjects thought about themselves at the time. Would the enhanced self-evaluation be found on a subsequent test of self-esteem, administered after the interview was complete? To test this the women were given, in private, a set of self-esteem items and asked to rate themselves as honestly as possible; they were advised that the interviewer would not be privy to these evaluations, and that their candor was important to the success of the project. When the self-ratings of the experimental group were examined, it was found that the interview had a marked and significant effect. These women retained the enhanced self-image developed in the interview. The control group showed no such effects.

Further illustrations of the ways in which social communication can alter self-conception are abundant in the social psychological literature.[5] One's identity in general, and self-evaluation in

[4] Gergen, K. J. Interaction goals and personalistic feedback as factors affecting the presentation of self. *Journal of Personality and Social Psychology*, 1965, 1, 413–24.

[5] Gergen, K. J. *The concept of self.* New York: Holt, Rinehart and Winston, 1971.

particular, thus seem importantly wedded to social circumstance. As the social environment shifts its definition of the individual, self-definition may be altered accordingly.

The Evidence of Action

. . . The view that our overt behavior furnishes us information about what we feel, believe, desire, will, and so on, has substantial empirical support. Over the past thirty years, social psychologists have provided numerous demonstrations of the effects of role playing on an individual's attitudes and feelings. If one can be induced (though not coerced) into taking a disagreeable public stance on an issue, one typically finds that his private opinion is subsequently changed in the direction of the public commitment.[6] In order to explore the relevance of this work for self-conception, my colleague, Margaret Gibbs, and I arranged a situation in which undergraduate females were to apply for a job.[7] In one condition, the women were asked to formulate a talk about themselves which would enable them to gain the positive regard of a prospective employer. They were encouraged to present themselves as positively as they could, and after spending fifteen minutes formulating their talks they recorded them for the ostensible purpose of later playing them to the prospective employer. Subsequently each participant was asked to help in validating some clinical test materials, including a standardized test of self-esteem; this test had been administered to the same group approximately six

weeks earlier in a large classroom setting. An examination of self-esteem change revealed that the role-playing subjects evidenced a striking increase in self-esteem ratings. This enhanced level of self-esteem was not found in a control group which did not participate in the role-playing procedure. Positive presentation seemed to generate positive self-conception.

Other research on self-observation has been concerned with the definition of one's emotional states. Traditionally, it had been supposed that various types of emotional states that we experience are coordinated with specific physiological states. Thus, one might expect that feelings of love can be differentiated in terms of physiological coordinates, from admiration, infatuation, and so on. To know what one is "truly" feeling from this viewpoint requires that one harken sensitively to his internal nudgings. Physiology tells no lies.

However, as arguments by Stanley Schachter and his colleagues demonstrate, there is little physiological support for this classic position.[8] Little physiological differentiation is revealed as one moves through the range of emotional experience, and it is virtually impossible to map a finely differentiated emotional vocabulary onto a set of physiologically discriminable states. Rather, the nervous system seems to operate primarily in terms of gross arousal. Differentiations may be made between positive and negative emotional states and between such states as intense fear and anger, but beyond such gross differences the physiologist is unable to predict, on the basis of information about the nervous system, when we experience hostility, as opposed to envy, vengefulness, or frustration. If such scant information regarding emotional state is furnished by the nervous system, what is the source of our differential experiences? The answer provided by Schachter and his col-

[6]Brehm, J. W. A dissonance analysis of attitude-discrepant behavior. In C I. Hovland & M. J. Rosenberg (Eds.), *Attitude organization and change.* New Haven: York University Press, 1960.

[7]Gergen, K. J. & Gibbs, M. S. Role playing and modifying the self-concept. Presented at the annual meeting of the Eastern Psychological Association, 1966.

[8]Schachter, G. & Singer, J. E. Cognitive, social and physiological determinants of emotional state. *Psychological Review*, 1962, 69, 379–99.

leagues is highly compatible with the present analysis. Through socialization, the individual comes to acquire an emotional vocabulary along with knowledge of the proper cues (either social or situational) concerning the proper utilization of such labels. Early work by Schachter and others indicated that precisely the same state of physiological arousal could give rise to experiences of anger or humor, depending on the situational context in which the arousal occurred. In effect, the situational cues provided the individual with the proper concepts to be used in understanding what he "truly" felt in the situation.

In one of the more interesting extensions of these investigations, males were exposed to slides of attractive, partially clothed females.[9] As they viewed the slides, they were also allowed to hear an amplification of what was purported to be their heartbeats. In actuality, the frequency of the heartbeat as controlled by the experimenter. By design, participants found that their heart appeared to undergo a rapid increase in rate on certain slide presentations, but not others. The particular instances in which such increases were experienced were randomly selected. Attractiveness ratings of the slides then revealed that those photographs which had ostensibly produced an increase in heart rate were viewed as more attractive; these effects remained when the participants were tested again two months later. Thus, subjects seemed to use their bodily cues to label their emotional reaction to the stimulus — they judged their preferences by observing and labelling their bodily reactions.

While highly compelling, this line of thinking does raise worrisome problems concerning the limits of the socio-cognitive approach. Our initial premise was that self-knowledge is primarily a socially mediated and essentially arbitrary construction of experience. Since such construc-

tions are virtually interchangeable, the notion of "true" knowledge of self becomes chimerical. However, if we admit that one's behavior furnishes information concerning the state of the self; then it might be concluded that some conceptual templates are superior to, or possess greater validity than, others. One's own behavior becomes the crucible against which we may assess the true value of various self-constructions.

Against this view, it may be proposed that one's own behavior, in itself, is not informative because it provides raw sensation that has no inherent meaning. Whatever meaning is found in the behavior must essentially be "read into" it. . . . Thus, comprehension depends on a pre-existing repertoire of concepts at the individual's disposal. What conclusions are reached regarding one's behavior depends on what concepts have been supplied through socialization and which happens to be salient at the time of behavior scanning.

This analysis suggests that, in principle, it should be possible for the individual to confirm virtually any concept of self at any time.[10] If I pause to consider the possibility that I am a passive person, not very comfortable in social situations, I can probably locate enough instances in my behavioral production to confirm this suspicion. Yet, at another time, I might be able to find evidence convincing me that I am active and socially at ease. The major limitation to complete relativism in self-understanding is provided by social consensus. That is, if a given behavioral act is univocally defined as active or passive, and the individual observes himself engaging in this behavior, he may be unable to reach any conclusions about himself other than that provided by the unanimous social milieu. Still, however compelling such self-evaluations

[9] Valens, S. Cognitive effects of false heart-rate feedback. *Journal of Personality and Social Psychology*, 1966, 4, 400–8.

[10] This line of argument is also consistent with Willard Day's reasoning . . . concerning the dependency of self-knowledge on the self-descriptive repertories engendered by the surrounding verbal community.

may appear, they do not constitute knowledge of "true self." A decade ago, a male who engaged in certain acts with others of his kind would have been labelled "homosexual" by virtually everyone, including himself. If he observed himself engaged in such actions, the conclusion that he was homosexual would be virtually inescapable. Today, the same acts may be labelled "bisexual," "self-actualizing," or "liberated"; the action is equivalent, but "self-knowledge" has been altered.

Self-Other Comparisons

Self-knowledge, the process of conceptualizing oneself, may be molded not only by direct communication from others and through self-labelling, but also by observations of other persons which have implications for self-labelling. It has been maintained that through learning, various concepts become associated with particular behavioral configurations. Such configurations may not only be evidenced in one's own behavior, but in the actions of others as well. When relating to others, much of our attention is focused on their behavior; we attempt to make sense of their actions by translating them into a conceptual structure. Intermittently we are also cognizant of our own actions, and the continuous shifting of attention between self and other lends itself to the ascription of similarity and difference. Such comparisons contain further implications as to how we might conceptualize our own behavior. For example, if we confront someone who seems jocular or waggish, and self-other comparison indicates strong differences in patterns of behavior, we may conclude that we are, after all, a more reasonable, circumspect, or unspontaneous sort of person. If we find a close match between the behavior patterns, we might conclude that we are also a jocular or waggish sort of individual.

This process has been documented in re-search conducted with Stanley Morse.[11] Participants in this research were students at the University of Michigan who answered an advertisement for part-time jobs in the Institute for Social Research. When each applicant arrived for the preliminary screening, he was seated in a room by himself and asked to complete a number of self-rating forms, including a battery of approximately thirty self-evaluation items carefully designed by Coopersmith to tap basic level of self-esteem. After each applicant had completed the various measures, the secretary entered the room, bringing with her another "applicant" for the job who was, in fact, a collaborator. For some forty applicants, the collaborator was obviously very desirable as a potential employee. He wore a dark business suit and carried an attache case which he opened to remove several sharpened pencils, at the same time revealing copies of books on statistics and philosophy. The remaining applicants were exposed to a dramatically different experience. Here the competitor entered wearing a smelly sweatshirt, torn trousers and no socks; he appeared generally dazed by the procedure and tossed onto the table a worn copy of a cheap paperback novel. After several minutes of silent exposure to the newcomer, the original applicant was given additional forms to complete, including a second battery of items assessing level of self-esteem.

This study showed that the mere presence of the other person was sufficient to alter the manner in which the applicants conceptualized their own self-worth. Applicants exposed to the impressive individual demonstrated a sharp drop in self-evaluation; those who sat face-to-face with the bumpkin showed a significant increase in their evaluations of self. The implications of such findings are far reaching, as they suggest that personal identity is in important measure dependent on the immediate or con-

[11] Morse, S. J. & Gergen, K. J. Social comparison, self-consistency and the presentation of self. *Journal of Personality and Social Psychology*, 1970, 16, 148–56.

tinuing social milieu. One need never come in direct communication with such surrounds; mere presence may be sufficient to cause elation or depression. What is "true" about self depends on those available for comparison. In the presence of the devout, we may "discover" that we are ideologically shallow; in the midst of dedicated hedonists, we may gain awareness of our ideological depths.

Concept Association: Identity by Implication

Concepts may become associated not only with particular experiential events but also with each other, a fact utilized in the free association method. When presented with a string of words and asked to respond to each with the first word that enters the mind, the split-second response that occurs reveals the underlying associational structure. In part, this structure may depend on the frequency of various associations within the language of the culture. If we hear a man described as "tall" and "dark," the word "handsome" is likely to come to the tip of our tongue. In addition, the configuration of associations may reflect patterns of behavior as they are commonly perceived. If we observe that behavior we term "aggressive" often produces behavior we term "anger" in the target of the aggression, a strong association between the concepts of aggression and anger may develop and influence our expectations. Thus, if we observe person X treating Y in an aggressive manner, we may be primed to anticipate that Y's subsequent behavior will reveal anger. As much early research on perceptual biases has shown, we may be inclined to label the behavior as "anger" even when a variety of other labels would be equally credible.

This enables us to understand additional influences on the way in which one interprets oneself: it may be that (1) we utilize others' behavior in order to interpret our reaction to them, and (2) we use others' reactions to us to understand our behavior or feelings toward them. In support of (1), it may be argued that we can often readily identify or label what another has done to us, but are less able to categorize our reaction. A person may realize that a friend is angry with him, but his reaction to this anger may be an emotional swim, unclear and diffuse. Since we have numerous associations regarding what type of behavior (A) leads to what reaction (B), the presence of A in another's behavior toward us may bring to mind its associated concept B which is then used in judging our reaction. If "fond expressions" on the part of one person have frequently been associated with "fond feelings" on the part of the individual to whom they are directed, then confronting an ardent suitor may cause one to label his or her diffuse emotional reaction as "fondness." The question is not whether one *actually* feels fond or not: it is misleading to ask about true feelings. The major issue is what concept has been called into play by the surrounding conditions.

We are hampered by a lack of direct empirical support for this particular line of reasoning. However, a study by Brehm,[12] concerned with the degree to which we like or dislike various foods lends itself to the case. Are such preferences intrinsic and knowable, or can they be understood as mobile conceptual constructions? High school students were offered a prize for eating a small amount of spinach, a vegetable for which they had previously expressed an antipathy. One group of students was then informed that they would be writing home indicating what vegetable they had eaten; the letter was stated in such a way that the student could

---

[12] Brehm, J. W. Increasing cognitive dissonance by a *fait accompli. Journal of Abnormal and Social Psychology*, 1959, *58*, 379–82.

fully expect to be served much more of this vegetable. Thus, through a *fait accompli*, they found themselves committed to a good deal of spinach eating in the future. The major question was whether this information about their "fated future" would have an effect on their subsequent liking for the vegetable. In terms of concept association, eating a great deal of any food is typically associated with liking it. If the environment is arranged so that we are to receive a great deal of spinach, we might well look at ourselves for evidence of a positive reaction; given the vagaries of human taste, we are most certain to find such evidence. Although multiple interpretations are possible, the results do lend ample support to this position. The knowledge of what they were to receive was sufficient to *decrease* the students' dislike of the vegetable as measured in subsequent ratings. No such change was found in a control group of students who did not receive the information about their future. Thus, the knowledge that the unwanted food was often to be served influenced the students to increase their liking for it.

What about (2), the claim that we use our categorizations of others' reactions to us in interpreting our behavior or feelings toward them? In most relationships, we speak without necessarily planning what we are going to say, and our feelings are often evanescent and ambiguous. We do not at each moment conceptualize our behavior and our feelings, but when we must decide what it is we are doing to the other or how it is we are feeling, the process of concept association may be quite important. If we are unable to identify our behavior *A* toward a person, but we can label his reaction, *B*, then relying on the structure of association including *A* and *B*, we may infer the existence of *A*, given the existence of *B*. If we observe another reacting to us in a "friendly" way, we may conclude that our behavior toward him has been friendly or that we are a friendly sort of person. If another reacts in a "submissive" manner, concept

association would suggest that we tend to be dominating. The actual state of our behavior or affect may be the same in all cases; our comprehension of it may vary markedly depending on inferences made from others' reactions.

Again, though there is no precise documentation, an experiment conducted with E. E. Jones and K. Davis provides interesting insight.[13] In this study, women students took part in a clinical interview about their academic life and various personal aspirations and values; after the interview, they learned the interviewer's impressions of them. These impressions were systematically constructed so that half of the students found the interviewer was uniformly impressed by them, conveying feelings of warmth, comfort and admiration in the written impression. For the remaining half of the participants, the interviewers' reactions were lukewarm and more carefully guarded. The participants were then asked to rate the honesty of their behavior during the interview. How candid were they; to what extent did they reveal a true picture of their personality in the interview? From the present standpoint, one's true personality is primarily a function of the label we happen to assign, and in this case, the label might be inferred through concept association. If the response is clearly guarded, it may be inferred that the picture one has presented has been less than accurate. This is precisely what the experimental results revealed. Those students who found the interviewer's reaction wholly positive, rated their presentation in the interview as significantly more honest and candid than those who received the neutral reactions. Essentially, one may not know whether he has been honest or authentic until he learns of others' reactions.

---

[13] Jones, E. E., Gergen, K. J. & Davis, K. Some reactions to being approved or disapproved as a person *Psychological Monographs*, 1962, *76*, Whole No. 521, No. 2.

Memory Scanning and Other Forms of Cognitive Processing

Thus far, we have viewed the process of self-conceptualization as actively molded by the actions and appearances of others and ourselves. However, self-conception may occur in relative isolation from the immediate givens of ongoing relations. That is, at any given point one may be moved to engage in some form of symbolic functioning, the results of which may yield an altered conceptualization of who one is, of one's true identity or true feelings. Such processing may serve to strengthen or weaken already existing conceptual structures, or it may provide altogether novel constructions of one's identity.

While complete account of such processing is beyond the scope of this paper, it may be useful to document the effects of one such process, namely memory scanning, in altering self-knowledge. While one may adopt a variety of different strategies in recalling the past, one mode of recall involves using a concept as a criterion of memory scanning. That is, the individual utilizes a given concept, such as "strong-principled," "intelligent," "physically attractive," or the like, and examines his or her memory for instances that may verify or falsify the application of the concept to self. Unless one is particularly systematic, there is good reason to suspect that the products of such memory scanning will be biased toward confirmation. Past experience is usually rich enough to provide confirming instance of virtually any self-relevant concept. Thus, if one commences his search with a given concept in mind, it should be relatively easy to discover confirming evidence and, once satisfied that the concept applies to the self go no further; if the concept is desirable, further search for disconfirmations may be less than appealing. In many cases, then, memory scanning may succeed in convincing the individual that the concept is an accurate description of self.

Evidence from an extension of the role playing study described earlier is relevant here.[14] As will be recalled, women in this study had to develop a speech that would impress a potential employer; women who presented the self-congratulatory talk subsequently came to evaluate themselves more positively. Within this experimental context, a further group of some fifteen women simply engaged in the process of developing the talk; it was never actually presented. In order to develop the talk, the women had to think of various accomplishments of the past which would enable them to present a positive image of themselves. The women were thus engaged in a biased scanning of their past history. Later, when a standardized test of self-esteem was administered, it was found that these women also evidenced a striking increase in self-esteem scores, an increase not found in a control group. It appeared, then, that the biased scanning of memory was sufficient to alter the conception of self operating at that moment. What we believe to be true of ourselves at any instant thus depends importantly on the particular machinations of memory in which we are engaged.

Memory scanning is only one of a number of cognitive processes through which self-conception may be fashioned; each of the environmentally dependent processes discussed thus far probably has an environmentally independent counterpart. Thus, just as others' opinions may influence self-conception at any given time, so may the memory of past communications from others, or the imagined communication that might take place should others witness our present or anticipated actions. Likewise, we may consider ourselves in comparison with groups that are not immediately present, groups from the past or from an imagined future. Each of these ratiocinative processes may yield a particular conception of self that may appear

---

[14] Gergen, K. J. & Gibbs, M. S., op. cit.

both compelling and valid at a particular time.[15] . . .

Summary and Implications for a Science of Self

We can now re-examine the assumptions which underlie the common quest for self-identity. The traditional view of self-knowledge is initially premised on the assumption that all human beings of normal constitution are capable of conscious experience or sensation. The present orientation is essentially similar in this respect. Traditionally such experience is subdivided into self (emotions, thoughts, memories, desires, etc.) vs. not self. At this point the present analysis began to deviate. Rather than viewing these experiences as intrinsically separated within experience, it was argued that such separations were accomplished through a conceptual process typically guided by social learning. The fact the emotions are singled out as part of oneself, the variety of emotions we believe to exist, and the conditions under which they are to be attributed to self, are all based on socially derived conceptualization. While the tradition emphasizes personal identity as a unified core of self-relevant experience which provides an essential criterion for conduct across time and circumstance, there is little reason to suspect such a core from the socio-cognitive standpoint. Rather, it appears that the individual harbors a multitude of self-relevant concepts, many of which are inconsistent if not diametrically opposed. Thus, the same experience of self may be coded differently from one situation to the next, or different self-experi-

ences may be conceptualized as similar. In this sense, the individual may feel at one moment that he is truly sensitive as a person, but at another that he is brutishly calloused in his relations with others. He may feel that each of these concepts of self is truly correct and experience full authenticity in each case.

This argument also challenges the traditional assumption regarding basic self-esteem. Rather than assuming that people possess some essential core level of self-evaluation, the present approach calls attention to the various ways in which an individual may evaluate himself as he moves through the social world. From the socio-cognitive viewpoint, therapy designed to enhance one's self-esteem is not likely to have long-term impact. Essentially, the individual may learn to adopt a particular conceptualization of self within the therapeutic hour, but whether this particular stance will be maintained as the individual confronts other groups whose opinions and characteristics are different, or who bring to mind other types of self-relevant memories, is quite another matter.

Finally, the present position differs from tradition in its assumptions about distortions in self-understanding. The tradition holds that beneath the patina of social circumstance lies a source of true knowledge about self. It is said that some of us have distorted images of ourselves, some defend against the truth, some have lost touch with themselves; and, according to the tradition, continued scientific study should reveal how such individuals might be helped to regain contact with themselves, to find true self-knowledge. From the present stance, that orientation is misguided. Self-conceptualization is essentially an arbitrary process, and to speak of valid or invalid self-perception is to do so primarily in terms of the social context. If the social rules dictate the application of particular concepts to particular experiences in specified situations, then rule violations may be said to constitute invalid or distorted self-perception. Such distortions must be viewed with a

[15] Other cognitive processes of potential significance in altering self-conception have been detailed [T. Mischel, ed., *The Self*, Basil Blackwell, 1977]. Charles Taylor's discussion of self-definition through radical choice is particularly relevant.

full appreciation for their social relativity. For other persons, at other times or at other places, those attributions favored within contemporary society would be viewed as invalid or distorted. "True self" is essentially a label and no intrinsic or objective criteria are available to guide the manner in which it is stuck.

This line of thinking has important implications regarding the potential for a science of self. It is commonly assumed that we may construct theoretical principles covering the development of self (including self-esteem) and its functioning within daily relationships. Such principles should be open to empirical test, and through continued study our knowledge of self should steadily be improved. Such an assumption is widely shared both in psychology and sociology, and has many adherents in psychiatry, anthropology, and political science. However, from the present standpoint, such assumptions are problematic. In traditional form, the ultimate crucible for scientific theory is provided by a common data base, that is, a series of relevant observables. While scientific theory may contain many terms which are not linked operationally to concrete particulars, a theory is not testable until such linkages are constructed. But the present analysis suggests that in the case of self-knowledge there is virtually nothing to know.[16] That is, there is little in the way of factual data that lies waiting to be discovered, explored or assessed. Rather than factual data, we are confronted with a series of social rules or intelligibility systems employed in the process of personal explanation. But such rule systems are tied imperfectly, if at all, to internal psychological or physiological events. From this view-

point, the proper concern of a science of self may be with the current intelligibility systems rather than with an underlying psychological data base.

To place this in a broader context, we may ask more generally what it means for a given experience to qualify in society as a fact. That is, we term some events factual, and consider them the proper subject of scientific study, while others are viewed as fiction, fantasy, myth and so on, and are ruled out of science. Science may concern itself with plants, trees, water, and neurons but not with the man in the moon, the spirit of God, or with unicorns. What is it about the former class of experiences which differentiates it from the latter? While the answer to this question may initially seem obvious, it is not. Closer scrutiny indicates that we are confronted, not with a simple bifurcation of fact vs. fantasy, but with a continuum. Some experiences clearly qualify as fact, and others as fancy, but between the two poles the applicability of scientific analysis is often in question. In the case of poltergeists, communication with plants, life after death, astrology, and communication with a divinity, to name but a few, it is simply unclear whether science should be brought to bear. In the case of flying saucers, for example, the American government has mounted major research into the question of whether there are any facts (outside of aberrant states of consciousness) worthy of scientific study. Given what we may view as a *continuum of factuality*, the question then arises as to what criterion or set of criteria are typically used in the placement of experiences or events along the continuum. By what standards do we in Western culture presently determine the degree to which a given experience is a reflection of reality?

The question of how we may trust our senses to map reality is, of course, an immensely complex one and has long been a chief concern within epistemology. However, for philosophers the question has primarily been one of establishing proper grounds for the determina-

[16] The contrary position is represented in this volume by D. W. Hamlyn, who posits a self-knowledge which is factually grounded and beyond mere belief or opinion (conceptualization). What he views as "true insight," I would consider the application of socially derived intelligibility systems; his conditions for "genuine self-knowledge" are primarily a formalization of our common rules for interpreting or describing social action.

tion of factuality: what *should* we take as the proper basis for establishing reality? But the question can also be asked descriptively: for good or ill, what criteria are currently pressed into service by the populace? Although such criteria may change from one historical era to another, they should be open to documentation. People do seem to sort experiences along a factuality continuum, and the following criteria seems to be operative, at least in our culture:

1. *Neural engagement.* The greater the engagement of the nervous system within a delimited period of time, the greater one's confidence in the factual basis of his experience. A loud roar, a bright flash, seem more indicative of factuality than a faint rumble or a brief flicker. 2. *Modality increment.* The greater the number of sensory modalities which are simultaneously engaged, the greater one's confidence in the factual basis of a given experience. One is most confident in the existence of a reality corresponding to his experiences when he can simultaneously see, taste, smell, touch, and hear. 3. *Discriminability.* The greater the degree to which a given experience may be differentiated spatio-temporally from other experiences, the greater one's confidence in its factuality. When the neural system is highly engaged, the accompanying experiential state typically (but not always) differs from its predecessors. If a given experience cannot be differentiated with certainty from its spatio-temporal surroundings, one may have little confidence that he is apprehending reality. 4. *Repeatability.* To the extent that an experiential state can be replicated, one's confidence in the factuality of the experience is increased. Since recurrence seems to enhance factuality, duration may be viewed as continuous repetition. The longer the duration of an experience, the greater one's confidence in its factual basis. 5. *Inter-observer exposure.* To the extent that a given experience can be replicated in the experience of other persons, our confidence in its factuality is increased.

In the case of flying saucers, factuality is in doubt because neural impact is often very meager and typically is limited to the visual modality; discriminability is often problematic because flying saucers may not be easily differentiated from comets, aircraft, etc.; the experience is seldom repeated for the same individual, is of brief duration, and is only available to a minor segment of the population.

In light of this, what are the prospects for a science of the self? In many respects, the saucer cults may have a stronger claim to scientific respectability. To the extent that self-psychology is concerned with internal states, that is, with evaluative feelings, wants, hopes, aversions, tastes, attitudes, emotions, beliefs, volition and the like, the prospects for a cumulative science seem dim. With the possible exception of emotions, neural engagement is often at a very low level; most sensory modalities are not called into play by internal states and one is virtually limited to interoceptive cues. Further, in the case of internal states, discriminability is often exceedingly difficult for the individual, and repeatability is often small. Finally, there is no opportunity for inter-observer exposure.

With so little in the way of factual underpinnings, the possibilities for an exact science of mental life in general, and a science of self-experience in particular, seem limited. In the main, those internal states bearing no reference to external events do not meet the common criteria for factuality. In an important sense, then, when considering self-knowledge it is unclear what there is to know. Yet, the search for self-knowledge continues, and people do experience "breakthroughs" in self-understanding. From the present vantage point, such breakthroughs are primarily in one's capacity to master an intelligibility system as it applies to one's own behavior.[17] Self-knowledge is not thereby increased; it is only constructed anew.

---

[17] In this sense, the man on the street may indulge in the kind of "diagnostic-descriptive" breakthroughs found within the scientific domain. . . .

24

ULRIC NEISSER
Five Kinds of Self-knowledge

Introduction

Considered as a unitary object, the self is full of apparent contradictions. It is simultaneously physical and mental, public and private, directly perceived and incorrectly imagined, universal and culture-specific. Although there is nothing with which we are more familiar, we are often enjoined to know ourselves better than we do. One way to clarify this puzzle may be to consider what makes it possible for individuals to know themselves at all, i.e. to analyse the information on which self-knowledge is ultimately based.[1] The analysis to be presented here distinguishes among several kinds of self-specifying information, each establishing a different aspect of the self. These aspects are so distinct that they are essentially different *selves*: they differ in their origins and developmental histories, in what we know about them, in the pathologies to which they are subject, and in the manner in which they contribute to human social experience. Here, in capsule form, is the list:

The *ecological self* is the self as perceived with respect to the physical environment: 'I' am the person here in this place, engaged in this particular activity.

The *interpersonal self*, which appears from earliest infancy just as the ecological self does, is specified by species-specific signals of emotional rapport and communication: I am the person who is engaged, here, in this particular human interchange.

The *extended self* is based primarily on our personal memories and anticipations: I am the person who had certain specific experiences, who regularly engages in certain specific and familiar routines.

The *private self* appears when children first notice that some of their experiences are not directly shared with other people: I am, in principle, the only person who can feel this unique and particular pain.

The *conceptual self* or 'self-concept' draws its meaning from the network of assumptions and theories in which it is embedded, just as all other concepts do. Some of those theories concern social roles (husband, professor, American), some postulate more or less hypothetical internal entities (the soul, the unconscious mind, mental energy, the brain, the liver), and some establish socially significant dimensions of difference (intelligence, attractiveness, wealth). There is a remarkable variety in what people believe about themselves, and not all of it is true.

These several 'selves' are not generally expe-

---

[1] The term 'information' is currently used by cognitive psychologists in two rather different ways. In J. J. Gibson's (1966, 1979) ecological theory of perception, information exists objectively, specifies the properties of objects and events by virtue of physical principles, and is 'picked up' by perceivers. In conventional theories of thinking and memory, information is thought of as stored in the brain and subject to such mental operations as 'recording' and 'retrieval' (see also footnote 13 below). Because the self is an object of thought as well as of perception, I will draw on both traditions in this paper.

rienced as separate and distinct, because there is stimulus information to specify their cohesion. (For example I can usually see that it is I, here, who am engaging in a particular social interaction.) In cases where such information is less salient, the unity of the self is correspondingly weakened. But unified or not, all five 'selves' are of fundamental importance. They all begin early in life, though not all at the same point or in the same way. They all exhibit some degree of continuity over time, and so each contribute to the universal experience of the continuity of self. They are all *experienced*, though perhaps not all with the same quality of consciousness. And they are all *valued*: people go to great lengths not only to save their lives but to preserve the personal relationships that establish their identities, to defend their interpretations of the past and their plans for the future, to keep inviolate the secret places of their minds, and to maintain the integrity of the culturally-defined self that they have adopted.

My analysis of the self will focus more on what we know and how we know it than on what we do and how we do it. Overt action is indivisible, or at least it only occasionally divides along the lines proposed here. I do not intend to suggest, for example, that some deeds are the responsibility of the ecological self and others of the conceptual self. The information on which a given action is based may be more or less weighted by what is known ecologically or interpersonally, publicly or privately, from personal memory or by acceptance of social norms; nevertheless it is the whole individual who acts in the real environment. This very fact provides further information for the coherence of the several 'selves,' or at least for those that are based on perceptual information.

The Ecological Self

A continuous flow of optical information anchors the visual system to its immediate environment. Any station point (i.e. any possible point of observation by an eye) in any illuminated environment can be thought of as surrounded by a 360° shell of optical structure—a structure that depends on the position of the point of observation and on the layout from which the light was reflected. This 'optic array' undergoes systematic changes as the point of observation moves through the environment. Under ordinary circumstances,[2] the resulting structure-over-time is unique to the particular layout of the immediate environment and to the actual path of the point of observation: it *specifies* the real situation that gives rise to it. The visual systems of animals have evolved to take advantage of this omnipresent veridical information.

Every movement of the point of observation produces a systematic flow pattern in the visual field. This flow is the basis of what J. J. Gibson called 'visual kinesthesis'—an optically produced awareness of one's own movement and posture (Gibson, 1979, p. 182). The simplest case occurs when an observer, looking straight ahead, walks toward an extended surface like a wall. Under these conditions every bit of optical texture flows outward from a single central point, and that focus of expansion is exactly the point toward which the observer is moving. This makes it possible, literally, for people to see where they are going.[3] Another important type of optical flow occurs when the observer moves *parallel* to an extended surface. The 'streaming' of texture elements that occurs under these conditions is a particularly effective source of infor-

[2] In this context, 'ordinary circumstances' refers to the conditions that prevailed during the evolution of the human visual system. Recent technologies such as film, television, and holography now make it possible to create optic arrays in the absence of the environments that they apparently specify.

[3] The analysis becomes rather more complicated if the environment is cluttered with objects and/or the observer is not looking forward (Regan & Beverley, 1982). Nevertheless, the wealth of egomovement-specifying information available in normally occurring patterns of optical flow cannot be disputed (Cutting, 1986).

mation, and can give rise to the experience of motion even in the absence of the corresponding central expansion pattern. (This is the basis of the illusion of egomotion often experienced in a stationary train or car when a neighbouring vehicle begins to move.) In normal movement, of course, the appropriate flow patterns occur everywhere in the visual field at once: they specify the position and movement of the entity I am calling the ecological self.[4]

The 'moving room' technique devised by David Lee and his associates (e.g. Lee & Lishman, 1975) makes it possible to present optical flow without any real motion of the individual. Although the subject is standing on the solid floor of the laboratory, s/he is surrounded by the walls of a small open-floored cubicle that hangs from the ceiling (or rides on rollers, as in Stroffregen, 1985) and is thus independently movable. Small children standing in this room can be 'knocked down' simply by moving the walls a short distance; their ability to remain upright depends on how long it has been since they first learned to stand (Butterworth & Cicchetti, 1978). Adults will sway a little, and fall if they are not securely balanced. What happens is that the optical flow created by moving the walls forward (for instance) specifies to the subjects that they themselves are swaying backwards; the muscular readjustments undertaken to compensate for this apparent sway cause them to fall.

The rapid radial expansion pattern produced by approach to a surface is called 'looming'. Although this pattern by itself does not distinguish movement of the observer from movement of the object, other information (the presence or absence of peripheral flow, the occlusion produced by the edge of the moving object) usually eliminates any ambiguity. In either case, looming specifies an imminent collision between the point of observation and the surface. Even very young infants apparently pick up this information: they blink, move their heads back, and generally behave as if they saw what was coming. But the looming expansion pattern does not merely suggest that a collision is coming sometime soon: it specifies the exact moment at which the impact will occur. David Lee (1980) has shown that the instantaneous value of the parameter *tau* (defined by the inverse of the rate of optical expansion) is a precise measure of the time remaining until the distance between the eye and the surface is reduced to zero. Of course, this principle applies only if there is no acceleration or deceleration; it will not hold if the owner of the eye slows down or moves out of the way. Both people and animals apparently use *tau* in the control of movement.

One surprising bit of evidence for the importance of optical flow for the ecological self comes from a phenomenon investigated by Flavell, Shipstead & Croft (1980). The phenomenon is amusing in its own right and has often been described: young children cover their eyes with their hands and say "You can't see me!" Prior to the work of Flavell *et al.* (1980), this behavior was typically interpreted in Piagetian terms: since the child cannot see anything, s/he assumes that you can't see anything either. Indeed, when these experimenters asked their eyes-covered subjects "Can I see you?," most 2- and 3-year-olds answered *No*. Surprisingly, however, the same subjects answered *Yes* to many other questions about what the experimenter could see. "Can I see Snoopy (a doll located nearby)?" *Yes*. "Can I see your leg?" *Yes*. "Can I see your head?" *Yes*. These results show that "You can't see me" does not reflect any egocentric misapprehension about other people's seeing; rather, it is a clue to the speaker's own conception of self. The child's 'me'—the entity to which the adult's question "Can I see you?" refers—is evidently somewhat near the eyes. To be sure, that localisation is not precise:

---

[4]George Butterworth (in press) has independently suggested that the optic flow field is an important determinant of the infant's emerging sense of self.

Flavell *et al.* got mixed results when they had their subjects cover only one eye, or stand behind a barrier with a hole in it so that nothing but an eye was visible. Nevertheless the implication seems clear: children locate the self at the point of observation, as specified by the optical flow field.[5]

Important as it is, optical flow is by no means the only determinant of the ecological self. The self is an embodied actor as well as an observer; it initiates movements, perceives their consequences, and takes pleasure in its own effectivity. Infants love to look at their own hands in action, and they can distinguish their own moving legs, seen in real time on a TV screen, from the moving legs of another baby (Bahrick & Watson, 1985). Many theorists have noted the importance of agency in establishing a sense of self. I can cause changes in the immediately perceptible environment, and those objects whose movements and changes I can inevitably and consistently control are parts of *me*. This kind of self-perception is precisely time-dependent and richly intermodal. I can see and feel what I do: the optical and kinesthetically-given structures that specify the consequences of movement are exactly synchronous, and both coincide with the efferent activity by which the action itself is produced. In general, then, the two principal aspects of the ecological self are defined by two distinguishable kinds of information. The existence of a perceiving entity at a particular location in the environment is most clearly specified by the optical flow field (though touch and hearing also contribute); the existence of a bounded, articulated and controllable body is specified not only by what we can

see of it but by what we feel and what we can do.[6]

The ecological self does not always coincide with the biological body. In particular, anything that *moves with* the body tends to be perceived as part of the self—especially if its movements are self-produced. This principle applies most obviously to the clothes we wear. It is *I* who kick the soccer ball, though in fact its only contact is with my shoe; when you touch my shoulder you are touching *me*, even when a shirt and a jacket interpose between your fingers and my skin. These experiences have nothing to do with my ownership of the clothes. The same jacket is not part of my ecological self when it hangs in my closet, or when I am carrying it home from the cleaners; to touch it in such cases is not to touch *me* at all. What matters is not possession or contact but agency and co-ordinate movement. The same principle explains why the practised wearer of an artificial limb so naturally perceives it as a part of the self. Such wearers have not mistakenly come to believe that the limbs are flesh-and-blood parts of their bodies. On the contrary, their perceptions are exactly correct: to the extent that the motion of a limb is responsive to one's intentions and is co-ordinated with movements of the point of observation, it belongs to the ecological self.

Any controllable object that moves together with the point of observation can become part of the ecological self. This principle even applies to automobiles—that's why we say "he ran into me" when we mean "he ran into my car." As in the case of clothing, such uses of the first person do not depend on ownership. I am just as likely to use 'me' when I have been driving a

[5] Selma Fraiberg (1977) reports that congenitally blind children are slow to develop an adequate sense of self; for example, they master the pronouns 'I' and 'you' much later than sighted children do. As E. G. Gibson (1976) has pointed out, this is to be expected if optical structure is an important source of self-specification.

[6] Passive bodily experiences such as pain are often mentioned in discussions of the self, but they contribute very little to the ecological self as defined here. Pain can disrupt everything we do, but it does not specify much about *us* unless we reflect upon it—an activity which belongs with the private or the conceptual self rather than with the self as perceived.

rented vehicle, and I would not use it about my own car if the collision occurred while a friend was at the wheel. The important point is not whether the car was mine but whether the two of us were moving together as an ecological unit when the crash occurred. This tendency is a special case of the principle that the Gestalt psychologists called 'common fate': objects that move together are perceived as belonging to a single coherent unit. (The collision example actually illustrates this principle in two different ways: "He ran into me" treats the *other* car and *its* driver as a unit too.) Kellman & Spelke (1983) have recently shown that common fate governs object perception even in early infancy; I am here suggesting that it governs self-perception as well.

The last 10 years have seen great advances in the study of infant perception (see Gibson & Spelke, 1983, for a review). Certainly by 3 months of age (and probably from birth), the infant perceives much the same sort of world that we do: a world of distinct, solid, and permanent objects of which she herself (or he himself) is one. The information that specifies the ecological self is omnipresent, and babies are not slow to pick it up. They respond to looming and optical flow from a very early age, discriminate among objects, and easily distinguish the immediate consequences of their own actions from events of other kinds. The old hypothesis that a young infant cannot tell the difference between itself and the environment, or between itself and its mother, can be decisively rejected. The ecological self is present from the first.[7] Indeed, it is not only present but *accurate*: except in rare pathological cases (pathologies of the ecological self include the 'phantom limbs' of amputees and the 'neglect' syndrome that

appears in some cases of brain damage), immediate perception of the self is more or less veridical at all ages. Although ecological self-perception certainly becomes more complete and more precise with development, it is almost never grossly in error.[8]

Of course, we do not perceive only the self: as J. J. Gibson (1979) put it, all perceiving involves co-perception of self and environment. Optical looming, for example, specifies an objective relationship (impending collision) between the two. What we perceive is ourselves as *embedded in* the environment, and acting with respect to it. Moreover, the distinction between perception and action can be made only at the level of theoretical analysis; in ordinary behavior they are inseparably fused. Except in special cases, we do not first perceive and only then proceed to move. We perceive *as* we act and *that* we act; often, our own actions constitute the very characteristics of the ecological self that we are simultaneously perceiving.

In summary, here are some of the characteristics of the ecological self:

The self, like the environment, exists objectively; many of its characteristics are specified by objectively-existing information. That information allows us to perceive not only the location of the ecological self but also the nature of its ongoing interaction with the environment.

Much of the relevant information is kinetic, consisting of structure over time. Optical structure is particularly important, but self-specifying information is often available to several perceptual modalities at once.

---

[7] The fact that children do not recognise themselves in the mirror till about 2 years old has often been taken to mean that they have no sense of self until that time (Lewis & Brooks-Gunn, 1984). In my view, however, what they achieve at 2 years is just an understanding of the optics of mirrors (Loveland, 1986); the self is present much earlier.

[8] The *conceptual* self usually includes (among other things) a representation of one's own body. These 'body-images' comprise an important subset of what we believe about ourselves, but they should not be confused with the ecological self. They are not based on perceptual information alone; partly for that reason, they can be quite inaccurate.

The ecological self is veridically perceived from earliest infancy; nevertheless self-perception develops and can become more adequate with increasing age and skill.

Are we *conscious* of our ecological selves? To answer this question in the negative would be to claim that ecological self-perception was phenomenally 'silent'. I believe, on the contrary, that it is often accompanied by a definite — and often powerful — kind of awareness.[9] This is presumably true not only of adults but of infants; indeed, of all animals whose perceptual systems pick up self-specifying information. Nevertheless, awareness of this kind is not what we would ordinarily call 'self-consciousness'. The ecological self *per se* is not an object of thought; very young infants have no internal self-representations to be conscious of or to think about. Such representations appear only in the extended, private, and conceptual selves. The ecological self, in contrast, is directly perceived.

The Interpersonal Self

The interpersonal self is the self as engaged in immediate unreflective social interaction with another person. Like the ecological self, it can be directly perceived on the basis of objectively existing information. Again like the ecological self, most of the relevant information is essentially kinetic, i.e. consists of structures over time. In this case, however, the information — and the state of affairs that it specifies — come into existence only when two (or more) people are engaged in personal interaction. If the na-

ture, direction, timing, and intensity of one person's actions mesh appropriately with the nature/direction/timing/intensity of the other's, they have jointly created an instance of what is often called *intersubjectivity*. The mutuality of their behaviour exists in fact and can be perceived by outside observers; more importantly, it is perceived by the participants themselves. Each of them can see (and hear, and perhaps feel) the appropriately interactive responses of the other. Those responses, in relation to one's own perceived activity, specify the interpersonal self.

What defines the responses of the other person as appropriate to our own? The underlying principles here are not those of ecological optics (Gibson, 1979); that is, they do not depend simply on the way that light is reflected to (moving) points of observation. Rather, they are species-specific. We take the expressions and gestures and vocalisations of other people as evidence of an ongoing intersubjectivity because, being human, we are genetically equipped to do so just as they are. We are not the only ones, of course: non-human animals also respond to their conspecifics. As Darwin put it, "When two young dogs in play are growling and biting each other's faces and legs, it is obvious that they understand each other's gestures and manners" (1904, p. 60). The communicative gestures of other species may resemble our own, but only to the extent that we are evolutionary kin.

Darwin's use of the term 'understand' in this context should not be misunderstood. He does not claim (or at least I do not claim) that puppies have an *intellectual* understanding of each other's behavior; their interactions do not necessarily involve a conceptual self or a conceptual other. What is going on between them is sometimes called 'non-verbal communication', but even that term can be misleading; it tends to suggest that each participant is somehow telling the other about his/her own mental states. If that were true, the achievement of intersubjectivity would depend on the accuracy with

[9] An account of the circumstances under which we are (or are not) explicitly conscious of what we perceive is beyond the scope of this paper. It is certain, however, that such consciousness is not primarily based on the use of language; everyone sees much more than they can possibly describe in words.

which we attribute thoughts and feelings to other people. While we do sometimes attempt such attributions in adult life, they can hardly be the basis of the smooth and immediate interpersonal co-ordination I am considering here.

The claim that intersubjectivity is based on direct perception rather than inference is most strongly supported by recent studies of infancy, especially of the interactions between infants and their mothers. These studies show that a very rich form of intersubjectivity is typically in place by the time the infant is 2 months old. Here is Colwyn Trevarthen's account:

In the second month infants become more precisely alert to the human voice and they exhibit subtle responses in expression to the flow of maternal speech. They are frequently content to engage in expressive exchanges for many minutes on end by means of sight and sounds alone . . . Definite eye contact is sought by most infants about 6 weeks after full term birth. Once this orientation is achieved, and in response to a complex array of maternal expressive signals, many 4- to 6-week-olds smile and coo . . .

Mothers align their faces with the baby, adjusting position to the least distance of clear vision for an adult, and making modulated vertical and horizontal head rotations. Their faces are exaggeratedly mobile in every feature and these movements are synchronized with gentle but rhythmically accentuated vocalizations. All this behavior responds to the infant's evident awareness and acts to draw out signs of interest and pleasure. The infants show intent interest with fixed gaze, knit brows and slightly pursed lips or relaxed jaw, and immobility of the limbs. They exhibit an affectionate pleasure, closely linked to fixation on the mother's face and responsive to her expression, with smiles of varied intensity, coos, and hand movements . . . When the mother makes her face immobile the baby ceases smiling and may exhibit distress with grimaces, pouting, wringing of the hands,

large forceful gestures with fisted hands, and gaze avoidance. [Trevarthen, 1983, p. 139]

These interactions illustrate what Trevarthen has called 'primary intersubjectivity'. The participants respond to each other immediately and coherently, in both action and feeling; their reciprocal activities are closely co-ordinated in time. The result is a shared structure of action —a structure that both of the participants enjoy, and that neither of them could have produced alone. Indeed, the contributions of the individual partners would be useless and foolish if they occurred by themselves. An elegant experiment by Lynne Murray (Murray & Trevarthen, 1985) demonstrates this point. Mothers and their 6 to 12 week-old babies, actually in separate rooms, interacted via double closed-circuit television. Each partner saw and heard a full-face, life-size video image of the other, with appropriate eye contact being made. As long as the video presentation was 'live', this system allowed interaction to proceed normally: the babies looked intently at their mothers with open and relaxed mouth, slightly raised eyebrows, and other signs of interest. The first minute of live interaction comprised the control condition. It was recorded on videotape; the tape of the mother was then rewound and immediately replayed on the infant's screen. This second (replay) minute comprised the experimental condition. Although what the infants saw and heard was identically the same in both conditions—the same mother, the same gestures, the same displays of affection—their responses were dramatically different. In the experimental condition, the babies who had been happy a minute ago now exhibited signs of distress: they turned away from the mother's image, frowned, grimaced, and fingered their clothing.[10] (A final control presentation ensured that they had not sim-

---

[10] If the procedure is reversed so that what the mother sees is only a replayed videotape of the baby, she too notices that something is wrong; she may wonder if she has unintentionally done something to disturb the relationship.

ply become tired of the situation itself.) The subjects' distress during the replay was evidently produced by some kind of mismatch between their mothers' responses and their own.

Murray's study shows that infants in normal face-to-face interactions are not just picking up information about their partners; they actually perceive the ongoing intersubjective relationship. J. J. Gibson's (1979) principle that all perceiving involves co-perception of environment and self applies also to the *social* environment and to the *interpersonal* self, i.e. the self that is established in these interactions. Just as the ecological self is specified by the orientation and flow of optical texture, so the interpersonal self is specified by the orientation and flow of the other individual's expressive gestures; just as the ecological self is articulated and confirmed by the effects of our own physical actions, so the interpersonal self is developed and confirmed by the effects of our own expressive gestures on our partner.

The stimulus basis of these interactions is still poorly understood. Murray's experiment does not imply that 2-month-old infants are exquisitively sensitive to variations in timing; for all we know at present, their distress in the experimental condition may have resulted simply from an inability to maintain eye contact. We do know, however, that the range of social responses available to babies increases dramatically during the first year. This development elicits a corresponding increase in the sophistication of the social behavior of their partners, so that very rich forms of intersubjectivity become possible. Consider, for example, the phenomenon that Daniel Stern calls *affect attunement*:

A 9-month-old girl becomes very excited about a toy and reaches for it. As she grabs it, she lets out an exuberant 'aaaah!' and looks at her mother. Her mother looks back, scrunches up her shoulders, and performs a terrific shimmy with her upper body, like a go-go dancer. The shimmy lasts only about as long

as her daughter's 'aaaah!' but is equally excited, joyful, and intense . . .

An 8½-month-old boy reaches for a toy just beyond reach. Silently he stretches toward it, leaning and extending arms and fingers out fully. Still short of the toy, he tenses his body to squeeze out the extra inch he needs to reach it. At the moment, his mother says "uuuuuh . . . uuuuuh!" with a crescendo of vocal effort, the expiration of air pushing against her tensed torso. The mother's accelerating vocal-respiratory effort matches the infant's accelerating physical effort. [1985, p. 140]

These examples (Stern gives many others) show again that intersubjectivity is an emotional business: the two partners are obviously sharing an affect. Nevertheless, the ordinary vocabulary of the emotions is not adequate to describe what is going on. It is not just that both are 'happy' or 'excited', but that the mother is precisely matching the pattern and temporal contour of the infant's activity with her own. Such 'vitality affects' (Stern, 1985) are specified by information in several sensory modalities: in visible movement, in the emphasis and modulation of the voice, in bodily contact. Their specification is so rich that they are readily perceived and shared, not only between mothers and infants but between any two individuals in social contact. The resulting experience is an immediate awareness of both the other person and the (interpersonal) self, as well as of the specific present relationship between them.

There is nothing inferential about this kind of interpersonal understanding, at least in its basic form. The information that specifies vitality affects is directly available in the optic array (and in the acoustic and haptic arrays), and anybody with the right kind of perceptual system can pick it up. As Solomon Asch noted a generation ago, ". . . the organised properties of experience are structurally similar to those of the corresponding actions . . . the emotion of joy and

the expressions of joy have identical characteristics . . . formally the same qualities are
present in the experience and movements of
tension, hesitation, and daring" (1952, p. 158).
That is why even very young infants can perceive and respond appropriately to the affective
gestures of other people.[11] The interpersonal
self begins just as early as the ecological self;
both are based on perceptually available information.

The close parallels between ecological and interpersonal self-perception should not be allowed to obscure certain important differences.
The successful achievement of intersubjectivity
depends not only on the operation of the perceptual and motor systems but on some additional, specifically human mechanism that permits us to relate to members of our own species.
The mechanism can fail, and it has often been
suggested that the dramatic condition called *infantile autism*, characterised from the outset by a
total lack of interest in relationships with people, results from just such a failure. Leo Kanner
made this point explicitly in the paper that established autism as a diagnostic category: "We
must, then, assume that these children have
come into the world with innate inability to
form the usual, biologically provided affective
contact with people, just as other children come
into the world with innate physical or intellectual handicaps" (1943, p. 250). Murray (1984)
has recently presented a similar argument, and
suggested that the effects observed in her double closed-circuit television paradigm may provide useful models for autism research.[12]

Both ecological and interpersonal perception
are soon supplemented by other forms of cognition. In the ecological case, we learn to make
inferences about the environment that go
beyond what we can see: for example, that the
faucet on the sink is not just a protuberance we
can grasp but a source of hot water as well. In
the interpersonal case, we learn that people are
not just participants in our interactions but have
beliefs, intentions, and feelings of their own.
Young children acquire what is nowadays called
a 'theory of mind' (Wellman, 1985; Leslie, 1987)
roughly between the ages of 2 and 4 years. They
begin to attribute mental states to other individuals: partly on the basis of what they have been
told, partly by analogy with their own private
experience, and perhaps partly by more detached consideration of the information available in personal interaction. Sometimes, the beliefs and emotions thus attributed to other
people concern ourselves. But despite the claims
of George Herbert (1934) and others, such inferences are certainly not the primary basis of
self-knowledge. Their effect is not on the self as
a whole but primarily on the conceptual self,
and even there it is modulated by other sources
of information.

Elaborating the interpersonal self (and the
'interpersonal other') in this way is necessarily
risky. Inference can go astray, not only through
our own lack of skill but also because our
partner may be deliberately presentating an in-
authentic image (Goffman, 1959). In contrast,
the *perception* of ongoing intersubjectivity is
necessarily veridical. Perhaps my partner only
pretends to like me, but s/he cannot pretend to
be intersubjectively engaged with me. Intersubjectivity is defined by an appropriate match between the nature/direction/timing/intensities
of two people's activities; it either occurs or it
does not. When it does occur, two distinct and
yet closely related interpersonal selves are
brought into existence along with it.

Awareness of the interpersonal self is almost
invariably accompanied by a simultaneous
awareness of the ecological self. A wealth of

---

[11] The fact that even newborn infants can apparently imitate facial expressions (Meltzoff & Moore, 1983) provides
further support for this view.

[12] I do not mean to suggest that every infant who fails to
exhibit affect attunement will necessarily become autistic. In
a follow-up study of 50 children who had originally been
diagnosed (at a median age of 18 months) as suffering from
Kanner's 'extreme aloneness', Knobloch & Pasamanick
(1975) found that three-fourths of them had lost their autistic symptoms a few years later.

information specifies their co-existence: I can see that the person to whom you are addressing yourself (the interpersonal me) is the very person who is located here, at this point of observation in this environment (the ecological me). For this reason, these two aspects of the self are rarely experienced as distinct. Such a separation can occur, however, if we attend exclusively to one class of information and ignore the other entirely. To attend only to ecological information structures, ignoring the interpersonal, is to treat another individual merely as a non-human object—perhaps to walk past him, or shove him aside, without engaging in any form of intersubjectivity. The opposite case can occur in very intimate personal contact, as between lovers or (as psychoanalysts have long suggested) between mothers and infants: one's attention is so fully directed to the ongoing intersubjective experience that one does not pick up any ecological-self-specifying information at all. This does not mean that lovers and infants have no ecological selves, but only that there are moments at which those aspects of their selves may go unnoticed.

The Extended Self

The objectively-existing kinds of information considered so far—optical flow, effective movement, other people's expressive gestures—specify only the present self. We can see what we are doing right now, and with whom, but how can we know what we did yesterday or last week? The answer, of course, is just that we *remember*: the information is in our own heads.[13] The extended self is the self as it was in

---

[13] At least, some of it is. Remembering is not like perceiving: the stored information does not specify the remembered state of affairs in the same unequivocal way that optical structure specifies the layout of the environment. Like the tree rings from which one can infer past variations in climate, information stored in memory is merely a record —generally an incomplete and fallible record—of the past.

the past and as we expect it to be in the future, known primarily on the basis of memory.

Not all uses of the past involve knowledge of the extended self. It is now well established that so-called procedural memory—'knowing how', as opposed to 'knowing that'—is substantially independent of memory for personal experiences. Perceptual and motor learning are obvious cases in point: performance gains are based on information stored in the past, but not necessarily information about the past *self*. (This is particularly dramatic in amnesics, who can acquire new skills without any recollection of the prior occasions on which those skilled were practised; *cf.* Parkin, 1982. Amnesia is, *par excellence*, the pathology of the extended self.) Even improvements in the ability to see how we ourselves are physically and socially engaged— i.e. in the articulation of the ecological and interpersonal selves—need not be accompanied by any experience of the self that transcends the present. In procedural memory the past *modulates* what we do in the present without standing apart from it.

Genuine remembering occurs when at least some information about the past is disentangled from the current situation. In many cases, that information is about *my* past, i.e. it is a record of some aspect of the extended self.[14] In remembering something that I did or experienced on some other occasion—by remembering *that* I did it rather than merely how to do it—I neces-

---

For convenience, I shall say that memory 'records' or 'encodes' or 'carries forward information about' certain events. What I mean is conventional enough: some (not all) of the information which originally specified those events to the perceiver was somehow stored, and some (not all) of that stored information is retrieved in the act of remembering.

[14] Not in all cases, of course. Everyone remembers a vast array of facts—e.g. that Columbus discovered America— that have no self-reference at all. Such facts are appropriately assigned to what Tulving (1972) called 'semantic memory'. Tulving's term cuts across the distinctions made here: my knowledge of my own familiar scripts and routines would also be classified as semantic memory, but they are clearly aspects of the extended self.

sarily became aware that my existence transcends the present moment. This can happen in two rather different ways. To the extent that what I recall is a unique and particular past event (say, presenting a colloquium talk at the University of Aberdeen in November 1987), I am having an *episodic memory* (Tulving, 1972). But to the extent that what I recall is a repeated and familiar routine (there is a script for colloquiua that includes arriving in town, talking to colleagues, being introduced, giving the talk, answering questions, etc.), I am using a general event representation (Nelson, 1986) or *script* (Schank & Abelson, 1977). Both kinds of memory contribute to the extended self. *I* am the person who gave that colloquium in Aberdeen: *I* am also a person who gives colloquium talks from time to time. While these two examples are certainly not among the most central components of my extended self (!), that self can be thought as a kind of cumulated total of such memories: the things I remember having done and the things I think of myself as doing regularly.

The notion that the sense of self depends on autobiographical memory is hardly new (for recent expositions see, e.g., Brewer, 1986; Baddeley, 1987; Fivush, 1988). What *is* new, however, is research on the development of that memory in early childhood. We now know that both script knowledge and episodic recall appear very early. Consider script knowledge: even 3-year-olds can readily answer such questions as "What happens when you make cookies?" Their answers—"Well, you bake them and eat them" (Nelson & Gruendel, 1986, p. 27)—are not very elaborate, but they almost always include a correctly-reported sequence of events. (By 4½, they can say "My mommy puts chocolate chips inside the cookies. Then ya put 'em in the oven; then we take them out, put them on the table and eat them.') These young children are not describing what happened on some particular occasion, but what regularly happens in a certain routine. At 3 years they already know a great many scripts: getting up, getting dressed,

having breakfast, and so on. What is important here is not merely being able to execute such routines—they have been doing that already for at least 2 years—but to remember one when it is *not* being executed. To do that is to be aware of oneself as existing outside the present moment, and hence of the extended self. In the case of script knowledge, however, that self does not belong so much to the past as to the timeless realm of regularities, rules, and roles; we say "This is what I *do*." The actual past self is more clearly established by episodic memory, when we can say "This is what I *did*."

Recent studies show that episodic recall, like script knowledge, is in place by the age of three. A 2½-year-old child will often fail to remember the particular 'target event' that an interviewer first asks about, but s/he will usually have at least some fairly accurate memories that go back 3 or more months (Todd & Perlmutter, 1980; Fivush, Gray & Fromhoff, 1987). Despite these findings, I doubt that episodic memory contributes very much to the sense of self at this early age. Children under 3 years are not very interested in the past, even when they can recall it. They would much rather talk about something in the present—or play and not talk at all—than spend effort in remembering earlier experiences (Galotti & Neisser, 1982).

That interest increases as the child comes to realise the social significance of autobiographical recall, i.e. its potential for extending relationships beyond the present moment. The most important adaptive function of memory may be that it makes permanent interpersonal relations possible, and thus vastly strengthens the coherence of human groups (Neisser, 1988). Note that even rather sloppy memories can serve this purpose: my recall of a shared event must be close enough to yours to avoid bizarre discrepancies, but it need not be accurate in every detail. Unsurprisingly, this is just the level of mnemonic accuracy that people generally achieve.

Although the development of the extended self is more or less inevitable—any child with a normal memory will sooner or later begin to reflect on its own past experiences—many families engage in activities that seem explicitly designed to stimulate and shape it. By talking to their children about shared experiences and future plans, parents deliberately try to create an increased awareness of the continuity of both the family and the self. Two examples from recent research illustrate this activity especially well. The father of Nelson's (1988) subject 'Emily' regularly spoke to her, just before bedtime, about family routines and plans for the next day. Emily's subsequent crib monologues (which were tape-recorded), often dealt with these very plans. For example:

Father: *You know what we're going to do, you know what we're going to do this weekend? We're going to go to Childworld and we're going to buy some diapers for Stephen and some diapers for Emily, and we're going to buy an intercom system so that we can hear Stephen in different parts of the house . . . When we go to Childworld and buy diapers for Stephen and diapers for Emily and what is called an intercom system that we plug in, Stephen, into Stephen's room and then we go downstairs and we plug it in and we get to hear Stephen! Making a, when Stephen wakes up we'll hear him cry, through the intercom system . . ."*

Emily *[later, in pre-sleep monologue]: . . . daddy said buy diapers for Stephen and Emily and buy some-thing for Stephen, plug in, and say ah-h-h [simulates baby cry] and put the in—. On Saturday go Childworld buy diaper for Emily and diaper for the baby and then buy something for the, and— see—for—that—baby, plug it in and get diapers for everybody, and . . . [Nelson, 1988, pp. 270–271].*

A different example of the role of the family in developing the extended self comes from the work of Edwards & Middleton (1988), who simply asked mothers to talk with their young children about pictures in the family photograph album. The resulting conversations, in which both partners were clearly interested in relating the past to the present, followed typical patterns. After a deliberate explication of what a given picture actually showed, the participants would usually go on to consider why it mattered: how they had felt, how the past event was related to present concerns, etc. Here are two examples (Paul is 4.3 years old):

Mother: *Look at you inside this photograph.*
Paul: *Is that our new car?*
Mother: *That was the car we hired. Oh look, you're pretending to drive it aren't you?*
Paul: *Mm. [Edwards & Middleton, 1988, p. 11].*

Or, more exlicitly:

Paul: *Is that me?*
Mother: *Yes, that's you. Mm.*
Paul: *Oh, that's nice. Did you love me there?*
Mother: *Oh I DID. Yes" [p. 15].*

The extended self becomes increasingly important as we grow older. Most adults develop a more or less standard life-narrative that effectively defines the self in terms of a particular series of remembered experiences. These accounts are continually being extended (and occasionally revised!), creating a narrative structure much like that of more formal autobiographies (Barclay, 1986). As in the case of social relationships, the memory that supports these narratives need not be highly accurate. It also need not deal in equal detail with every epoch of life. Recent studies suggest that elderly people have particularly rich and accessible memories for the period of adolescence and young adulthood (Rubin et al., 1986).

The extended self and ecological selves are linked by objectively available stimulus information. Even in the act of recollecting the past, I can still see that I am here in the circumstances of the present. But their coherence is not always salient: I do not *need* to know those circumstances in order to recall effectively. It is possible, then, for the remembered self to be somewhat detached from the self experienced in the present. This possibility gives rise to wide individual and cultural differences. Some people are not much concerned with the past, and spend relatively little time in retrospection; others, of whom Marcel Proust is the best-known example, seems to value the past much more highly.

Although our knowledge of the extended self is based on stored information, access to that information is not unproblematic. Memory is typically reconstructive (Bartlett, 1932); what we recall depends on what we now believe as well as on what we once stored. This means that the remembered self is not independent of the conceptual self; our self-theories affect what we choose to recall as well as how accurately we recall it. (Those theories even affect what we perceive, ecologically and interpersonally, by focusing our attention on some aspects of the available information to the neglect of others.) Because the information we have for the extended self is private and limited rather than public and indefinitely rich, it is especially vulnerable to misconstrual.

The Private Self

Each of us has conscious experiences that are not available to anyone else. Some of these are the inner aspects of perception and action; others (dreams, for example) are quite independent of the individual's actual present circumstances. These personal experiences are an important source of self-knowledge.[15] When are

---

[15] I am reluctant to call private conscious experience a 'form of information' (like stimulus structure, or the stored contents of memory) because it does not specify anything beyond itself in the way that optical information (say) specifies the layout of the environment. Some conscious experiences do 'refer' to the environment, but the sense in which they do so is beyond the scope of this paper; other conscious experiences do not 'refer' at all.

they first used for that purpose? While even the youngest children surely have a conscious mental life (including an awareness of the ecological and interpersonal selves!), I suspect that they do not yet take the *immediacy* of their experience as an important line of demarcation between themselves and the rest of the world. They do not need to: such a line already exists for them, established by ecologically available information. Although each of us certainly "dichotomizes the Kosmos in a different place," as William James put it (1890, p. 290), we first do so by exterospection rather than by introspection.

Sooner or later, children notice that certain experiences are exclusively their own. It is hard to be sure just when this happens. Although phrases like 'It hurts' and 'I'm hungry' appear well before the age of 2 years (Bretherton *et al.*, 1981), they may not yet have the introspective reference we accept as adults. ('I'm hungry', for example, may only be a way of asking for food.) Whatever may be true at earlier ages, however, many studies show that children are aware of the privacy of mental life before the age of 5 years. The 4-year-olds tested by Mossler *et al.* (1976), for example, clearly understood the notion of a 'secret': if A and B agree on something by gesture while C is not looking, then C will not know it unless he is subsequently told. More recent studies by Wimmer & Perner (1983) have confirmed this point.

We not only *have* private experience but *remember* it, recalling dreams we had last night or thoughts we had last week and thus augmenting the extended self. The importance of this contribution varies substantially from one person to another, perhaps in part because memory for mental experiences is relatively poor. Pains are notoriously difficult to recall; we remember that we were in pain, but cannot easily recapture the quality of the experience. Most people forget most of their dreams almost immediately. William Brewer (1988) has recently shown that this principle also applies to everyday waking thoughts. The subjects of his ecological memory study carried 'beepers' that went off randomly several times a day; at the sound of the beep they wrote down where they were, what they were doing, and what they were thinking. In later tests, recall of the recorded thoughts was far below recall of actions.

Although the varieties of phenomenal experience cannot easily be catalogued, it is easy to list familiar examples. Some, like dreams and memories, are virtually independent of the ecological and interpersonal selves. I can be asleep in Atlanta and dreaming of London, or talking to Peter and thinking of Paul. In many belief systems, such experiences are taken as support for a dualistic distinction between mind and body —i.e. for the existence of an entirely bodiless conceptual self. Logically, of course, this evidence is not compelling. The fact that private experience is essentially independent of the ecological self does not at all imply that it is independent of the material brain.

Philosophers in the Western tradition— indeed, in many traditions—have often treated the private self as the only self worth knowing. Descartes is primarily responsible for the further claim that it is the only self we can be sure about, all other experiences being subject to error and delusion. I have argued, in contrast, that the ecological and interpersonal selves are perceived effectively and surely from the beginning of life. (This argument does not dispute the *value* of the private self, only its epistemiological priority.) In any case it is worth noting that individuals differ widely in the value and importance they attach to inner experience. This was roughly Jung's original distinction between *extraverts* and *introverts*. In the extravert, ". . . thinking is oriented by the object and objective data" (Jung, 1921/1971, p. 342), while introverted thinking ". . . is neither determined by objective data nor directed to them; it is a thinking that starts from the subject and is directed to subjective ideas or subjective facts" (p. 344). These are essentially differences in the allocation of attention. All such forms of infor-

mation and experience are available to everyone, but within the normal range they are not all equally noticed, equally used, or equally valued. Outside the normal range are the pathologies of the private self, which include obsessive thinking, repression and denial of feelings, multiple personality, and related conditions.

There are also individual differences in concern with another, less detached aspect of the private self. Perceiving and doing—'being in the world'—are typically associated with particular subjective experiences, and one can take those experiences themselves as objects of attention. In addition to seeing a pencil and picking it up (say), one can attend to the *experience* of seeing it and picking it up. Although this particular example is trivial, what is gained from private experience can be rich and deep. In an eloquent passage, Isaiah Berlin attributes the discovery of this kind of knowledge to the Italian philosopher Giambattista Vico:

> *He [Vico] uncovered a sense of knowing that is basic to all humane studies: the sense in which I know what it is to be poor, to fight for a cause, to belong to a nation, to join or abandon a church or a party, to feel nostalgia, terror, the omnipresence of a god, to understand a gesture, a work of art, a joke, a man's character, that one is transformed or lying to oneself . . . The sense in which [one] claims to know this is quite different from that in which I know that this tree is taller than that, or that Caesar was assassinated on the Ides of March . . . In other words, it is not a form of 'knowing that.' Nor is it like knowing how to ride a bicycle or win a battle or what to do in case of fire . . . That is to say, it is not a form of 'knowing how' (in Gilbert Ryle's sense). What then is it like? It is a species of its own. It is a knowing founded on memory and imagination. [Berlin, 1969, pp. 375–376].*

Vico was not the first person to have this form of knowledge and self-knowledge, only the first to theorise about it. He also believed that one could have valid knowledge of the same kind about *other* people, and even about other epochs in history, by an effort of the imagination. An evaluation of that hypothesis is beyond the scope of this paper. Like many similar claims, however, it remains significant whether or not it is true. To the extent that we believe in such a capacity, or in other private capacities, they become parts of our conceptual selves.

The Conceptual Self

Each of us has a concept of him/herself as a particular person in a familiar world. These self-concepts originate in social life, and so they vary widely across different societies and cultures. A few concepts of my own can serve as convenient examples: I am an American, a husband, and a professor. I assume that I have certain social obligations and political rights; that I have a liver and a spleen and a distinctive pattern of nuclear DNA; that I am a fast reader, poor at remembering names, and neither handsome nor ugly; that in general I do not think enough about the future consequences of my actions. Everyone could make such a list, and no two lists would be the same. Even the relevant dimensions need not be the same: a member of the Lohorung Rai in East Nepal would include the state of his *Niwa* (Hardman, 1981), and a medieval Englishman the state of his soul.[16]

In the face of this complexity, it is useful to begin by considering concepts and categories of other kinds. What do we mean, for example, when we say that something is a 'dog'? The

[16]Even in our own culture, individuals can differ substantially in what they take as relevant dimensions of self-description. Markus (1977) has pointed out that a characteristic which is central for one individual may be a matter of indifference to another; her research shows that these differences have predictable consequences for what each is likely to notice and remember.

so-called classical theory of concepts, which would claim that the class *dog* is defined by certain necessary and sufficient features, no longer seem adequate: it is too difficult to think of really definitive features, and those that do come to mind (e.g. 'has four legs') are just as hard to define as *dog* itself (Murphy & Medin, 1985). The classical theory also fails to explain the typicality effects discovered by Eleanor Rosch (1978); in most categories, some members function as 'prototypes' while others are more marginal. But category membership cannot just be a matter of similarity to the prototype either: besides the difficulty of defining 'similarity', such a definition would miss the point that many categories, including *dog*, are conceptually all-or-none. (Any given animal either is or isn't a dog.) These difficulties are resolved by realising that concepts do not stand alone: each is defined with reference to a network of others, i.e. to a *theory*.[17]

Many linguists, philosophers, and psychologists have made this point (e.g. Lakoff, 1987; McCauley, 1987; Medin & Wattenmaker, 1987). To call something a dog is to assign it to a place in our theory of animals in general and dogs in particular, i.e. to assert that it occupies space, has internal organs, must eat or starve to death, is likely to behave in certain ways, is bigger than a mouse and smaller than an elephant, should be treated in a particular manner appropriate to dogs, had two parents who were dogs and will (if it becomes a parent) have puppies, etc. These beliefs are components (not all equally central) of our implicit theory of doghood—of what George Lakoff (1987) would call an 'idealised cognitive model'. Children have such models quite early, at least where animals are concerned (Carey, 1985).

Where do cognitive models come from? Like all other theories, they are based on a mixture of

[17]As I have suggested elsewhere (Neisser, 1987), Rosch's 'basic-level' categories are based on perception, and hence comprise a partial exception of this rule.

instruction and observation. We acquire concepts from our parents and our peers and our culture, and in some cases from reading and schooling as well. We also see things for ourselves, and do our best to co-ordinate those observations with what we have heard and read. As in science proper, however, observation is often shaped by theory. What we notice and how we interpret it depends substantially on what we already believe, so that fundamental changes are rare after a theoretical framework has once been established.

These principles apply equally to the concept of self. My notion of what I am, like your notion of what you are, reflects a cognitive model embedded in a theoretical network. It too is based primarily on what I have been told, not only in the form of general cultural assumptions but also of communications addressed to me in particular. Like other concepts it tends to govern what I notice; in this case, what I notice about myself. Like other theories, it is not necessarily correct; all of us know people whose self-theories seem off the mark in certain respects. Nevertheless most self-theories do work fairly well, at least in areas where they make predictions about real experience. (Where this is not the case—e.g. in paranoia—we tend to classify them as pathological.) When Epstein (1973) proposed that psychologists should think of the self as a theory rather than as an independently-existing entity, he was talking about the conceptual self.

Although the self-concept can usefully be regarded as a single cognitive model, it usually comprises several more or less distinct subtheories. Three of these deserve specific mention, although they cannot be considered in detail here. *Role theories*, which have been much studied by sociologists, are our own notions of how we fit into society: of what we should do and how we should be treated. They originate, I think, in children's understanding of the scripts in which they participate; hence they are in place very early. *Internal models*, in contrast,

concern our bodies and our minds. In modern Western culture, self-theories of the body (like my firm belief that I have an internal organ called the liver[18]) are mostly based on biology and medicine. Theories of the mind, in contrast, are the province of psychology, philosophy, and religion. Children are presented with these theories by the people around them, and do their best to interpret their own lives in terms of what they have been told. When and what they are told depends, of course, on the particular culture in which they are growing up.

Trait attributions are an important class of self-theories that straddle the boundary between social roles and internal models. We may believe, for example, that we are clever or stupid, handsome or ugly, fortunate or unlucky. Although these dimensions are essentially conventional—not all cultures classify along the same importance. In this vein, Carol Dweck (1986) has shown that children's beliefs about intelligence affect their actual performance in school. Those who believe that intelligence is a fixed quantity (and that they themselves are stupid) learn much less from school experience than those who have a self-concept that allows for intellectual growth and development. Although such attributions are acquired early, they are not impervious to change.

Self-theories are distinguished from the other four aspects of the self by being based primarily on socially established and verbally communicated ideas. As we elaborate our own conceptual selves, however, we often try to take other kinds of experience into account. Thus our self-concepts typically include ideas abut our physical bodies, about interpersonal communication, about what kinds of things we have done in the past and are likely to do in future, and especially about the meaning of our own thoughts and feelings. The result is that each of the other

---

[18]Under ordinary circumstances, internal bodily organs do not belong to the ecological self: they cannot be directly perceived and are not subject to intentional movements.

four kinds of self-knowledge is also represented in the conceptual self. These 'meta-selves' are never quite accurate, but they make a difference. Just as our concepts of intelligence can affect what we learn in school, for example, so our conception of our own body and its movements may affect our physical activity and motor skill. Social behavior is shaped not only by the directly perceived quality of real social interactions but by our own theories of how we relate (and how we should relate) to other people. Our memories of past experiences depend on our self-conceptions as well as on originally-stored information (*cf.* Greenwald, 1980; Neisser, 1981). Even our interpretations of our own private experience are partly shaped by what we believe experience should be like; that is one reason why introspection is such an uncertain source of psychological understanding. While it is a mistake to suppose that the conceptual self is the only self we have, it would also be a mistake to underestimate its scope and importance.

Conclusion

What we know about ourselves seems paradoxical: it is both objective and subjective, social and private, definite and vague, abstractly theoretical and firmly concrete. One claim of this paper has been to dispel that air of paradox and replace it with a set of clear distinctions. But I have done so at the risk of creating what may seem to be a new puzzle: if there are five cognitively different 'selves', why do we (usually) experience ourselves as unitary and coherent individuals? The answer, again, is in terms of information. The fact that the ecological and interpersonal self are aspects of the same person can be directly perceived: they are located in the same place and engaged in the same activities. The extended self is linked to both of them, not only because what we recall are ecological and interpersonal experiences but because we can

see where we are even in the act of remembering.[19] In the private self at least one form of consciousness—explicit awareness of what we are doing—is intimately linked to our present situation. It is true that dreams and other detached mental phenomena tend to fractionate the self, but most cultures have theories to deal with such phenomena. Some of these self-theories maintain that there is only one self, others that there are two or perhaps three; in Buddhism, there is said to be no self at all (Kolm, 1986). Whatever the theory on which it is based, the conceptual self still helps to hold all the others together. It does so by providing a roughly coherent account of ourselves as persons in interaction with our neighbors; an account that is almost always similar in structure, though different in detail, from the one that our neighbors would give of us.

We know our neighbors (and they know us) in much the same ways that we know ourselves. If there are many kinds of self-knowledge, there are many kinds of other-knowledge too. We get information about other people ecologically by seeing what they do and interpersonally through direct engagement; we remember our previous encounters with them; we think about them, as about ourselves, in ways that depend on our general conceptions of human nature. To be sure, we typically have *less* information about other individuals than about ourselves. Optical flow most fully specifies our own movements, memory records many more of our own actions than anyone else's, and our private experience is exclusively our own. This wealth of information must be one of the reasons why children (and many adults) are so naturally self-centered; why it is so easy to pursue one's own interests from one's own point of view. But though it is easy, it is not necessary. Information about other people is also available from earliest

---

[19] As noted earlier, this link is not always compelling: we can 'lose ourselves' in a memory to the extent that we are no longer aware of our present ecological and interpersonal situation.

infancy: the same interactions that specify a real interpersonal self also specify a real interpersonal other. Even more such information is available conceptually, at least in cultures with beliefs that define *man* and *woman* and *person* to include others equally with the self. Self-knowledge is inherent in the human condition, but self-centredness is not.

The principle that all concepts are embedded in more general theoretical schemes applies also to the ideas presented in this paper. Most of those ideas have their roots in cognitive and perceptual psychology: I have drawn particularly on the ecological approach to perception, on recent naturalistic studies of memory, and on the notion — familiar to philosophers but relatively new to psychologists — that concepts can only be defined with respect to larger conceptual systems. Perhaps because of this cognitive focus, certain traditional questions about the self have been given rather short shrift. The most obvious omission concerns the identity of the doer as opposed to the knower: who is it that thinks, acts, and feels? If I do something that later seems incomprehensible to me, who was responsible? If I produce an egocentrically distorted memory, who has distorted it? The answer to all such questions is brutally simple: I was, and I have. There is no internal agent to whom I can realistically delegate the responsibility.[20] The inner man, the unconscious mind,

---

[20] This principle applies even to reflexive cases, as when I admire myself or despise myself, although the *object* of such sentiments may only be an aspect of the conceptual self.

and the alternate personality are not real entities but aspects of the conceptual self. They are defined only with reference to particular theories of motivation and action, and it seems unlikely that any of the theories currently popular will turn out to be correct.

The theory of self-knowledge presented here is also a version of the conceptual self — or at least, it becomes one to the extent that it is believed. My hope is that it *will* turn out to be correct, in outline if not in detail. While there are certainly other ways to classify the information we have about ourselves, there is no way to deny its multiplicity. We know ourselves not only as objects of thought and experience but also as objects of perception, genuinely engaged with our fellow human beings and our shared environment.

Acknowledgments

Preparation of this paper was supported by a Fellowship from the John Simon Guggenheim Memorial Foundation; it was written while the author was in residence at the MRC Cognitive Development Unit in London. (A preliminary version was presented at the International Society for Ecological Psychology in Atlanta on May 23, 1987.) Reprints may be obtained from Ulric Neisser, Department of Psychology, Emory University, Atlanta GA 30322, U.S.A.

References

Asch, S. E. (1952) *Social Psychology* (Englewood Cliffs, NJ, Prentice-Hall).

Baddeley, A. (1987) But what the hell's it for? in: M. M. Gruneberg, P. M. Morris & R. N. Sykes (Eds) *Practical Aspects of Memory II* (London, Academic Press).

Bahrick, L. E. & Watson, J. S. (1985) Detection of intermodal proprioceptive-visual contingency as a potential basis of self-perception in infancy, *Developmental Psychology*, 21, pp. 963–973.

Bartlett, F. C. (1932) *Remembering* (Cambridge University Press).

Berlin, I. (1969) A note on Vico's concept of knowledge, in: G. Tagliocozzo & H. V. White (Eds.) *Giambattisto Vico: an international symposium* (Baltimore, Johns Hopkins Press).

Bretherton, I., McNew, S. & Beeghly-Smith, M. (1981) Early person knowledge as expressed in gestural and verbal communication: when do infants acquire a 'theory of mind'? in: M. E. Lamb & L. R. Sherrod (Eds) *Infant social cognition: Empirical and social considerations* (Hillsdale, NJ, Erlbaum).

Brewer, W. F. (1986) What is autobiographical memory? in: D. C. Rubin (Ed.) *Autobiographical Memory* (New York, Cambridge University Press).

Brewer, W. F. (1988) Memory for randomly sampled autobiographical events, in: U. Neisser & E. Winograd (Eds) *Remembering Reconsidered: ecological and traditional approaches to the study of memory* (New York, Cambridge University Press).

Butterworth, G. E. (in press) Self-perception in infancy, in: D. Cicchetti & M. Beeghly (Eds) *The Self in Transition* (University of Chicago Press).

Butterworth, G. E. & Cicchetti, D. (1978) Visual calibration of posture in normal and motor retarded Down's syndrome infants, *Perception*, 7, pp. 513–525.

Carey, S. (1985). *Conceptual change in childhood* (Cambridge, Ma, MIT Press).

Cutting, J. E. (1986) *Perception with an Eye for Motion* (Cambridge, Ma, MIT Press).

Darwin, C. (1904) *The Expression of Emotion in Man and Animals* (London, John Murray).

Dweck, C. S. (1986) Motivational processes affecting learning, *American Psychologist*, 41, pp. 1040–1048.

Edwards, D. & Middleton, D. (1988) Conversational remembering and social relationships: how children learn to remember, *Journal of Social and Personal Relationships*, 5, 3–25.

Epstein, S. (1973) The self-concept revisited: a theory of a theory, *American Psychologist*, 28, pp. 404–416.

Fivush, R. (1988) The functions of event memory, in: U. Neisser & E. Winograd (Eds) *Remembering Reconsidered: ecological and traditional approaches to the study of memory* (New York, Cambridge University Press).

Fivush, R., Gray, J. T. & Fromhoff, F. A. (1987) Two-year-olds talk about the past, *Cognitive Development*, 2, pp. 393–409.

Flavell, J. H., Shipstead, S. G. & Croft, K. (1980) What young children think you see when their eyes are closed, *Cognition*, 8, pp. 369–387.

Fraiberg, S. (1977) *Insights From the Blind* (New York, Basic Books).

Galotti, K. M. & Neisser, U. (1982) Young children's recall of Christmas, *Quarterly Newsletter of the Laboratory of Comparative Human Cognition* (San Diego, California), 4, pp. 72–74.

Gibson, E. J. (1976) A few thoughts inspired by the papers of Fraiberg, Bellugi, and Sinclair,

Paper presented at the Eric Lenneberg Memorial Symposium, Ithaca, NY.

Gibson, E. J. & Spelke, E. S. (1983) The development of perception, in: P. H. Mussen (Ed.) *Handbook of Child Psychology, Vol. III* (J. H. Flavell & E. M. Markman, Eds) *Cognitive Development* (New York, Wiley).

Gibson, J. J. (1966) *The Senses Considered as Perceptual Systems* (Boston, Houghton Mifflin).

Gibson, J. J. (1979) *The Ecological Approach to Visual Perception* (Boston, Houghton Mifflin).

Goffman, E. (1959) *The Presentation of Self in Everyday Life* (New York, Doubleday).

Greenwald, A. G. (1980) The totalitarian ego: fabrication and revision of personal history, *American Psychologist*, 35, pp. 603–618.

Hardman, C. (1981) The psychology of conformity and self-expression among the Lohorung Rai of East Nepal, in: P. Heelas & A. Lock (Eds) *Indigenous Psychologies: the anthropology of the self* (London, Academic Press).

James, W. (1890) *Principles of Psychology* (New York, Holt, 1890). [Reprinted by Dover Press, 1950.]

Jung, C. G. (1921/1971) *Psychological Types* (First published 1921); [Translated as (1971) *Collected Works of C. G. Jung*, Vol. 6. (Princeton University Press).]

Kanner, L. (1943) Autistic disturbances of affective contact, *Nervous Child*, 2, pp. 217–250.

Keil, F. C. (1987) Conceptual development and category structure, in: U. Neisser (Ed.) *Concepts and Conceptual Development* (New York, Cambridge University Press).

Kellman, P. J. & Spelke, E. S. (1983) Perception of partly occluded objects in infancy, *Cognitive Psychology*, 15, pp. 483–524.

Knobloch, H. & Pasamanick, B. (1975) Some etiologic and prognostic factors in early infantile autism and psychosis, *Pediatrics*, 55, pp. 182–191.

Kolm, S.-C. (1986) The Buddhist theory of 'no-self', in: J. Elster (Ed.) *The Multiple Self* (Cambridge University Press).

Lakoff, G. (1987) Cognitive models and prototype theory, in: U. Neisser (Ed.) *Concepts and Conceptual Development* (New York, Cambridge University Press).

Lee, D. N. (1980) The optic flow field: the foundation of vision, *Philosophical Transactions of the Royal Society of London*, B 290, pp. 169–179.

Lee, D. N. & Lishman, J. R. (1975) Visual proprioceptive control of stance, *Journal of Human Movement Studies*, 1, pp. 87–95.

Leslie, A. M. (1987) Pretense and representation: the origins of 'theory of mind', *Psychological Review*, 94, pp. 412–426.

Lewis, M. & Brooks-Gunn, J. (1984). The development of early visual self-recognition, *Developmental Review*, 4, pp. 215–239.

Loveland, K. A. (1986) Discovering the affordances of a reflecting surface, *Developmental Review*, 6, pp. 1–24.

Markus, H. (1977) Self-schemata and the processing of information about the self, *Journal of Personality and Social Psychology*, 35, pp. 63–78.

McCauley, R. N. (1987) The role of theories in a theory of concepts, in: U. Neisser (Ed.) *Concepts and Conceptual Development* (New York, Cambridge University Press).

Mead, G. H. (1934) *Mind, Self, and Society* (University of Chicago Press).

Medin, D. L. & Wattenmaker, W. D. (1987) Category cohesiveness, theories, and cognitive archaeology, in: U. Neisser (Ed.) *Concepts and Conceptual Development* (New York, Cambridge University Press).

Meltzoff, A. N. & Moore, M. K. (1983) Newborn infants imitate adult facial gestures, *Child Development*, 54, pp. 702–709.

Murphy, G. L. & Medin, D. L. (1985) The role of theories in conceptual coherence, *Psychological Review*, 92, pp. 289–316.

Murray, L. (1984) Emotional regulation of intersubjective encounters: implications for the theory of autism, in: *Contributions a la recherche scientifique sur l'autisme: Aspects cog-*

nitifs (Paris, Association pour la recherche sur l'autisme et les psychoses infantiles).

Murray, L. & Trevarthen, C. (1985) Emotional regulation of interactions between two-month-olds and their mothers, in: T. M. Field & N. A. Fox (Eds) *Social Perception in Infants* (Norwood, NJ, Ablex).

Neisser, U. (1981) John Dean's memory; a case study, *Cognition*, 9, pp. 1–22.

Neisser, U. (1987) From direct perception to conceptual structure, in: U. Neisser (Ed.) *Concepts and Conceptual Development* (New York, Cambridge University Press).

Neisser, U. (1988) Time present and time past, in: M. M. Gruneberg, P. M. Morris & R. N. Sykes (Eds) *Practical Aspects of Memory II* (London, Academic Press).

Nelson, K. (1986) *Event Knowledge: structure and function in development* (Hillsdale, NJ, Erlbaum).

Nelson, K. (1988) The ontogeny of memory for real events,in: U. Neisser & E. Winograd (Eds) *Remembering Reconsidered: ecological and traditional approaches to the study of memory* (New York, Cambridge University Press).

Nelson, K. & Gruendel, J. (1986) Children's scripts, in: K. Nelson (Ed.) *Event Knowledge: structure and function in development* (Hillsdale, NJ, Erlbaum).

Parkin, A. J. (1982) Residual learning capacity in organic amnesia, *Cortex*, 18, pp. 417–440.

Regan, D. M. & Beverly, K. I. (1982) How do we avoid confounding the direction we are looking and the direction we are moving? *Science*, 215, pp. 194–196.

Rosch, E. (1978) Principles of categorisation, in: E. Rosch & B. B. Lloyd (Eds) *Cognition and Categorisation* (Hillsdale, NJ, Erlbaum).

Rubin, D. C., Wetzler, S. E. & Nebes, R. D. (1986) Autobiographical memory across the lifespan, in: D. C. Rubin (Ed.) *Autobiographical Memory* (New York, Cambridge University Press).

Schank, R. C. & Abelson, R. P. (1977) *Scripts, Plans, Goals and Understanding* (Hillsdale, NJ, Erlbaum).

Stern, D. N. (1985) *The Interpersonal World of the Infant* (New York, Basic Books).

Stoffregen, T. A. 9185) Flow structure versus retinal location in the optical control of stance, *Journal of Experimental Psychology: human perception and performance*, 11, pp. 554–565.

Todd, C. & Perlmutter, M. (1980) Reality recalled by preschool children, in: M. Perlmutter (Ed.) *New Directions in Child Development, vol. 10: Children's Memory* (San Francisco, Jossey-Bass).

Trevarthen, C. (1983) Emotions in infancy: regulators of contacts and relationships with persons, in: K. Scherer & P. Ekman (Eds) *Approaches to Emotion* (Hillsdale, NJ, Erlbaum).

Tulving, E. (1972) Episodic and semantic memory, in: E. Tulving & W. Donaldson (Eds) *Organization of Memory* (New York, Academic Press).

Wellman, H. M. (1985) The child's theory of mind: the development of conceptions of cognition, in: S. R. Yussen (Ed.) *The Growth of Reflection in Children* (London, Academic Press).

Wimmer, H. & Perner, J. (1983) Beliefs about beliefs: representation and constraining function of wrong beliefs in young children's understanding of deception, *Cognition*, 13, pp. 103–128.

25

FRITHJOF BERGMANN
Freedom and the Self

Our relationship to the idea that we possess a permanent "real" self is strange in its extreme ambivalence. When we discuss childhood development, we find it natural and easy to imagine a consciousness which does not yet possess a self. That the self is not a given, but has to be achieved, that is not fixed, but fluid and precarious, seems then a quite innocuous thought. But beyond that, if we are asked to identify and to locate the "real" inner self, or to describe it we quickly come to the confession that we imagined a complete but disembodied duplicate of ourselves, a ghost-dwarf that observes our minds from the inside—and then we laugh at our childishness, for surely that homunculus comes from a fairy tale.

Yet nonetheless the idea persists.

To "refute" this notion seems ineffectual. Arguments only prune the stem, but leave the root intact. Our strategy is therefore different. We developed from the very start an alternative interpretation, that was designed radically to undercut and literally to replace this image of an inner core, of the old Substance-Subject. We meant to substitute for this Gestalt the concept and the picture of identification, the pattern of a shifting, moving weight. In this view the "real" self is only a grouping into this or that configuration. The underlying thought has been that the inherited metaphor has to be supplanted, that we cannot expect our thinking to abandon its old home, until another place has been prepared. . . .

But how can we then conceive and understand the self?

Logic points onward from the contrast that has now emerged. We must no longer suppose that the self is something that we ever simply find. We have to free ourselves not just from the idea that it is a peculiarly baffling core-entity, which is always still one step beyond our grasp, but we must also abandon the notion that it is any special entity at all—and saying this is easy, but really thinking it is hard.

It means that the fantasy of our searching through a great many masks where we look and examine and then discover that this is sham or spurious, while that is genuine and authentic, does not apply. Nothing corresponds to it. There are no characteristics which we have to detect, as when we have in front of us ten paintings and know that nine are fake while one is an actual Monet. The real self from which we have to act in order to be free is basically not something endowed with certain qualities which make it "real." And even our metaphors of "further back" and "deeper down" are misleading, for they substitute a location, or an order of discovery for the possession of inherent properties. To deny all this and to emphasize in contrast that the self does not pre-exist, but is brought into being only through an act is part of the import of the idea of identification, and making this explicit should begin to clarify its meaning.

To go further: the stress is not on the aspect that we ourselves perform this act since this might generate the confusion of some self already being there to undertake this act which brings the real self into being. Nor are we in the main concerned to bring out that this is an active rather than a passive process or that some "decision" is involved, that "we chose to be what we are." These are all *under*statements that fall short of our target.

An analogy might bring us closer to it: numerous writers have remarked that in the case of the emotions a peculiar *intimacy*, a special connectedness exists between our investigating judgment on the one side, and the object of this judgment (that which it purports to describe) on the other. We think that we are in love, or angry, but our opinion is not a detachable and separate fact. That thought or conviction is itself a part of the event. Our believing that we are in love is itself a proof of the actuality of our love, just as a doubt also does not remain apart, but itself can be an indication that our feeling has begun to cool. This inclusion of the observer in the phenomenon observed has led some to say that in the realm of the emotions reality cannot be separated from appearance, that in this special case our "thinking so" indeed does "make it so," that our perception and the fact perceived merge into one.

One can obviously raise objections to this view. (What I believe may be part of the emotion, but it is not the whole, and therefore my perception can be mistaken: I may believe that I am in love, but still be wrong.) Yet for our purposes this is irrelevant; the remaining element of truth will still serve us as an illustration and at the moment this is all we want.

What is useful is the general conception of "self-constitutiveness"—which is proposed. How widely it applies, whether only to some minor portions of the emotions, or more likely, to many different aspects of the mind is not the issue. We are interested only in the principle involved, namely, that a mental phenomenon may be so constituted that it and our perception of it are not two separate components, but coincide, so that the phenomenon comes into being through our apprehension of it and has no existence apart from it. This exemplifies in general

terms the more particular characteristic of the self which we are trying to explain.

The point of our insisting that we must set aside the image of an inspection through which the authentic or the sham reveals itself should now make itself felt: there is nothing there to be discovered. If we observed the river of experience and waited for something bearing a special mark to come floating past, we would be disappointed. Our identity, or our self, is not a collection of such premarked bits. The qualities in virtue of which something becomes part of the real self are not there beforehand, but are only brought into existence when the self is formed.

Yet it would be a disastrous misunderstanding to suppose that a mere opinion, or a judgment, or a thought were enough to "create" the self. It would be laughable to imagine that a child did not have a self or a sense of identity until it at some point thinks: "Ah, this must be me!" and that then, touched by the wand of this reflection, a self suddenly materializes. And it would be equally absurd to allege that every momentary judgment, or passing doubt, radically changes the identity of an adult. That would make the self too fickle and would rob it of all permanence.

No, the picture we are trying to create is best seen in two halves: on the one hand there is "self-constitutiveness"—to that extent the analogy to what we said about the emotions holds—but on the other hand it is not just a "thinking" that constitutes the self: it is the act that we from the outset called identification. It is crucial to understand that the self is literally "constituted" through this act of identification. There is no self apart from this or prior to it. The self—if we may put it so—has its being only in the fact that something is given that significance.

To render this thought more concrete one could envision a flow of elements that are initially "neutral." Then, gradually, some of these undergo a process of "attachment" and are invested with a special status; they receive an added significance. In a fashion analogous to this, the self is by degrees eventually constructed.

That the self is "built up" in this manner, and that this is its status should now throw some light on a terminological concern: we have been speaking of "the self" and of "the real self," but also of "the sense of self," and again of "identify" and "the sense of identity" as if they meant nearly the same. This was not unintentional, but was one expression of the contention we have just advanced. Despite all the finer-grained distinctions which can be drawn, we wanted to underscore that all of these are far more intimately related than one normally assumes.

This interpretation of the status of the self runs in many ways parallel to important psychological discussions, most prominently perhaps to those of Erickson and of Piaget, and this, too, is not accidental. It has been one of our aims to draft a philosophical perspective that would be more in harmony with the psychology of our own century than with that of three hundred years ago. But there are of course close kinships also to contemporary philosophic writings.

Sartre, both in the *Transcendence of the Ego* and in *Being and Nothingness*, elaborated a similar view of the self in incomparably greater detail. His notion of "pre-personal" experience is especially close to some thoughts we have just put forth, yet there are nonetheless major divergencies. For one, Sartre believed that the self is generated by "reflection," i.e., by the act of becoming aware of our consciousness, and we would disagree with this; but Sartre also, and importantly, places an "emptiness at the heart of Being" and often identifies consciousness with this "lack," this "nothingness." For us this represents essentially a remnant, an element which Sartre inherited from earlier philosophical positions which he transformed when he should have abandoned it completely. An accurate (let alone a "presuppositionless") phenom-

enological description does not discover any "emptiness" from which experience is perceived. This "hole in the core of Being" is either the hollow shell of the Subject otherwise repudiated by Sartre, or it is the postulated refuge to which the wholly alienated (disassociated) self withdraws. . . . Experience, therefore, does not enclose a vacuum into which it threatens to collapse, but is more like a compact, evenly supporting ground. From the essential sameness of this plain some things are gradually "raised" to become the self.

The actual process of this "personalization" of consciousness could be compared to an aspect of our relationship to language. Especially in traditional, still unspoiled settings, in mountain villages or among farmers, one frequently encounters an intriguing contrast: in their own speech, when they tell jokes or stories, these people often express themselves with marvelous vitality and color. But it is quite different when they turn to writing. Suddenly their tongues are tied, and only strangely stilted, bureaucratic phrases reach the page.

There is an analogy in this to how all of us experience language: at first it confronts us as a finished building made by others. The sentences we form, the words we overhear ourselves speak seem awkward and inflexible. We are like a farmer writing. Our medium of thought is still impersonal and copied. Then starts the arduous and never quite successful process of moving this crust back. One opens cracks, experiments and rearranges and gradually bits take on a character that is more private, until through continuous alterations we slowly make what we are saying more nearly our own. Some great writers persist in this effort till even a single sentence out of context is recognizable as Kafka or as Brecht.

Our experience is similarly impersonal at first. We do not progress outward from the private but grow in the reverse direction: away from a neutral, anonymous and glaringly public world that is not yet experienced from a point of view and is not yet divided into a self and its opposite.

The absence of any inherent self and the fact that it arises only when that significance is attached to some parts of an otherwise neutral experience lead us to speak of its "self-constitutiveness," but this does not mean that the self (or an identification) exists only in the thoughts we have about it, that it comes into being only through reflection, or that it is as we think or imagine it to be. The genesis of the self involves a rearranging of experience, and that reorganization exists and is real whether we are aware of it or not. In other words, the self is genuinely mental, it exists only in our minds and not apart from it, but it would simply be a blunder to confuse this with "the next level higher up," and to imagine that this reorganization has its being only in what we think about our minds — in the consciousness we have of our minds. Our identification does not appear in the instant in which we recognize it, and it does not vanish when we close our eyes.

From this it follows immediately that we can be mistaken about our own identifications. Not only that; in actual fact we never have a secure and settled sense of what our identity or our real self is. It remains elusive and unstable, and is always seen as through a veil. We guess at it, suspect an error, and grope in a new place.

This is of course not in conflict with our earlier contention that there is no self which could be discovered or detected. To put the difference concisely: we then said that there is no inherent "self-characteristic" — like a color, or a flashing red light — and that it would be folly to look for one. All we are now saying is that once this significance has been given to a content, or that reorganization of it has indeed occurred, then that different fact can be either missed or grasped. The process involved, however, is once again not an "inspection." We cannot discover who we are by something analogous to a mere "look," but only through certain kinds of actions.

The self crystallizes behind our back. Meanings attach themselves, experience is organized into new structures, and no announcements of the progress are made to us. It happens unobtrusively and in the background. To determine what we feel or want or hope or think is often hard enough, but these are ropes compared to cobwebs when the questions are: Is this feeling truly my own, or is it copied, borrowed from a book, invented or only a wish? Is this what I want, or is it a Pavlovian response, a knee-jerk of the brain? So the lines are blurred and seem to shift, and only fragments come into view and then disappear.

The actual "shape" of our identity is therefore more like the inkblots of a Rorschach test than the neat circles in our opening diagrams. The exact geometry of these drawings made the important logical relationships explicit, but in real life we do not actually identify with all of our reason and with nothing else, nor with the whole person, nor with none of the parts of our person, but more nearly with irregularly broken pieces of some or all of these. We also do not identify either totally or not at all. It is rather a matter of increasing and diminishing degrees, and even these are anything but permanent. At most the fluctuating patterns develop in a gradually stabilizing way.

Still, we should not suppose that we are trying to lay hold of nebulous and mocking wisps. On the contrary, the self, from one perspective, is for us in the end a simple and quite ordinary concept precisely because we think of it merely in terms of a set of identifications.

What we mean by the distinction between an element with which we identify and from which we disassociate — and only this inclusion or exclusion has a direct relationship to freedom . . . [is often] described [in] situations in which we disassociate from our thoughts. A . . . very ordinary example in which the . . . division plays a role . . . would be the case of an adolescent whose upbringing may have been extraordinarily puritanical and strict. Under such a tutelage an identification with one's sexual impulses would very likely not occur. During the onset of puberty the insurgence of these desires would then be experienced as an invasion by external forces, and the resulting actions would concomitantly signify the suffering of defeats and of compulsions.

The familiarity of what we mean by identifications can be brought home still more if we consider the manner in which they most commonly are changed by us. That, too, is at least in certain contexts a quite straightforward undertaking which, under different names, we all have performed many times. We know the steps and the extended strategies and procedures which someone might adopt so as to "accept" his sexuality more fully; they range from ordinary resolutions, to small deliberate changes in all sorts of patterns of behavior to various forms of therapy—and this would be the general picture of how many identifications can be altered.

The emphasis on the homespun, however, should also not be overdone. A very different illustration is needed to balance our picture. In his well-known "The Case of Ellen West," Ludwig Binswanger portrays a highly intelligent young woman. In her teens she was impatient with much of the dreariness of philistine everyday living, and was given to flights of romantic exuberance, but was otherwise "normal" enough. Yet around her twentieth year she developed with relative suddenness a most bizarre and wholly overpowering obsession for the eating of every kind of food. Her craving became so intense that after waking in the morning, she would wait for its arrival as a prisoner locked in a tin box might wait for the heat of the rising sun. But she attached at the same time a truly religious fervor to the thin and weightless and the fragile, and felt an intense loathing for anything suggesting the obese. Her struggle between these opposites took ever more desperate forms, and Binswanger's account traces the stages of her descent over several years, though extended periods of nearly total abstinence,

close to starvation, interrupted by stretches in which she is wholly in the grip of her unnatural hunger, to her death at the age of 26.

We mention this case partly because the differentiation into self and non-self is in this instance so sharp and clear. In one sense Ellen West's original personality remains quite untransformed throughout her whole ordeal. She observes the subtlest changes in herself with astonishing lucidity, and reasons with acute intelligence about her situation. She is even quite aware of the macabre humor of her unusual affliction. Whatever advice is given to her she invariably has already considered. And this makes her utter helplessness more graphic. She is extremely conscious but is nonetheless moved by forces which she cannot control. And this is one aspect most immediately at issue: that this division, this "organization of experience" can be so powerful—that the phenomenon of identification can be so real.

But it is also true that nothing in this poignant story can be easily explained. We certainly do not imagine that the entire syndrome was caused by a particular identification, or that some change in it, perhaps the "acceptance" of her inhuman appetite, would have produced a cure. It is precisely the mysteriousness, the fact that we often do not understand how such splits are engendered, and that their shape can be so baffling which we mean to stress. So from a different perspective the phenomenon of identification is dark and obscure. Nothing in regard to it is "simple" except for the bare division drawn by it, but this is the only part of it that is to our purpose.

Our conception, though, would still be too one-sided unless we recognized that this example represents one extreme on an extended spectrum. The dividing line between that with which we identify and that from which we disassociate can be as overpowering and fixed as in the case of Ellen West, but the phenomenon itself reaches through subtly graduated steps to another pole, where it can be quite fluid and mobile, and where the area of identification or the locus of the self can be displaced with ease, through a sheer effort of our will. That end of this continuum is of special interest to our concern with freedom and we shall therefore illustrate it rather fully.

We can think of a relationship, perhaps a marriage, which one of the partners resisted form the start. Conceivably something established itself in the man's mind in the original encounter: this woman was not a "serious possibility" for him—why is quite unimportant; doors were shut, that is all. Every growth of the relationship was from then on for him an incursion, every demand an imposition, the whole a steadily increasing servitude. That might have been the situation up to the point at which the man experienced a kind of conversion. Having taken stock of his life, he realizes the absurdity of his reluctance, assesses his marriage and decides that it is good, and thus commits himself to it and identifies with it. Such a turn is within our power, and it can reverse the position of the self so abruptly that one has an acute experience as of a weight that suddenly is being lifted. It is as if one were now running downhill and no longer climbing upwards through the snow.

In a smaller form I have sometimes witnessed similarily immediate redirections in some of my students. To some, all facets of university life occasionally seem uniformly bleak; they feel that kindergarten was the beginning of a conveyor belt on which their parents laid them at the age of five and that so far they have been only holding still, while the hands they passed performed their operations. They themselves remained asleep, feeling dimly but one thing: that what was being done to them was ghastly. They are apt to say: "Everything I do is always accompanied by a monotonous, dull sound that keeps repeating: 'All of it should be different, none of this has any connection to what I really want.'"

The alternative thus is blank, a sheer negation. And just this sometimes opens the door, for an abrupt change can be effected by simply filling in the other options. As soon as the fantasies of a completely different life are spelled out, their seductiveness starts to pale—combing beaches in Hawaii becomes less attractive once the sand is real enough to get into one's food. With this the realization dawns that one's present life, as it is now, corresponds much more closely to what one oneself wants than one had supposed. And this can be decisive. For this, too, produces sometimes a reversal. One says: "Yes, this is part of me. What I am doing is not just due to outside pressures. It is something that I want and I am doing." And this can make the same startling difference as in the marriage we described.

This brings us back to the episode from my own life to which I referred in the last chapter. During the first few years in my profession I surrendered my time and energy to the demands of teaching philosophy with a sense of deprivation. I experienced it as a concession. The space I gave to it curtailed what I had meant to do. But then I gradually had to acknowledge that I never felt as alive as when I was discussing a question in philosophy. It seemed a grotesque admission: real aliveness was found not in love, not with nature, but in this—in the rearranging of abstractions. For a time I still resisted, and the more territory I gave over to philosophy the more barricaded in and corralled I felt. Eventually it came to a kind of crisis, for the disproportion had grown too absurd: the things I really wanted to do had shrunk to the point that everything else, which comprised nearly my whole life, was suspended, was placed between brackets, and rendered negative by a mere prefix. The change happened quickly. In one sense it was like leaping into the air and making in the fall of severed limbs a whole new body, but in another sense it was like simply putting one's pen from the left hand into the right one. I went on as before. Only the prefix was different—and yet nothing was the same.

This should not be misconstrued. There was no "real" self in the cellar. The idea is not that under false surface layers a more genuine self had all the time been hidden, one "destined" to teach philosophy from the very start, and that I came to terms with this inner essence. It was not as if some impulses were more "real" than others. One might better think in almost quantitative terms. It was just that my mind when left alone found itself spinning philosophic webs more and more of the time, and that these thickened and usurped increasingly more space until the significance attached to them had become a paradox which was resolved when their meaning was converted, and I said: "They and not the rest represent myself."

Inherent in these relatively sudden adoptions of a new identity is also the possibility of a cynical abuse. For if the locus of the self can be so wilfully displaced, if it can sometimes be shifted almost by command, then this creates the option of executing these dispositions calculatingly, like maneuvers in a war game. If in certain situations the opposing forces happen to be very strong then the conflict can be preempted and reversed through a crude sleight-of-hand. I simply join the stronger side, or even better, I pronounce it to be me (a mode of conquest that leaves even generals behind) and I now dismiss the former identity without so much as a skirmish.

These relatively rare instances in which the sense of what I really am can be maneuvered by my will, in which I can, so to speak, slip my identity under what I have been doing all along and can thereby reinforce and free in one fell swoop a region so far resisted and held down, capture once more the thrust of our whole discussion of the self and guide it further. For the general perspective in which the self is not originally given, where it comes into being only through the organization of experience, can be seen in a still different light. It is an irritation, a tongue stuck out at our intellects. It is somewhat humiliating to admit that there should be any such dichotomy between what we accept and what we reject about ourselves when both are, of course, part of the whole and when both

sides obviously are entangled in much more complex relationships. That we in so many situations want, on top of that, to cleave along such school-boyish straight lines—as when we set reason on one side and the emotions on the other—makes it still worse. Yet, the real wound to our narcissicism is the realization that it is our self that is involved. We are deprived even of a place to rest, and only the shifting sands of a problematical "significance" remain.

The "radical reversals" in the marriage, student and philosophy teaching examples thus have a disturbing implication. How much weight can we attach to an identity that is so readily manipulated? What if no more than a phantom had been rearranged? Yet this, too, is only one face of a coin: for without the organization supplied by the self our experience would remain an inchoate sprawling flood.

But the entirety of this discussion of the self and of identification was for us in a sense preliminary. It should have clarified the base, or the source from which we must act in order to be free. Now we can develop the implications that this has for the idea of freedom. For to make it more palpable has all along been our main concern.

In the simplest terms we propose to think of a person as free to the extent to which his actions correspond to the identity, or to the self, which has all the various characteristics that we have been endeavoring to define. We have turned away from the envisioning of freedom as an absence, as the smoothing out of obstacles, as the removal of hindrances till the air becomes too thin to breathe, in favor of pursuing a very different goal: that of reaching, making contact with and even of submitting to the forces of the self, so that they may be expressed and released.

Everything that we have said about the self and about identification should now be applied, and should narrow down and clarify what is meant by these "inner forces" or this "nature" that must be expressed if we are to be free. Most obviously we do not accept the notion that man is endowed with an inner, let alone an eternal, essence, and we deny this even for the individual. When we speak of the "real self" we simply are not talking about an underlying, or hidden, or mysterious "inner nature"—either of man, or of the individual person—but only about the plain and, as it were, surface identifications. Freedom for us is the expression of what we are, of the qualities and characteristics we possess, but in an unpretentious sense: it is the expression of qualities with which we identify, and the totality of the section just concluded should have rendered sufficiently specific what this means.

This protects us at once against the situation in which someone else begins to dictate to us in the name of freedom; where we are told that our own experience of oppression is not to be trusted, that our mysterious real self is in fact extremely free, though some coercion of our lesser self unfortunately seemed required to force us into line with our truer nature. We are shielded against this kind of Newspeak by the categorical denial of any general, hidden human nature, which could be known or invoked by those who want to control us, while we ourselves are ignorant of it. (Even if there were a universal human nature, freedom according to our definition still would not be the expression of it, but would be action from our individual identification.) The fact that our identities are highly individuated thus puts a hurdle in the way or anyone who presumes to speak sweepingly for a great number. The fact is that it is extremely difficult for each of us to discover our areas of identification, and anyone else is at an incommensurately greater disadvantage.

But this also undergirds the critical dimension of our whole account of freedom, for a further implication is that freedom is now understood to be "no more" than the acting out of these diverse identities; and what we have said about their problematic status now affects—and was of course intended to affect—the status which freedom itself can claim.

But to sever the idea of freedom from any possible core-subject also places it on firmer ground, for it now can no longer fall together with that doubtful entity. Freedom for us, in other words, is viable and genuine—is not merely an illusion, but a reality to be reckoned with—even if the core-self with its traditional attributes cannot be defended. We have taken that millstone from freedom's neck. For us the phenomenon of identification is sufficient; if it is granted, then man can be free.

We have said that the simple idea of a correspondence should take the place of the customary associations of freedom with the absence of hindrances and that in their stead we now think fundamentally of a matching—our outward life has to match our identity or our self if we are to attain freedom. We have to achieve something like a geometrical congruence, a mutual fit, a kind of attunedness, like a harmony between two tones. There should therefore be a basic sense of ease, as when two gears spin without friction in a prearranged synchronization. The usual stress on the difficulty of freedom, on its weight-lifting muscularity and lonely heroism, should begin to have some slight ring of melodrama and of pathos, and just the reverse side should make itself felt: the absence of strain, the collapse of tension, the lightness of freedom, glorious as that of pure play. The now appropriate connections might be with the superb effortlessness of Bach's or Mozart's music, though the reverence and respectfulness can be dispensed with; one picture of the free person might be the figure of a baker, twirling soft disks of pizza-dough in a shop window, juggling elegantly to keep three of them simultaneously in the air.

Freedom should connote a natural flow, neither cramped nor forced, a shift away from the need to control, to compensate and to correct, and toward the exuberance of actions and words at last taking shape quite effortlessly, as if by themselves. This is, in the end, the most authentic prototype of the experience of freedom, and is at the same time the one most revealing tell-tale signal of where the boundaries of one's "real" self may lie. For nothing offers itself to the traveling glance of a mere introspection. No booms are lowered and no red flashing light says "self, self, self." We discover ourselves only indirectly, and often from the "feel" of certain actions. It is this increase in vitality and surefootedness, this undertaking of a shift that ends with the definite impression of one's now "having found one's stride," of one's now "functioning" that is by all accounts one of the surest indications that an accord with our nature has been found.

This in effect reverses the process of our self-discovery. We do not start from an unstably floating image of the self and then systematically close in on this elusive source. It is not as if the circle of the self were originally given, and some other circle, like in an experiment in perception, gradually had to be superimposed on the first. It is more the other way around: we first become aware of this experience of a "free flow," of a natural, heightened functioning and then work backwards from many observations of its appearance and its absence to the tentative formulation of what may be our self. This fact, that our identity, or our self, is largely discovered (and perhaps even comes into being) only through the process of an "acting out," that the possibility for expression is thus in a very stringent sense the necessary precondition for the very having of a self, is packed with social, political and also educational implications. But even now it should give us a new sense of how very intimately the self and freedom are related: the paradigmatic experience of freedom is not just a consequence, or a by-product of the expression of our nature; it is in fact the principal guide to the discovery of our identifications: we fashion our self from the mirror image of our freedom.

This close relationship between the self and freedom has of course everything to do with the extravagant valuation that is sometimes placed on freedom. The fact that the spontaneous flow of action is at once a signal of the self and our most immediate realization of freedom points toward some of the deeper reasons for the special relationship that artists and intellectuals have to freedom. Freedom often matters much more to them than to farmers and to workers, and the reason is not just that they are in many cases simply better off, let alone that they are more far-sighted or more idealistic. The kind of freedom which we have moved into the center of the stage is an indispensable necessity for their everyday work. For most serious writers, for example, it is an either/or over which they have not much control. Their writing either suits themselves, and is quite stringently a self-expression, which regardless of the arduous work it may require, nonetheless in some sense naturally flows from them, or it simply cannot be done at all. The degree to which this is not a matter of "principles" or of "integrity" is surprising. Quite often a writer may even want to write a casual potboiler, but it turns out to be impossible. He either writes in "his own style," or the individual sentences simply refuse to come. Thus artists and intellectuals in insisting on freedom defend more nearly the very thing that makes it possible for them to do their work, while the need of others to be attuned to the requirements of their nature is very much less, mainly because their work is of a fundamentally different kind, and can still be done even if the connection with the self has been disrupted. (I can build a table according to your specifications, and I can even write a doctoral dissertation in this way, but if I try this with a book for which I care, the conflict will become intolerable: either I stop altogether or I become a hack.)

The process through which an artist finds his own style or his own "voice" could thus be a symbol for much of what we have tried to say. His experimenting and rejecting, the feeling-out of alternative modes of expression, and still more, of course, the eventual hours of "inspiration" where the otherwise foot-by-foot advance finally becomes a dance, a swift and flying rush, incarnates the concept we have tried to define.

If this is an embodiment of what freedom

means, then it should be quite apparent that I can be in a situation in which I "have a choice," or in which I even can participate, by voice vote and quite directly, in the making of the rules that now govern me, where for all this I still do not experience anything like freedom, but may still be like an insect trapped in amber. The conditions which either make freedom possible or preclude it are therefore subtler and much more complex than the mere presence or absence of opportunities to choose or vote, and the notion that in arranging for these privileges one has done enough, that they are synonymous with freedom, cannot be defended.

Deeper than this still lies the general preconception that "order" or "community" somehow share a common quantity with freedom so that a measure of one of these must be taken away from the other, that they exist at their mutual expense; or again the similar presumption that an increase of freedom always risks the possibility of chaos and the disintegration of society into isolated atoms. Since this is one of the most facile justifications of those who rush at opportune occasions (often coinciding with moments at which their most material interests are at stake) to the defense of an abstract "order" it is important to say flatly that this opposition is in general terms entirely unreal. The analogies we have introduced make this palpably apparent: Why should an artist who has found his voice or style produce work which must be inimical in principle to "order"? Or why should the artist who comes closer to self-expression than his fellows be either more isolated, or with his actions put greater strain on the communal bonds? How easily one could argue just the reverse: namely, that the work of such an artist will be less erratic, and will be consonant with a "deep," "organic" order; or that his art, as it grows more authentic will at the same time speak more penetratingly to others, and will emanate from layers that are shared and common, if not "universal." And if for artists, then why not for ordinary mortals? The fact that my

everyday actions accord with my own nature in no way suggests that they are in principle opposed either to order or to anything communal, but on the contrary holds out the promise of a harmony with others.

But of course there is an opposition, only it is specific and not general: a society naturally can mold a type and encourage in him a specific set of identifications which will, if acted out, produce perhaps not exactly chaos, but will at any rate oppose and undermine the social, and engender the hackneyed war of each against all others. But this does not inhere in freedom; it is a consequence of one peculiar identification — with those individual desires whose satisfaction perversely always spells another's loss. And this puts one aspect of our own society into the proper critical perspective: we have substituted "human nature" for an unfortunate type that the institutions of our culture foster; the calamity of this type comes to the surface in the paradox that he finds his freedom only in the antisocial. For him the exclusion indeed holds: he is so constituted that the communal always represents oppression, and his identity is expressed only in the advancement of his individual advantage. The opposition between freedom and community or order is thus not a general boundary of freedom, but is the symptom of a disease from which we suffer. Or it is an accusation: forces in our society have malformed us to the point where this is our freedom.

The same is true of the relationship between freedom and one's individual uniqueness: advocates of "autonomy" often sound as if all conformity is shameful, and as if sheer difference were already admirable. But even a crude common sense can see that this is comic: for in the name of independence from all others one ends up being guided by them. What others do is automatically precluded; the prevalent is ruled out, no matter how right or appropriate for oneself it actually might be, and one imagines oneself a gourmet while in fact feeding only on leftovers. But this is no requirement of freedom. If some accepted norms happen to accord with one's own nature, then their adoption does not diminish one's own freedom. If they really fit they may enhance one's self-expression and also make one more genuinely independent. The force of one's energies for resistance and rebellion can then concentrate on rules or customs which really do violence to one's nature—and there will be no dearth of those.

Part of the point of this "concretization" is to have done with empty praise of freedom. To throw around its shoulders a cloak of glittering superlatives is as fatuous as showering warm adjectives all over love, except that it is more of a travesty, since blind veneration begins to undo freedom, while love survives inanity.

A first step towards a genuine appraisal of freedom's actual value, relative to other goods, might be the realization that freedom is not just a matter of degree, that to think in terms of a continuum from less to more is to oversimplify. The facts approximate more closely the familiar bellshaped curve: a small proportion of our actions or of our lives approach the two extremes, and are genuinely one or the other, but the preponderant majority lie somewhere near the middle, neither coerced nor free but to roughly similar degrees both at once. In most everyday situations we would be hard put to deliver a clear verdict; and significantly not so much because the pros and cons balance each other out, but because the individual factors are themselves gray instead of black and white. This in a sense confirms what we earlier said about identifications, namely, that our identity is often vague, that only fragments crystallize and that the locus of the self is shifted as we hesitate and change. In modern culture this hedging of one's bets becomes in fact endemic so that even the occasional experience of real freedom or real oppression is bleached out. One no longer has a clearly defined identity, and therefore both enthusiasm and rejection are so toned down that

one lives in a twilight world to which the categories of the free and the coerced hardly still apply.

But even aside from this vision of a grey apocalypse, people in their ordinary lives probably never felt particularly free. And this is important only because it stresses once more the contrast between rhetoric and truth: when we decide on a career or on a marriage the quantity of freedom we gain or lose is just one of many factors that can be easily outweighed. In these contexts we rather casually surrender some of our freedom in exchange for the greater fascination for the greater usefulness of a certain job, and we of course make such decisions in our personal relationships at every point. To recall these homey truths might be of some help when freedom-or-death oratory threatens to sweep us off our feet.

To gain a better notion of the relative worth of freedom we might give more body to its counterpart, and see whether we cannot render, concretely and briefly, the meaning of being unfree. Here, too, we reject the commonly accepted picture which raises hurdles, piles up obstacles and pressures, and sees the unfree man essentially as a man "boxed in." We have been suggesting that these words as they stand conceptualize much more adequately what they represent than any translation into degrees of diminished freedom would. But we also advanced the consideration that freedom should not be identified with the mere smoothing out of obstacles, since liberation then dissolves into mere ease. But if we are not to imagine the unfree man as fenced in then how shall we picture him?

We can outline him with an inversion: if freedom could be symbolized as a correspondence, as a harmony, and if the free man basically expresses what he really is, then unfreedom is a conflict, a dissonance. The outward life and conduct of the unfree man are unattuned and grate against his inner nature. If the free man has found the channels through which his forces can flow out, so that his gestures are animated with an energy that comes from within, then the vitality of the unfree man either lies unused and fallow, a pool of stagnant, brackish water, or it is bottled up and kept under pressure, while the outward conduct is disconnected from it, shaped by unassimilated, arbitrary and external strictures which render it mechanical and dessicated.

The analogy to Freud's concept of repression is here consciously intended, but a major difference should be observed at once. We have already indicated that the sense of self comes into existence only through its expression, that the sense of identity develops and becomes known to us only as it is acted out. The exact opposite is true of Freud's libidinal forces. The main burden of Freud's conception is that these forces have a permanent existence so that they will manifest themselves in the form of neurotic symptoms if other avenues are blocked. Our vision of the self is radically different. The self is extremely fragile; it can wither from sheer lack of use, a little dust can suffocate it. The problem of freedom is in large part the problem of how to keep the self alive, how to devise a mode of education and a society which do not extinguish it.

There can be no question of an absence of influence or pressures, and a free man in any case might encounter obstacles with exuberance or contempt. What renders a man unfree is therefore not constraints — these are inevitable — but the increasing distance from, and the eventual loss of a foundation in himself, the less motivated and organic, the more arbitrary the controlling forces are, the less relationship they have to anything within the self and the more freedom is crushed.

In proportional terms, freedom decreases as the dominion of the forces which I can integrate and accept is reduced and as the controlling forces become more alien and remote. If there is an absolute, a Black Mass of oppression, it would be the final betrayal of the self; the moment in which what is most loathed conquers the last defended sanctity: an act like the one in George Orwell's novel, when Winston screams that they should hold Julia's face into the cage with the rats.

One general understanding, that really should be obvious, nonetheless has to be made explicit at this point: what value I should place on freedom has to be at the very least a complex question that one flip of the oar cannot decide. Maybe every language needs some sound to signify the last resolution and the placid sea, but freedom in any case is not its name. So the where and when and what kind of freedom must be delicately calculated. And not just because "circumstances vary" but for deeper reasons that bear spelling out.

For one thing there is no "correct" identity — not even in the individual case. How could there be? It is not as if an original self lay there, waiting as a measure, so that my identification can approximate its contours till the two eventually coincide. My acts can fit my identification, but for my identity there is no model to be copied. The slowly forming pattern is therefore never simply right or wrong. I can never say: this is me, here I stand, I cannot help it, this I must express — it is instead a tenuous construction whose benefits and disadvantages call for elaborate evaluations. . . . And in our own case we similarly have to ask: What will be the whole web of psychological and other consequences if I accept this or that as my self, and how will these compare to the freedom obtained by acting this self out?

This suspendedness, even of the very self, the fact that it is included in the calculation and in the flux that knows no ultimate firm ground, separates our framework most sharply from all forms of a wistful "return to nature." It precludes any abdication to a mysterious, primordial source whose outflow could be of overshadowing importance, and demands instead a restless care and circumspection that is aware of the duality we faced before: that the self whose release is freedom is both, a mere shadow, and nonetheless also the pulse of our life.

But any simple lifting of freedom unto a shield, or plunging forward with a cry of "Freedom at any price" is ruled out by a still more powerful consideration. To say it harshly, parts of myself or of my nature are bound to be unappealing or mean or retrograde or evil, and the chances are that I simply will not want to act these out. Expressing those would not just be a slight and easily outweighed advantage, but would be a straight detriment. It is the hindrance or the extirpation of these impulses that represents the immediate gain. So freedom needs to be limited not only for the sake of others. The requirement to curtail it originates in each of us alone and is determined by our own individual evaluation.

This does mean that we are a battleground. And it is downright curious that the idea of freedom responds with such obtuseness to this toddler's truth. For despite the habitual association of freedom with the upward rising and the transcendence of the self, these are precisely the aspirations with which freedom seems to reckon least. To give the reins to all my facets, alike to the attractive and to the repugnant, might maximize my freedom but it would also signify the end of any further growth. It is this and not just compromises with the social order or the rights of others that imposes limits on my freedom. The more basic question is: With what value is a particular identification, or more simply, a given impulse endowed? If it is generous or beneficial, then giving expression to it is (if I hold these values) good; but if it is mean or ugly or destructive, then providing for its unhindered expression is plainly bad.

The evaluation of the identification (or of my nature) by moral, human or whatever other standards is therefore always primary and dominant. And this means that freedom is anything but a categorical or unquestionable good. How great or small its value is depends decisively on the value of the force that is to be released.

This, it seems to me, is how each of us individually almost has to think, and we are also, in my judgment, entitled to apply this mode of adjudication when it comes to others. This implies (to give, for now, just one example) that the free pursuit of one's material gain deserves perhaps only a very lowly status. And with that one of the classical reasoning-tricks, astounding in its artlessness, should be exposed: the invocation of the general sanctity of freedom whenever property runs the danger of being in some way restricted. The whole gamut of restraints placed on "free" enterprise, from the basic right to ownership down to graduated income taxes, were all along protested from the high plank of freedom's inviolability. Could society in the abstract or particular citizens ever interfere with the full exercise of this impulse to acquire, and how could such intrusion possibly be justified? The tacit assumption behind this question is almost farcical, since there is not a single thought or wink of our eye that is not influenced and shaped by the environment in which we move. We are constantly "interfered with." So why not in regard to what we own — especially since large accumulations are wholly interwoven with complex social arrangements, and with the contributions made by others? To take advantage of every manner of interdependencey while one acquires, but then to shout "freedom" at the sign of the first claim by others should by now provoke a laugh, or maybe anger — but not a philosophical debate.

But let us nonetheless point to another premise which lies behind these ratiocinations: it is the assumption that the very high significance of freedom applies with equal force to all parts of the self that want to be acted out. Would the trepidations when limits on property are to be "justified" have any motive if one did not believe that with the frustration of any impulse freedom is equally at stake? But we know from our own individual case that one or another part of us has to be checked at every moment, and, more decisively, we know that the exercise of some specific inclinations represents anything but an awesome value. On the contrary, they may be wretched to begin with so that it is their discouragement (and not their freedom) which represents a good. Why then can we not think more sanely about others— and about society? Every expression of the self is obviously not of equal value, and to limit some may be hardly ever, or even never, justified, but in the case of other impulses this may not be true. We might place small value on the desire for excessive property. Or we may decide that it is baleful in itself and that its exhibition is a lapse which we should combat in ourselves and help others to avoid.

In short: it is not true or legitimate to say simply, "The more freedom the better." I know that some parts of me are pretty vile and that expressing those will make me worse. And the same goes for others: they, too, have some foul qualities and it is natural that these should be restrained. A great deal more about how, and by whom, this would have to be decided needs to be said, but by now we at least should be prepared to resist those who use the idea of freedom as an instrument of intimidation. If some people can express their identifications only through the manipulation of great economic power, then we might point out to them that not every expression of the self is sacred. If the identifications of some happen to be such that the social discouragement of these impulses would cramp their self-expression, then the time may have come where they should cultivate a different self.

One can think of freedom as a luxury. None of the qualities it stands for— neither the consonance between my life and my nature or my identifications, nor the richer flow of energy released by this, nor any of the other signs it might bring in its train are brutal, bare necessities. In many cultures most have lived their lives in hostile circumstances, and were cramped and misshapen by their molds. To demand otherwise is in a sense presumptuous; to want more than others were content with rings of being spoiled. For most people the advantages of freedom do not come first, nor should they. Naturally this, too, can be frivolously misconstrued.

But if survival itself is at stake, if the example is that of a man looking for food and shelter, then the expression of his individual nature, and the attunedness to his self can wait. Freedom becomes a consideration only after the few brute needs of life are met; it belongs to the plenitude of the "superfluous" that gives life splendor.

But I mean the word luxury to have also another and more ominous overtone. Think of two boys in a fairly serious fight, evenly matched. One of them knows that staying close to his own style might mean that he will lose, while forgetting this, and concentrating on what seems to work might give him the upper hand. We know that he will decide that this is not the time to experiment with self-expression, that he cannot afford this luxury just now. And this is the point: the freedom is a subtle and refined attunement, easily lost and speedily abandoned by most when things get raw. Very few are clearheaded and controlled enough to know what their nature is and to stay close to it, not only under strain, but even just in the confusion and the "too much" of modern culture. And this has serious implications. For if one is tired of calloused exhortations but actually wants ordinary people to possess some freedom, then the creation of a general setting which makes this possible will have to be among the first and main requirements. This would have to be like a benevolent, mild climate, with long and pleasant summers and winters not too harsh; the soil would have to be fertile and harvests easy. Only in a milieu corresponding to this image— with the necessities provided, and sustenance secured, with the calamities muted as far as can be— will most men find it possible to act more nearly in accord with what they really are. Certainly they will be forced away from this in the middle of a "struggle for survival." And this shows that the conception of freedom which our society adopted is on this score reversed: for we link the idea of freedom to the Darwinian jungle, and imagine that any moderation of it limits freedom, when it is just the other way around: freedom becomes possible only after the fight over the bare necessities has stopped.

Our version of freedom is in some ways less presuming than others. We do not see man as solitary, autonomous, or independent; he is for us inseparable form his culture. In other respects, however, our concept demands much more and places freedom higher; that his actions cannot be predicted, that he makes choices, that he is self-conscious, does not distinguish man and does not make him free. It is not obvious that every detail of how a plant will grow can be predicted either; even a dog chooses one food and refuses others, and that we alone are self-conscious is a curious claim: it is constantly repeated with bland self-certainty, and yet, if the capacity to be aware of one's experience is meant by this, then this too is patently not a prerogative of man. No cat and no mouse could survive a single hour if it did not experience its own pain. So these cannot be the unique attributes on which freedom rests. All of these fall short and lie on too low a level. What we have singled out is by comparison rarer, subtler and more mysterious: that man forms a self, that he creates an image of his own identity and acts this out—nothing less than this is the foundation of his freedom.

The idea of freedom does not ask us to pass beyond the limits, and to transcend the fixedness of the self. It represents a warning not to lose touch with our nature. As we move on from one embodiment to others, it writes on the wall the place from where we have come. That is its power, but also its worst failing. For the will to self-transformation, the hope to travel far into the distance must conflict with it. Freedom advocates the expression of what we already are. Since this includes the struggle among the parts which make us up, it does not enjoin the surrender to any one of these, or the pretense of a false consensus. Yet it also does not teach us to burn bridges, to leave whatever we are now behind,

to become "arrows of longing for the other shore." In the face of such departures it warns of calamities. And the refusal to embark with us on these high journeys, the fact that it wants to stay at home, is probably its most disenchanting trait.

Still, freedom is nonetheless entitled to a superbly high rank among other values, and the full force of its great claim becomes most clearly felt when the absolute extinction, the total loss of freedom is conjured up, not as a hyperbolic phrase, but as a fact. Perhaps one can imagine it like an encirclement: despite one's mute or clamorous resistance one is quite gradually driven back. A force, in no way affected by us, deprives us slowly of more and still more ground. It moves like a wall of ice, takes from us this and then another area of our life, till nothing is any longer our own: till even the last refuge is surrendered and the ice has closed.

Freedom thus is, but it is also *not*, a "luxury." One place of self-expression can be exchanged for others rather lightly. In this it is similar to food: whether we eat bread or rice is of debatable importance, and to have both is finally to have more than we need. But we must eat; and in the same way we must have some self, and something that is our own, and some small area in which what we are can be expressed.

The extinction of freedom, when it is complete, thus spells much more than just the loss of the privilege to be different, or to be unique. Gone would be not merely the recognition of oneself as an individual or as a person. The deprivation would be more absolute. At stake is not only the ease with which the self can be singular, or the acknowledgment of its high status—at stake is its existence: if everything is taken from the self, nothing remains.

One image of a truly unfree person would be that of a human being who can no longer say: this is a bench that I have made, this is my feeling, this is a moment I have for myself. It would be someone who has nothing left after the sham and trash of life has been discarded.

26

MARK JOHNSTON
Self-Deception and the Nature of Mind*

When paradox dominates the description of a widespread phenomenon, dubious presuppositions usually lurk. Paradox dominates the philosophical treatment of bad faith or self-deception.[1] Part of the explanation is that the descriptive content of any claim that someone has deceived himself can be made to seem paradoxical. Such paradox mongering is not a fetish found only among analytic philosophers. Here is J. P. Sartre:

One does not undergo one's bad faith; one is not infected with it . . . but consciousness affects itself with bad faith. There must be an original intention and a project of bad faith: this project implies a comprehension of bad faith as such and a pre-reflective apprehension of consciousness as affecting itself with bad faith. It follows first that the one to whom the lie is told and the one who lies are one and the same person, which means that I must know in my capacity as deceiver the truth which is hidden from me in my capacity as the one deceived.[2]

This suggests *the surface paradox of self-deception*. If bad faith or self-deception is lying to oneself then a self-deceiver must stand to himself as liar to liar's victim. As liar he knew or strongly suspected that, as it might be, he was too drunk to drive home safely; as victim of the lie he did not know or strongly suspect this. If the same subject of belief or knowledge is both liar and liar's victim, we have a simple contradiction in *our* description of his condition: he both knew and did not know that he was too drunk to drive home safely.

There is a natural homuncularist response to this surface paradox of self-deception.[3] Distinct

---

*In writing this paper I have been helped by John Cooper, Raymond Guess, Gilbert Harman, Richard Jeffrey, David Lewis, Alison McIntyre, Michael Smith, and Bas van Fraassen.

[1] See Raphael Demos, "Lying to Oneself," *Journal of Philosophy* 57 (1960):588–595; John Canfield and Patrick McNally, "Paradoxes of Self-Deception," *Analysis* 21 (1961):140–144; Herbert Fingarette, *Self-Deception* (New York: Humanities Press, 1969); David Pears, "The Paradoxes of Self-Deception," *Theorema* 1 (1974). John Turk Saunders, "The Paradox of Self-Deception," *Philosophy and Phenomenological Research* 35 (1975):559–570; Richard Reilly, "Self-Deception: Resolving the Epistemological Paradox," *Personalist* 57 (1976):391–394; Jeffrey Foss, "Rethinking Self-Deception," *American Philosophical Quarterly* 17 (1980):237–243; David Kipp, "On Self-Deception," *Philosophical Quarterly* 30 (1980):305–317; Mary Haight, *A Study of Self-Deception* (London: Harvester Press, 1980).

[2] J. P. Sartre, *Being and Nothingness*, trans. Hazel Barnes (New York: Philosophical Library, 1956), chap. 2.

[3] The loci classici of the resort to homuncularist models to explain irrational mental processes are S. Freud, "Repression" (1915), *The Ego and the Id* (1923) and "Splitting of the Ego in the Process of Defence" (1938), all in *The Standard Edition of the Complete Psychological Works*, ed. James Strachey, Anna Freud, Alix Strachey, and Alan Tyson (London: Hogarth Press and The Institute of Psychoanalysis, 1954–

subsystems that play the distinct roles of deceiver and deceived are located within the self-deceiver. So no single subject of belief is required to both believe (know) a proposition and not believe (know) it.

The homuncularist picture has some independent appeal. For there is another sort of epistemic duality in self-deception which the homuncularist picture can capture. There is a sense in which the self-deceiving drunkard who believes and claims he will make it home safely also knows he may very well not, but this latter knowledge is suppressed, unacknowledged, or inoperative. When he is drunk it does not find useful expression in his thought or speech. When he sobers up or comes out of his self-deception he might plausibly say that he knew all along that it would be disastrous for him to drive. The self-deceptive belief that he will make it home safely can be located in the deceived system, and the knowledge that he probably won't can be located in the deceiving system. One snag remains. If the deceiving system is actively to deceive, then its knowledge of the facts must be operative and available to it. But then the homuncularist must also find a privileged sense in which knowledge is inoperative in self-deception. A strategy suggests itself. Let the deceived system be the analogue of the Freudian ego—the locus of the person's conscious thought, perception, decision, and voluntary control of the body. What is stored in the deceiving system is then hypothesized as not accessible to consciousness and so inoperative and inaccessible from the point of view of the ego or main system. So the homuncularist not only avoids contradiction in his description of the self-deceiver but also appears to be able to explain, in terms of mental compartmentaliza-

tion, how it is that the self-deceiver could believe propositions that are contradictory.

If another model of self-deception were produced then this account of the duality involved in self-deception might seem forced. One can make perfectly good sense of conscious belief that *p* and unacknowledged knowledge of the contrary without thinking that there are particular loci within the mind which are the respective subjects of attitudes of these sorts, as if "consciousness," "preconsciousness," and "unconsciousness" were names for layers or compartments of the mind.

One reason for thinking that another model should be produced is that the homuncular explanation replaces a contradictory description of the self-deceiver with a host of psychological puzzles. How could the deceiving subsystem have the capacities required to perpetrate the deception? For example, do such deceiving subsystems have a much higher alcohol tolerance than their hosts? Is that why they seem particularly active when one is drunk? Why should the deceiving subsystem be interested in the deception? Does it like lying for its own sake? Or does it suppose that it knows what it is best for the deceived system to believe?

Again, how does the deceiving system engage in an extended campaign of deception, employing various stratagems to alter the beliefs of the deceived system, without the deceived system's somehow noticing? If the deceived system somehow notices then the deception cannot succeed without the collusion of the deceived system. However, to speak of the collusion of the deceived system in its own deception simply reintroduces the original problem. The deceived system is now both (partial) agent and patient in the deception. Must we now recognize within the deceived system a deceiving subsystem and a deceived subsystem? If so, we face a dilemma: either a completely unexplanatory regress of subsystems of subsystems or the termination of the regress with a deceived subsystem stupid enough not to notice the strategies of deception

---

1974). David Pears develops a homuncularism specifically tailored to deal with self-deception in *Motivated Irrationality* (Oxford: Oxford Univ. Press. 1985). Both Fingarette and Haight consider the homuncularist response to the surface paradox.

and so one for which the question of collusion does not arise. The latter may always seem to be the way out until we reflect on the fact that the knowing, *complex*, and deceiving subsystem must have a curious kind of self-effacing motivation both to deceive the stupid and *simple* subsystem *and* to let it speak for and guide the whole person on the issue in question. Often self-deception involves a matter vital to the self as a whole, e.g., whether one will survive the drive home tonight. It is hard then to see why the wiser, deceiving subsystem should stand aside and let its foolish victim's belief control subsequent inference and action.

In fact homuncularism is a premature response to the surface paradox of self-deception. A dubious presupposition does lurk behind the familiar construal of the paradox. To be deceived is sometimes just to be *misled* without being *intentionally* misled or lied to. The self-deceiver is a self-misleader. As a result of his own activity he gets into a state in which he is misled, at least at the level of conscious belief. But the presupposition that generates the paradox is that this activity must be thought of as the intentional act of lying to oneself so that self-deception is just the reflexive case of lying. Evidently, *as the surface paradox shows*, nothing could be *that*. The homuncularist holds to the presupposition that the intentional act of lying is involved but drops the strict reflexive condition. If self-misleading is to be lying then the best one can do is to have parts of the self play the roles of liar and liar's victim. (Some have suggested that temporal parts of the self over time could play this role, but as we shall see this will not provide a general account.)[4]

The suggestion I wish to explore is that the surface paradox and deeper paradoxes of self-deception (i.e., those developed by Bernard Williams, by Sartre in a different passage, and

by Donald Davidson)[5] arise because as theorists of self-deception we tend to over-rationalize mental processes that are purposive but not intentional. These are processes that serve some interests of the self-deceiver, processes whose existence within the self-deceiver's psychic economy depends upon this fact, but processes that are not necessarily initiated by the self-deceiver for the sake of those interests or for any other reason. If we call mental processes that are purposive but not initiated for and from a reason *subintentional* processes then we can say that our over-rationalization of self-deception consists in assimilating subintentional processes to intentional acts, where an intentional act is a process initiated and directed by an agent because he recognizes that it serves a specific interest of his.[6] Faced with the subintentional processes of division, denial, repression, removal of appropriate affect, wishful perception, wishful memory, and wishful thought, the theorist whose only model for things done by an agent is that of the intentional act will multiply subagents complete with their own interests and action plans. Self-deception is an important test case for such a theorist since the very characterization of someone as self-deceived suggests both mental division and self-directed agency. If the subagency or homuncularist picture applies anywhere it should apply here. However, as I shall argue, little in the way of plausible interests and action plans can be constructed in order to carry out the program of

---

[4]R. A. Sorenson, "Self-Deception and Scattered Events," *Mind* 94 (1985):64–69.

[5]B. Williams, "Deciding to Believe," reprinted in *Problems of the Self* (Cambridge: Cambridge Univ. Press, 1973); J. P. Sartre, *Being and Nothingness*, chap. 2; D. Davidson, "Paradoxes of Irrationality," in *Philosophical Essays on Freud*, ed. R. Wollheim and J. Hopkins (Cambridge: Cambridge Univ. Press, 1982).

[6]For a discussion of subintentional bodily processes and their significance for a theory of the will, see Brian O'Shaughnassey, *The Will* (Cambridge: Cambridge Univ. Press, 1981), vol. 2, chap. 10.

representing self-deception as an intentional act of a lying subagency. In any case, this would misrepresent what we are censuring when we censure someone for self-deception. For in censuring the self-deceiver we do not blame any subagency for simply lying, nor are we mixing such blame with sympathy for an innocent victim of the lying subagency. . . .

Self-Deception

· ·

In wishful thought there need not be any appearance of a split within the agent. Someone may simply exploit the slack between inductive evidence and conclusion and wishfully think that the evidence that his wife is unfaithful to him is misleading and is to be otherwise explained. That this was wishful thought on his part rather than conservative thought need not be shown by the existence of some unacknowledged recognition in him that the evidence more or less establishes her infidelity. It can be shown by the fact that when presented with corresponding evidence about other married women he makes the judgment of infidelity.

Once one is no longer theoretically committed to understanding wishful thought as something intentionally done, one need not postulate some degree of recognition in the wishful thinker of what he has done, recognition that then has to be taken as somehow dissociated or sequestered from the mainstream of consciousness in order to avoid having the mainstream entertain what seems an impossible combination, i.e., both the wishful belief and the belief that this belief is wishful and so is not supported by anything that would suggest that it is true. Here we have a prima facie theoretical advantage of the subintentionalist treatment of wishful thought, since there is no direct implication of mental division in the accusation of mere wishful thought.

Things seem otherwise with self-deception strictly so-called. To the extent that the self-deceiver is to be distinguished from the mere wishful thinker by his perversely adopting the wishful belief *despite* his recognition at some level that the evidence is to the contrary, we have reason to regard the self-deceiver as divided. For it is hard to see how anxiety could be reduced by a wishful belief if the wishful belief is copresent in consciousness with the recognition that the evidence is strongly against it. Indeed it is hard to see how the wishful belief could persist in consciousness under these conditions. So it seems that some play must be given to the concept of *repression* in discussing self-deception. If anxiety that not-p produced by recognition of telling evidence for not-p is to be reduced, not only must the wishful belief that p arise, but the recognition of the evidence as more or less establishing the contrary must also be repressed, i.e., the subject must cease consciously acknowledging it. The strategies by which one ceases consciously to acknowledge that one recognizes the evidence to be against one's wishful belief are manifold. One may selectively reappraise and explain away the evidence (rationalization). One may simply avoid thinking about the touchy subject (evasion). One may focus one's attention on invented reasons for p and spring to the advocacy of p whenever opportunity presents itself (overcompensation). Where repressive strategies abound, it is plausible to postulate a repressive strategist. But the strategist cannot be the main system, in which the wishful belief allays anxiety. For then the main system would have to aim to put down the threatening belief or recognition of the import of the contrary evidence *in order* that it should cease to be aware of the threatening belief. Consciousness of its reason for repression makes the main system's task of forgetting impossible. Ignorance of its reason makes the task uninteresting. So we seem driven to recognize a subagency distinct from the main system, a subagency that, like Freud's censor or super-ego, is active in repression.

However, as Sartre maintained in his attack on Freud, it can appear that the Freudian account of repression in self-deception, e.g., the account of repression in self-deceptive resistance to the probings of the analyst, represents no advance over having the main system play the role of repressive agency.[7] If the censor who controls the border traffic between unconsciousness and consciousness is to successfully repress condemned drives and so resist the analyst, it must be aware of the drive to be repressed in order not to be conscious of these repressed drives. So it seems that the censor's putative project or intention is an impossible one—at the same time to be aware and not to be aware of the repressed desire. Now even if there is reason to doubt this objection of Sartre's to Freud's resort to the censor, say because it is unclear why the *censor* should have to be unaware of the repressed material, Sartre has still highlighted a real difficulty about repression. And this difficulty generalizes, so that we may speak of *a paradox of repression*. No project or action plan can satisfy the condition of simultaneously including awareness and ignorance of the repressed material. Given Sartre's ambition to use the paradox of repression to undermine Freudian pessimism about the scope of conscious choice in our mental life, it is ironic that the way out of the paradox seems to be the same as the way out of the paradox of wishful thought and the surface paradox of self-deception. We should not treat repression, even in its complex manifestations, as an intentional act of some subagency guided by its awareness of its desire to forget. On the contrary, we should understand repression as subintentional, i.e., not guided by reasons but operating for the purpose of reducing anxiety. For where we can

find neither a coherent intention in acting nor a coherent intention to be acted upon we cannot discern intentional action.

But before we take this way out of the paradox of repression we must deal with an alternative solution and then . . . with an alternative account of the role of the censor or protective system in self-deception, an account developed by David Pears.

First, why should the condition of *simultaneously* including awareness and ignorance of the repressed material be a natural condition to impose on any repressor's action plan? Surely there are cases of deceiving oneself in which the shadow of forgetfulness falls between the intention and the act.

Forgetfulness can sometimes be planned around. Certain powerful sleeping pills cause retroactive amnesia. One's memory of what one did in the hour or so before taking the pill is very indistinct and sometimes apparently erased completely. Knowing this, one could get up to mischief during such a period and avoid the guilt of the morning after by taking the precaution of rearranging things so that in the morning one will be misled about what one did the night before. This is certainly intentional activity, and if it succeeds it results in the deception of one's later self by an earlier self. Similarly, taking to holy water and rosary beads, i.e., acting as if one accepted the tenets of Catholicism, was Pascal's suggested method of bringing about the belief in those tenets. This is certainly intentional activity, and it can result in the production of a desired belief in one's later self, presumably because it gradually inclines one to view the favorable evidence more sympathetically and not attend to the countervailing evidence. Here we have self-deceptive action plans involving repression and forgetting, and yet nothing paradoxical.

Indeed, it has been suggested[8] that in general

---

[7]Sartre, *Being and Nothingness*, chap. 2.

[8]Sorensen, "Self-Deception and Scattered Events," and D. W. Hamlyn, "Self-Deception," *Proceedings of the Aristotelian Society* 45 (1971):45–60.

the way to avoid the surface paradox of know-ing deceiver and unknowing victim's being em-bodied in the one agent is to exploit the fact that self-deception takes time: in the interim the de-ceiver can forget what he knew and forget that he set out to mislead himself. This time-lag strategy, however, not only leaves the most puzzling cases of self-deception untreated but also leaves unexplained the most puzzling fea-tures of many of the cases it seems to render unparadoxical.

Not all self-deception takes a form in which stages of the self-deceiver's history are succes-sively stages of deceiving, forgetting, and being the victim of deceit. One can simultaneously develop as deceiver and deceived. A case of progressive and self-deceptive alcoholism might be of this sort. As the alcoholic's case worsens and more evidence accumulates, his self-decep-tive denials develop concurrently.

Moreover, it cannot be the mere fact that self-deception takes time (if it does take time) that allows the self-deceiver to forget what he knew and forget that he set out to mislead himself. Rather, what is crucial to the cases in which the time delay seems to allow a nonparadoxical de-scription is that the self-deceiver explicitly em-ploys a means to achieve his motivated belief, a means whose operation does not require that the self-deceiver attend to it under the descrip-tion "means of producing in me the desired belief" or something equivalent. Let us call a means that does not require this kind of moni-toring, an *autonomous* means. In the case of nocturnal mischief, the autonomous means is a combination of a process in the external world, the persistence of misleading evidence, and the intended outcome of a drug-induced process of forgetting, a process that is not itself an inten-tional act and so does not require directive monitoring after the taking of the pill. In the case of Pascal's method, the means is the adop-tion of a practice itself sufficiently engaging so that past a certain point one need not think of one's participation under the description

"means of getting me to believe in the tenets of Catholicism in the absence of sufficient evi-dence" in order to intend to participate. Past a certain point one just gets carried along.

The phrase "past a certain point" itself masks a puzzling feature of the case. Around the point in question there must be a transition from in-tending one's participation in the practice under the description "means of getting me to believe in the tenets of Catholicism in the absence of sufficient evidence" to doing it habitually and perhaps under more particular descriptions in-ternal to the practice, e.g., "asking for God's forgiveness." This very transition, which might be called "falling in with the practice," may be compared to getting lost in a fantasy or a pre-tense, not in order to belittle it but in order to point out that the transition in question involves a kind of forgetfulness that cannot itself be rep-resented as an intentional act, something done from and for a reason. For this forgetfulness simply *occurs* at a certain point, and to represent it as something done for a reason is to allow that it could be monitored as something tending to satisfy and ultimately satisfying an intention. The intention would have to be something like "to forget that my only reason for engaging in this practice is as a means of producing in me belief in the tenets of Catholicism." The para-dox of repression simply recrystalizes at the point at which I recognize that this intention is satisfied. I would have to recognize some con-current act of mine as forgetting that my only reason for engaging in the practice is as a means to produce in me belief in the tenets of Catholi-cism. That is, I would have to be lucidly aware of what I am supposed to be concurrently forgetting.

The time-lag theory does not illuminate the nature of self-deception, and when it provides a way out of the surface paradox of self-deception it does this by admitting that only subinten-tional forgettings could produce the intended or desired outcome of having forgotten. But it might be thought that the theory at least has served dialectically to force us to formulate the concept of an autonomous means, which now allows us to qualify our main thesis appropriately. That is, we should say that motivated believings and cessations of conscious belief *that do not employ autonomous means* are not intentional acts but are nonintentional outcomes of mental tropisms.

The restriction does not render the main thesis uninteresting, since it points to a large class of cases that cannot be explained in a certain way. More important, the cases omitted are those in which the means of producing the desired belief operates without one's attending to it. Indeed it is important that one does not intend or monitor the process throughout. But then the operation of the means, although intended to occur, is not itself an intentional act, and neither is the outcome produced by the means, although it is an intended outcome of a process one set in motion. One can describe what one does in the case of nocturnal mischief as "deceiving oneself by arranging misleading evidence and taking the amnestic drug." The description corresponds to a statement of intention that captures one's reason for arranging the misleading evidence and taking the amnestic drug. One intended to deceive oneself by arranging misleading evidence and taking the amnestic drug. But what one *did* in arranging the evidence and taking the drug did not itself constitute self-deception. Only the cooperation of future events made what one did deserve the name of *deceiving oneself* by arranging misleading evidence and taking the amnestic drug. So the main thesis can be stated without restriction: nothing that itself constitutes motivated believing or motivated cessation of (conscious) belief is an intentional act. In the cases of self-deception and repression in which autonomous means are employed, the motivated believing and accompanying repression are constituted by the intentional acts of setting the means in motion *plus* the brute operations of those means culminating in the belief and the forgetting.

And this captures the peculiar opacity to intention that self-deception and its associated repressions exhibit. Even when there is a self-deceptive or repressive action plan, no intentional act is intrinsically a self-deception or a forgetting. So at least things currently seem to stand.

Homuncularism Revisited

David Pears has recently offered a response to Sartre's paradox of repression by way of providing a new model of the role of the censor or protective system in self-deception.[9] Pears offers a model in which self-deception is constituted by an intentional act of a lying subagency.

Sartre's mistake, according to Pears, is to suppose that the subagency that does the deceiving and repressing and monitors its success in these projects needs itself to be deceived. Instead, Pears proposes that we should take quite literally a model that locates a protective system as the agent in self-deception, a protective system that operates like a paternalistic liar, protecting the main system or ego for what the protective system takes to be the ego's good. The lying protective system need never deceive itself and so need never be engaged in the contradictory project of trying to believe what it knows to be false. The lying protective system need never produce forgetfulness in itself and so need never aim at forgetting something that having this aim forces it to keep in mind. . . .

I suggest that if the segregation, within distinct subsystems, of the relevant mental cause and effect is to do anything to resolve the alleged paradox of irrationality associated with wishful thinking and self-deception, then one must follow Pears and understand these processes as the suggestive implantation of belief in

---

[9]Pears, *Motivated Irrationality*, chap. 6.

the main system by a protective system. Only then will one have an appropriate analogue of the perceptual link, namely, one person saying something to another who hears what he said and believes it. (The analogy has some appeal. Thomas Reid actually took the receiving of testimony to be a sort of perception via conversation.)[10] In this way the theoretical division of a person into a protective, lying system and a main system that is its gullible victim allows us to reestablish a chain of rational causes. The main system is aware of and reasonably accepts the testimony of the protective system. The protective system's reason for offering this testimony is to allay the anxiety of the main system. So also the protective system may go in for distracting the main system from its anxiety-producing beliefs.

Here we have a homuncularism that solves all the paradoxes of self-deception we have encountered and which seems to represent self-deception (and wishful thinking) as constituted by intentional acts of protective systems. The surface paradox is solved by having distinct subsystems play the respective roles of liar and victim of the lie. The paradox of wishful thinking is solved by having the protective system altruistically set out to allay the main system's anxiety that not-p by inculcating the belief that p in the main system. The paradox of repression is solved by having the protective system altruistically set out to allay the main system's anxiety that p by distracting it from its anxiety-producing belief that not-p. The paradox of irrationality is solved by modeling self-deception (and wishful thought) on interpersonal testimony. If the main strategy of this paper is to work, that is, if we are to use the paradoxes of self-deception to support a tropistic and anti-intentionalist account of the processes involved, then we must discredit the account of self-de-

ception in terms of protective and main subsystems.

This account can be discredited so long as we do not allow its advocates the luxury of hovering noncommittally between the horns of a dilemma: either take the subsystem account literally, in which case it implausibly represents the ordinary self-deceiver as a victim of something like multiple personality, or take it as a metaphor, in which case it provides no way to evade the paradoxes while maintaining that intentional acts constitute self-deception and wishful thinking.

The several difficulties for the subagency account literally construed may be stated as objections to Pears's explicitly worked-out model of a protective system influencing a main system. (It should be emphasized that Pears is not committed to the *general* applicability of this model.)

The main system may be thought of as having the desire for some outcome p and the anxiety that p will not occur. Somehow, as a result of these conditions, a protective system is either generated or set into operation, a protective system that has its own internal rationality directed toward the quasi-altruistic manipulation of the main system. Whereas the inferential processes of the main system are typically introspectable by the self-deceiving person and thereby constitute *his* conscious feelings, thoughts, memories, etc., those in the protective system are not, so that the self-deceiver is not aware of the protective system's manipulation of his beliefs.

Although the system's operations are not introspectable by the self-deceiver and so are not in that sense part of his consciousness, they are not mere instinctual drives, like hunger and thirst, unconsciously pushing the self-deceiver toward outcomes that in fact constitute their satisfaction. The protective system has rather complex beliefs and desires about the main system. In the light of these the protective system acts on the main system by means of various stratagems until it produces the protective belief. That is, the protective system has to have

---

[10]Thomas Reid, "Of Social Operations of Mind," essay 1, chap. 8 in *Essays on the Powers of the Human Mind*.

the capacity to manipulate its representations of the main system in practical inference that issues in action on the main system, action that the protective system monitors for its effectiveness. This is Pears's motive for referring to the protective system's operations as *preconscious*, i.e., as involving complex manipulations of representations, manipulations that are not introspectable to the main system and so not part of the self-deceiver's conscious life. The question arises how the protective system could do all this without being conscious of (introspecting) its own operations. After all, it has to compare the outcome it is producing with the outcome it aimed for and act or cease to act accordingly. Any consciousness by the protective system of its own operation is "buried alive," i.e., is not accessible to the consciousness of the main system.

Pears suggests that in wishful and self-deceptive thought such a protective system is either generated or set into operation by the main system's desire for some outcome. The protective system "crystallizes around" the main system's desire. This is puzzling. For it is unclear how the main system's desire that *p* could give the protective system any reason to produce in the main system the belief that *p*. The belief that *p* does not satisfy the desire that *p*. At most it can reduce the concurrent disturbing anxiety that not-*p* will obtain. So if any desire of the main system gives the quasi-altruistic protective system a reason to aim to produce in the main system the belief that *p*, it is the main system's understandable desire to be rid of its anxiety that not-*p*.

This desire of the main system gives the protective system a reason to aim to produce the wishful belief in the main system only if the protective system is altruistically disposed to the main system. But whence this altruism? Surely *not* from a history of sympathetic identification born of recognition of likeness and fellow feeling. Pears calls it quasi-altruism, thereby suggesting that this is the altruism of

concern for the larger unit—the self-deceiver—which includes both the protective, deceiving altruist and the deceived subsystem. But then it must be objected that in many cases of self-deception all but the self-deceived person can see that he would be better off without the protective belief. In such cases the putative actions of the protective system cannot be represented as the outcome of lucid concern for the whole system, which includes it and the main system as parts. Indeed in many such cases the main system and the person as a whole suffer considerably as a result of the putative actions of the protective system, so that the protective system must have a curiously narrowed focus of quasi-altruistic concern.

Take for example the sort of case Freud discusses in the essay "Mourning and Melancholia."[11] One very much wants to love one's mother, and yet one feels hostility toward her for the pain she caused. This conflict generates anxiety that is relieved by the repression of one's hostility toward one's mother. Such repression can be seen as self-deceptive blocking of thought. One ceases to acknowledge or actively entertain one's hostile beliefs, and perhaps one comes to believe that one simply loves one's mother. But as Freud points out, the repressed or unacknowledged hostile beliefs can nonetheless operate to produce unacknowledged guilt experienced as objectless depression and a desire for self-punishment which prompts self-destructive behavior. Here we have a familiar case of self-deceptive resolution of conscious ambivalence and associated anxiety by repression of one's hostile attitudes, with subsequent hell to pay. If a protective system is intentionally repressing the hostile, anxiety-generating belief, and if the effects of repression are often considerably worse than the anxiety produced by the original conflict in the main system, then either the protective system must have a cur-

[11]Freud, "Mourning and Melancholia" (1915), in *The Standard Edition of the Complete Psychological Works*.

iously sadistic concern for the main system, involving a readiness to get the main system out of the psychic frying pan and into the fire, or the protective system, despite its otherwise excellent monitoring of the main system, must itself have a curious blind spot that prevents it from seeing the destructive effects of its own characteristic way of reducing anxiety in the main system.

Suppose somehow that these difficulties are solved without making the protective system so limited that it collapses into a tropistic anxiety-reducer, too simple to have motives or intentions.[12] So somehow the protective system's motives are plausibly made to mesh with what it is supposed to do. Concentrate instead on what it is supposed to do, i.e., get the main

system to adopt the protective belief. Notice that we invite a regress if we say what is nevertheless plausible, namely, that this is all too easy because the main system is all too ready to accept the protective belief. Such collusion by the main system would itself be wishful acceptance of belief, reproducing within the main system the kind of duality that the intentionalist-gone-homuncularist is trying to keep outside. Instead it must be that the protective system somehow slips the protective belief into the main system, even though the main system's acquiring that belief does not satisfy the main system's ordinary standards of belief acquisition. After all, the main system must be inclined to recognize that the belief does not come from the main system's perceptual input or from its memory or from inference from its other beliefs. The protective belief just pops up. Why does the main system so happily tolerate this?

Moreover, it is clear that getting the main system to adopt the protective belief cannot be something the protective system does directly without employing any particular means. One agency cannot will as a *basic* act of its own that another adopt a belief or ignore evidence or not acknowledge its beliefs. Given this, it is hard to see how wishful thought that involves wishfully exploiting the slack between inductive evidence and conclusion could be brought about simply by the protective system. For the crucial move in such a process is the main system's failing to see that the evidence is sufficient to make the anxiety-provoking conclusion believable. How is this act of the main system explained by anything that the protective system could intentionally do? Well, we may allow for purposes of argument that the protective system can distract, suggest, and cajole, but this leaves the worrying question why the main system is so distractable, suggestable, and biddable in this matter. At a certain point, the protective system's suggestions to the effect that, despite the evidence, p, are supposed to be accepted by the main system as sufficient to believe p. Why?

[12]When is a system too simple to have intentions, in particular the intention to deceive? This is a complicated matter, but I think that if a system is to be correctly ascribed intentions then the system should have some capacity for practical reasoning and have a means of representing its own desires and beliefs, a means of representing possible outcomes of action and the extent to which they serve its desires, and a capacity to act upon what it has judged to be the best alternative. Call such a system a *primary homunculus*. Now Daniel Dennett, among others, has suggested that we might take the intentional stance even towards things that are not primary homunculi, e.g., plants. That is to say we might explain the plant's turning toward the sun by attributing to it a desire for sunlight on its leaves and a belief that turning will make this more likely (see his "Intentional Systems"). In some quarters this is called 'homuncular explanation'. Evidently, this sort of homuncular explanation is not at issue in this paper. If any explanatory end is served by understanding a plant as if it has beliefs and desires, as much could be done by so understanding a tropistic anxiety-reducer. However, it is obvious that those who invite the paradoxes of self-deception by explaining self-deception on the model of other-deception are driven to postulate *primary* homunculi, i.e., systems that are rich enough to have intentions, in particular the intention to deceive. In "Machines and the Mental," *Proceeding and Addresses of the American Philosophical Association* 59 (1985), Fred Dretske presents what amounts to an argument that the attributions of beliefs and desires to systems that lack internal representation cannot be literally true. So there may well be problems with taking the intentional stance toward plants or tropistic anxiety-reducers.

The main system has no reason to regard these suggestions as reliable testimony. So why does it accept them? The tempting answer is: because it wants to believe *p* and so is all too ready to collude in its own deception. But "collude" is an intentionalist idiom that raises the very difficulties the protective system was postulated to deal with. Should we then postulate within what we were taking to be the main system a second protective system and a more primary system? This would be to make any explanation of self-deceptive and wishful thought forever recede as we try to grasp it. For the very same problems would arise for the actions of the second protective system. We can take as many turns as we want on the intentionalist roundabout, but we will still be left with our original problem: how is it that some main or primary system's desire to believe *p* leads it to accept suggestions that *p* as grounds for believing *p* even though that system has no reason to believe that they are reliable indications that *p* is true? In short, how could the desire that *p* lead the main or primary system to be favorably disposed toward believing *p*? And there seems no other answer but the anti-intentionalist and tropistic one: this is the way our minds work; anxious desire that *p* simply leads one to be disposed to believe that *p*.

Finally, the anti-intentionalist and tropistic account does better than the homuncularist account in enabling us to explain the kind of censure involved in accusations of self-deception. On the homuncularist account the deceived and noncolluding main system, a system that has good claim to be the analogue of the Freudian ego, the active controller of the person's conscious thought, speech, and bodily action, is an innocent victim of deception. It is simply lied to. Correspondingly, the protective system is a straightforward, albeit paternalistic, liar. But our accusations of self-deception seem to be accusations of a sort of failure not unlike that involved in cowardly flight from the frightening. For example, in that part of Augustine's orgy of self-accusation in which he confesses his past self-

deceptions, he explicitly employs the metaphor of mental flight from horrific features of himself.

> *Ponticianus told us this story [of a conversion] and as he spoke, you, O Lord, turned me back upon myself. You took me from behind my own back, where I had placed myself because I did not wish to look upon myself. You stood me face to face with myself, so I might see how foul I was, how deformed and defiled, how covered with stains and sores. I looked, and I was filled with horror but there was no place for me to flee from myself. If I tried to turn my gaze from myself, he still went on with the story that he was telling, and once again you placed me in front of myself and thrust me before my own eyes, so that I might find out my iniquity and hate it. I knew what it was, but I pretended not to; I refused to look at it and put it out of my memory.*[13]

Here the self-directed accusation of self-deception is an accusation of mental cowardice, of flight from anxiety (or angst), a failure to contain one's anxiety, a lack of courage in matters epistemic. The homuncularist picture of the self-deceiver prevents us from rationally reconstructing a fitting subject for this sort of censure. The protective system is simply lying. The main system is simply the victim of a paternalistic liar. This does not add up to anything like mental cowardice.

The anti-intentionalist and tropistic account does better. Though mental flight, like physical flight, is typically subintentional, one can still be held responsible for lacking the ability to contain one's anxiety and face the anxiety-provoking or the terrible. The accusation of self-deception is a familiar case of being held responsible

---

[13]St. Augustine, *Confessions* VIII, 7–16. I thank Bas van Fraassen for drawing my attention to this passage. It is quoted and discussed in his paper. "The Peculiar Effects of Love and Desire," chap. 5 in B. McLaughlin and A. Rorty, eds., *Perspectives on Self-Deception*, Berkeley: University of California Press, 1988.

for an episode that evidences a defect of character, in this case a lack of the negative power that is reason, i.e., the capacity to inhibit changes in beliefs when those changes are not well grounded in reasons.

Tropisms and Reason

The presupposition that drives the paradoxes of self-deception or bad faith is succinctly expressed by Sartre at the beginning of his statement of the surface paradox: "one does not undergo one's bad faith, one is not infected with it. . . . But consciousness affects itself with bad faith. There must be an original intention and a project of bad faith."[14] This is to assume that if self-deception is something *done* rather than merely undergone it must be something intentionally done. We know already from the case of bodily activity that this assumption is false. For example, running our eyes predominantly over the tops and not the bottoms of printed words is something many of us do, since many of us read *by* running our eyes predominantly over the tops of printed words. A way to make this vivid to oneself is to cover the bottom half of a line of print and try to read it and then cover the top half of a similar line of print and try to read it. Now it would be absurd to suggest that using our eyes this way must be something we do intentionally, e.g., for and from the reason that this makes it possible to read more quickly. For many of us, performing the little experiment just outlined gives us the first inkling of what we were up to. But of course the explanation of why this method of reading is unwittingly used by many of us has to do with the fact that it helps us to read faster. The method, once hit upon, persists because it serves a purpose; it is not intentionally employed for that purpose.

Similar things need to be said about the mental process of self-deception by which anxiety that one's desire that p will not be satisfied is reduced by one's acquisition of the belief that p (wishful thinking) and one's ceasing to acknowledge one's recognition of the evidence that not-p (repression). This process is not mediated by intention; rather, processes of this kind persist because they serve the end of reducing anxiety. Hence I speak of a mental tropism, a characteristic pattern of causation between types of mental states, a pattern whose existence within the mind is no more surprising, given what it does for us, than a plant's turning toward the sun.

In fact mental tropisms abound. When the victim of Korsakoff's syndrome confabulates or spontaneously and without deceptive intent fills in the considerable gaps in his memory, we see in operation a process that produces a needed coherence in the patient's remembering of his past, but a process that is not carried on for and from this reason.[15] When we encounter an instance of the phenomenon of so-called "sour-grapes," in which the subject's desires are tailored to what he can get in an ad hoc way that reduces the chances of frustration, we see the securing of a comprehensible goal but not intentional activity.[16] When at a reception one's attention suddenly and automatically shifts from the weary discussion of comparative mustards in which one has been idly involved to the nearby conversational group that happens to be discussing one's secret passion, one need not be intentionally turning one's attention to the more interesting exchange. More typically, one has been served by an automatic filtering process that is ordinarily inaccessible to introspection and which determines that what is

[14]Sartre, *Being and Nothingness*, chap. 2.

[15]See Nelson Butters and Laird S. Cermak, *Korsakoff's Syndrome* (New York: Academic Press, 1980).

[16]This is effectively argued in Jon Elster, *Sour Grapes* (Cambridge: Cambridge Univ. Press, 1983).

salient in perception will be what answers to one's interests.

Dogmas die hard, so it is natural to suppose that such tropisms either are peripheral to the mind or represent breakdowns in the otherwise smooth working of the reason machine, the movements of which are properly mediated or guided by reason and are *therefore* different in nature from irrational processes. But this too can be made to seem like a quaint fantasy.

What is it for the normal operations of the mind to be mediated by reason? I suggest that it is just for causal relations to hold between mental states one of which in fact is a reason for another. What is it for mental operations to be *guided* by reason? Just for the reasoner to employ a certain inhibitory capacity—the capacity to inhibit conscious changes in attitude when he recognizes that those changes are not well grounded in reason. Here too we have mental tropisms, characteristic causal processes leading from one kind of attitude to another, tropisms that qualify as rational processes not because of some sui generis manner—rational causation—in which the one attitude causes another but because the one attitude is in fact a reason for the other.

Consider a case of intentional and rational belief change. I explicitly reason from my belief that p and my belief that if p then q to a belief that q. Thanks to my good schooling there takes place in me a causal process the terms of which are mental states whose contents, taken together, conform to *modus ponens*. Indeed, I might have explicitly aimed to guide my thought in accord with *modus ponens*. Then, thanks to my good schooling, there takes place in me a causal process leading *from* my desire so to guide my thought, my belief that p, my belief that if p then q, and my belief that *modus ponens* prescribes that I come to believe q, to my coming to believe q. This causal process is relevantly different from the mental tropisms we have been discussing only in involving as antecedent causes mental states that are reasons for my coming to believe q. Given this fact about the

terms of the causal process, that causal process *constitutes* my explicitly guiding my thoughts in accord with *modus ponens*. No special kind of event intervening between reasons and my response to them, no special kind of intrinsically rational causation, is needed to make a causal process between mental states a case of rational, and intentional, belief change. Wayward causal cases aside,[17] the existence of a causal process connecting mental states that conform to a rational pattern can itself constitute rational and intentional belief change.

For suppose that what is required over and above causation by states that are in fact reasons for the states or changes they cause is as follows. First, the agent must recognize that he has reasons that support the drawing of a certain conclusion or the performance of an intentional act; second, the agent must will the drawing of the conclusion or will the performance of the act; and third, as a result of the willing, draw the conclusion or perform the act. The special something extra distinguishing rational causal processes from the mere mental tropisms that constitute irrational changes in belief is then supposed to be an intervening act of will rationalized by recognition of sufficient reason. This *could* on occasion go on in a person—he recognizes that he has sufficient reason for an act and he wills that he perform the act in question and he does perform it. But it cannot capture a general condition on rational inference or intentional action. For now we have a causal connection between someone's recognizing that he has reasons to perform a certain act and his willing or coming to intend to perform that act. This is a rational connection—the recognition of reasons rationalizes or gives a point to the willing or the forming of an intention to act. But if a condition on its being a rational connection is its including an intermediate forming of an

[17]In wayward causal cases, states that rationalize other states or events cause them, but cause them by a tortuous route employing processes not typical of willing (i.e., that do not typically constitute willing). See D. Davidson, "Freedom to Act," in *Essays on Actions and Events*.

intention to intend or a willing to will, we are launched on a regress we can never stop without at some point abandoning the general demand for an intervening willing to constitute a rational connection. At some point we must recognize an intentional act that is constituted merely by attitudes causing activity that they rationalize. So in particular, the case of intentionally drawing the logical conclusion from one's beliefs must ultimately turn on the operation of tropisms connecting the attitudes in question. Thanks to innate dispositions, training, and employment of the capacity to inhibit competing irrational operations, certain mental operations conform to good inferential rules but are as blind as the operations of the tropisms that do not conform. If we are to be able to draw any conclusions at all we must in the relevant sense draw some conclusions blindly, which is not to say unintentionally but rather to say without there occurring in us anything more than an automatic response to those reasons, a response that is in fact rationalized by them.

Just as a condition of understanding is that one must at some point respond appropriately to representations without interpreting them in terms of further representations,[18] a condition

[18]This is surely part of the lesson of L. Wittgenstein's *Philosophical Investigations*, section 201, though I shy away from saying what else is going on there.

of reasoning is that one must at some point allow one's reasons to work on one in the appropriate fashion. Better, one's allowing them to work on one in accord with reason is one's reasoning from them, just as responding to one's representations in accord with convention constitutes one's understanding of them.

If this is the truth about rational connections among mental states, then the operations of mental tropisms (blind but purpose-serving connections between mental state types) are not peripheral phenomena but are the basic connections that constitute rationality and irrationality alike. Rational connections are not constitutive and exhaustive of the mental. Rationality could hardly be constitutive and exhaustive, given that minds evolved under conditions in which rational mental tropisms conferred only limited advantages. That a creature whose environment is too complicated for it to get by on the strength of its instincts does better in some ways if it can monitor its desires and rationally exploit means to their satisfaction is no surprise. But it should be no more surprising that such a creature, fallen from simple harmony with nature, does better in other ways if its frequent and debilitating anxieties that its desires will not be satisfied are regularly dealt with by doses of hopeful belief. Though we specially prize reason, it is just one adaptive form mental processes can take.

27

MARTHA NUSSBAUM
Love's Knowledge

> And if a cataleptic impression does not exist, neither
> will there be any assent to it, and thus there will not
> be any certainty either. And if there is no certainty,
> neither will there be a system of certainties, that is to
> say a science. From which it follows that there will be
> no science of life either.
> —Sextus Empiricus, *Adversus Mathematicos* vii, 182

> As we examine this view closely, it looks to us more
> like a prayer than like the truth.
> —Sextus, ibid., xi, 401

Françoise brings him the news: "Mademoiselle
Albertine has gone." Only a moment before, he
believed with confidence that he did not love
her any longer. Now the news of her departure
brings a reaction so powerful, an anguish so
overwhelming, that this view of his condition
simply vanishes. Marcel knows, and knows
with certainty, without the least room for doubt,
that he loves Albertine.[1]

We deceive ourselves about love—about
who; and how; and when; and whether. We
also discover and correct our self-deceptions.
The forces making for both deception and un-
masking here are various and powerful: the un-
surpassed danger, the urgent need for protec-
tion and self-sufficiency, the opposite and equal
need for joy and communication and connection. Any of these can serve either truth or falsity, as the occasion demands. The difficulty
then becomes: how in the midst of this confusion (and delight and pain) do we know what
view of ourselves, what parts of ourselves, to

trust? Which stories about the condition of the
heart are the reliable ones and which the self-
deceiving fictions? We find ourselves asking
where, in this plurality of discordant voices with
which we address ourselves on this topic of
perennial self-interest, is the criterion of truth?
(And what does it mean to look for a criterion
here? Could that demand itself be a tool of
self-deception?)

Proust tells us that the sort of knowledge of
the heart we need in this case cannot be given
us by the science of psychology, or, indeed, by
any sort of scientific use of intellect. Knowledge
of the heart must come form the heart—from
and in its pains and longings, its emotional responses. I examine this part of Proust's view,
and its relation to the "scientific" opposition.
The view raises a number of troubling questions, which are only partially answered by the
more elaborate account of emotion's interaction
with reflection that Proust develops in his final
volume. I then examine an alternative view of
knowledge of love, one that opposes the scientific account in a more radical way. I find this
view in a short story by Ann Beattie. Finally, I
ask about the relationship between these views
of love's knowledge and the styles in which
they are expressed, and make some remarks
about a philosophical criticism of literature.

Knowledge of the Heart
by Intellectual Scrutiny

1. We need to begin with a picture of the view
that Proust is opposing when he offers his account of how we come to know our own love. It

---

[1] I have discussed this passage and its view of knowledge
in "Fictions of the Soul," *Philosophy and Literature* 7
(1983):145–161. The present discussion modifies many of
the views expressed in that article, and expands on others.

is important to recognize from the beginning that this is not simply a rival alternative account of the matter, incompatible with Proust's as one belief is incompatible with another. It is also, according to Proust, a form of activity that we engage in, a commitment we make, when we wish to avoid or block the sort of knowledge that he will describe. It is a practical barrier to this knowledge as well as a theoretical rival. To believe in the theoretical rival and live accordingly is not just to be in error; it is to engage in a fundamental form of self-deception.

The rival view is this. Knowledge of whether one loves someone—knowledge of the condition of one's heart where love is concerned—can best be attained by a detached, unemotional, exact intellectual scrutiny of one's condition, conducted in the way a scientist would conduct a piece of research. We attend carefully, with subtle intellectual precision, to the vicissitudes of our passion, sorting, analyzing, classifying. This sort of scrutiny is both necessary and sufficient for the requisite self-knowledge.[2] Proust's Marcel is deeply attached to this view. Just before he receives the news of Albertine's departure, he has, accordingly, been surveying the contents of his heart in the scientific manner: "I had believed that I was leaving nothing out of account, like a rigorous analyst; I had believed that I knew the state of my own heart" (III:426).[3] This inspection convinces him that no love for Albertine is present. He is tired of her. He desires other women.

This view of knowledge has, it hardly needs to be said, powerful roots in our entire intellectual tradition, and especially our philosophical tradition. It is also a view on which much of the thought about method and about writing in that tradition relies. The view (as it is defended by thinkers otherwise as diverse as Plato and Locke)[4] holds that our passions and our feelings are unnecessary to the search for truth about any matter whatever. What is more, feelings can easily impede that search, either by distracting the searching intellect or, still worse, by distorting its view of the world. Desire, as Plato puts it in the *Phaedo*, binds the soul to its bodily prison house and forces it to view everything from within that distorting enclosure. The result is that intellect is "bewitched," distorted in its function; a captive, it "collaborates in its own imprisonment." In short, self-deception about our condition, when it occurs, is the result of the corruption of reason by feeling and desire. Intellect "itself by itself" is never self-deceptive. Though of course it may fail to reach its goal for some external reason, it never presents a biased or one-sided view of truth. It is never internally corrupt or corrupting. Nor does it require supplementation from any other source. "Itself by itself" it reaches the truth.

This view has implications for questions of method and style. Locke has, of course, an altogether different view from Plato's about the relationship between intellect and bodily sense-perception, but is no more charitable to the passions and their role in the search for truth. His attack on rhetorical and emotive features of style (which I have discussed further elsewhere) presupposed that the passions are never necessary to the grasp of truth, and are usually pernicious. I quote it as typical of a prejudice that runs through much of our philosophical tradition:

> But yet, if we would speak of things as they are we must allow that all . . . the artificial

---

[2]On this point there is a longer discussion in my "Fictions," with reference to Plato.

[3]My references to Marcel Proust's *Remembrance of Things Past* will be to the volumes and pages of the translation by C. K. Scott Moncrieff and A. Mayor, as revised by Terence Kilmartin (New York, 1981). In several cases I have retranslated the French myself, in order to bring out more clearly some aspect of the original, but I still give the pages of the Kilmartin edition.

[4]On this comparison and related issues, see my "Fictions" and my *The Fragility of Goodness: Luck and Ethics in Greek Tragedy and Philosophy* (Cambridge, 1986), especially chap. 1, Interlude 1: on Plato see chaps. 5–7.

*and figurative application of words eloquence
hath invented, are for nothing else but to in-
sinuate wrong ideas, move the passions, and
thereby mislead the judgment, and so indeed
are perfect cheat; and therefore . . . they are
certainly, in all discourses that pretend to inform or instruct, wholly to be avoided, and,
where truth and knowledge are concerned,
cannot but be thought a great fault either of
the language or person that makes use of
them. (Essay, bk. 3, chap. 10)*[5]

Notice especially the inference: "move the passions and *thereby* mislead the judgment"; notice
also the explicit claim that the emotive elements
in style have no good or necessary function and
that they can and should be altogether dropped.
Intellect is a sufficient criterion of truth; we
have no other veridical elements. Therefore a
discourse that claims to search for truth and
impart knowledge must speak in the language
of the intellect, addressing itself to (and, as Plato
might say, encouraging the separation of) the
reader's own intellect. Using this view of
knowledge and of discourse as our (somewhat
simplified) target, we can now proceed to explore Proust's counterproposal.

The Cataleptic Impression: Knowledge in Suffering

2. Self-assured and complacent, carrying out
his analytical scrutiny of the heart. Marcel hears
the words, "Mademoiselle Albertine has gone."
Immediately the anguish occasioned by these
words cuts away the pseudotruths of the intellect, revealing the truth of his love. "How much
further does anguish penetrate in psychology,"
he observes, "than psychology itself" (III:425).
The shock of loss and the attendant welling up
of pain show him that his theories were forms

[5]On this passage, see also Paul de Man, "The Epistemology of Metaphor," *Critical Inquiry* 5 (1978):13–30.

of self-deceptive rationalization—not only *false*
about his condition but also manifestations and
accomplices of a reflex to deny and close off
one's vulnerabilities that Proust finds to be very
deep in all of human life. The primary and most
ubiquitous form of this reflex is seen in the
operations of habit, which makes the pain of
our vulnerability tolerable to use by concealing
need, concealing particularity (hence vulnerability to loss), concealing all the pain-inflicting
features of the world—simply making us used
to them, dead to their assaults. When we are
used to them we do not feel them or long for
them in the same way; we are no longer so
painfully afflicted by our failure to control and
possess them. Marcel has been able to conclude
that he is not in love with Albertine, in part
because he is used to her. His calm, methodical
intellectual scrutiny is powerless to dislodge this
"dread deity, so riveted to one's being, its insignificant face so incrusted in one's heart"
(III:426). Indeed, it fails altogether to discern the
all-important distinction between the face of
habit and the true face of the heart.

In various ways, indeed, intellect actively aids
and abets habit, concealing that true face. First,
the guided tour of the heart conducted by intellect treats all landmarks as on a par, pointing
out as salient and interesting many desires that
are actually trivial and superficial. Like the account of social life offered in the parody journal
of the Frères Goncourt (in which the color of the
border on a dinner plate has the same importance as the expression in someone's eyes), intellect's account of psychology lacks all sense of
proportion, of depth and importance. Accordingly, it is inclined to reckon up everything in
terms of the numbers, "comparing the medioc-
rity of the pleasures that Albertine afforded me
with the richness of the desires which she prevented me from realizing" (III:425). This cost-
benefit analysis of the heart—the only comparative assessment of which intellect, by itself, is
capable—is bound, Proust suggests, to miss
differences of depth. Not only to miss them, but

to impede their recognition. Cost-benefit analysis is a way of comforting oneself, of putting oneself in control by pretending that all losses can be made up by sufficient quantities of something else. This stratagem opposes the recognition of love—and, indeed, love itself.[6] Furthermore, we can see that not only the content of the intellectual account but the very fact of engaging in intellectual self-scrutiny is, here, a distorting source of comfort and distance. The very feeling that he is being subtle and profound, that he is "leaving nothing out of account, like a rigorous analyst," leads Marcel into complacency, deterring him from a richer or deeper inquiry, making him less likely to attend to the promptings of his own heart.

What is the antidote to these stratagems? To remove such powerful obstacles to truth, we require the instrument that is "the subtlest, most powerful, most appropriate for grasping the truth." This instrument is given to us in suffering.

Our intelligence, however lucid, cannot perceive the elements that compose it and remain unsuspected so long as, from the volatile state in which they generally exist, a phenomenon capable of isolating them has not subjected them to the first stages of solidification. I had been mistaken in thinking that I could see clearly into my own heart. But this knowledge, which the shrewdest perceptions of the mind would not have given me, had now been

[6]On these issues, see the further discussion in my *Fragility*, chap. 10. On the modification of our emotional life by a belief in commensurability, see chap. 4, parts of which have also been published as "Plato on Commensurability and Desire," *Proceedings of the Aristotelian Society*, supp. vol. 58 (1984):55–80. In a Matchette Lecture. "The Discernment of Perception: An Aristotelian Model for Public and Private Rationality." I have discussed the relationship between Aristotle's attack on commensurability and some models of rationality in contemporary economic theory. Part of this manuscript appears under the title "The Discernment of Perception" in *Proceedings of the Boston Area Colloquium in Ancient Philosophy* I (1985):135–178, with a commentary by Dan Brock.

brought to me, hard, glittering, strange, like a cyrstallised salt, by the abrupt reaction of pain. (III:426).

The Stoic philosopher Zeno argued that all our knowledge of the external world is built upon the foundation of certain special perceptual impressions: those which, by their own internal character, their own experienced quality certify their own veracity.[7] From (or in) assent to

[7]The cataleptic impression is an enormously complex historical issue. For the main ancient sources, see J. von Arnim, *Stoicorum Veterum Fragmenta* I (Stuttgart, 1905), 52–73, and II (1903), 52–70. The most important texts are: Diogenes Laertius, *Lives of the Philosophers* VII (Zeno), 45–46, 50–54; Sextus Empiricus, *Adversus Mathematicos* (hereafter M). VII.227ff., 236ff., 248ff., 426; Cicero, *Academica Priora* II. 18, 77, 144; and Cicero, *Academica Posteriora* I.41. The view I articulate here—that the impression itself compels assent by its own intrinsic character—is the view most commonly taken by the ancient expositors (two of whom, however, are quite hostile to the view). This is surely the idea that Marcel, as a reader of Sextus and of Cicero, would have absorbed. Modern commentators have tried to find in the evidence a more complex and sophisticated position, and it has at least become clear that later Stoics modified the original simple Zenonian view. For discussions of all the evidence, see: J. Annas, "Truth and Reality," in *Doubt and Dogmatism*, ed. J. Barnes et al. (Oxford, 1980), pp. 84–104; M. Frede, "Stoics and Skeptics on Clear and Distinct Impressions," in *The Skeptical Tradition*, ed. M. Burnyeat (Berkeley, 1983), pp. 65–94: J. Rist, *Stoic Philosophy* (Cambridge, 1969), chap. 8; and F. Sandbach, "Phantasia Kataleptike," in *Problems in Stoicism*, ed. A. A. Long (London, 1971), pp. 9–21.

"Cataleptic" is the Greek *kataleptike*, an adjective from the verb *katalambanein*, "apprehend," "grasp," "firmly grasp." It is probably active rather than passive: "apprehensive," "firmly grasping (reality)." In the epigraphs I have translated the associated noun *katalepsis* (the condition of the person who has such an impression) as "certainty." This seems to me appropriate: it brings out the essential point that this person now has an absolutely indubitable and unshakable grasp of some part of reality, a grasp that could not have been produced by nonreality. However, it is important to note that only an orderly system (*sustema*) of such *katalepseis* will constitute scientific understanding or *episteme*.

One further point about these impressions should be borne in mind as we consider Proust's analogue: they can be, and very frequently are, propositional—i.e., impressions *that* such-and-such is the case.

such impressions, we get the cataleptic condition, a condition of certainty and confidence from which nothing can dislodge us. On the basis of such certainties is built all science, natural and ethical. (Science is defined as a system of *katalēpseis*.) The cataleptic impression is said to have the power, just through its own felt quality, to drag us to assent, to convince us that things could not be otherwise. It is defined as a mark or impress in the soul, "one that is imprinted and stamped upon us by reality itself and in accordance with reality, one that could not possibly come from what is not that reality."[8] The experience of having one is compared to a balance scale being weighed down by a very heavy weight—you just have to go along with it; it compels assent.[9] Again, Zeno compares its closure and certainty to a closed fist: it's that firm; there's no room for opposition.[10] It seems to me that Marcel—who elsewhere reveals his serious interest in the Hellenistic philosophers[11]—is working out a (highly non-

Stoic)[12] analogue to Zeno's view for our knowledge of the inner world. Knowledge of our heart's condition is given to us in and through certain powerful impressions, impressions that come from the reality itself of our condition and could not possibly come from anything else but that reality. Indeed he uses explicitly Zenonian language of the way in which we gain self-knowledge through these experiences. He tells us that the impression is "the only criterion of truth" (III:914); that all our understanding of our life is built up on the basis of the text "that reality has dictated to us, whose impression in us has been made by reality itself" (III:914). The cataleptic impressions in this case, however, are emotional impressions: specifically impressions of anguish.

What it is about the impressions of suffering that makes them cataleptic? Why do they convince Marcel that truth is *here*, rather than in the deliverances of intellect? We are conscious, first of all, of their sheer *power*. The suffering is "hard, glittering, strange"; "an anguish such that I felt I could not endure it much longer" (III:425); an "immense new jolt" (429); a "physical blow . . . to the heart" (431); "like . . . a

---

[8]For the definition, see Sextus, *M* VII.248, 426; Sextus, *Outlines of Pyrrhonism* II.4; Diogenes, *Lives* VII.50; and Cicero, *Acad. Pr.* II.18, 77. The point of the last clause seems to be not only that the impression couldn't come from what is altogether unreal or nonexistent but also that it couldn't come from anything else but the very reality that it claims to represent. For the definition of science (*technē*) as a "system of *katalēpseis* ordered together for some useful practical purpose," see reference in von Arnim. *SVF* I.73.

[9]See Cicero, *Acad. Pr.* II.38; cf. Sextus, *M* VII.405.

[10]Cicero, *Acad. Post.* I.41 and *Acad. Pr.* II.144 (*Technē* itself is like a hand grasping the closest fist.)

[11]See Proust, *Remembrance*, especially I:768, where the anxiety aroused in Marcel by the sight of a beautiful girl prompts the following remark:

and I found a certain wisdom in the philosophers who recommend us to set a limit to our desires (if, that is, they refer to our desire for people, for that is the only kind that leads to anxiety, having for its object something unknown but conscious. To suppose that philosophy could be referring to the desire for wealth would be too absurd.)

The connection between setting a limit to desire and the avoidance of anxiety is an individuating feature, promi-

nently stressed, in Hellenistic ethical thought (both Epicurean and Stoic), and in Skepticism as well, with slight variation. (It should also be borne in mind that the Hellenistic philosophers were central in Marcel's curriculum in a way that they are not for us; were read more widely than Cicero and Plutarch above Aristotle, and the Skeptics too enjoyed continuous prominence.) Only a short time after this interesting remark, Marcel meets Albertine.

[12]The true Stoic could never countenance an emotional cataleptic impression. This would come close to being a contradiction in terms, since the Stoics argued that emotions are forms of false judgment. However, as one looks into this more closely, the difference grows narrower. The false judgments with which emotions are identical for the Stoic are judgments about the value of external uncontrolled objects: thus love—*if* we understand by this an emotion involving a high valuation of the loved one, seen as a separate being—is a false emotion in their terms. But it is not at all clear that Marcel's conception of love would be objectionable to the Stoic in this way (see below).

thunderbolt" (431); it makes "an open wound" (425). The power of this impression simply overwhelms every other impression. The superficial impressions of the intellect "could no longer even begin to compete . . . , had vanished instantaneously" (425).

These passages show us that, in addition to sheer force, there are also surprise and passivity. The impression comes upon Marcel unbidden, unannounced, uncontrolled. Because he neither predicts nor governs it, because it simply gets stamped upon him, it seems natural to conclude that it is authentic and not a stratagem devised by self-assuaging reason. Just as the Stoic perceptual impressions drag the perceiving agent to assent not only by their vividness but also by their unbidden and external character—they seem such as could not have been made up; they must have come from reality itself—so too with these emotional impressions. For Proust it is especially significant that surprise, vivid particularity, and extreme qualitative intensity are all characteristics that are systemically concealed by the workings of habit, the primary form of self-deception and self-concealment. What has these features must have escaped the workings of self-deception, must have come from reality itself.

We notice, finally, that the very painfulness of these impressions is essential to their cataleptic character. Our primary aim is to comfort ourselves, to assuage pain, to cover our wounds. Then what has the character of pain must have escaped these mechanisms of comfort and concealment; must, then, have come from the true unconcealed nature of our condition.

We now confront an ambiguity in Marcel's account.[13] He has told us that certain self-impressions are criterial of psychological truth about ourselves. But this picture can be understood in more than one way. On one interpretation, the impression gives us access to truths that could *in principle* (even if not in fact) be grasped in other ways, for example, by intellect. We, perhaps, cannot so grasp them because of certain obstacles in human psychology. But they exist in the heart, apart from the suffering, available for knowledge. Marcel's love is the sort of thing that some superior being—say, a god—could see and know without pain. Pure intellectual knowledge of the heart as it is in itself is possible in principle, apart from emotion; it is not in the very nature of the knowledge itself that it involves suffering. On this reading, Marcel will be taking issue with the intellectualist only about the instrumental means to knowing; also, in some cases, about the content of the knowledge gained. But he will not be taking issue in a fundamental way about what knowing *is*, what activity or passivity of the person constitutes it.

There is, however, another possibility. For the Stoic the cataleptic impression is not simply a route to knowing; it *is* knowing. It doesn't point beyond itself *to* knowledge; it goes to constitute knowledge. (Science is a system *made up of katalēpseis*.) If we follow the analogy strictly, then, we find that knowledge of our love is not the fruit of the impression of suffering, a fruit that might in principle have been had apart from the suffering. The suffering itself is a piece of self-knowing. *In* responding to a loss with anguish, we are grasping our love. The love is not some separate fact about us that is signaled by the impression; the impression reveals the love by constituting it. Love is not a structure in the heart waiting to be discovered; it is embodied in, made up out of, experiences of suffering. It is "produced" in Marcel's heart by Françoise's words (III:425).

This reading is borne out by Marcel's chemical analogy. A catalyst does not reveal chemical compounds that were there all along. It brings

---

[13]This discussion closely follows the treatment of this contrast in my "Fictions," but with some significant changes, especially concerning the relationship between creation and discovery. I now say that there are both creation and discovery on both the particular and general levels, whereas before I said that the particular love was created, the general discovered.

about a chemical reaction. It precipitates out the salt. The salt was not there before, or not in that state or form. The words, like the catalyst, both reveal a chemical structure and create something that was not there in the same way. Françoise's words are like the catalyst. They do not simply remove impediments to scientific knowledge, as if some curtains were pulled back and Marcel could now see exactly what he could have seen before had the curtains not been there. They bring about a change, which *is* the suffering; and this suffering is not so much an object of scientific knowing as an alternative to that knowing. In place of scientific knowing is substituted something that *counts* as knowing himself in a way that the scientific sort of grasping didn't—because it is not a stratagem for mastery of anything, but simply a naked case of his human incompleteness and neediness. Its relation to self-deception is not that of a rival and more accurate account of standing structures in the heart. It *is* the thing from which the deception was protecting him, namely the love, the needy, painful reaching out that is not only a specific condition of his heart now towards Albertine but also a fundamental condition of the human soul.

Marcel is brought, then, by and in the cataleptic impression, to an acknowledgment of his love. There are elements of both discovery and creation here, at both the particular and general levels. Love of Albertine is both discovered and created. It is discovered, in that habit and intellect were masking from Marcel a psychological condition that was ready for suffering, and that, like the chemicals, needed only to be affected slightly by the catalyst in order to turn itself into love. It is created, because love denied and successfully repressed is not exactly love. While he was busily denying that he loved her, he simply was not loving her. At the general level, again, Marcel both discovers and enacts a permanent underlying feature of his condition, namely his neediness, his hunger for possession and completeness. That too was there in a sense before

the loss, because that's what human life is made of. But in denying and repressing it. Marcel became temporarily self-sufficient, closed, and estranged from his humanity. The pain he feels for Albertine gives him access to his permanent underlying condition by being a case of that condition, and no such case was present a moment before. Before the suffering he was indeed self-deceived—both because he was denying a general structural feature of his humanity and because he was denying the particular readiness of his soul to feel hopeless love for Albertine. He was on the verge of a precipice and thought he was safely immured in his own rationality. But his case shows us as well how the successful denial of love is the (temporary) extinction and death of love, how self-deception can aim at and nearly achieve self-change.

We now see exactly how and why Marcel's account of self-knowledge is no simple rival to the intellectual account. It tells us that the intellectual account was wrong: wrong about the content of the truth about Marcel, wrong about the methods appropriate for gaining this knowledge, wrong, as well, about what sort of experience of the person knowing is. And it tells us that to try to grasp love intellectually is a way of not suffering, not loving; a practical rival, a stratagem of flight.

Cataleptic Impressions and the Science of Life

3. Marcel's cataleptic view is a powerful alternative to its theoretical and practical rival. And most of us have had such experiences, in which the self-protective tissue of rationalization is in a moment cut through, as by a surgeon's knife. Zeno's picture seems more compelling, in fact, as a story about emotional knowing than as an account of perceptual knowledge, its intended function. And yet, as we reflect on Marcel's story, mining, as Proust urges, our own experi-

ence for similar material, we begin to feel a certain discontent.

This blind, unbidden surge of painful affect: is it really the "subtle and powerful" instrument Marcel believes it is? Can't it too be deceptive—occasioned, for example, by egocentric needs and frustrations that have little to do with love? Isn't it, moreover, in its very violence and rage—qualities that were important to its cataleptic status—a rather coarse and blunt instrument, lacking in responsiveness and discrimination?

There are several different worries here; we need to disentangle them. They fall into two groups: worries that Marcel has picked the wrong impressions to be the cataleptic ones, and more general worries about the whole cataleptic idea. First, then: if there are cataleptic feelings where love is concerned, why must they be feelings of suffering? We understand why Marcel thinks this: these are the only ones we would never fake. But still, as I consider my own experiences here, I find myself asking, Why not feelings of joy? Or some gentler passions, such as the feeling of tender concern? Why not, indeed, experiences that are more essentially relational in nature—experiences of the exchange of feeling, the mutual communication of emotion; experiences that cannot be characterized without mention of the other person's awareness and activity? If we accept Marcel's claim that our natural psychological tendency is always towards self-insulation and the blunting of intrusive stimuli, then it does seem reasonable to suppose that a feeling of intense suffering wouldn't be there if it weren't in some sense true, an emanation from depths that we usually conceal. But should we accept this story? And even if we do, does it give us reason to think that other feelings could not also have depth?

We notice, further, that if suffering is the only reliable impression where the heart is concerned, and if suffering *is* love, then the only reliable answer to the question "Do I love?" must always be "yes." We can see why

Proust wishes to say this, but it seems peculiar nonetheless. Aren't there possibilities of self-deception on both sides?

This brings us to our second group of questions. Can any feeling, taken in isolation from its context, its history, its relationship to other feelings and actions, really be cataleptic? Can't we be wrong about it and what it signifies? Emotions are not, nor does Proust believe they are, simply raw feelings, individuated by their felt quality alone. Then to be sure that this pain is love—and not, for example, fear or grief or envy—we need to scrutinize the beliefs and the circumstances that go with it, and their relation to our other beliefs and circumstances. Perhaps this scrutiny will disclose that Marcel was simply ill or lacking sleep; perhaps he is really feeling discouragement about his literary career, or a fear of death—and not love at all. The impression does not seem to come reliably labeled with the name of the emotion it is. And even if it is love, can one impression inform him, beyond doubt, that it is a love of Albertine (and not longing for his grandmother, or some more general desire for comfort and attention)? Impressions, in short, require interpretation. And reliable interpretation may well be impossible if we are given only a single experience in isolation. Even an extended pattern might be wrongly understood. But to concede this much is to give up cataleptic impressions.

All this leads us to ask whether Marcel has not been too hasty in (apparently) dismissing intellect and its scrutiny from the enterprise of self-knowing. He may perhaps have shown that it is not sufficient for knowledge of love; he has not shown that it is not necessary. We shall shortly see that Proust later concedes this point—in a limited way.

But now we come upon a deeper criticism, which we borrow from Sextus Empiricus' attack on the Stoic cataleptic impression. This is that Marcel's whole project has about it an odd air of circularity. How do we know love? By a cataleptic impression. But what is this thing, love, that gets known? It is understood to be, is more or less defined as, the very thing that is revealed to us in cataleptic impressions. We privilege the impressions of suffering as the criterion, and then we adopt an account of love (hardly the only possible account) according to which love is exactly what this criterion reveals to us. We suspect that Marcel will not allow love to be something that cannot be cataleptically conveyed, something toward which we cannot have the certainty of the single and solitary impression. We suspect that at the root of his emphatic rejection from the account of love of many aspects of what we usually call love— say, mutuality, laughter, well-wishing, tenderness—is the thought that there is, for these things, no catalepsis. Even so, the Stoic defines the cataleptic impression as "that which is imprinted and impressed by what is real," etc., and then defines "what is real" as "that which produces a cataleptic impression."[14] In this way, the science of life is established on a sure foundation.

Marcel's relation to the science of self-knowledge now begins to look more complex than we had suspected. We said that the attempt to grasp love intellectually was a way of avoiding loving. We said that in the cataleptic impression there is acknowledgment of one's own vulnerability and incompleteness, an end to our flight from ourselves. But isn't the whole idea of basing love and its knowledge on cataleptic impressions itself a form of flight—from openness to the other, from all those things in love for which there is in fact no certain criterion? Isn't his whole enterprise just a new and more subtle expression of the rage for control, the need for possession and certainty, the denial of incompleteness and neediness that characterized the intellectual project? Isn't he still hungry for a science of life?

For consider a remarkable consequence of the project. Proustian catalepsis is a solitary event. This is emphasized in the narrative, where true knowledge of love arrives in Albertine's absence, indeed at a time when, although he doesn't know it, Marcel will never see her again. The experience does not require Albertine's participation or even awareness; it has no element of mutuality or exchange. And it certainly does not presuppose any knowledge of or trust in the feelings of the other. It coexists here with the belief that he does not and cannot know whether she loves him. In fact, the cataleptic experience seems to possess even object-directed intentionality only in a very minimal way. What Marcel feels is a gap or lack in himself, an open wound, a blow to the heart, a hell inside himself. Is all of this really love of Albertine? And isn't it clear that the determination to have cataleptic certainty, together with the recognition that the separateness and independence of the other gives no purchase in the other for such certainty, is what has led him to portray the nature of love in this highly peculiar manner?

The result is actually more disturbing still. We said that the cataleptic impression can coexist with skepticism about the feelings of the other. In fact, it implies this skepticism. For on the cataleptic view an emotion can be known if and only if it can be vividly experienced. What you can't have you can't know. But the other's will, thoughts, feelings are, for Marcel, paradigmatic of that which cannot be had. They beckon to him out of Albertine's defiant, silent eyes at Balbec, a secret world closed to his will, a vast space his ambitious thoughts can never cover.[15] His projects of possession, doomed before they begin, satisfied only in their own self-undercutting—as when he guards a sleeping Albertine, who at that moment no longer eludes him, but who, in having become merely "a being that breathes," does not inspire love either—teach him that the heart and mind of another are unknowable, even unapproachable,

[14]See Sextus, *M* VII.426. A different and extremely interesting account of Marcel's error is in Richard Wollheim, *The Thread of Life* (Cambridge, Mass., 1984), pp. 191ff.

[15]See Proust, *Remembrance* I:847ff.

except in fantasies and projections that are really elements of the knower's own life, not the other's. "The human being is the being who cannot depart from himself, who knows others only in himself, and, if he says the contrary, lies." Albertine can never be for him anything more than "the generating center of an immense construction that rose above the plane of my heart" (III:445). In short: "I understood that my love was less a love for her than a love in me. . . . It is the misfortune of beings to be for us nothing else but useful showcases for the contents or our own minds" (III:568).[16]

This condition is their misfortune; in a sense it is also ours. But skepticism is not just an incidental and unfortunate consequence of Marcel's epistemology. It is at the same time its underlying motivation. It is because this is a suspicious man who can be content with nothing less than full control, who cannot tolerate the other's separate life, that he demands cataleptic impressions and a certainty that the other can never give him. It is because he wishes not to be tormented by the ungovernable inner life of the other that he adopts a position that allows him to conclude that the other's inner life is nothing more than the constructive workings of his own mind. The skeptical conclusion consoles far more than it agonizes. It means that he is alone and self-sufficient in the world of knowledge. That love is not a source of dangerous openness, but a rather interesting relation with oneself.

Catalepsis Ordered by Reflection: Proust's Final View

4. Before we turn away from Proust, we should recognize that this is not Marcel's final word on the knowledge of love. The position he articulates in the novel's last volume complicates the cataleptic view, apparently in response to some

[16]There are many other similar statements; for only a few examples, see Proust, *Remembrance* III:656, 908–909, 950.

of our criticisms. I think we shall see, however, that our deepest worries remain unaddressed.

Intellect, Marcel still insists, must begin its work from unbidden nonintellectual truths, "those which life communicates to us against our will in an impression which is material because it enters through the senses but yet has a spiritual meaning which it is possible for us to extract" (III:912). Intellect, using cataleptic impressions, and above all impressions of suffering, as its basic material, extracts from them the general "laws and ideas" to which they point. We *think* what we had "merely felt" before. Reflection achieves this generality by drawing on a number of impressions and linking them together in an artistic way. "It is our passions which draw the outlines of our books, the ensuing intervals of repose that write them" (III:945).

What truths about love does reflection deliver that would not have been perspicuous in and through feeling alone? First of all, the general form and pattern of one's loves:

A work, even one that is directly autobiographical, is at the very least put together out of several interrelated episodes in the life of the author—earlier episodes which have inspired the work and later ones which resemble it just as much, the later loves being traced after the pattern of the earlier. For to the women whom we have loved most in our life we are not so faithful as we are to ourself, and sooner or later we forget her in order—since this is one of the characteristics of that self—to be able to begin to love again. At most our faculty of loving has received from this woman whom we so loved a particular stamp, which will cause us to be faithful to her even in our infidelity. We shall need, with the woman who succeeds her, those same morning walks or the same practice of taking her home every evening or giving her a hundred times too much money . . . These substitutions add then to our work something that is disinterested and more general. (III:145–146)

But this generalizing power does more: it shows us that love is not simply a repeated experience; it is a permanent structural feature of our soul. "If our love is not only love of a Gilberte (the one who is causing us so much suffering), it is not because it is also love of an Albertine, but because it is a portion of our soul . . . which must . . . detach itself from beings to restore its generality" (III:933). At this level of depth, love unites in itself and shows us the unity in different disappointments and sufferings that we might previously not have called forms of love at all. In reflection we see that the suffering of love and the suffering of travel, "were not different disappointments at all but the varied aspects which are assumed, according to the particular circumstances which bring it into play, by our inherent powerlessness to realize ourselves in material enjoyment or in effective action" (III:911). In other words, we know this love for Albertine as an instance of our loving, and our loving as the general form of our permanent finitude and incompleteness—in this way deriving a far more complete and correct understanding of love than we could have had in the impression alone.

Finally, reflection shows us "the intermittences of the heart"—the alternations between love and its denial, suffering and denial of suffering, that constitute the most essential and ubiquitous structural feature of the human heart. In suffering we know only suffering. We call our rationalizations false and delusive, and we do not see to what extent they express a mechanism that is regular and deep in our lives. But this means that in love itself we do not yet have full knowledge of love—for we do not grasp its limits and boundaries. Sea creatures cannot be said to know the sea in the way that a creature does who can survey and dwell in both sea and land, noticing how they bound and limit one another.[17]

[17]Here I am responding to criticisms of my account of Proust in "Fictions" made at the time of its first presentation, in different ways, by Peter Brooks and Richard Wollheim.

This reformulation of the cataleptic view appears to answer some of our worries: for reflection permits the critical assessment of impressions, their linking into an overall pattern, their classification and reclassification. Proust now concedes that about certain impressions we can be wrong: we do not notice that the pain of travel and the pain of love are one and the same emotion. Interpretation begins to play the role we sought for it. But caution is needed here. First, we still cannot be wrong about *love*. We go wrong only in failing to pick out as love another pain that is really love. The revision that takes place consists in noticing love's ubiquity as *the* basic form of desire, not in becoming more subtle and selective concerning which experiences to count as love. Second, it is essential to notice that the cataleptic impressions of love are still the unchallenged foundations of all knowledge. Reflection and art may fill in the outline; they can never challenge or revise it. "The impression is the only criterion of truth," therefore the only source for truths of reflection (III:914). The emotional impression is to the artist, Marcel continues here, what observational data are to a Baconian scientist: although in some sense the data are not really and fully known until they are integrated into a theory, still the scientist starts from them alone, and relies on them implicitly. Thus the revised view does not really answer our questions about suffering—whether it is the best guide, whether any solitary impression is really evidence of *love*.

And it has a further consequence. The connection between self-knowledge and skepticism about the other is actually reinforced in the complex view. Built upon cataleptic data and trusting these alone, reflection can never penetrate to the thoughts and feelings of the other. And, being reflection, it turns this fact into a theoretical conclusion, an "austere lesson." The greatest courage of the artist. Marcel announces, lies in his or her willingness to acknowledge the truth of skepticism, "abrogating his most cherished illusions, ceasing to believe in the objectivity of that which one has oneself created, and, instead of cradling oneself for the hundredth time with the words, 'She was very sweet,' reading *through* them, "I enjoyed kissing her'" (III:932). Belief in the other is a weakness, a form of consoling self-deception.

And yet, we can hardly help feeling that there is something more consoling still in the austere lesson of solipsism, certified and pinned down and made scientific by the operations of thought. Sextus seems to be right: this view looks more like a wish or a prayer for something than like a statement of truth. And isn't it perhaps a wish for the very thing the intellectualist sought: freedom from disturbance and pain?[18]

Learning to Fall

5. I turn now to a view that shares Proust's criticisms of intellectualism but locates love's knowledge in an altogether different place. It says, in effect, that knowing love is knowing how to go beyond Proustian skepticism and solitude. And how is skepticism to be overcome here? By love.

Unlike Proust's view, this view does not simply substitute for the activity of the knowing intellect some other single and simple inner attitude or state of the person, holding that knowl-

edge consists in this. It insists that knowledge of love is not a state or function of the solitary person at all, but a complex way of being, feeling, and interacting with another person. To know one's own love is to trust it, to allow oneself to be exposed. It is, above all, to trust the other person, suspending Proustian doubts. Such knowledge is not independent of evidence. Typically it is built upon a good deal of attention over time, attention that delivers a lot of evidence about the other person, about oneself, about patterns of interaction between the two. Nor is it independent of powerful feelings that have real evidential value. But it goes beyond the evidence, and it ventures outside of the inner world.

It is in the nature of this view that it is difficult to say much about it in the abstract. Its message is that there are no necessary and sufficient conditions, that knowledge of love is a love story. The best way to explore it seems to be to turn to stories ourselves. We could find it in many places (I think above all of Henry James and Virginia Woolf). But I have chosen instead a contemporary example that exemplifies the view with a remarkable compression and intensity of focus. This is Ann Beattie's story "Learning to Fall"[19] As its title announces, it is the story of a woman who learns to know her own love and not to fear her own vulnerability. I want to let this woman's voice, whose shifting rhythms are themselves part of her emerging knowledge, tell the story as far as possible. So I shall sketch the "plot" crudely, then comment on three passages.

The narrator is a woman in her thirties, a Connecticut housewife, unhappily married to a dry and successful professional man. She had a lover named Ray, in New York. She broke up with him some time before, "when I decided that loving Ray made me as confused as disliking Arthur, and that he had too much power

---

[18]Here I am obviously not pursuing all the relevant aspects of Proust's account of our knowledge of others. Above all, I am not pursuing the claim of the last volume that we *can* have knowledge of the mind of another in one case: we can know the mind of the artist through reading a work of literary art. I therefore ascribe both the simple and the complex cataleptic views to the character Marcel without drawing any official conclusions about Proust's overall view, even of our knowledge of those we love. But I do think it fair to say that the novel as a whole discourages optimism about knowledge of another within personal love and appears to endorse Marcel's solipsistic conclusion, by showing all apparently more hopeful cases of loving to be based upon some kind of self-deception.

[19]Ann Beattie, "Learning to Fall," in *The Burning House* (New York, 1979), pp. 3–14.

over me and that I could not be his lover any-more" (p. 12). Now when she goes into the city, she avoids Ray by taking with her the son of her best friend, Ruth. The boy is a lonely, slightly brain-damaged third grader with a drooping mouth and unusual capacities of perception. This day she takes him to various places in the city, all the while thinking about Ray but not calling him. Then, discovering that she has (perhaps intentionally) made them late for the train back to Connecticut, she does call. He joins them for coffee. The end of this story I shall discuss in detail, but first we need the beginning.

> *Ruth's house, early morning: a bowl of apples on the kitchen table, crumbs on the checkered tablecloth. "I love you," she says to Andrew. "Did you guess that I loved you?" "I know it," he says. He's annoyed that his mother is being mushy in front of me. He is eager to seem independent, and cranky because he just woke up. I'm cranky too, even after the drive to Ruth's in the cold. I'm drinking coffee to wake up. If someone said that he loved me at this moment, I'd never believe him; I can't think straight so early in the morning, hate to make conversation, am angry at the long, cold winter. (p. 3)*

Ruth is the trusting and trusted, the one most capable of love, the one whose poor messy warm house is for the narrator the antithesis of the opulent sterility of her own marriage. ("She earns hardly any money at the community college, but her half-gallons of wine taste better than the expensive bottles Arthur's friends uncork. She will reach out and touch you to let you know she is listening when you talk, instead of suggesting that you go out to see some movie for amusement" [p. 8].) We begin in Ruth's house, situated as by a stage direction, surrounded by her presence. For Ruth, asking a question about love is — can only be — a loving game, a way of saying I love you gently and playfully. "Did you guess," she can ask, be-

cause their whole life is so far beyond guessing. (The boy's father left her abruptly, shortly before the birth, and has had no contact with them since. Even at that, she's "not bitter," just "angry at myself. I don't often misjudge people that way" [p. 9].) The little boy has never thought of asking a real skeptical question. To him all the question means is that his mother's being mushy. "I know it" is the reply the game demands: but for him as for her, it has nothing to do with really seeking for knowledge. He isn't examining his (or his mother's) psychology: he isn't looking for or experiencing any cataleptic anything. He's just eating his breakfast, saying the usual things. Knowledge of love is his whole way of life with his mother. We see that he isn't sure he likes this knowledge. He wants to separate himself, learn not to say those words. He may already think of male adulthood as requiring that repudiation.[20] To repudiate it, however, would not be to discover some new facts about her heart or his. It would be simply to stop playing that game, living that life.

The narrator is a skeptic. She wouldn't believe a claim of love. She wouldn't believe it because she is angry, confused, sleepy, ill-at-ease with conversation. She doesn't have Ruth's grace at touching and being touched. She holds herself to one side, aloof, wondering. She drinks

---

[20] It is perhaps worth mentioning that discussion with Brown University undergraduates (taking my course on Philosophy and the Novel) showed that male students overwhelmingly sympathized with the cataleptic view, while female students stressed the importance of time and a pattern of interaction. (Were they talking about the same phenomenon? Were they, like Marcel, shaping the definiendum in accordance with epistemological convictions? Does the gap between the two groups pose new epistemological problems of its own?) I do not believe at all that one view is in any deep or necessary way a male view and the other a female view. But it may be that the emphasis on autonomy and control in the education of males in this culture leads many of them in the direction of a view of love that promises such self-sufficiency. This is borne out by the portrait of Andrew here. Also see the related observations of Carol Gilligan, in *In a Different Voice* (Cambridge, Mass., 1982).

coffee a lot, and Andrew knows she doesn't eat "during the day" (p. 4). She has to control everything, her thinness, her lover, the time. Always early, hurrying for the train, fascinated with the food she refuses.

This brings me to her watch.

I look at my watch. The watch was a Christmas present from Arthur. It's almost touching that he isn't embarrassed to give me such impersonal presents as eggcups and digital watches. To see the time, you have to push in the tiny button on the side. As long as you hold it, the time stays lit, changes. Take away your hand and the watch turns clear red again. (p. 7).

The watch is impersonal time, time scrutinized, controlled, and intellectualized: the time of the skeptic. (Ruth just takes the time, feeling there's "plenty of" it, hand on your back, not on her watch.) Hand always on the time, she won't let the things happen that take time. It took eight years, she remembers, for Andrew to trust someone other than his mother.[21] Only with Andrew—because she has fun with him, because she "know[s] him so well," because he is not alarming and she pities him—does she take her hands off the watch sometimes, "I almost love him." Her whimsical fantasy of Superman launching himself from the Superman patch on Andrew's knee and flying a foot above the ground, disconcerting the passers by (p. 4)— this has a charm, an unguarded quality of en-

joyment and humor, that we haven't seen in this woman before. It's possibly the first time she hasn't had a thought for herself.

It's after she has been walking down the street with Andrew, swinging hands, that she realizes that they are late. The watch is wrong and she knew it. (It wasn't even good at its impersonal job.) Andrew "thinks what I think —that if I had meant to, we could have caught the train" (p. 11). While she was relying on it to distance her from love, to keep her from that knowledge by precise knowledge, another part of her was using its untrustworthiness to work towards trust of another sort. She goes to a pay phone in Grand Central and calls Ray.

For the intellectualist view, knowledge of love is measured by the clock like everything else. It is in measured time, and it is itself a measuring, assessing activity, very like the measuring of the watch. (It weighed and measured one pleasure against another counting costs and benefits.) Proust shows us how the temporality of the heart breaks with the rhythms of measuring devices. The full story of love—its intermittences, its rhythms of pain and avoidance—can be comprehended only by a reflection that observes the specifically human temporality of desire and habit, which proceeds by its own laws of felt duration. And the blinding moment of cataleptic knowledge, like any other break in the walls of habit, has the feeling of eternity, of the whole of a life: mysterious and momentary, instantaneous yet forever, "hard, glittering, strange," with the precipitous finality of death. It is not a progress or a sequence; it is not a relation evolving over time. In fact, it's because it is not a relation at all—it has really nothing to do with the other, it's a chemical reaction in oneself—that it can have this instantaneous character. Proust moves us from clock time to human time, but to human time that will not take time for things to happen—because they might happen, and then one would perhaps not be alone. Beattie's narrator turns from her digital watch to a different sort of human time—to

---

[21]The story depicts love of a lover as continuous with, and yet infinitely more difficult and risky than, love of the parent. Andrew's difficulty in turning from the safe reliability of home to the outer world of children and strangers is extreme, born of his handicap. But his self-consciousness, unusual for a child, is here an image of what the narrator takes to be true for adult love in general—the difficulty of allowing oneself to be exposed, the fear of being criticized, deceived, and mocked. She doesn't feel any more at home in her body than Andrew does in his, and she too is afraid of being rejected. Also, and more, she is afraid of being accepted.

a trust that evolves over time, that is learned, that must be permitted, in time, through missing a train and taking the time, to happen.[22]

What do we know about this man? More, I find, in the story's ten pages than about Albertine in three thousand. That's already a sign of something. He makes himself felt from the first, long before we see him, as an intrusive, confusing presence—with his soft voice, his laconic speech, his boots, his joy in physical objects, his beautiful hands, and his patience. His sexual power, intense yet gentle, is everywhere she goes—the Guggenheim, the loft in Soho, the station phone booth. From the beginning this is a story about two people, the story of a knowledge that resides in the other and in the space between them. "I used to sleep with him and then hold his head as if I believed in phrenology. He used to hold my hands as I held his head. Ray has the most beautiful hands I have ever seen." She's using the present tense, watching them. "Want to stay in town?" he says (p. 12).

The moment that's comparable to and so different from Proust's is precipitated by the boy,

catalyst with a Superman patch on his knee—omnipotence, a foot above the ground. They are sitting in a restaurant booth. Andrew is eating as always, drinking a milkshake. More coffee for her. Ray wanted a drink, but he has to put up with coffee. The story ends this way:

> *Andrew shifts in the booth, looks at me as if he wants to say something. I lean my head toward him. "What?" I say softly. He starts a rush of whispering.*
>
> *"His mother is learning to fall," I say.*
> *"What does that mean?" Ray says.*
> *"In her dance class," Andrew says. He looks at me again, shy. "Tell him."*
> *"I've never seen her do it," I say. "She told me about it—it's an exercise or something. She's learning to fall."*
> *Ray nods. He looks like a professor being patient with a student who has just reached an obvious conclusion. You know when Ray isn't interested. He holds his head very straight and looks you right in the eye, as though he is.*
> *"Does she just go plop?" he says to Andrew.*
> *"Not really," Andrew says, more to me than to Ray. "It's kind of slow."*
> *I imagine Ruth bringing her arms in front of her, head bent, an almost penitential position, and then a loosening in the knees, a slow folding downward.*
> *Ray reaches across the table and pulls my arms away from the front of my body, and his touch startles me so that I jump, almost upsetting my coffee.*
> *"Let's take a walk," he says. "Come on. You've got time."*
> *He puts two dollars down and pushes the money and the check to the back of the table. I hold Andrew's parka for him and he backs into it. Ray adjusts it on his shoulders. Ray bends over and feels in Andrew's pockets.*
> *"What are you doing?" Andrew says.*
> *"Sometimes disappearing mittens have a way of reappearing," Ray says. "I guess not."*

---

[22]On the importance of time for the trust required in love and friendship, see Aristotle, *Nicomachean Ethics* 1156b25ff. See also Stanley Cavell's reading of *It Happened One Night* in *Pursuits of Happiness* (Cambridge, Mass., 1982), chap. 2. Several motifs in Cavell's discussion of this film intersect with the reading of Beattie here: see particularly the discussion of eating. Diogenes tells us that Zeno, famed in general for iron self-control, didn't like to be publicly associated with the humbler bodily functions. To cure him of this shame, the Cynic philosopher Crates

gave him a potful of lentil-soup to carry though the Ceramicus: and when he saw that he was ashamed and tried to keep it out of sight, with a blow of his staff he broke the pot. As Zeno took to flight with the lentil-soup flowing down his legs. Crates said, 'Why run away, my little Phoenician? Nothing terrible has befallen you.'" (*Lives* VII.3, trans. Hicks, with my revisions)

Diogenes also reports that at parties Zeno liked to sit at the far end of the couch, so as not to be too near others (VII.14).

Ray zips his own green jacket and pulls on his hat. I walk out of the restaurant beside him, and Andrew follows.

"I'm not going far," Andrew says. "It's cold."

I clutch the envelope. Ray looks at me and smiles, it's so obvious that I'm holding the envelope with both hands so I don't have to hold his hand. He moves in close and puts his hand around my shoulder. No hand-swinging like children—the proper gentleman and the lady out for a stroll. What Ruth has known all along: what will happen can't be stopped. Aim for grace. (pp. 13–14)

She knows what Ruth knew all along: what will happen can't be stopped. But what this means is that she lets herself not stop it, she decides to stop stopping it. She discovers what will happen by letting it happen. Like Ruth, slowly falling in the class exercise that teaches and manifests trust, she learns to fall. As Andrew says, she doesn't just go plop (as Marcel did, abruptly plunging): she gently, slowly yields to her own slow folding, to the folding of his arm around her. She lets that touch not startle her. Like Ruth's bodily fall and, as she sees, like prayer, it's something done yet, once you do it, fundamentally uncontrolled; no accident, yet a yielding; an aiming, but for grace. You can't aim for grace really. It has so little connection, if any, with your efforts and actions. Yet what else can you do? How else are you supposed to pray? You open yourself to that possibility.

Is this discovery or creation? Both, we have to say. A pattern is there already; it vibrates through the story. The final moment has the conviction, the power, the crazy joy it does because it is the emerging of something that has been there all along and has been repressed. We can talk of self-deception here just as we could in Marcel's case, because she has been denying the power Ray continuously exerts over her imaginings and her actions. Andrew knew

about her what she denied to herself. But of course she is loving Ray now as she didn't before. Love feared and avoided is not just sitting there beneath the skin waiting to be laid bare, any more than Ruth's slow fall Platonically inhabits the narrator's stiff, thin, coffee-drinking body. It has to be created. The removal of self-deception is also a change in the self. Both discovery and creation are present on the general level too, as she both finds a vulnerable and passionate side of herself that had been denied and makes herself evolve into a more trusting woman. She decides to let those elements flourish, be actualized.[23]

The cataleptic view has its role to play inside these experiences. There's no doubt that she was missing him, that she missed the train because she was missing him. There's no doubt either of the power of her arousal, and also her fear, when he reaches across the table and takes her hand. All this has some role in her knowledge of love, and the power of those impressions is a part of what prepares her love. But that's the point: they prepare it, they aren't it. The knowing itself is a relation, a dizzy elated falling. There are powerful feelings here—sexual feelings, feelings, I think, of profound joy and nakedness and giddiness and freedom: the feelings of falling. But he's too intrinsic to it all for us to say that those feelings just *are* the falling, the loving. The loving is about him, an opening toward him; as prayer in her image, would be an opening toward God. She could also say that faith is a certain strong feeling in the region of the heart. Proust's prayer, the cataleptic prayer, is that this should be all there is to say.

[23]I have been asked whether this story and the view I find in it depend on Ray's being this sort of secure, strong, (apparently) non-neurotic person, towards whom she can safely quite simply fall. Could we talk of falling, and so forth, if he was as complex and neurotic as she? The answer, I believe, is yes; we could in that case speak of learning to fall on both sides. But then it would have to be a much longer story.

Knowledge of her own condition and knowledge of him are inextricable here. Not in the sense that she has succeeded in doing phrenology, in getting a scientific account of his head that's beyond doubt. Not in the sense that she possesses his experiences or feels them herself. She could be wrong, that's clear. Evidence is not for nothing, either in her view or in ours about her. It's not for nothing that she has this history with him, that she knows how he makes jokes, that he has waited so patiently for her. But none of this puts her, or us, beyond doubt of him. Ruth misjudged someone and was betrayed. Faith is never beyond doubt; grace can never be assured. The enterprise of proving God's existence has little to do with it. You aim for it by not asking to prove it. What puts her beyond doubt is the absence of the demand for proof, the simple fact that she allows his arm to stay around her back. (We must add: in this she allows herself to be tender and attentive toward him, to notice and respond to what he is doing, in a way that she hadn't before, caught up as she was in her own anxiety.)

I find myself returning again, as I consider this pair, to their jokes, to the entire role of jokes and humor in separating this view of love from Proust's. Ray thinks it is very important to make this woman laugh. "You know what, lady?" he says, after his first success; "I do better amusing you over the phone than in person" (p. 12). He knows, as we do when she laughed then (for the first time in the story), that her laughter is a yielding, a surrender of that tight control. And at the end her yielding comes in a smile, responding to his smile. She shares with him the joke of her own tightness as she holds the envelope so she doesn't have to hold his hand. The "proper gentleman and the lady out for a stroll" are, I imagine, laughing together (as that phrase indicates, so comically inappropriate for an improper, adulterous woman and her lover with his black boots and his language so unlike Arthur's — yet so appropriate, too, to their gentleness with one another, to their relationship that goes so far beyond eggcups and digital watches) — laughing at the comedy of control and uncontrol, self-sufficiency and yielding. Laughter is something social and relational, something involving a context of trust, in a way that suffering is not. It requires exchange and conversation; it requires a real live other person — whereas Marcel's agonies go on in a lonely room and distract him from all outward attentions. To imagine love as a form of mourning is already to court solipsism; to imagine it as a form of laughter (of smiling conversation) is to insist that it presupposes, or is, a transcendence of solipsism, the achievement of community.[24] It is worth adding here: we imagine that this pair have a happy sexual life together, whereas Marcel's view implies that there is really nothing but masturbation. "The beings whom we love . . . are nothing but a vast vague space where we can externalize our own desires" (III:505). As Cary Grant once said, "Why that's no good. That's not even conversation."

And why do we trust Ray, and not wonder who he is really, with his boots and his ballet tickets, what his intentions really are? Because we follow her. For that matter, why do we trust her? Why do we suppose without doubt that she is telling us the truth? Because, like her, we have learned to fall. Reading a story is like that. Like her love, it takes time; you learn it from childhood. And if your mother asked you, "Did you guess that that character was really feeling what I said she was?" you'd be as amused, or mystified, or annoyed, or embarrassed as Andrew at the breakfast table. . . .

[24]Cf. Cavell, *Pursuits*, esp. chap. 2, pp. 80ff., and also the chapter on *The Philadelphia Story*, from which film the remark at the end of this paragraph is quoted.

28

ALLEN STAIRS
Quantum Mechanics, Mind, and Self

In 1961, the physicist Eugene Wigner published an essay called "Remarks on the Mind–Body Question." I will have more to say below about the contents of Wigner's essay, but for the moment, the title of the collection in which Wigner's essay appeared is more significant: *The Scientist Speculates: An Anthology of Partly-Baked Ideas*.[1] There is a warning there that applies equally to this essay, and that the reader should take seriously: all of this is half-baked. It *has* to be. Quantum mechanics is puzzling enough in its own right. Trying to draw out any implications it might have for the philosophy of mind is a more than usually speculative enterprise.

Before we can get anywhere at all, we will have to spend some time talking about quantum mechanics itself, and especially about the concept of *superposition*. My guess is that many of you have very little familiarity with quantum mechanics, let alone superposition, and I will try hard to keep that in mind in what follows. But for those of you who already know a little or even a lot, let's make a sort of shopping list of topics that will hint at what comes later. Quantum mechanics has variously been seen as providing arguments for the splitting (and remerg-

[1]I. J. Good (ed.), Heineman, London (1962) pp. 284–302. My references to Wigner will be to the reprint of the essay in *Quantum Theory and Measurement*, John Archibald Wheeler and Wojciech Hubert Zurek (eds.), Princeton (1983), pp. 168–181.

ing) of the self, for some form of mind–body dualism, for the dependence of the universe on the existence of minds, and has even been seen as having theological implications of one sort or another. For those who like to speculate, quantum mechanics provides plenty of material. So speculate away. But pause every once in a while, poke your fork into the dough, and take a good look at what sticks to it when you pull it out.

You won't go too far wrong if you begin by thinking of quantum mechanics as the physics of the very small—of electrons, atoms, molecules, and such. In fact, quantum mechanics also has important implications for middle-sized bodies and ultimately even for the structure of the whole universe. But quantum effects are most pronounced at the level of the microcosm. The entities that make up the world at that level are very different from what classical physics and our experience with ordinary objects would lead us to expect.

Classical physics is the physics of Isaac Newton—Newtonian mechanics. In classical *and* quantum physics, the concept of the *state* is very important. The state of a body in Newtonian physics is given by saying what position it occupies and what its momentum is (momentum being just mass times velocity). If we have a collection of bodies (for example, the planets and the sun), then the state of the whole collection is given by setting forth the position and momentum of each one of them. The state changes deterministically in classical physics: given the state of a collection of bodies at a particular moment of time, and given the forces acting on them, the equations of classical physics determine the state at every other moment. So the classical world is a world in which things have a definite character and in which change takes place in accord with completely rigid laws.

Quantum mechanics is like this in some ways, and very different in others. We can talk about the state of a quantum system (i.e., one or more electrons, protons, or whatnot in various combinations), though we will see that this has a rather strange meaning. Given the state of a quantum system, and given the forces acting on it, there is a deterministic law that tells us what the state will be at any other time. So far, so much the same. But in classical physics, we specify the state of a particle by giving its momentum and position. In quantum mechanics, there are no allowable states that do both at once. If a quantum state is highly specific about the momentum of a particle, it will be extremely vague about its position, and vice versa. This may lead you to ask why we don't just combine a state description that is precise about position with one that is precise about momentum. The answer, in a nutshell, is that the theory will not let us. We can't say what we want in a form that fits the equations of quantum mechanics. This may suggest that we simply need to find some way of expanding the theory—of getting it to include more detailed state descriptions. This is a large topic, but for now I will simply remark that this may very well be impossible in principle, and one symptom of this is reflected in measurement. If I try to *measure* the precise position and the precise momentum of a quantum system at the same time, I will be unable to do so.[2] And things get worse. Our earlier remark

that quantum states change deterministically needs to be qualified: quantum states change deterministically *only so long as you don't look.* This odd remark will take a bit of explaining.

Rather than talking about position and momentum, let's talk about a purely quantum mechanical property called *spin*. Although quantum spin is in some mathematical respects like the spinning of a top, there are important differences, and there is no clear way of "picturing" electron spin. On the other hand, spin can be measured. If I pick a particular direction in space, call it *x*, I can measure the component of the spin of an electron in that direction. I will always get one of two possible results, either "up" or "down." (The fact that there are only two possibilities, rather than the infinitely many I would expect for a classical spinning body, means that spin is *quantized*. It also is part of the difficulty in "picturing" spin.) Although the spin doesn't completely specify the electron's state, for some purposes we can proceed as though it did. In fact, let's introduce some shorthand. We will let $|x_+>$ represent the state in which the electron has spin up in direction *x*, and let $|x_->$ represent the state in which the electron has spin down in direction *x*, and we will use a similar notation for other directions. Now suppose we have an electron in the state $|x_+>$, and we measure the spin component in direction *y*, where *y* is at right angles to *x*. The theory doesn't tell us what will happen. What it *does* tell us is with a certain probability, we will find spin up, and with a certain probability we will find spin down.

What should we make of the fact that the theory won't allow us to predict the electron's spin? Here is one common suggestion: Like a classical spinning body (think of a globe, for instance), an electron has a preferred axis of spin. With a classical spinning body, knowing the quantity of spin around the preferred axis determines how fast the body is spinning around any other axis. Because quantum spin is "quantized," however, things are different with

---

[2]There is some controversy about this, but in the end, nothing that matters for our purposes will turn on it.

electrons. If an electron is definitely spinning "up" around the x axis, then it doesn't have a definite spin around the y axis. Rather, if you *measure* the spin in direction y, the electron will randomly flop its spin axis onto the new direction either up or down. The state $|x_+>$ will transform suddenly into either $|y_+>$ or $|y_->$, but exactly which is a matter of chance.

In fact, there is a way of calculating the chance. The states $|x_+>$, $|x_->$, etc., behave like the vectors that you studied in high school math and physics: You can multiply them by numbers, and you can add and subtract them. It so happens that the "state vector" $|x_+>$ can be written as a sum of $|y_+>$ and $|y_->$:

$$|x_+> = 1\sqrt{2}|y_->.$$

We say that $|x_+>$ is a *superposition* of $|y_+>$ and $|y_->$—a concept about which we will have much more to say. If our electron starts out in state $|x_+>$, and hence if its spin is definitely up in direction x, then we derive the probability of finding spin up in direction y by taking the number $1\sqrt{2}$ that multiplies $|y_+>$ and squaring it. This gives ½, or 50 percent. Similarly, we find the probability of seeing spin down in direction y by taking the number that multiples $|y_->$—in this case, also $1\sqrt{2}$—and squaring. Thus, we get the same probability of ½. If y had not been perpendicular to x, the numbers would have been different, but the principle would have been the same. So on the present suggestion, the numbers that multiply $|y_+>$ and $|y_->$ are measures of the strength of the electron's disposition to jump into one of the states $|y_+>$ or $|y_->$ on measurement.

It is crucial not to confuse the state $|x_+> = 1\sqrt{2}|y_+> + 1\sqrt{2}|y_->$ with a case in which the electron is either definitely in the state $|y_+>$ or definitely in the state $|y_->$, but we don't know which. Unlike a particle in state $|x_+>$, a particle that is *either* in state $|y_+>$ *or* in state $|y_->$ is not guaranteed to have spin up in direction x. Superpositions are *not* cases in which we are simply ignorant of which of the superposed states

really describes the system, and this difference has experimental consequences.

The interpretation of spin measurements described above is often spoken of as positing the *collapse of the wave-packet*, or the *collapse of the state*. We will call it the *quantum jump* interpretation, because it says that sometimes the quantum state jumps discontinuously from one state to another. The quantum jump interpretation may sound reasonable at first. However, it accounts very badly for some situations. One of the most famous problem cases is Schrödinger's cat. Imagine we have a box containing a cat, a tiny bit of radium, and a geiger counter. The geiger counter is hooked up to a Rube Goldberg device that will break open a capsule of poison gas if the geiger counter clicks. We seal the box and wait. Simplifying greatly, we can say that there are two possible states for the cat: alive (which we will write as $|cat_+>$) and dead ($|cat_->$). And there are two possible states for the radium: decayed ($|rad_+>$) and undecayed ($|rad_->$). When we seal the box, its contents are in a state that we can write as $|cat_+>|rad_->$— cat alive and radium undecayed. What does quantum mechanics say about later times? Suppose the probability is 50 percent that if we looked after one minute, we would find that the radium had decayed, and thus 50 percent that it would not have decayed. If we *don't* look, then what quantum mechanics tells us is that after one minute the quantum state is the superposition

$$|\Psi> = 1\sqrt{2}|cat_+>|rad_-> + 1\sqrt{2}|cat_->|rad_+>.$$

This means that if *we looked*, there would be a probability of ½, i.e., $(1\sqrt{2})^2$, that we would find a live cat and undecayed radium, and a probability of ½ that we would find a dead cat and decayed radium. But remember! This state is a superposition. Quantum mechanics does *not* say that there is a 50 percent chance that the state is $|cat_+>|rad_->$ and a 50 percent chance that it is $|cat_->|rad_+>$. Rather, quantum mechanics says that (so long as we don't look) the state after one minute will be the strange amalgam $|\Psi\rangle = 1\sqrt{2}|cat_+\rangle|rad_-\rangle + 1\sqrt{2}|cat_-\rangle|rad_+\rangle$. But now we have a problem. The quantum jump story applied to electron spin said that if the state of an electron is $|x_+\rangle = 1\sqrt{2}|y_+\rangle + 1\sqrt{2}|y_-\rangle$, then the spin of the electron is neither up nor down in direction y, but rather, the electron has a certain propensity to jump into an up or down state for y when we "look" — when we make a measurement. Applying this reasoning to the present case, we would have to say that if the state of the cat-plus-radium is $|\Psi\rangle = 1\sqrt{2}[vt.cat_+\rangle|rad_-\rangle + 1\sqrt{2}|cat_-\rangle|rad_+\rangle$, then the cat is neither alive nor dead (and the radium neither decayed nor undecayed), but the total system has a certain propensity to make a quantum jump into a state in which the cat is alive and the radium undecayed and a certain propensity to make a jump into a state in which the cat is dead and the radium decayed if we open the box and look. However, this seems crazy. Whatever we may want to say about something as esoteric as radioactive decay, surely the cat is either alive or dead, *whether or not* we look!

This suggests a different interpretation of quantum states and quantum probabilities. Return to the electron. Perhaps what we should say is that if the state is $|x_+\rangle = 1\sqrt{2}|y_+\rangle + 1\sqrt{2}|y_-\rangle$, the electron really *does* have a definite spin in direction y. It is just that the state $|x_+\rangle$ doesn't fix the spin in other directions: quantum mechanical systems are somehow "looser" than classical systems. What the coefficients of $|y_+\rangle$ and $|y_-\rangle$ tell us is the distribution of spin values in a large ensemble of electrons. More precisely, the coefficient of $|y_+\rangle$ is $1\sqrt{2}$. The square of this number gives us a statistical prediction.[3] Roughly, it means that in a very large collection of electrons, all in state $|x_+\rangle$, approximately 50 percent of them, would have spin up in direc-

tion y. We interpret the coefficient of $|y_-\rangle$ similarly.

We will call this the *statistical interpretation of quantum states*.[4] With this view we can solve the problem of Schrödinger's cat. The state

$$|\Psi\rangle = 1\sqrt{2}|cat_+\rangle|rad_-\rangle + 1\sqrt{2}|cat_-\rangle|rad_+\rangle$$

gets interpreted in terms of ensembles. It tells us that in a very large collection of duplicates of the cat experiment, about half the boxes would contain live cats and undecayed radium, while the other half would contain dead cats and decayed radium. And this would be true whether or not we looked. This may sound as though it ignores our earlier remarks about the difference between superpositions and mere ignorance of the state. It doesn't. It amounts to saying that we can't confuse *having a certain property* with *being in the corresponding quantum state*. In this view, there are more facts about quantum systems than the quantum state alone discloses. If the state says that an electron has a certain property with certainty, then it has the property. Thus, if the state is $|x_+\rangle$, the electron definitely has spin up in direction x. But even though the state only assigns a probability of $\frac{1}{2}$ to spin up in direction y, the electron may still have this property. In other words, on this view, a quantum state does two things: it picks out a particular definite property, say spin up in direction x, and assigns it to the system, *and* it provides a particular set of statistics for other properties.

The statistical interpretation is tempting, but it is subject to tremendous technical and conceptual problems. A particularly intriguing difficulty has to do with the phenomenon of *interference*. Here we need to talk about a striking experiment called the *two-slit experiment*. The set-up is simple. We have a barrier with two small slits, appropriately arranged, and on the

---

[3]Technically, the square of the *norm*, since in quantum mechanics we sometimes have complex coefficients

[4]I would add, however, that there are many views called "the statistical interpretation," and some of them differ crucially from this one.

Figure 1
After Niels Bohr.

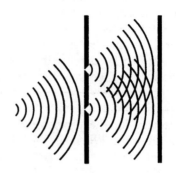

Figure 2
Also after Bohr.

other side of the barrier at an appropriate distance there is a photographic plate. First we cover one hole and shine a beam of light against the barrier. The result will be a beam of light spreading out from the uncovered hole and leaving a blur on the photographic plate, a blur that is most intense in front of the hole, and shades off gradually. Figure 1 should give the rough idea.

If we cover the first hole, open the second, and install a new photographic plate, the result will simply be the mirror image of what we just described. If we open both slits, however, the pattern on the plate will not just be the "sum" of the patterns; it will exhibit a distinct pattern of interference fringes. This is not puzzling by itself. Light as we usually conceive of it is a wave phenomenon. When both slits are open, two waves head toward the plate. They can reinforce and cancel one another at various points, and that is how classical physics explains the interference pattern. Figure 2 suggests the general idea.

The beam of light that reaches the plate when both slits are open is a *superposition* of two different beams. (It is no coincidence that the same word "superposition" is used here as for the combining of quantum states.) The photographic plate will look something like Figure 3.

The connection this has with our problem comes out when we consider what quantum mechanics has to say about light. Light comes in discrete clumps, or "quanta," called *photons*. We can turn the intensity of the source of light down so low that only one photon is emitted at a time. Each single photon that makes it past the barrier will hit the plate at a definite (though unpredictable) spot, leaving a single dot on the developed plate. But over time, a pattern will build up. And that pattern will be like Figure 3. But this is puzzling. Since the photon ends up in one spot, it presumably only goes through one hole. So how does the interference pattern arise?

Figure 3
Bohr once more.

Here we have the famed "wave-particle duality" of quantum mechanics. Single photons behave like particles in some ways, but they somehow interfere with themselves. The same, in fact, can be said for electrons: The two-slit experiment can be done with electrons, and the results will be the same. How this happens is a mystery that won't be solved here. Rather, I want to draw out the implications of the two-slit experiment for the problem of understanding quantum states. When slit no. 1 is the only one open, we would assign a certain definite quantum state to any photon that got past the barrier. Let us denote this state by $|1\rangle$. When slit no. 2 is the only one open, we would once again assign a definite quantum state to any photons that got past the barrier. Let us call this state $|2\rangle$. When *both* slits are open, however, we don't say that the photon is either in state $|1\rangle$ or state $|2\rangle$, but we don't know which; rather, the photon is in state

$$|\Phi\rangle = 1\sqrt{2}|1\rangle + 1\sqrt{2}|2\rangle.$$

(Actually, the numbers will depend on the exact details of the arrangement, but let's keep things simple.) A beam of photons in state $|\Phi = 1\sqrt{2}|1\rangle + 1\sqrt{2}|2\rangle$ is not the same as a beam of photons, half of which are in state $|1\rangle$, and half of which are in state $|2\rangle$. The physical effects that arise when both slits are open suggest that there is a genuine contribution from each of the states $|1\rangle$ and $|2\rangle$—that the coefficients don't represent simply the degree of our ignorance about which slit the electron went through, but represent the "contribution" of two distinct possibilities to the final, actual state of affairs.

There is some intriguing metaphysics here, but rather than savor the puzzle, let's see how the two-slit experiment bears on our earlier problems. We tentatively rejected the quantum jump interpretation because it seemed to imply that before we looked, Schrödinger's cat was neither alive nor dead, and this seemed ridiculous. So we moved to the statistical interpretation of the state: the state provides the statistics

of the way in which properties (such as spin up or down in direction y) would be distributed in large ensembles. However, the two-slit experiment suggests that things can't be so simple. The superposition $|\Phi\rangle = 1\sqrt{2}|1\rangle + 1\sqrt{2}|2\rangle$ seems to involve some real contribution from both $|1\rangle$ and $|2\rangle$; it seems to be a genuine amalgam of these states and not just a way of expressing our ignorance about what is really going on. But if this is so, the coefficients in $|x_+\rangle = 1\sqrt{2}|y_+\rangle + 1\sqrt{2}|y_-\rangle$ don't just represent the degree of our ignorance; they represent the "contribution," however that is to be understood, of the states $|y_+\rangle$ to the state $|x_+\rangle$. In that view, however, it is as though in the state $|\Psi\rangle = 1\sqrt{2}|cat_+\rangle|rad_-\rangle + 1\sqrt{2}|cat_-\rangle|rad_+\rangle$, the actual state of affairs in the unopened box is a ghostly mingling of cat-alive and cat-dead.

But when we look, we see no ghosts! The cat is either alive or dead! So it is. This may suggest that the cat is different in some crucial respect from the photon—that quantum mechanics doesn't apply to cats in the usual way. In the end this may be so, and we will return to the point later. On the other hand, it isn't just obvious that cats aren't quantal. The problem of Schrödinger's cat is just a particularly striking example of the general problem of understanding superpositions. We can raise difficulties about electrons themselves that are just as puzzling to common sense.

There is another problem with the statistical interpretation of quantum mechanics, and even though it is rather abstract, it is worth talking about briefly. It is that the statistical interpretation is inconsistent, at least in its most obvious version. Briefly, when we examine the mathematics of the way in which quantum mechanics represents various physical quantities, it appears that there ought to be various connections among the values of different quantities— even, in some cases, between quantities that can't be measured simultaneously. These connections have the result that for quantum systems of even modest complexity, there are no consistent assignments of values to all the quantities. In a little more detail, there might be a quantity Q with, say, three different values, say +1, −1, and 0. As I attempt to relate its values to other quantities, I need to make certain assumptions at each stage in order to preserve consistency. But these assumptions accumulate in such a way that if, for instance, I start out by saying that $Q = +1$, I end up having to say that $Q = −1$, and surely both can't be true at once! If we try to work out the statistical interpretation in full detail, the quantum world starts to look like an Escher print in which one and the same part of the drawing must be assigned inconsistent properties as we try to make sense of the whole. So the statistical interpretation appears to collapse into inconsistency, at least if we read the apparent connections among different physical quantities in the most "natural" way.[5]

There are variations on all these themes and nuances of interpretation that we have ignored, but you have seen enough to see that quantum mechanics is a deeply puzzling theory. What is probably less clear is what any of this has to do with problems in the philosophy of mind. We now turn to that question.

Recall where our troubles began. Quantum mechanics makes statistical predictions about what will happen when we make measurements, but when we try to interpolate a story about what is going on at the deep level, we run into severe difficulties. These difficulties all have a common source. It is the existence of *superpositions*—of states like $|\Phi> = 1\sqrt{2}|1> + \frac{1}{2}|2>$. For classical waves such states abound. For classical particles, they make no sense. (What would it mean for a classical particle to be in a superposition of position states?) But quantum systems are not classical waves, and

they are not classical particles. A cynic might say that they embody the worst of both. One reaction to these difficulties is to deny that quantum mechanics is anything more than a calculating device for predicting the statistics of experiments. However, even this retreat isn't entirely satisfactory. Presumably there is *something* going on out there behind the experiments, even if we don't know just what. And (partly for reasons I haven't gone into) the fact that quantum mechanics is so successful empirically already gives us reason to suspect that whatever the world is really like, it is far stranger than we might have expected. So intellectual courage suggests that we make a stab at making sense of superposition. But immediately upon setting this course, we run into something puzzling.

If there is anything that is clear about the actual application of quantum mechanics to the world, it is that experiments have results. If I measure an electron's spin, I will either find it to be up or down, or, at worst, it will fail to register (due, perhaps, to the inefficiency of my equipment). But quantum mechanics leaves *this* puzzling. A measuring instrument, after all, is simply a big physical device. Ultimately, it is composed of subatomic particles. So in principle, it seems, quantum mechanics ought to be able to give an internal account of measurement; classical physics certainly can do this. The difficulty is that the very same problems of superposition that have dogged us all along come back to haunt us when we consider measurement from the point of view of quantum mechanics. Suppose I intend to measure the spin of an electron in direction y, and I intend to do so by a bit of gadgetry that will register the result with a red light for spin up and a blue light for spin down. The device starts out in some (huge) quantum state which we will simply call $|$ready$>$, indicating that the device is "ready" to make a measurement. The two states that are relevant to the outcome will be written as $|$red$>$ and $|$blue$>$. (I am ignoring the case in

---

[5]This is essentially the content of Kochen and Specker's no-hidden-variable theorem. See S. Kochen and E. P. Specker, "The Problem of Hidden Variables in Quantum Mechanics," *Journal of Mathematics and Mechanics* 17 (1967) 59–87.

which we don't get an answer. From the internal point of view of quantum mechanics, it won't help.) If the electron begins in the state $|y_+>$, then the electron + device will end up in the state $|y_+>|red>$. If the electron begins in the state $|y_->$, then the electron + device will end up in the state $|y_->|blue>$. But what if the electron starts out in the state $|x_+> = 1\sqrt{2}|y_+> + 1\sqrt{2}|y_->$? The laws of quantum mechanics as embodied in the *Schrödinger equation* tell us that the electron + device must end up in the state

$$|\Phi> = 1\sqrt{2}|y_+>|red> + 1\sqrt{2}|y_->|blue>.$$

By now, we are quite familiar with the problems of states like $|\Phi>$ above. They seem either to require quantum jumps, or else to require the statistical interpretation, and neither seems to work. But perhaps there is an escape. Perhaps there is something special about *us*, so that when we look at the device, we no longer have a superposition.

Here the problem is that we ourselves seem to be very complicated physical systems. We start out as very complicated but thoroughly physical bits of genetic material and grow from there. So it seems that we are just other measuring devices. Suppose, then, that we add *you* to the story. After the measurement is made, you look at the result. If you are essentially just a complicated physical object subject to the laws of quantum mechanics, Schrödinger's equation tells us to replace the state $|\Phi>$ just set forth with the state

$$|\Phi'> = 1\sqrt{2}$$
$$|y_+>|red>|"red"> + 1\sqrt{2}$$
$$|y_->|blue>|"blue">.$$

Here $|"red">$ and $|"blue">$ are states in which you see either a red or a blue light, respectively. The reason that this is the correct state is that the laws of quantum mechanics have a property called *linearity*, which doesn't allow us to get from a superposition to a nonsuperposition. Nonetheless, we know that *you* will see either a red or a blue light.

We seem to have reached a branch point. If we maintain that the laws of standard quantum

mechanics are universally valid—in particular that Schrödinger's equation is universally valid—then we have great difficulty explaining how measurements can have results. But if we deny the universal validity of Schrödinger's equation, we need to find some acceptable replacement, or at least an acceptable general story about how the failures come about. Otherwise, or so the story goes, we are simply making an ad hoc move to get ourselves out of trouble. So what can we do?

I want to begin with the most extravagant answer to the question. It is called the *many worlds interpretation*, and it is due to the physicists Hugh Everett III and John Wheeler.[6] If the Schrodinger equation is correct, then after you look at the measuring device in the spin experiment, the wave function has two terms:

$$1\sqrt{2}| y_+>| red>"red">$$
$$\text{and}$$
$$1\sqrt{2}| y_->| blue>| "blue">.$$

According to the many-worlds interpretation, the universe has literally branched! There is one branch corresponding to $|y_+>|red>|"red">$ and another corresponding to $|y_->|blue>|"blue">$. But if that is so, then your consciousness has split! So if the many worlds interpretation is true, quantum mechanics has truly startling implications for our concepts of self and personal identity. Fission of the self—a possibility that philosophers had considered only as a conceptual device for testing the limits of our notion of personal identity—would be an everyday occurrence.

This may seem to be a fatal objection to the many-worlds interpretation. We simply have no experience of the fissioning of our "selves," and neither do the physicists who perform the exotic experiments of quantum mechanics. But this objection rests on a misunderstanding. What

[6]Everett's original paper, entitled "'Relative State' Formulation of Quantum Mechanics," appeared in *Reviews of Modern Physics* 29 (1957) 454–462. A very useful nontechnical presentation can be found in Paul Davies' book *Other Worlds* (1980), first published by J. M. Dent and Sons Ltd. The paperback by Touchstone appeared in 1982.

would our experience be like if the many-worlds interpretation were true? The answer is that it would be just as it actually is. The many-worlds interpretation is intended as an *interpretation* of quantum mechanics. It is intended to make sense out of the way things actually *are* if the theory is true. The reason we are not aware of a fissioning of our consciousness is that the branches don't coexist in one space–time. Under normal circumstances, the branches don't interfere with one another. And the circumstances in which they do are so rare and remote as to be of no practical interest.

What are the advantages of this view? For one thing, it allows us to keep the laws of quantum mechanics, in particular Schrodinger's equation, intact. It simply requires a very striking understanding of those laws. For another, it explains the appearance of quantum jumps. Within each branch, you, or your continuant, will observe a definite result, and thus it will seem as though a quantum jump has occurred. But the original superposition will still persist. Finally, this interpretation goes some way to making sense of the idea that a superposition is an amalgam of the superposed states.

The most obvious *apparent* disadvantage of the view is its metaphysical extravagance. In fact, this isn't a very convincing objection by itself. If quantum mechanics is true, then *whatever* the world is like, it is very strange. My worries about the many-worlds interpretation are humdrum and technical. The many-worlds interpretation provides a rule for telling us how the world will branch. But it turns out that the rule is very sensitive to the details of the physics. In the case of *ideal* "perfect" measurements, the universe will branch in just the way we want to solve our problem: There will be a well-defined branch corresponding to each outcome of the experiment.[7] However, no real-world

measurements are ideal. And for nonideal measurements, the rule for determining the "axes" of branching would leave each branch as a *superposition* of measurement results. Thus, suppose we want to measure the spin of an electron in direction x. If our measurement is ideal, then the branching rule of the many-worlds interpretation gives us what we want. The world will divide into two branches. In one, there will be a spin-up electron and a measuring instrument that *says* the spin is up. In the other, there will be a spin-down electron, and a measuring instrument that says the spin is down. But *no* actual measurements are ideal. In a real-world measurement, the branching rule would create two branches, each of which is a *superposition* of the states in which the electron has spin up and the apparatus says it has spin up with the state in which the electron has spin down and the measuring device says it has spin down. So the many-worlds interpretation doesn't explain the fact that real-world measurements have results![8]

We turn, then, to a different thought. By now, it should be clear that all of the problems we have seen are a result of the existence of quantum superpositions. To be a little more precise, the problem arises from a combination of the superposition of states and the rules of the quantum mechanical game, which always take us from one damn superposition to another. But there is one case of superposition that cries out for special attention: the superposition of mental states. The state =

$$| \Phi> = 1\sqrt{2}|y_+>|\text{red}> = 1\sqrt{2}|y_->|\text{blue}>$$

---

[7]Actually, there is a technical problem here: if the coefficients of the expansion of $|Y>$ contain any duplication, there will be no clear answer to the question of which way things will branch. But I waive that problem, since it might be argued that the set of cases in which this actually occurs is a set of measure zero.

[8]For those familiar with the technical details, what I have in mind is this. The obvious "rule" for determining branching is to use the bi-orthogonal decomposition of $|\Psi>$, and let each vector in this decomposition determine a branch. But in real-life measurements, there will always be *some* probability, however low, that the answer we get is "incorrect." That is, the correlation between eigenstates of the measured observable and states of the measuring device will be imperfect. So the bi-orthogonal decomposition will *not* be in terms of the indicator states of the measuring device.

only makes sense—indeed, can only be written down—if there are superpositions of |red> and |blue>. But likewise, the state

$$|\Phi'> = 1\sqrt{2}$$
$$|y_+>|red>|''red''> + 1\sqrt{2}$$
$$|y_->|blue>|''blue''>$$

only makes sense if there are superpositions of the *mental* states |''red''> and |''blue''>.

The possibility that we may undergo fission by the splitting of worlds is striking, but for my money, it is metaphysically tame beside the possibility that our mental states superpose. However, if we are going to take this stranger possibility seriously, we need to look at it more closely.

The first question, perhaps, is why we might believe it. We already suggested the answer earlier. Our bodies, it seems, are just complicated collections of quantum systems. To this we can add that our mental life seems to be grounded in and inextricably tied to our physical side—particularly to our brains and nervous systems. So on the face of it, it seems hard to escape the idea that we are governed by the laws of physics, and in particular by the laws of quantum mechanics. Whether this argument is strong enough to do its job is something we will return to. Right now, another question is more urgent.

What would it mean for two mental states to be in superposition? The most blunt response is that there is nothing *for* this to mean. Focus on the cognitive states—belief, doubt, etc. What would it *mean* to be in a state of superposition between believing, say, that the next president will be a Republican and that the next president will be a Democrat? Notice that being uncertain about which will happen is *not* a superposition of these two states. For one thing, if it really were a superposition, then we would expect it to have the character of standard superpositions. If I measure the y spin of a particle in state $|x_+>$, I get a definite answer, though I can say only with some probability what the answer will be. If uncertainty about the politics of the next president were a matter of superposition, then when

you "measured" by belief, presumably by getting me to state it honestly, I would say either "Republican" or "Democrat." But that is precisely what I *won't* do if I am uncertain. There seems to be no independent reason to treat uncertainty or indecision as a superposition of belief states. More generally, there is probably a continuum from firm belief to strong disbelief, and various shades of doubt and uncertainty occupy various points on the continuum. But the mere fact that belief states are graded—come in degrees—is not in any way nonclassical. We can program computers to model states of indecision, and at the program level, computers are thoroughly classical.

Let us carry this analogy with the computer a little further. One of the growth industries of the present-day intellectual world is the so-called *computational theory of the mind* in cognitive science. A little too crudely, the aim is to think of the operation of the mind on the model of the running of a *program* in a computer. Now the structure of programs, and more importantly, the "logic" of a computational view of the mind, is thoroughly classical. There is no room in our usual conception of a computer program for the superposition of two different computational states. And to the best of my knowledge, there is no room for anything of this sort in the "computational paradigm" that many people working in cognitive science are pursuing.

How does this bear on our problem? Suppose the computational approach to the mind is essentially correct and suppose this implies that there are no superpositions of mental states. In that case, there is no such state as

$$|\Phi'> = 1\sqrt{2}$$
$$|y_+>|red>|''red''> + 1\sqrt{2}$$
$$|y_->|blue>|''blue''>.$$

because such a state requires the possibility of superposing the mental states |''red''> and |''blue''>. But in that case, we get a quantum jump. The argument, in outline, is as follows. In general, measurement is treated as a process in which certain states of the measured object are correlated with certain states of the measuring device. When the states of the measuring device can be superposed, the correlation takes the form of a superposition. But when they can't, we will have to settle for the next best thing. And that will be a "mixture" of states. That is, the superposition will disintegrate into one or another to two distinct states, but we won't be able to predict which beforehand. Or more precisely, the superposition

$$|\Phi> = 1\sqrt{2}|y_+>|red> + 1\sqrt{2}y_->|blue>$$

may occur, but it will disintegrate when the physical system couples with a mind, because the superposition

$$|\Phi'> = 1\sqrt{2}|y_+>|red>|"red"> + 1\sqrt{2}|y_->|blue>|"blue">$$

can't exist. Thus, the end state will be either $|y_+>|red>|"red">$ or $|y_->|blue>|"blue">$, in this case, each with probability ½.

If this is correct, then it is not so much that quantum mechanics has implications for our view of the mind as that our view of the mind has implications for quantum mechanics. The facts about our minds require that the usual laws of quantum mechanics break down at a certain point. Something like this view was argued by Eugene Wigner in the article referred to in the opening paragraph of this essay, and more generally has been part of a tradition of interpretation that goes back at least to von Neumann's 1932 *Mathematical Foundations of Quantum Mechanics*. I want to turn first to Wigner's argument.

Wigner begins his argument with a striking statement. He writes: "Until not many years ago, the 'existence' of a mind or soul would have been passionately denied by most physical scientists"—the implication being that this is no longer so (or, at least, wasn't in 1961, when the article was written). The main reason offered by Wigner for the acceptance of mind by the physicists is that "it[is] not possible to formulate the laws of quantum mechanics in a

fully consistent way without reference to consciousness."[9] At the most general level, the view lying behind this comment is that quantum mechanics is not a theory about the "quantum world"; rather, it is a theory about the probabilistic connections among our *impressions*. This may sound like mere bad philosophy. It isn't. Without endorsing Wigner's view, it is important to understand that it grows out of the peculiarities of quantum mechanics itself. In classical physics *and* in quantum physics, when we make a measurement, our state of knowledge changes, and the predictions that we make about future measurements are thereby changed. But in classical physics, we can treat the change of our knowledge as just that—as coming to know something that was already true, but that we simply didn't know before.[10] Furthermore, in classical physics, we can use classical physics itself to describe the process of measurement in a way that makes clear why measurements have definite results. However, as our discussion of superposition should have made clear, it is hard to see how we can say anything like this about measurement in quantum mechanics.

Wigner's specific point about consciousness is this: When we come to know something about a quantum mechanical system as a result of making a measurement, this alters the predictions that we make about future measurements—it brings about a change in the statistics. Corresponding to this change in the statistics will be a new quantum state in which the old superposition is resolved into one if its components. (For instance, a transition from

$$|\Phi> = 1\sqrt{2}|y_+>|red> + 1\sqrt{2}|y_->|blue>$$
$$\text{to just}$$
$$|y_+>|red>.)$$

But this is a "quantum jump"; it is just the sort

[9]Wigner, p. 168. See note 1 for the complete reference.

[10]For the mathematically sophisticated, we can treat classical *statistical* states as statistical mixtures of pure states, and we can treat the change in a statistical state that comes about through measurement as mere conditionalization.

of change that Schrödinger's equation can't predict. Now we could blame the change on the measuring device itself, but the measuring device is clearly just a large physical device, and Wigner strongly suspects that we will be forced to say in the end that *all* ordinary physical systems are subject to the laws of quantum mechanics. So the change of state is apparently a result of our becoming *conscious* of the outcome of the measurement. Thus, reference to consciousness appears to enter physics in a fundamental way.

This is the first half of Wigner's point: the laws of physics must make reference to consciousness. Wigner goes on to argue that consciousness *influences* physical processes. This would seem to be implicit in what he has already said, but Wigner elaborates by considering the case in which you make a measurement by, in effect, having a *friend* make the measurement and then asking him what the result was. If we treat the friend merely as another physical system, you might believe that the state of electron + apparatus + friend was

$$|\Phi'> = 1\sqrt{2}|y_+>|red>|''red''> + \\ + 1\sqrt{2}|y_->|blue>|''blue''>$$

before you asked the friend for a result. *You* complete your measurement by asking the friend what he saw. Suppose he says "I saw a red light." At that point, you conclude that the state of electron + apparatus + friend is $|y_+>|red>|''red''>$. But then you ask the friend, "What were your impressions like before I asked you?" The friend will reply "I already told you. I saw a red light." Unless you are prepared to give yourself an exalted place in the universe, you will conclude that the friend *already* had reduced the superposition, before you asked. So Wigner concludes that consciousness —yours or anyone else's—has an influence on matter. Note that this gives us a way of holding the "quantum jump" interpretation. Quantum jumps occur only in special circumstances: when a quantum system interacts with a conscious being. And note that this gives us a reply

to the original objection to the quantum jump interpretation. Schrödinger's cat, being a conscious being, will not end up in a superposition.

I want to emphasize that this argument is fraught with uncertainty. In many ways, understanding quantum measurement is *the* central problem in the foundations of quantum mechanics, and there is nothing like agreement about how it ought to be solved. In particular, there is no general agreement that quantum states change as a result of measurement, even though it *is* admitted that the result so measurement can't be predicted by applying Schrödinger's equation. But let us leave this aside and press Wigner's argument further. Does it prove the existence of an independent, nonphysical *entity*—a separate mind or soul? In spite of some of his remarks, it isn't at all clear that Wigner intends the argument this way. For one thing, Wigner certainly doesn't deny that consciousness has a physical basis. He writes "it is very likely that, if certain physical-chemical conditions are satisfied, a consciousness, *that is, the property of having sensations, arises*" (italics mine).[11] Wigner also refers to the physical conditions as the *substrate*.[12] This doesn't suggest a separate mental *substance* so much as the view that consciousness is a surprising *property* of our bodies, brains or what not. What makes the property surprising is that systems that possess it don't follow the usual laws of quantum mechanics.

We now have two arguments for the conclusion that mind is relevant to quantum mechanics. Both seem to be to be problematic, but for different reasons. Wigner's is problematic because it begins from an assumption that, even though it is not just gratuitous, is very controversial: that quantum mechanics makes essential reference to consciousness. In the end, we may be forced into this position, but there is a venerable tradition of attempts to avoid it. The problem with the argument from the computa-

[11]Ibid., p. 175.
[12]Ibid., p. 175.

tional theory is different. Let us grant for the moment that there are no *mental* states that are superpositions of other mental states. This is a view that might be shared by many accounts of the mind, and has nothing in particular to do with computationalism. But it simply doesn't follow that there are no *states* that are superpositions of mental states. An analogy: we can't superpose position states and get another *position* state. But we *can* superpose position states. So for the argument from the computer view of the mind (or any other theory of the mind) to establish that Schrödinger's equation breaks down, we would need the stronger thesis that mental states don't superpose, *period*.

Perhaps we could argue that no states of the *self* are superpositions of other states of the self. But how would we establish this? Here is one possible approach. The self is always in one of two states: conscious or unconscious. There is no reason to think that unconscious states are superpositions of conscious states. But by our earlier considerations, there is no reason to think that any *conscious* states are superpositions of conscious states. So no states of the self are superpositions.

I hope no one is persuaded by this! To begin with, why believe that there are only two sorts of mental states, conscious and unconscious? Trivially, I suppose, there are these two sorts of states: those of which we are aware, and those of which we aren't. But it is not clear that we are *aware* of all conscious states — after all, we don't introspect continuously — and thus, it is not clear that all states of which we are unaware are unconscious states in the usual sense of "unconscious." We can go further. Whatever virtues the computational approach may have, there are other ways of looking at the mind, or at least some of its aspects, and these other ways should make us hesitate before simply attributing a classical structure to the mind. Abner Shimony[13] has pointed to various characteristics of

mentality that are at least suggestive of superposition.[13] One phenomenon is perceptual vagueness, which is reminiscent of the fact that in a superposition, quantities seem to have indefinite values. Another is the possible role of what Freud calls the "preconscious," which even seems to involve superposition-like phenomena, "for instance," as Shimony writes, "the image of a parent and that of a spouse may be superposed."[14]

In fact, Shimony is skeptical that any of this amounts to genuine superposition in the sense of quantum mechanics. One reason is that for mental states to exhibit quantum mechanical superposition, they would have a certain definite mathematical character, and the vague *analogies* with quantum superposition that we have noted do not rise to anything like that level of precision. Nonetheless, there is a caution here. Given how rudimentary our understanding of the mind remains, and given our bafflement about the nature of quantum superposition, we should be leery of simply claiming that the mind has a thoroughly classical structure, and that there is no such thing as superposition of mental states. But there is another sin of which we should be equally wary. That is the sin of unthinking reductionism — in particular, of thinking that all phenomena can and must be explained in terms of the fundamental laws of physics.

Recall the reason noted above for the claim that mental states can be superposed. It was that our mental life seems to be well and thoroughly grounded in our bodily, especially our neurophysiological, functioning. But our bodies are just large and complex arrangements of quantum systems, and so are subject to Schrödinger's equation and the principle of superposition. If this were treated as a strict argument, it would have to be counted as a fallacy: The ultimate constituents that make up our bodies are each subject to the laws of quantum mechanics; therefore, the resulting assemblage is

[13]"Role of the Observer in Quantum Theory," *American Journal of Physics* 31 (1963) 755–773.

[14]Ibid., p. 760.

subject to the laws of quantum mechanics. Compare this with a more patent fallacy: The ultimate constituents that make up our bodies are not living; therefore, the resulting assemblage is not living. Unfortunately, even if we admit that this argument is, strictly speaking fallacious, we can't simply dismiss its conclusion. That is because it is part of quantum mechanics to tell us, at least in principle, how to do the physics of large collections of quantum systems, and quantum mechanics is very successful at this job. Macroscopic phenomena explained by quantum mechanics include the behavior and growth of crystals, superconductivity, and the functioning of your solid state TV set. Indeed, it seems to be of the nature of fundamental theories in physics that they try to be all-encompassing.

We are in tricky territory. The ambitions of fundamental physics may be global, and perhaps even necessarily so. Furthermore, it is not as though physics has no goods to back up its ambitions. But does that mean we should simply acquiesce in reductionism? Interestingly enough, there is a fair amount of consensus that the answer is no. Without in any way trying to summarize the debate, let me give a (somewhat idiosyncratic) account of reasons for this.

There are two sorts of ways in which we might understand the claim that all empirical facts are ultimately explainable in terms of physics. One is a claim about the relationships among various *sciences*, the other claim about reality itself. The first way would be to say that sciences such as chemistry, biology, psychology, and economics can ultimately be reduced to the science of physics. This would presumably mean that the laws of these higher-level sciences could be derived from the laws of physics, together with appropriate background assumptions. This is the claim about which people are most skeptical. Most *actual* higher-level sciences have a high degree of autonomy from physics. To mention just one problem, the basic concepts and categories of higher-level sciences

are far removed from physics, and have no obvious theoretical connection with physics. This seems obvious enough in the case of concepts such as *species* in biology, but is even more glaring in the case of an economic concept such as *inflation*.

The topic of theoretical reduction is an interesting one, but we will pursue it no further. Many philosophers would claim that we can do without reduction and make our point with the more ontologically inclined thesis of *supervenience*.[15] The idea can be put crudely but simply as follows: There can be no difference at a higher level (say, at the psychological level) without a difference at the physical level. The difference between supervenience and reductionism is that reductionism requires the existence of all manner of "bridge laws" and other connections that in effect permit the higher-level theory to be derived from the lower-level theory. Supervenience doesn't ask for any of this. It merely says that differences at higher levels (psychological, economic, etc.) depend in some unspecified way on differences at the level of physics. This makes supervenience seem like a way of having your cake and eating it too.

What does supervenience tell us about the superposition of mental states, or more broadly, of states of the self? Let's try to proceed by example. Consider the two states |"red"> and |"blue"> (i.e., *seeing* that the light is red versus *seeing* that it is blue) discussed above. Supervenience does *not* require us to say that there is some *one* physical state that corresponds to |"red"> and another that corresponds to |"blue">. There would no doubt be very many different physical conditions that would amount to my being in the state |"red"> and very many that would amount to my being in

---

[15]For an excellent discussion of supervenience, see Paul Teller, "A Poor Man's Guide to Supervenience and Determination," *Southern Journal of Philosophy* 22 (1984), Supplement: Spindell Conference) 137–159.

the state |"blue"⟩. Furthermore, the physical states that would amount to my seeing that the light is red might be a diverse and motley lot form the point of view of physics. (The same goes, of course, for |"blue"⟩.) So even as an approximation, it might not make sense to talk of *the* physical state that is a superposition of |"red"⟩ and |"blue"⟩. But nonetheless, there would be a collection (probably infinite) of physical states such that if any one of them held, I would be in the state |"red"⟩, and a collection of physical states (again, probably infinite) such that if any of *them* held, I would be in the state |"blue"⟩. Further, these sets of states would have no members in common. And if these are "ordinary" quantum states, then any state in the first set could be superposed with any state in the second set. So in this roundabout way, we come to the conclusion that any particular way of being in the state |"red"⟩ could be superposed with any particular way of being in the state |"blue"⟩. But what this would be like or what implications it has for our view of ourselves is something that I think we don't understand *at all*. Consequently, the relationship between mind and microphysics is still a mystery.

In spite of this, the thesis of supervenience has considerable charm. It is no doubt true that economics can't be reduced to physics. In fact, it can't be reduced to psychology either. But our sense is that even if this is so, economic facts depend, in some sense, on quite ordinary facts about the behavior of individual and groups. In particular, we can't make sense of the idea that there could be two societies that were indistinguishable at the purely physical and behavioral level, but different economically—say, one undergoing inflation, the other not. This suggests that we think economic facts, for instance, supervene on facts at lower levels. Nonetheless, there are limits to how far this gets us. It *may* be true that the mental supervenes on the physical. Part of the problem is that the notion of "the physical" is extremely amorphous. Chairs, for

instance, are clearly physical objects. So are electrons, protons, and such. But this would remain so *even if the facts about chairs did not supervene on the facts about elementary particles and fundamental forces.* This is a point that is highly significant for our purposes. What is at issue is not whether the mental supervenes on the physical. What is at issue, if you will, is whether the mental supervenes on the *quantum mechanical*. The two questions aren't the same. Furthermore, oddly enough, quantum mechanics helps us understand *why* they aren't the same.

Let's consider a different supervenience thesis. Jaegwon Kim points out that much of our thinking on matters of supervenience is deeply rooted in the idea that wholes are completely determined by their parts—that if you made an atom-for-atom copy of an object, the result would be an object that was an exact duplicate of the first object at *all* levels. But it is a striking fact about quantum mechanics that on one natural reading, this thesis is false *even for a single pair of electrons.* This is just one more manifestation of superposition. The example that has been studied most extensively is the so-called *singlet* or *spin-zero* state of two electrons. Here is how it works. Suppose we have two electrons, one in state $|x_+⟩$, the other in state $|x_-⟩$. Then the pair is in state $|x_+⟩|x_-⟩$, and the total spin is zero in direction x. The same would be true if the first electron were in state $|x_-⟩$ and the second in state $|x_+⟩$, giving us an overall state of $|x_-⟩|x_+⟩$. But now consider the superposition:

$$| \Psi⟩ = 1\sqrt{2}| x_+⟩| x_-⟩ - 1\sqrt{2}| x_-⟩| x+⟩.$$

This state doesn't specify a definite spin for the first electron, nor for the second. It is not a mere "product" or "conjunction" of states of the two electrons. Rather, it is irreducibly a state of the pair itself. Here is how the state works. Suppose you pick *any* direction d, and measure the spin of one of the electrons in that direction. Then I measure the other electron's spin in the same direction *d*. I will get the opposite result—e.g., "+" if you got "−"—no matter how far apart the electrons are. This might lead you to think that there is a simple explanation: each electron already had a spin in direction *d*, and in every other direction. It is just that the spins are oppositely aligned. Unfortunately, this explanation won't work. If we assume that the electrons already have spins, this leads to certain statistical predictions for cases in which the spin measurements on the two electrons aren't made in the same direction. As it turns out, however, quantum mechanics gives predictions incompatible with this assumption, and nature bears quantum mechanics out. Thus, we have a very strange situation. If two electrons are in the singlet state, then their total spin is zero *in every direction*. Nonetheless, neither electron has a definite spin *in any direction*.

What I have just done is to give a very brief, qualitative statement of a famous result known as Bell's theorem. Although the proof is extremely simple, I won't reproduce it here.[16] What matters for our purposes is this: the singlet state is irreducibly a state of the *pair* of electrons. The information it contains simply cannot be thought of as a summing up of facts about the individual electrons. Thus, even in this extremely simple case, the facts about the whole are not determined by the facts about the parts, and thus, an intuitively plausible supervenience thesis turns out to be false.

What is the significance of this? Here we need to be careful. On the one hand, the result should drastically weaken our intuitive tendency to accept supervenience principles. An "obvious" supervenience principle fails at a

[16]There are many excellent elementary accounts of Bell's Inequality. I will mention just one: it is N. David Mermin's "Quantum Mysteries for Anyone," *Journal of Philosophy 78* (1981) 397–408. For some interesting more general philosophical discussion that explicitly invokes the concept of supervenience, I would direct your attention to Paul Teller, "Relation Holism and Quantum Mechanics," *The British Journal for the Philosophy of Science 37* (1986) 71–81.

very low level of complexity: the facts about pairs of quantum systems simply do not supervene on the facts about the individuals. On the other hand, this failure of supervenience is not a surprise from within quantum mechanics; it is built into the very mathematical structure of the theory. Consequently, it is not a license to claim that the whole is greater than the sum of its parts whenever this suits our taste. But if there is anything that is made clear by the history of the attempts to make sense of quantum mechanics, it is that the relationship between the microworld, in which quantum mechanical superposition is the order of the day, and the everyday world, from which it appears all but absent, is deeply mysterious. When this fact is combined with the general difficulties that stand in the way of reductionism, we are simply in no position to claim that the facts about our mental life supervene on facts about the microworld. On this question the jury is out, and is likely to stay out for a long time.

Suppose, then, that the mental does not supervene on the quantum mechanical. Where does that leave us? As we have already noted, it doesn't necessarily mean that there is a separate mental *substance*, detached from ordinary physical things. More likely, it would mean that mentality involves higher-order *properties* that are unpredictable from within quantum mechanics. This does not mean that mental properties would float free of physics. The quantum mechanical facts would no doubt constrain the mental. But just as the singlet state has consequences for the behavior of the individual electrons, even if it doesn't supervene on the facts about them, so the mental might have consequences for the quantum level in general, even if it doesn't supervene on that level. In particular, if the mental doesn't supervene on the quantum mechanical, this *could* enter into an explanation of how quantum superpositions sometimes collapse, and hence of why measurements have definite results.

I am not claiming that this is actually so, but I

don't think we have reason enough to deny it. For the moment, I want to talk about an apparent odd consequence of the view that the mental affects the physical by bringing about the collapse of the wave function. There is a variant of the two-slit experiment due to John Wheeler that is called the *delayed choice experiment*. In this variant, we can choose *after the photons have passed the barrier* whether to observe the interference pattern, or to find out which slit the photon went through. As Wheeler sees it, this amounts to saying that we can decide *after the fact* whether the photon went through one slit or both, and that there is no fact of the matter before an observation is made. His view is summed up by a tidy slogan: "No elementary phenomenon is a phenomenon until it is a registered (observed) phenomenon."[17] But as Wheeler sees it, this means that we live in a universe in which the observer participates in the very coming-into-being of the past! And while this may delight you or appall you, it is surely a lot to swallow.

However shocking this idea of Wheeler's may seem on the surface, when it is examined a little more closely it takes on a different character. In the first place, Wheeler is very clear about one thing. He is *not* saying that it is *consciousness* that is responsible for this "coming-into-being" of the past. What he is saying is that certain facts are not definite until there is what he calls "an irreversible act of amplification,"[18] and this would include such nonconscious processes as the blackening of a photographic plate. This suggests something that has no doubt occurred to many of you already: In spite of Wigner's remarks, it is not at all clear that mentality per se has anything to do with the problem of superposition, even though the problem may raise interesting questions about mentality. The problem, rather, has to do with some ill-defined and ill-understood distinction

between a purely quantum level and some other level that may not be purely quantal. The other point is that Wheeler's language in explaining his slogan is actually very guarded, and is seen by Wheeler himself as a development of the "Copenhagen interpretation" of Niels Bohr, one of the founders of quantum mechanics. Bohr's writings on this subject are notoriously obscure, and just what the Copenhagen interpretation really amounts to is a question much too big to be taken up here. However, at least in the version that Wheeler presents, it seems to be a way of saying that physics doesn't really tell us about reality as such. Superficially, the delayed choice experiment makes it sound as though we literally *cause* the past in some robust, physical sense, but that is almost certainly a bad interpretation. Let us look more closely at some of the things Wheeler actually says.

First, it is worth remarking that the word "phenomenon," which Wheeler takes over from Bohr, is reminiscent of the philosopher Kant. For Kant, "phenomena" were, roughly speaking, things *as known by us*. This is borne out in such remarks of Wheeler's as "we are inescapably involved in bringing about that which *appears* to be happening" (emphasis mine).[19] He writes

> In the delayed choice version of the split-beam experiment, for example, we have no right to say what the photon is doing in all its long course from point of entry to point of detection. Until the act of detection the phenomenon-to-be is not yet a phenomenon.[20]

In fact, Wheeler says that "what we call 'reality' . . . consists of an elaborate papier maché construction of imagination and theory fitted in between a few iron posts of observation."[21] The central idea seems to be this. We can pose certain questions to nature by performing certain

---

[17]Wheeler, op. cit., p. 184.
[18]Ibid., p. 185.

[19]Ibid., p. 185.
[20]Ibid., p. 185.
[21]Ibid., p. 195.

experiments. These experiments will issue in "phenomena," which allow us to talk about nature in certain ways. Had we asked different questions, we would have brought different and incompatible phenomena into being. But this doesn't seem to mean, in Wheeler's view, that we are literally creating nature, past and present. Rather, we, with the help of nature, are bringing about "what we have the right to say"[22] about nature.

I remarked when we were discussing Wigner that his attempt to bring consciousness into the very formulation of quantum mechanics was not just bad philosophy. I want to say the same thing about Wheeler's "participatory universe." What Wheeler's lyrical rhapsodies and Bohr's tortured prose both point to is the extreme difficulty of giving a satisfactory realist interpretation of quantum mechanics—of finding a way to see it as telling us the true story of an independent quantum world. Of course, if quantum mechanics resists a realist interpretation, then the question of the relationship between quantum mechanics and the mind might seem to be moot: if quantum mechanics isn't really telling us something about the world as it is in itself, then it doesn't have anything to say about the nature of those aspects of the world that we describe in the vocabulary of mentality.

In fact, I suspect that this is too simple. If quantum mechanics continues to be successful, then if we decide that quantum mechanics can't be interpreted as telling us about an independent, real world, we would be in the interesting position of having deep scientific reasons for thinking that science isn't telling us how things are in themselves. Here we have reached a never-never land of nebulous speculation. In spite of this, I would like to venture a little further.

In the last fifteen or more years, a philosophical view has come into vogue that has obvious resonances with these speculations about quan-

tum mechanics. Especially as developed by Hilary Putnam[23] and Nelson Goodman[24] the view emphasizes the idea that there are many distinct ways of representing the world. And on Putnam's view, this stress on distinct representations is combined with an understanding of *truth* in terms of what we can *know*. Now quantum mechanics as understood along the lines suggested by Wheeler and, ultimately, Bohr, might seem to provide the clearest and most convincing examples of this idea.[25] We can put certain questions to nature. When we do, we will get answers. But the answers will depend on the kind of question asked, and the answers to different questions will not fit together into a unified whole—to use a phrase of Putnam's they will not form a "common text." Thus, I can talk about an electron in terms of position, and I can come to know its position. *Or* I can talk about it in terms of momentum and come to know *that*. But I can't know both, nor even *ascribe* both a position and a momentum to the electron at the same time. As Putnam would almost certainly stress, this sounds like an extreme and especially precise example of the idea that there are distinct, incompatible, but *equally valid* ways of representing the world.

This has a suspiciously relativist sound about it. I will confess that my overall philosophical sentiments are realist and antirelativist. Putnam thinks that people like me are committed to the existence of the "one true theory." And it is certainly true that belief in one great, overarching, internally consistent, independently true theory would be one way of avoiding relativism. But I will also confess a lot of sympathy for the idea that there may be distinct ways of look-

---

[22]Ibid., p. 194.

[23]See, for example, *Reason, Truth and History*, Cambridge: Cambridge University Press (1981).

[24]See *Ways of Worldmaking*, Hackett (1978).

[25]Indeed, Putnam explicitly defends a view of quantum mechanics along these lines in "Quantum Mechanics and the Observer," *Erkenntnis* 16 (1981) 193–219, although he insists that his view differs from the Copenhagen interpretation.

ing at the world that are "equally valid," but don't fully mesh with one another. So I would like to see if there is any way in which these two tendencies can somehow be reconciled.

In certain ways, the answer is yes. If you don't believe in reductionism, but you do believe in some sort of supervenience thesis,you already believe something of this ilk. You may think that cognitive psychology is a perfectly good scientific discipline that is telling us true and important things about the mind. You may also not believe that there is the slightest hope for mapping the categories and laws of cognitive psychology onto the categories and laws of physics. But you may believe that the facts described by cognitive psychology supervene on physical facts. I'm not saying whether this is right or wrong. But it *is* a view that is held by many people who think of themselves as realists.

On the other hand, one might have some suspicions. No doubt there are lots of connections between facts at various levels. But the strong version of belief in supervenience presupposes, I think, something quite a bit stronger. It presupposes a common, unified level of fact on which all else supervenes. And I must confess that I don't quite know why I should believe in this. Surely it can't be on scientific grounds! Here some remarks of Nancy Cartwright's should cause us to hesitate. Cartwright says:

Look at any catalogue for a science or engineering school. The curriculum is divided into tiny, separate subjects that irk the interdisciplinist. Our knowledge of nature, nature as we best see it, is highly compartmentalized. Why think nature itself is unified?[26]

One way in which nature may not be unified is that there may be no grand, overarching laws

that tie all the various more specific laws together. As Cartwright points out;

[Some philosophers think] there is a law to cover every case. I do not. I imagine that natural objects are much like people in societies. Their behaviour is constrained by some specific laws, and by a handful of general principles, but it is not determined in detail, even statistically. We do not know whether we are in a tidy universe or an untidy one.[27]

I suggest that to the extent that this is true, the point—let alone the truth—of the supervenience theses so popular these days is a lot less clear than meets the eye. And if we do live in an "untidy" universe, then the question of the relationship between the mind and the quantum world would seem to me to be entirely open. But the point is not restricted to the mind. If our world is "untidy," then we simply have no reason to accept the hegemony of the usual laws of orthodox quantum mechanics. They may well break down or run out of their proper domain long before we get to the level of the mind.

I would like to close by considering a more extreme suggestion. We noted above that believers in certain sorts of supervenience claims think there are distinct, "equally valid" ways of looking at the world that don't entirely mesh. That is because supervenience theorists agree that reductionism fails. But quantum mechanics presents a more interesting challenge than the mere failure of the reductionist program. The "differing perspectives" that are contained within quantum mechanics aren't reconciled by some tidy, well-behaved deeper level of fact. When both slits are open in the two-slit experiment, we can't simply say that the photon either went through this slit or that, nor can we simply deny this. We have to make room for the fact that somehow the states associated with each slit each make a real contribution to the superposition, *and* we have to make room for the fact

---

[26]*How the Laws of Physics Lie*, Oxford: Clarendon Press (1983), p. 13.

[27]Ibid., p. 49.

that if we force the issue, we can get an answer to the question "which slit," though if we do, we will have chosen not to observe the interference pattern. In the end, it seems, this is *not* like the supervenience relationships we have considered so far. Quantum mechanics suggests to me something much more radical. It suggests that reality itself has a richness that, so to speak, "spills over" when one attempts to contain it within a single point of view.[28] To put it in a vocabulary that has a little more common coinage among philosophers, we might say that if quantum mechanics is right, even in some appropriately restricted domain, then the possible and the actual are in much closer contact than we are used to thinking. (You may recall a remark along these lines much earlier in our discussion of the two-slit experiment.) And if that is right, all the usual bets in metaphysics are off.

Here I think the reader may justifiably complain that I have reached the end of my speculative rope. I would agree, but I would like to draw a moral from this discussion. It is that quantum mechanics should induce in us both a sense of humility and a sense of excitement. The humility should come from the realization that there is much that we don't understand about the fundamental nature of reality. After more than sixty years, the quantum world is still mysterious. But the excitement should come from the fact that whatever the best way of understanding quantum mechanics is, the possible structures of reality are almost certainly much richer than we thought. This includes, I believe, the possibilities for the structure of mind and self themselves, and the possibilities for the relationship of these to the rest of reality.

---

[28]The sorts of analogies that are apt to occur to the nonreligious reader are religious paradoxes, for example, the Christian doctrine of the Holy Trinity—that God is one Being, but three Persons—or the more general idea that God is transcendent and yet immanent. Both are attempts to express a conception of a reality that cannot be captured by a single, nonparadoxical description.

Bibliography
(Pre-1980)

Adler, Alfred, *The Individual Psychology of Alfred Adler*, edited by Heinz L. Ansbacher and Rowena R. Ansbacher, New York: Harper and Row, 1964.

Alexander, Peter, "Wishes, Symptoms and Actions," *Proceedings of the Aristotelian Society* 48 (1974) 119–134.

Alexander, S., "The Self as Subject and Person," *Proceedings of the Aristotelian Society* 11 (1910–1911).

Allison, Henry E., "Locke's Theory of Personal Identity: A Reexamination," *Journal of the History of Ideas* 27 (1966) 41–58.

Allport, G., *The Person in Psychology*, Boston: Beacon Press, 1968.

Anderson, Susan Leigh, "Coconsciousness and Numerical Identity of the Person," *Philosophical Studies* 30 (1976) 1–10.

Anderson, Thomas C., *The Foundation and Structure of Sartrean Ethics*, Lawrence: Regents Press of Kansas, 1979.

Anscombe, G.E.M., "The Principle of Individuation," *Proceedings of the Aristotelian Society*, supp. vol. 27 (1953) 83–96.

Anscombe, G.E.M., "Pretending," in Stuart Hamshite, ed., *Philosophy of Mind*, New York: Harper and Row, 1966.

Anscombe, G.E.M., and Peter, Geach, *Three Philosophers*, Ithaca: Cornell University Press, 1961.

Aristotle, *De Anima*, Books 2 and 3, *Metaphysics*, Book 7, and *Nichomachean Ethics*, in Richard McKeon, ed., *The Basic Works of Aristotle*, New York: Random House, 1941.

Arlow, J. A. and Brenner, C., *Psychoanalytic Concepts and the Structural Theory*, New York: International Universities Press, 1964.

Armstrong, D. M., *Belief, Truth and Knowledge*, Cambridge: Cambridge University Press, 1973.

Audi, Robert, "The Limits of Self-Knowledge," *Canadian Journal of Philosophy* 4 (1974) 253–267.

Audi, Robert, "The Epistemic Authority of the First Person," *Personalist* 56 (1975) 5–15.

Audi, Robert, "Epistemic Disavowals and Self-Deception, "The Personalist 57 (1976) 378–385.

Ayer, A. J., *The Foundations of Empirical Knowledge*, New York: Macmillan, 1940.

Ayer, A. J., *Language Truth and Logic*, New York: Dover, 1946.

Ayer, A. J., "Individuals," *Mind* 61 (1952) 441–457.

Ayer, A. J., "Myself and Others," in *The Problem of Knowledge*, A. J. Ayer Harmondsworth: Penguin Books, 1956, Ch. 5.

Ayer, A. J., *The Concept of a Person*, London: Macmillan, 1963.

Baier, Kurt, "Guilt and Responsibility," in Peter A. French, ed., *Individual and Collective Responsibility*, Cambridge, Mass.: Schenkman Publishing Co., 1972, pp. 35–61.

Becker, Ernest, *The Denial of Death*, New York: Free Press, 1975.

Bell, Linda, "Sartre, Dialectic, and the Problem of Overcoming Bad Faith," *Man and World* 10 (1977) 292–302.

Bellow, Saul, "Interview with Saul Bellow," in George Plimpton, ed., *Writers at Work: The Paris Review Interviews*, 3rd series, New York: Penguin Books, 1967, pp. 175–196.

Beloff, John, *The Existence of Mind*, New York: Citadel Press, 1962, Ch. 2.

Bennett, Jonathan, "The Simplicity of the Soul," *Journal of Philosophy* 64 (1967) 648–660.

Bogen, J., "Identity and Origin," *Analysis* 26 (1966).

Bogen, J. E., "Further Discussion on Split-Brains and Hemispheric Capabilities," *British Journal for the Philosophy of Science* 28 (1977) 281–284.

Bogen, J. E., D. D. Fisher, and P. J. Vogel, "Cerebral Commissurotomy: a Second Case Report," *Journal of the American Medical Association* 194 (1965) 1328–1329.

Bosanquet, Bernard, "The Philosophical Importance of a True Theory of Identity," *Essays and Addresses*, London, 1891.

Boyers, Robert, "Observations on Lying and Liars," *Review of Existential Psychiatry* 13 (1974) 150–168.

Bradley, F. H., *Appearance and Reality*, Oxford: Oxford University Press, 1930.

Bradley, F. H., *Ethical Studies*, Oxford: Oxford University Press, 1962.

Branden, Nathaniel, *The Disowned Self*, New York: Bantam Books, 1973.

Broad, C. D., "The Unity of Mind," in *The Mind and Its Place in Nature*, Ch. 13, London: Routledge and Kegan Paul, 1925.

Broad, C. D., *Examination of MacTaggart's Philosophy*, 2 vols., Cambridge: Cambridge University Press, 1933, 1938.

Brody, Baruch, "Is There a Philosophical Problem about the Identity of Substances?" *Philosophia* 1 (1971) 43–59.

Brody, Baruch, "Locke on the Identity of Person," *American Philosophical Quarterly* 9 (1972) 327–334.

Burrell, David, and Stanley Hauerwas, "Self-Deception and Autobiography: Theological and Ethical Reflections on Speer's *Inside the Third Reich*," *Journal of Religious Ethics* 2 (1974) 99–117.

Butchvarov, P., "The Self and Perceptions: A Study in Human Philosophy," *Philosophical Quarterly* 9 (1959) 97–115.

Butler, Joseph, "Upon the Character of Balaam," "Upon Self-Deceit," and Sermon 3 of the Six Sermons, in W. E. Gladstone, ed., *The Works of Joseph Butler*, vol. 2, Oxford: Clarendon Press, 1896, pp. 121–135, 168–184, 317–338.

Butler, Joseph, "Of Personal Identity," in J. H. Bernard, ed., *The Works of Bishop Butler*, Vol. 2, London, Macmillan 1900; reprinted in Flew, ed., *Body, Mind and Death*, 1964, and also in Perry, ed., *Personal Identity*, 1975.

Campbell, C. A., "On Selfhood and Godhood," *Lecture VI*, London: 1957.

Canfield, John V., and Don F. Gustafson, "Self-Deception," *Analysis* 23 (1962) 32–36.

Canfield, John V., and Patrick McNally, "Paradoxes of Self-Deception," *Analysis* 21 (1961) 140–144.

Care, Norman S., and Robert H. Grimm, *Perception and Personal Identity*, Cleveland: Case Western Reserve Press, 1969.

Cartwright, Helen, "Heraclitus and the Bathwater," *Philosophical Review* 74 (1965) 466–485.

Cartwright, Helen, "Quantities," *Philosophical Review* 79 (1970) 25–42.

Castaneda, Hector-Neri, "On the Logic of Self-Knowledge," *Nous* 1 (1967) 9–21.

Cavell, Stanley, "The Avoidance of Love: A Reading of King Lear," in *Must We Mean What We Say?* New York: Charles Scribner's Sons, 1969, pp. 267–353.

Champlin, T. S., "Double Deception," *Mind* 85 (1976) 100–102.

Champlin, T. S., "Self-Deception—A Reflexive Dilemma," *Philosophy* 52 (1977) 281–299.

Champlin, T. S., "Self-Deception: A Problem About Autobiography," *Proceedings of the Aristotelian Society*, supp. vol. 53 (1979) 77–94.

Chandler, Hugh, "Shoemaker's Arguments Against Locke," *Philosophical Quarterly* 19 (1969) 263–265.

Chandler, Hugh, "Wiggins on Identity," *Analysis* 29 (1969).

Chappell, V. C., ed., *Hume: A Collection of Critical Essays*, Garden City, N.Y.: Doubleday, 1966.

Chappell, Vere, "Sameness and Change," *Philosophical Review* 69 (1960) 351–362.

Chisholm, Roderick M., *Perceiving*, Ithaca: Cornell University Press, 1957.

Chisholm, Roderick M., "Identity Through Possible Worlds, Some Questions," *Nous* 1 (1967) 1–8.

Chisholm, Roderick M., "The Loose and Popular and the Strict and Philosophical Senses of Identity and Reply," in Care and Grimm, eds., *Perception and Personal Identity*, 1969, pp. 82–139.

Chisholm, Roderick M., "Identity Through Time," in Kiefer and Munitz, eds., *Language, Belief, and Metaphysics*, 1970, pp. 163–182.

Chisholm, Roderick M., "Problems of Identity," in Munitz, ed., *Identity and Individuation*, 1971, pp. 3–30.

Chisholm, Roderick M., *Person and Object*, New York: George Allen & Unwin, 1976.

Chisholm, Roderick M., and Thomas Feehan, "The Intent to Deceive," *Journal of Philosophy* 74 (1977) 143–159.

Churchland, Paul, *Scientific Realism and the Plasticisty of Mind*, Cambridge: Cambridge University Press, 1979.

Cioffi, Frank, and Peter Alexander, "Symposium: Wishes, Symptoms and Actions," *Proceedings of the Aristotelian Society* 48 (1974) 97–134.

Collins, Arthur W., "Unconscious Belief," *Journal of Philosophy* 66 (1969) 667–680.

Condon, W. S., W. D. Ogston, and L. V. Pacoe, "Three Faces of Eve Revisited: A Study of Transient Microstrabismus," *Journal of Abnormal Psychology* 74 (1969) 618–620.

Congdon, M. H., J. Hain, and I. Stevenson, "A Case of Multiple Personality Illustrating the Transition from Role-Playing," *Journal of Nervous and Mental Disease* 32 (1961) 497–504.

Cook, John W., "Wittgenstein on Privacy," *Philosophical Review* 74 (1965) 281–314.

Cowley, Fraser, "The Identity of a Person and His Body," *Journal of Philosophy* 68 (1971) 678–683.

Daniels, Charles B., "Personal Identity," *American Philosophical Quarterly* 6 (1969) 226–232.

Daniels, Charles B., "Self-Deception and Inter-personal Deception," *The Personalist* 55 (1974) 244–252.

Danto, A. C., "Basic Actions," *American Philosophical Quarterly* 2 (1965) 141–8.

Davidson, Donald, "How Is Weakness of Will Possible?" in Joel Feinberg, ed., *Moral Concepts*, New York: Oxford University Press, 1970, pp. 93–113.

Davidson, Donald, "Mental Events," in L. Foster and J. W. Swanson, eds., *Experience and Theory*, Amherst: University of Massachusetts Press, 1970, pp. 79–101.

Demos, Raphael. "What Is It that I Want?" *Ethics* 55 (1945) 182–195.

Demos, Raphael, "Lying to Oneself," *Journal of Philoslophy* 56 (1960) 588–595.

Dennett, Daniel C., "Intentional Systems," *Journal of Philosophy* 68 (1971) 87–106.

Dennett, Daniel C., "Conditions of Personhood," in Rorty, ed., *The Identities of Persons*, 1976, pp. 175–196.

Dennett, Daniel C., "Towards a Cognitive Theory of Consciousness," in C. Wade Savage, ed., *Minnesota Studies in the Philosophy of Science*, vol. 9, Minneapolis: University of Minnesota Press 1978, pp. 201–228.

Dennett, Daniel C., *Brainstorms*, Hassocks: Harvester Press, 1979.

Descartes, René, *The Philosophical Works of Descartes*, edited and translated by E. S. Haldane and G.T.R. Ross, Cambridge: Cambridge University Press, 1967.

de Sousa, Ronald B., "Review of *Self-Deception* by Herbert Fingarette," *Inquiry* 13 (1970) 308–321.

de Sousa, Ronald B., "Rational Homunculi," in Rorty, ed., *The Identities of Persons*, 1976, pp. 217–238.

de Sousa, Ronald B., "Self-Deceptive Emotions," *Journal of Philosophy* 75 (1978) 684–697, reprinted in A. O. Rorty, ed., *Explaining Emotions*, Berkeley: University of California Press, 1980, pp. 283–297.

Deutscher, Max, and C. B. Martin, "Remembering," *The Philosophical Review* 75 (1966) 161–197.

DeWitt, L., "Consciousness, Mind, and Self: The Implications of Split-Brain Studies," *British Journal for the Philosophy of Science* 26 (1975) 41–60.

Dilman, Ilham, and D. Z. Phillips, *Sense and Delusion*, Atlantic Highlands, N.J.: Humanities Press, 1971.

Drengson, Alan R., "Critical Notice" in H. Fingarette, *Self-Deception, Dialogue: Canadian Journal of Philosophy* 12 (1973) 142–147.

Eck, Marcel, *Lies and Truth*, translated by Bernard Murchland, New York: Macmillan, 1970.

Edgley, Roy, *Reason in Theory and Practice*, London: Hutchinson University Library, 1969.

Ellenberger, Henri F., *The Discovery of the Unconscious*, New York: Basic Books, 1970.

Emmet, D., *Rules, Roles and Relations*, New York: Macmillan, 1966.

Enc, Berent, "Numerical Identity and Objecthood," *Mind* 84 (1975) 10–26.

Engelhardt, H. Tristram, "Mind-Body Quandaries," *The Journal of Medicine and Philosophy* 2 (1977).

Ettinger, R.C.W., *The Prospect of Immortality*, New York: Macfadden, 1966.

Evans, Donald, "Moral Weakness," *Philosophy* 50 (1975) 295–310.

Exdell, John, and James R. Hamilton, "The Incorrigibility of First-Person Disavowals," *The Personalist* 56 (1975) 389–394.

Factor, R. Lance, "Self-Deception and the Functionalist Theory of Mental Processes," *The Personalist* 58 (1977) 115–123.

Falk, W. D., "Morality, Self, and Others," in Hector-Neri Castaneda and George Nakhnikian, eds., *Morality and the Language of Conduct*, Detroit: Wayne State University Press, 1965, pp. 25–66.

Feldman, Fred, "Geach and Relative Identity," *Review of Metaphysics* 22 (1969) 547–555.

Feldman, Fred, "A Rejoinder," *Review of Metaphysics* 22 (1969) 560–561.

Festinger, Leon, *The Theory of Cognitive Dissonance*, Stanford, Calif.: Stanford University Press, 1957.

Fingarette, Herbert. *The Self in Transformation*, New York: Basic Books, 1963, and New York: Harper Torchbooks, 1965.

Fingarette, Herbert, *On Responsibility*, New York: Basic Books, 1967.

Fingarette, Herbert, *Self-Deception*, Atlantic Highlands, N.J.: Humanities Press, 1969.

Fingarette, Herbert, *The Meaning of Criminal Insanity*, Berkeley: University of California Press, 1974.

Fingarette, Herbert, and Ann F. Hasse, *Mental Disa-*

bilities and Criminal Responsibility, Berkeley: University of California Press, 1979.

Flew, Antony, "Locke and the Problem of Personal Identity," *Philosophy* 26 (1951).

Flew, Antony, "The Soul of Mr. A. M. Quinton," *Journal of Philosophy* 60 (1963) 337–343.

Flew, Antony, ed., *Body, Mind and Death*, New York: Macmillan, 1964.

Fox, Michael, "On Unconscious Emotions," *Philosophy and Phenomenological Research* 34 (1973) 151–170.

Fox, Michael, "Unconscious Emotions: A Reply to Professor Mullane's Unconscious and Disguised Emotions," *Philosophy and Phenomenological Research* 36 (1976) 412–414.

Frankfurt, Harry, "Freedom of the Will and the Concept of a Person," *Journal of Philosophy* 68 (1971) 5–20.

Frenkel-Brunswik, Else, "Mechanisms of Self-Deception," *Journal of Social Psychology* 10 (1939) 409–420.

Frondizi, R., *The Nature of the Self*, New Haven: Yale University Press, 1953.

Fuller, Gary, "Other Deception," *Southwestern Journal of Philosophy* 7 (1976) 21–31.

Gale, Richard M., "A Note on Personal Identity and Bodily Continuity," *Analysis* 29 (1969) 193–195.

Gallie, Ian, "Is the Self a Substance?" *Mind* 45 (1936) 28–44.

Gallup, Gordon, "Self-Recognition in Primates: A Comparative Approach to the Bidirectional Properties of Consciousness," *American Psychologist* 32 (1977) 329–338.

Gardiner, Patrick, "Error, Faith and Self-Deception," *Proceedings of the Aristotelian Society* 70 (1969–70) 221–243, reprinted in Jonathan Glover, ed., *The Philosophy of Mind*, New York: Oxford University Press, 1976, pp. 35–52.

Gazzaniga, M., *The Integrated Mind*, New York: Plenum Press, 1978.

Gazzaniga, M. S., J. E. Bogen, and R. W. Sperry, "Observations on Visual Perception after Disconnection of the Cerebral Hemisphere in Man" *Brain* 88 (1965) 221–236.

Gazzaniga, M. S., and R. W. Sperry, "Language after Section of the Cerebral Commissures," *Brain* 90 (1967) 131–148.

Geach, P. T., *Mental Acts*, New York: Humanities Press, 1957.

Geach, P. T., *Reference and Generality*, Ithaca: Cornell University Press, 1962.

Geach, P. T., "Identity," *Review of Metaphysics* 21 (1967) 3–12.

Geach, P. T., *God and Soul*, London: Routledge and Kegan Paul, 1969.

Geach, P. T., "A Reply," *Review of Metaphysics* 22 (1969) 556–560.

Geach, P. T., *Logic Matters*, Ithaca: Cornell University Press, 1972.

Gert, Bernard, "Personal Identity and the Body," *Dialogue* 10 (1971) 458–478.

Glover, Jonathan, *Responsibility*, London: Routledge and Kegan Paul, 1970.

Glover, Jonathan, "Freud, Morality and Responsibility," in Jonathan Miller, ed., *Freud: The Man, His World, His Influence*, Boston: Little, Brown and Co., 1972, pp. 152–163.

Goffman, Erving, *The Presentation of Self in Everyday Life*, Garden City, N.Y.: Doubleday, 1959.

Goffman, Erving, *Frame Analysis*, New York: Harper and Row, 1974.

Gordon, C., and K. Gergen, eds., *The Self in Social Interaction*, 2 vols., New York: John Wiley, 1968.

Grant, C. K., *Belief and Action*, Durham: University of Durham, 1960.

Green, Marjorie, "Authenticity: An Existential Virtue," *Ethics* 62 (1952) 266–274.

Greenwood, Terence, "Personal Identity and Memory," *Philosophical Quarterly* 17 (1967) 334–344.

Grice, H. P., "Personal Identity," *Mind* 50 (1941) 330–350, reprinted in Perry, ed., *Personal Identity*, 1975.

Gunderson, Keith, "Content and Consciousness and the Mind–Body Problem," *Journal of Philosophy* 69 (1975) 591–604.

Gur, Ruben C., and Harold A. Sackheim, "Self-Deception: A Concept in Search of a Phenomenon," *Journal of Personality and Social Psychology* 37 (1979) 147–169.

Hamlyn, D. W., "Self-Deception," *Proceedings of the Aristotelian Society* 45 (1971) 45–60.

Hampshire, Stuart, "Sincerity and Single-Mindedness," in Stuart Hampshire, *Freedom of Mind and Other Essays by Stuart Hampshire*, ed., Princeton, N.J.: Princeton University Press, 1971, pp. 232–256.

Hart, H.L.A., *Punishment and Responsibility*, New York: Oxford University Press, 1968.

Hartmann, H., *Ego Psychology and the Problem of Adaptation*, New York: International Universities Press, 1958.

Hausman, Carl R., "Creativity and Self-Deception," *Journal of Existentialism* 7 (1967) 295–308.

Haydon, Graham, "On Being Responsible," *Philosophical Quarterly* 28 (1978) 46–57.

Hegel, G.W.F., *The Phenomenology of Mind*, translated

by J. B. Baillie, New York: Harper Torchbooks, 1967.

Henry, Jules, *On Sham, Vulnerability, and Other Forms of Self-Destruction*, New York: Vintage Books, 1973.

Henry, Jules, *Pathways to Madness*, New York: Vintage Books, 1973.

Hildegard, E., "Human Motives and the Concept of Self," in R. S. Lazarus and E. Opton, Jr., eds., *Personality*, Harmondsworth and Baltimore: Penguin Books, 1967, pp. 255–258.

Hilgard, Ernest, *Divided Consciousness: Multiple Controls in Human Thought and Action*, New York: Harcourt, 1977.

Horney, Karen, *Neurosis and Human Growth*, New York: W. W. Norton, 1950.

Hospers, John, "What Means This Freedom?" in Sydney Hook, ed., *Determinism and Freedom in the Age of Modern Science*, New York: Collier Books, 1958, pp. 126–142.

Hospers, John, "Personal Identity," in *Introduction to Philosophical Analysis*, Englewood Cliffs, N.J.: Prentice-Hall, 1967, pp. 410–415.

Hospers, John, "Free-Will and Psychoanalysis," in Wilfrid Sellars and John Hospers, eds., *Readings in Ethical Theory*, 2nd ed., Englewood Cliffs, N.J.: Prentice-Hall, 1970, pp. 633–645.

Hume, David, *An Enquiry Concerning Human Understanding*, edited by L. A. Selby-Bigge, 2nd ed., Oxford, 1902.

Hume, David, *A Treatise of Human Nature*, Book I, Part IV, sects. 1, 5, 6, esp. sect. 6, "Of Personal Identity," Oxford: Clarendon Press, 1964.

Ishiguro, Hide, "A Person's Future and the Mind–Body Problem," in W. Mays and S. Brown, eds., *Linguistic Analysis and Phenomenology*, London: Macmillan, 1972.

James, William. *The Principles of Psychology*, esp. Ch. 10, "The Consciousness of Self," New York: Dover Press, 1950.

Jones, J. R., "The Self in Sensory Cognition," *Mind* 58 (1949) 40–61.

Jones, J. R., and T. R. Miles, "Self-Knowledge," *Proceedings of the Aristotelian Society*, supp. vol. (1956).

Kant, Immanuel, *Critique of Pure Reason*, esp. the Transcendental Deduction (Ch. 2 of Book I of the Transcendental Analytic), the First and Second Analogies (in sect. 3 of Ch. 2 of Book II of the Transcendental Analytic), and the Paralogisms of Pure Reason (Ch. 1 of Book II of the Transcendental Dialectic), translated by Norman Kemp Smith, New York: St. Martin's Press, 1965.

Kant, Immanuel, *Anthropology from a Pragmatic Point of View*, translated by Victor Lyle Dowdell, edited by Hans H. Rudnick, Carbondale: Southern Illinois University Press, 1978.

Kaufmann, Walter, *Nietzsche: Philosopher, Psychologist, Antichrist*, 4th ed., Princeton, N.J.: Princeton University Press, 1974.

Kaufmann, Walter, ed., *Existentialism from Dostoevsky to Sartre*, New York: New American Library, 1975.

Keen, Ernest, "Suicide and Self-Deception," *Psychoanalytic Review* 60 (1973/74) 575–585.

Kiefer, Howard E., and Milton K. Munitz, *Language, Belief, and Metaphysics*, Albany: State University of New York Press, 1970.

Kierkegaard, Soren, *Fear and Trembling and The Sickness Unto Death*, translated by Walter Lowrie, Garden City, N.Y.: Doubleday Anchor Books, 1954.

Kierkegaard, Soren, *Purity of Heart Is to Will One Thing*, translated by Douglas Steere, New York: Harper Torchbooks, 1956.

Kierkegaard, Soren, *Either/Or*, translated by Walter Lowrie, 2 vols., Princeton, N.J.: Princeton University Press, 1959.

King-Farlow, John, "Self-Deceivers and Sartrian Seducers," *Analysis* 23 (1963) 131–136.

King-Farlow, John, "Review of Herbert Fingarette's *Self-Deception*," *Metaphilosophy* 4 (1973) 76–84.

King-Farlow, John, "Philosphical Nationalism: Self-Deception and Self-Direction," *Dialogue* 17 (1978) 591–615.

Knox, John, Jr., "Can the Self Survive the Death of Its Mind?" *Religious Studies* 5 (1969) 85–97.

Kovar, Leo, "The Pursuit of Self-Deception," *Review of Existential Psychology and Psychiatry* 13 (1974) 136–149.

Laing, R. D., *Self and Others*, New York: Pantheon Books, 1969.

Laing, R. D., *The Divided Self*, Baltimore: Penguin, 1973.

Lang, Berel, "The Neurotic as Moral Agent," *Philosophy and Phenomenological Research* 29 (1968) 216–231.

Lazarus, R. S., "Cognitive and Coping Processes in Emotion," in Alan Monat and Richard S. Lazarus, eds., *Stress and Coping*, New York: Columbia University Press, 1977, pp. 145–158.

Lazarus, R. S., and E. M. Opton, eds., *Personality*, Harmondsworth and Baltimore: Penguin Books, 1967.

LeDoux, J. E., D. H. Wilson, and M. Gazzaniga, "A Divided Mind: Observations on the Conscious Properties of the Separated Hemispheres," *Annals of Neurology* 2 (1977) 417–421.

Lee, Vernon, *Vital Lies*, 2 vols., London: John Lane, 1912.

Leibniz, G. W., *New Essays On Human Understanding*, esp. Book II, Ch. 27, translated by Peter Remnant and Jonathan Bennett, New York: Cambridge Univ. Press 1981.

Leibniz, G. W., *Discourse on Metaphysics*, esp. 34, in Philip P. Wiener, ed., *Leibing Selections*, New York: Charles Scribner's Sons, 1951, pp. 290–344.

Leibniz, G. W., *Mondalogy*, 9, 10, 14, 22, 47, 62, 71. Translated by Robert Lotta, New York: Garland, 1985.

Levy-Agresti, J., and R. W. Sperry, "Differential Perceptual Capacities in Major and Minor Hemispheres," *Proceedings of the National Academy of Sciences* 61 (1968) 1151.

Levy-Bruhl, L., *The "Soul" of the Primitive*, London: Allen & Unwin, 1965, pp. 86–95.

Lewis, David D., "Counterparts of Persons and their Bodies," *Journal of Philosophy* 68 (1971) 203–211.

Lewis, H. D., *The Elusive Mind*, London: Allen & Unwin, 1969.

Locke, John, *An Essay Concerning Human Understanding*, edited by P. H. Nidditch, Book II, Ch. 27, reprinted in Perry, ed., *Personal Identity*, 1975.

Lovejoy, Arthur O., *Reflections on Human Nature*, Baltimore: Johns Hopkins University Press, 1961.

MacDonald, G. F., ed. *Perception and Identity*, Ithaca: Cornell University Press, 1979.

MacIntyre, Alasdair, *The Unconscious*, New York: Humanities Press 1958.

Mackie, John, *Problems from Locke*, Oxford: Clarendon Press, 1976.

Marcel, Gabriel, *Homo Viator: Introduction to a Metaphysic of Hope*, New York: Harper and Row, 1951.

Margolis, J., "Puccetti on Brains, Minds, and Persons," *Philosophy of Science* 42 (1974) 275–280.

Martin, Mike W., "Immorality and Self-Deception," *Dialogue* 16 (1977) 274–280.

Martin, Mike W., "Sartre on Lying to Oneself," *Philosophy Research Archives* 4 (1978) 1–26.

Martin, Mike W., "Factor's Functionalist Account of Self-Deception," *The Personalist* 60 (1979) 336–342.

Martin, Mike W., "Morality and Self-Deception: Paradox, Ambiguity or Vagueness?" *Man and World* 12 (1979) 47–60.

Martin, Mike W., "Self-Deception, Self-Pretence, and Emotional Detachment," *Mind* 88 (1979) 441–446.

McTaggart, J. M., *The Nature of Existence*, 2 vols. Cambridge: Cambridge University Press, 1927.

Mead, G. H., *Mind, Self and Society*, Chicago: University of Chicago Press, 1934.

Melden, A. I., *Rights and Persons*, Berkeley: University of California Press, 1977.

Menne, Albert, "Identity, Equality, Similarity," *Ratio* 4 (1962) 50.

Mill, James, *Analysis of the Phenomena of the Human Mind*, Vol. II, London, 1878.

Minkus, P. A., *Philosophy of the Person*, Oxford: Basil Blackwell, 1960.

Miri, Mrinal, "Memory and Personal Identity," *Mind* 82 (1973) 1–21.

Miri, Mrinal, "Self-Deception," *Philosophy and Phenomenological Research* 34 (1974) 576–585.

Mischel, T., ed., *The Self*, Oxford: Basil Blackwell, 1977.

Monts, Kenneth J., A. Louis, and Rudy Nydegger, "Interpersonal Self-Deception and Personality Correlates," *Journal of Social Psychology* 103 (1977) 91–99.

Mortimore, G. W., ed., *Weakness of Will*, New York: St. Martin's Press, 1971.

Mounce, H. O., "Self-Deception," *Proceedings of the Aristotelian Society* 45 (1971) 61–72.

Muehlmann, Robert, "Russell and Wittgenstein on Identity," *Philosophical Quarterly* 19 (1969) 221–230.

Munitz, M. K., ed., *Identity and Individuation*, New York: New York University Press, 1971.

Murphy, Gardner, "Experiments in Over-coming Self-Deception," *Psychophysiology* 6 (1970) 790–799.

Murphy, Gardner, *Outgrowing Self-Deception*, New York: Basic Books, 1975.

Murphy, Gardner, and Wendell M. Swenson. "Outgrowing Self-Deception," *American Journal of Psychiatry* 133 (1976) 115–128.

Nagel, Thomas, "Physicalism," *Philosophical Review* 74 (1965) 339–356.

Nagel, Thomas, *Mortal Questions*, Cambridge University Press, 1979.

Nemiah, John C., *Foundations of Psychopathology*, Oxford: University Press, New York, 1961, and New York: Jason Aronson, 1973.

Neu, Jerome, *Emotion, Thought and Therapy*, Berkeley: University of California Press, 1977.

Niebuhr, Reinhold, "The Nature and Destiny of Man," Vol. 1, *Human Nature*, New York: Charles Scribner's Sons, 1964.

Nisbett, Richard E., and Timothy D. Wilson, "The Halo Effect: Evidence for Unconscious Alteration of Judgements," *Journal of Personality and Social Psychology* 35 (1977) 250–256.

Odegard, Douglas, "Personal and Bodily Identity," *Philosophical Quarterly* 19 (1969) 69–70.

Odegard, Douglas, "Identity Through Time," *American Philosophical Quarterly* 9 (1972) 29–38.

Palma, A. B., "Memory and Personal Identity," *Australasian Journal of Philosophy* 42 (1964) 53–68.

Palmer, Anthony, "Self-Deception: A Problem About Autobiography," *Proceedings of the Aristotelian Society*, supp. vol. 53 (1970) 61–76.

Palmer, Anthony, "Characterizing Self-Deception," *Mind* 88 (1979) 45–58.

Paluch, Stanley, "Self-Deception," *Inquiry* 10 (1967) 268–278.

Pascal, Blaise, *Pensées*, translated by A. J. Krailsheimer, Baltimore: Penguin Books, 1973.

Parfit, Derek, "On The Importance of Self-Identity," *Journal of Philosophy* 68 (1971) 683–690.

Parfit, Derek, "Personal Identity," *Philosophical Review* 80 (1971) 3–27, reprinted in Perry, ed., *Personal Identity*, 1975, pp. 199–226.

Parfit, Derek, "Lewis, Perry, and What Matters," in Rorty, ed., *The Identities of Persons*, 1976, pp. 91–108.

Paskow, Alan, "Towards a Theory of Self-Deception," *Man and World* 12 (1979) 178–191.

Paton, H. J., "Self-Identity," in *Defense of Reason*, London: Hutchinsons, 1951, pp. 99–116.

Pears, D. F., "Critical Study of Strawson," *Philosophical Quarterly* 11 (1961) 172–185, 262–277.

Pears, D. F., "Hume on Personal Identity," in D. F. Pears, ed., *David Hume: A Symposium*, London: Macmillan, 1963.

Pears, D. F., "Freud, Sartre and Self-Deception," in R. Wollheim, ed., *Freud*, Garden City, N.Y.: Anchor Books, 1974.

Penelhum, Terence, "Hume on Personal Identity," *Philosophical Review* 64 (1955) 571–589.

Penelhum, Terence, "Personal Identity, Memory, and Survival," *Journal of Philosophy* 56 (1959) 882–903.

Penelhum, Terence, "Hume on Personal Identity," in V. C. Chappell, ed., *Modern Studies in Philosophy: Hume*, New York: Doubleday and Co., 1966, pp. 213–239.

Penelhum, Terence, "Pleasure and Falsity," in Stuart Hampshire, ed., *Philosophy of Mind*, Harper and Row, New York (1966) 242–266.

Penelhum, Terence, "Personal Identity," in Paul Edwards, ed., *Encyclopedia of Philosophy*, New York: Macmillan, 1967, pp. 95–106.

Penelhum, Terence, *Survival and Disembodied Existence*, London: Routledge and Kegan Paul; New York: Humanities Press, 1970.

Penelhum, Terence, "The Importance of Self-Identity," *Journal of Philosophy* 68 (1971) 667–677.

Penelhum, Terence, W. E. Kennick, and Arnold Isenberg, "Symposium: Pleasure and Falsity," *American Philosophical Quarterly* 1 (1964) 81–91.

Perry, John, "The Same F," *Philosophical Review* 79 (1970) 181–200.

Perry, John, "Can the Self Divide?" *Journal of Philosophy* 69 (1972) 463–488.

Perry, John, "Personal Identity, Memory, and the Problem of Circularity," in Perry, ed., *Personal Identity*, 1975, pp. 135–155.

Perry, John, "The Problem of Personal Identity," in Perry, ed., *Personal Identity*, 1975, pp. 3–30.

Perry, John, "The Importance of Being Identical," in Rorty, ed., *The Identities of Persons*, 1976.

Perry, John, review of Bernard Williams, "Problems of the Self," *Journal of Philosophy* 73 (1976) 416–428.

Perry, John, "Frege on Demonstratives," *The Philosophical Review* 86 (1977) 474–497.

Perry, John, *A Dialogue on Personal Identity and Immortality*, Indianapolis: Hackett, 1978.

Perry, John, "The Problem of the Essential Indexical," *Nous* 13 (1979) 3–21.

Perry, John, ed., *Personal Identity*, Berkeley: University of California Press, 1975.

Peyre, H., *Literature and Sincerity*, Yale University Press, New Haven, 1963.

Peyre, Henri, *Literature and Sincerity*, New Haven: Yale University Press, 1963.

Pike, Nelson, "Hume's Bundle Theory of the Self," *American Philosophical Quarterly* 17 (1967) 159–165.

Pole, David, "The Socratic Injunction," *Journal of the British Society for Phenomenology* 2 (1971) 31–40.

Popper, K., and J. C. Eccles, *The Self and Its Brain*, London: Routledge and Kegan Paul, 1977.

Price, H. H., "Belief and Will," in Stuart Hampshire, ed., *Philosophy of Mind*, New York: Harper and Row, 1966, pp. 91–116.

Price, H. H., *Belief*, New York: Humanities Press, 1969.

Prince, Morton, *The Unconscious*, 2nd ed., New York: Macmillan, 1929.

Prior, A. N., "Report on Analysis Problem #11," *Analysis* 17 (1957) 121–123.

Prior, A. N., "Opposite Number," *Review of Metaphysics* 11 (1957–1958) 196–201.

Prior, A. N., "Time, Existence, and Identity," in *Papers on Time and Tense*, Oxford: Clarendon Press, 1968.

Puccetti, Roland, "Can Humans Think?" *Analysis* 26 (1966) 198–202.

Puccetti, Roland, "Mr. Strawson's Concept of a Person," *Australasian Journal of Philosophy* 45 (1967) 321–328.

Puccetti, Roland, "Brain Transplantation and Personal Identity," *Analysis* 29 (1969) 65–77.

Puccetti, Roland, "Brain Bisection and Personal Identity," *British Journal of the Philosophy of Science* 24 (1973) 339–355.

Puccetti, Roland, "Multiple Identity," *The Personalist* 54 (1973) 203–215.

Puccetti, Roland, "Remembering the Past of Another," *Canadian Journal of Philosophy* 2 (1973) 523–532.

Puccetti, Roland, "Brains that Think," *Dialogue* 13 (1974) 99–104.

Puccetti, Roland, "Neural Plasticity and the Location of Mental Events," *Australasian Journal of Philosophy* 52 (1974) 154–162.

Puccetti, Roland, "A Reply to Professor Margolis," *Philosophy of Science* 42 (1975) 281–285.

Puccetti, Roland, "The Mute Self," *British Journal for the Philosophy of Science* 27 (1976) 65–73.

Puccetti, Roland, "Robinson on My Views: A Correction," *British Journal for the Philoslophy of Science* 27 (1977) 171.

Puccetti, Roland, "Sperry on Consciousness: A Critical Appreciation," *Journal of Medicine and Philosophy* 2 (1977) 127–144.

Puccetti, Roland, "Borowski on the Relative Identity of Persons," *Mind* 87 (1978) 262–263.

Puccetti, Roland, "Ontology vs. Ontogeny," *Dialogue* 17 (1978) 128–131.

Pugmire, David, "'Strong' Self-Deception," *Inquiry* 12 (1969) 339–346.

Purtill, R. L., "About Identity Through Possible Worlds," *Nous* 2 (1968) 87–90.

Quine, W.V.O., "Review of Identity and Individuation," ed. M. K. Munitz, *Journal of Philosophy* 69 (1972) 488–497.

Quinton, Anthony, "Two Conceptions of Personality," *Revue Internationale de Philosophie* 22 (1958) 387–402.

Quinton, Anthony, *The Nature of Things*, London: Routledge and Kegan Paul, 1973, Part I.

Quinton, Anthony, "The Soul," *Journal of Philosophy* 59 (1962) 393–409; reprinted in Perry, ed., *Personal Identity*, 1975.

Rank, Otto, *Truth and Reality*, translated by Jessie Taft, New York: W. W. Norton, 1978.

Reichenbach, Hans, *The Direction of Time*, edited by Maria Reihenbach, Ch. 2, esp. sect. 5, Berkeley: University of California Press, 1956.

Reid, Thomas, *Essays on the Intellectual Powers of Man*, Chs. 4 and 6, Edinburgh, 1785, edited by A. D. Woozley, London: Macmillan, 1941.

Reid, Thomas, *Essays on the Active Powers of the Human Mind*, Essay 5, Ch. 4, Cambridge, Mass.: MIT Press, 1969.

Reid, Thomas, "Of Memory," "Of Identity," "Of Mr. Locke's Account of Our Personal Identity," in *Essays on the Intellectual Powers of Man*, 1785, reprinted in Perry, ed., *Personal Identity*, 1975.

Reik, Theodor, *Listening with the Third Ear*, New York: Arena Books, 1972.

Reilly, Richard, "Self-Deception: Resolving the Epistemological Paradox," *The Personalist* 57 (1976) 391–394.

Ripley, Charles, "Sperry's Concept of Consciousness," *Inquiry* 27 (1984) 399–423.

Riviere, Jacques, *The Ideal Reader*, Meridian Books, New York, 1960.

Robinson, D., "What Sort of Persons are Hemispheres?" *British Journal for the Philosophy of Science* 27 (1976) 73–78.

Rogers, Carl, "A Theory of Therapy, Personality, and Interpersonal Relationships as Devleoped in the Client-Centered Framework," in S. Koch, ed., *Psychology: A Study of a Science*, Vol. 3, New York: McGraw-Hill, 1959, pp. 184–256.

Rogers, Carl, *On Becoming a Person*, Boston: Houghton Mifflin, 1961.

Rorty, Amélie Oksenberg, "Belief and Self-Deception," *Inquiry* 15 (1972) 387–410.

Rorty, Amélie Oksenberg, "Persons, Policies, and Bodies," *International Philosophical* Quarterly 13 (1973) 63–80.

Rorty, Amélie Oksenberg, "The Transformations of Persons," *Philosophy* 48 (1973) 261–275.

Rorty, Amélie Oksenberg, "Adaptivity and Self-Knowledge," *Inquiry* 18 (1975) 1–22.

Rorty, Amélie Oksenberg, ed., *The Identities of Persons*, Berkeley: University of California Press, 1976.

Rorty, Richard, "Incorrigibility as the Mark of the Mental," *Journal of Philoslophy* 67 (1970) 399–424.

Rorty, Richard, "Cartesian Epistemology and Changes in Ontology," in J. E. Smith, ed., *Contemporary American Philosophy*, London: George Allen & Unwin, 1970, pp. 273–292.

Ruddock, R., *Six Approaches to the Person*, London: Routledge and Kegan Paul, 1972.

Russell, Bertrand, "The Philosophy of Logical Atomism," *The Monist* (1918), reprinted in R. C. Marsh, ed., *Logic and Knowledge*, London: Allen & Unwin, 1956.

Russell, J. Michael, "Saying, Feeling, and Self-Deception," *Behaviorism* 6 (1978) 27–43.

Ryle, Gilbert, *The Concept of Mind*, New York: Barnes and Noble, 1949.

Sackheim, Harold A., "Self-Deception, Self-Confrontation, and Consciousness," in Gary E. Schwartz and David Shapiro, eds., *Consciousness and Self-Regulation: Advances*, New York: Plenum Press, 1978.

Sackheim, Harold A., and Ruben C. Gur, "Self-Deception, Other-Deception, and Self-Reported Psychopathology," *Journal of Consulting and Clinical Psychology* 47 (1979) 213–215.

Sanford, David, "Locke, Leibniz and Wiggins on Being in the Same Place at the Same Time," *Philosophical Review* 79 (1970) 75–82.

Santoni, Ronald E., "Sartre on 'Sincerity': Bad Faith? or Equivocation?" *The Personalist* 53 (1972) 150–160.

Santoni, Ronald E., "Bad Faith and 'Lying to Oneself,'" *Philosophy and Phenomenological Research* 38 (1978) 384–398.

Sartre, Jean-Paul, *No Exit and Three Other Plays*, translated by Stuart Gilbert and Lionel Abel, New York: Vintage Books, 1949.

Sartre, Jean-Paul, *The Transcendence of the Ego*, New York: Noonday Press, 1957.

Sartre, Jean-Paul, *Anti-Semite and Jew*, translated by George J. Becker, New York: Schocken Books, 1965.

Sartre, Jean-Paul, *Being and Nothingness*, translated by Hazel E. Barnes, New York: Washington Square Press, 1966.

Sartre, Jean-Paul, "Existentialism Is a Humanism," translated by Philip Mairet, in Walter Kaufmann, ed., *Existentialism from Dostoevsky to Sartre*, New York: New American Library, 1975, pp. 345–369.

Saunders, John Turk, "The Paradox of Self-Deception," *Philosophy and Phenomenological Research* 35 (1975) 559–570.

Schechter, D., "Identification and Individuation," *Journal of American Psychoanalytic Association* 16 (1968) 48–80.

Scheler, Max, *Ressentiment*, edited by Lewis A. Coser, translated by William W. Holdheim, New York: Schocken Books, 1972.

Schopenhauer, Arthur, *The World as Will and Representation*, translated by E.F.J. Payne, New York: Dover, 1966, Vol. 2, Chapter 19.

Schutz, A., *Collected Papers*, The Hague: Nijhoff, 1962.

Scott-Taggart, M. J., "Socratic Irony and Self Deceit," *Ratio* 14 (1972) 1–15.

Sellars, Wilfred, "Metaphysics and the Concept of a Person," in K. Lambert, ed., *The Logical Way of Doing Things*, New Haven: Yale University Press, 1969.

Shafer, Roy, *A New Language for Psychoanalysis*, New Haven: Yale University Press, 1976.

Shaffer, J., "Personal Identity: The Implications of Brain Bisection and Brain Transplants," *Journal of Medicine and Philosophy* 2 (1977) 147–161.

Shapiro, Gary, "Choice and Universality in Sartre's Ethics," *Man and World* 7 (1974) 20–36.

Shlien, John M., "A Client-Centered Approach to Schizophrenia: First Approximation," in Arthur Burton, ed., *Psychotherapy of the Psychoses*, New York: Basic Books, 1961.

Shoemaker, Sydney, "Personal Identity and Memory," *Journal of Philosophy* 56 (1959) 868–882, reprinted in Perry, ed., *Personal Identity*, 1975, pp. 119–134.

Shoemaker, Sydney, *Self-Knowledge and Self-Identity*, Ithaca: Cornell University Press, 1963

Shoemaker, Sydney, "On Knowing Who One Is," *Common Factor* 4 (1966) 49–56.

Shoemaker, Sydney. "Self-Reference and Self-Awareness," *Journal of Philosophy* 65 (1968) 555–567.

Shoemaker, Sydney, "Comments," in Norman S. Care and Robert H. Grimm, eds., *Perception and Personal Identity*, Cleveland: Case Western Reserve Press, 1969.

Shoemaker, Sydney, "Identity, Properties and Causality," in Peter French et al., eds., *Midwest Studies in Philosophy* 4 (1969) 321–342.

Shoemaker, Sydney, "Persons and their Pasts," *American Philoslophical Quarterly* 7 (1970) 269–285.

Shoemaker, Sydney, "Wiggins on Identity," *The Philosophical Review* 79 (1970) pp. 529–544, reprinted in Munitz, ed., *Identity and Individuation*, 1971, pp. 103–107.

Shorter, J. M., "More about Bodily Continuity and Personal Identity," *Analysis* 22 (1962) 79–85.

Shorter, J. M., "Personal Identity, Relationships, and Criteria," *Proceedings of the Aristotelian Society* Suppl. vol. (1970–71) 165–186.

Siegler, Frederick A., "Demos on Lying to Onself," *Journal of Philosophy* 59 (1962) 469–475.

Siegler, Frederick A., "Self-Deception," *Australasian Journal of Philosophy* 41 (1963) 29–43.

Siegler, Frederick A., "Self-Deception and Other Deception," *Journal of Philosophy* 60 (1963) 759–764.

Siegler, Frederick A., "Unconscious Intentions," *Inquiry* 10 (1967) 251–267.

Siegler, Frederick A., "An Analysis of Self-Deception," *Nous* 2 (1968) 147–164.

Smart, Brian, "How Can Persons Be Ascribed M-Predicates?" *Mind* 86 (1977) 49–66.

Smith, Adam, "Of the Nature of Self-Deceit," in *The*

Theory of Moral Sentiments, New York: Kelley, 1966.

Sperry, R. W., "Cerebral Organization and Behavior," *Science* 133 (1961) 1749–1757.

Sperry, R. W., "The Great Cerebral Commissure," *Scientific American* 210 (1964) 42–52.

Sperry, R. W., "Brain Bisection and Mechanisms of Consciousness," in J. Eccles, ed., *Brain and Conscious Experience*, New York: Springer-Verlag, 1966.

Sperry, R. W., "Mental Unity Following Surgical Disconnection of the Cerebral Hemispheres," *Harvey Lectures* 62 (1968) 293–323.

Sperry, R. W., Michael Gazzaniga, and J. E. Bogen, "Interhemispheric Relationships," in P. J. Vinken and G. W. Bruyn, eds., *Handbook of Clinical Neurology*, New York: North-Holland, 1969, pp. 273–290.

Sperry, R. W., "Forebrain Commissurotomy and Conscious Awareness," *Journal of Medicine and Philosophy* 2 (1977) 101–125.

Sperry, R. W., "Reply to Professor Puccetti," *Journal of Medicine and Philosophy* 2 (1977) 145–146.

Spinoza, Baruch, *Ethics*, translated by R.H.M. Elwes, in *Benedict de Spinoza*, New York: Dover Publications, 1955, Book 1, sects. 3, 5, 6, 8, 13.

Stern, Laurent, "On Make-Believe," *Philosophy and Phenomenological Research* 28 (1967/68) 24–38.

Strawson, P. F., *Individuals*, Garden City, N.Y.: Anchor Books, 1963.

Strawson, P. F., *The Bounds of Sense*, London: Methuen, 1966.

Strawson, P. F., "Self, Mind, and Body," *Common Factor* 4 (1966) 5–13.

Strawson, P. F., "Chisholm on Identity Through Time," in Kiefer and Munitz, eds., *Language, Belief, and Metaphysics*, 1970, pp. 183–186.

Stroll, Avrum, "Identity," in Paul Edwards, ed., *The Encyclopedia of Philosophy*, New York: Macmillan, 1967.

Stroud, B., *Hume*, London: Routledge and Kegan Paul, 1977.

Swinburne, Richard, "Personal Identity," *Proceedings of the Aristotelian Society* 74 (1973/74) 231–48.

Swinburne, Richard, *Space and Time*, London: Macmillan, 1968, Ch. 1.

Szabados, Bela, "Wishful Thinking and Self-Deception," *Analysis* 33 (1973) 201–205.

Szabados, Bela, "The Morality of Self-Deception," *Dialogue* 13 (1974) 25–34.

Szabados, Bela, "Rorty on Belief and Self-Deception," *Inquiry* 17 (1974) 464–473.

Szabados, Bela, "Self-Deception," *Canadian Journal of Philosophy* 4 (1974) 51–68.

Szabados, Bela, "Fingarette on Self-Deception," *Philosophical Papers* 6 (1977) 21–30.

Szabados, Bela, "Hypocrisy," *Canadian Journal of Philosophy* 9 (1979) 195–210.

Taylor, Richard, "Spatial and Temporal Analogies and the Concept of Identity," *Journal of Philosophy* 52 (1955); reprinted in J.J.C. Smart, ed., *Problems of Space and Time*, London: Macmillan, 1964.

Taylor, Richard, "DeAnima," *American Philosophical Quarterly* 10 (1973) 61–64.

Thomson, J. Jarvis, "Time, Space and Objects," *Mind* 74 (1965) 1–27.

Trilling, Lionel, *Sincerity and Authenticity*, Cambridge, Mass.: Harvard University Press, 1971.

Unger, Peter, "I Do Not Exist," in G. F. MacDonald, *Perception and Identity*, London: Cornell University Press, 1979.

Unger, Peter, "Why There Are No People," in Peter French et al., eds., *Midwest Studies in Philolsophy*, 1979.

Vaihinger, Hans, *The Philosophy of "As-If"*, 2nd ed., translated by C. K. Ogden, New York: Barnes and Noble, 1952.

Vesey, Godfrey, *Personal Identity: A Philosophical Analysis*, Ithaca: Cornell University Press, 1974.

Walker, A.D.M., "The Ideal of Sincerity," *Mind* 87 (1978) 481–497.

Wallace, James D., *Virtues and Vices*, Ithaca: Cornell University Press, 1978.

Watson, Gary, "Skepticism about Weakness of Will," *Philosophical Review* 86 (1977) 316–339.

White, A. R., *Attention*, Basil Blackwell, Oxford, 1964.

Wiggins, David, *Identity and Spatio-Temporal Continuity*, Oxford: Basil Blackwell, 1967.

Wild, John, "Authentic Existence," in W. K. Frankena and J. T. Granrose, eds., *Introductory Readings in Ethics*, Englewood Cliffs, N.J.: Prentice-Hall, 1974, pp. 356–366.

Wilkes, K. V., "Consciousness and Commissurotomy," *Philosophy* 53 (1978) 185–199.

Williams, Bernard, *Problems of the Self*, Cambridge: Cambridge University Press, 1973.

Wilshire, Bruce, "Self, Body and Self-Deception," *Man and World* 5 (1972) 422–451.

Wittgenstein, Lugwig, *Philosophical Investigations*, translated by G.E.M. Anscombe, 3rd ed., New York: Macmillan, 1953.

Wittgenstein, Lugwig, *The Blue and Brown Books*, Oxford: Blackwell, 1958.

Wittgenstein, Lugwig, *On Certainty*, G.E.M. Anscombe and B. H. von Wright, eds., Oxford: Blackwell, 1969.

Zemach, Eddy, "Sensations, Raw Feels, and Other

Minds," *The Review of Metaphysics* 20 (1966) 317–340.

Zemach, Eddy, "Personal Identity Without Criteria," *Australasian Journal of Philosophy* 47 (1969) 344–353.

Zemach, Eddy, "The Unity and Indivisibility of the Self," *International Philosophical Quarterly* 10 (1970) 542–555.

Zemach, Eddy, "The Reference of 'I'," *Philosophical Studies* 23 (1972) 65–75.

Zemach, Eddy, "Time and Self," *Analysis* 39 (1979) 143–147.

Bibliography
(Since 1980)

Aboulafia, Mitchell, *The Mediating Self: Mead, Sartre, and Self-Determination*, New Haven: Yale University Press, 1986.

Adams, E. M., "The Concept of a Person." *The Southern Journal of Philosophy* 23 (1985) 403–412.

Allen, N. J., "The Category of the Person," in Carrithers et al., eds., *The Category of the Person*, 1985, pp. 26–45.

Anderson, Scott W., "Dasein As Self: Some Implications of Heideggerian Ontology," *Kinesis* 14 (1985) 106–129.

Armstrong, D. M., "The Nature of Mind" in Block, ed., *Readings in Philosophy of Psychology*, vol. 1, 1980, pp. 191–199.

Audi, Robert, "Self-Deception, Action, and Will," *Erkenntnis* 18 (1982) 133–158.

Audi, Robert, "Self-Deception and Rationality," in Martin, ed., *Self-Deception and Self-Understanding*, 1985.

Audi, Robert, "Self-Deception, Rationalization, and Reasons for Acting," in McLaughlin and Rorty, eds., *Perspectives on Self-Deception*, 1988, pp. 99–122.

Ayer, A. J., *Freedom and Morality and Other Essays*, Oxford: Clarendon Press, 1984.

Bach, Kent, "An Analysis of Self-Deception," *Philosophy and Phenomenological Research* 41 (1981) 351–370.

Barnes, Hazel, "Sartre's Concept of the Self," *Review of Existential Psychology and Psychiatry* 17 (1980–1981) 41–66.

Baron, Marcia, "What is Wrong with Self-Deception?" in McLaughlin and Rorty, eds., *Perspectives on Self-Deception*, 1988, pp. 431–449.

Barresi, John, "Prospects for the Cyberiad: Certain Limits on Human Self-Knowledge in the Cybernetic Age," *Journal for the Theory of Social Behavior* 17 (1987) 19–46.

Barrett, William, *Death of the Soul: From Descartes to the Computer*, Garden City: Anchor Press, 1987.

Bastow, David, "Self-Construction in Buddhism," *Ratio* 28 (1986) 97–113.

Baumeister, Roy F., *Public Self and Private Self*, New York: Springer-Verlag, 1986.

Beahrs, John, *Unity and Multiplicity: Multilevel Consciousness of Self in Hypnosis, Psychiatric Disorder, and Mental Health*, New York: Brunner/Mazel, 1982.

Beehler, Rodger, "Moral Delusion," *Philosophy* 56 (1981) 313–331.

Bellah, Robert N., "The Quest for the Self," *Philosophical Theology* 2 (1988) 374–386.

Benhabib, Seyla, "The Generalized and the Concrete Other: The Kohlberg-Gilligan Controversy and Feminist Theory," *Praxis International* 5 (1986) 402–424.

Bergoffen, Debra, "Sartre and the Myth of Natural Scarcity," *Journal of British Social Phenomenology* 13 (1982) 15–25.

Bernal, Ellen W., "Immobility and the Self: A Clinical-Existential Inquiry," *Journal of Medicine and Philosophy* 9 (1984) 72–92.

Bittner, Rüdiger, "Understanding a Self-Deceiver," in McLaughlin and Rorty, eds., *Perspectives on Self-Deception*, 1988, pp. 535–552.

Blakemore, C., and S. Greenfield, eds., *Mindwaves: Thoughts on Intelligence, Identity and Consciousness*, Oxford: Basil Blackwell, 1987.

Blanchot, Maurice, "Who?" translated by Eduardo Cadava, *Topoi* 7 (1988) 99–100.

Bliss, Eugene, *Multiple Personality, Allied Disorder, and Hypnosis*, New York: Oxford University Press, 1986.

Block, Ned, ed., *Readings in Philosophy of Psychology*, 2 vols., Cambridge, Mass.: Harvard University Press, 1980.

Blum, Roland Paul, "Deconstruction and Creation," *Philosophy and Phenomenological Research* 46 (1985) 293–306.

Boer, Stephen E., and William G. Lycon, *Knowing Who*, Cambridge, Mass.: MIT Press, 1986.

Bok, Sissela, "The Self Deceived," *Social Science Information* 19 (1980) 905–922.

Bok, Sissela, *Secrets*, New York: Pantheon Books, 1982.

Bowes, Kenneth, and Donald Meichenbaum, eds., *The Unconscious Reconsidered*, New York: John Wiley and Sons, 1984.

Bosart, William, "Sartre's Theory of Consciousness and the Zen Doctrine of No Mind," in Casey and Morano, eds., *The Life of the Transcendental Ego*, 1986, pp. 126–150.

Braude, Stephen, *The Limits of Influence: Psychokinesis and the Philosophy of Science*, New York: Routledge and Kegan Paul, 1986.

Braude, Stephen, "Mediumship and Multiple Personality," *Journal of the Society of Psychical Research* 55 (1988) 177–195.

Braude, Stephen, *First Person Plural: Multiple Personality and the Philosophy of Mind*, New York: Routledge, forthcoming.

Brennen, Andrew, "Personal Identity and Personal Survival," *Analysis*, 42 (1982) 44–50.

Brennan, Andrew, "Survival," *Synthese* 59 (1984) 339–362.

Brennan, Andrew, "Best Candidates and Theories of Identity," *Inquiry* 24 (1986) 423–438.

Brennan, Andrew, "Discontinuity and Identity," *Nous* 21 (1987) 241–260.

Brennan, Andrew, "Survival and Importance," *Analysis* 47 (1987) 225–230.

Brennan, Andrew, *Conditions of Identity*, Oxford: Clarendon Press, 1988.

Brody, Baruch, *Identity and Essence*, Princeton, New Jersey: Princeton University Press, 1980.

Brown, Robert, "Integrity and Self-Deception," *Critical Review* 25 (1983) 115–131.

Broyles, James E. "Wittgenstein on Personal Identity," *Philosophical Investigations* 9 (1986) 56–65.

Brueckner, Anthony L., "Humean Fictions," in *Philosophy and Phenomenological Research* 46 (1986) 655–664.

Buchanan, Allen, "Advance Directives and the Personal Identity Problem," *Philosophy and Public Affairs* 17 (1988) 277–302.

Buford, Thomas O., "Person, Identity, and Imagination," *Personalist Forum* 5 (1989) 7–25.

Burke, Michael, "Cohabitation, Stuff and Intermittent Existence," *Mind* 89 (1980) 391–406.

Callan, Eamonn, "The Moral Status of Pity," *Canadian Journal of Philosophy* 18 (1988) 1–12.

Campbell, Keith, "Can Intuitive Psychology Survive the Growth of Neuroscience?" *Inquiry* 29 (1986) 143–152.

Carrithers, Michael, Steven Collins, and Steven Lukes, eds., *The Category of the Person: Anthropology, Philosophy, History*, Cambridge: Cambridge University Press, 1985.

Carruthers, P., *Introducing Persons: Theories and Arguments in the Philosophy of Mind*, Albany: State University of New York, 1986.

Carruthers, Peter, "Brute Experience," *Journal of Philosophy* 86 (1989) 258–269.

Carter, W. R., "Death and Bodily Transfiguration," *Mind* 93 (1984) 412–418.

Cavell, Stanley, *The Claim of Reason: Wittgenstein, Skepticism, Morality and Tragedy*, Oxford: Oxford University Press, 1982.

Casey, Edward, and Donald V. Morano, eds., *The Life of the Transcendental Ego: Essays in Honor of William Earle*, Albany: SUNY Press, 1986.

Canowitz, Benzion, and Ellen Langer, "Self-Protection and Self-Inception," in Martin, ed., *Self-Deception and Self-Understanding*, 1985, pp. 117–135.

Cherry, Christopher, "Self, Near-Death and Death," *International Journal of the Philosophy of Religion* 16 (1984) 3–12.

Cherry, Christopher, "Mind and Mattering," *Philosophy and Phenomenological Research* 47 (1986) 297–304.

Chessick, Richard D., *Psychology of the Self and the Treatment of Narcissism*, Northvale, N.J.: Aronson, 1985.

Christman, John, ed., *The Inner Citadel: Essays on Individual Autonomy*, New York: Oxford University Press, 1989.

Churchland, Patricia Smith, "Consciousness: The Transmutation of a Concept," *Pacific Philosophical Quarterly* 64 (1983) 80–95.

Churchland, Patricia Smith, *Neurophilosophy*, Cambridge, Mass.: MIT Press, 1986.

Churchland, Paul, *Matter and Consciousness*, Cambridge, Mass.: MIT Press, 1984.

Churchland, Paul, "Reduction, Qualia, and the Direct Introspection of Brain States," *The Journal of Philosophy* 82 (1985) 8–28.

Churchland, Patricia Smith, "Replies to Comments," *Inquiry* 29 (1986) 241–272.

Churchland, Paul, and Patricia Smith Churchland, "Functionalism, Qualia, and Intentionality," *Philoslophical Topics* 12 (1981) 121–145.

Clark, A., *Psychological Models and Neural Mechanisms*, Clarendon Press, Oxford, 1980.

Clark, Peter, and Crispin Wright, eds., *Mind, Psychoanalysis and Science*, New York: Basil Blackwell, 1988.

Clark, Romane, "Self Knowledge and Self Consciousness: Thoughts About Oneself," *Topoi* 7 (1988) 47–55.

Coburn, Robert C., "Personal Identity Revisited," in *Canadian Journal of Philosophy* 15 (1985) 379–403.

Confer, W. N., and Ables, B. S., *Multiple Personality: Etiology, Diagnosis, and Treatment*, New York: Human Sciences Press, 1983.

Cook, Deborah, "Self Knowledge as Self Preservation," in Green, ed., *Spinoza and the Sciences*, 1986, pp. 191–210.

Cook, Deborah, "The Turn Toward Subjectivity: Michel Foucault's Legacy," *The Journal of the British Society for Phenomenology* 18 (1987) 215–225.

Cooper, David E., *Authenticity and Learning: Nietzsche's Educational Philosophy*, Boston: Routledge and Kegan Paul, 1983.

Cosentino, Dante A., "Self-Deception without Paradox," *Philosophy Research Archives* 6 (1980) 443–465.

Cowley, Fraser, "The Identity of a Person and His Body," *Journal of Philosophy* 68 (1971) 678–683.

Crabtree, Adam, *Multiple Man: Explorations in Possession and Multiple Personality*, New York: Praeger Publishers, 1985.

Daniels, Charles, "Personal Identity," in C. Brown and P. French, eds., *Puzzles, Paradoxes and Problems*, New York: St. Martin's Press, 1987, pp. 49–63.

Darwall, Stephen L., "Self-Deception, Autonomy, and Moral Constitution," in McLaughlin and Rorty, eds., *Perspectives on Self-Deception*, 1988, pp. 407–430.

Dauenhauer, Bernard P., "I and Mine," in Welton, ed., *Critical and Dialectical Phenomenology*, 1987, pp. 216–229.

Davey, Nicholas, "Nietzsche, the Self, and Hermeneutic Theory," in *The Journal of the British Society for Phenomenology* 18 (1988) 272–284.

Davidson, Donald, "Paradoxes of Irrationality," in Wollheim and Hopkins, eds., *Philosophical Essays on Freud*, 1982.

Davidson, Donald, "First Person Authority," *Dialectica* 38 (1984) 101–112.

Davidson, Donald, "Deception and Division," in Elster, ed., *The Multiple Self*, 1985, pp. 79–92.

Davie, William E., "Hume on Perceptions and Persons," *Hume Studies* 10 (1984) 125–138.

Delius, Harold, *Self-Awareness: A Semantical Inquiry*, München: Beck, 1980.

Dennett, Daniel C., "How to Study Consciousness Empirically: Or, Nothing Comes to Mind," *Synthese* 12 (1982) 159–182.

Dennett, Daniel C., *Elbow Room: The Varieties of Free Will Worth Wanting*, Cambridge, Mass.: MIT Press, 1984.

Dennett, Daniel C., "Consciousness," in Richard L. Gregory, ed., *Oxford Companion to the Mind*, Oxford: Oxford University Press, 1987.

Dennett, Daniel C., "The Self as the Center of Narrative Gravity," in Kessel et al., eds., *Self and Consciousness*, forthcoming.

Desmond, William, *Desire, Dialectic, and Otherness: An Essay on Origins*, New Haven: Yale University Press, 1987.

de Sousa, Ronald B., "Emotion and Self-Deception," in McLaughlin and Rorty, eds., *Perspectives on Self-Deception*, 1988, pp. 324–344.

Detweiler, Robert, *Story, Sign, and Self: Phenomenology and Structuralism as Literary-Critical Methods*, Philadelphia: Fortress Press, 1988.

Deutsch, Eliot, *Personhood, Creativity, and Freedom*, Honolulu: University Press of Hawaii, 1982.

Dewhurst, David, "How Can I Know Myself?" *Philosophy* 59 (1984) 205–218.

Dilman, Ilham, *Freud and the Mind*, Oxford: Basil Blackwell, 1984.

Dilman, Ilham, *Love and Human Separateness*, New York: Basil Blackwell, 1987.

Donagan, A., A. Perovich, Jr., and M. V. Weldin, eds., *Human Nature and Natural Knowledge*, Dordrecht: Reidel, 1985.

Double, Richard, "Brain Bisection: Philosophy Meets Science," *Dialogos* 43 (1984) 39–48.

Douglas, W., and K. Gibbins, "Inadequacy of Voice Recognition as a Demonstration of Self-Deception," *Journal of Personality and Social Psychology* 44 (1983) 589–592.

Duhan, Laura, "Ambiguity of Time, Self, and Philosophical Explanation in Merleau-Ponty, Husserl, and Hume," *Auslegung* 13 (1987) 126–138.

Dworkin, Gerald, *The Theory and Practice of Autonomy*, Cambridge: Cambridge University Press, 1988.

Eccles, John C., *Evolution of the Brain: Creation of the Self*, New York: Routledge, 1989.

Edidin, Aron, "Fearing for Our Mental Lives," in French et al., eds., *Midwest Studies in Philosophy* 12 (1988) 335–360.

Ehring, Douglas, "Mental Identity," *The Southern Journal of Philosophy* 22 (1984) 189–194.

Ehring, Douglas, "Personal Identity and the Causal Theory of Memory," *The Modern Schoolman* 63 (1985) 65–69.

Ehring, Douglas, "Personal Identity and Time Travel," *Philosophical Studies* 52 (1987) 427–433.

Ehring, Douglas, "Survival and Trivial Facts," *Analysis* 47 (1987) 50–54.

Eldridge, Richard, *On Moral Personhood*, Chicago: University of Chicago Press, 1989.

Elliot, R., "How to Travel Faster than Light?" *Analysis* 41 (1981) 4–6.

Elster, Jon, ed., *Sour Grapes: Studies in the Subversion of Rationality*, Cambridge: Cambridge University Press, 1983.

Elster, Jon, ed., *The Multiple Self*, Cambridge: Cambridge University Press, 1985.

Erwin, Edward, "Psychoanalysis and Self-Deception," in McLaughlin and Rorty, eds., *Perspectives on Self-Deception*, 1988, pp. 228–245.

Fang, Wan Chuan, "Hume on Identity," *Hume Studies* 10 (1984) 59–68.

Fields, Lloyd, "Parfit on Personal Identity and Desert," *Philosophical Quarterly* 37 (1987) 432–441.

Filice, Carlo, "Sustained Causation and the Substantial Theory of the Self," *International Philosophical Quarterly* 26 (1986) 137–145.

Filice, Carlo, "Non-Substantial Streams of Consciousness and Free Action," *International Studies in Philosophy* 20 (1988) 1–11.

Fisher, David D. V., "A Conceptual Analysis of Self-Disclosure," *Journal for the Theory of Social Behavior* 14 (1984) 277–296.

Fisher, David D. V., "Experential Being and the Inherent Self: Towards a Constructivist Theory of the Self," *Journal for the Theory of Social Behavior* 18 (1988) 149–167.

Flanagan, Owen J., *The Science of the Mind*, Cambridge, Mass.: MIT Press, 1986.

Flay, Joseph C., "Experience, Nature, and Place," *Monist* 68 (1985) 467–480.

Flew, Antony, "Personal Identity and Imagination: One Objection," *Philosophy* 60 (1985) 123–126.

Floistad, Guttorm, ed., *Contemporary Philosophy: A New Survey*, vol. 4, *Philosophy of Mind*, The Hague: Nijhoff, 1983.

Follesdal, Dagfinn, "Sartre on Freedom," in Paul Arthur Schilpp, ed., *The Philosophy of Jean-Paul Sartre*, LaSalle, Ill.: Open Court, 1981, pp. 392–407.

Fontinell, Eugene, *Self, God, and Immortality: A Jamesian Investigation*, Philadelphia: Temple University Press, 1986.

Ford, Norman, *When Did I Begin?* Cambridge: Cambridge University Press, 1988.

Foss, Jeffrey, "Rethinking Self-Deception," *American Philosophical Quarterly* 17 (1980) 237–243.

Foucault, Michel, *Politics, Philosophy, Culture: Interviews and Other Writings of Michel Foucault, 1977–1984*, ed. Lawrence D. Kritzman, New York: Routledge, 1988.

Foucault, Michel, *Technologies of the Self*, Amherst: University of Massachusetts Press, 1988.

Frankfurt, Harry, "Identification and Wholeheartedness," in Schoeman, ed., *Responsibility, Character, and the Emotions*, 1988, pp. 27–45.

Frankfurt, Harry, *The Importance of What We Care About*, New York: Cambridge University Press, 1988.

French, Peter A., "Kinds and Persons," *Philosophy and Phenomenological Research* 44 (1983) 241–254.

French, Peter, Theodore E. Ulhling, Jr., and Howard K. Wettstein, eds., *Midwest Studies in Philosophy*, Minneapolis: University of Minnesota Press, 1986, 1988.

Friedman, Marilyn A., "Autonomy and the Split-Level Self," *The Southern Journal of Philosophy* 24 (1986) 19–35.

Garrett, Brian, "Best-Candidate Theories and Identity: Reply to Brennan," *Inquiry* 31 (1988) 79–85.

Garrett, Brian, "Identity and Extrinsicness," *Mind* 97 (1988) 105–109.

Garrett, Brian, review of Noonan's *Personal Identity*, New York: Routledge, 1989, in *Nous*, forthcoming.

Garrett, Brian, "Personal Identity and Extrinsicness," *Philosophical Studies* (1990), 59, 177–194.

Garrett, Brian, "Personal Identity and Reductionism," *Philosophy and Phenomenological Research*, 1990, forthcoming.

Garrett, Brian, "Can There Be Vague Identity Statements?" *Nous*, 1990, forthcoming.

Garrett, Brian, "Personal Identity and Animal Identity," *Logos*, 1990.

Gauthier, J. D., et al., trans., "The Ethic of Care for the Self as a Practice of Freedom: An Interview With Michael Foucault," *Philosophy and Social Criticism* 12 (1987) 112–131.

Gazzaniga, M., *The Social Brain: Discovering the Networks of the Mind*, New York: Basic Books, 1985.

Gergen, Kenneth J., "Toward Self as Relationship," in Yardley and Honess, eds., *Self and Identity: Psychosocial Perspectives*, 1987, pp. 53–63.

Geschwind, Norman, and Albert M. Galaburda, *Cerebral Lateralization*, Cambridge, Mass.: MIT Press, 1987.

Gilbert, Daniel T., and Joel Cooper. "Social Psychological Strategies of Self-Deception," in Martin, ed., *Self-Deception and Self-Understanding*, 1985, pp. 75–94.

Gillett, G. R., "Brain Bisection and Personal Identity," *Mind* 95 (1986) 224–229.

Gillett, G. R., "Disembodied Persons," *Philosophy* 61 (1986) 397–386.

Gilligan, Carol, *In a Different Voice: Psychological Theory and Women's Development*, Cambridge, Mass.: Harvard University Press, 1982.

Gilligan, S., and G. Bower, "Cognitive Consequences of Emotional Arousal," in C. Izard, J. Kagan, and R. Zajonc, eds., *Emotions, Cognition and Behaviour*, Cambridge: Cambridge University Press, 1984.

Ginet, Carl, and Sydney Shoemaker, eds., *Knowledge and Mind: Philosophical Essays*, New York: Oxford, 1983.

Glass, James M., *Private Terror/Public Life: Psychosis and the Politics of Community*, New York: Oxford University Press, 1989.

Glenn, Jr., John D., "The Definition of the Self and the Structure of Kierkegaard's Work," in Perkins, ed., *The Sickness Unto Death*, 1987, pp. 5–21.

Glover, Jonathan, *I: The Philosophy and Psychology of Personal Identity*, London: Penguin Books, 1988.

Goleman, Daniel, *Vital Lies, Simple Truths: The Psychology of Self-Deception*, New York: Simon and Schuster, 1985.

Gollwitzer, P., W. Earle, and W. Stephan, "Affect as a Determinant of Egotism: Residual Excitation and Performance Attributions," *Journal of Personality and Social Psychology* 43 (1982) 702–709.

Green, Marjorie, ed., *Spinoza and the Sciences*, Dordrecht: Kluwer, 1986.

Greene, David B., "Where Am I in the Story: Reflections on the Reader's Location and the Encounter with Fictive People," *Man and World* 22 (1989) 163–183.

Gruzalski, Bart, "Parfit's Impact on Utilitarianism," *Ethics* 96 (1986) 721–745.

Guthrie, Jerry L., "Self-Deception and Emotional Response to Fiction," *British Journal of Aesthetics* 21 (1981) 65–75.

Haight, David, and Marjorie Haight, "Time, Memory, and Self-Remembering," *Journal of Speculative Philosophy* 3 (1989) 1–11.

Haight, Mary, *A Study in Self-Deception*, Atlantic Highlands, N.J.: Humanities Press, 1980.

Haight, Mary, "Tales from a Black Box," in Martin, ed., *Self-Deception and Self-Understanding*, 1985, pp. 244–260.

Haldane, John, "Psychoanalysis, Cognitive Psychology and Self-Consciousness," in Clark and Wright,

eds., *Mind, Psychoanalysis and Science*, 1988, pp. 113–129.

Hamlyn, D. W., *Metaphysics*, Cambridge: Cambridge University Press, 1984.

Hampshire, Stuart, *Morality and Conflict*, Cambridge, Mass.: Harvard University Press, 1983.

Hamrick, William, ed., *Phenomenology in Practice and Theory*, Dordrecht: Nijhoff, 1985.

Hannay, Alastair, "Hamlet Without the Prince of Denmark: Porn on Kierkegaard and the Self," *Inquiry* 28 (1985) 261–272.

Hannay, Alastair, "Spirit and the Idea of the Self as a Relexive Relation," in Perkins, ed., *The Sickness Unto Death*, 1987, pp. 23–38.

Hanson, Karen, *The Self Imagined: Philosophical Reflections on the Social Character of Psyche*, New York: Routledge and Kegan Paul, 1987.

Harré, Rom, *Social Being: A Theory for Social Psychology*, Totowa, N.J.: Littlefield, Adams, 1980.

Harré, Rom, and Roger Lamb, eds., *The Encylopedic Dictionary of Psychology*, Cambridge, Mass.: MIT Press, 1982.

Harré, Rom, *Personal Being: A Theory for Individual Psychology*, Cambridge, Mass.: Harvard University Press, 1984.

Harré, Rom, *Social Construction of Emotions*, New York: Basil Blackwell, 1986.

Harré, Rom, "The Social Context of Self-Deception," in McLaughlin and Rorty, eds., *Perspectives on Self-Deception*, 1988, pp. 364–379.

Harré, Rom, and Peter Muhlhauser, *Pronouns and People*, Oxford: Basil Blackwell, 1990.

Harrington, Anne, "Nineteenth-Century Ideas on Hemisphere Differences and Duality of Mind," *Behavioral and Brain Sciences* 8 (1985) 617–653.

Hartle, Ann, *The Modern Self in Rousseau's 'Confessions': A Reply to St. Augustine*, Notre Dame: University of Notre Dame Press, 1983.

Harvey, J., and G. Weary, "Current Issues in Attribution Theory and Research," *Annual Review of Psychology* 35 (1984) 427–459.

Heckmann, Heinz-Dieter, "What a Res Cogitans Is—And Why I Am One," *Ratio* 25 (1983) 121–136.

Heil, J., "Doxastic Incontinence," *Mind* 93 (1984) 56–70.

Hellige, J. B., ed., *Cerebral Hemisphere Asymmetry*, New York: Praeger Publishers, 1983.

Hellman, Nathan, "Bach on Self-Deception," *Philosophy and Phenomenological Research* 44 (1983) 113–120.

Hewitt, John P., *Deliverance of the American Self*, Philadelphia: Temple University Press, 1989.

Hirsch, Eli, *The Concept of Identity*, New York: Oxford University Press, 1982.

Hofstadter, Douglas, *Metamagical Themas: Questing for the Essence of Mind and Pattern*, New York: Basic Books, 1985.

Hofstadter, Douglas, and Daniel C. Dennett, eds., *The Mind's I*, Bantam Books, 1982.

Hollis, Martin, "Of Masks and Men," in Carrithers et al., eds., *The Category of the Person*, 1985, pp. 217–233.

Holyer, Robert, "Belief and Will Revisited," *Dialogue: The Canadian Philosophical Review* 22 (1983) 273–290.

Honig, B., "Arendt, Identity, and Difference," *Political Theory* 16 (1988) 77–98.

Horowitz, Gad, "The Foucaultian Impasse: No Sex, No Self, No Revolution," *Political Theory* 15 (1987) 16–80.

Humphrey, N. A., *Consciousness Regained: Chapters in the Development of Mind*, Oxford: Oxford University Press, 1983.

Hundert, Edward M., *Philosophy, Psychiatry and Neuroscience, Three Approaches to the Mind: A Synthetic Analysis of the Varieties of Human Experience*, Oxford: Clarendon Press, 1989.

Imlay, Robert A., "Descartes, Russell, Hintikka and the Self," *Studia Leibnitiana* 17 (1985) 77–86.

Jahn, Robert G., "Consciousness, Quantum Mechanics, and Random Physical Processes," in Papanicolaou, ed., *Bergson and Modern Thought*, 1987, pp. 271–303.

Johnston, Mark, "Human Beings," *Journal of Philosophy* 84 (1987) 59–83.

Johnston, Mark, "Is There a Problem about Persistence?" *Proceedings of the Aristotelian Society*, Supplementary Volume (1987).

Johnston, Mark, "Review of Shoemaker and Swinburne's *Personal Identity*," *Philolsophical Review* 96 (1987) 123–128.

Johnston, Mark, "Fission and the Facts," in *Philosophical Perspectives*, Berkeley: University of California Press, 1989.

Johnston, Mark, "Relativism and the Self," in Krausz, ed., *Relativism*, University of Notre Dame Press, 1989.

Johnston, Mark, "Reasons and Reductionism," *Philosophical Review*, forthcoming.

Jones, Royce P., and George J. Agich, "Personal Identity and Brain Death: A Critical Response," *Philosophy and Public Affairs* 15 (1986) 267–274.

Joseph, R., "Awareness, The Origin of Thought, and The Role of Conscious Self-Deception in Resistance and Repression," *Psychological Reports* 46 (1980) 767–781.

Kenney, Anthony, *The Self*, Milwaukee: Marquette University Press, 1988.

Kessel, F., P. Cole, and D. Johnson, eds., *Self and Consciousness: Multiple Perspectives*, Hillsdale, N.J.: Erlbaum, forthcoming.

Ketchum, Sara Ann, "Moral Re-description and Political Self-Deception," in Mary Vetterling-Braggin, ed., *Sexist Language*, Totowa, N.J.: Littlefield, 1981.

Kihlstron, John, "Conscious, Unconscious, Subsconscious: A Cognitive Perspective," in Bowes and Meichenbaum, eds., *The Unconscious Reconsidered*, 1984, pp. 149–211.

Kim, Jaegwon, "Self-Understanding and Rationalizing Explanations," *Philosophia Naturalis* 21 (1984) 309–320.

King-Farlow, John, "Akrasia, Mastery and the Master-Self," *Pacific Philosophical Quarterly* 62 (1981) 47–60.

King-Farlow, John, "Deceptions? Assertions? or Second-String Verbiage?" *Philosophy* 56 (1981) 100–105.

Kipp, David, "On Self-Deception," *Philosophical Quarterly* 30 (1980) 305–317.

Kipp, David, "Self-Deception, Inauthenticity, and Weakness of Will," in Martin, ed., *Self-Deception and Self-Understanding*, 1985, pp. 261–283.

Kitcher, Patricia, "Kant on Self-Identity, *Philosophical Review* 91 (1982) 41–72.

Kitcher, Patricia, "Kant's Real Self," in Wood, ed., *Self and Nature in Kant's Philosophy*, 1984, pp. 113–147.

Kittay, Eva Feder, "On Hypocrisy," *Metaphilosophy* 13 (1982) 277–289.

Kleinig, J., *Ethical Issues in Psychosurgery*, London: George Allen and Unwin, 1985.

Kohlenbach, Margret, "Error or Self-Deception? The Case of Eduard in Goethe's *Elective Affinities*," in McLaughlin and Rorty, eds., *Perspectives on Self-Deception*, 1988, pp. 515–534.

Kolak, Daniel, *I Am You: A Philosophical Explanation of the Possibility That We Are All the Same Person*, Ph.D. diss., Ann Arbor: University Microfilms International, 1986.

Kolak, Daniel, "Art and Intentionality," in *The Journal of Aesthetics and Art Criticism* 48 (1990) 158–162.

Kolak, Daniel, "The Experiment," in Kolak and Martin, eds., *The Experience of Philosophy*, 1990, pp. 232–243.

Kolak, Daniel, and Raymond Martin, "Personal Identity and Causality: Becoming Unglued," *American Philosophical Quarterly* 24 (1987) 339–347.

Kolak, Daniel, and Raymond Martin, "Who," "Values," in *Wisdom Without Answers*, 2nd ed., Belmont, Calif. Wadsworth, 1991.

Kolak, Daniel, and Raymond Martin, eds., *The Expe-*

rience of Philosophy, Belmont, Calif.: Wadsworth, 1990.

Krausz, Michael, *Relativism: Interpretation and Confrontation*, Notre Dame: University of Notre Dame Press, 1989.

Kupperman, Joel J., "Investigations of the Self," *Philosophy East and West* 34 (1984) 37–52.

LaCentra, Walter, *Authentic Self: Toward a Philosophy of Personality*, New York: P. Lang, 1987.

Lachs, John, "Is There an Absolute Self?" *Philosophical Forum* 19 (1988) 169–181.

Lamiell, James, *The Psychology of Personality: An Epistemological Inquiry*, New York: Columbia University Press, 1987.

Lancaster, Sandra, and Margaret Foddy, "Self Extensions: A Conceptualization," *Journal for the Theory of Social Behavior* 18 (1988) 77–94.

Langan, William J., "The Life of Spirit," in Casey and Morano, eds., *The Life of the Transcendental Ego*, 1986, pp. 68–91.

Lapsley, D. K., and Powers, F. C., eds., *Self, Ego, and Identity*, New York: Springler-Verlag, 1988.

Leder, Drew, "Troubles with Token Identity," *Philosophical Studies* 47 (1985) 79–94.

LeDoux, J. E., and Michael Gazzaniga, "The Brain and the Split Brain: A Duel with Duality as a Model of Mind," *The Behavioral and Brain Sciences* 4 (1985) 109–110.

Lee, J. Roger, "Self," in *Reason Papers* 13 (1988) 152–165.

Letwin, Oliver, *Ethics, Emotion and the Unity of the Self*, London: Croon Helm, 1987.

Levin, David M., *The Opening of Vision: Nihilism and the Postmodern Situation*, New York: Routledge, 1988.

Lewis, David, *Philosophical Papers*, 2 vols., New York: Oxford University Press, 1983.

Lewis, Delmas, "Dualism and the Causal Theory of Memory," *Philosophy and Phenomenological Research* 44 (1983) 21–30.

Lewis, H. D., *Elusive Self*, Philadelphia: Westminster Press, 1982.

Linehan, Elizabeth A., "Ignorance, Self-Deception and Moral Accountability," *Journal of Value Inquiry* 16 (1982) 101–115.

Lockard, J., and D. Paulhus, eds., *Self-Deception*, Englewood Cliffs, N.J.: Prentice-Hall, 1988.

Lockwood, Michael, *Mind, Brain and the Quantum: The Compound "I"*, Oxford: Basil Blackwell, 1989.

Lyons, William, *The Disappearance of Introspection*, Cambridge, Mass.: MIT Press, 1986.

MacKay, David M., "Divided Brains—Divided Minds?" in Blakemore and Greenfield, eds., *Mindwaves*, 1987, pp. 5–18.

Mackay, David M., and Valerie Mackay, "Explicit Dialogue between Left and Right Half-Systems of Split Brains," *Nature* 295 (1982) 690–691.

Madell, Geoffrey, *The Identity of the Self*, Edinburgh: The University Press, 1981.

Madell, Geoffrey, "Derek Parfit and Greta Garbo," *Analysis* 45 (1985) 105–109.

McInerney, P., "Person Stages and Unity of Consciousness," *American Philosophical Quarterly* 22 (1985) 197–209.

McLaughlin, Brian, "Exploring the Possibility of Self-Deception in Belief," in McLaughlin and Rorty, eds., *Perspectives on Self-Deception* 1988, pp. 29–62.

McLaughlin, Brian, and Amélie Rorty, eds., *Perspectives on Self-Deception*, Berkeley: University of California Press, 1988.

Manser, Anthony, "The Presidential Address: Problems With the Self," *Proceedings of the Aristotelian Society* 84 (1984) 1–13.

Manser, Anthony, ed., *The Philolsophy of F. H. Bradley*, Oxford: Clarendon Press, 1984.

Margolis, Joseph, *Philosophy of Psychology*, Englewood Cliffs, N.J.: Prentice-Hall, 1984.

Margolis, Joseph, *Science Without Unity*, Oxford: Basil Blackwell, 1987.

Margolis, Joseph, "Minds, Selves, and Persons," *Topoi* 7 (1988) 31–45.

Marks, C., *Commissurotomy, Consciousness and Unity of Mind*, Cambridge, Mass.: MIT Press, 1986.

Marsella, Anthony, George De Vos, and Francis L. Hsu, eds., *Culture and Self: Asian and Western Perspectives*, New York: Tavistock, 1985.

Marshall, Sandra, "Public Bodies, Private Selves," *Journal of Applied Philosophy* 5 (1988) 147–158.

Martin, Mike W., "Demystifying Doublethink: Self-Deception, Truth and Freedom in 1984," *Social Theory and Practice* 10 (1984) 319–331.

Martin, Mike W., ed., *Self-Deception and Self-Understanding: New Essays in Philosophy and Psychology*, Lawrence: University Press of Kansas, 1985.

Martin, Mike W., *Self-Deception and Morality*, Lawrence: University Press of Kansas, 1986.

Martin, Raymond, "Memory, Connecting, and What Matters in Survival," *Australasian Journal of Philosophy* 65 (1987) 82–97.

Martin, Raymond, "Identity's Crisis," *Philosophical Studies* 53 (1988) 295–307.

Martin, Raymond, *The Past Within Us*, Princeton: Princeton University Press, 1989.

Martin, Raymond, "Personal Identity and Survival: Becoming the Persons We Most Want to Be," in Kolak and Martin, eds., *The Experience of Philosophy*, 1990, pp. 97–108.

Martin, Luther, Huck Gutman, and Patrick H. Hutton, eds., *Technologies of the Self: A Seminar with Michel Foucault*, Amherst: University of Massachusetts Press, 1988.

McGinn, Colin, *The Character of Mind*, Oxford University Press, 1982.

Measor, Nicholas, "On What Matters in Survival," *Mind* 89 (1980) 406–411.

Meiland, Jack W., "What Ought We to Believe? or The Ethics of Belief Revisited," *American Philosophical Quarterly* 17 (1980) 15–24.

Mele, Alfred R., "Self-Deception," *Philosophical Quarterly* 33 (1983) 365–377.

Mele, Alfred R., "Incontinent Believing," *Philosophical Quarterly* 36 (1986) 212–222.

Mele, Alfred R., "Self-Deception, Action and Will: Comments," *Erkenntnis* 18 (1982) 159–164.

Mele, Alfred R., "Self-Control, Action, and Belief," *American Philosophical Quarterly* 22 (1985) 169–176.

Mele, Alfred R., *Irrationality: An Essay on Akrasia, Self-Deception, and Self-Control*, New York: Oxford University Press, 1987.

Mendola, Joseph, "Parfit on Directly Collectively Self-Defeating Moral Theories," *Philosophical Studies* 50 (1986) 153–165.

Mendus, Susan L., "Kant's Doctrine of the Self," *Kantstudien* 75 (1984) 55–64.

Meyers, Diana, *Self, Society, and Personal Choice*, New York: Columbia University Press, 1989.

Midgley, Mary, *Wickedness, A Philosophical Essay*, Boston: Routledge and Kegan Paul, 1984.

Miller, Izchak, "Husserl and Sartre on the Self," *Monist* 69 (1986) 534–545.

Miller, Izchak, "Husserl on the Ego," *Topoi* 5 (1986) 157–162.

Miller, Thomas G., "Goffman, Positivism and the Self," *Philosophy of Social Science* 16 (1986) 177–195.

Millikan, Ruth Garrett, *Language, Thought, and Other Biological Categories*, Cambridge, Mass.: MIT Press, 1984.

Milo, Ronald D., *Immorality*, Princeton, N.J.: Princeton University Press, 1984.

Minsky, Marvin, *The Society of Mind*, New York: Simon and Schuster, 1986.

Moor, James, "Split Brains and Atomic Persons," *Philosophy of Science* 49 (1982) 91–106.

Moran, Richard, "Making Up Your Mind: Self-Interpretation and Self-Constitution," *Ratio* 30 (1988) 135–151.

Moreland, J. P., "An Enduring Self: The Achilles' Heel of Process Philosophy," *Process Studies* 17 (1988) 193–199.

Morris, Phyllis Sutton, "Self-Deception: Sartre's Resolution of the Paradox," in Hugh J. Silverman and Frederick A. Elliston, eds., *Jean-Paul Sartre*, Pittsburgh: Duquesne University Press, 1980.

Morton, Adam, "Partisanship," in McLaughlin and Rorty, eds., *Perspectives on Self-Deception*, 1988, pp. 170–182.

Mukherjee, Deba Prasad, "Does Ayer's Doctrine of Personal Identity Lead to No-Ownership Doctrine?" *Teoria* 8 (1988) 147–151.

Muller, Rene J., *The Marginal Self: An Existential Inquiry into Narcissism*, Atlantic Highlands, N.J.: Humanities Press, 1987.

Nagel, Thomas, "The Objective Self," in Ginet and Shoemaker, eds., *Knowledge and Mind*, 1983, pp. 211–232.

Nagel, Thomas, *The View From Nowhere*, New York: Oxford University Press, 1986.

Natsoulas, Thomas, "The Experience of a Conscious Self," *The Journal of Mind and Behavior* 4 (1983) 451–478.

Nehamas, Alexander, *Nietzsche: Life As Literature*, Cambridge, Mass.: Harvard University Press, 1985.

Nelkin, Norton, "Pains and Pain Sensations," *The Journal of Philosophy* 83 (1986) 129–148.

Nelkin, Norton, "What Is It Like to Be a Person?" *Mind & Language* 2 (1987) 221–242.

Nisbett, Richard, and L. Ross, *Human Inference: Strategies and Shortcomings of Social Judgment*, Englewood Cliffs, N.J.: Prentice-Hall, 1980.

Noonan, Harold W., "Reply to Garrett's 'Noonan, "Best-Candidate" Theories and the Ship of Theseus'," *Analysis* 46 (1986) 205–211.

Noonan, Harold W., *Personal Identity*, New York: Routledge, 1989.

Nozick, Robert, *Philosophical Explanations*, Cambridge, Mass.: Harvard University Press, 1981.

Nozick, Robert, *The Examined Life: Philosophical Meditations*, New York: Simon and Schuster, 1989.

Oaklander, L. Nathan, "Nietzsche on Freedom," *The Southern Journal of Philosophy* 22 (1984) 211–222.

Oaklander, L. Nathan, "Perry, Personal Identity and the 'Characteristic' Way," *Metaphilosophy* 15 (1984) 35–44.

Oaklander, L. Nathan, "Parfit, Circularity, and the Unity of Consciousness," *Mind* 96 (1987) 525–529.

O'Brien, Gerard J., "Eliminative Materialism and Our Psychological Self-Knowledge," *Philosophical Studies* 52 (1987) 49–70.

Oderberg, David S., "Johnston on Human Beings," *Journal of Philosophy* 86 (1989) 137–141.

Oderberg, David S., "Reply to Sprigge on Personal and Impersonal Identity," *Mind* 98 (1989) 124–133.

O'Neill, John, "The Specular Body: Merleau-Ponty and Lacan on Infant Self and Other," *Synthese* 66 (1986) 201–217.

Ornstein, R., *The Psychology of Consciousness*, New York: Penguin Books, 1986.

Ornstein, R., and R. Thompson, *The Amazing Brain*, Boston: Houghton Mifflin, 1984.

Owens, Joseph, "The Self in Aristotle," *Review of Metaphysics* 41 (1988) 707–722.

Papanicolaou, Andrew C., ed., *Bergson and Modern Thought*, New York: Harwood, 1987.

Parfit, Derek, "Rationality and Time," *Proceedings of the Aristotelian Society* 84 (1984) 47–82.

Parfit, Derek, *Reasons and Persons*, Oxford: Clarendon Press, 1984.

Parfit, Derek, "Comments," *Ethics* 96 (1986) 832–872.

Patten, St. C., "Kant's Cogito," *Kantstudien* 66 (1985) 331–341.

Pears, David, "Motivated Irrationality, Freudian Theory and Cognitive Dissonance," in Wollheim and Hopkins, eds., *Philosophical Essays on Freud*, 1982.

Pears, David, *Motivated Irrationality*, New York: Oxford University Press, 1984.

Penelhum, Terence, "Reasons, Spirits and Criteria," *Dialogue* 22 (1983) 579–586.

Perkins, Robert L., ed., *The Sickness Unto Death*, Macon: Mercer University Press, 1987.

Perrett, Roy W., "Egoism, Altruism and Intentionalism in Buddhist Ethics," *Journal of Indian Philosophy* 15 (1987) 71–85.

Perry, John, "Personal Identity and the Concept of a Person," *Contemporary Philosophy: A New Survey* 4 (1983) 11–43.

Peterman, James, "Self-Deception and the Problem of Avoidance," *Southern Journal of Philosophy* 21 (1983) 565–574.

Philips, Michael, ed., *Philosophy and Science Fiction*, Buffalo: Prometheus Books, 1984.

Phillips, D. Z., "Bad Faith and Sartre's Waiter," *Philosophy* 56 (1981) 23–31.

Piper, Adrian M. S., "Two Conceptions of the Self," *Philosophical Studies* 48 (1985) 173–178.

Piper, Adrian M. S., "Personal Continuity and Instrumental Rationality in Rawl's *Theory of Justice*," *Social Theory and Practice* 13 (1987) 49–76.

Piper, Adrian M. S., "Pseudorationality," in McLaughlin and Rorty, eds., *Perspectives on Self-Deception*, 1988, pp. 297–323.

Popper, Karl, and John Eccles, *The Self and Its Brain: An Argument for Interactionism*, originally published in Berlin: Springer-Verlag, 1977; republished, London: Routledge and Kegan Paul, 1983.

Puccetti, Roland, "The Duplication Argument Defeated," *Mind* 89 (1980) 582–586.

Puccetti, Roland, "On Saving Our Concept of a Person," *Philosophy* 55 (1980) 403–307.

Puccetti, Roland, "The Case for Mental Duality: Evidence from Split-Brain Data and Other Considerations," *The Behaviorial and Brain Sciences* 4 (1981) 93–123.

Puccetti, Roland, "Rigterink on Mental Division," *Canadian Journal of Philosophy* 12 (1982) 75–76.

Quattrone, George, and Amos Tversky, "Causal versus Diagnostic Contingencies: On Self-Deception and the Voter's Illusion," *Journal of Personality and Social Psychology* 46 (1984) 237–248.

Ray, C. "Can We Travel Faster Than Light?" *Analysis* 42 (1982) 50–52.

Rey, Georges, "Toward a Computational Account of *Akrasia* and Self-Deception," in McLaughlin and Rorty, eds., *Perspectives on Self-Deception* 1988, pp. 264–299.

Rhees, Rush, ed., *Recollections of Wittgenstein*, New York: Oxford University Press, 1984.

Rigterink, R. "Puccetti and Brain Bisection: An Attempt at Mental Division," *Canadian Journal of Philosophy* 10 (1980) 429–452.

Robinson, Denis, "Re-Identifying Matter," *Philosophical Review* 91 (1982) 317–341.

Robinson, Denis, "Can Amoebae Divide Without Multiplying?" *Australasian Journal of Philosophy* 63 (1985) 299–319.

Robinson, Hoke, "The Spatiality of Inner Sense," *Southwestern Journal of Philosophy* 2 (1985) 55–66.

Robinson, John, "Personal Identity and Survival," *Journal of Philosophy* 85 (1988) 319–328.

Robinson, William S., *Brains and People: An Essay on Mentality and its Causal Conditions*, Philadelphia: Temple University Press, 1988.

Rorty, Amelie Oksenberg, "Self-Deception, Akrasia and Irrationality," *Social Science Information* 19 (1980) 905–922.

Rorty, Amelie Oksenberg, "Akratic Believers," *American Philosophical Quarterly* 20 (1983) 175–183.

Rorty, Amelie Oksenberg, "The Deceptive Self: Liars, Layers, and Lairs," in McLaughlin and Rorty, eds., *Perspectives on Self-Deception*, 1988, pp. 11–28.

Rorty, Richard, *Philosophy and the Mirror of Nature*, Oxford: Basil Blackwell, 1980.

Rorty, Richard, "Should Hume Be Answered or By-Passed?" in Donagan et al., eds., *Human Nature and Natural Knowledge*, 1985, pp. 341–352.

Rorty, Richard, *Contingency, Irony and Contingency*, New York: Cambridge University Press, 1989.

Rosenberg, Jay F., *Thinking Clearly About Death*, Englewood Cliffs, N.J.: Prentice-Hall, 1983.

Rosenberg, Jay F., "Bodies, Corpses, and Chunks of Matter—A Reply to W. R. Carter's 'Death and Bodily Transfiguration,'" *Mind* 93 (1984) 419–422.

Rosenberg, Jay F., *The Thinking Self*, Philadelphia: Temple University Press, 1986.

Roth, John K., ed., *The Philolsophy of Josiah Royce*, Indianapolis: Hackett, 1982.

Roth, Robert J., "Locke On Ideas and the Intuition of the Self," *International Philosophical Quarterly* 28 (1988) 163–169.

Rovane, Carol A., "The Epistemology of First-Person Reference," 84 (1987) 147–167.

Ruddick, William, "Social Self-Deceptions," in McLaughlin and Rorty, eds., *Perspectives on Self-Deception*, 1988, pp. 380–389.

Russell, J. Michael, "Reflection and Self-Deception," *Journal for Research in Phenomenology* 11 (1981) 62–74.

Sabini, John, and Maury Silver, *Moralities of Everyday Life*, New York: Oxford University Press, 1982.

Sacks, Oliver, *The Man Who Mistook His Wife for a Hat*, New York: Harper and Row, 1987.

Salmon, Nathan, *Reference and Essence*, Oxford: Basil Blackwell, 1982.

Sanford, David H., "Self-Deception as Rationalization," in McLaughlin and Rorty, eds., *Perspectives on Self-Deception*, 1988, pp. 157–169.

Scarre, Geoffrey, "What Was Hume's Worry About Personal Identity?" *Analysis* 43 (1983) 217–221.

Schenck, David, "Operative Dimensions of Zaner's Context of Self," *International Studies in Philosophy* 16 (1984) 58–64.

Schick, Theodore W., "Computers and Self-Knowledge," *Thought* 64 (1989) 137–145.

Schleichert, Hubert, "On the Concept of Unity of Consciousness," *Synthese* 64 (1985) 411–420.

Schmitt, Frederick F., "Epistemic Dimensions of Self-Deception," in McLaughlin and Rorty, eds., *Perspectives on Self-Deception*, 1988, pp. 183–206.

Schoeman, Ferdinand, ed., *Responsibility, Character, and the Emotions*, New York: Cambridge University Press, 1987.

Schroeder, Craig, "Levels of Truth and Reality in the Philosophies of Descartes and Sankara," *Philosophy East and West* 35 (1985) 285–294.

Segalowitz, Sid, *Two Sides of the Brain*, Englewood Cliffs, N.J.: Prentice-Hall, 1983.

Sereno, Martin, "A Program for the Neurobiology of Mind," *Inquiry* 29 (1986) 217–240

Shklar, Judith, "Let Us Not Be Hypocritical," *Daedalus* 108 (1979) 1–25, reprinted in Judith N. Shklar, *Ordinary Vices*, Cambridge, Mass.: Belknap Press of Harvard University Press, 1984, pp. 45–86.

Shoemaker, Sydney, "On an Argument for Dualism," in Ginet and Shoemaker, eds., *Knowledge and Mind*, New York: Oxford University Press, 1983.

Shoemaker, Sydney, *Identity, Cause and Mind*, New York: Cambridge University Press, 1984.

Shoemaker, Sydney, "Critical Notice of Parfit's *Reasons and Persons*," *Mind* 44 (1985).

Shoemaker, Sydney, "Introspection and the Self," in Peter French et al., eds., *Midwest Studies in Philosophy*, 1986, pp. 101–120.

Shoemaker, Sydney, and Richard Swinburne, *Personal Identity*, Oxford: Basil Blackwell, 1984.

Shultz, Bart, "Persons, Selves, and Utilitarianism," *Ethics* 96 (1986) 721–745.

Silverman, Hugh J., "The Self in Question," in Hamrick, ed., *Phenomenology in Practice and Theory*, 1985, pp. 153–160.

Sirgy, M. Joseph, *Self-Congruity: Toward a Theory of Personality and Cybernetics*, New York: Praeger, 1986.

Skarda, Christine A., "Explaining Behavior: Bringing the Brain Back In," *Inquiry* 29 (1986) 187–202.

Smith, A. D., "The Self and the Good," *Proceedings of the Aristotelian Society* 85 (1984–1985) 101–117.

Smith, Aaron, "Brain-mind Philosophy," *Inquiry* 29 (1986) 203–215

Smith, Holly, "Culpable Ignorance," *Philosophical Review* 92 (1983) 543–571.

Smith, Peter, and O. R. Jones, *The Philosophy of Mind*, Cambridge: Cambridge University Press, 1986.

Smook, Roger, "Does Remembering Doing the Deed Presuppose Personal Identity?" *Dialogue* 25 (1986) 363–365.

Snyder, C., "Collaborative Companions: The Relationship of Self-Deception and Excuse Making," in Martin, ed., *Self-Deception and Self-Understanding*, 1985.

Snyder, Mark, *Public Appearances, Private Realities*, New York: W. H. Freeman, 1987.

Solomon, Robert, *The Passions*, Notre Dame, Ind.: University of Notre Dame Press, 1983.

Sorensen, R., "Self-Deception and Scattered Events," *Mind* 94 (1985) 64–69.

Sorensen, Roy, *Blindspots*, Oxford University Press, 1988.

Sosa, Ernest, "Persons and Other Beings," *Philosophical Perspectives* 1 (1987) 155–187.

Sosa, Ernest, "Surviving Matters," *Noûs* 24 (1990) 305–330.

Sprigge, T.L.S., "The Self and Its World in Bradley

and Husserl," in Manser, ed., *The Philosophy of F. H. Bradley*, 1984, pp. 285–302.

Sprigge, T.L.S., "Personal and Impersonal Identity," *Mind* 97 (1988) 29–49.

Springer, S., and G. Deutsch, *Left Brain, Right Brain*, New York: W. H. Freeman and Co., 1985.

St. Clair, Michael, *Object Relations and Self Psychology: An Introduction*, Belmont, Calif.: Wadsworth, 1986.

Stern, Cindy D., "Hume and the Self at a Moment," *History of Philosophy Quarterly* 4 (1987) 217–233.

Stone, Jim, "Why Potentiality Matters," *Canadian Journal of Philosophy*, 17, 1987.

Stone, Jim, "Parfit and the Buddha: Why There Are No People," *Philosophy and Phenomenological Research*, 48, 1988.

Stone, Robert V., "Sartre on Bad Faith and Authenticity," in P. A. Schilpp, ed., *The Philosophy of Jean-Paul Sartre*, LaSalle, Ill.: Open Court, 1981.

Storr, Anthony, *Solitude: A Return to the Self*, New York: The Free Press, 1988.

Swann, William J., and Stephen J. Read, "Self-Verification Processes: How We Sustain Our Self-Conceptions," *Journal of Experimental Social Psychology* 17 (1981) 351–372.

Swinburne, Richard, and Sydney Shoemaker, *Personal Identity*, Oxford: Basil Blackwell, 1984.

Swoyer, Chris, "Causation and Identity," in French et al., eds., *Midwest Studies in Philosophy* 8 (1984).

Szabados, Bela, "Review of M. R. Haight's 'A Study of Self-Deception,'" *Canadian Philosophical Review* 1 (1982) 259–263.

Szabados, Bela, "The Self, Its Passions and Self-Deception," in Martin, ed., *Self-Deception and Self-Understanding*, 1985, pp. 143–168.

Taber, John, *Transformative Philosophy: A Study of Sankara, Fichte, and Heidegger*, Honolulu: University of Hawaii Press, 1983.

Taylor, Charles, "The Person," in Carrithers et al., eds., *The Category of the Person*, 1985, pp. 257–281.

Taylor, Charles, *Sources of the Self*, Cambridge, Mass.: Harvard University Press, 1989.

Taylor, E., ed., *William James on Exceptional Mental States*, Amherst: University of Massachusetts Press, 1984.

Taylor, Gabriele, *Pride, Shame, and Guilt*, Oxford: Clarendon Press, 1985.

Taylor, Gordon Rattray, *The Natural History of the Mind*, New York: Penguin Books, 1981.

Theron, Stephen, "Other Problems about the Self," *Sophia* 24 (1985) 11–20.

Tov-Ruach, Leila, "Freud on Unconscious Affects, Mourning, and the Erotic Mind," in McLaughlin and Rorty, eds., *Perspectives on Self-Deception*, 1988, pp. 246–263.

Traiger, Saul, "Hume on Finding an Impression of the Self," *Hume Studies* 11 (1985) 47–68.

Trigg, Roger, *Ideas of Human Nature: An Historical Introduction*, Oxford: Basil Blackwell, 1988.

Trigg, Roger, "The Metaphysical Self," *Religious Studies* 24 (1988) 277–289.

Tugendhat, Ernst, *Self-Consciousness and Self-Determination*, translated by Paul Stern, Cambridge, Mass.: MIT Press, 1986.

Tversky, Amos, "Self-Deception and Self-Perception," in Elster, ed., *The Multiple Self*, 1985.

Unger, Peter, "Toward a Psychology of Common Sense," *American Philosophical Quarterly* 19 (1982) 117–129.

Unger, Peter, "Consciousness and Self-Identity," in French et al., eds., *Midwest Studies in Philosophy*, 1986, pp. 63–100.

Unger, Peter, "Conscious Beings in a Gradual World," in French et al., eds., *Midwest Studies in Philosophy*, 1988, pp. 287–333.

Unger, Peter, *Identity, Consciousness and Value*, New York: Oxford University Press, 1990.

Vailati, Ezio, "Leibniz's Theory of Personal Identity in the *New Essays*," *Studia Leibnitiana* 17 (1985) 36–43.

Van Cleve, James, "Three Versions of the Bundle Theory," *Philosophical Studies* 47 (1985) 95–108.

van Fraassen, Bas C., "The Peculiar Effects of Love and Desire," in McLaughlin and Rorty, eds., *Perspectives on Self-Deception*, 1988, pp. 123–156.

Van Inwagen, Peter, *Material Beings*, Ithaca: Cornell University Press, forthcoming.

Wachsberg, Milton, *Personal Identity, The Nature of Persons, and Ethical Theory*, Ph.D. diss., Princeton University, 1983.

Wald, George, "Consciousness and Cosmology: Their Interrelations," in Papanicolaou, ed., *Bergson and Modern Thought*, 1987, pp. 343–352.

Ward, Andrew, "Hume, Demonstratives, and Self-Ascriptions of Identity," *Hume Studies* 11 (1985) 69–93.

Warner, Richard, "Deception and Self-Deception in Shamanism and Psychiatry," *International Journal of Social Psychiatry* 26 (1980) 41–52.

Warner, Richard, "Hume, Demonstratives, and Self-Ascriptions of Identity," *Hume Studies* 11 (1985) 69–93.

Warner, Richard, *Freedom, Enjoyment, and Happiness: An Essay on Moral Psychology*, Ithaca: Cornell University Press, 1987.

Wedeking, Gary, "Locke's Metaphysics of Personal Identity," *History of Philosophy Quarterly* 4 (1987) 17–31.

Weiskrantz, L., *Blindsight: A Case Study and Implications*, Oxford: Clarendon Press, 1986.

Welker, David, "Logical Problems for Lockean Persons," *Grazer Philosophische Studien* 21 (1984) 115–132.

Welles, Jim, "The Socio-biology of Self-Deception," *Human Ethology Newsletter* 3 (1981) 14–19.

Welton, Donn, ed., *Critical and Dialectical Phenomenology*, Albany: SUNY Press, 1987.

Weston, Drew, *Self and Society: Narcissism, Collectivism, and the Development of Morals*, New York: Cambridge University Press, 1985.

White, Marjorie T., and Marcella V., Weiner, *The Theory and Practice of Self Psychology*, New York: Brunner-Mazel, 1986.

White, Stephen L., "What Is It Like to Be an Homonculus?" *Pacific Philosophical Quarterly* 68 (1987) 148–174.

White, Stephen L., "Self-Deception and Responsibility for Self," in McLaughlin and Rorty, eds., *Perspectives on Self-Deception*, 1988, pp. 450–486.

White, Stephen L., "Metapsychological Relativism and the Self," *Journal of Philosophy* 86 (1989) 298–323.

Wigan, A. L., *The Duality of the Mind* (republished) Malibu, Ca., Joseph Simon, Publisher, 1985.

Wiggins, David, *Sameness and Substance*. Oxford: Basil Blackwell, 1980.

Wilkes, Kathleen V., "More Brain Lesions," *Philosophy* 55 (1980) 455–470.

Wilkes, Kathleen V., "Is Consciousness Important?" *British Journal for the Philosophy of Science* 35 (1984) 223–243.

Wilkes, Kathleen V., *Real People: Personal Identity Without Thought Experiments*, Oxford: Clarendon Press, 1988.

Williams, C.J.F., *What Is Identity?* Cambridge: Cambridge University Press, 1990.

Wilshire, Bruce, *Role Playing and Identity: The Limits of Theatre as Metaphor*, Bloomington: Indiana University Press, 1982.

Wilshire, Bruce, "Mimetic Engulfment and Self-Deception," in McLaughlin and Rorty, eds., *Perspectives on Self-Deception*, 1988, pp. 390–406.

Wilson, Catherine, "Self-Deception and Psychological Realism," *Philosophical Investigations* 3 (1980) 47–60.

Wilson, Catherine, "Morality and the Self in Robert Musil's *The Perfecting of a Love*," *Philosophy and Literature* 8 (1984) 222–235.

Wolf, Susan, "The Importance of Free Will," *Mind* 90 (1981) 386–405.

Wolf, Susan, "Self-Interest and Interest in Selves," *Ethics* 96 (1986) 704–720.

Wollheim, Richard, *The Thread of Life*, Cambridge, Mass.: Harvard University Press, 1984.

Wollheim, Richard, and J. Hopkins, eds., *Philosophical Essays on Freud*, Cambridge: Cambridge University Press, 1982.

Wood, Allen, ed., *Self and Nature in Kant's Philosophy*, Ithaca: Cornell University Press, 1984.

Wood, Allen, "Ideology, False Consciousness, and Social Illusion," in McLaughlin and Rorty, eds., *Perspectives on Self-Deception*, 1988, pp. 345–363.

Wood, Allen, "Self-Deception and Bad Faith," in McLaughlin and Rorty, eds., *Perspectives on Self-Deception*, 1988, pp. 207–227.

Worthington, B. A., *Selfconsciousness and Selfreference: An Interpretation of Wittgenstein's Tractatus*, Aldershot: Avebury, 1988.

Yardley, K., and T. Honess, *Self and Identity: Psychosocial Perspectives*, New York: John Wiley and Sons, 1987.

Zemach, Eddy, "Unconscious Mind or Conscious Minds," in French et al., eds., *Midwest Studies in Philosophy*, 1986, pp. 121–149.

Zimmerman, Michael E., *Eclipse of the Self: The Development of Heidegger's Concept of Authenticity*, Athens, Ohio: Ohio University Press, 1981.

Zuboff, Arnold, "The Story of a Brain," in Hofstadter and Dennett, eds., *The Mind's I*, New York: Basic Books, 1981; reprinted in Kolak and Martin, eds., *The Experience of Philosophy*, 1989 pp. 289–296.

Zuboff, Arnold, "One Self: The Logic of Experience," *Inquiry*, 1990.

Notes on Contributors

Julian Jaynes is professor of psychology at Princeton University.

Daniel C. Dennett is professor of philosophy at Tufts University, where he is Director of the Center for Cognitive Studies.

Jonathan Miller received his M.D. from University College in London and is a Research Fellow in Cognitive Science, University of Sussex, England.

R. W. Sperry was Hixon Professor of Psychology at the California Institute of Technology, where currently he is Trustee Professor Emeritus. In 1981 he won the Nobel Prize for Physiology or Medicine "for his discoveries concerning the functional specialization of the cerebral hemispheres."

Roland Puccetti is professor of philosophy at Dalhousie.

Thomas Nagel is professor of philosophy and law at New York University.

Derek Parfit is a Research Fellow of All Souls College, Oxford.

Ernest Hilgard taught psychology at Yale and at Stanford University, where he is professor emeritus of psychology.

Kathleen Wilkes is Fellow and Tutor in philosophy at St. Hilda's College, Oxford.

Stephen Braude is professor of philosophy at the University of Maryland, Baltimore County.

Nicholas Humphrey received his Ph.D. in psychology from Cambridge University, where from 1970–1982 he was Assistant Director of Research, Sub-Department of Animal Behavior.

Bernard Williams is Knightsbridge Professor of Philosophy at Cambridge, a Fellow of King's College, and also teaches at the University of California at Berkeley.

Peter Unger is professor of philosophy at New York University.

Robert Nozick is Arthur Kingsley Porter Professor of Philosophy at Harvard University.

Sydney Shoemaker is Susan Linn Sage Professor of Philosophy at Cornell.

David Lewis is professor of philosophy at Princeton University.

Raymond Martin is professor of philosophy at the University of Maryland.

Christine Korsgaard is associate professor of philosophy and General Studies in the Humanities at the University of Chicago.

Rom Harré is fellow in Linacre College, Oxford, and professor of psychology at Georgetown University.

Kenneth Gergen is professor of psychology at Swarthmore.

Ulric Neisser is Robert W. Woodruff Professor of Psychology at Emory University.

Frithjof Bergman is professor of philosophy at University of Michigan, where he is also professor of anthropology and director of the Center for New Work in Flint, Michigan.

Mark Johnston is associate professor of philosophy and Richard Stockton Bicentennial Preceptor at Princeton University.

Martha Nussbaum is university Professor of Philosophy, Classics, and Comparative Literature at Brown University.

Allen Stairs is associate professor of philosophy at the University of Maryland.

Index

Names listed only where they appear in the text